D0365818

Time Out

Weekend
Breaks
from London

Edited and designed by
Time Out Guides Limited
Universal House
251 Tottenham Court Road
London W1T 7AB
Tel + 44 (0)20 7813 3000
Fax + 44 (0)20 7813 6001
guides@timeout.com
www.timeout.com

Editorial
Editor Ros Sales
Deputy Editor Peter Watts
Researcher Alix McAlister
Proofreader Tamsin Shelton
Indexer Jonathan Cox

Editorial/Managing Director Peter Fiennes
Series Editor Sarah Guy
Deputy Series Editor Cath Phillips
Guides Co-ordinator Anna Norman
Accountant Sarah Bostock

Design
Art Director Mandy Martin
Acting Art Director Scott Moore
Acting Art Editor Tracey Ridgewell
Senior Designer Averil Sinnott
Designers Astrid Kogler, Sam Lands
Digital Imaging Dan Conway
Ad Make-up Charlotte Blythe

Picture Desk
Picture Editor Kerri Littlefield
Deputy Picture Editor Kit Burnet
Picture Researcher Alex Ortiz
Picture Desk Trainee Bella Wood

Advertising
Sales Director & Sponsorship Mark Phillips
Sales Manager Alison Gray
Advertisement Sales Simon Davies
Copy Controller Oliver Guy
Advertising Assistant Sabrina Ancilleri

Marketing
Marketing Manager Mandy Martinez
US Publicity & Marketing Associate Rosella Albanese

Production
Guides Production Director Mark Lamond
Production Controller Samantha Furniss

Time Out Group
Chairman Tony Elliott
Managing Director Mike Hardwick
Group Financial Director Richard Waterlow
Group Commercial Director Lesley Gill
Group Marketing Director Christine Cort
Group General Manager Nichola Coulthard
Group Art Director John Oakey
Online Managing Director David Pepper

Contributors

KENT **North Kent Coast** Will Hodgkinson. **Canterbury** Anna Norman. **Sandwich to Sandgate** Abby Aron. **North Kent Downs** Sarah Jacobs. **Rye, Dungeness & Romney Marsh** Yolanda Zappaterra. **The Heart of Kent** Lesley McCave. **The Kent Weald** Simon Radcliffe.

SUSSEX & SURREY **Battle & Hastings** Janice Fuscoe. **The Ashdown Forest** Dean Irvine. **Lewes & Around** Chris Moore. **Brighton** Cathy Limb. **South-west Sussex** Dorothy Boswell. **North Surrey Downs** Sharon Lougher. **The Three Counties** Michael Flexer.

HAMPSHIRE & ISLE OF WIGHT **Around Newbury** Andrew White, Arabella Keatley. **Winchester & Around** Abby Aron. **The New Forest** Caroline Taverne. **Isle of Wight** Dorothy Boswell. **Bournemouth & Poole** Hugh Graham.

WILTSHIRE & BATH **Salisbury & Stonehenge** Cath Phillips. **Bradford-on-Avon & Around** Natalia Marshall. **Bath** Ismay Atkins. **Chippenham to Avebury** Will Fulford-Jones. **Malmesbury & Around** Peter Watts.

THE COTSWOLDS **Cirencester to Gloucester** Lucy Muss. **Cheltenham to Stow** Cyrus Sharad. **North Cotswolds** Dean Irvine. **Stratford & Warwick** Derek Hammond. **Oxford** Peter Watts. **South Oxfordshire** Andrew White, Arabella Keatley. **Woodstock to Burford** Ruth Jarvis. **Chipping Norton to Banbury** Susie Grimshaw.

THE CHILTERNS TO YORK **Windsor & Around** Cyrus Sharad. **North Chilterns** Cyrus Sharad. **Hertfordshire** Natalia Marshall. **Rutland** Derek Hammond. **Lincoln** Anna Smith. **York** Christi Daugherty.

EAST ANGLIA **Cambridge** Janice Fuscoe. **West Essex** David Hall. **Lower Stour Valley** Tony Mudd. **Upper Stour Valley** Tony Mudd. **Bury St Edmunds & Around** Emma Perry. **The Suffolk Coast** Caroline Taverne.

For photography credits, see page 316.

Maps by JS Graphics (john@jsgraphics.co.uk). Maps based on data supplied by Lovell Johns Ltd.

Published by the Penguin Group
Penguin Books Ltd, 80 Strand, London, WC2R 0RL, England
Penguin Group (USA) Inc, 375 Hudson Street, New York, NY10014, USA
Penguin Books Australia Ltd, 250 Camberwell Road, Camberwell, Victoria 3124, Australia
Penguin Books Canada Ltd, 10 Alcorn Avenue, Toronto, Ontario, Canada M4V 3B2
Penguin Books (NZ) Ltd, cnr Rosedale and Airborne Roads, Albany, Auckland, New Zealand

Penguin Books Ltd, Registered Offices: Harmondsworth, Middlesex, England

First published 1999
Second edition 2001
Third edition 2003
10 9 8 7 6 5 4 3 2 1

DOES MY BUM LOOK BIG IN THIS?

Leave the stress of the city behind in 600 acres of countryside filled with elephants and tigers and penguins and more at

WHIPSNADE WILD ANIMAL PARK

LONDON ZOO
ZSL

www.whipsnade.co.uk
or call 01582 872 171
Junction 9 off the M1

Whipsnade
WILD ANIMAL PARK

Contents

Page 6: Make the most of your weekend with our money-saving offers.

Introduction

England is nothing if not diverse. A journey of two hours from London by road or rail brings you to countryside green, rolling and quintessentially 'English' enough to be an Ealing film set; or to eerily desolate marshland; or to a resort shedding a reputation as an old colonels' retirement home to emerge as a beacon of style (that's Bournemouth, by the way). Or it might bring you to a seaside town where the empty arcades and dilapidated seafront tell a story of a time before package holidays abroad (that's Margate, where the beach is still gorgeous and there's plenty of fun for kids). Or it might take you to the landscape that inspired Constable. Not to mention some of England's iconic sights – Canterbury Cathedral, York Minster, more or less the whole of Bath, Stonehenge, the White Cliffs of Dover.

We've tried to reflect this diversity. Our writers have visited sights, stayed in hotels, drunk in pubs and eaten in restaurants in 45 very different destinations. They've uncovered quirky and fascinating details about places and the people who lived in them: the castle with a collection of dog collars; the story of the diver who saved Winchester Cathedral by wallowing amid the waterlogged foundations to dig out rotting beams; the singularly unglamorous reality of highwayman Dick Turpin; the place where the first photographic negative was produced.

There seems to be a new-found consciousness of the countryside among city-dwellers. After all, these days people want to know where their food comes from. We found this concern about the quality and provenance of our food reflected on restaurant menus everywhere, with a growing number of places serving locally sourced produce. We've tended to ignore hotel restaurants of the more glacial and cheerless type in favour of places where good food is part of an all-round enjoyable experience. We found plenty, as well as good pubs serving top-class pub food. And fine hotels and comfy B&Bs. And amazing countryside that's itching to be explored. It really is a green and pleasant land; why not go out and enjoy it?

How the book is arranged

For ease of use, we have divided this book into seven sections, some roughly corresponding to counties, others covering areas such as the Cotswolds. Within each section, we've based the breaks around areas that are explorable

Town Maps legend

▨ Place of interest	▨ Restricted road
▢ College or University	🚾 Toilet with disabled access
▦ Station	🚾 Toilet without disabled access
▨ Park	🅿 Car park

Area Maps legend

— Major footpath	– – County boundry
▪ Place of interest	– – Ferry route

over a weekend, so while some are county-based, others slip over county boundaries. This has led to a few anomalies in the names of sections and breaks in various parts of the book, but we felt this was preferable to unwieldy chapter titles or breaks strictly divided by county boundaries.

Accommodation rates and booking

Unless otherwise stated, breakfast is included in room prices. Where breakfast is extra, we indicate this and give prices: 'Eng' for a full English breakfast, 'cont' for a continental breakfast. Many hotels offer special rates for weekends, often including dinner. It's always worth checking when booking.

Booking accommodation in advance is always recommended; most of the places we feature in this book are very popular, and at least several weeks' (and often months') notice is required, particularly during the high season. Also, bear in mind that many establishments close for a couple of weeks during the year, so it is always risky to turn up without phoning first. If you are unable to find a room in any of the places we feature, most Tourist Information Centres we list should be able to help you find somewhere to rest your head.

Things to check when booking

We have attempted to find out most of the following accommodation information for you, but always double-check if you don't want the risk of an unwelcome surprise.

Children – We have shown where children are not admitted, where there are age restrictions or places where they are particularly welcome.

Dogs – We have indicated places that are happy to take dogs.

Maps and directions – The maps in this book are intended (with the exception of the town plans) for general orientation and you

will need a road atlas or other detailed map to find your way around. We have included instructions of how to find your way to the hotels, guesthouses and B&B establishments we list, unless their location is easy to find without directions.

Minimum stay – Some hotels and B&Bs insist on a minimum stay of two nights or more (usually over a Friday and Saturday).

No-smoking policies – Many places (hotels less so than B&Bs) have strict no-smoking policies in their bedrooms and/or throughout the building. We've indicated this in the listings.

Sponsors and advertisers

We would like to thank our sponsor MasterCard for their involvement in this book. We would also like to thank the advertisers. However, we stress that they have no control over editorial content. No establishment has been included because it has advertised, and no payment of any kind has influenced any review. The opinions given in this book are those of *Time Out* writers and entirely impartial.

Listings

All the listings information was fully checked and correct at the time of going to press, but owners and managers can change their arrangements at any time, and prices can rise. Therefore, it is always best to check opening times, admission fees and other details before you set off. Bear in mind that some sights may open on certain bank holidays in addition to the days listed. While every effort and care has been made to ensure the accuracy of the information contained in this book, the publishers cannot accept responsibility for any errors it may contain.

Credit cards

In the 'Where to stay' and 'Where to eat & drink' sections, the following abbreviations have been used – **AmEx**: American Express; **DC**: Diners Club; **MC**: MasterCard; **V**: Visa.

Let us know what you think

We hope you enjoy this book and welcome any comments or suggestions you might have. A reader's reply card is included at the back of the book, or you can email us at guides@timeout.com.

Overview

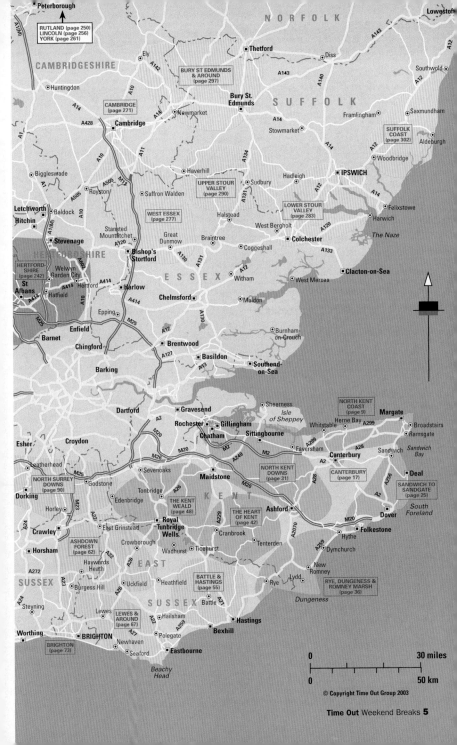

Special offers

To make your Weekend Break even more of a treat we've once again exclusively negotiated some great offers for our readers. All the hotels participating in these offers are cross-referenced in the guide and are signposted with the OFFER symbol.

As always your comments are of great help to us. Help us to continue creating great guides by filling in our readers survey card at the back of this guide. Plus you could win ten guides from our City Guides series or a copy of the next edition of Weekend Breaks.

Westover Hall

Granville Hotel

AROUND NEWBURY

Esseborne Manor
Hurstbourne Tarrant (01264 736444) *See page 104*
Offer:	Three nights for the price of two
Rate:	Between £95 (single) and £180 (deluxe double)
Conditions:	Minimum two nights, based on two sharing
Valid until:	Oct 2004

Newbury Manor
Newbury (01635 528838) *See page 104*
Offer:	Three nights for the price of two
Rate:	Between £115 (single) and £275 (master suite)
Conditions:	Subject to availability
Exclusions:	Christmas, New Year & Hennessy Racing Weekend
Valid until:	Oct 2004

BRIGHTON

Granville Hotel
Brighton (01273 326302). *See page 77*
Offer:	Three nights for the price of two
Rate:	Between £55 (single) and £185 (double/suite)
Conditions:	None
Exclusions:	Christmas & New Year
Valid until:	Oct 2004

NEW FOREST

Westover Hall
Milford on Sea. (01590 643044) *See page 117*
Offer:	Three nights for the price of two
Rate:	Between £120 (single) and £260 (superior double), including dinner
Conditions:	Excludes Saturday night
Exclusions:	Easter, Christmas & New Year
Valid until:	Oct 2004

NORTH COTSWOLDS

Lygon Arms
Broadway (01386 852255) *See page 159*
Offer:	Three nights for the price of two
Rate:	Between £159 (single) and £495 (king suite)
Conditions:	Sun-Thur only subject to availability (room only)
Exclusions:	Christmas & New Year
Valid until:	Oct 2004

LINCOLN

Courtyard by Marriott
Broadway (01522 544244) *See page 259*
Offer:	Three nights for the price of two
Rate:	Between £65/£89 midweek (single) and £90/£99 midweek (superior double)
Conditions:	None
Exclusions:	Christmas & New Year
Valid until:	Oct 2004

WOODSTOCK TO BURFORD

The King's Arms Hotel
Woodstock (01993 813636) *See page 217*
Offer:	Three nights for the price of two
Rate:	Between £70 (single) and £150 (superior double)
Conditions:	None
Exclusions:	Christmas & New Year
Valid until:	Oct 2004

WINDSOR & AROUND

Sir Christopher Wren House Hotel
Windsor (01753 861354) *See page 232*
Offer:	Three nights for the price of two
Rate:	Between £120 (single) and £275 (superior double)
Conditions:	Valid Fri/Sat/Sun only
Exclusions:	Christmas & New Year
Valid until:	Oct 2004

The Lygon Arms Spa

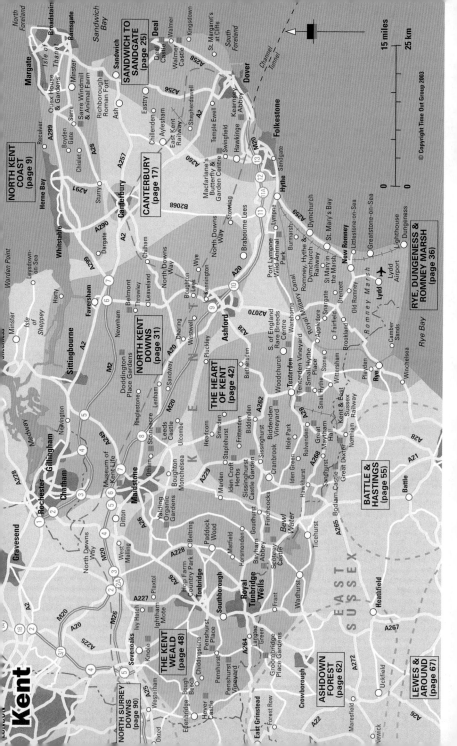

North Kent Coast

The British seaside at its best.

Nowhere in Britain offers a better guide to English society than the North Kent Coast. From the gaudy but decrepit charms of Margate to the lifestyle bohemiania of Whitstable and the respectable Victorian gentility of Broadstairs, the area is like a geographical class system. It occupies the **Isle of Thanet**, an actual island at the time of the Roman conquest that was separated from the rest of the country by the Wantsum Channel, until silt filled the channel up and turned it into an indistinct drainage ditch currently about six feet across.

From then on Thanet was first port of call for anyone wishing to invade, rape and pillage England: the Vikings combined invasions with their annual summer holidays throughout the 440s, while smugglers favoured the 26 miles of the Thanet Coastal Path for its myriad caves and alcoves in the centuries that followed. The smugglers are long gone, leaving behind some of the best beaches that England has to offer, with fine golden sands, white cliffs and some beautiful surrounding countryside. There are quiet, peaceful beaches such as **Herne Bay** near Whitstable and **Kingsgate Bay** at Cliftonville; and traditional family beaches such as **Margate Main Sands** and **Viking Bay** at Broadstairs. Inland there are some good walks to enjoy including the **Wantsum Walk** and **St Augustine's Trail**, which take in a few good country pubs along the way.

Margate

Once upon a time Margate was the pride of Kent, a pleasure palace brimming with life, colour and hedonism. It was Britain's first seaside resort, with donkey rides, deckchair attendants and boarding houses as long ago as the 1730s. Until the 1960s Margate remained the cockney summer breaker's premier holiday destination and, accordingly, it had a reputation as a place for unpretentious fun and saucy humour: a slap, a tickle, and a toffee apple for the little ones was all part of the day out.

That was a long time ago. Margate's has been a gradual but steady decline. It began in the 1970s when holidaymakers discovered 'abroad'; the demise of Margate Pier, destroyed by storms in 1978, marked the end of the good old days. While the façade of the seafront Tivoli amusement arcade is still a glorious example of multicoloured kitsch, the boarded-up milk bars and fish and chip restaurants further along the front are evidence of a town in a slump. A fire in 2003 put paid to two seafront amusement parks. Groups of pimply lads in baseball caps sit on the seafront railings and pass the hours whistling at girls, while asylum seekers, living in Margate's many B&Bs, wander up and down the front. Many beautiful buildings are falling ever more into decay and small local businesses are clearly struggling to survive.

Despite it all, Margate remains a romantic place. Local girl Tracey Emin has stated that 'Margate made me what I am', and strolling along the seafront you can see what she means. The town has a melancholic touch of parochial eccentricity that makes a refreshing change from the chain Starbucks- and Pizza Express-dominated regularity of England's supposedly more illustrious towns. The beaches themselves are still glorious: vast stretches of glistening sand studded with pockets of childish fun – a bouncy castle here, a miniature train there, and a few donkeys to get from one to the other on. The **Dreamland Fun Park** is a fantastically old-fashioned leisure complex, dominated by a huge and ancient rollercoaster built on a rickety wooden frame, which enjoys the status of being the first fairground attraction to become a Grade II-listed building. Unfortunately, a fall in the number of rides has given much of Dreamland the look of a deserted car park. The park's days could well be numbered; owner Jimmy Godden has sold the site, making a retail development seem likely.

As for the town itself, grand Regency squares sit alongside the dilapidated streets of the old town, and beautiful, ancient oddities such as the **Shell Grotto** and **Margate Caves** are buried down unassuming neighbourhood roads. In fact, Margate's rougher edges only make its hidden charms all the more exciting to find.

By train from London

Trains run from **Victoria** to **Ramsgate** every 20-30mins, and take 1hr 50mins. Most stop at **Whitstable**, **Margate** and **Broadstairs**. Info: www.connex.co.uk. (Services will be taken over by South Eastern Trains in 2004; timetables should not be affected.)

Broadstairs

The old seaside town of Broadstairs couldn't be more different to Margate. Viking Bay – with its rows of blue and yellow beach huts, old wooden swingboats, Punch & Judy show, donkey rides and golden sands – looks like a Victorian seaside resort transplanted to the modern age. One feels almost indecent wearing modern swimming attire in such a place: knee-length bathing costumes for the gents and bloomers for the ladies seem more appropriate. Even the sailing boats seem old-fashioned. The

harbour itself looks as if it belongs to a quaint 19th-century fishing village; no wonder Dickens loved it here so much (*see p15* **What the Dickens?**). Elsewhere the town has touches of the 1950s (the tiny pebble-dashed **Windsor Cinema** under the harbour's York Gate, with its collection of old film posters in the foyer and retro £3 admission charge); and the 1960s (**Chiappini's** coffee bar on the Promenade that looks over Viking Bay). Sadly, the formica-topped 1960s milk bars have now gone, to be replaced by nondescript pizza and pasta joints.

This is a wonderful town in which to spend a day. While Whitstable has the best restaurants and hotels, Broadstairs has the beaches with the best atmosphere. Head for the end of Viking Bay and you'll find a walkway carved into the cliff that takes you round to the quiet **Louisa Bay**, which has a tiny stretch of sand and chalets for hire. The Promenade also makes for a good walk, and the town itself, with its old-fashioned sweet shops, handful of decent restaurants and obsession with all things Dickensian, can be covered in an afternoon. The town is particularly lively during **Broadstairs Folk Week**, which begins on 8 August.

Whitstable

They don't call it Islington-on-Sea for nothing. Over the past few years this little fishing village has been undergoing a remarkably successful gentrification, with stressed Londoners finding the beach huts a great place to relax and the native oyster trade a good reason to come here for a long Sunday lunch. The whole town has been styled in weathered tastefulness, from the bleached-out colours of the High Street shopfronts to the creosote-sealed wooden huts at the harbour to the thousands of seashells that are washed up

Punch & Judy and trampolines keep children busy at nostalgic **Broadstairs** beach.

at the point where the sea gently laps the pebbled shore. Whitstable is one seaside town that actually benefits from rainy, windy weather: traversing the windbreakers on a winter's day really does feel quite romantic.

The oysters themselves make for a pretty good excuse for a visit. Whitstable's harbour, which opened in 1832, is still operating, and you can watch the oystermen gathering their catch in traditional yawls before sampling their wares at some of the counry's best oyster restaurants. It takes about five years for an oyster to reach maturity, and if you have only ever had oysters from the supermarket before, the superiority of the ones here is something to behold.

Ramsgate

After the saucy fun of Margate, the nostalgic charm of Broadstairs and the stylish gourmet delights of Whitstable, it has to be said that Ramsgate doesn't really match up, but there are still some reasons to visit this solid working town. The long, well-maintained **Ramsgate Main Sands** have an Edwardian lift up the white cliffs and there is also a faithful replica of a Viking longboat that has been around since 1949. The **Model Village** in Westcliff has a good location on the clifftop promenade. Ramsgate also has its own **Green Festival**, held on the first weekend of June, which features the world's only solar-powered circus.

What to see & do

Tourist Information Centres

6B High Street, Broadstairs, CT10 1LH (01843 583333/www.tourism.thanet.gov.uk). **Open** *Jan-Apr, Oct-Dec* 9.15am-1pm, 1.45-4.45pm Mon-Fri; 10am-1pm, 1.45-4.45pm Sat. *May-Sept* 9.15am-1pm, 1.45-4.45pm Mon-Fri; 10am-1pm, 1.45-4.45pm Sat; 10am-4pm Sun.

12-13 The Parade, Margate, CT9 1EY (01843 583333/www.tourism.thanet.gov.uk). **Open** *Jan-Apr, Oct-Dec* 9.15am-1pm, 1.45-4.45pm Mon-Fri; 10am-1pm, 1.45-4.45pm Sat. *May-Sept* 9.15am-1pm, 1.45-4.45pm Mon-Fri; 10am-1pm, 1.45-4.45pm Sat; 10am-4pm Sun.

17 Albert Court, York Street, Ramsgate, CT11 9DN (01843 583333/www.tourism.thanet.gov.uk). **Open** *Jan-Apr, Oct-Dec* 9.15am-4.45pm Mon-Fri; 10am-4.45pm Sat. *May-Sept* 9.15am-4.45pm Mon-Fri; 10am-4.45pm Sat; 10am-4pm Sun.

7 Oxford Street, Whitstable, CT5 1DB (01227 275482/www.visitwhitstable.co.uk/www.canterbury.co.uk). **Open** *Sept-June* 10am-4pm Mon-Sat. *July, Aug* 10am-5pm Mon-Sat.

Bleak House Museum

Fort Road, Broadstairs, CT10 1EY (01843 862224/www.bleakhouse.ndo.co.uk). **Open** *Apr-Sept* 10am-6pm daily. *Oct-Mar* 10am-4pm daily. **Admission** £3; £2-£2.80 concessions. **No credit cards.**

This castle-like turreted house overlooking the coast is where Dickens escaped to for long summer holidays, entertaining family and friends and writing *David Copperfield* when he wasn't taking bracing afternoon constitutionals along Viking Bay. Now the author's holiday home is used as a maritime museum, dominated by a grisly exhibition documenting the many ships and lives lost at the perilous Goodwin Sands, reputed to be the most dangerous stretch of water in the world. Don't miss a trip down to the cellars, where there is an exhibition on the golden age of smuggling.

Dickens House Museum

2 Victoria Parade, Broadstairs, CT10 1QS (01843 861232/863453/www.dickenshouse.co.uk). **Open** *Apr-June, Sept, Oct* 2-5pm daily. *July, Aug* 11am-5pm daily. Closed Nov-Mar. **Admission** £2; £1 concessions. **No credit cards.**

Not actually Dickens's house, but the home of Miss Mary Pearson Strong, the inspiration for Miss Betsey Trotwood in *David Copperfield*. Now it is a museum commemorating Dickens' association with Broadstairs.

Dreamland Fun Park

Belgrave Road, Margate, CT9 1XG (01843 227011). **Open** *Mar-June, Sept* 11am-5pm daily. *July, Aug* 11am-9pm daily. Closed Oct-Feb. **Admission** free. **Credit** *Rides* MC, V.

This wonderfully dilapidated old theme park features the Scenic Railway, a huge wooden rollercoaster built in 1920 that is the oldest in Europe and a listed building. There is also a more modern, much more terrifying Wild Mouse rollercoaster, a log flume and all the usual ghost trains, dodgems, waltzers and amusements. On the day we visited half the rides were shut, but if you asked an attendant they would start them up for you. Locals have a lot of affection for Dreamland – have a look at www.savedreamland.co.uk to see why.

Margate Caves

1 Northdown Road, Cliftonville, CT9 2RN (01843 220139). **Open** *Easter-Oct* 10am-5pm daily. *Nov-Easter* 10am-4pm Sat, Sun. **Admission** £2; £1-£1.50 concessions. **No credit cards.**

Formerly used as a refuge from invaders, these 1,000-year-old, man-made chalk tunnels have an entrance on a residential street and contain a secret church, a prison, a torture chamber and a smugglers' store.

Margate Local History Museum

The Old Town Hall, Market Place, Margate, CT9 1ER (01843 231213). **Open** *Apr-Sept* 10am-5pm Tue-Sun. *Oct-Mar* 10am-4pm Thur-Sun. Last entry 1hr before closing. **Admission** £1; 50p concessions. **No credit cards.**

The history of the town from the 18th century onwards, with Victorian seaside souvenirs, Edwardian bathing costumes and model vessels. It's not hugely interesting.

Quex House & Gardens/ Powell-Cotton Museum

Quex Park, Birchington, CT7 0BH (01843 842168/www.sealtd-development.co.uk/quex/www.powell-cottonmuseum.co.uk). **Open** *Apr-Oct* 11am-5pm Tue-Thur, Sun. *Nov, Mar* 11am-4pm Sun. Closed Dec-Feb. **Admission** £4; £3 concessions. *Gardens only* £1; 50p concessions. **Credit** MC, V.

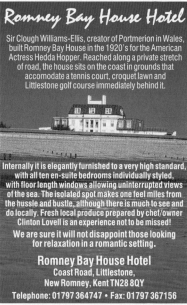

The **Fishermen's Huts** offer unorthodox accommodation on Whitstable seafront. *See p14.*

Major Powell-Cotton was a Victorian ethnographer and scientist who collected animal skins and skeletons from around the world. His collection, much of it fashioned into animal dioramas, is on show here. The house is set in 15 acres of lovely woodland.

Ramsgate Maritime Museum

Clock House, Pier Yard, Royal Harbour, Ramsgate, CT11 8LS (01843 570622/587765/www.ekmt. fsnet.co.uk). **Open** *Apr-Oct* 10am-5pm daily. *Nov-Mar* 10am-4.30pm Thur-Sun. Last entry 30mins before closing. **Admission** £1.50; 75p concessions. **No credit cards**.

Housed in an early 19th-century clock house, this small museum documents Thanet's maritime heritage, and has an attached dry dock and floating exhibits.

Ramsgate Motor Museum

West Cliff Hall, The Paragon, Ramsgate, CT11 9JX (01843 581948/www.thanetonline.com/Ramsgate MotorMuseum). **Open** *Easter-Sept* 10.30am-5.30pm daily. *Oct-Easter* 10.30am-5pm Sun. **Admission** £3.50; £1-£2.50 concessions; free under-6s. **No credit cards**.

This collection of cars and motorcycles is based on a clifftop above the town with views overlooking the Channel. The exhibits date back to 1900 and the most recent is from the present day. There are ten cars from every decade including of-their-time oddities such as a 1960s bubble car and a 1980s Sinclair C5.

Shell Grotto

Grotto Hill, off Northdown Road, Margate, CT9 2BU (01843 220008). **Open** *Easter-Oct* 10am-5pm daily. *Nov-Easter* 11am-4pm Sat, Sun. **Admission** £2; £1 concessions. **Credit** MC, V.

One of Britain's most remarkable discoveries is hidden down a steep and narrow sidestreet, at the back of what looks like a shell gift shop with an original 1960s façade outside. Go to the back of the shop, however, and a small flight of circular stone stairs leads you to a mysterious subterranean shell temple, unearthed in 1835 by a young

boy who climbed down a hole at the bottom of his garden. Nobody really knows the meanings of the beautiful shell patterns, which form phallic symbols, rams' heads, solar constellations and skeletons, but H G Wells believed that the temple is around 3,000 years old. The grotto consists of a circular passage and a chamber at the back. Although small, this really is a fascinating – and ancient – pagan oddity.

Spitfire & Hurricane Memorial Building

The Airfield, Manston Road, Ramsgate, CT12 5DF (01843 821940/www.spitfire-museum.com). **Open** *Apr-Sept* 10am-5pm daily. *Oct-Mar* 10am-4pm daily. **Admission** free, donations welcome.

This patriotic museum houses Spitfires and Hurricanes, the fighter aircraft that defended the country in the Battle of Britain. There is also a Battle of Britain tapestry, exhibits that tell the story of the Dambusters, and a close view of planes taking off from Manston airstrip.

Where to stay

There are plenty of places to stay throughout the Thanet area. Margate and Ramsgate have large hotels, Broadstairs has plenty of B&Bs and there are some nice country places in the villages inland, but we recommend Whitstable as the town with the best, most characterful accommodation.

Crown Inn

Ramsgate Road, Sarre, CT7 0LF (01843 847808/ fax 01843 847914/www.shepherd-neame.co.uk). **Rates** £55 single occupancy; £75 double/twin; £110 four-poster; £90-£110 family room; £120 suite. **Rooms** (all en suite) 5 double; 3 twin; 1 four-poster; 3 family; 1 suite. **Credit** AmEx, MC, V.

A very old inn – it was built in 1492 – the Crown is a Grade I-listed building restored to its former glory as a very traditional pub and hotel with no fruit machines,

Dog-tired outside the **Royal Albion Hotel.**

jukeboxes, pub quizzes or anything brash and modern. Some of the 12 en suite bedrooms have four-poster beds, and just think, you might be sleeping in the bed that was once host to Douglas Fairbanks, Lloyd George, Mary Pickford, Room 14's ghost or, of course, Charles Dickens (that must have been one hell of a party). The fish served in the adjacent restaurant is, as you might expect, locally caught. Children welcome.

Fishermen's Huts
On the seafront near the harbour, Whitstable (01227 280280/fax 01227 280257/www.hotelcontinental. co.uk). **Rates** £85-£130 2-person hut; £100-£150 4-person hut; £150-£250 6-person hut. **Rooms** (all en suite) 2 2-person huts; 6 4-person huts (2 adults, 2 children); 1 6-person hut (4 adults, 2 children). **Credit** AmEx, DC, MC, V.
Don't be misled into thinking that this is a primitive affair: these wooden 1860s fishermen's huts, saved from dilapidation six years ago, have been turned into stylish, minimalist holiday homes complete with their own bathrooms, sofa beds, pine tables, director's chairs and cafetières. They are also based in Whitstable's prime location: slap bang on the seafront in the centre of the town, right next to many of the best restaurants. Prices include a good breakfast at the Hotel Continental (*see below*) restaurant next door (owned by the same people as the Whitstable Oyster Fishery Company). Highly recommended – and you will most likely have to book well in advance due to their popularity. All huts are no smoking and children are welcome.

Hanson Hotel
41 Belvedere Road, Broadstairs, CT10 1PF (01843 868936). **Rates** £22-£27 per person. **Rooms** 2 single; 2 twin (1 en suite); 3 double (2 en suite); 2 family (1 en suite). **No credit cards.**
Once owned by Admiral Sutherland, a contemporary of Horatio Nelson and hero of myriad seafaring battles, this is a small and friendly hotel in a Georgian mansion block. Rooms are fairly drab, but the hotel is right in the centre of town, and has the added advantage of a tiny basement bar (albeit with even more drab decor). Children and dogs welcome.

Hotel Continental
29 Beach Walk, Whitstable, CT5 2BP (01227 280280/fax 01227 280257/www.hotelcontinental. co.uk). **Rates** £49.50-£69.50 single occupancy (weekdays only); £55-£135 double; £100-£150 family room. **Rooms** (all en suite) 20 double; 3 family. **Credit** AmEx, DC, MC, V.
Whitstable's most illustrious hotel is owned by the Whitstable Oyster Fishery Company, so you are guaranteed a decent seafood dish in the restaurant here. Hidden up a small street that looks out to sea, the Continental has a garden that meets the beach, and rooms with balconies that offer a wonderfully balmy way to finish off an evening thanks to their sea view. It also has a modern, unfussy feel that makes a change from twee B&Bs or corporate country house hotels. Children welcome. All rooms are no-smoking.

Royal Albion Hotel
Albion Street, Broadstairs, CT10 1AN (01843 868071/fax 01843 861509/www.albionbroadstairs. co.uk). **Rates** £57-£79 single; £89-£112 double/ family room. **Rooms** (all en suite) 2 single; 14 double/twin; 2 family. **Credit** AmEx, DC, MC, V.
Once patronised by Charles Dickens, this is a very traditional hotel with three AA stars that could deceive you into thinking it's better than it really is: our room was drab, characterless and small. Still, staff are accommodating and friendly, and the hotel has the best location of anywhere in Broadstairs: on the promenade overlooking Viking Bay, with a garden that stretches down to the sea. The connected Marchesi's Restaurant (*see p16*), a couple of doors down, is regarded as the best in town; it gets rammed on weekends. Children welcome.

Walpole Bay Hotel
Fifth Avenue, Cliftonville, Margate, CT9 2JJ (01843 221703/fax 01843 297399/www.walpolebay hotel.co.uk). **Rates** £40-£75 single occupancy; £60-£75 double/twin/family room; £95 suite/family room; £105 four-poster/suite. **Rooms** (all en suite) 29 double/twin/family; 5 suite/family; 3 four-poster/suites. **Credit** AmEx, DC, MC, V.
This elegant, slightly kitsch seafront hotel is full of old-fashioned charm. It has its own 1920s museum, open fireplaces and ancient gas lamps in the period bedrooms, three of which have four-poster beds. Even if you don't fancy staying in Margate – and this is the best hotel in the town – it's worth dropping in for a classic cream tea. There is also a library and a picture gallery. Children and dogs welcome.

Where to eat & drink

There aren't too many pubs in the touristy part of Broadstairs, but worth visiting – in addition to the places reviewed below – are the **Dolphin** on Albion Street (01843 861056), which has live music and big screen football, and **Neptune's Hall**, on Harbour Street (01843 861400), which serves local Kentish bitter Shepherd Neame. Places to eat include **Broadstairs Tandoori** (41 Albion Street, 01843 865653) and **Chiappinis** (236 Northdown Road, Cliftonville, 01843 299388), a 1960s-style Italian café with

What the Dickens?

The good folk of Broadstairs would have you believe that Charles Dickens could not bear to be anywhere else. It's true that he described the little seaside town as 'our English watering place', but he would surely be surprised to see how boldly the town now wears its Dickens connection: there's Dickens Walk, the Old Curiosity Shop, Dickens' Pantry, Bill Sykes' Market, the Barnaby Rudge Pub, Dodgers and Quilp's restaurants... Surely one man's summer holidays have never since produced so much cottage industry.

Dickens first visited Broadstairs in 1837, at the age of 25. He was already a famous author and completed *The Pickwick Papers* while staying at 12 High Street. He returned regularly over the summers that followed.

He was certainly inspired by provincial life. He wrote most of *David Copperfield* while staying in Bleak House – then known as Fort House – and found a strong-willed local spinster, Miss Mary Pearson Strong, to be the ideal model for David Copperfield's aunt, the vitriolic but loving Betsey Trotwood. Miss Pearson Strong was a kindly old woman, who Dickens visited for tea and cakes, and who informed the author of her right to stop any donkeys that passed in front of her cottage. The incident made it into *David Copperfield*, as did a description of a cottage filled with old-fashioned furniture and a square gravelled garden

abundant with flowers, which matched Miss Pearson Strong's. Dickens did, however, move the location of Betsey Trotwood's cottage to Dover, in order to avoid any embarrassment to his friend. Known as Dickens House since the 19th century, Miss Pearson Strong's old cottage is now a museum devoted to her literary guest.

Dickens also wrote about the upper classes taking to the waters for a bathing party, while local washerwomen, given the task of washing the pantaloons of the local gentry, discuss in distinctly negative terms the nature of the strange new items they have been given to wash, 'not to mention those low-line dresses that the so-called "ladies" wear to their posh do's – talk about revealing!'

While every day is Dickens day in Broadstairs, the town really pushes out the crinoline during the Broadstairs Dickens Festival, held for nine days in mid June. Everybody dresses up in Victorian finery, and there are promenades along the seafront, croquet on the lawn and Victorian bathing parties (complete with pantaloons). It isn't only the Victorian upper classes who come to visit, though: Scruff's Day allows vagabonds and rascals to invade the town, while ladies of ill-repute, rat-catchers and stale bread-sellers entice the public to sample their dubious wares as they parade up and down the High Street.

great decor, good cappuccinos and quite nice sandwiches. The **Fish Inn** on the High Street (01843 860106) does fresh fish and chips.

Whitstable has a great pub in the **Old Neptune** (Marine Terrace, 01227 272262), which is on the seafront near the harbour. The **Harbour Street Café** (48 Harbour Street, 01227 772575) does brilliant breakfasts and an eclectic range of lunch dishes.

Margate is a town filled with fish and chip restaurants and sweet shops; try **Ye Olde Humbug & Honeycomb Shoppe** on 16 Marine Drive (01843 226745) to get into the tooth-rotting spirit. The Marketplace in the Old Town has some good restaurants, including the **Mad Hatter** (9 Lombard Street, Old Market Place, 01843 232626, only open 11.30am-3pm Sat), a blue-rinse tearoom complete with large pots of tea, 1920s tea dance music, and

year-round Christmas decorations. Right on the end of the East Pier at Margate is the **Harbour Lights Café** (01843 592224).

Ramsgate has the **Queen's Head** on Harbour Parade (01843 853888), another advantageously positioned seafront boozer with a pretty Victorian tile and sculpted brick façade, while the nearby **Harvey's Crab & Oyster House** (Harbour Parade, 01843 591110) is a pub with the best seafood in town.

Dove Inn

Plum Pudding Lane, Margate, ME13 9HB (01227 751360). **Food served** noon-2pm Tue; noon-2pm, 7-9pm Wed-Sat; noon-2pm Sun. **Main courses** £10.95-£18. **Credit** MC, V.

The Dove is one of the best gastropubs in Kent, and has a Michelin star to prove it. The scrubbed interior has modernised the Victorian building in some measure, but it still retains a country pub atmosphere. The cooking, too, retains this balance, with imaginative modern dishes that are nevertheless firmly rooted in the French classical tradition. A fresh, well-presented main of whole plaice with capers, and another of guinea fowl came with new potatoes and a selection of vibrant vegetables. Moderate-sized servings left room for cherry clafoutis. Ordering à la carte isn't cheap, although less expensive options are available from the blackboard menu. Still, the quality of food and wine is high, Shepherd Neame ales are available on tap, there's a beautiful garden and the owners are welcoming.

Gate Inn

Marshside, Chislet, CT3 4EB (01227 860498). **Food served** 11am-2pm, 6-9pm Mon-Sat; noon-2pm, 7-9pm Sun. **Main courses** £3.35-£5.95. **No credit cards.**
Another Shepherd Neame pub, this country inn is dominated by a huge open hearth at the centre of the bar and has a large, secluded garden that ends in a stream populated by geese and ducks. Along with traditional home-cooked bar meals, there are dominos inside and games of rounders outside. On most weekends a large number of birdwatchers and ramblers take a break from patrolling the nearby Chesney Marshes to pop in for a pint. About as close to the popular imagination's idea of a country pub as you could hope for.

Marchesi's Restaurant

16-18 Albion Street, Broadstairs, CT10 1LU (01843 862481/www.marchesi.co.uk). **Food served** noon-2pm, 6.30-9.30pm Tue-Sat; noon-2pm Sun. **Main courses** £9.95-£19.50. **Credit** AmEx, MC, V.
Established in 1866, this Broadstairs institution claims to be England's oldest family-owned restaurant and is still the most popular place in town for the locals. The decor is very traditional and not hugely inspiring, but the views of the sea are magnificent, and on a warm summer's evening the balcony tables make for a romantic evening rendezvous. The menu is solidly Franco-British: starters include salmon gâteau topped with smoked salmon and lemon dressing, and Caesar salad with seared chicken breast; mains might feature pan-fried calf's liver with bacon and garlic butter, and roast fillet of local cod in a mild curried sauce.

Osteria Posillipo Pizzeria

14 Albion Street, Broadstairs, CT10 1LU (01843 601133). **Food served** *Jan-May, Sept-Dec* noon-3pm, 6-10.30pm daily. *July, Aug* noon-3pm, 6-10.30pm Mon, Wed-Sun. **Main courses** £6.95-£15.95. **Credit** AmEx, DC, MC, V.
Sandwiched between Marchesi's (*see above*) and the Royal Albion (*see p14*) is this decent Italian restaurant, which specialises, naturally, in seafood, and has an unpretentious rustic feel. Linguini Posillipo – with clams, king prawns and mussels in a white wine sauce – is the best bet for a local catch, while the Dover sole in olive oil and lemon was delicate and well cooked. It's well positioned for an after-dinner stroll, too: Viking Bay is just below. Broadstairs used to have a large Italian community; this is one of its last remaining outposts.

Pearson's Crab & Oyster House

Horsebridge, Whitstable, CT5 1BT (01227 272005/ fax 01227 282115). **Food served** noon-2.30pm, 6.30-10pm Mon-Sat; noon-10pm Sun. **Main courses** £8.95-£21.95. **Credit** MC, V.

The first-floor restaurant of this traditional seafront pub has stiff competition. It is right next door to the Whitstable Oyster Fishery Company (*see below*), but its own take on local seafood is pretty good, and many favour it for a more intimate meal. The young staff are keen, and the seafood and fish are superb: a huge platter features the best oysters you could wish for, plus wonderful langoustines, crab, clams, king prawns and cockles, served with rice and salad. A swordfish steak with salsa was fresh – which swordfish often isn't – and delicate. The pub itself is fairly uninspiring, but don't be put off by initial appearances: this is a lovely place.

Tartar Frigate

Harbour Street, Broadstairs, CT10 1EU (01843 862013). **Food served** noon-2pm, 7-9.30pm Mon-Sat; noon-4pm Sun. **Main courses** £13-£17. **Set meals** (Mon-Fri) £13 2 courses, £16 3 courses, (Sun lunch) £14.95 3 courses. **Credit** AmEx, MC, V.
On Broadstairs' little harbour and at the beginning of Viking Bay, this 17th-century flint inn specialises in fish. Many of the dishes have Mediterranean tinges, such as mozzarella and skate or pan-fried monkfish, and all of the fish is fresh and locally caught.

Wheelers Oyster Bar

8 High Street, Whitstable, CT5 1BQ (01227 273311/www.whitstable-shellfish.co.uk). **Meals served** 1-7.30pm Mon, Tue, Thur-Sat; 1-7pm Sun. **Main courses** £5-£18. **No credit cards.**
The pink façade is a Whitstable landmark, and Wheelers has been a purveyor of native oysters for 150 years. When Mark Stubbs took over the kitchen, locals struggled to keep secret his wonderful way with fish. Why? The seafood bar seats four people, while the back-room restaurant has just three tables. Here lobster ravioli with baby leeks, aged parmesan and broad bean cappuccino or pan-fried skate wing, beurre noisette, salsa verde croquettes and steamed vegetables stuffed with mint and basil ratatouille are delivered with a cosmopolitan finesse. No licence (but no corkage) keeps the bill in line, and if it's fully booked there's consolation in seafood tarts, fish cakes and fresh shellfish to take away.

Whitstable Oyster Fishery Company

The Royal Native Oyster Stores, Horsebridge, Whitstable, CT5 1BU (01227 276856/www. oysterfishery.co.uk). **Lunch served** noon-1.45pm Tue-Sat; noon-2.30pm Sun. **Dinner served** 7-8.45pm Tue-Sat; 6.30-8.15pm Sun. **Main courses** £12.50-£25. **Credit** AmEx, DC, MC, V.
The Oyster Fishery restaurant was the old company headquarters and is now the most atmospheric place in town to sample the local speciality. The restaurant's reputation is deserved, but the draw is as much the setting as the food, with a sublime sea view (and stunning sunsets). And there's the classic yet modern decor – red and white checked tablecloths, exposed brickwork and old photos of fishermen on the walls. The menu changes regularly. This time around, scallops, for starters, were perfectly cooked in garlic butter. Mains were also good: skate was simply but classically prepared with black butter and capers; organic salmon was char-grilled and accompanied by a salsa verde. Chocolate and walnut brownie was generous in flavour, but stingy in size.

Canterbury

Join the pilgrims.

Canterbury has a long history as a short-break destination. Its distinct character has been shaped by the need to accommodate the thousands of pilgrims who converged on the city throughout the Middle Ages. Visitors still flock here in vast numbers to explore the city, and particularly its magnificent cathedral, which dominates the skyline.

It was also shaped by a need to protect itself from attack. Parts of its city wall still survive, along with the Westgate at the end of St Dunstan's Street, constructed in the 14th century and originally one of eight gates that were built into the wall.

Even a brief introduction to Canterbury's history reveals its profound religious and cultural significance. The revival of Christianity (after its rapid decline when the Romans left in the fifth century) took place here, when Pope Gregory of Rome sent St Augustine to Canterbury in 596 to convert the Anglo-Saxon peoples who had settled in the ruins of the Roman town. The city thereafter became the nucleus of religious activity in England, and a place of great power and wealth, as well as an important centre of learning. It was the murder of Thomas Becket in the cathedral in 1170, and his subsequent elevation to sainthood, that turned it into a major centre of pilgrimage (see p23 **To be a pilgrim**). Its crucial role in religious, educational and economic life continued for centuries.

Despite all this, the city today can feel surprisingly provincial. It sank out of national prominence in the late 1500s (when Henry VIII dissolved the monasteries) and became a quiet market town; its atmosphere today is paradoxically both small-town and cosmopolitan. The University of Kent, built on the outskirts in the 1960s, draws many international students to the city, and has re-established it as a centre of learning, but the place still seems to lack the refinement of other great historical cities. However, it's precisely the absence of pretension, as well as its manageable size, that make Canterbury's historical treasures so enticing. The place has also had an air of renewal over the past decade, with the biggest project to date – the £10 million Whitefriars development – currently in full swing. Ugly concrete buildings knocked up in this quarter after the devastating German

bombing of 1942 have now been demolished, with buildings more sensitive to Canterbury's environment being constructed in their place. In the process, archaeologists have been busy uncovering artefacts from the layers below, and with Canterbury as a settlement dating back to pre-Roman times, the pickings have been rich.

Visitors today can enjoy improved museums, ancient buildings, copious numbers of pubs and restaurants, a mix of mainstream and quirky shopping, and extensive pedestrianisation. Any visit will be rewarding, but it's best to come off-season to avoid the hordes of language-school students who saturate the centre, although pretty gardens and quiet backstreets such as Palace Street and Stour Street make peaceable escapes from the fray in the summer months.

What to do and see

Tourist Information Centre
12/13 Sun Street, The Buttermarket, CT1 2HX (01227 378100/www.canterbury.co.uk). **Open** *Jan-Mar* 9.30am-5pm Mon-Sat. *Apr-Dec* 9.30am-5pm Mon-Sat; 10am-4pm Sun.

Canterbury Castle
Castle Street (info line 01227 378100/www. canterbury.co.uk). **Open** 8am-dusk daily. **Admission** free.
The shell is all that remains of the Norman castle, built after William the Conqueror's invasion. But the brick-work still provides clues to where the various doorways, dungeons and staircases once stood, evoking the once-great structure that was attacked by Wat Tyler and his revolting peasants in 1381.

Canterbury Cathedral
The Precincts, CT1 2EH (01227 762862/ www.canterbury-cathedral.org). **Open** *Cathedral & crypt* Easter-Sept 9am-5pm Mon-Sat; 12.30-2.30pm,

By train from London

Trains to **Canterbury East** leave **Victoria** every half-hour (journey time 1hr 25mins). Trains to **Canterbury West** leave **Charing Cross** hourly (journey time 1hr 25mins). Info: www.connex.co.uk. (In 2004 services will be taken over by South Eastern Trains; timetables should not be affected).

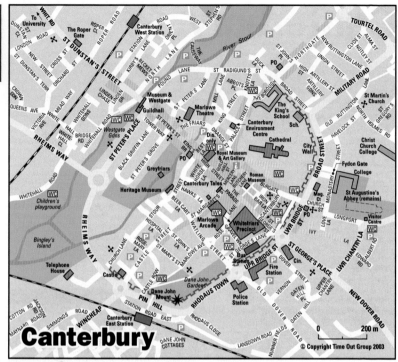

Canterbury

DANE JOHN
COTTAGES

© Copyright Time Out Group 2003

0   200 m

4.30-5.30pm Sun. Oct-Easter 9am-4.30pm Mon-Sat; 12.30-2.30pm, 4.30-5.30pm Sun. During evensong certain parts of cathedral are closed. **Admission** £4; £3 concessions; free under-5s. **Credit** MC, V.

The cathedral is the centrepiece of the city, and justifiably so. From the splendour of the 16th-century Christ Church Gate in the Buttermarket, which serves as the entry point, the cathedral rises up before you, with Bell Harry tower soaring heavenward some 250ft. Augustine first established a cathedral here in AD 602; the current incarnation was begun by Archbishop Lanfranc in 1070. To see what remains, descend to the huge crypt to view the fine pillars with intricate capitals and carved columns.

On reappearing in the north transept, note the Altar of the Sword's Point, the site of Becket's gruesome end (amputation *and* scalping) at the hands of those four cursed knights. The main nave of the building dates from around 1400; its intricate lierne vaulting (a complex form of ribbed vaulting) is its finest feature, although this is more than matched by the magnificent fan vaulting beneath Bell Harry. Other essential viewing includes the tombs of the Black Prince and Edward the Confessor in the Trinity Chapel at the eastern end, and, outside, the magnificent cloisters and Green Court overlooked by King's School. The cathedral is at its most magical just before dusk, with a recital reverberating from within, and the otherwise ubiquitous coach parties long gone.

Canterbury Tales

St Margaret's Street, CT1 2TG (01227 454888/ info line 01227 479227/www.canterburytales.org.uk). **Open** *Mid Feb-June, Sept, Oct* 10am-5pm daily. *July, Aug* 9.30am-5pm daily. *Nov-mid Feb* 10am-4.30pm daily. **Admission** £6.75; £5.25-£5.75 concessions; free under-4s. **Credit** MC, V.

Chaucer's tales brought to life by waxwork models, medieval smells and Bernard Cribbins reading through your headset as you stroll around. Clunking mechanical sets cleverly evoke the spirit of the tales, and although young children might struggle to concentrate on the actual storytelling the sound and lighting effects should hold the attention of most. An excellent introduction to Chaucer's work. Lasts 45 minutes.

Dane John Garden

Entrance on Watling Street.

Music festivals and French markets are sometimes held in this historic park. It's bordered on one side by the city wall and on the other by some lovely Georgian houses; a tree-lined path cuts through the centre. Another path spirals up a grass-covered 'mound' (a former motte) next to a children's play area.

Eastbridge Hospital

25 High Street, CT1 2BD (01227 471688). **Open** 10am-4.45pm Mon-Sat. **Admission** £1; 50p-75p concessions; free under-5s. **No credit cards**.

A hospital in the original sense of the word (a place of hospitality), the Eastbridge was established in the 12th century to provide lodging for poor pilgrims and, remarkably, it still provides accommodation for the elderly and disadvantaged of today. Basic display boards explain the hospital's history and the chapel upstairs contains a 12th-century mural of Christ. The medieval atmosphere that reverberates around the stone walls is by itself worth the paltry entrance fee.

Greyfriars
Entrance on Stour Street (01227 471688). **Open** *Easter-Sept* 2-4pm Mon-Sat. Closed Oct-Easter. **Admission** free; donations welcome.
This 13th-century structure, on the edge of a well-kept garden, straddles the River Stour. It's the only part of the original Franciscan monastery that's still standing and its isolated position contributes to a sense of the spiritual that can be hard to feel in the beautiful but often crowded cathedral.

Museum of Canterbury
Stour Street, CT1 2NR (01227 475202/01227 452747/www.canterbury-museums.co.uk). **Open** *June-Sept* 10.30am-5pm Mon-Sat; 1.30-5.30pm Sun. *Oct-May* 10.30am-5pm Mon-Sat. Last entry 1hr before closing. **Admission** £3; £2 concessions; free under-5s. **No credit cards**.
The best museum devoted to Canterbury's history. A series of well laid-out displays documents the emergence of the modern city, beginning with the establishment of the Roman town, and ending with the destruction of significant areas of the city during World War II. There are also displays dedicated to less well-known historical events, such as the establishment of the Canterbury to Whitstable steam railway in 1830 (the first passenger railway in the world). The 30-minute video on Becket's life and death is entertaining and informative. The Rupert Bear room, in honour of his creator, Canterbury-born Mary Tourtel, is slightly overdone. More on Joseph Conrad (who lived in Canterbury) and Christopher Marlowe (who was born here) would have been just as apt but more interesting.

Roman Museum
Butchery Lane, CT1 2JR (01227 785575/www. canterbury-museums.co.uk). **Open** *Nov-May* 10am-5pm Mon-Sat. *June-Oct* 10am-5pm Mon-Sat; 1.30-5pm Sun. Last entry 1hr before closing. **Admission** £2.70; £1.70 concessions; free under-5s. **No credit cards**.
A record of Durovernum Cantiacorum (the Roman name for Canterbury), this carefully arranged museum focuses as much on the archaeological process as the finds themselves. Built around the mosaic floor of a Roman townhouse (excavated during the Longmarket development a decade or so ago), it features computer displays, waxwork installations depicting Roman life and a 'hands-on' area, with samples and replicas of Roman artefacts.

Royal Museum & Art Gallery
High Street, CT1 2RA (01227 452747/www. canterbury-museums.co.uk). **Open** 10am-5pm Mon-Sat. **Admission** free; donations welcome.
Porcelain, Roman glass, military memorabilia and a chaotic collection of paintings take up the first floor of the Beaney Institute, an eccentric Victorian building that

also houses the public library. Thomas Sydney Cooper's 19th-century cattle portraits are the most notable of the permanent works, and temporary exhibitions display work by local artists.

St Augustine's Abbey
Longport, CT1 1TF (01227 767345/www.english-heritage.org.uk). **Open** *Apr-Sept* 10am-6pm daily. *Oct* 10am-5pm daily. *Nov-Mar* 10am-4pm daily. **Admission** (EH) £3; £1.50-£2.30 concessions; free under-5s. **Credit** MC, V.
The remains of this historic abbey are laid out in a site outside the city walls. Following King Ethelbert's conversion to Christianity by St Augustine in the sixth century, he gave land to the Benedictine monk to found this abbey. Archbishop Lanfranc rebuilt the abbey in the 11th century, and it flourished until the dissolution of the monasteries by Henry VIII in 1538, when it was converted into royal lodgings. An informative audio tour escorts you around the ruins (now protected by English Heritage), drawing a picture of the monastery in its prime. The remarkably tranquil setting gives a good opportunity to reflect on where it all began. The abbey, along with the cathedral and St Martin's Church, was pronounced a UNESCO World Heritage Site in 1988. The three sites make up Queen Bertha's walk, named after King Ethelbert's Christian wife.

St Martin's Church
North Holmes Road, CT1 3AR (01227 768072). **Open** 10am-3pm Tue, Thur; 10am-1pm Sat. Other times by arrangement. Sun services 9am, 6.30pm. **Admission** free; donations welcome.

Canterbury Cathedral. *See p17.*

This beautiful small church is reputed to be the oldest parish church in continuous use in England. It is thought to have been established in the sixth century, when Bertha, the Christian wife of the Anglo-Saxon King of Kent, Ethelbert, sought a place to worship. What remains is mainly 13th and 14th century – look out for the font and the replica Chrismatory (a tiny chest for holy oils, set into the north wall). In the stepped graveyard are buried Mary Tourtel (the creator of Rupert Bear; directions to the grave are pinned up in the church) and Thomas Sydney Cooper (artist).

Westgate Museum

St Peter's Street (01227 789576/452747/ www.canterbury-museums.co.uk). **Open** 11am-12.30pm, 1.30-3.30pm Mon-Sat. **Admission** £1; 65p concessions. **No credit cards.**

Although there's been a gate on this site since the third century, the current twin towers were erected in 1380, when fear of a French invasion prompted stronger fortification. As the last remaining example of the gates of the medieval walls (the other seven were demolished in 1787), the Westgate survived because of its conversion into a prison (its cells were still in use until 1829). Climb the spiral steps to the roof for fine views of the city.

Where to stay

Despite all those medieval buildings begging to have tasteful, quirky – or just plain historic – hotels, Canterbury's accommodation options are pretty run of the mill. Staying in is not the point here. That said, it's worth paying more for a berth within or near to the walls, as neither parking nor public transport are much fun.

It's not a good idea to arrive in town without a reservation, but if you find yourself stuck, your best bet is to cruise the strip of B&Bs that run along London Road, or the more institutional B&Bs and hotels at the town end of the New Dover Road.

Acacia Lodge & Tanglewood

39-40 London Road, CT2 8LF (01227 769955/ fax 01227 478960/www.acacialodge.com). **Rates** £30-£40 single occupancy; £43-£50 double/twin. **Rooms** (all en suite) 2 double; 1 twin. **Credit** MC, V.

Maria Cain, affable proprietor of Tanglewood, took over the neighbouring Acacia Lodge in 2000, combining the 1880s farm cottages into a single B&B. The properties share a living area and dining room, where a proper breakfast (lots of choice, with different diets catered for) is served. Rooms are not large, but they're homely, traditionally furnished and spotlessly clean. Self-catering accommodation is also available in an old school building (Dunstan's Court) on the opposite side of the road. It's a ten-minute walk to the centre of town, but low prices compensate, and Maria used to work as a guide, so information and recommendations come free. Children over three welcome. No smoking throughout.

Cathedral Gate Hotel

36 Burgate, CT1 2HA (01227 464381/fax 01227 462800). **Rates** £25-£44 single; £48-£88 double; £68-£111 triple; £58-£111 family. Breakfast £7 (Eng).

Rooms 10 single (4 en suite); 8 double (4 en suite); 3 triple (1 en suite); 2 family (both en suite). **Credit** AmEx, DC, MC, V.

Short of taking the cloth, you won't get to sleep a lot closer to the cathedral than here. In fact, if the bells are ringing, you won't get to sleep at all. The building is historically significant, being part of the old Sun Inn, popular with medieval pilgrims. It could be argued that the Cathedral Gate is resting on its location laurels: although its winding corridors and plainly decorated rooms with random original features are charming, some of the furnishings are a little scruffy, the facilities ageing, not all the bathrooms are en suite and breakfast is only continental if you stump up an extra £7. Such quibbles pale into insignificance if you're one of the lucky ones with a cathedral view, for which there's no extra cost. Another downside: there's no private parking; the nearest car park is on Broad Street, at the end of Burgate. Children and dogs are welcome.

Coach House

34 Watling Street, CT1 2UD (01227 784324). **Rates** £30-£35 single occupancy; £45-£50 double; £65-£80 family room. **Rooms** 2 double; 4 family. **No credit cards.**

A plain, graceful Georgian building near the Whitefriars development, the Coach House is something of an antidote to the city's other institutionalised B&Bs. It has an unaffected personal touch: staying here is a bit like staying with friends, if, that is, your friends have pleasantly magpie tastes. A 'lived-in' atmosphere is provided by the cat and young children. The rooms are large (particularly the family rooms) and clean, and there's a sweet garden where you can have breakfast. Good value. Children and dogs welcome.

County Hotel

High Street, CT1 2RX (01227 766266/fax 01227 451512/www.macdonaldhotels.co.uk). **Rates** £70-£112 single; £80-£120 double/twin; £100-£150 four-poster/deluxe; £120-£160 suite. **Rooms** (all en suite) 1 single; 27 twin; 31 double; 4 four-poster; 10 deluxe; 1 suite. **Credit** AmEx, DC, MC, V.

The County achieves comfort rather than greatness: with mainly Victorian origins it is neither particularly historically significant nor architecturally interesting. But the bedrooms are tastefully done in restrained rusts, ochres and woods, the dressing gowns are fluffy, and Sully's restaurant, beloved of wedding groups (late-night revellers are an occupational hazard in the bar) is a comfortable place for breakfast if a little institutional for dinner. And you're smack bang in the centre of town too. Children and dogs (£10 per stay) welcome.

Falstaff Hotel

8-10 St Dunstan's Street, CT2 8AF (01227 462138/fax 01227 463525/www.corushotels.co.uk). **Rates** £100 single; £110 double/twin; £140 four-poster/family/suite rooms. Breakfast £10.50 (Eng); £7.50 (cont). **Rooms** (all en suite) 9 single; 23 double/twin; 3 four-poster/suite; 1 family. **Credit** AmEx, DC, MC, V.

Canterbury's loveliest historic hotel – a 15th-century coaching inn just outside the Westgate – has done a fine job of reconciling its chain-hotel present with its manifold period charms. Peep through the little lead-lined windows into the tastefully countrified beamed lounge

Waxing lyrical at the **Canterbury Tales**, where life-size models take on Chaucer. *See p18*.

and you'd expect to find a handful of charmingly wonky oak-lined rooms off creaky corridors. As indeed you do, 25 of them (three with four-posters), and lots more at the back in two converted annexes, all furnished in modern comfortable style. All the usual hotel facilities are available – plus good-value room service of simple dishes. And if there's no genial innkeeper of the kind Falstaff would have appreciated, at least there are well-trained staff. The main complaint is that the dining room doesn't have the seating capacity to serve increased guest numbers, resulting in too-long waits. Children welcome.

Magnolia House

36 St Dunstan's Terrace, CT2 8AX (tel/fax 01227 765121/http://freespace.virgin.net/magnolia. canterbury). **Rates** £55-£65 single; £85-£110 double/twin; £125 four-poster. **Rooms** (all en suite) 1 single; 4 double; 1 twin; 1 four-poster. **Credit** AmEx, DC, MC, V.

The Magnolia is the doyenne of Canterbury B&Bs, with stars and awards aplenty, accommodating hosts who really look after you, a small but tranquil garden with many tropical plants, and bristling standards of cleanliness. You get tea on arrival, and there are generous home-cooked breakfasts too. The rooms are all a bit floral, but are comfortable and reasonably sized (the largest, the Garden Room, has a four-poster bed and corner bath). Magnolia House's great bonus is its location: St Dunstan's Terrace, ten-minutes' walk from the centre, is one of the loveliest residential streets in the city. Children over 12 welcome. No smoking throughout.

Miller's Arms

2 Mill Lane, CT1 2AW (01227 456057/fax 01227 452421/www.shepherdneame.co.uk). **Rates** £45 single; £60 double/twin; £70 kingsize/family room;

£80 suite. **Rooms** (all en suite) 2 single; 3 double; 3 twin; 1 kingsize; 1 family; 1 four-poster suite. **Credit** AmEx, MC, V.

Situated in a calm yet central area of the city, on the site of the old water mill, this popular Shepherd Neame pub provides accommodation in the relaxed upper floors of the house. The rooms look out on to the cathedral, or, on the opposite side, the river (not as idyllic as it could be, due to the amount of rubbish it traps). All 11 rooms are clean and pleasantly furnished, all have TVs, and although the pub below is often heaving on Friday and Saturday nights, the noise doesn't reach upstairs. Children welcome.

Where to eat & drink

Eating options in Canterbury are plentiful and varied, and although the overall quality isn't especially high, the recently opened Goods Shed, together with Augustine's (now firmly established), have started a positive trend. Most of the chain and touristy restaurants, of the likes of Pizza Express, Zizzi's, ASK and Café Uno, are huddled together around Best Lane and King's Bridge (where St Peter's Street turns into the High Street). Some of the hotels mentioned above, such as the **Falstaff** (*see p21*) and the **County** (*see p21*), have decent menus if rather bland dining rooms.

In addition to our selections below, best central bets for lunch are **Jacques** (71 Castle Street, 01227 781000), a cosy bistro with an imaginative menu, **Bar 11** (11-12 Burgate, 01227 478707), which has an extensive meat-heavy selection, and **Café St Pierre** (41 St Peter's Street, 01227 456791), a small French bakery with a few tables at the back. Or try **Il Pozzo** (15 Best Lane, 01227 450154), **Tue E Mio** (16 The Borough, 01227 761471) or **Lloyds** (89-90 St Dunstan's Street, 01227 768222) for upmarket evening dining.

Since the opening of a club on the university campus, the city centre can be eerily quiet, even on a Friday or Saturday evening. However, with a pub-based nightlife, it's still possible to have a good night out in Canterbury. Needless to say, the city hasn't escaped the purchasing power of the big chains, but best bets for historic boozers that still have some genuine atmosphere are the **Thomas Becket** on Best Lane, the **White Hart Inn** just off Castle Row (very popular on sunny days due to its big beer garden), the recently refurbished **Blind Dog** on Rosemary Lane, the **Canterbury Tales** down the Friars, and a handful of pleasant pubs around St Radigund's Street, most notably **Simple Simon's**. All serve food. Outside the city walls, best bets are the **Bishop's Finger** on St Dunstan's Street, popular despite looking a bit newer on the inside than its 16th-century origins suggest; and the low-key local the **Unicorn**, a bit further on.

For late-night drinking, **Alberry's** on St Margaret's Street, with its cellar bar, is still a magnet for the post-pub crowd due to its late licence (you'll have to queue to get in if you arrive after 10.30pm). **Ha! Ha! Bar & Canteen** (01227 379800) opposite is popular with the Ben Sherman shirts brigade.

Augustine's

1-2 Longport, Canterbury, CT1 1PE (01227 453063). **Food served** noon-1.30pm, 6.30-9pm Tue-Sat; noon-1.30pm Sun. **Main courses** £9.50-£15.90. **Set lunch** (Tue-Sat) £10.95, (Sun) £19.50, 3 courses. **Credit** AmEx, MC, V.

This family-run restaurant gets everything right, offering one of the finest dining experiences to be found in the city. Friendly and unobtrusive service, culinary expertise and beautifully presented dishes (at reasonable prices) ensure maximum satisfaction levels. After ordering from the reassuringly short menu in the bar area, you're escorted to your table in the formal yet homely dining area decorated with attractive paintings. On a recent visit, moules normande (mussels with Breton cider and cream) was wonderfully fresh, and the juices provided an excellent mopping-up opportunity. Next, pan-fried sea bass with a crisp potato crust came with a tasty tomato fondue and lemon butter sauce, while confit of duck was served on a rich mushroom risotto. Dessert didn't let the side down: the tangy lemon tart (the house speciality) was sublime.

To be a pilgrim

'And specially, from every shires ende Of Engelond, to Caunterbury they wende...'

The murder of Thomas Becket, Archbishop of Canterbury, in 1170, by four knights hoping to curry favour with King Henry VII is one of the most graphically recounted events in European history. A story of a conflict of power between Crown and Church, one of its most interesting aspects is the affect of Becket's death on the city.

Within a few years of the murder, it had became the most important place of pilgrimage in Europe, as thousands flocked to Becket's shrine in the cathedral seeking absolution or miracles from the martyr. A pilgrimage was also the chance to enjoy a change of scene – the medieval equivalent of a holiday. Dozens of inns were built to accommodate the visitors, and new eateries and souvenir shops opened, turning Canterbury into a crowded and prosperous commercial centre.

The pilgrimages continued for over 300 years (until Becket's tomb was destroyed during the Reformation), and have been immortalised by Geoffrey Chaucer in his 14th-century classic of English literature *The Canterbury Tales*, which depicts the journey from Southwark to Canterbury Cathedral made by a diverse group of everyday medieval characters.

The presence of such pilgrims transformed Canterbury, and created a legacy that survives to this day. Many medieval buildings that housed pilgrims' inns are still standing (there are several in the Buttermarket area), and Chaucer's contribution to the city's reputation is hard to avoid. The city's tourist industry is currently being given a big push, with the Kent Tourism Alliance seeking to recreate the past by making Canterbury the capital of short breaks once again.

So the city has come full circle, with visitors flocking here to visit the cathedral, wander the streets and to shop and eat – following in the footsteps of pilgrims past.

Join the merry throng at the **Goods Shed**, a cavernous restaurant and farmers' market.

Bistro Vietnam

The Old Linen Store, Whitehorse Lane, CT1 2RU
(01227 760022). **Food served** noon-2pm, 7-9.30pm
Mon-Sat; 7-9pm Sun. Phone to confirm last orders.
Main courses £8.75-£10. **Credit** AmEx, DC, MC, V.
Although something has been lost, atmospherically,
since Bistro Vietnam's move from Castle Street to its
current location – the lemon walls, orange wooden
beams, pine floor and modern art are more IKEA than
Vietnam – it's still a popular choice for locals. The standard of the cooking is often nothing more than adequate,
but the ingredients are fresh and the staff friendly and
obliging. When ordering mains, you'll be asked how
spicy you'd like your dish on a scale of 1 to 10. Best to
stay on the side of caution, as even a 4 has plenty of kick.
The highlight of a recent meal came at the end: the own-
made pear ice-cream was delicious.

Café des Amis du Mexique

95 St Dunstan's Street, CT2 8AA (01227 464390).
Food served noon-10pm Mon-Sat; noon-9.30pm
Sun. **Main courses** £6.95-£14.95. **Credit** AmEx,
MC, V.
A long-standing favourite, the draw here is as much the
upbeat atmosphere as the food. However, the zest of the
dishes surpass standard Mexican fare, and the occasional French twist adds originality: seafood and lamb
dishes can be found next to enchiladas and burritos.
Several dishes are made with sharing in mind. It's best
to book in the evening as the place gets very busy.

The Goods Shed

Station Road West, CT2 8AN (01227 459153).
Food served noon-2.30pm, 6-9.30pm Tue-Fri; noon-
3pm, 6-9.30pm Sat; noon-3pm Sun. **Main courses**
£8-£16. **Credit** MC, V.

A disused Victorian engine shed has been renovated to
house this appealing restaurant and attendant farmers'
market. The high-vaulted ceiling, exposed brickwork
and huge cream doors create a huge and harmonious
space that reflects the ethos of the place. Wooden tables
overlook the market from a raised platform, and the gentle activity from those perusing the stalls coupled with
natural light from big, arched windows creates the perfect mood for a leisurely lunch. When we ate here
recently we loved the fresh and creamy moules
marinière, although another starter of mushroom soup
was a little thin. For mains, roasted red mullet was
carefully prepared and flavourful, and the generous
vegetable platter – the only vegetarian option – was delicious. The Goods Shed is a propelling force behind the
city's burgeoning food scene.

Tapas

13 Palace Street, CT1 2DZ (01227 762637).
Food served noon-3pm, 6-10pm Mon-Fri;
noon-10pm Sat, Sun. **Main courses** £4.95-£8.75.
Credit AmEx, MC, V.
The atmosphere here is authentic (think stone floors,
low-beamed ceilings and Spanish guitar music) and the
menu traditional, with patatas bravas, Spanish omelette,
paella (strangely, *sin mariscos*) and calamaras fritos all
present and correct. None of the dishes was outstandingly fresh when we called in, but all were tasty enough,
and this is a good venue if you need to satisfy a range
of appetites (there are three size choices for each dish
making sharing an option). The waitresses seemed
strangely tired when we visited (there were two plate
crashes, and our coffee didn't materialise); we wondered
if they could have been at the rioja. Despite that, Tapas
is still a reasonable bet for lunch, with a decent wine list
and sangria by the pitcher.

Sandwich
to Sandgate

The white cliffs of Dover and beyond.

Not many places can boast such a rich heritage as this historically significant stretch of coastline – England's front line. Celt warriors fended off a Roman invasion by Julius Caesar in 55 BC; it was not until AD 43, under the rule of Emperor Claudius, that the Romans succeeded in establishing themselves on British soil. **Dover** was their most strategic naval fort. To this day, the remains of the lighthouse, fort and *vicus* (hotel) are in evidence.

In the 14th century Dover was one of the Cinque Ports, a series of Kentish coastal towns that provided ships and men to protect against invasion, in return for privileges such as exemptions from tax. During the Napoleonic Wars, it became a garrison town. The castle defences were altered to hold heavy guns, and in 1804 gun batteries and deep brick-lined ditches were built, which remain to this day.

Sandwich: it's better bred

At the north end of this region is **Sandwich**. Sitting on the River Stour, this now-landlocked former port is still very much a small medieval town, with half timber-framed houses lining the narrow streets. Overlooking the grassy banks of the Stour is the town's most celebrated building, the fine 16th-century Barbican. Not far away are the golden sands and famous Royal St George's golf course of Sandwich Bay. North of the town, set in bleak Pegwell Bay, are the remains of **Richborough Roman Fort**, one-time sentinel over the southern entrance of the Wantsum Channel, which once cut off the Isle of Thanet from the rest of Kent.

By train from London

Trains for **Sandwich** leave **Charing Cross** every 30mins, passing through **Dover Priory** (journey time 1hr 40mins). Trains to **Dover** also run from **Victoria** hourly (journey time 1hr 50mins) and pass through Canterbury East. Info: www.connex.co.uk. (Services will be taken over by South Eastern trains in 2004; timetables should not be affected.)

Moving south, the contiguous low-key resort towns of **Deal** and **Walmer** are notable chiefly for their Tudor castles (Henry VIII added both to the list of Cinque Ports). It's a fine 45-minute coastal walk between the two of them. Deal's winding streets – although now lined with antiques emporiums, hardware stores, an old-fashioned sweet shop and an excellent second-hand bookshop – bring to mind its reputation as an erstwhile smugglers' den.

Those white cliffs

During World War II, Dover's cliffs concealed the wartime operations unit where Admiral Ramsey and Winston Churchill planned the Dunkirk evacuation. The tunnels beneath the striking castle can be explored and are one of the area's most worthwhile attractions. The **Dover Museum** (01304 201066/www. dovermuseum.co.uk) traces the history of the town from the Bronze Age to the present day with dioramas, paintings, models and artefacts. There is also a new Bronze Age boat gallery, centred on the remains of a 3,500-year-old boat. Close by, the **Roman Painted House** (New Street, 01304 203279), discovered in 1970, is impressively well preserved with chunks of frescoed walls, hypocaust heating system and brickwork. Also worth a visit is the **Old Town Gaol** (Biggin Street, 01304 242766), where staff will happily let you try out a cell and lock the door. Somewhat surprisingly, there's also decent shopping at **De Bradelei Wharf** (01304 226616), where designer wear is sold at huge discounts. Despite these historical and consumer attractions, the town has a decided lack of charm and down-at-heel feel; poverty and publicity surrounding conflicts between residents and asylum seekers have combined to create a picture of a town with problems.

A few miles up the coast, **St Margaret's Bay**, with its villas clinging to the chalk cliffs, is a splendidly dramatic spot from which to watch the sea, best enjoyed off-season when the car park and the neighbouring pub are empty. Beware the precipitous drive down, though. The village just above it, **St Margaret's at Cliffe**, is very pretty and quiet and has several venerable inns. Away from the coast, **Kearsney Abbey** at River, on the road between Dover and Folkestone, is a great spot for walks (it has no ecclesiastical connections at all, having been built for a banker in 1820).

Folkestone and Sandgate

Folkestone and **Sandgate** are virtually one and the same, though Sandgate, with its antiques shops and rows of bright Victorian villas facing the sea, is more well-to-do. After the crippling decline of its ferry crossings, and despite the proximity of the entrance to the Channel Tunnel, Folkestone is struggling to get back on track. The town is in limbo, caught between trendification and recession – with once-charming shops closing down amid garish new cafés and bars. One reminder of days gone by is Rowlands Confectionery in Old High Street, where the rock is still rolled out and cut. A more offbeat attraction is the **Russian Submarine** moored on the south quay (01303 240400). It can be hired for parties.

Otherwise stroll along the Leas, the town's main attraction. It's a magnificent Edwardian boardwalk, full of entertainment sites, including the **Rotunda** (01303 245245), a quaint 1950s amusement complex, and the **Metropole Arts Centre**, which offers brilliant children's activities and events (01303 255070). Then take the quirky water-powered chairlift down to the shingle below.

What to see & do

If you're looking for picturesque, you'll have to look elsewhere than Dover and Folkestone: these are functional port towns (and ones that have seen better days at that). Better to head for Sandwich or, at a pinch, Deal, which offers attractive streets among the seaside Victoriana.

Tourist Information Centres

Deal Library, Broad Street, Deal, CT14 6ER (01304 369576/www.whitecliffscountry.org.uk). **Open** 9.30am-5.30pm Mon, Tue, Thur-Sat; 9.30am-1pm Wed.
Townwall Street, Dover, CT16 1JR (01304 205108/www.whitecliffscountry.org.uk). **Open** 9am-5.30pm daily.
Harbour Street, Folkestone, CT20 1QN (01303 258594). **Open** 10am-5.30pm Mon-Sat; noon-5pm Sun.
Guildhall, Sandwich, CT13 9AH (01304 613565/ www.open-sandwich.co.uk). **Open** *Apr-Sept* 10am-4pm daily. Closed Nov-Mar.

Bike hire

Deal Prams & Cycles *30 Mill Hill, Deal, CT14 9EW (01304 380680).*
One mile from the railway station.

Caesar's Camp & the Warren

These chalk downs at Folkestone were once accessible from the town on foot by passing through the golf course. Now access is via a major road, which passes straight through the hillside, somewhat lessening the ambience of Caesar's Camp and Sugarloaf Hill. Nevertheless, the wilds of the Warren are great for walking, with spectacular views on a clear day and access to quiet beaches.

Dover's **white cliffs**.

Deal Castle

Victoria Road, Deal, CT14 7BA (01304 372762/ www.english-heritage.org.uk). **Open** *Apr-Sept* 10am-6pm daily. *Oct* 10am-5pm daily. *Nov-Mar* 10am-4pm Wed-Sun. **Admission** (EH) £3.50; £1.80-£2.60 concessions. **Credit** MC, V.

Built by Henry VIII in the shape of a Tudor rose, the castle is a warren of dank, spooky corridors that seem to go on for miles. In the centre is a fine display of the castle's history and other coastal fortifications.

Deal Maritime Museum

St George's Road, Deal, CT14 6BA (01304 381344 /http://home.freeuk.com/deal-museum). **Open** *Easter-Sept* 2-5pm Mon-Sat. Closed Oct-Easter. **Admission** £1.50; 50p-£1 concessions. **No credit cards.**

The main gallery depicts the life and times of local sailors on this famously treacherous stretch of coast where the Goodwin Sands have claimed many a vessel. There are also displays on local history, including the naval yard and the military importance of the town.

Dover Castle

Castle Hill, Dover, CT16 9HU (01304 211067/www. english-heritage.org.uk). **Open** *Apr-Sept* 10am-6pm daily. *Oct* 10am-5pm daily. *Nov-Mar* 10am-4pm daily. **Admission** (EH) £8; £4-£6 concessions. **Credit** AmEx, DC, MC, V.

This vast, brooding monument against European integration dominates the landscape. 'The key to England', it has been the front line in the defence against invasion since the 12th century and even had a military role in World War II. The only time Dover Castle has ever fallen was when the Parliamentarians successfully besieged the Royalists during the Civil War. William the Conqueror laid down the foundations, it was improved by Henry II and additions have been made regularly since. This is an extraordinary place and there is much to see, including the Georgian tunnels that were used as a command centre in 1940 and again during the Cuban missile crisis of 1962. There are also regular re-creations of sieges, all of which culminate in thrilling mock battles.

East Kent Railway

Station Road, Sheperdswell, nr Dover, CT15 7PD (01304 832042/www.eastkentrailway.com). **Open** *Static viewing at Sheperdswell station* 11am-3pm daily. *Train rides* Sun, bank hols; phone or check website for timetable. **Tickets** £5; £2.50-£4 concessions. **No credit cards.**

Enjoy a round trip on a steam train. You can also eat birthday teas or Sunday roasts on some services and hire an entire (static) train for parties. For the serious train nut, steam locomotive driving courses are offered.

Richborough Roman Fort

Richborough Road, Sandwich, CT13 9JW (01304 612013/www.english-heritage.org.uk). **Open** *Apr-Sept* 10am-6pm daily. *Oct* 10am-5pm daily. *Mar* 10am-4pm Wed-Sun. *Nov-Feb* 10am-4pm Sat, Sun. **Admission** (EH) £3; £1.50-£2.30 concessions. **Credit** MC, V.

The site of Britain's first Roman fortress, which marks the likely spot of the AD 43 landing. The invasion of the rest of Britain was orchestrated from here. Not much remains now, but the ruins of the triumphal arch built to signal the might of the Roman forces are still visible.

Samphire Hoe

01304 225688. **Open** 7am-dusk daily. **Admission** free.

Five million cubic metres of chalk were dug up during the building of the Channel Tunnel. Much of it went to create this expansive area of land, accessible only through a deep tunnel, and landscaped with flowers and grasses. Samphire Hoe is surrounded by sheer white cliffs and attracts all kinds of wildlife. Visitors come to walk, fish, picnic and cycle.

St Margaret's Museum & Pines Garden

Beach Road, St Margaret's Bay, Dover, CT15 6DZ (01304 852764/fax 01304 853626/www.bay trust.org.uk). **Open** *Pines Garden* 10am-5pm daily. *Museum* Easter weekend, May bank hols, June-Sept 2-5pm Wed-Sun. **Admission** *Museum* £1; free under-16s. *Garden* £3.50; 50p-£3 concessions. **No credit cards.**

Just past the sleepy village of St Margaret's, on the road down to the bay, this somewhat bizarre yet imaginative six-acre garden was created in 1970, and includes a lake with waterfall, Romany caravan, wishing well and Oscar Nemon's statue of Churchill. The museum is equally eclectic, with a large collection of local curios.

South Foreland Lighthouse

The Front, St Margaret's Bay, Dover, CT15 6HP (01304 852463/www.nationaltrust.org.uk). **Open** *Mar-Oct* 11am-5.30pm Mon, Thur-Sun. Open at these times every day during school hols. **Admission** (NT) £2; £1 concessions. **No credit cards.**

Built in 1843, the lighthouse commands the Dover Straits. It was from here that Marconi made the world's first international radio transmission to Wimereux in France. Learn about the history of the tower on the short tour and marvel at the view.

Walmer Castle & Gardens

Kingsdown Road, Walmer, Deal, CT14 7LJ (01304 364288/ www.english-heritage.org.uk). **Open** *Apr-Sept* 10am-6pm daily. *Oct* 10am-5pm daily. *Nov, Dec* 10am-4pm daily. *Jan, Feb* 10am-4pm Sat, Sun. *Mar* 10am-4pm Wed-Sun. **Admission** (EH) £5.50; £2.80-£4.10 concessions. **Credit** MC, V.

The most attractive and well-preserved of the Cinque Ports fortifications. Walmer is still official home to the Lord Warden; past incumbents include William Pitt the Younger and the Duke of Wellington (whose life is celebrated inside).

Where to stay

There are hundreds of B&Bs along the coast. Wear Bay Road in **Folkestone** is the main drag for comfy accommodation, while the ship-shaped Grand Hotel Burstin dominates the harbour – it tends to draw the older generation down for the sea air. **Dover**'s waterfront area offers the best views and standards – but be warned, there are some grotty dives here. **Deal** is an attractive alternative with some reasonably priced waterfront inns with rooms. **Sandwich** and **Sandgate** are altogether classier.

The Bell Hotel

The Quay, Sandwich, CT13 9EF (01304 613388/
fax 01304 615308/www.princes-leisure.co.uk).
Rates £75 single; £100 double/twin; £155 deluxe
double; £110 family room. **Rooms** (all en suite) 8
single; 17 double/twin; 7 deluxe double/twin; 1
family. **Credit** AmEx, DC, MC, V.
Three hundred years old and starting to show its age, the
Bell is in dire need of a makeover. Heavy wood furnishings, once grand, are now dowdy; carpets are in need of
replacement; staff are terse. So why come here? For the
27-hole golf course and top location as the centrepiece of
Sandwich. Each room is reasonably sized and bathrooms
are carpeted; there's room service too. Meals are served
in the Honfleur, a silver service restaurant with ornate
chandeliers and embroidered dining chairs; note the dress
code. Magnums Wine Bar, with seats outside, is more
casual, serving real ales and pub grub. Children and dogs
welcome. All rooms are no-smoking.

The Churchill Hotel

The Waterfront, Dover, CT17 9BP (01304 203633/
fax 01304 216320/www.churchill-hotel.com). **Rates**
£62 single; £82 double/twin; £98 deluxe double; £97
family room. Breakfast £9. **Rooms** (all en suite) 4
single; 37 double; 20 twin; 5 deluxe double; 4 family.
Credit AmEx, DC, MC, V.
Reminiscent of the Royal Crescent in Bath, the curving
Regency terrace that houses the Churchill was built in
1834 so visitors could indulge in the new craze for sea-
bathing. After World War I, a number of houses here
were converted into hotels, which promptly closed at
the outbreak of World War II. Reopened in peacetime
and renamed the Churchill, the exterior has been restored
sympathetically. The interior is spotless, if rather uninspiring, though the long glass terrace for promenade
gazing is an attractive feature. A major attraction is the
very well-equipped gym, spa, sauna, steam and heated
pool. Children welcome.

Dunkerley's Hotel

19 Beach Street, Deal, CT14 7AH (01304 375016/
fax 01304 380187/www.dunkerleys.co.uk). **Rates**
£55-£75 single; £45-£65 per person double/twin/
family room; £60 per person four-poster/suite.
Rooms (all en suite) 12 double; 4 twin; 1 four-poster;
1 suite; 2 family. **Credit** AmEx, DC, MC, V.
Each of the 16 rooms at Dunkerley's is simply furnished
but spacious, with red carpets, solid wood beds and
satellite TV. Try and get one with a sea view if you can;
or, if you're feeling self-indulgent, go for the suite, which
has a jacuzzi and four-poster. The wood-panelled bar
has comfy leather armchairs, a grand piano and an old-
fashioned hooded porter's chair.

Loddington House

East Cliff, Marine Parade, Dover, CT16 1LX
(tel/fax 01304 201947). **Rates** £45 single;
£54-£70 double; from £70 family room.
Rooms 1 single (en suite); 5 double (3 en suite).
Credit AmEx, MC, V.
Located in a crumbling row of Victorian townhouses,
Grade II-listed Loddington House backs right on to the
cliffs so ask for rooms facing away from the sea if you
want to gaze up at the dramatic chalk face. These are
also quieter, because just 200 yards away is the main
thoroughfare from the ferry terminal, frequented by

heavy goods lorries. Each of the six rooms is spotless
but basic (four rooms are en suite). Children welcome.
No smoking throughout.

Park Inn

1-2 Park Place, Ladywell, Dover (01304 203300/
www.theparkinnatdover.co.uk). **Rates** (per person)
£35 single; £27 double/twin; £32 four-poster.
Rooms 1 single; 3 double/twin; 1 four-poster. **Credit**
AmEx, DC, MC, V.
Five accessibly priced rooms in downtown Dover, opposite the town hall. Each is spotlessly clean, brightly
painted in ornate greens and pinks, with bathrooms en
suite. One also has an elaborately draped four-poster.
All come with Sky TV, tea- and coffee-making facilities
and large marble-effect bathrooms. Accommodation is
above a pub, which is big and busy with hearty fare that
includes starters of prawn cocktail or stuffed potato
skins, and mains such as salmon supreme or mixed grill.

Sandgate Hotel

8-9 Wellington Terrace, The Esplanade, Sandgate,
CT20 3DY (01303 220444/fax 01303 220496/
www.sandgatehotel.com). **Rates** £45 single; £55-£70
double/twin. **Rooms** (all en suite) 2 single;
4 double/twin; 4 deluxe double (with balcony).
Credit AmEx, DC, MC, V.
Reopened in March 2003 under new management, the
Sandgate is now a family-run, contemporary hotel where
beige is all the rage. The rooms are smallish but clean
and elegant, with big baths and powerful showers,
though soundproofing of the paper-thin walls would be
a good addition. Best are those with balconies at the
front offering spectacular views of the sea. During the
summer, dining extends on to the split-level terrace.

Wallett's Court Country House Hotel

Westcliffe, St Margaret's at Cliffe, CT15 6EW
(01304 852424/fax 01304 853430/www.
wallettscourt.com). **Rates** £75-£115 single; £90-£150
double/twin/deluxe; £150 four-poster; £150 suite;
£110 family room. **Rooms** (all en suite) 9 double;
1 twin; 2 deluxe; 2 four-poster; 2 suites. **Credit**
AmEx, DC, MC, V.
Former home of William Pitt the Younger, this country
house hotel is a jewel in the east Kent countryside. The
main accommodation is in the substantial whitewashed
farmhouse where Queen Eleanor of Castile and Edward
the Black Prince lay claim to occupancy of the rooms (as
noted on plaques on the doors). Rooms are beautifully
furnished with antique dressers and carved four-poster
beds. Outside in the grounds are a sauna, steam room,
heated pools, spa and tennis courts, further chalet-style
rooms, a wooden tree house and a bench swing. It also
has a fine restaurant. Need we say more? Children
welcome. All bedrooms are no-smoking. No dogs allowed.
A2 from Canterbury; take A258 towards Deal for half a
mile; 1st right after Swing Gate pub; Wallett's Court is
opposite church on right.

Where to eat & drink

High-quality restaurants or pubs are yet to hit
this stretch of the East Kent coast, though if
you can tolerate the rarified hotel atmosphere,

Wallet's Court Country House Hotel (*see p28*) is a good bet for high-quality cooking using locally sourced ingredients.

But a trip inland can reveal lovely foodie pubs hidden away in the smallest villages with more than a usual quota of thatched cottages. Some of the best include the **Griffin's Head** for great summer barbecues (Chillenden, 01304 840325), the **Hare & Hounds** in Northbourne, near Deal (01304 365429), **Lydden Bell** at Lydden (near Dover, 01304 830296) – look out for specialities such as roasted squirrel – and the tiny **Old Lantern Inn** in Martin near St Margaret's Bay (01304 852276). The **Coastguard Pub** in St Margaret's Bay (01304 853176) is an unattractive pebbledash building

on the beach, but it serves a delicious 'catch of the day'. Meanwhile, the **Clarendon Inn** (01303 248684) in Sandgate, just behind the Sandgate Hotel, doles out good, unpretentious fare. Cheap and cheerful comes no better than at **Goodwin's Restaurant** (01304 374257) at the far end of Deal Pier, with burgers, omelettes or full English breakfast, to be enjoyed with views over Deal's colourful seafront. **Blakes** (Castle Street, Dover, 01304 202194) and **Fisherman's Wharf** (The Quay, Sandwich, 01304 613636) are good for hearty seafood dishes and nautical paraphernalia. Upstairs at **Dickens' Corner** (Market Square, Dover, 01304 206692) home-made cakes and traditional cream teas are served by waitresses in 19th-century garb.

Literary connections

Proximity to London and the lure of the seaside have drawn various literary figures to the stretch of coast between Sandgate and Sandwich. In 1900, H G Wells moved into Spade House (it was named after the spade-shaped letterbox) in Sandgate. The house had been built specifically for him at a cost of £1,760 as somewhere to convalesce from a kidney infection. Being originally from Bromley, a place Wells condemned as 'swallowed up by seedy urbanisation', he chose Sandgate for the healthy sea air and because it enabled him to 'feel free'. Inspired by his surroundings, he penned *Sea Lady* in 1902 and *Kipps* in 1905, both based around life in Folkestone.

Frequently visited by writers such as George Bernard Shaw, Henry James and Joseph Conrad, Spade House became a centre of literary sparring. It was so well known as a social hub that D H Lawrence named it 'Dostoevsky's Corner', claiming it was filled with 'tortured artists'. Conrad, who wrote *Heart of Darkness* at Pent Farm a few miles up the road, would drop by in a ferociously driven little black carriage, cracking his whip and yelling at his puny Kent pony in his native Polish, much to the fascination of the locals.

In 1945 the celebrity spotlight moved north to St Margaret's Bay where Noel Coward bought the derelict White Cliffs. The house was hidden in a secluded bay, with sheer white cliffs climbing up behind it, and it was so close to the sea that seagulls would fly in through the windows. It became a haven for famous guests

such as Katharine Hepburn, who was partial to swimming in the freezing sea, along with Daphne du Maurier and Spencer Tracy.

Coward's most favoured guest, however, was Ian Fleming, creator of James Bond. The two used to race one another from London to convene for drinks at the Swingate Arms on the Deal Road (01304 204043/www.swingate.com). Fleming's love affair with the region centred around the Royal St George's golf course in Sandwich (01304 613090), which he claimed was the 'best seaside golf course in the world'. It was between the cliffs of St Margaret's and Kingsdown, en route to Walmer, that Fleming sited the missile in *Moonraker*, while Royal St George's is the location of the famous golf scene in *Goldfinger*.

In the early 1950s the appearance of celebrity-hunting daytrippers forced Coward to leave St Margaret's Bay, claiming the beach to be 'crowded with noisy hoi polloi'. In December 1951 he sold White Cliffs to Ian Fleming and wife Ann Rothermere, but continued to be a regular guest.

The legacy of these writers and their Kentish links are preserved at the annual Folkestone Literary Festival, which takes place in the third week of September (20-25 Sept 2004, ticket sales and information 0800 056 5086/ www.folkestonelitfest.com). During the festival, there are visits and tours of White Cliffs, Spade House, Pent Farm and the homes of other literary figures.

Tudor defence at **Deal Castle**. *See p27.*

The Arlington

161 Snaregate Street, Dover, CT17 6BZ (01304 209444/www.thearlington.co.uk). **Food served** noon-2.30pm, 6.30-9.30pm Tue-Sat. **Main courses** £3-£5.50 lunch; £13.95-£16.50 dinner. **Credit** MC, V.
Kent's tiniest pub reopened in March 2003 as a restaurants for 20 diners. It's so spanking new that there's the temptation to rough it up a bit: splash colour on the bleak yellow walls, crumple the linen. However, the enthusiasm of the friendly young couple who run it is infectious. The menu, rolled up and tied with ribbon, is accessible both in content and price. Food is fairly trad: minute steaks or sausage and mash can be followed by the likes of crème brûlée and Dutch apple tart. No smoking.

Cullins Yard

11 Cambridge Road, Wellington Dock, Dover, CT17 9BY (01304 211666). **Food served** noon-11pm daily. **Main courses** £5.50-£21. **Credit** MC, V.
Loud and lively, this dockside restaurant leaves you in no doubt as to its fishy theme. Every inch of the wood interior, decked out like a boat, is filled with bric-a-brac: giant crabs in glass cases, masts and sails draped across the ceiling, grandfather clocks and nautical paintings. While some may find this a bit much, there's no doubting the focus on fish freshness, demonstrated by the live lobsters and the fact that every dish takes 30 minutes to prepare. Cullins is well known for its bouillabaisse, Dover sole and gravadlax, served with homely classics like bubble and squeak, chunky chips and crusty bread.

Dunkerley's

Beach Street, Deal, CT14 7AH (01304 375016/www. dunkerleys.co.uk). **Food served** noon-2.30pm, 7-9.30pm Mon-Fri; noon-2.30pm, 6-10pm Sat; noon-3pm, 7-9.30pm Sun. **Set lunch** £11.95 3 courses. **Main courses** £11.95-£21.95. **Credit** AmEx, DC, MC, V.
Slap bang on the seafront, Dunkerley's is loved for its seafood. Starters include shrimp pagoda piled high on tiers of Melba toast and caramelised scallops served

with bacon. Main dishes have a choice of six fish, including roast sea bass on saffron mash and Sandwich Bay plaice fillet seared on banana and sweet potato. There are also game and meat options. Complimentary palate-cleansers of asparagus soup in an espresso cup and ice-cold Bramley apple stew are unexpected touches that go towards making the experience one up from the special.

Quayside Bar & Brasserie

Bell Lane, The Quay, Sandwich, KT13 9EN (01304 619899/www.quaysidebar.co.uk). **Food served** noon-2.30pm, 6-9.30pm Mon-Sat; noon-4pm Sun. **Main courses** £3.95-£14.95. **Credit** AmEx, MC, V.
Quayside is airy, bright and open-plan with light walls, a long bar and spot lit columns. Colourful art depicting seaside huts and Miami city scenes fills the walls alongside blackboards that list cocktails, food specials and jazz performances (last Sunday of every month). Light meals include baguettes or tapas (hot chorizo salad, marinated anchovies). Main courses could be calf's liver with crispy bacon, fillet of pork with prune and apricot mousse or a choice of risottos. Service is chatty.

Sandgate Hotel Restaurant

The Esplanade, Sandgate, CT20 3DY (01303 220444/www.sandgatehotel.com). **Food served** 12.15-1.30pm, 7.15-9.15pm Tue-Sat; 12.15-1.30pm Sun. **Set lunch** (Tue-Fri, Sun) £22 3 courses. **Set meal** (dinner Fri; lunch, Sat, Sun) £31 5 courses. **Credit** AmEx, DC, MC, V.
Simply decorated and overlooking the sea, the new restaurant at the Sandgate (opened March 2003) serves good Modern European food. There were still teething problems when we visited (starters took forever to arrive with no explanation). But gripes aside, there was plenty that was positive. Presentation was faultless: a tian of provençal vegetables was colourfully stacked and dressed with a hazel-nut salad – shame it tasted a little bland. Much better was a fillet of beef, served with a rich pesto, chilli, mustard and Swiss chard sauce.

North Kent Downs

Progress with pilgrims or be king of the castle in this corner of Kent.

The **Harty** delights of the Isle of Sheppey. *See p32.*

Once the trudging ground for 12th-century pilgrims on their way to Canterbury, the North Kent Downs is now a place of worship for dedicated outdoorists and village lovers. Don't be put off by the motorways that dissect the region – they make access to the area easy and once you're off them, the peace of chalky escarpments, rolling hills, hopfields, orchards and ancient country pubs will engulf you.

The Downs, a well-maintained 153-mile stretch from the Surrey hills to the white cliffs of Dover, has been a main thoroughfare since neolithic times. The Victorians dubbed part of the route the **Pilgrim's Way**, after those who went to honour the shrine to Thomas à Beckett in Canterbury Cathedral. Navigation on the trail is facilitated by acorn symbols (01622 696185/ www.nationaltrails.gov.uk).

By train from London

Trains to **Maidstone East** leave **Victoria** every half an hour (journey time approx 1hr). Trains to **Ashford** leave **Victoria** hourly and pass through **Lenham** and **Charing** (journey time to Ashford **1hr 25mins**). Trains to **Faversham** leave from **Victoria** every 25mins and pass through **Chatham** and **Sittingbourne** (journey time to Faversham is around 1hr to 1hr 30mins). Info: www.connex.co.uk. (Services will be taken over by South Eastern Trains in 2004; timetables should not be affected.)

Beyond the satisfaction of country pub beer and food after a hard walk on the Downs, there is little in this area to draw you indoors. Two historic highlights are just outside the county seat of Maidstone: the fairytale **Leeds Castle** is one of Kent's main tourist attractions, and two miles further west is the lesser-known **Stoneacre**, a delightful yeoman's house.

Royal connections

The area isn't bursting with major draws, but it does have plenty of lovely villages. The majority are stretched along an axis that follows the **North Downs Way** (and to the south, the M20) between **Maidstone** and **Ashford**; a country tour, taking in a handful of them, is an enjoyable way to pass a leisurely day.

Despite the heavy traffic traversing it, the centre of **Lenham** (nine miles south-east of Maidstone) has retained its village character. A few miles further south-east is **Charing**, not so much a village as an attractive tiny town with a main street lined with mellow walls and roofs. An **archbishop's palace** was built here in 1333, the last in a chain that began at Otford. The ivy-covered ruins can still be seen by the parish church of **St Peter and Paul**. Henry VIII stayed here on his way to the famous meeting with the French king Francis I at the Field of the Cloth of Gold near Guisnes in 1520. Another mile or so south-east is **Westwell**, nestling beneath the Downs. Although not far from the M20, it feels well off the beaten track.

About the same distance south-east again, you can walk to **Eastwell** and **Boughton Lees**. En route is the bomb-damaged, 15th-century church of **St Mary's**, which remains sacred ground despite being in ruins. The churchyard contains a number of impressive tombs, including that of Richard III's bastard son, who fled to Kent after his father's death at the Battle of Bosworth and worked as a stonemason at nearby **Eastwell Manor**.

Two miles to the east is **Wye**. On the hillside to the north of the village is a white chalk crown, carved for the coronation of Edward VII in 1902. Wye is a charming place, though not essentially Kentish; it has a Georgian look, with many of its 17th-century houses unusually uniform, radiating from the 13th-century church.

Tiny **Chilham** (eight miles north-east of Ashford) is one of the most visited villages in the county, with half-timbered houses leading to a picture-perfect square. Between Wye and Chilham, just off the A28, is the tiny village of **Godmersham**, where Jane Austen was a regular visitor. Her brother, Edward, owned Godmersham Park, and it is thought she based some of *Mansfield Park* on her experiences there.

Windy walks and marshy marches

For those who like wide open spaces, the Swale, on the north-west Kent coast, is the place for estuary walks. The modern market town of **Sittingbourne** and pretty **Faversham** are the major towns of the area, but it's the **Isle of Sheppey**, the Swale estuary that divides it from the mainland and along the nearby coastal **Saxon Shore Way** that are the draw. Avoid the caravan horrors of Leysdown or Sheerness and head to **Harty** in the south-east of the island. If you fancy a dip, the beaches east beyond **Leysdown** are reasonably quiet.

Medway awayday

In the area north of the North Kent Downs where the Medway, Thames and Swale rivers meet, sit the sprawling towns of Rochester, Gillingham and Chatham. Though there's much to be found here for lovers of castles, Charles Dickens and all things maritime, the area lacks noteworthy accommodation or places to eat. Highlights in **Rochester** include the castle and cathedral, plus a number of Dickens heritage sites – his writing chalet behind the **Charles Dickens Centre** on Rochester High Street (01634 844176) was the model for Miss Havisham's jolly abode in *Great Expectations* and, in nearby Higham-by-Rochester, is Dickens' final home at **Gad's Hill Place** (01474 822366).

Nautical types shouldn't miss the historic dockyards at **Chatham** (Dock Road, 01634 823800/www.chdt.org.uk) or a trip on the paddle steamer the **Kingswear Castle** (01634 827648/www.pskc.freeserve.co.uk); for their military counterparts, there's an award-winning museum devoted to the work of the **Royal Engineers** at Gillingham (Prince Arthur Road, 01634 822839/www.royalengineers.org.uk).

What to see & do

Tourist Information Centres

18 The Church Yard, Ashford, TN23 1QG (01233 629165/www.ashford.gov.uk). **Open** *Easter-Oct* 9.30am-5.30pm Mon-Sat. *Nov-Easter* 9.30am-5pm Mon-Sat.

95 High Street, Rochester, ME1 1LX (01634 843666/ www.medway.gov.uk). **Open** 9am-5pm Mon-Fri; 10am-5pm Sat; 10.30am-5pm Sun.

The Fleur de Lis, Preston Street, Faversham, ME13 8NS (01795 534542/www.faversham.org.uk). **Open** 10am-4pm Mon-Sat; 10am-1pm Sun.

Bike hire

Ken James *22A Beaver Road, Ashford (01233 634334).*
Close to the rail station.

Belmont House & Gardens

Belmont Park, Throwley, nr Faversham, ME13 0HH (01795 890202/www.belmont-house.org). **Open** *Apr-Sept* House (guided tours) 2-5pm Sat, Sun. Last entry

4.15pm. Gardens 10am-6pm Mon-Thur, Sat, Sun. **Admission** *House & gardens* £5.25; £2.50-£4.75 concessions. *Gardens only* £2.75; £1 concessions. **No credit cards.**
This beautiful neo-classical 18th-century mansion, the work of Samuel Wyatt, has stunning grounds and views of Kent. It was bought by General George Harris in 1802 – later Lord Harris – with proceeds from his successful military career in India. Inside are family mementoes including Indian silverware and the most extensive private collection of clocks in the country.

Doddington Place Gardens
Doddington, nr Sittingbourne, ME9 0BB (01795 886101). **Open** *Easter-June* 2-6pm Sun. Closed July-Easter. **Admission** £3.50; 75p concessions. **No credit cards.**
During the summer, this private Victorian mansion throws open its magnificent landscaped gardens to the public. The ten acres of ground, lined with fantastic yew hedges, include a woodland garden, a large Edwardian sunken rock garden, a formal sunken garden (best in late summer) and a flint and brick folly. There's a café, and next to Doddington Place is an enchanting and well-maintained church, one of two in England dedicated to the beheading of St John the Baptist.

Godinton House & Gardens
Godinton Lane, Ashford, TN23 3BP (01233 620773/ www.godinton-house-gardens.co.uk). **Open** *Easter-early Oct* House (guided tours) 2-5.30pm Fri-Sun, last tour 4.30pm. Garden 2-6pm Mon, Thur-Sun. Closed early Oct-Easter. **Admission** *House & garden* £6; free under-16s. *Garden only* £3; free under-16s. **No credit cards.**
This delightful Jacobean house has fabulous grounds with views across extensive parkland. The yew hedges, formal topiary, pond and lawns were Sir Reginald Blomfield's first garden design in 1890, and you can also wander in the softer wild garden, 1920s Italian garden and 18th-century walled garden.

Rochester Cathedral
Garth House, The Precinct, Rochester, ME1 1SX (01634 401301/www.rochester.anglican.org). **Open** 8am-6pm daily. **Admission** free; suggested donation of £3 welcome.
The second-oldest in England, this small cathedral has a fine collection of medieval wall paintings, charming floor tiles and some very old graffiti. You can also see the first fresco to be commissioned in an English cathedral for 800 years, painted by Russian artist Sergei Fyodorov on the theme of baptism (it's due to be finished at the end of 2003).

Shepherd Neame Brewery
Court Street, Faversham, ME13 7AX (01795 542016/ www.shepherdneame.co.uk). **Tours** most weekdays & evenings plus selected weekends, phone for exact times, booking essential. **Admission** *Day tour & tasting* (3 x half-pint) £5.20; £2.60-£3.80 concessions. *Evening tour, finger buffet & tasting* (5 x half-pint) £9.25. **Credit** AmEx, MC, V.
If you want to find out more about the Shepherd Neame sign that swings above most pubs in the area, go for a tour of this famous Faversham brewery. It takes an hour and a half and you'll experience the whole process from

barley to bottle, learning about the company's 300-year history and tasting some of its finest Kentish ales, such as Spitfire and Bishop's Finger.

Stoneacre
Ortham, nr Maidstone, ME15 8RS (01622 862871/ www.nationaltrust.org.uk). **Open** *mid Mar-mid Oct* 2-6pm Wed, Sat. Last entry 5pm. **Admission** (NT) £2.60; £1.30 concessions. **No credit cards.**
At the north end of Ortham village, three miles southeast of Maidstone, is this National Trust property – a half-timbered yeoman's house. Stoneacre's attractions include a great hall and crownpost dating from the late 15th century, delightful gardens and a new rose garden.

Where to stay

If you're looking for convenience, the functional **Harrow Hill Hotel** near Lenham (Warren Street; 01622 858727, doubles £85) has 14 rooms. A base for superb walking is **Little Mystole**, a small Georgian house near Chatham (Little Mystole, nr Canterbury, 01227 738210, doubles £70), or the delightful **Frith Farm House** (Otterden, nr Eastling, 01795 890701/www.frithfarmhouse.co.uk, doubles £65-£70) just south of Newnham, which boasts its own orchards and heated indoor pool.

Barnfield
Charing, nr Ashford, TN27 0BN (tel/fax 01233 712421). **Rates** £26-£30 single; £46-£48 double/twin. **Rooms** 3 single; 2 double; 1 twin. **No credit cards.**
The cosy 15th-century home of Phyllida and Martin Pym is set in 30 acres of land and houses five simple bedrooms. Each has its own washbasin, but guests have to share one bathroom (guests are limited to six at any one time). There is also a comfortable, book-lined sitting room and tennis court. The Pyms are outstandingly helpful, and are on standby to provide local knowledge and advice. Children welcome. No smoking throughout.

Chilston Park
Sandway, Lenham, ME17 2BE (01622 859803/fax 01622 858588/www.handpicked.co.uk/chilstonpark). **Rates** £100-£130 double/twin; £160-£295 four-poster; £210-£295 suite. Breakfast £12.95 (Eng/cont). **Rooms** (all en suite) 41 double/twin; 10 four-poster; 2 suites. **Credit** AmEx, DC, MC, V.
The new owners of this fabulous 17th-century mansion have decided to abandon the concept of staff in period costume. However, it's still got all the trimmings: acres of parkland, wood-panelled drawing rooms and formal restaurant, as well as rooms decorated by theme such as 'Gothic' and 'Raj'. Children and dogs welcome.

Eastwell Manor Hotel
Eastwell Park, Boughton Lees, TN25 4HR (01233 219955/reservations 0500 526735/ fax 01233 635530/www.eastwellmanor.co.uk). **Rates** £200-£265 double/twin; £265-£355 suite. *Self-catering cottages* £200 per night per room or £500-£900 per wk. **Rooms** *Hotel* (all en suite) 18 double/twin; 5 suites. *Cottages* 4 1-bed; 10 2-bed; 5 3-bed. **Credit** AmEx, DC, MC, V.

If you're after the luxury of a full country house experience, head for the panelled drawing rooms, sweeping staircases and open fires of this beautiful Tudor house. Stately grandeur is balanced by exquisite service, and there are indoor and outdoor pools, tennis courts and a formal restaurant. The self-contained mews cottages with kitchen, sitting room and ISDN line offer privacy and value. The manor's spa and conference facilities are minor blips on its otherwise picturesque landscape of manicured lawns and topiary displays. But it does mean you can enjoy a facial after an exhausting game of croquet. Children and dogs (£15 per night) welcome.

Howfield Manor

Chartham Hatch, CT4 7HQ (01227 738294/ www.howfieldmanor.co.uk). **Rates** £79.50 single; £99.50 double/twin; £115 four-poster. **Rooms** (all en suite) 2 single; 11 double/twin; 2 four-poster. **Credit** AmEx, MC, V.
Howfield is protected from the noise of the A2 by a buffer of five acres of garden. The site of this 15-room, family-run hotel once belonged to the 12th-century Priory of St Gregory and part of the original chapel still stands, now housing the manor's pleasant restaurant. Rooms in the original house are more characterful, with sloping floors and exposed beams, although those in the tastefully rendered extension are equally comfortable. Children over ten welcome.

Ringlestone Farmhouse

Ringlestone Hamlet, nr Harrietsham, Maidstone, ME17 1NX (01622 859900/fax 01622 859966/ www.ringlestone.com). **Rates** £89 single occupancy; £99-£110 double/twin/four-poster; £10 supplement for child sharing parents' double. Breakfast £15 (Eng); £12 (cont); £6 (tray). **Rooms** (all en suite) 2 double/ twin; 1 four-poster. **Credit** AmEx, DC, MC, V.
Across the leafy road from the Ringlestone Inn (*see p35*) is its sister farmhouse, which houses three airy and comfortable en suite bedrooms. Rustic oak beams, heavy cottons, fresh flowers and homely ornaments give it a fresh but lived-in feel, and guests can make use of the communal sitting room and dining room with its ancient oak table. Children are welcome. All rooms no-smoking.

Stowting Hill House

Stowting, nr Ashford, TN25 6BE (01303 862881/ fax 01303 863433). **Rates** £35 single occupancy; £60-£70 twin. **Rooms** 1 double; 2 twin (en suite). **No credit cards.**
An 18th-century family house with views over the Downs, substantial gardens and a tennis court, Stowting has three twin-bedded rooms for B&B. The service is unfussy and pleasant, and there's a conservatory area and separate living room for guests. All rooms are no-smoking. Children over ten welcome.

Wife of Bath

4 Upper Bridge Street, Wye, TN25 5AF (01233 812540/812232/fax 01233 813033/www.w-o-b. demon.co.uk). **Rates** £45 single occupancy; £75-£95 double. Breakfast £5 (Eng). Closed 1 wk after Christmas. **Rooms** (all en suite) 3 double; 2 twin. **Credit** AmEx, DC, MC, V.
Staying at the Wife of Bath is an idyllic experience. Each of the five rooms in the 18th-century timber-framed house is named after a pilgrim in

Chaucer's *Canterbury Tales*, and combines wormy old beams with fresh paint and power showers. The Knight's and Miller's rooms, housed in converted stables in the lovely back garden, share a small kitchen. The restaurant is worth a visit even if you're not staying here. All rooms are no-smoking. Children welcome.

Where to eat & drink

Apart from a couple of top-notch restaurants (at **Eastwell Manor**, *see p33* and **Wife of Bath** *above*), the richest gastronomic pickings are to be found in the area's lovely pubs. The **Tickled Trout** on the river at Wye (2 Bridge Street, 01233 812227) provides the perfect outdoor setting, and the **Carpenter's Arms** at Eastling (The Street, 01795 890234), the **Flying Horse** by the cricket green in Boughton Lees (01233 620914), the **Windmill** in Hollingbourne (Eyhorne Street, 01622 880280) and the **Pepperbox Inn** at Fairbourne Heath (nr Ulcombe, 01622 842558) are all good foodie bets. For a smarter and pricier experience, try the **Lime Tree** restaurant and hotel in Lenham (8-9 The Square, 01622 859509).

Froggies at the Timber Batts

School Lane, Bodsham, TN25 5JQ (01233 750237). **Food served** noon-2.30pm, 7-9.30pm Tue-Sat; noon-2.30pm Sun. **Main courses** £12-£19. **Set lunch** (Sun) £14 2 courses, £18 3 courses. **Credit** MC, V.
The charisma and cooking of French chef Joel Gross has turned the 15th-century Timber Batts pub into one of the area's most popular and boisterous restaurants. The self-taught chef takes pride in substantial and unpretentious dishes, specialising in fish and seafood (vegetarians are scantily catered for but Joel will whip up a dish of your choice if warned a day in advance). Expect classics such as onion soup, fantastic stuffed mussels, great confit of duck, fillet of beef with roquefort sauce, profiteroles and tarte tatin. Unsurprisingly, the cheeses and wine are French only, with a house wine made by Joel's cousin in the Loire.

The George Inn

The Street, Newnham, ME9 0LL (01795 890237). **Food served** noon-2.30pm, 7-9.30pm Mon-Thur; noon-2.30pm, 7-10pm Fri, Sat; noon-2.30pm, 7-9pm Sun. **Main courses** £7.50-£14.95. **Credit** AmEx, MC, V.
A packed car park bears testament to the success of the George Inn, which draws locals and visitors with its extensive gastro menu and animated atmosphere. Pricier dishes such as pan-fried calf's liver with red wine jus or sea bass with fresh asparagus are on offer, alongside simpler pub fare and an impressive range of roasts, including a veggie option. Dried flowers and fairy lights hang from the low-beamed ceiling, and friendly and attentive waiters man both the main room and the darker, cosier restaurant area.

Read's

Macknade's Manor, Canterbury Road, Painter's Forstal, nr Faversham, ME13 8XE (01795 535344/www.reads.com). **Food served** noon-2pm,

Animal attractions

Most ancient fortresses harbour the odd spider or two, but it is rather larger animals that play a major part in the history – and attraction – of **Leeds Castle**. While the deer park that once surrounded this 12th-century castle would have provided hunting recreation for the string of kings that lived here (Edward I, Richard II and Henry VIII among others), Leeds' creaturely connections are mostly due to its last owner, the late Lady Baillie. An American heiress, she bought the castle in 1926 and set about restoring its older parts, building her own rooms and indulging her passion for all things ornithological. Her feathered friends appear in watercolours, carvings and tapestries throughout the castle, and the small aviary she set up in the early 1950s has now become an award-winning collection that houses more than 100 species, including parrots all the shades of Smarties, parakeets and macaws. For those not so keen on cages, ducks, geese and peacocks strut around the 500-acre grounds, and the moat is home to a colony of the rare black swan, now the symbol of the castle.

Dog devotees won't be disappointed either. Besides the rumour that a large black hound haunts the castle, Leeds – rather surreally – plays kennel to the world's finest collection of dog collars. Try for size the fearsome 16th-century boar-hunting collar with spikes or, in contrast, the brass model fit for a pup, which is engraved 'I am Mr Pratt's Dog, Kind Wokingham, Berkshire. Whose dog are you?'

Leeds Castle
Broomfield, nr Maidstone, ME17 1PL (01622 765400/www.leeds-castle.com). **Open** *Mar-Oct* 10am-6pm daily. *Nov-Feb* 10am-4pm daily. Last entry 1hr before closing. **Admission** *Nov-Feb* £9.50; £6-£8 concessions. *Mar-June, Sept, Oct* £11; £7.50-£9.50 concessions. *July, Aug* £12; £8.50-£10.50 concessions. **Credit** MC, V.

7-9pm Tue-Sat. **Set lunch** £19.50 3 courses. **Set dinner** £42 3 courses. **Credit** AmEx, DC, MC, V.
Run by Michelin-starred chef David Pitchford and his wife Rona, the restaurant has recently moved to a splendid Georgian mansion with an airy drawing room (used for pre-dinner drinks), a dining room overlooking the garden and a small terrace. Ingredients are locally sourced: fish from Whitstable, lamb from Romney Marsh and vegetables from their own kitchen garden. If you can't choose between hand-rolled gnocchi with asparagus, brill with seared scallops, cabbage and sweetcure bacon, or roasted Kentish lamb with fondant potatoes, then try the tasting menu, which offers smaller portions of four dishes. Presentation is beautiful and the friendly service faultless. Stay the night in one of their six rooms: that way you get to have breakfast as well.

Ringlestone Inn
Ringlestone Hamlet, nr Harrietsham, Maidstone, ME17 1NX (01622 859900/fax 01622 859966/ www.ringlestone.com). **Food served** noon-2pm, 7-9.30pm Mon-Thur; noon-2pm (bar food 2-7pm), 7-9.30pm Fri-Sun. **Main courses** £11.50-£15.50. **Credit** AmEx, DC, MC, V.
'No thieves, fakirs, skulking loafers or flee-bitten tramps' are allowed inside the dark and cosy Ringlestone Inn, so you'll be safe to sample the speciality pies, fruit wines (cowslip, walnut, elderberry) or imaginative country fare (country chicken, pistachio-stuffed duck). Built in 1533 as a hospice for monks, the inn became an ale house in 1615, and original flint walls, inglenooks and beams lend a real sense of history. The emphasis at Ringlestone is on taking your time and it's a lovely place to do just that, particularly in the pleasant garden.

Rye, Dungeness & Romney Marsh

Another country.

Cobbled streets, sandy beaches and a desolate promontory combine here to create one of the eeriest coastlines in England, a fact due in no small way to the almost year-round peacefulness of large parts of **Romney Marsh**, which stretches a few miles inland from the coast. But other factors contribute too; the strange architectural mix, for example, is defined by centuries of defensive constructions such as the Royal Military Canal (the sleepy waterway that idles from Rye in the west to Hythe in the east and was built against the threat of invasion by Napoleon), Norman and Tudor castles, Martello towers, concrete radar devices and army rifle ranges.

Combine these with the frankly grim and garish architecture of amusement arcade towns such as Dymchurch and Camber Sands, the quiet beauty of the marsh's medieval churches, some of them no bigger than a shack, houses converted from boats and railway carriages at Dungeness and a slew of historic pubs dating back 700 years, and you have the unique mix that gives this part of Kent its very individual charm. This is something filmmaker Derek Jarman was well aware of when he bought a little cabin here. His book *Derek Jarman's Garden* describes his battles with the elements; the fruits of his labours – and influence – can still be seen on the road to the Old Lighthouse.

Starting over in the west of the area, **Rye** is a lovely town that's almost too quaint to be true. A gorgeous jumble of Norman, Tudor and Georgian architecture scrambles over one of the area's few hills; the narrow, cobbled streets are chock-full of antiques shops, tearooms and pubs. Of course, it's too popular, but at least Rye is a living town, with real shops and a lively Thursday market. The best antiques and curio shops are on High Street, where there's also a great old record shop in the Old Grammar School (built 1636) and the second-hand bookshop Chapter & Verse (105 High Street, 01797 222692). Slightly twee pottery shops are everywhere (particularly towards the recently revamped Strand Quay), but you can at least keep the kids busy making their own at Paint Pots (Cinque Ports Pottery, The Monastery, Conduit Hill, 01797 222033).

Apart from simply wandering the streets, it is worth taking a look at **St Mary's Church** (dating from 1150), the pithy **Castle Museum** and 13th-century **Ypres Tower** (both Gun Garden, 3 East Rye Street, 01797 226728), and the medieval Landgate gateway (built in 1329).

Rye's prosperity was founded on its port; the town's fine state of preservation is partly thanks to the loss of that port when the coast retreated a couple of miles. It's worth driving to Rye Harbour to enjoy some windswept walks, past a bird sanctuary and the ruins of Henry VIII's Camber Castle.

Winchelsea, a couple of miles south-west of Rye, was built on a never-completed medieval grid pattern when 'old' Winchelsea was swept into the sea in the storms of 1287. The place is proud of its status as England's smallest town, but really it's a sleepy village with a jaw-dropping wealth of medieval (and later) architecture, a pub, a shop, a tiny local museum stuffed with bits of broken pottery and old photos, and a tearoom. The church of St Thomas à Becket contains some fine medieval carvings (including the head of Edward I). A further mile or so south-east of here is pebbly Winchelsea beach, which is sandy at low tide. Heading east from Rye, along the coastal road, is popular **Camber Sands**, a vast and glittering sandy beach that's hard-pressed by the wind and caravan parks. The Pontins

By train from London

Trains leave for **Rye** from **Charing Cross** hourly. They also pass through **Waterloo East**, **London Bridge** and **Tunbridge**. Passengers must change at **Ashford** (journey time 1hr 45mins) or **Hastings** (journey time 2hrs). Info: www.connex.co.uk. (Services will be taken over by South Eastern Trains in 2004; timetables should not be affected.)

Holiday Centre (0870 6010475) occasionally gets taken over for music festivals, so it's worth checking in advance whether the town will be inundated with goths, crusties and indie kids.

A place unlike any other

It's hard to imagine a greater contrast to the tame pleasures of Rye than desolate **Dungeness**, only a few miles to the east. A thousand years ago Dungeness Point didn't even exist. Longshore drift has built up huge banks of flint shingle, some of them 57 feet deep, which stretch miles out into the sea in a unique promontory. The light on this remote, gloriously bleak patch of land is odd, reflected from the sea on both sides, and the surreal quality of the landscape is enhanced by the presence of the massive **Dungeness Nuclear Power Station**. Sited almost on the tip of Dungeness Point, it dominates the horizon; at night its lights make it look like the Pompidou Centre. The hum is audible for miles, and was used as a backing soundtrack for Jarman's film *The Garden*. Until recently a visitor centre welcomed the public, but the power station recently shut its doors to visitors. The power station is linked to the seaside developments straggling away to the north towards Folkestone by the dinky **Romney, Hythe and Dymchurch Railway**.

The best place to stop on the coast before you reach Hythe, is **Dymchurch**, which is proud to proclaim itself as a 'Children's Paradise' – the presence of MW's Amusement Park, with its dodgems and arcades, is the best explanation we can find for this. There's also a sandy beach and a fine example of a Martello tower (topped by a restored 26-pounder gun). Further north, **Hythe** is the end-stop of the miniature railway and the **Royal Military Canal**; the latter lends charm to a town centre of fine buildings but busy roads and random housing developments. The high street has been pedestrianised and has some decent shops. In the summer, the hollyhock-packed little streets that meander up the steep hill to the Church of St Leonard are charming and a welcome respite from the frenetic seafront. The 11th-century church is another of the area's triumphs, complete with bone-packed crypt. Inland is Romney Marsh and a score of interesting villages. Away from the marsh, **Lympne** is worth visiting (for its castle and Wild Animal Park), as are **Warehorne**, **Stone** and **Appledore**. The latter used to be a Jute and then Norman port on the English Channel; now it's around six miles inland. It's here that you can find the best walks along the Royal Military Canal: trudge north along either bank, or drive south along the road to Rye.

Cathedrals of the marsh

The strange, low, wind-scoured area south of the Royal Military Canal is at its most bleak on Dungeness Point, but the inland area north and west of Dymchurch has a weird intensity. It is justly famous for its tiny medieval churches, of which there are 14 still standing (plus a few ruins). Among the most notable are **All Saints** at Lydd (known as the Cathedral of the Marsh) and **St Augustine's** at Brookland, with its extraordinary detached wooden bell tower. North of here is **St Thomas à Becket** at Fairfield, which many consider to be the epitome of the isolated Romney Marsh church (look for the sign and approach via a causeway). **St Clement** in Old Romney has a particularly lovely interior, with a magnificent minstrels' gallery. And **St Mary the Virgin** at St Mary in the Marsh carries the understated gravestone of Edith Nesbit, author of *The Railway Children*, who loved the area and died in the village.

What to see & do

Tourist Information Centre

Rye Heritage Centre, Strand Quay, Rye, TN31 7AY (01797 226696/www.visitrye.co.uk). **Open** *Mar-Oct* 9.30am-5pm Mon-Sat; 10am-5pm Sun. *Nov-Feb* 10am-4pm daily.
The Heritage Centre houses the Heritage Exhibition and the Story of Rye, a 20-minute sound and light show (£2.50, £1-£1.50 concessions). An audio tour of the town is available (£2.50, £1-£1.50 concessions) and the Heritage Centre also runs two tours – a historical and a ghost tour.

Bike hire

Rye Hire *1 Cyprus Place, Rye, TN31 7DR (01797 223033).*
A few minutes' walk from the station.

Brenzett Aeronautical Museum

Ivychurch Road, Brenzett, Romney Marsh, TN29 0EE (01797 344747/www.kent2do.com/brenzett aeronautical). **Open** *Easter-Oct* 11am-5.30pm Sat, Sun. *July-Oct* 1-5.30pm Wed-Fri; 11am-5.30pm Sat, Sun. Closed Nov-Easter. **Admission** £3; £2 concessions; free under-16s. **No credit cards**.
A couple of cowsheds (well, hangars) in a field don't look that inspiring, but this is a thrilling treat for World War II enthusiasts: a lovingly compiled collection of aircraft and memorabilia, much of it salvaged from the region.

Lamb House

West Street, Rye, TN31 7ES (NT regional office 01372 453401/www.nationaltrust.org.uk). **Open** *Apr-Oct* 2-6pm Wed, Sat. Closed Nov-Mar. **Admission** (NT) £2.60; £1.30 concessions. **No credit cards**.
The novelist Henry James lived in this stately townhouse from 1898 to 1916, at which point the writer G F Benson moved in, closely followed by his brother, A C (1922-25). Lamb House is now a small museum. The garden house where James wrote most of his novels, including *The Ambassadors* and *The Golden Bowl*, was destroyed by bombing in 1940.

Steaming in with the typically eccentric miniature **Romney, Hythe & Dymchurch Railway**.

Lydd Airport

Lydd, Romney Marsh, TN29 9QL (01797 322411/ www.lydd-airport.co.uk/www.lyddair.com). **Open** 9am-5.30pm Mon-Thur, Sun; 9am-7pm Fri, Sat. **Admission** free.

Ordinarily, we wouldn't recommend an airport as a tourist attraction, but Lydd Airport is no ordinary airport. Here are hand-painted murals from the 1960s decorating an 'aviation theme bar restaurant' and scores of tiny planes to watch from a nice conservatory or terrace. The crowning glory has to be the fly 'n' dine (Lyddair 01797 320000) experience; for £20 (plus lunch £39, dinner £59) you get champagne and canapés followed by a low-level flight over Kent and lunch or a five-course candlelit dinner. And if that doesn't appeal you could take a flying lesson instead.

Old Lighthouse

Dungeness Road, Dungeness, TN29 1NA (01797 321300/www.dungenesslighthouse.com). **Open** *Mar-June, mid Sept-Oct* 11am-5pm Sat, Sun. *July-mid Sept* 10.30am-5pm daily (phone to check). Closed Nov-Feb. **Admission** £3; £2 concessions. **No credit cards.**

The lighthouse is no longer operational, but climb the 169 steps for fine views over the Ness.

Port Lympne Wild Animal Park

Lympne, nr Hythe, CT21 4PD (01303 264647/ www.howletts.net). **Open** *Easter-Oct* 10am-6pm daily. Last entry 4.30pm. *Nov-Easter* 10am-5pm or dusk. Last entry 1½hrs before closing. **Admission** £11.95; £8.95 concessions; free under-4s. **Credit** AmEx, DC, MC, V.

Amble round Sir Philip Sassoon's sumptuous mansion (complete with a fine muralled room by Rex Whistler), then head off into the extensive grounds and get close

to the wild beasts. This collection was started and idiosyncratically run by the late John Aspinall and it's particularly good for gorillas, wolves and big cats. The views over Romney Marsh are sensational.

Romney, Hythe & Dymchurch Railway

New Romney Station, TN28 8PL (01797 362353/ www.rhdr.demon.co.uk). **Open** *Easter-Sept* 9.15am-6pm daily. *Mar, Oct* 9.15am-6pm Sat, Sun. Closed Nov-Feb. **Tickets** (all day) £9.60; £4.80 concessions. Phone to check other ticket prices. **Credit** MC, V.

A miniature railway barrels merrily from Dungeness Point to Hythe, stopping at the small beach towns along the coast. It passes some fine, flat scenery and seems to sweep through any number of back gardens. The railway was built by the millionaire racing driver Captain Howey in 1927 and everything (track, engines and the sweetest carriages) is one-third standard size.

Rye Art Gallery

107 High Street, Rye, TN31 7JY (01797 222433). **Open** 10.30am-1pm, 2-5pm daily. **Admission** free.

A constantly changing series of exhibitions, encompassing photography, paintings, pottery, glasswork, jewellery and crafts, mostly by locals and to a consistently high standard. The white walls and sympathetic lighting set off the exhibits well. Prices are reasonable.

Where to stay

Most of the good accommodation is clustered around Rye and Winchelsea and the best places tend to be booked out weeks ahead. If the options listed below are full, try the ancient **Mermaid Inn** (Mermaid Street, 01797 223065, doubles £100-£160) in Rye. **Wickham Manor**, a National Trust farmhouse outside Winchelsea, is also worth trying (Pannel Lane, 01797 226216/07885 790597/www.wickham manor.co.uk, doubles £60-£70). You can also stable your horse here.

Hope Anchor Hotel

Watchbell Street, Rye, TN31 7HA (01797 222216/ fax 01797 223796/www.thehopeanchor.co.uk). **Rates** £50-£85 single occupancy; £85-£130 double/twin; £125-£135 four-poster; £100-£155 family room. **Rooms** (all en suite) 9 double/twin; 1 four-poster; 1 family. **Credit** AmEx, DC, MC, V.
The Hope Anchor prides itself on being a family hotel, a rarity among the establishments in the area. It boasts very individual rooms, all furnished and fitted to very high standards, with lovely bedlinen and sherry on the welcome tea tray. All rooms have great views. Children and dogs welcome. All rooms are non-smoking.

Jeake's House

Mermaid Street, Rye, TN31 7ET (01797 222828/ fax 01797 222623/www.jeakeshouse.com). **Rates** £35-£75 single; £65-£75 single occupancy; £80-£88 double; £100-£112 four-poster. **Rooms** 1 single; 5 double (4 en suite); 3 four-poster (all en suite). **Credit** MC, V.
Wonderfully located in the heart of historic, cobbled Rye, the atmospheric 17th-century Jeake's House is heavy on the mahogany and damask but light in touch, with pale walls, white linen and views over a lovely garden keeping the decor the right side of chintzy. Each of the 11 rooms is individually decorated by proprietor Jenny Hadfield, daughter of Rye-born novelist John Burke. Service is attentive and an honesty bar completes the feeling of bonhomie. Children over 12 and dogs (£5 per night) welcome.

Little Orchard House

3 West Street, Rye, TN31 7ES (tel/fax 01797 223831/www.littleorchardhouse.com). **Rates** £50-£70 single occupancy; £70-£100 double. **Rooms** (both en suite) 2 four-poster. **Credit** MC, V.
Little Orchard House's two bedrooms are tastefully and comfortably decorated with antiques and paintings, as is the rest of Sara Brinkhurst's delightful Georgian townhouse. The overall feeling is one of welcoming informality, from the sitting room with its open fire through to the book and games room for wet days. There's also a large walled garden with an 18th-century smuggler's watchtower and secluded corners for balmy summer days. No smoking throughout.

The Old Vicarage

66 Church Square, Rye, TN31 7HF (01797 222119/ fax 01797 227466/www.oldvicaragerye.co.uk). **Rates** £74-£90 double/twin; £124 family room. **Rooms** (all en suite) 3 double/twin; 1 family. **No credit cards.**
Even if the four rooms weren't lovingly fitted and decorated with ash furniture and off-white decor, the attention to detail would make Julia and Paul Master's picturesque Georgian house stand out from the crowd: home-made cake and tea on your arrival; local handmade fudge and biscuits on your tea tray; sherry in the

evening and breakfasts that are fully deserving of the hotel's AA Best Breakfast in England Award. Children over eight welcome. No smoking throughout.

Romney Bay House Hotel

Coast Road, Littlestone-on-Sea, New Romney, TN28 8QY (01797 364747/fax 01797 367156). **Rates** £60-£95 single occupancy; £80-£140 double/twin; £125 four-poster. **Rooms** (all en suite) 2 twin; 6 double; 2 four-poster. **Credit** AmEx, MC, V.
The only really good place to stay on the Dungeness peninsula and it's bang on a pebble beach at the end of a bumpy track, enveloped by the Littlestone golf course. The house was originally designed for Hollywood gossip columnist Hedda Hopper by Sir Clough Williams-Ellis, who built Portmeirion. The rooms are spotless and the house is filled with antique furniture. All bedrooms are no smoking. Children over 14 welcome.
Littlestone-on-Sea is on B2071 off A259 at New Romney.

Rye Lodge Hotel

Hilders Cliff, Rye, TN31 7LD (01797 223838/fax 01797 223585/www.ryelodge.co.uk). **Rates** £90-£170 double/twin. Family rooms available, phone for details. **Rooms** (all en suite) 18 double/twin. **Credit** AmEx, DC, MC, V.
Just beyond the quaint cobbles of olde worlde Rye and a stone's throw from the Landgate Bistro (*see p41*) is Rye Lodge, an independent hotel with an indoor swimming pool, spa bath, sauna and steam room along with its 19 spacious bedrooms – perfect for those days when the rain won't let up. What it lacks in guesthouse charm it makes up for in facilities and comfort, including an award-winning restaurant. The staff are helpful without being intrusive. Children and dogs welcome.

White Horses Cottage

180 The Parade, Greatstone-on-Sea, Romney Marsh, TN28 8RS (01797 366626/www.folkstonehotels. uk.com/details/whitehorses.html). **Rates** £25 single occupancy; £40 double; £50 twin/four-poster. **Rooms** 1 double (private shower room); 1 twin (en suite); 1 four-poster (en suite). **No credit cards.**
This idiosyncratic Gothic pile overlooking the sea may not be quite as delightful a find as Romney Bay House (*see above*), but at half the price it's definitely a bargain, and it makes a great base for exploring Dungeness and Romney Marsh. Once part of a Sussex farmhouse and still with its oak beams, leaded windows and original doors, the house was relocated here in 1928. Its three double rooms all have a sea view and share a balcony, making it perfect for a group of friends. Children are welcome. No smoking throughout.
From the A259 in New Romney take the Station Road to the seafront then turn right; follow the road for a mile and a half. The hotel is on the right-hand side.

White Vine House

24 High Street, Rye, TN31 7JF (01797 224748/fax 01797 223599/www.whitevinehouse.co.uk). **Rates** £50-£60 single; £60-£85 single occupancy; £80-£110 double; £115-£125 four-poster; £95-£155 family. **Rooms** (all en suite) 1 single; 3 double; 2 four-poster; 1 family. **Credit** AmEx, DC, MC, V.
From the outside, White Vine House looks rather like a vertical version of the Chelsea Flower Show, with blooms covering every available inch of the Georgian

Walk on the weird side

Romney Marsh is without doubt one of the most surreal places in southern England. Classified as Britain's only desert and boasting the world's largest area of shingle, the combination of sea, vast flat open space (the area was an island until 300 years ago) and that pervasive, permanent hum of the Dungeness power station makes you feel as if you're in an episode of *The Prisoner*. Then, when the miniature Romney, Hythe and Dymchurch Railway train tootles by, you *know* you're in an episode of *The Prisoner*.

That feeling of dislocation and disorientation is best experienced by getting out of the car and walking the area – and there is plenty of wonderful walking to be done here. The **Dungeness RSPB Nature Reserve**, the oldest of the RSPB's reserves, is the best place to start your exploration and experience the fragile ecology of Dungeness Point. Built around huge gravel pits, here you can see scores of wildfowl species including, in late spring, terns, reed and sedge warblers, whitethroats and yellow wagtails migrating north. But you don't have to be an avid birdwatcher to enjoy yourself on the reserve's trails; hire some binoculars at the visitors' centre, pick up a trail leaflet and head off to explore 2,000 acres housing a quarter of Britain's plant species and 1,550 species of invertebrates, some unique to the area. Rest stops can be had in the reserve's five hides, where the silence is interrupted only by the lonely call of a marsh frog or bird.

You can do walks on the reserve too. The **Romney Marsh Countryside Project** (01797 367934/www.rmcp.co.uk) organises walks and events, most of which are free. There is a good range, all weird enough to do justice to the mood of the area: evening walks, minibeast safaris, moth walks, pond-dipping for grown-ups or an introduction to the plants of Dungeness. The Marsh's Listening Ears is one of the most interesting. This walk takes place only a few times a year and it's well worth making a special trip to

take part in it. The 'listening ears' in question are three bizarre concrete constructions, including a 200-foot-long curved wall rising up some 25 feet. They were built in the 1930s as part of an early warning system to detect enemy aircraft approaching from the Channel and were frankly rubbish, as the walk's guide will admit if pressed; at best, their range was only about 15 miles, and even the sound of a car in the area could easily throw the fragile equipment's reading out completely. As structures they are bizarre to say the least – and the subject of work by various artists, including Tacita Dean – yet their presence is another piece of the jigsaw that makes the marsh the strange, desolate and unique place it is.

Dungeness RSPB Nature Reserve
Dungeness Road, Lydd, TN29 9PN (01797320588/www.rspb.org.uk/reserve s/dungeness). **Open** *Reserve 9am-dusk daily. Visitors' centre Apr-Oct 10am-5pm daily. Nov-Mar 10am-4pm daily. Phone for details of events.* **Admission** (RSPB) £3; £1-£2 concessions. **Credit** MC, V.

façade. The flower theme continues inside, where the breakfast room features hand-painted sunflowers growing up the walls. Florals are dropped in the seven bedrooms, however. Here plush red carpets and embroidered linens create an air of luxury and quiet calm that is carried through into the beautiful mahogany-panelled residents' room. Children and dogs (£5 per night) welcome. All rooms are no smoking.

Where to eat & drink

Good food isn't a strong point in these parts and really good restaurants are few and far between, but there are some decent pubs with fantastically atmospheric interiors and two very good restaurants, the **Landgate Bistro** and **Romney Bay House**. Romney Bay House only accepts non-residents with prior bookings and you'll need to book ahead for the Landgate too. If you're craving spices, Rye offers Indian fare at **Tiger Coast** (5 High Street, 01797 224222), and Thai food at the **Lemongrass** (1-2 Tower Street, 01797 222327).

The cottagey **Peace & Plenty** pub in Playden (01797 280342) offers decent food and good beer. If you're in Winchelsea, try the **New Inn** (German Street, 01797 226252) for locally caught fish and seafood, while the **Black Lion** in Appledore (15 The Street, 01233 758206) offers stronger brews than anything you'll find in the omnipresent tearooms.

Bayleaves

33-5 The Street, Appledore, TN26 2BU (01233 758208). **Food served** 10am-5.30pm Tue-Fri, Sun; 9.30am-5.30pm Sat. **Main courses** £4.75-£8.75. **No credit cards.**
The impossibly quaint and tiny Bayleaves offers a welcome change from the (admittedly above par) pub grub that's ubiquitous in the Romney Marsh area. It's obviously popular with plummy locals of a certain age, who enjoy the banter that comes with the homely lunches and cream teas. These are as sumptuous as you'd expect, and well priced too: smoked haddock and spring onion fish cakes were two inches high and revealed slivers of roasted peppers as they crumbled on our forks; pork pie came with a tangy pickle and local salad, and a strawberry meringue was moist, sticky and irresistible.

Hythe Bay Fish Restaurant & Bar

Marine Parade, Hythe, CT21 6AW (01303 267024). **Food served** 12.30-2.15pm Tue; 12.30-2.15pm, 6.30-9.30pm Wed-Sat; 12.30-2pm Sun. **Main courses** £12.50. **Set lunch** (Tue-Fri) £10.95 2 courses. **Credit** AmEx, MC, V.
With the English Channel lapping at the door, this is the place to indulge in seafood, whether it be a dozen oysters and a glass of wine in the bar, or osso bucco of cod with garlic and thyme risotto in the restaurant. This unpretentious place has a modestly ambitious streak running through the kitchen, yet still satisfies traditionalists with fish and chips. Plate-glass windows keep the sea in view and the staff are friendly and efficient. The short lunch menu offers outstanding value for money.

The Landgate Bistro

5 Landgate, Rye, TN31 7LH (01797 222829/ www.landgatebistro.co.uk). **Food served** 7-9.30pm Tue-Fri; 7-10pm Sat. Closed 2wks at Christmas. **Set dinner** (Tue-Thur) £17.90 3 courses. **Main courses** £9.90-£12.90. **Credit** DC, MC, V.
Ask anyone in Rye for the best restaurant in town and the verdict is unanimous: it's the Landgate Bistro, a small, unprepossessing and unpretentious place that's as affordable as it is good. The menu majors on top-class ingredients prepared with a simplicity that allows the quality to shine through; fairly robust choices include mains of marinated chump of Romney Marsh lamb with onions and thyme or rabbit with white wine and rosemary. There's plenty of fish on the menu too: starters could include salmon and salt cod fish cakes; mains a traditional baked sea bass with hollandaise sauce. Desserts are mouthwatering. A good bottle of Chablis at £16 was the perfect accompaniment. The Landgate was packed out on our visit, so do book ahead.

The Pilot

Battery Road, Lydd, Dungeness, TN29 9NJ (01797 320314/www.thepilot.uk.com). **Food served** *Summer* noon-2.30pm, 6-9pm Mon-Fri; noon-9pm Sat; noon-8pm Sun. *Winter* noon-2.30pm, 6-9pm Mon-Fri; noon-2.30pm Sat; noon-8pm Sun. **Main courses** £5.50-£8.70. **Credit** MC, V.
The place to come for fish and chips on Romney Marsh is the Pilot, a seafront pub on the Dungeness promontory serving crisply battered, melting cod nestling on a bed of chips. While the huge portions, excellent service and friendly atmosphere doubtless contribute to its popularity, we suspect the glorious traditional seaside puds – towering knickerbocker glories, long banana splits and custard-drowned pies and crumbles – have a lot to do with it too, not to mention good children's meals, a covered veranda and a good range of beers.

Woolpack Inn

Beacon Lane, nr Brookland, TN29 9TJ (01797 344321). **Food served** noon-2pm, 6-9pm daily. **Main courses** £5.45-£11.95. **Credit** MC, V.
This lovely 15th-century Romney Marsh pub is hugely popular with locals, so get there early if you want some of the good-quality pub grub before last orders. The menu's a wide-ranging one: ploughman's – cheddar, pâté, stilton or ham – come piled high; the dish of the day on a recent visit was a platter of tender liver and bacon. Accompany it with a strong selection of beers and wines, the latter starting at £8.50 a bottle.

Ypres Castle Inn

Gun Garden, Rye, TN31 7HH (01797 223248/ www.ryetourism.co.uk/ypres/index.htm). **Food served** *July-Sept* noon-2.30pm, 7-9pm daily. *Oct-June* noon-2.30pm, 7-9pm Mon, Wed-Sat; noon-2.30pm Sun. **Main courses** £6.95-£12.50. **Credit** AmEx, MC, V.
Situated at the base of the 13th-century Ypres Tower, built to protect Rye from French invaders and just below the even older Church of St Mary, the Ypres Castle Inn serves an eclectic mix of superior pub food at moderate prices. There are locally produced steaks and lamb served with a choice of potatoes, whole grilled plaice, cod wrapped in prosciutto and a decent range of vegetarian dishes. Friendly service, nice-looking pub, a great selection of beers – what more could you ask for?

The Heart of Kent

An old-fashioned idyll just outside London.

As clichéd as it sounds, the heart of the Garden of England really is a vision of gentle rolling hills, restored windmills and time warp villages. While other parts of the country stomp brazenly into the 21st century, resistance is strong in this neck of the woods. OK, the modern world has had some impact – new-fangled restaurants keep springing up, and family-run farms and B&Bs may be feeling the pinch in increasingly difficult economic times – but the reasons for coming here remain the same: whether you want to ramble through scenic fields, gain inspiration from the many public gardens, or simply to eat, drink and be merry, it's all here.

The region began to prosper in the 14th century when Edward III invited Flemish weavers to settle in the area to teach the English a thing or two about producing good-quality cloth. It was a great success and the area became the centre for the manufacture of broadcloth, the export of which was greatly helped by the close proximity of nearby sea ports. The towns of Cranbrook and Tenterden and their surrounding villages thrived for the next 350 years until the silting up of many of the Channel ports led to the industry's decline.

Agriculture took over, especially hops and fruit, although today there are fewer hop gardens and orchards than there used to be, and many oasts, with their distinctive white cowls, have been transformed from dried hop storage to quirky homes. Nonetheless, fruit-picking opportunities abound, and this part of the county also has some of the most promising vineyards in south-east England (see p47 **A vine romance**).

Local highlights

The attractive town of **Cranbrook** is dominated by its array of Wealden architecture, particularly the **Union Windmill**. To the north-east lies the pretty white-weatherboarded village of **Sissinghurst**, known nationwide for the splendour of **Sissinghurst Castle Garden** on its outskirts (see p43 **Bi Vita**). Directly north, between peaceful Frittenden and Staplehurst, is **Iden Croft Herbs** (Frittenden Road, 01580 891432), an interesting garden for cooking and herbal enthusiasts.

East of Staplehurst is **Headcorn**. Formerly one of the area's major cloth-making centres,

today's town has little to offer the visitor, except conveniences such as a train station, a supermarket and a cash dispenser. It's a good base from which to explore, though.

Around here, the fabulous rolling countryside begins to flatten out, and heading south you come to a series of beautiful villages, including the unspoilt **Biddenden**, whose village sign depicts the Chulkhurst sisters, England's first recorded conjoined twins. Further east and north-east are **Smarden**, **Bethersden** and **Pluckley**, which rises high above the surrounding countryside and is reputed to be the most haunted village in the South-east. Pluckley is also known as the place where much of the H E Bates-inspired *Darling Buds of May* series was filmed. Its welcoming pub, the Black Horse (01233 840256), boasts a large peaceful beer garden where you can enjoy good pub food and cask ales.

The delightful market town of **Tenterden**, south-east of Biddenden, with its wide tree-lined thoroughfare, is filled with antiques shops. The station is the main jumping-on point for the **Kent and East Sussex Railway**. Trains run all the way from Tenterden to the moated 13th-century **Castle** (see p55), in East Sussex.

Leaving Tenterden to the south, the hills gradually descend with the approaching marshlands. Arriving at the village of Small Hythe, you'll find the charming 16th-century country house **Small Hythe Place**, once home to the actress Ellen Terry. Wine tastings, tours and tea can be had at **Tenterden Vineyard** across the road.

Just over the border with East Sussex at Northiam is the beautiful house and gardens of **Great Dixter** (see p55). Returning towards Cranbrook, **Sandhurst Vineyards** is well worth a tasting or two, while the eccentric cars

---

By train from London

Trains to **Headcorn** leave **Charing Cross** about every 30mins; the journey time is just over 1hr. Info: www.connex.co.uk. (From 2004 services will be taken over by South Eastern Trains; timetables should not be affected.)

Bi Vita

Remembered as both a keen gardener who lovingly restored the grounds of Sissinghurst Castle (*see p45*) and a prolific writer, Vita Sackville-West was an unlikely pioneer of gay rights. Born Victoria Mary Sackville-West in 1892, she was writing ballads by the age of 11. And even at this early age, Vita was infatuated by her childhood friend Rosamund Grosvenor. Nonetheless, she met and married the diplomat and art critic Harold Nicolson in 1913.

Despite an apparently happy marriage, which produced two children, Ben and Nigel, both Vita and Harold had homosexual affairs. Of Vita's various lesbian lovers, Virginia Woolf is perhaps the most famous, and she based the eponymous character in her novel *Orlando* (1928) on her. But Vita's most scandalous affair was undoubtedly the one she had with Violet Keppel, another childhood friend. The two women travelled together to Cornwall and France, Vita dressing as a man and calling herself 'Julian'. Later, Keppel went on to marry, but this didn't deter Vita – on the contrary, the two women eloped to France together, and were pursued by their husbands, who took a private plane and persuaded them to return home.

Some of Vita's works include veiled references to her bisexuality – in *Challenge* (1923), she wrote a fictional account of her affair with Keppel, moving the action to a Greek island and depicting the relationship between 'Julian' and 'Eve' as heterosexual. Vita seemed to find solace in her writing – penning 55 books, and writing a long-term weekly gardening column for the *Observer*.

Indeed, it was only in her secret diary, discovered some years after her death in 1962 by her son Nigel, that she felt free to explore her troubled mind. In the diary, which formed the basis for *Portrait of a Marriage* (1973), Nicolson's novel about his parents' life together, she claimed that if she could understand her dual personality, she would be able to leave a useful record for the future, when 'the psychology of people like myself will be a matter of interest, and... it will be recognised that many more people of my type do exist than under the present-day system of hypocrisy is commonly admitted'.

at the **CM Booth Collection of Vehicles** in **Rolvenden** is an added attraction in the pretty village. Between Rolvenden and the tranquil village of **Benenden** is **Hole Park**, a fabulously peaceful garden.

What to see & do

Tourist Information Centres
The Vestry Hall, Stone Street, Cranbrook, TN17 3HA (tel/fax 01580 712538/www.cranbrook.org.uk). **Open** *Apr-Sept* 10am-5pm Mon, Wed-Sat; noon-5pm Tue. Closed Oct-Mar.

Tenterden Town Hall, High Street, Tenterden, TN30 6AN (01580 763572/fax 01580 766863/ www.ashford.gov.uk). **Open** *Apr-Oct* 9.30am-1.30pm, 2-5pm Mon-Sat. Closed Nov-Mar.

CM Booth Collection of Historic Vehicles
63 High Street, Rolvenden, TN17 4LP (01580 241234). **Open** 10am-5.30pm Mon-Sat. **Admission** £2; £1 concessions. **No credit cards.**
This small collection is housed in a Tardis-like garden shed behind an antiques shop. There's an emphasis on three-wheeled classic Morgans, plus a wealth of auto-mobile memorabilia and toy and model cars.

Cranbrook Museum

Carriers Road, Cranbrook, TN17 3JX (01580 715542/ www.localmuseum.freeserve.co.uk). **Open** *Apr-Oct* 2-4.30pm Tue-Sat. Closed Nov-Mar. **Admission** £1.50; 50p concessions. **No credit cards.**

This timber-framed brick-fronted house, parts of which date from the late 15th century, is home to a collection of exhibits. The museum tells the history of the manufacture of broadcloth, the industry on which the town thrived; there's also material on the Royal Academy artists who made the area their home. There's quirky stuff too, such as exhibits about the Frittenden Forgers – a group who made coins out of siphon tops stolen from local pubs – plus an underwear collection of early 'drawers' and a signed photo of Elizabeth Taylor, who lived in Cranbrook as a child.

Cranbrook Union Windmill

The Hill, Cranbrook, TN17 3AH (01580 712984/ www.argonet.co.uk/users/tonysing/Union/). **Open** From spring 2004 *Apr-June, Sept* 2.30-5pm Sat. *July-Aug* 2.30-5pm Sat, Sun. Closed Oct-Mar. **Admission** free, donations welcome.

A local landmark, the Union Windmill is the largest and one of the best preserved smock mills in the country, so called because from a distance it was said to resemble a farmer's smock. The windmill is closed for renovations until spring 2004, after which it may open during the week as well as at weekends. More windmills can be found in Rolvenden (no tours, no phone), Woodchurch (01233 860649, tours by arrangement) and Wittersham (01797 270364, tours May-Sept 2.30-5pm Sun & bank hols).

Great Maytham Hall

Off A28 in Rolvenden, Cranbrook, TN17 4NE (01580 241346/www.cha.org.uk). **Open** *May-Sept* 2-5pm Wed, Thur; also National Garden Scheme days. Closed Oct-Apr. **Admission** *House & gardens* £4; £2 concessions. *Gardens only* £2; £1 concessions. **No credit cards.**

The house was designed by Sir Edwin Lutyens in 1910, although the 18-acre estate dates back to Saxon times; it includes the walled garden that was the inspiration for Frances Hodgson Burnett's *The Secret Garden.*

Headcorn Aerodrome

Shenley Road, Headcorn, TN27 9HX (01622 890226/ www.headcornaerodrome.co.uk). **Open** 9am-dusk daily. Old buildings and gardens may not appeal to adrenaline junkies, who'd prefer to go skydiving with the Headcorn Parachute Club (01622 890862, or check out their website at www.headcornparachuteclub.co.uk), have flying lessons with Weald Air Services (01622 891539/www.headcornaerodrome.co.uk) or take a trip in a Tiger Moth with the Tiger Club (01622 891017/ www.tigerclub.co.uk). This could be the most exhilarating way of exploring the heart of Kent.

Hole Park

Rolvenden, Cranbrook, TN17 4JB (01580 241251). **Open** *Apr-Oct* 2-6pm Wed; by appointment Thur. Closed Nov-Mar. Guided tours with tea by arrangement. **Admission** £3.50; 50p concessions. **No credit cards.**

This large, privately owned estate and garden is a beautiful and peaceful place to escape from the crowds at the better-known gardens in the Weald (where solitude is practically impossible). Walled and terraced areas add a certain distinction and a sunken garden is thrown in for good measure. Hole Park is also open on occasional Sundays as part of the National Gardens Scheme.

Kent & East Sussex Railway

Tenterden, TN30 6HE, Bodiam & Northiam, East Sussex stations (01580 765155/www.kesr.org.uk). **Open** School holidays daily, other dates phone for details. Closed Jan, Nov. **Admission** (return fare) £9; £4.50-£8 concessions; free under-3s. **Credit** MC, V. Chug back into the past with a journey on a steam train between Tenterden and Bodiam, East Sussex. There are family events throughout the year, such as Thomas the

Go bats in **Pluckley**. See p42.

Tank Engine fun days. The luxury Pullman also plays host to dinners, lunches, murder mystery evenings and even an annual *Fawlty Towers*-style evening.

Sissinghurst Castle Garden

Sissinghurst, Cranbrook, TN17 2AB (01580 712850/www.nationaltrust.org.uk/sissinghurst).
Open *Mid Mar-Nov* 11am-6.30pm Mon, Tue, Fri (last admission 5.30pm); 10am-6.30pm Sat, Sun (last admission 5.30pm). Closed Dec-mid Mar.
Admission (NT) £6.50; £3 concessions.
Credit AmEx, MC, V.
The most popular attraction in the area, Sissinghurst is famous not only for its inspirational gardens but also for its celebrity creators – poet and novelist Vita Sackville-West and her husband, diplomat Harold Nicolson – who rescued the property from near-ruin in 1930. There's tremendous individuality in the gardens, which have something to offer whatever the season. Visitors can also visit the 15th-century library and tower, where Sackville-West wrote 20 books, including *All Passion Spent*, and her gardening column. *See also p43* **Bi Vita**.

Small Hythe Place & Ellen Terry Memorial Museum

Small Hythe, nr Tenterden, TN30 7NG (01580 762334/www.nationaltrust.org.uk/smallhytheplace).
Open *Late Mar-mid Nov* 11am-5pm (last entry 4.30pm) Mon-Wed, Sat, Sun. Closed mid Nov-late Mar. **Admission** (NT) £3.40; £1.70 concessions; free under-5s. **No credit cards**.
Set in beautiful walking country, Small Hythe Place was the final home of Victorian actress Ellen Terry, who lived here from 1899 to her death in 1928. During her successful 24-year partnership with actor-manager Henry Irving, Terry came to be recognised as the leading Shakespearean actress of the English stage. The timber-framed house, which dates from the 15th century, is now a fascinating theatre museum depicting Terry's life and times. There is a small theatre in the garden, where

plays are staged and where Terry's great-nephew John Geilgud once performed. (Note that you have to be a member of the Barn Theatre Society to see the shows, but the general public can enjoy productions of Shakespeare, classical music and so on during July and August at the on-site open-air theatre). Exhibits include a message from Sarah Bernhardt, a visiting card from Alexandre Dumas and a letter from Oscar Wilde begging Terry to accept a copy of his first play. Upstairs are some of the actress's lavish costumes.

South of England Rare Breeds Centre

Highlands Farm, Woodchurch, TN26 3RJ (01233 861493/www.rarebreeds.org.uk). **Open** *Apr-Sept* 10.30am-5.30pm daily. *Oct-Mar* 10.30am-4.30pm Tue-Sun. **Admission** £5; free under-5s. **Credit** MC, V.
Opened in 1992, the South of England Rare Breeds Centre is home to, and has breeding programmes for, historic breeds of farm animal that are in danger of dying out, such as the Belted Galloway cow and Manx Loghtan sheep. Children in particular jump at the chance to pet the animals and ride on tractor trailers. You can even spot some celebs while you're here – namely Butch and Sundance – aka the Tamworth Two, saved from slaughter after they absconded from the abattoir a few years back. The *Daily Mail* still pays for their upkeep.

Where to stay

Bishopsdale Oast

Cranbrook Road, Biddenden, TN27 8DR (01580 291027/fax 01580 292321/www.bishopsdaleoast.co.uk). **Rates** £56.40 single occupancy; £70.50-double/twin. **Rooms** 5 double/twin (4 en suite, 1 with private bath). **Credit** MC, V.
Garden enthusiasts will delight in this 18th-century oasthouse, tucked down a country lane. With so many attractions nearby (and plenty of leaflets on hand to help you

plan your day), it's an ideal and relaxing base for touring. In summer you can eat outside in the garden (planted with wild flowers and herbs), or in winter lounge by the log fire. The decent-sized rooms retain their original beams, but are kept reassuringly up to date with a TV, tea- and coffee-making facilities and other mod cons. The Oast Room is the largest and most atmospheric. Bishopsdale offers an optional evening meal, which, like the breakfasts, is prepared using fresh ingredients (organic where possible) from the garden. All bedrooms are no-smoking.
A28 from Ashford to Tenterden; right at Cranbrook Road; after 2¹/2 miles, follow sign on left for Bishopsdale Oast.

Folly Hill Cottage
Friezley Lane, Hocker Edge, Cranbrook, TN17 2LL (tel/fax 01580 714299/www.follyhillcottage.co.uk). **Rates** £30-£32 single occupancy; £46-£50 twin. **Rooms** 2 twin (1 en suite, 1 with private shower room). **No credit cards.**
A great place to unwind. At the end of a narrow private lane dotted with stunning listed houses in the heart of a wooded valley, this welcoming house is the perfect choice for those looking for peace and quiet. Rooms are modern in style (one even has its own fridge), and owners Sonia and John de Carle are friendly and accommodating. Guests have use of the small communal TV lounge (there are TVs in the rooms too) and the pool in summer. Breakfast is an excellent spread, including cheese, meats, cereals and organic bread; there's an optional three-course evening meal (£17.50) if all that relaxing has taken its toll and you can't move. Children over ten welcome. No smoking throughout.
N of A262 between Goudhurst and Sissinghurst.

Hallwood Farm Oasthouse
Hallwood Farm, Hawkhurst Road, Cranbrook, TN17 2SP (01580 712416/www.hallwoodfarm.co.uk). **Rates** £55-£65 double/twin. **Rooms** (both en suite) 1 double; 1 twin. **No credit cards.**
At the end of a long private lane, this oasthouse is part of a working farm that has been in the Wickham family for 50 years. The two rooms (one twin, one double) are in the former hop-cooling part of the building. Both are tastefully decorated, with good-quality furnishings and books to browse. Breakfast is the only meal offered, but it's a showcase of local ingredients, and finding somewhere local for dinner won't be a problem. Should you gather the energy to leave your room, you're free to explore the farm's 230 acres. The lovely, lazy dogs, Bill and Moby, make this place feel like a real home – this is what all B&Bs should be like. No smoking throughout.

Sissinghurst Castle Farm
Biddenden Road, Sissinghurst, Cranbrook, Kent TN17 2AB (01580 712885/www.kent-esites.co.uk/ sissinghurstcastlefarm). **Rates** £28-£30 single; £56-£60 double. **Rooms** 2 single (shared bathroom); 5 double (1 en suite, 4 shared bathrooms). **No credit cards.**
This 19th-century property, which sits comfortably between a B&B and country house hotel, couldn't be better situated for fans of Sissinghurst Castle Garden. Owned by the Stearns family for decades (the current owner, James, was born in the house), it has a homely feel, with chandeliers, rugs and antiques, not to mention a sweeping staircase dominating the hall. Rooms are creaky and cosy, with attractive florals and books to browse. The

bathrooms – one of which has a huge sofa in it – are stocked with bottles of everyday toiletries. And if all those gardens at Sissinghurst Castle Garden weren't enough, this place also has its own, which guests are free to wander. Weekend house parties, including dinner, are a speciality in winter. Children over nine welcome.
Follow signs to Sissinghurst Castle Gardens; farm is in the grounds of castle.

Where to eat & drink

Good local boozers abound, with the odd decent restaurant thrown in for good measure. Fish lovers, in particular, will be spoilt for choice. Among the rural pubs worthy of a journey are the **Woodcock** at Iden Green (south of Benenden, 01580 240009), the rambling 16th-century **Bell** at Smarden (01233 770283) or the **Wild Duck** in Marden Thorn (Pagehurst Road, between Marden and Staplehurst, 01622 831340), popular for its interesting grub. The town pubs pale by comparison, but if you are staying in or near Tenterden, head down to the inviting **William Caxton** (West Cross, 01580 763142). Tenterden also has an Indian, **Badsha** (10 West Cross, 01580 765151), and the **Thai Orchid** (75 High Street, 01580 763624); for a meze fix, try the popular Turkish restaurant **Ozgur** (126 High Street, 01580 763248).

Dering Arms
Station Road, Pluckley, TN27 0RR (01233 840371). **Food served** noon-2pm, 7-9pm daily. **Main courses** £8.45-£21.95. **Credit** AmEx, DC, MC, V.
Fish and seafood are the mainstay at this atmospheric former hunting lodge, complete with flagstones, wood floors and high ceilings. It can be hard to find if you're coming by car (it's tucked away by the train station), and the dining room can get so busy that there are lapses in service, but staff are friendly and the food is a cut above the rest (as evidenced by the many awards the pub has picked up). Expect starters such as grilled sardines with rosemary butter or garlic king prawns; typical main courses might be pan-fried scallops with basil spaghetti and saffron sauce, or breast of duck with potato and celeriac purée and port sauce. The wine list features some choice bottles – should they prove too tempting, you can stagger upstairs afterwards and stay in one of the bedrooms (good value at £40 for a double).

Rankins Restaurant
The Street, Sissinghurst, TN17 2JH (01580 713964/ www.rankinsrestaurant.com). **Food served** 7.30-9pm Wed-Sat; 12.30-2pm Sun. **Set dinner** £24.50 2 courses; £29.50 3 courses. **Main courses** (Sun lunch only) £12.50. **Credit** MC, V.
The interior of Hugh and Leonora Rankins' restaurant won't win any design awards with its step-back-in-time look, but it's good to see such a friendly and self-assured place. The menu is short but well executed, and local produce features strongly, with lamb from Frittenden and Romney Marsh, and fish from Rye. Stand-out dishes include a starter of Rankins' oak-smoked haddock baked in a cheddar glazed creamy lemon sauce, and coffee

A vine romance

Don't knock it till you've tried it – English wine is gaining a reputation. A good one, that is. Many of the country's 400-odd vineyards are in the South-east, and below is our pick of the bunch. The best time to visit the Kentish vineyards is September and October, when the vines are full and harvesting begins. All the following have free admission and tastings, though some charge a small fee for tours.

Biddenden Vineyards
Little Whatmans, Gribble Bridge Lane, Biddenden, TN27 8DF (01580 291726/ www.biddendenvineyards.com). **Open** *Mar-Dec* 10am-5pm Mon-Sat; 11am-5pm Sun. *Jan, Feb* 10am-5pm Mon-Sat. Tours by arrangement, phone for details. Kent's oldest commercial vineyard is also home to some CAMRA award-winning ciders.

Harbourne Vineyard
Wittersham, TN30 7NP (01797 270420/ www.harbournevineyard.co.uk). **Open** 2-6pm daily (phone to check).

A small, friendly vineyard that also includes vegan and vegetarian wines in its repertoire.

Sandhurst Vineyards & Hop Farm
Hoads Farm, Crouch Lane, Sandhurst, TN18 5PA (01580 850296). **Open** *Apr-Dec* 2-6pm Mon-Fri; 11.30am-6pm Sat; noon-5pm Sun (phone to check). Closed Jan-Mar. Tours by arrangement for groups only, phone for details.
A friendly, family-run vineyard with some award-winning wines. The owners also run a B&B in their beautifully restored 16th-century farmhouse.

Tenterden Vineyard
B2082, Small Hythe, Tenterden, TN30 7NG (01580 763033/www.newwave wines.com). **Open** 10am-5pm daily. **Tour & tasting** *Easter-Oct* £4; £1-£3.50 concessions; free under-12s.
The second-largest winery in the UK is home to Chapel Wines. It has the added attractions of a small museum, a plant centre, a herb garden and a bistro.

---

fudge pudding. Prices aren't the lowest in the world, or indeed the area, but the wine list has plenty of bottles to choose from for under £20. An enjoyable experience.

Restaurant 23
23 Stone Street, Cranbrook, TN17 3HF (01580 714666). **Food served** 7-9.30pm Tue; noon-2pm, 7-9.30pm Wed-Sat. 12.30-2.30pm Sun. **Main courses** £12.50-£17.50. **Set lunch** (Sun) £23.95 3 courses. **Credit** MC, V.
This restaurant, formerly Soho South, is another one to watch. The decor is heavy on beams and dried hops, and the atmosphere is low-key. Food in upmarket Modern European food. Typical starters from the frequently changing menu include fried goat's cheese with pear and ginger chutney and rocket salad; main courses might be loin of pork with black pudding crust, velouté of peas and broad beans, or fillet of Sussex beef with sun-blushed tomato relish, roast provençal vegetables and olive gravy. Desserts, such as apple tarte tatin with vanilla ice-cream, are worth holding out for. Booking recommended.

Three Chimneys
Just off the A262, west of Biddenden, TN27 8LW (01580 291472). **Food served** noon-2.50pm, 6.30-9.50pm Mon-Sat; noon-2.50pm, 7-9pm Sun. **Main courses** £10.95-£18.95. **Credit** MC, V.
This deservedly popular country pub dates back to 1420 (though the restaurant out back is a mere 25 years old). The friendly service can be on the slow side and prices are high, but portions are generous and standards impressive. Typical starters include deep-fried brie with

Cumberland sauce and crusty bread. Among the mains are fillet of smoked haddock on a bacon, parmesan and spring onion mash with grain mustard butter sauce. Those generous portions mean you may have no time for dessert, though you'll be hard pressed to refuse the likes of sticky toffee pudding and raspberry and vanilla brûlée. Well-kept ales include Adnams, Shepherd Neame and Harveys Best. Booking is advisable (but not possible for Sunday lunch, so get here early).

The West House
28 High Street, Biddenden, TN27 8AH (01580 291341). **Food served** noon-2pm, 7-9.45pm Tue-Fri; 7-9.45pm Sat; noon-2pm Sun. **Set dinner** £24.50 3 courses. **Main courses** (lunch only) £11.95-£14.95. **Credit** MC, V.
With Graham Garrett – who trained under Richard Corrigan – at the helm, the West House is a showcase for superlative Modern European cooking. The airy interior is enticing, with beams, wooden floors and candles, and the mood relaxed. The menu is inventive and brimming with local produce – starters might be dab fillets and steamed mussels in Biddenden cider, cream and tarragon, or potted mackerel, marinated cucumber and toast; mains could include a generous portion of monkfish wrapped in parma ham, with sprouting broccoli and smoked anchovy butter, or roast spring lamb, new season garlic, verdina beans and basil. Desserts tread the line between comfort food and inventiveness, with a smooth and tangy prune and Armagnac brûlée, and strawberry and orange soup with yoghurt panna cotta (part of the fixed-price dinner menu). The wine list is extensive – and not too expensive.

The Kent Weald

Quiet byways lead to delightful villages, superb castles and immaculate gardens.

Wooded valleys, hop gardens, fruit orchards, ancient half-timbered pubs; the dreamy landscape of *The Darling Buds of May* (actually filmed in Pluckley, *see p42*) is to be found in the Kent Weald. Although the Weald is often thought of as specifically Kentish, the term does, in fact, refer to the entire basin between the North and South Downs and thus stretches from the south Kent coast all the way through Sussex, even spilling over into Hampshire. This chapter only covers part of the Kent Weald (for the more southerly section, *see p42* **The Heart of Kent**; for the Sussex Weald, *see p62* **The Ashdown Forest**).

The term 'weald' – meaning forest and taken from the Anglo-Saxon 'Wald' – refers to the immense swathe of oak and beech that once stretched from Hythe to Winchester. The Anglo-Saxons, while searching for hog pastures, were the first to establish permanent settlements within the Weald, and Anglo-Saxon terms are still the most frequent suffixes found on Wealden place names – 'hurst' means a wooded knoll, '-den' a clearing in a wood, '-ley' a meadow and '-ham' a small homestead. By the early 14th century, much of the forest had been cleared and the familiar landscape of hedged, cultivated fields punctuated by small, neat, green woods was established.

The Weald became the major manufacturing area of the country from the Middle Ages until the 18th century and was renowned for iron ore production. This declined as industrialisation got seriously ugly, leaving the Weald with an unparalleled collection of late medieval and Tudor buildings. Weather-boarded and tile-hung houses are another distinctive feature, as are the ubiquitous oast houses; at one time more than 30,000 acres of Kent countryside were devoted to growing hops. Once – before the full-scale mechanisation of agriculture in the 1960s – working-class Londoners would travel to Kent to stay on hop farms for a working holiday. Today not one of Kent's oast houses is used for it's original purpose of pressing and drying – even those of Britain's oldest brewer, Shepherd Neame in Faversham, are now redundant. At **Hop Farm Country Park** in Beltring, however, you can see how it was done.

A right royal spa

Tunbridge Wells (more properly and pompously known, since 1909, as Royal Tunbridge Wells) exists chiefly in the public imagination as the upright, uptight home of 'disgusted' *Times* letter-writers. It's actually a rather appealing town, if a touch staid, basking in a typically Wealden wooded valley. It makes an excellent base for exploring the region. As Kentish towns go, it's something of an upstart, dating back only as far as the 17th century, when Lord North discovered the Chalybeate Spring in 1606, declared himself cured of consumption and set in train a development that left the town second only to Bath in the fashionable spa circuit. The spring, at the end of the Pantiles, the town's most famous street (and attraction), still draws tourists today, who come to drink a glass of the iron-bearing, apparently revolting-tasting, waters. The Pantiles were once described by John Evelyn as 'a very sweet place… private and refreshing'. This colonnaded late 17th-century shopping street is still rather sweet and thankfully not yet totally overwhelmed by tacky trinket shops.

A favourite family outing from here is to the **High Rocks**, a couple of miles south-west of the town. This series of sandstone rocks, linked by 11 bridges and set in a wooded valley, is a lovely spot for a stroll and a pleasant picnic. It isn't exactly undiscovered, though – the steam-powered **Spa Valley Railway** (01892 537715) regularly passes through the area (between March and October, from West station close to the Pantiles, phone for details).

By train from London

Trains to **Tunbridge Wells** and **Tonbridge** leave from **Charing Cross** approximately every 15-30mins and pass through **Waterloo East** and **London Bridge** (55mins journey time). Trains to **Edenbridge** leave from **London Bridge** hourly and take 50mins. Info: www.connex.co.uk. (Services will be taken over by South Eastern Trains in 2004; timetables should not be affected).

Hop Farm Country Park. *See p51*.

Weald in motion

The Weald is perfect country for gentle touring, either by car or bike, or walking. There are marked cycle and motoring routes and a plethora of walking trails (leaflets available at Tourist Information Centres). In between Tunbridge Wells and Sevenoaks is the workaday town of **Tonbridge**, with a main feature of a striking ruined Norman castle. West is **Chiddingstone**'s much photographed single street (entirely owned by the National Trust) – an open-air museum of 15th- and 16th-century domestic architecture. Neighbouring **Penshurst** is also exceptionally pretty and has the added attractions of **Penshurst Place and Gardens** and **Penshurst Vineyard** (01892 870255). Also close by is exquisite and popular **Hever Castle**.

South of Tunbridge Wells, on the border with East Sussex, is **Groombridge Place Gardens** (Groombridge, 01892 861444/ www.groombridge.co.uk) with award-winning kid paradise Enchanted Forest. East lies **Bewl Water**, the largest body of water in the South-

east. It's actually a reservoir and a popular spot for watersports, fishing, walking, horse riding and cycling. For the latter, bikes can be hired from the visitors' centre off the A21 between Lamberhurst and Flimwell. Nearby is the evocative ruined medieval **Bayham Abbey**, the extensive keyboard instruments collection at **Finchcocks** and the effortlessly romantic **Scotney Castle Gardens**.

At the point north-east of Tunbridge Wells where the High Weald tumbles down into the Low (also known as the Vale) is a clutch of stunning little villages, such as **Goudhurst**, **Horsmonden** and **Matfield**. The country gently flattens towards where the Medway flows down to Maidstone. Nearby **Leeds Castle**, more remarkable for its setting than its interior, is a major draw.

On the flanks of the Greensand Ridge that runs from Maidstone to Sevenoaks and beyond are yet more cutesy villages (such as **Plaxtol**), along with yet more fine noble piles and gardens, chief among them the medieval/Tudor manor house of **Ightham Mote** (*see p50* **Ightham Mote**) and the vast Sackville family gaff of **Knole**.

The Weald has a wealth of gardens. In addition to those listed (*see below*), other fine examples include **Marle Place Gardens and Gallery** near Brenchley (Marle Place Road, 01892 722304), **Great Comp Garden** at Platt near Sevenoaks (Comp Lane, 01732 886154/ www.greatcomp.co.uk), **Owlhouse Gardens** in Lamberhurst (Mount Pleasant Lane, 01892 890230), **Stoneacre** at Otham near Maidstone (Stoneacre Lane, 01622 862871/www.national trust.org.uk), **Broadview Gardens** at Hadlow (Hadlow College, Hadlow Road, 01732 853211) and the world's finest collection of conifers at the **Bedgebury National Pinetum and Forest Gardens** near Goudhurst (Park Lane, 01580 211044/www.forestry.gov.uk).

What to see & do

Tourist Information Centres

Stangrove Park, Station Road, Edenbridge, TN8 5LU (01732 868110/www.sevenoaks.gov.uk). **Open** 9.30am-4pm Mon-Sat.

The Town Hall, Middle Row, High Street, Maidstone, ME14 1TF (01622 602169/602048/www.heartofkent. org.uk). **Open** 9am-5pm Mon-Sat; 10am-4pm Sun.

Buckhurst Lane, Sevenoaks, TN13 1LQ (01732 450305/www.heartofkent.org.uk). **Open** *Apr-Sept* 9.30am-5pm Mon-Sat. *Oct-Mar* 9.30am-5pm Mon-Fri; 9.30am-4.30pm Sat.

Old Fish Market, The Pantiles, Tunbridge Wells, TN2 5TN (01892 515675/www.visittunbridgewells. com). **Open** *June-Sept* 9am-6pm Mon-Sat; 10am-5pm Sun. *Oct-May* 9am-5pm Mon-Sat; 10am-4pm Sun.

Ightham Mote

Tucked away down a winding lane in a deep wooded valley, where the River Bourne begins its journey to the Medway, is **Ightham Mote**, a moated medieval manor house that is one of the finest in the country. The original part of the house (the great hall, chapel, crypt and kitchen) dates back to the early 14th century. The house has undergone a complex series of alterations and additions over the years, including the building of garden cottages (pictured), and has had some brushes with dramatic events in English history.

The first recorded owner, a Staffordshire knight called Sir Thomas Carne, moved in around 1360, although

Bike hire

Cycle-ops.co.uk *5 Bank Street, Tonbridge, TN9 1BL (01732 500533/www.cycle-ops.co.uk).* Four hundred yards from the railway station.

Finchcocks

Riseden, nr Goudhurst, TN17 1HH (01580 211702/ www.finchcocks.co.uk). **Open** *Easter-July, Sept* 2-6.30pm Sun (music concerts starts at 2.45pm in Sept). *Aug* 2-6pm Wed, Thur, Sun. *Oct-Easter* only by appointment. **Admission** *House, gardens & music* £7.50; £4-£5 concessions. *Gardens only* £2.50. **No credit cards.**

A popular venue for weddings parties due to its attractive setting, this early Georgian manor house has a collection of around 100 historical keyboard instruments. Behind the house are four acres of gardens with shrub borders and there is also a walled garden containing a circle of immaculately clipped flowers. The house and its grounds make a perfect setting for the Finchcocks September Festival (call or details).

Hever Castle

Hever, nr Edenbridge, TN8 7NG (01732 865224/ www.hevercastle.co.uk). **Open** *Castle & gardens* Mar-Nov 11am-6pm daily. Closed Dec-Feb. **Admission** *Castle & gardens* £8.40; £4.60-£7.10 concessions. *Gardens only* £6.70; £4.40-£5.70 concessions. **Credit** MC, V.

The childhood home of Henry VIII's ill-fated second wife Anne Boleyn, the 13th-century Hever Castle is surrounded by a double moat and has a water maze with jets for visitors to negotiate. The castle was bought and restored by William Waldorf Astor in 1903 and it was he who constructed the 'Tudor' village that lies behind it and also who created the magnificent gardens and lake. Other main attractions inside the house include a model houses exhibition and a rather gruesome display of instruments of execution and torture dating back over a few hundred years – the kind of things kids will dig, in other words. Special events take place throughout the year and include Easter Egg trails, jousting and archery tournaments, and music festivals.

research suggests the original part of the house was built before then. Despite its grandeur, life in medieval Mote would not have been comfortable by today's standards. It would have been dark, draughty and chilly in winter. Privacy was hard to find, with most members of the household sleeping on straw pallets in the hall or kitchen. The Carnes would have had the only beds in the place.

A series of owners made alterations and additions during the 15th and 16th centuries. Edward Hault (1487-1519) not only enclosed the courtyard but also built a three-storey gatehouse tower complete with medieval letterbox. The courtier Sir Richard Clement bought the house in 1521 and wasted no time showing his devotion to the Tudor crown by covering it with symbolic ornamentation.

The house passed on to Sir William Selby in 1591 and stayed in the staunchly Catholic family for three centuries. The Selbys are said to be responsible for ghostly goings-on at La Mote. There is a theory that Dame Dorothy Selby was the sender of the letter that led to the uncovering of the Gunpowder Plot in 1605. The letter was delivered to Lord Monteagle, a 'reformed' Catholic and Dorothy Selby's cousin, warning him to stay away from the opening of parliament on 5 November.

A suspicious Monteagle showed the letter to Secretary of State Robert Cecil. A search was made of the cellars beneath the House of Lords and Guy Fawkes was arrested, the plot thwarted, and the other conspirators hunted down. Legend has it that outraged friends of the conspirators seized Dame Dorothy and walled her up in a small room in the tower. A female skeleton was found in a sealed room in 1872, and it is said that a strange chill persists there to this day.

In the 20th century American industrialist Charles Henry Robinson became the saviour of a deteriorating Ightham Mote. He bought the house in 1953 and made vital repairs over the next 30 years, before bequeathing it to the National Trust in 1985.

Ightham Mote is currently undergoing the largest conservation project ever undertaken by the National Trust on a house of this age and fragility. The phased programme of conservation and repair began in 1988 and is now nearing completion.

Ightham Mote

Mote Road, Ivy Hatch, Sevenoaks, TN15 0NT (01732 810378/information line 01732 811145/www.national trust.org.uk/ighthammote). **Open** (2003) *Mar-10 Nov,* (2004) *28 Mar-7 Nov* 10am-5.30pm Mon, Wed-Fri, Sun, bank hols. Last entry 5pm. **Admission** (NT) £6.50; £3.50 concessions. *Tour* 10.30am, additional £2.50; £1 concessions. **No credit cards**.

Hop Farm Country Park

Maidstone Road, Beltring, Paddock Wood, TN12 6PY (01622 872068/www.thehopfarm.co.uk). **Open** 10am-5pm (last entry 4pm) daily. **Admission** £6.50; £5.50 concessions. *Special events* £7.50; £6.50 concessions. **Credit** MC, V.

The largest surviving collection of Victorian oast houses is the centrepiece of this multifaceted family attraction, which includes a children's activity centre and adventure playground, the Hop Story exhibition and the Shire Pottery. There are also special family events that take place during the holidays.

Knole

Sevenoaks, TN15 0RP (01732 450608/www. nationaltrust.org.uk). **Open** *House* Mar-Nov 11am-4pm Wed-Sun. Closed Dec-Feb. *Gardens* May-Sept 11am-4pm (last entry 3pm) 1st Wed of mth. Closed Oct-Apr. **Admission** (NT) *House* £5.50; £2.75 concessions. *Gardens only* £2; £1 concessions. *Parking* £2.50 for visitors. **Credit** MC, V.

Set in a magnificent deer park, the birthplace of the writer Vita Sackville-West was also the setting for Virginia Wolfe's novel *Orlando*. This original 15th-century house was enlarged and embellished in 1603 by the first Earl of Dorset, one of Queen Elizabeth's 'favourites', and has remained unaltered ever since. There are 13 staterooms open to the public, containing furnishings, art, textiles and portraits.

Museum of Kent Life

Lock Lane, Sandling, nr Maidstone, ME14 3AU (01622 763936/www.museum-kentlife.co.uk). **Open** *Mar-Oct* 10am-5.30pm daily (last entry 4pm). *Nov-Feb* 10am-3pm Sat, Sun (last entry 2pm). **Admission** £5.50; £3.50-£4 concessions. **Credit** MC, V.

Kent's fascinating and family-friendly open-air museum is home to a collection of historic buildings; they house both conventional and interactive exhibitions covering the past 100 years. Visitors can explore an oast house, a thatched barn or the Larkin's kitchen and lounge, recreated from the *Darling Buds of May* TV series.

Penshurst Place & Gardens

*Penshurst, nr Tonbridge, TN11 8DG (01892
870307/www.penshurstplace.com).* **Open** *House*
Apr-Oct noon-5.30pm Mon-Fri, Sun; noon-4.30pm
Sat. Closed Nov-Mar. *Grounds* Apr-Oct 10.30am-6pm
daily (last entry 5pm). Closed Nov-Mar. **Admission**
House & gardens £7; £5-£6.50 concessions; free
under-5s. *Gardens only* £5.50; £4.50-£5 concessions;
free under-5s. **Credit** MC, V.

This finely preserved medieval masterpiece has been
home to the Sidney family since 1552 and little has
changed over the centuries. Additions to the house have
seen it grow into an imposing stately home displaying
features of at least eight different architectural periods,
as well as an 11-acre Elizabethan garden. Visitors can
also enjoy the Toy Museum or walk the Woodland Trail.

Scotney Castle Gardens

*Lamberhurst, nr Tunbridge Wells, TN3 8JN (01892
891081/www.nationaltrust.org.uk).* **Open** *Castle*
May-mid Oct 11am-6pm Wed-Sun (last entry 5pm).
Closed mid Oct-Apr. *Garden* mid Mar-Oct 11am-6pm
Wed-Sun. Closed Nov-mid Mar. **Admission** (NT)
£4.40; £2.20 concessions. **Credit** AmEx, DC, MC, V.

One of England's most romantic gardens, designed in
picturesque style around the ruins of a 14th-century
moated castle. Rhododendrons and azaleas are plentiful, with wisteria and roses rambling over the old ruins.
A viewing paradise with lovely woodland and walks.

Tonbridge Castle

*Castle Street, Tonbridge, TN9 1BG (01732 770929/
www.tmbc.gov.uk).* **Open** *Apr-Oct* 9am-4pm Mon-Sat;
10.30am-4pm Sun. *Nov-Mar* 9am-3pm Mon-Sat;
10.30am-3pm Sun. **Admission** £4.20; £2.10
concessions; free under-5s. **Credit** MC, V.

Set on the banks of the Medway river, this 13th-
century castle is surrounded by 14 acres of gardens and
castle walls. It offers seasonal tours as well as events in
the castle lawns, including summer concerts.

Yalding Organic Gardens

*Benover Road, Yalding, ME18 6EX (01622 814650/
www.hdra.org.uk).* **Open** *Apr, Oct* 10am-5pm Sat,
Sun. *May-Sept* 10am-5pm Wed-Sun. Closed Nov-Mar.
Admission £3; free under-16s. **Credit** MC, V.

There's a historical theme to these unusual gardens near
Maidstone. Visitors can walk through 'ancient' woodlands as well as medieval, psychic, knot and paradise
gardens. There's also a 19th-century artisan's plot, and
a 1940s 'Dig for Victory' allotment. The rest of the garden is devoted to the 'organic future of horticulture'.

Where to stay

Becketts

*Pylegate Farm, Hartfield Road, Cowden, Edenbridge,
TN8 7HE (01342 850514/www.becketts-bandb.
co.uk).* **Rates** £35-£48 single occupancy; £55-£65
twin; £58-£68 four-poster. **Rooms** 2 twin (shared
bathroom); 1 four-poster (en suite). **No credit cards.**
Set among several properties at Pylegate Farm, this
charming, heavily beamed Grade II-listed barn conversion is situated in an ideal spot, less than a mile from
Cowden station (one hour to Victoria), within spitting
distance of numerous watering holes and convenient for

a host of Wealden attractions. Upstairs there are two
comfortable twin rooms that share a bathroom, while on
the ground floor there's a cute little four-poster room
with en suite bathroom. The friendly, chatty host Jacqui
Wilcox is most welcoming. All bedrooms are no smoking. Vegetarian and vegan breakfasts available.

Hoath House

*Chiddingstone Hoath, nr Edenbridge, TN8 7DB
(tel/fax 01342 850362).* **Rates** £25-£27.50 single
occupancy; £50-£55 double/twin; £60-£80 family
(sleeps 4-5). **Rooms** 2 double (en suite); 1 twin; 1
twin/family room. **No credit cards.**

The friendly Streatfield family have lived in exquisite
Chiddingstone village (three miles away) for 400 years.
Their extraordinary current home – a mishmash of
architectural styles from Tudor onwards – is as far from
a typical B&B as it's possible to imagine. Guests are
housed in the Edwardian wing, complete with shared
art deco bathrooms, but eat breakfast in the oak-beamed
and panelled Tudor dining room and can lounge in the
neighbouring beamed sitting room with a wood-
burning fire. Decent food is available in nearby pubs.
Children welcome. No smoking throughout.

Hotel Du Vin and Bistro

*Crescent Road, Tunbridge Wells, TN1 2LY (01892
526455/fax 01892 512044/www.hotelduvin.com).*
Rates £89-£165 single occupancy/double/twin.
Rooms (all en suite) 16 double; 18 double/twin.
Credit AmEx, DC, MC, V.

A perfect base for visiting and exploring Tunbridge
Wells and the surrounding countryside. The 36 individually decorated bedrooms feature magnificent beds
and there are CD players, minibars and satellite television for that special home-from-home feeling. Power
showers, oversized baths, robes and fluffy towels add
to the comfort, as does the well-mannered service.
There's even a billiard room, complete with Armagnac
bar. Breakfast costs £13.50 for a full English or £9.50
for croissant and juice. The hotel is part of the small and
flourishing Hotel Du Vin chain of boutique hotels.
Children welcome. For restaurant, *see p53.*

Jordans

Sheet Hill, Plaxtol, TN15 0PU (01732 810379).
Rates £42-£45 single; £68-£72 double. **Rooms**
1 single; 2 double (en suite). **No credit cards.**

This B&B was originally a yeoman farmer's house. It
dates from the 15th century, and is deeply atmospheric,
with oak beams, inglenook fireplaces, leaded windows,
antiques and paintings. Many of these are by the owner,
Jo Lindsay, a Blue Badge guide who can also help plan
your tour of the area. Breakfast is a bargain £3. This is
a real B&B, so check-in isn't until 6pm and the house is
closed during the day. No smoking throughout. Children
over 12 welcome.

The Old Parsonage

*Church Lane, Frant, TN3 9DX (tel/fax 01892
750773/www.theoldparsonagehotel.co.uk).* **Rates**
£75-£95 four-poster/twin. **Rooms** (all en suite)
2 four-poster; 1 twin. **Credit** MC, V.

Voted the best B&B in south-east England, this pretty
but grand Georgian country house set in three acres of
gardens offers luxury accommodation. Owned by Tony
and Mary Dakin, the house features antiques and

chandeliers. An atrium at its centre provides ample natural light, and guests have the use of the comfortable drawing room, conservatory and terrace. Children over seven and pets welcome. All bedrooms are no smoking.

Scott House
37 High Street, West Malling, ME19 6QH (01732 841380/fax 01732 522367/www.scott-house.co.uk). **Rates** £59 single occupancy; £79 double/twin. **Rooms** (all en suite) 1 twin; 3 double. **Credit** AmEx, DC, MC, V.

In the heart of West Malling is this Grade II-listed Georgian townhouse. While the owners have retained a small interior design business on the ground floor, much of the upstairs has been tastefully converted into B&B accommodation including a spacious resident's lounge. The five rooms are styled and immaculate, and service from the immensely likeable Ernie and Margaret Smith is attentive but low-key. No smoking throughout.

Where to eat & drink

The shortage of quality restaurants in this area is compensated for by some cracking pubs. Many, such as the ones listed here, serve good food. Try the **Wheatsheaf Inn** (Hever Road, Bough Beech, 01732 700254), a former hunting lodge renowned for its ales; the stereotypically picturesque **Crown Inn** at Groombridge (The Walks, 01892 864742); the rambling **Castle Inn** in Chiddingstone (The Street, 01892 870247/ www.castleinn.co.uk), which boasts the village's own-brewed Larkins. There's also the creeper-clad **Harrow Inn** on Common Road, Ightham Common (01732 885912); the **Papermakers Arms** in Plaxtol (The Street, 01732 810407) and the **Bottle House Inn** in Penshurst (Coldharbour Lane, Smarts Hill, 01892 870306).

The Hare
Langton Road, Langton Green, TN3 0JA (01892 862419/www.hare-tunbridgewells.co.uk). **Food served** noon-9.30pm Mon-Sat; noon-9pm Sun. **Main courses** £6.95-£15.95. **Credit** MC, V.

The spacious dining rooms at this popular pub packs diners in. Food is inventive. 'Little things' (aka starters) might include a light mushroom and port pâté with toasted brioche and smoked cheese, or a cajun salmon, mango and rocket filo tart with vanilla dressing. Mains ('big things') are the likes of smoked haddock and salmon fish cakes, or grilled halibut with spring vegetable and prawn risotto and salsa verde – superb on a recent visit. Puds are traditional and gorgeous: ginger sponge pudding with golden syrup and cream. There's dining on the terrace in fine weather.

Hotel Du Vin & Bistro
Crescent Road, Tunbridge Wells, TN1 2LY (01892 526455/fax 01892 512044/www.hotelduvin.com). **Food served** noon-1.30pm, 7-9.45pm Mon-Sat; 12.30-2pm, 7-9pm Sun. **Set lunch** (Sun) £23.50 3 courses. **Main courses** £11-£15.50. **Credit** AmEx, DC, MC, V.

With stiff competition from Thackeray's (*see below*) for the title of Tunbridge Wells' most stylish venue, the bare floorboarded Hotel Du Vin bistro make a good platform for the mainly modern, Mediterranean-inspired food. Typical starters include crab croquettes with spinach and velouté, pan-seared scallops with vanilla vinaigrette. For mains, deep fried fillet of cod with pea purée and pommes frites was an excellent rendition on a recent visit, as was a simple smoked trout salad. Pudding was a succulent mango cheesecake. The amiable service was slow but apologies and free drinks softened the blow.

Plough at Ivy Hatch
High Cross Road, Ivy Hatch, TN15 0NL (01732 810268). **Food served** noon-2pm, 6.30-10pm Mon-Sat; noon-3pm, 6.30-8.30pm Sun. **Main courses** £15. **Credit** MC, V.

A long-standing favourite for seafood in the area, the Plough looks more like a homely village pub than a restaurant. The extensive and ambitious menu is brimming with marine life in a variety of forms and while some dishes lack panache, the fresh flavours deliver. Mouth-watering Irish oysters, anchovies on bruschetta and a seafood chowder make good starters, while grilled lemon sole and fresh halibut with mustard and herb crust are decent mains. Service is friendly, and there's a beer garden if a drink and snack are all that is required.

Swan
35 Swan Street, West Malling, ME19 6JU (01732 521910). **Food served** noon-2.30pm, 6.30-10pm Mon-Sat; noon-4pm Sun. **Main courses** £9-£14. **Credit** AmEx, DC, MC, V.

The total makeover of this boozer reveals an eye for metropolitan sophistication. The clean lines of the bar and eating areas are as spare and attractive as the food. The menu is lively, with imaginative pairings, and raises the stakes from pub food to restaurant with starters of delicately flavoured leek and gruyère tart, as well as a zippy fresh crab linguine with chilli and basil. Main courses range from classic smoked haddock and chive fish cakes with mustard sauce to roast rump of lamb with roasted root vegetables and rosemary sauce. Desserts are their equal, especially a silky lemon crème brûlée.

Thackeray's Restaurant
85 London Road, Tunbridge Wells, TN1 1EA (01892 511921/www.thackeraysrestaurant.co.uk). **Food served** noon-2.30pm, 6.30-10.30pm Tue-Sat; non-2.30pm Sun. **Main courses** £16-£22.50. **Set lunch** £11.50 2 courses, £12.50 3 courses. **Set dinner** £48 6 courses. **Credit** AmEx, MC, V.

The white timber-fronted former home of novelist William Thackeray is now home to one of the area's best restaurants. Awarded a Michelin star in 2003, talented chef Richard Phillips has brought a wealth of experience from London's gastronomic beacons. The charming exterior leads into a melting pot of extravagant interiors: two minimalist, stylish and elegant dining rooms on the ground floor contrast with the upstairs gold leaf bar. There's even a Japanese-inspired outdoor dining area. The pricey Modern French food delivers on all fronts. Highlights include a starter of duck salad with toasted brioche and a main course of roast monkfish tail, stuffed courgette flower and red wine sauce. A raspberry soufflé with hazelnut ice-cream and warm raspberry coulis confirmed what a fine kitchen this is.

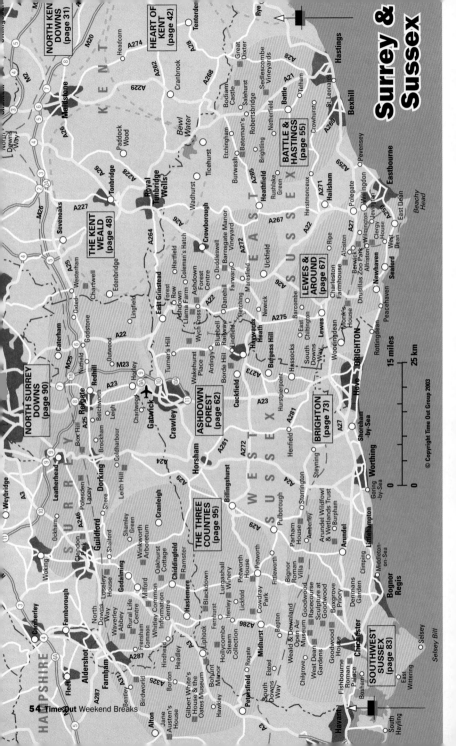

Surrey & Sussex

© Copyright Time Out Group 2003

Battle & Hastings

Come and conquer these lovely seaside towns.

The quaint villages of East Sussex exhibit little evidence of the blood spilled more than 900 years ago when Norman hordes laid waste to thousands of Saxons on 14 October 1066. Outside those Ealingesque centres of Little England, however, are plenty of castles, imposing abbeys and even the odd re-enactment of the battle itself to remind you that this was the scene of the event that set England's history on a different course.

War...

The beautiful medieval town of **Battle** is dominated by the remains of the **abbey** that William the Conqueror built in 1067 at the very spot where his troops defeated Harold's army. One of the most pleasant walks is around the battlefield itself, taking in the 14th-century **St Mary's Church** and ending up at the Chequers Inn on Lower Lake (*see p60*) for a pint, or sampling the fine food at the Pilgrim (*see p61*). Also worth a quick visit is **Battle Museum of Local History**, a few minutes' walk away from the abbey.

... and peace

Close by are a host of little villages that can be reached by travelling a few miles in any direction along pretty, winding roads lined with wild hedgerows and open fields. Five miles north of Battle is **Salehurst**, a good place to look at after visiting the medieval **Bodiam Castle** or the 15th-century manor house of **Great Dixter**. To the north-east near **Robertsbridge** lies **Sedlescombe**, where you can sample wines from the **Sedlescombe Organic Vineyard** (Cripps Corner, 0800 980

2884/www.englishorganicwine.co.uk), which bills itself as England's premier organic vineyard. To the north-west is **Netherfield**, home to foxes, deer and water birds – much of the land around here is owned by the Forestry Commission. Just off the A265 at Burwash is **Bateman's**, long-time home of writer and poet Rudyard Kipling.

Hastings

The history of Hastings as a maritime centre goes back more than 1,000 years. The shingle beach, in the lee of the West Hill, gave shelter to fishing boats and trade vessels. It became known as the **Stade** (a medieval word for 'landing place') and led to Hastings becoming a key Cinque Port, providing the Crown with naval craft before the Royal Navy existed. In the early 19th century it was a base for smugglers, and now the town boasts a thriving fishing industry, still possessing one of the only fleets in Europe that launches boats directly from the beach.

Hastings was once favoured by royalty (Queen Victoria was a visitor), and was placed firmly on the map by architect James Burton, whose wonderful Georgian buildings gave the area a sense of gentility. Over the years the area steadily declined but, happily, Hastings is now having something of a revival and, if you avoid the tawdry amusement arcades, the town manages to combine a bohemian quality with a kiss-me-quick seaside feel. The intriguing little alleyways all over the old town are known locally as 'twittens'. Just a little way along the seafront is the **Rock-a-Nore** area (thought to mean 'rock of the north' or 'Black Rock') where you'll find a profusion of tall, wooden, windowless huts. First built in 1834 to house fishing gear, the huts were only allowed to occupy eight or nine square feet each so, in order to dry their nets thoroughly, the fishermen built upwards, resulting in a multi-storey effect. Local fishermen still sell their catches from the huts – a reminder that the **Stade** remains a working beach.

The steepest funicular railway in Britain traverses the East Hill Cliff face here. You'll also find the award-winning **Shipwreck Heritage Centre** (Rock-a-Nore Road, 01424 437452, admission free but donations appreciated), **Underwater World**

By train from London

The fastest trains from **Charing Cross** (leaving approximately every half hour) take between 1hr 15mins and 1hr 25mins to reach **Battle** and **Hastings**. There are some additional trains from **Cannon Street**, taking 1hr 38mins, that leave around every hour. Info: www.connex.co.uk. (Services will be taken over by South Eastern Trains in 2004; timetables should not be affected.)

The Great Gatehouse of **Battle Abbey**. *See p57.*

(Rock-a-Nore Road, 01424 718776/www.
underwaterworld-hastings.co.uk, admission
£3.65-£5.75), and the **Hastings Fishermen's
Museum** (Rock-a-Nore Road, 01424 461446,
admission free but donations welcome). A
miniature railway can take you back along the
seafront towards the centre of town. Hastings is
also famed for its antiques shops along George
Street where you might find anything from
17th-century sea chests to 1960s furniture, at
much lower prices than in London or Brighton.
From George Street the **West Hill Cliff
Railway** travels up to St Clement's Caves,
home of **Smugglers Adventure**. A short walk
away are the remains of Hastings Castle. The
Hastings Museum and Art Gallery (John's
Place, Bohemia Road, 01424 781155, admission
free) is worth a look for its spectacular Durbar
Hall, built for the Indian and Colonial
Exhibition of 1886. West of Hastings lies the
sedate town of **Bexhill**, home to the **De La
Warr Pavilion** (Marina, 01424 787949,
admission free), one of the most significant
modernist buildings in England, designed by
Erich Mendelsohn in 1935.

What to see & do

Tourist Information Centres

*Battle Abbey Gatehouse, High Street, Battle,
TN33 OAD (01424 773721/www.battletown.
co.uk).* **Open** *Apr-Sept* 9.30am-5.30pm daily.
Oct 9am-5pm daily. *Nov-Mar* 10am-4pm Mon-Sat;
11am-3pm Sun.
*Queens Square, Priory Meadow, Hastings, TN34
ITL (01424 781111/www.1066country.com/
www.hastings.gov.uk.* **Open** 8.30am-6.15pm Mon-Fri;
9am-5pm Sat; 10am-4.30pm Sun.

Bike hire

Hastings Cycle Hire *St Andrew's Market, St
Andrew's Square, South Terrace, Hastings, TN34
1SJ (01424 444013).*
A few minutes' walk from the station.

Bateman's

*Bateman's Lane, Burwash, Etchingham, TN19 7DS
(01435 882302/www.nationaltrust.org.uk/places/
batemans).* **Open** *House* Apr-Oct 11am-5pm Mon-
Wed, Sat, Sun (last entry 4.30pm). *Grounds* Apr-Oct
11am-5.30pm Mon-Wed, Sat, Sun (last entry 4.30pm).
Admission (NT) £5.20; £2.20 concessions.
Credit AmEx, DC, MC, V.

The family home of Rudyard Kipling has been maintained just as it was in his day, even down to his 1928 Rolls-Royce in the garage. The gardens and the house are beautiful, and room stewards are present to offer information and keep the masses in order. Bateman's is closed until the end of September 2003 for renovation.

Bodiam Castle

Bodiam, Robertsbridge, TN32 5UA (01580 830436/ www.nationaltrust.org.uk/places/bodiamcastle). **Open** *Mid Feb-Oct* 10am-6pm daily. *Nov-mid Feb* 10am-4pm Sat, Sun (last entry 1hr before closing). **Admissions** (NT) £4; £2 concessions. **Credit** AmEx, MC, V.

A wonderful 14th-century medieval castle, with four round towers and ramparts that are reflected dramatically in the moat below. Inside, a museum charts the castle's history and its beautiful grounds are set on the banks of the River Rother. Unfortunately, your movements inside the castle are restricted, but there's still plenty to see.

Great Dixter House & Gardens

Northiam, nr Rye, TN31 6PH (01797 252878/ www.greatdixter.co.uk). **Open** 2-5.30pm Tue-Sun, bank holidays (last entry 5pm). **Admission** *House & gardens* £6.50; £2 concessions. *Gardens only* £5; £1.50 concessions. **Credit** MC, V.

Before Alan Titchmarsh there was Christopher Lloyd, a horticulturalist who devoted much of his life to creating one of the most experimental gardens of our time here. The main part of the stunning house dates back to the 15th century and boasts the largest remaining timber-framed hall in the country. In 1910, Lloyd's family commissioned Edwin Lutyens to enlarge the property and, using materials from derelict homes, he seamlessly blended the new with the old. Needless to say, the gardens are absolutely magnificent.

Hastings Castle & the 1066 Story

Castle Hill Road, West Hill, Hastings, TN34 3RG (01424 781112/www.discoverhastings.co.uk/castle/). **Open** *Apr-Sept* 10am-5pm daily. *Oct-Mar* 11am-3.30pm daily. **Admissions** £3.20; £2.10-£2.60 concessions. **No credit cards**.

A multimedia exploration of the events leading up to the battle (what do you mean, 'what battle?') takes place in a medieval siege tent within the ruins of Britain's first castle constructed by the Norman conquerers. Don't miss the 'whispering dungeons'.

Herstmonceux Castle & Gardens

Herstmonceux, Hailsham, BN27 1RN (01323 834444/www.herstmonceux-castle.com). **Open** *Castle tours* Easter-Oct noon-2.30pm Mon-Fri, Sun. *Grounds* Easter-Oct 10am-6pm daily. *Both* Closed Nov-Easter. **Admission** *Castle tours* £2.50; £1 concessions. *Grounds* £4.50; £3.50 concessions. **Credit** AmEx, MC, V.

Now a conference and business centre, this wonderful 15th-century brick-built moated castle is only open to the public for guided tours (when there's no function taking place, phone to check for details) in addition to one-off concerts and festivals. But the 500 acres of Elizabethan gardens surrounding the castle are definitely worth a visit in themselves. Open-air concerts complete with fireworks are held here in the summer; again, phone Herstmonceux for details.

St Mary in the Castle Art Centre

7 Pelham Crescent, Hastings, TN34 3AF (01424 781624/www.1066.net/maryinthecastle).

One of the great successes of Hastings' promising recent revitalisation is this spanking new art centre, that stands on the seafront among the decrepit amusement arcades. A former Church of England church, the once derelict building was thoroughly restored and then reopened, holding its first concert in October 1997. The theatre has an emphasis on music, but also hosts poetry readings, comedy nights, film screenings and more. The café is open from 10am to 5pm daily.

Smugglers Adventure

St Clement's Caves, West Hill, Hastings, TN34 3HY (01424 422964/www.discoverhastings.co.uk/ smugglers). **Open** *Easter-Sept* 10am-5.30pm daily. *Oct-Easter* 11am-4.30pm daily. **Admission** £5.75; £3.65-£4.75 concessions. **Credit** MC, V.

A labyrinth of tunnels filled with menacing-looking smugglers, 'rotting corpses' chained to walls and 'skeletons' with fierce, sharp daggers lodged between their ribs. Oh, and there's a tearoom.

1066 Battle of Hastings & Battle Abbey

High Street, Battle, TN33 0AD (01424 773792/ www.battle-abbey.co.uk/www.1066country.com). **Open** *Apr-Sept* 10am-6pm daily. *Oct* 10am-5pm daily. *Nov-Mar* 10am-4pm daily. **Admission** £5; £2.50-£3.80 concessions. **Credit** MC, V.

This is where the epic battle between the Normans and the Saxons took place almost 950 years ago. Here, too, are the remains of the abbey that William the Conqueror built soon afterwards. English Heritage has done an excellent job with the site: visitors are allowed to wander freely through the buildings and grounds while interactive audio tours recall the events of 1066 from the perspective of a bitter Saxon foot soldier, a Norman officer and Harold's widow. Battle re-enactments take place at the abbey on the weekend nearest 14 October, with a much larger event (with more than 1,000 re-enactors) every five years. Phone for more information.

1066 Country Walk

Pevensey–Rye, 31 miles in total.

William of Normandy and his army landed at Pevensey and marched to what is now Battle, and you can too. This country walk retraces William's route and takes in some of the most beautiful areas of the East Sussex Downs, including marshlands that are home to herons, warblers, grebes and other water birds. You will need an Ordnance Survey map, some stout boots and several days to undertake the entire journey; there are 17 pubs along the route and a number of guesthouses. Battle Tourist Information Office has details of the route.

Where to stay

The seafront at Hastings is full of B&Bs and seaside hotels, ranging from the basic to the swanky (in price at least), but the best places to stay are situated in the little villages that surround Battle and Hastings. If you don't have a car, **Parkside House** (59 Lower Park Road,

Festival fun

Given their eventful pasts, it should come as little surprise that the towns of Battle and Hastings like to kick up a fuss. Throughout the year, both towns host a wide range of events, usually celebrating an aspect of their history. Hastings' proud maritime history is captured in the annual **Walking the Fish** procession every July – a parade of spectacular fish and other sea creatures that are created by local schoolchildren, with the help of Radiator Group (01424 435711), an arts company that works directly with the community. Radiator helps to put on various large-scale innovative public events, often at local historical sites (keep an eye out for performances by them at Bodiam, Herstmonceux and Hastings castles).

Other festivals hark back to England's folk traditions and pagan pre-Christian past. The **Jack-on-the-Green Festival** is inspired by May Day celebrations dating to the Celtic Beltane. May Day celebrations, sometimes including Jack as a symbol of fertility and renewal, survived well into the 19th century, often associated with parades of chimney sweeps or milkmaids. Hastings' Jack in the Green was paraded annually until 1889. The festival was revived in 1979 by Mad Jack's Morris Dancers. Hastings Information Centre (01424 781111/www.hastings.gov.uk) has more information, or visit www.jack-in-the-green.co.uk.

Coastal Currents (www.coastalcurrents.org.uk) is perhaps the largest festival organiser of all, putting on events from September to the end of October that take place all along the coast from Bexhill as far as Dungeness. In Hastings, the contemporary arts festival comprises street theatre, stunning outdoor sound and light spectaculars, and a film festival, as well as visitor access to artists in their studios and working environments. Check the website for details of events.

01424 433096, doubles £50-£60) in Hastings is in a quiet residential area away from the seafront, overlooking Alexandra Park.

Fox Hole Farm
Kane Hythe Road, Battle, TN33 9QU (tel/fax 01424 772053). **Rates** £29-£33 single occupancy; £49-£59 double. **Rooms** (all en suite) 3 double. **Credit** MC, V.
One of the best mid-range guesthouses in the area. Paul and Pauline Collins's converted 18th-century woodcutter's cottage is homely and relaxed, with individually decorated rooms. Hidden away at the end of a long dirt track, the only neighbours being foxes, deer, chickens, geese and moorhens, this is as cosy as it gets: Pauline bakes her own bread and pies, the eggs are free range (naturally), and the dogs are usually found lazing by the hearth. Children over ten and dogs are welcome. No smoking throughout.
Take first right on A271 west of Battle on to B2096. Farm is 0.7 miles on right.

King John's Lodge
Sheepstreet Lane, Etchingham, TN19 7AZ (01580 819232/fax 01580 819562). **Rates** £50-£55 single occupancy; £70-£80 double/twin. **Rooms** 3 double (2 en suite); 1 twin (en suite). **No credit cards**.
Fourteenth-century French King John didn't so much lodge here as be kept prisoner – but the fact that he was here in any capacity gives some idea of the historical pedigree of this wonderful house. With architectural styles running the gamut from medieval to Victorian, it makes interesting viewing. Bedrooms vary in size and shape but all of them are packed with beamy character. Children are welcome, and one of the double bedrooms even has a special annexe where children can stay in relative privacy – it costs £20-£25 per child. All bedrooms are no-smoking.
A21 Flimwell then B2087 to Ticehurst. In Ticehurst, take first left after church on to Sheep Street. King John's Lodge is about 1 mile along on right.

Lavender & Lace
106 All Saints Street, Old Town, Hastings, TN34 3BE (tel/fax 01424 716290). **Rates** £28-£45 single occupancy; £50-£55 double/twin. Closed Jan, Feb. **Rooms** 2 double (1 en suite); 1 twin (en suite). **No credit cards**.
This charming 16th-century guesthouse is a few hundred yards up from the fishing huts and close to all that Hastings has to offer. It's a very traditional establishment, so as you'd expect, all three rooms are frilly, nicely scented and clean. The breakfast sets you up for a day exploring the area. Children over ten welcome; all bedrooms are no-smoking.

Little Hemingfold
Telham, Battle, TN33 0TT (01424 774338/fax 01424 775351). **Rates** £44-£69.50 single occupancy; £92-£96 double/twin. **Rooms** (all en suite) 7 double; 4 twin; 1 four-poster. **Credit** AmEx, DC, MC, V.
Set in 40 acres of grounds near Battle and beside a lake packed with trout is this lovely farmhouse, parts of which date back to the 17th century. The bedrooms are simple, and some have log-burning stoves. Fishing, rowing, tennis and other sporting activities are available, as is a four-course dinner for £24.50. Children over seven and dogs are welcome.
12 miles south of Battle on A2100; follow sign for hotel by sharp right road sign; Little Hemingfold is up short track.

Powdermills

*Powdermill Lane, Battle, TN33 0SP (01424
775511/fax 01424 774540/www.powdermills
hotel.co.uk).* **Rates** £85-£105 single; £110-£140
double/twin; £185 suite. **Rooms** (all en suite)
2 single; 8 twin; 24 double; 6 suites.
Credit AmEx, DC, MC, V.
This grand 18th-century country house sits in well-
maintained grounds backing on to Battle Abbey. The
owners are keen collectors of antiques and have decorated the house along traditional lines with lots of bits
and bobs crowding every available mantlepiece and
table top. Staff are attentive without being overbearing.
The Orangery Restaurant (also open to non-residents)
offers good-value Modern European food with a global
twist in a smart but relaxed country house atmosphere,
and the hotel's grounds are at your disposal for an after-
coffee walk. Children are welcome; those under ten aren't
allowed in the restaurant in the evening, but high tea is
served between 5.30pm and 6.30pm. Dogs are accepted
by arrangement.
*Powdermill Lane is opposite Battle rail station; Powdermills
is 1 mile along on right.*

Royal Victoria Hotel

*Marina, St Leonards on Sea, TN38 0BD (01424
445544/fax 01424 721995/www.royalvichotel.co.uk).*
Rates £110 single; £130 double/twin; £130-£150
suite; £140 family room. **Rooms** (all en suite)
44 double/twin; 5 suites; 3 family. **Credit** AmEx,
DC, MC, V.
Taking its name from its most famous visitor, the old
queen herself, the Royal Vic (now run by the Best
Western group) is looking a little down-at-heel these
days, though it's clearly still popular with the corporate
crowd. With the exception of its grand marbled staircase, there are few reminders of the hotel's glory days.
That said, rooms are satisfyingly clean and spacious,
and a cooked full English breakfast for an additional £9
can be taken overlooking the sea, which is as pleasant
a way of starting the day as any. For drinks come
evening time (or as soon as the sun's slipped past the
yard arm), move to the Piano Bar, which also has a great
sea view. Children and dogs (£10 charge) are welcome.

Stone House

*Rushlake Green, Heathfield, TN21 9QJ (01435
830233/fax 01435 830726/www.stonehouse
sussex.co.uk).* **Rates** £115-£180 double/twin;
£195-£225 four-poster/suite. **Rooms** (all en suite)
3 double/twin; 2 four-poster; 1 suite. **Credit** MC, V.
The jewel in the East Sussex crown of country hotels,
this large stately home has been occupied by the Dunn
family for more than 500 years. Family portraits line the
walls, the Elizabethan staircase is still in use, priceless
antiques inhabit corners of rooms, and a library, a billiards room and 1,000 acres of private land are at the
guests' disposal. It's like Noel Coward without the jokes.
Children over nine and dogs are welcome.
*B2096 from Heathfield to Battle; take 4th turn on right to
Rushlake Green. Take first left by village green (keep green
on your right) to crossroads; house is on far left-hand
corner and is signposted.*

Where to eat & drink

With the catch being netted just yards from
here, fish and chips from Rock-a-Nore has to
be on the menu. As well as selling fresh fish,
Rock-a-Nore Fisheries (3 Rock-a-Nore
Road, 01424 445425) serves a portion of moules
marinière with French bread for a mere £2.95.
Also in Hastings, **Gannets** (45 High Street,
01424 439678) does all-day breakfasts and
fabulous omelettes. **Sundial Restaurant**
(Gardner Street, Herstmonceux, 01323 832217)
is a traditional village restaurant serving
classic French cuisine in a 17th-century inn.

The **Chequers Inn** (Lower Lake, Battle,
01424 772088) specialises in trad country
cooking and has an intimate atmosphere, while
the **Bell** on the High Street in Burwash (01435
882304) serves a good local ale before a huge
fireplace. The **Netherfield Arms** (Netherfield
Road, Netherfield, 01424 838282) is a friendly
pub/restaurant just a short walk from Fox
Hole Farm (*see p59*); its good staple dishes and

laid-back atmosphere are popular with locals as well as visitors. **Salehurst Halt** (Church Lane, 01580 880620) is a lovely freehouse dating back around 150 years that serves good British cooking along with its real ales.

The Curlew

Junction Road, Bodiam, TN32 5UY (01580 861394/ 861396/www.thecurlewatbodiam.co.uk). **Food served** 11.30am-3pm Tue-Sat; 6-9.30pm Sun. **Main courses** £12.95-£19.95. **Credit** MC, V.

In the heart of 1066 country and a stone's throw from imposing Bodiam Castle, the local Sussex cognoscenti are treading the well-worn Roman Road (aka the A229) to the Curlew. The pub may look olde worlde, but the food served in the restaurant is not. A cheery welcome from Australian front-of-housers is backed up with good knowledge of the food and wine. The Roux brothers-trained chef exerts a Mediterranean influence on the seasonally changing menu, which includes starters such as succulent diver-caught scallops, plus the occasional global twist with the likes of spicy Thai soup. Mains range from traditional ribeye steak served with field mushrooms and fries to a more adventurous teaming of pan-fried red mullet with green beans, crushed niçoise potatoes, roast tomatoes, peppers and chive oils. Both were a complete success on a recent visit. Desserts are heavenly, but why opt for one when the miniature dessert plate gives you a bite-size portion of each? A good global selection of wine includes reasonably priced Australian, Chilean and Spanish bottles. Bon appetit.

Eurasia

The Royal George, 54 London Road, Hurst Green, TN19 7PN (01580 860200). **Food served** noon-2pm, 5.30-10.30pm Mon, Wed-Sun; 5.30-10.30pm Tue. **Main courses** £5.50-£12.80. **Set meals** £16.30-£23.80 2 courses. **Credit** AmEx, MC, V.

Inauspiciously located on the A21, a Georgian house has been tastefully converted into a local pub/restaurant. The atmosphere is relaxed, service prompt, and the cooking of a high standard, with the kitchen making good use of quality ingredients and local produce, including organic vegetables. The extensive menu, featuring many nonya-style dishes (nonya is a fusion of Chinese and Malay cooking), promises 'east meets west'. In truth the food is more east than west, but that's no cause for complaint. Starters include prawns cooked in cream and sprinkled with coconut or satay chicken, with Eurasia's wonderful home-made sauce. An impossibly long list of mains includes some real treats: a particularly fine two-ways duck (aromatic duck roasted with Malaysian herbs), Nonya Mama Chicken (fruity), or steamed sea bass, this time with an aromatic black bean sauce. The extensive wine list even includes a dry white from China (£12.80). You can, of course, settle for a pint of beer, at pub prices. This is a deservedly popular pub and restaurant and well worth your time.

Food Rooms

The Chapel, 53-5 High Street, Battle, TN33 OEN (01424 775537/fax 01424 775950/www.food rooms.co.uk). **Food served** 8.30am-5.30pm Mon-Sat; 8.30am-4.30pm Sun. **Main courses** £7.50-£18.50. **Set lunch** (Sun) £16.50 2 courses, £19 3 courses. **Credit** MC, V.

Bright and airy, the entrance to the Food Rooms is taken up with a delicatessen-cum-takeaway, leading into an informal, child-friendly eating area beyond. Local farmers provide fresh, often organic, produce (even the coffee is roasted locally), and there's always a decent vegetarian option. The creative menu is well presented and unbelievably priced for such great food. The set Sunday lunch is a particular bargain (booking essential). Service is attentive, informative and friendly.

Maggie's

Above the fish market, Rock-a-Nore Road, Hastings (01424 430205). **Main courses** £3.20-£5.90. **No credit cards**.

Opening at 5am to provide the local fishermen with breakfast (they'll have been out since 2am), Maggie Banford reputedly serves the best fish and chips in Hastings, perhaps the world. Locals and fans from further afield crowd into the check tableclothed café, located in one of the old fishermen's huts, sit beneath grainy black-and-white photos of fishing fleets of yore and look out over the sea. The menu has plenty of options but to have anything other than fish would be criminal: it's perfectly cooked in whisper-light batter, accompanied by a heap of hand-cut chips and optional mushy peas. Be warned: a 'standard' portion fills the plate. A mug of tea is a mere 55p (but you can get a glass of wine too). Come early; it packs out at lunchtime, even during the week.

Mermaid

2 Rock-a-Nore Road, Hastings, TN34 3DW (01424 438100). **Food served** 6.30am-3pm Mon, Tue; 6.30am-7.30pm Wed-Sun. **Main courses** £4.75-£5.85. **No credit cards**.

Fishermen and tourists sit inside at wooden tables and chairs, or outside under umbrellas in fine weather (you'll need to look beyond the car park for a glimpse of the sea). The menu is chalked on a blackboard: big breakfasts are served early on, giving way to fish and chip lunches (cod, huss and skate), all served with hand-cut chips. Home-made pies are also available, as are children's meals. Drinks include steaming stripy mugs of Bovril. Follow up with treacle pudding or spotted dick. It's always busy here and there's a ten-minute cooking time for the fish – but it's worth the wait.

The Pilgrim

1 High Street, Battle, TN33 OAE (01424 772314/fax 01424 775950/www.foodrooms.co.uk). **Food served** *June-Sept* noon-9.30pm Mon-Sat; noon-4pm Sun. *Oct-May* noon-3pm, 3-7pm (tea), 7-9.30pm Mon-Sat; noon-4pm Sun. **Main courses** £9.80-£32. **Set lunch** £12.50 2 courses, £16.50 3 courses. **Set dinner** £14.75 2 courses, £19.50 3 courses. **Credit** AmEx, MC, V.

On the site of a 12th-century monastic hospital, this sister restaurant to the Food Rooms (*see above*) is impressive on many levels – from the beautiful vaulted hall, period furniture and open fire, to the attentive service, inventive Modern European menu, and warm and relaxed atmosphere. Starters might be smoked fish chowder or garlic cappuccino with shaved truffles, with mains such as pan-fried fillet of whiting with a coriander, chilli and star anise butter or Brightling venison with field mushrooms, pancetta and gratin dauphinois. Desserts are heavenly – try the chocolate parfait – and the well-chosen wine list manages a decent bottle under £12. Not to be missed, but you'll have to book.

Ashdown Forest

Woodland meets heathland in Pooh country.

Ancient woodland and endangered lowland heath span this northern corner of East Sussex. For some, the area has an edge of mystery: it was home to Sir Arthur Conan Doyle and witnessed secret wartime MI5 operations as well as the occult rituals of 'the wickedest man in the world', Aleister Crowley. But it's the charms of homely country pubs, beautiful landscaped gardens and the paw print of A A Milne's *Winnie the Pooh* that leave the largest impression on most visitors today.

The Ashdown Forest area makes up the Sussex portion of the High Weald, a huge sweep of rolling countryside between the North and South Downs, which also spans Surrey, Hampshire and Kent. Don't expect too much from its towns: large conurbations such as Crawley, East Grinstead and Haywards Heath principally attract commuters heading for London or Gatwick.

This part of the Weald is refreshingly tourist-free – a prime spot for getting away from it all. While serious hikers can walk all day, there's plenty for the less energetic to do too: exploring historic houses and gardens, indulging in cream teas and wandering round lost-in-time villages.

A healthy alternative
The main draw of the area is ancient **Ashdown Forest** itself, 6,000 acres of heathland broken up by wooded valleys and copses. Used for deer hunting in medieval times by Edward I, the forest later became an important centre for the ship-building and iron industries, activities that contributed to considerable deforestation.

Now the largest area of heathland in the South-east, the landscape is latticed by thousands of gorse-lined walks, and is also popular for cycling and horse riding. Although the forest has no identifiable centre, the **Ashdown Forest Centre** (01342 823583) near Wych Cross is a good place to start.

More than Pooh
In addition to the attractions of Winnie the Pooh (*see p64* **Pooh's corner**), there's plenty else to excite and exhaust children. Once they've run around in the forest, the **Ashdown Llama Park** makes for an out-of-the-ordinary afternoon. Kids (and certain adults) will also love the **Bluebell Railway**, which steams its way from Sheffield Park to East Grinstead through flower-strewn woodland, while **Wilderness Wood** has some good nature trails. Watersports are on offer throughout the year at the reservoir at **Ardingly** (pronounced 'Arding-lie'; 01444 892549/ www.ardinglyactivitycentre.co.uk); the village also hosts the South of England agricultural show every June. Nearby is **Wakehurst Place**, one of the many country houses and gardens in the area open to the public.

To escape the tourists, take a drive to a quieter part of the forest to see the **Nutley Windmill** (off the A22; 01435 873367). Another restful site is the **Airman's Grave** (www.thisisworthing.co.uk), a memorial marking the spot where a Wellington bomber crashed in 1941. The grave is about a mile south of the village of Marlpits, which is on Danehill Road west of the B2026, just north of Duddleswell.

The fairies of Tom Tit's Lane
Many of the forest's surrounding villages harbour hidden histories. The former Tiger Inn (now Church House) in the pretty village of **Lindfield**, just outside Haywards Heath, once played host to smugglers, who would sail their contraband up the River Ouse from the Cuckmere Valley to hide it in false graves in the neighbouring churchyard. The church in the delightful village of **Fletching** was where Simon de Montfort spent a night of vigil before defeating Henry III in the Battle of Lewes, while fairies have reputedly been spotted in **Tom Tit's Lane** in the small town of Forest Row.

By train from London

Trains for **East Grinstead** leave Victoria about every half hour (journey time 50mins). Trains to **Uckfield** leave **Victoria** and **London Bridge** every hour, with a change at Hurst Green or Oxted (taking 1hr 30mins). Trains to **Haywards Heath** leave from **Farringdon**, **Blackfriars**, **Kings Cross Thameslink**, **London Bridge** and **Victoria** about every 15-30mins, and take 45mins to 1hr 10mins. Info: www.connex.co.uk. (Services will be taken over by South Eastern Trains in 2004; timetables should not be affected).

Tourist Information Centres

There is a tourist office at the **Ashdown Forest Llama Park** (01825 712040). Other nearby offices include **Burgess Hill** (01444 247726/www.burgesshill.gov.uk), **Lewes** (01273 483448/www.lewes-town.co.uk) and **Royal Tunbridge Wells** (01892 515675/www.heartofkent.org.uk). For additional information try www.sussex-country-tourism.co.uk.

Bike hire

Future Cycles *Lower Square, London Road, Forest Row, RH18 5HD (01342 822847).*
Two miles from East Grinstead station.

Ashdown Forest Centre

Wych Cross, Forest Row, RH18 5JP (01342 823583). **Open** *Oct-Mar* 11am-5pm Sat, Sun. *Apr-Sept* 2-5pm Mon-Fri; 11am-5pm Sat, Sun.
This information centre is the place to pick up walk leaflets and learn about the forest's history, flora and fauna. Interactive displays and games will entertain children, and there's a temporary exhibition space used by conservation groups and local artists.

Ashdown Forest Llama Park

Wych Cross, nr Forest Row, RH18 5JN (01825 712040/www.llamapark.co.uk). **Open** 10am-5pm daily. **Admission** £3.50; £3 concessions. **Credit** MC, V.
If you've got kids, a visit to this unusual farm is a fun half-day excursion. If not, once you've seen one llama, you've seen them all. The farm's 32 llama-dotted acres make for pleasant walking, and a new visitors' centre and café have been added to the World of Wool exhibition and gift shop. Don't expect a petting zoo – the 70-strong woolly herd is more interested in grazing than socialising, although the farm's cashmere and angora goats are quite approachable.

Barnsgate Manor Vineyard

Herons Ghyll, nr Uckfield, TN22 4DB (01825 713366). **Open** *Vineyard, shop & tearoom* 10am-5pm daily. *Restaurant* noon-2pm daily. **Admission** free. **Credit** *Restaurant* MC, V.
Barnsgate's three friendly donkeys greet visitors to this working vineyard, which has extensive views over the whole forest. After a walk round the grounds (watch out for the grazing llamas!), choose between the airy manor house or the large patio for some hearty English refreshment – tearoom titbits include a selection of scones and cakes. Barnsgate vintages are on sale in the gift shop.

Bluebell Railway

Sheffield Park Station, on A275 between Lewes & East Grinstead, TN22 3QL (01825 720800/talking timetable 01825 722370/www.bluebell-railway.co.uk). **Operates** *May-Sept* 11am-3.50pm daily. *Oct-Apr* 11am-3.50pm Sat, Sun, school hols, bank hols. **Tickets** £8.50; £4.20-£6.80 concessions; free under-3s. **Credit** DC, MC, V.
One look inside the Bluebell's packed trains and you'll see that this restored steam railway isn't just for train-spotters. The track runs from Sheffield Park, via Horsted Keynes to Kingscote, and each station is restored according to a different era: Victorian, the 1930s

Ashdown Forest Llama Park.

and the 1950s respectively. From Kingscote you can take a bus to East Grinstead while the line link is being extended. Events run through the year, including Thomas the Tank Engine days in June and a Santa Special at Christmas. Train anoraks can join a course on how to drive a steam engine (01273 731873), while the more gastronomically minded might prefer to dine in style on the Golden Arrow Pullman. The railway also has two museums and a locomotive collection.

Borde Hill Gardens

Balcombe Road, Haywards Heath, RH16 1XP (01444 450326/www.bordehill.co.uk). **Open** 10am-6pm daily, or dusk if earlier. **Admission** £5; £2.50 concessions; free under-3s.
Adults can enjoy an award-winning collection of azaleas, rhododendrons, magnolias and camellias while the kids are occupied by the pirate adventure playground. Begging the question, who is going to have more fun?

Leonardslee Gardens

Lower Beeding, nr Horsham, RH13 6PP (01403 891212/www.leonardslee.com). **Open** *Apr-Oct* 9.30am-6pm daily. **Admission** £5-£7; £3 concessions; free under-5s.
Sometimes described as the most beautiful garden in Europe, Leonardslee offers more than just a massive range of wonderful flowers and plants. There's also the wallabies that have lived semi-wild here for more than 100 years, the carp-filled lakes and the collection of Victorian motorcars to ogle.

Nymans Garden

Handcross, nr Haywards Heath, RH17 6EB (01444 400321). **Open** *Mar-Oct* 11am-6pm or sunset Wed-Sun. *Nov-Mar* 11am-4pm Sat, Sun. **Admission** (NT) £6; £3 concessions; free under-5s.
Near-theatrical landscaping designed by Ludwig Messel in 1980. Highlights include a sunken garden with a stone loggia, a laurel walk, a pinetum and beautiful herbaceous borders.

Priest House

North Lane, West Hoathley, RH19 4PP (01342 810479). Open Mar-Oct 10.30am-5.30pm Tue-Sat; noon-5.30pm Sun. Closed Nov-Feb. **Admission** *House & garden £2.60; £1.30-£2.30 concessions. Garden only £1.* **No credit cards.**

A peacefulness pervades this delightful 15th-century farmhouse; as you wander round its beautiful cottage garden, you can really begin to feel lost in time. The house has been a museum ever since 1908; the beamed rooms contain an array of 17th- and 18th-century household items and furniture, as well as a series of themed temporary exhibitions.

Sheffield Park Gardens

Sheffield Park, TN22 3QX (01825 790231/ www.nationaltrust.org.uk). Open Jan, Feb 10.30am-4pm Sat, Sun. Mar-Oct 10.30am-6pm Tue-Sun, bank holidays. Nov, Dec 10.30am-4pm Tue-Sun. Last entry 1hr before dusk. **Admission** *(NT) £4.60; £2.30 concessions; free under-5s.*

This park has 120 acres that were landscaped by 'Capability' Brown in 1776 and encompass four lakes linked by cascades and waterfalls. Cleverly planted springtime daffodils and bluebells give way to rhododendrons and the national collection of Ghent azaleas (more than 40 varieties in summer, followed by flowering shrubs in autumn).

Wakehurst Place

Ardingly, nr Haywards Heath, RH17 6TN (01444 894066/www.kew.org.uk). Open Feb 10am-5pm daily. Mar, Oct 10am-6pm daily. Apr-Sept 10am-7pm daily. Nov-Jan 10am-4pm daily. **Admission** *(NT) £6.50; £4.50 concessions; free under-16s.*

Pooh's corner

The Ashdown Forest's lowland heath might be home to some rare species, but it's a silly old bear named Pooh that's the area's most famous animal. A A Milne lived just north of the forest with his family in the 1920s, and it provided the inspiration for his famous fictional character. His, or rather Pooh's, mark has been left on the area, with many of the places featured in *Winnie the Pooh* and *The House on Pooh Corner* based upon real locations that his son Christopher visited with his nanny. The whole area has been Pooh-ified, so many of these 'enchanted places' can be visited.

Tracking down Pooh and Christopher Robin's favourite places is a popular project with young children and should begin with a trip to Pooh Corner (01892 770678), a 300-year-old, low-ceilinged shop in the village of Hartfield where Christopher used to go shopping with his nanny. It's now packed with oodles of gifts and Pooh-phernalia, mostly of the cartoonish variety. Once you and your children are thoroughly merchandised out, pick up a free map from the shop staff and head out into Pooh country.

Galleon's Lap and Roo's Sandypit (actually an old quarry) are both within easy walking distance of Gill's Lap car park, just off the B206. A memorial plaque laid by Christopher to his father and E H Shepard, the illustrator of the stories, can be found not far away at the Enchanted Place. Also nearby is the site of the North Pole, although there's really nothing to see apart from a small pond.

Instead, head north past Five Hundred Acre Woods (inspiration for Hundred Acre Wood in the books) and, between Marsh Green and Chuck Hatch, you'll find what is perhaps the area's most famous Pooh attraction, Poohsticks Bridge. The bridge was rebuilt in 1979 and in itself is nothing special, but the 15-minute walk from Poohsticks Bridge car park along bluebell-strewn paths and bridleways provides the chance to pick up enough sticks for games to keep the most hyperactive Tiggers and laziest Eeyores in the family entertained.

The Magical POP-UP World of WINNIE -THE- POOH

From the stories by A.A. Milne with illustrations by Andrew Grey

Fruitful times at **Gravetye Manor**. *See p66.*

The country home of London's Kew Gardens. Once you've observed the scientists at work cleaning and preparing seeds for freezing, you can wander round grounds that include water gardens and a unique glade of specials – usually found in the Himalayas, they were transported here because a yeti kept stepping all over them.

Where to stay

Accommodation ranges from a number of top-class hotels to a profusion of B&Bs, with not much on offer in between. In addition to the places listed below, luxurious but pricey options include **Ockendon Manor** in Cuckfield (01444 416111/www.hshotels.co.uk, doubles £155-£320) and **Newick Park Hotel** (01825 723633/www.newickpark.co.uk, doubles £165-£235). Cheaper choices in the area include **Broom Cottage** in Fairwarp (01825 712942, doubles £50-£55) and **Bolebroke Mill** (01892 770425, doubles £68-£79) in Hartfield.

Ashdown Park Hotel

Wych Cross, Forest Row, RH18 5JR (01342 824988/ fax 01342 826206/www.ashdownpark.com). **Rates** £135-£325 single occupancy; £165-£355 double/twin; £355 four-poster/suite. **Rooms** (all en suite) 6 single; 95 double/twin; 6 four-poster/suites. **Credit** AmEx, DC, MC, V.

If the idea of a formal country estate is something you'd hate, then Ashdown Park Hotel may just change your opinion. The emphasis is on efficient but understated service; the staff are adept at making guests feel very welcome without any uncomfortable bowing and scraping. Additional wings have been added to the impressive Victorian building, and most rooms are of a generous size, and equipped with satellite TV and Molton Brown toiletries. The restaurant and lounge are a little drab, although the stunning views across Ashdown Forest and 186 acres of landscaped gardens more than make up for it. Popular with wedding parties (there's a chapel attached to the main building) and

conferences (these take advantage of the nearby golf and country club, which guests have access to).
From junction 6 of M25, take A22 S through East Grinstead, then through Forest Row for a further 2 miles. At crossroads with traffic lights, turn left (signposted Ashdown Park Hotel and Hartfield). Hotel is three-quarters of a mile down the road on the right.

Copyhold Hollow

Copyhold Hollow, Copyhold Lane, Borde Hill, Haywards Heath, RH16 1XU (01444 413265/ www.copyholdhollow.freeserve.co.uk). **Rates** £45 single; £60 double. **Rooms** (all en suite) 1 single; 1 twin; 1 double. **No credit cards**.

You could be forgiven for thinking you were staying in someone's private home while at Copyhold Hollow – after all, there are only three guest rooms. Owner Frances Druce invites guests to treat the place as their own, and even allows pets (as long as they're well behaved). The building is 16th-century Grade II listed; the inglenook fireplace in the lounge is its centrepiece. Rooms are comfortable and simply furnished. With the woods nearby for bracing constitutionals and a roaring fire to come home to, a stay in this hollow won't leave an empty feeling.
Take M23/A23 S, following signs E to Cuckfield; then signs for Borde Hill Gardens; over brow of hill, turn right into Copyhold Lane; B&B is half a mile down the road on the right.

Gravetye Manor Hotel

Vowels Lane, East Grinstead, RH19 4LJ (01342 810567/www.gravetyemanor.co.uk). **Rates** £160 single occupancy; £200-£310 double. Breakfast £16 (Eng); £14 (Cont). **Rooms** (all en suite) 17 double; 1 single. **Credit** MC, V.

With a driveway that seems as long as the A22, Gravetye exudes a stately detachment that suits its secluded location. That very seclusion once made it popular with smugglers looking for a place to hide contraband, but these days there's nothing suspect about this ivy-covered Tudor manor house. It boasts some of the most beautiful gardens in England, landscaped by William Robinson, one of the pioneers of the natural English style. Bedrooms are decorated in an understated style with antique furnishings, in keeping with the handsome oak-panelled interior of the lounge and restaurant (*see p66*). Bentleys and Jags fill the car park during Glyndebourne, although the idyllic croquet lawn provides less highbrow pursuits. No children allowed under seven.

Griffin Inn

Fletching, nr Uckfield, TN22 3SS (01825 722890/ fax 01825 722810/www.thegriffininn.co.uk). **Rates** £60 single occupancy; £70 twin; £85-£120 double/ four-poster. **Rooms** (all en suite) 1 twin; 7 double/ four-poster. **Credit** AmEx, MC, V.

All of Fletching seems to gather here at weekends to enjoy the great pub banter or sample some of the very accomplished cooking in the restaurant (*see p66*), but visitors can also linger longer at this 17th-century coaching inn by staying in one of the Griffin's eight guest rooms. Rooms have four-poster beds and exposed beams and are refreshingly free of too much chintz; the bathrooms are Victorian-style with free-standing baths. There are barbecues and live jazz performances to entertain customers on some summer evenings.

Hooke Hall

250 High Street, Uckfield, TN22 1EN (01825 761578/fax 01825 768025). **Rates** from £55 single occupancy; from £70 double; £125 four-poster. Breakfast £8.50 (Eng); £6.50 (cont). **Rooms** (all en suite) 8 doubles; 2 suites. **Credit** MC, V.

With keys provided to the front door but not the rooms, the trusting instincts of the owners pervade this ten-room Queen Anne townhouse and the place has a relaxed, laid-back atmosphere. Curios, antiques and botanical paintings by the owner enliven the spacious high-ceilinged interior. Take one of the rooms on the first floor if you can, as the ones on the top floor are a good deal pokier (former servants' quarters). All the rooms have been named after famous mistresses and lovers – who could resist the charms of Mme de Pompadour?

Where to eat & drink

Ashdown Forest harbours a good selection of rural pubs and tearooms, as well as expensive restaurants. Cuckfield's **Ockenden Manor** (01444 416111) and the **Alexander House Hotel** in Turner's Hill (01342 714914) both have notable eateries. For a relaxed meal and pint of local brew, try the **Cat** (01342 810369) in peaceful West Hoathley, **Gallipot Inn** (01892 770268) in Upper Hartfield, the popular **Chequer's Inn** (01342 823333) in Forest Row or the small **Half Moon** in Friar's Gate near Hartfield (01892 661270), where on a fine day you can watch hot air balloons taking off from the field behind. For a wider choice of cuisine, drive out of the forest to one of the area's small towns. Newick is famous for its **Newick Village Tandoori** (01825 723738). The **Anchor Inn** (Church Street, Hatfield, 01892 770424), where seafood dominates, is popular.

Coach & Horses

Coach and Horses Lane, Danehill, RH17 7JF (01825 740369). **Food served** 10am-2pm, 7-9pm Mon-Thur; 10am-2.30pm, 7-9.30pm Fri, Sat; noon-2.30pm Sun. **Main courses** £8.50-£12.95. **Set meal** £16 2 courses. **Credit** MC, V.

This place can be a bit tricky to find, but once discovered it won't be forgotten. The splendid front garden is a boon in the summer when locals and rambling tourists scramble for the best spots. There's also more than just pub grub available from the kitchen, with home-made traditional British and Italian dishes complementing a brace of pan-Asian offerings such as stir-fried chilli beef. When the weather closes in, the light and airy main dining area, complete with hanging baskets, provides most of the shelter, while more intimate evenings can be spent in the cosy, candlelit upstairs room.

Duddleswell Tea Rooms

Duddleswell, Fairwarp, TM22 3BH (01825 712126). **Food served** *Summer* 10am-5pm Tue-Sun. *Winter* 10am-4.30pm. **No credit cards.**

There can be few finer places to take high tea or scones than this venerable tearoom. A twee cottage, decorated granny-style in pink with lace curtains and doilies, you'd

be forgiven for thinking you'd stepped back into the 1950s when you pay a visit. It's conveniently situated at the southern end of the forest, so ramblers can refuel on the hearty lunches that are now also offered; more sedentary customers can gently walk off the clotted cream in the woods.

Gravetye Manor

Vowels Lane, nr East Grinstead, RH19 4LJ (01342 810567/www.gravetyemanor.co.uk). **Food served** noon-1.45pm, 7-9.30pm daily. **Main courses** £30. **Set lunch** £27. **Set dinner** £37. **Set meal** £52. **Credit** MC, V.

The oak-panelled interior and impeccably trained staff provide the perfect backdrop for a meal in this formal yet unstuffy hotel restaurant. From the canapés served while you peruse the menu to the coffee and Cognac taken in the lounge after dining, the whole experience is entirely relaxing. With the bill easily topping £45 a head, you'd expect nothing less. Dishes are often as pleasing on the eye as they are the stomach, and, where possible, use vegetables from Gravetye's own kitchen garden. Starters may include ballotine of wild smoked salmon with avocado jus, followed by mains such as an excellent fillet of beef with oyster mushrooms in a mild stilton sauce or red mullet and seared scallops with a piquant olive salsa. The wine cellar boasts around 400 wines and is suitably grand, in keeping with the surroundings – the landscaped gardens making the perfect place to get some air after such a rarefied atmosphere.

Griffin Inn

Fletching, nr Uckfield, TN22 3SS (01825 722890/www.thegriffininn.co.uk). **Food served** noon-2.30pm, 7-9.30pm Mon-Sat; noon-2.30pm, 7-9pm Sun. **Main courses** £7.50-£14.90. **Credit** AmEx, DC, MC, V.

The Griffin is a focal point for locals of all generations, united in stoking up a boisterous vibe on long-opening weekend nights. The pub has a cricket theme throughout and is split into a saloon (Pavilion End) and lounge bar (Nursery End) offering Harvey's and Tangle Foot on tap and a bar menu of ciabatta sandwiches and pasta dishes. The restaurant is a more sedate affair and overlooks the sizeable garden, itself a great feature with views stretching towards the Ouse Valley. Roasted local venison and sea bass with a vine and tomato risotto are just two examples of the confident cooking emanating from the kitchen.

Hatch Inn

Coleman's Hatch, nr Hartfield, TN7 4EJ (01342 822363/www.hatchinn.co.uk). **Food served** noon-2pm Mon; noon-2pm, 7-9pm Tue-Sat; noon-3pm, 6-8pm Sun. **Main courses** £5.50-£14. **Credit** AmEx, MC, V.

It's not hard to believe that this place was frequented by smugglers in the 16th century (as is reputed). The dark, low-ceilinged bar helps create an atmosphere that lends itself to hushed discussions and clandestine meetings. These days, however, the bar is more likely to be home to gossipy locals and tourists. Behind the horse brasses and decorative dried hops, visitors will find a lively menu that's traditional with an occasional Mediterranean twist. Roasts are a favourite; Caesar salads practically spill off the plate (all portions are generous). The spacious gardens provide an overflow for busy summer weekends. Ales are from Harvey's.

Lewes & Around

Virginia Woolf and burning Bushes – genteel Lewes
has hidden depths.

Between sleepy Downland villages and the gaudy bacchanalia of Brighton is Lewes, East Sussex's county town. Knowledgeable old architecture buff Alec Clifton-Taylor named it one of the *Six English Towns* in his 1980s TV series. A quintessential Englishness comes in the form of cutesy cobbled lanes (known locally as 'twittens'), leaning buildings and ragged roofs up on a hill. Much of the centre is even older than it looks – many beamed Tudor buildings are encased in Georgian façades. There's even a Norman castle, built by William de Warenne, a leading Norman noble and henchman of William the Conqueror. Unlike the implausibly twee surrounding villages, this is a proper working town that remains relatively free of tourists, while refugees from London and Brighton give a bohemian edge to the olde worlde surroundings. Tofu is a mainstay on local menus, and second-hand bookshops and craft stalls are ten-a-penny. Yet the place was always a little town that liked to think big. Revolutionary writer and libertarian Tom Paine lived here before crossing the Atlantic, the Bloomsbury Group were all over the nearby countryside like a rash and weighty doctrinal arguments pepper the town's history (*see p72* **For Fawkes' sake, burn it**).

The castle and the High Street are the focal points. Some of the shops along the High Street feel as if they've been preserved in aspic: the **Fifteenth Century Bookshop** (100 High Street, 01273 474160) is one, with racks of second-hand books in tumbledown wattle-and-daub environs. Winner of the picture postcard competition is the cobbled and phenomenally steep **Keere Street**, down which the Prince Regent reputedly took his horse and carriage for a wager. The prince's headlong flight would have taken him past an attractive clutter of 15th-century timbered houses and, later, flint cottages. Right at the bottom of the hill is **Southover Grange**, built in 1572 and later inhabited by the diarist John Evelyn. The expansive gardens are open to the public and are a lovely place to waste a sunny summer's afternoon: a secluded hatch serves tea, cakes and ice-cream. Nearby you will find **Anne of Cleves House and Museum**. The house was given to her by Henry VIII who decided poor Anne was not a beauty fit to wed, but more of a 'Flandres Mare'. Henry's influence is also apparent at William de Warenne's **Lewes Priory**, founded in 1077. Closed during the dissolution of the monasteries, all that now remains is an atmospheric array of flint stacks.

Downs time

The **South Downs** surrounding Lewes are an alluring mix of smooth chalk hills, chocolate box villages and country pubs and churches.

The most visited of the villages is **Alfriston**, whose thatched cottages, narrow lanes and magnificent church make it almost a cartoon version of the rustic idyll. Although undeniably beautiful, it's way overcrowded with trippers. Less touristy are docile **Alciston** and flinty **West Dean**. The twin villages of **Firle** and **Glynde** are also worth a visit, each with its own manor house – the latter is home to the famous **Glyndebourne Opera House**, so time your visit carefully. Just off the A27 is the village of **Wilmington**. The draw of this fairly nondescript but pleasant little village is nearby **Windover Hill**, home to a colossal chalk carving of a man carrying a couple of staffs. His origins are uncertain – traditionalists see a pilgrim; wiccan types see the midsummer man of pagan folklore; cynics see a practical joke by a Victorian farmer. Whatever he is, he's big, and can be found only a walk away from the village.

When the Downs meet the sea, it is with spectacular results. Towering **Beachy Head** is the largest cliff in the area. You can gaze up from the bottom just outside Eastbourne, or gaze out to sea from the top as you wander through the windswept gorse-strewn landscape. At **Seven Sisters Country Park** you can

---

By train from London

Direct trains from **Victoria** to **Lewes** leave approximately every half hour and the journey takes 1hr 5mins. Info: www.connex.co.uk. (Services will be taken over by South Eastern Trains in 2004; timetables should not be affected).

trample down the gorgeous Cuckmere Valley to the foot of the famous cliffs, although the view is actually better from Hope Gap.

East Sussex is also Bloomsbury Group territory and there's no better way to bore your children than by dragging them around the former haunts of this 1920s self-elected cultural elite. The entirely restored **Charleston**, the farmhouse discovered by Virginia Woolf that became home to her sister Vanessa Bell, the artist Duncan Grant and the novelist David Garnett, is a short drive away from **Monk's House**, a small converted farmhouse that was Virginia and Leonard Woolf's country retreat. It was at the banks of the nearby River Ouse that Virginia drowned herself in 1941, wading into the water, her pockets filled with stones.

What to see & do

Tourist Information Centre

187 High Street, Lewes, BN7 2DE (01273 483448/ fax 01273 484003/www.lewes.gov.uk). **Open** *Apr-Sept* 9am-5pm Mon-Fri; 10am-5pm Sat; 10am-2pm Sun. *Oct-Mar* 9am-5pm Mon-Fri; 10am-2pm Sat, bank hols.

Anne of Cleves House

52 Southover High Street, Lewes, BN7 1JA (01273 474610/www.sussexpast.co.uk). **Open** 11am-5pm Mon, Sun; 10am-5pm Tue-Sat. **Admission** (EH) £2.80; £1.10-£2.10 concessions. **Credit** MC, V.
When Henry VIII divorced his fourth wife in 1540, this timber-framed house was given to her as part of the settlement. Having undergone a few changes over the ensuing 400 years, the house has now been restored as near as possible to its former Tudor glory, with a Tudor kitchen, a bedroom recreated as the spurned Anne's boudoir and pieces of original furniture. The Lewes Folk Museum keeps its exhibits within the timbered walls and there's a well-kept herb garden too.

Charleston House

Signposted off A27 halfway between Lewes & Eastbourne, between Firle & Selmeston, BN8 6LL (01323 811265/www.charleston.org.uk). **Open** *Apr-June, Sept, Oct* 2-6pm (last entry 5pm) Wed-Sun. *July, Aug* 11.30am-6pm (last entry 5pm) Wed-Sat; 2-6pm (last entry 5pm) Sun. Closed Nov-Mar. **Admission** £6; £4.50 concessions; free under-6s. **Credit** MC, V.
Virginia Woolf came across this beautiful old farmhouse in 1916 and decided that it would be the perfect place for her sister Vanessa Bell to live with the artist Duncan Grant, the novelist David Garnett and Vanessa's two sons. Bell and Grant lived there for the rest of their lives, decorating every surface with their post-Impressionist daubings and using the house as a gallery for their own paintings, those of their friends and some by Picasso, Cézanne, Sickert and Pissaro. Now the house has been restored as a testament to their work and lives. Nearby, **Monk's House** in Rodmell (National Trust 01892 890651; open Apr-Oct 2-5.30pm Wed, Sat) is the more understated home of Woolf and her husband Leonard – packed with books and near the site of Virginia's suicide.

Visitors to **Lewes** can do it by the book.

Drusillas Park

Alfriston, BN26 5QS (01323 874100/www.drusillas. co.uk). **Open** *Apr-Oct* 10am-6pm daily (last entry 5pm). *Nov-Mar* 10am-5pm daily (last entry 4pm). **Admission** £9.49; £8.49 concessions; free under-3s. **Credit** MC, V.
This small zoo and adventure park is one of the most imaginatively interactive of Britain's children's parks, with the chance to meet a meerkat, handle a snake, go on a monkey walk or feed a mongoose. Children and adults brave enough to follow them can climb through tunnels and over scrambling walls to come face to face with animals that are kept in imaginatively designed enclosures. Beyond the animal adventures there's a miniature train ride, bouncy castles, a jungle adventure golf course, Monky Kindom, an SAS-style assault course of bridges, ropes and chutes and Explorers Lagoon, a paddling pool and sandpit for younger kids. It all adds up to a frantic, exhilarating, educational day out that is guaranteed to tire out the little 'uns.

Glynde Place

Glynde, Lewes, BN8 6SX (01273 858224/www. glyndeplace.com). **Open** *June-Sept* 2-5pm Wed, Sun. **Admission** £5; £2.50 concessions.
No credit cards.
A huge Elizabethan manor house built in 1589 from local flint as well as stone brought over from Normandy, Glynde Place has been occupied by the same family for the past 400 years – they have been documented in numerous stern-looking oil portraits. There is also a collection of 18th-century Italian works, Elizabethan furniture and large grounds in which to wander.

Don't get ruffled at John Evelyn's lovely and secluded **Southover Grange**. See p67.

Lewes Castle & Barbican House Museum

169 High Street, Lewes, BN7 1YE (01273 486290/ www.sussexpast.co.uk). **Open** 11am-5.30pm/dusk Mon, Sun; 10am-5.30pm/dusk Tue-Sat. **Admission** (EH) £4.20; £2.10-£3.70 concessions. **Credit** AmEx, MC, V.

Lewes Castle was built by William de Warenne, William the Conqueror's right-hand man, after the Battle of Hastings. It was extended during the next 300 years and today its outline dominates the town. It's worth a visit if only for the views of the Downs. The admission price includes entrance to Barbican House at the Castle Gate, which contains many remnants of the Norman conquest.

St Andrew's Alfriston & St Michael's and All Angels Berwick Church

St Andrew's, The Tye, Alfriston (01323 870376/ www.alfriston-churches.co.uk). **Open** 9am-6pm/dusk daily. **Admission** free.

St Michael's and All Angels, Berwick, off A27, halfway between Lewes & Eastbourne, Alciston (01323 870512/www.inn-quest.co.uk/berwick). **Open** 9am-dusk daily. **Admission** free.

St Andrew's, known as the Cathedral of the South Downs, is a 13th-century church built in the shape of a Greek cross, with a tall and spacious interior crowned by a stunning oak-beamed ceiling. At nearby Alciston is the tiny Berwick Church, a limestone building with an exuberant interior courtesy of Bloomsbury artists Duncan Grant and Vanessa Bell.

Seven Sisters Country Park

Exceat, Seaford, BN25 4AD (01323 870280/ www.vic.org.uk). **Open** *Park* 24hrs. *Visitors' centre* Easter-end Oct 10.30am-4.30pm Mon-Fri; 10.30am-5pm Sat, Sun. *Nov-Easter* 11am-4pm Sat, Sun. **Admission** free.

There is a car park and information centre, from where you can walk down the meandering River Cuckmere to the famous chalk cliffs. The idyll is rather spoiled on summer weekends by hordes of tourists.

Visit **Anne of Cleves House**, where the 'Flandres Mare' wallowed after rejection. *See p68*.

Where to stay

Crossways Hotel

Lewes Road, Wilmington, nr Polegate, BN26 5SG (01323 482455/fax 01323 487811/www.crossways hotel.co.uk). **Rates** £55 single; £80-£95 double/twin. **Rooms** (all en suite) 2 single; 3 double; 2 twin. **Credit** MC, V.

On the A27, this large white house with blue shutters resembles a French country hotel. Set in well-tended gardens, complete with duck pond, the idyll is rather spoiled by the incessant traffic at the front. Inside, however, this friendly and well-established family-run venture is calm enough. Rooms are a little small but clean and comfortingly traditional: floral patterns and pot pourri aplenty with tea bags and fresh milk arranged on formica trays. Dinner in the downstairs restaurant costs £30.95 for four courses and features locally reared meat, fish and game.

Millers

134 High Street, Lewes, BN7 1XS (01273 475631/ fax 01273 486226/www.hometown.aol.com/millers 134). **Rates** £57 single occupancy; £63 double. **Rooms** (both en suite) 2 double. **No credit cards**.

Behind the Georgian façade, this town centre building is actually a timber-framed 16th-century townhouse and home to Lewes's most idiosyncratic lodgings. Still very much a family home, with two rooms given over to guests, bed down here and you'll be sleeping with Lewes's colourful history. Named after an inn that was once part of the house, the Victorian Rose Room comes complete with mahogany four-poster and en suite bath.

The gloriously beamed Studio Room, meanwhile, was once the workplace of the Ladies of Millers, eccentric sisters and Bloomsbury groupies who bought the house in 1939 and curated no fewer than 40 art exhibitions in the stables behind. The room even houses a link to modern Lewes's Bonfire Night celebrations, with a shower room that was once a priest hole. Sectarianism in Elizabethan Lewes meant much more than throwing a few bangers at Guy Fawkes, and quivering Catholics would stow themselves away here during anti-Papal witch-hunts. No smoking throughout.

Shelley's Hotel

The High Street, Lewes, BN7 1XS (01273 472361/ fax 01273 483152). **Rates** £95-£140 single; £120-£180 double/twin; £235 suite; £260 four-poster. **Rooms** (all en suite) 1 single; 9 double/twin; 2 suites; 1 four-poster. **Credit** AmEx, DC, MC, V.

Housed in an elegant 17th-century manor, this is the aristocrat of the town's hotels. Once home to the Shelley family, links with the poet are tenuous. Open a door in the corner of the austere drawing room, however, and you'll find the pencilled heights of the esteemed romantic's relatives as they grew up. In the crooked-beamed bar guests chat amiably with locals, and the formal restaurant overlooks a fabulous garden and is home to Lewes's most consistently upmarket cuisine. However, the grandeur bestowed on the place by its associations – along with the hotel's active courting of business and Glyndebourne-bound clientele – leaves a hole where the atmosphere ought to be. But this is compensated for by the rooms: stylish and luxurious in a genteel country house way. Children and dogs welcome.

White Hart Hotel

55 High Street, Lewes, BN7 1XE (01273 476694/fax 01273 476695/www.whitehartlewes.co.uk). **Rates** £65 single; £94 double/twin/family room; £102 four-poster. **Rooms** (all en suite) 3 single; 47 double/twin/family; 2 four-poster. **Credit** AmEx, DC, MC, V.

Originally a Tudor coaching inn, the White Hart has everything you'd expect from a big hotel in a small town. The place has an unpretentious charm; locals huddle round the fire in the fuggy bar while out the back a carvery serves meat and two veg. Altogether different in character is the extension (in 'Roman' style, with palm trees), which houses a swimming pool and gym complex. Many of the 50 rooms are in a new wing; try for one in the original building, which come complete with beamed ceilings and creaky floorboards. Children and dogs welcome.

White Lodge Country House Hotel

Sloe Lane, Alfriston, BN26 5UR (01323 870265/ fax 01323 870284/www.whitelodge-hotel.com). **Rates** £60 single; £120-£130 double/twin/family room; £130 four-poster/kingsize; £150 suite. **Rooms** (all en suite) 3 single; 11 double/twin; 2 four-poster/kingsize; 1 suite. **Credit** MC, V.

With its immaculate drawing rooms, studies and bars – varied in style but equal in chintz – this place puts you in mind of a cosy Miss Marple mystery. There's something strangely romantic about this old-school family hotel. Service is attentive without being stuffy and adds to the generally slow-paced charm. Rooms, many named after the proprietor's children, come individually decorated and some offer gorgeous views across the Downs. Entertainment is served in attractively old-fashioned packages: board games in the social areas and there's the occasional murder mystery evening or gourmet night. There's also plenty for kids to do – with games rooms, family areas and manicured grounds. Children and small dogs welcome.

Where to eat & drink

The restaurant at **Shelley's** (*see p70*) is the only truly upmarket place to eat in Lewes but there are numerous brasseries, pizzerias, Indian and oriental restaurants to fill up at. Of the pubs, the **Lamb** (10 Fisher Street, 01273 470950) is modern and attracts a young local crowd. Quiet pints of real ale are to be had at the **Black Horse** (55 Western Road, 01273 473653) and the **Gardner's Arms** (46 Cliffe High Street, 01273 474808). But the best of the bunch is the tiny **Lewes Arms** (1 Mount Place, 01273 473152), up in the castle ramparts and home to some of the town's most venerable beards. Out in the country, the **Sussex Ox** at Milton Street (01323 870840) weighs down hikers with enormous 'Ox Burgers', while the **Ram** at Firle (01273 858222) is a lovely village pub with good food. The **Anchor** at Barcombe (Anchor Lane, 01273 400414) is wonderfully isolated, offers decent pub grub and hires out boats for a spin on the River Ouse. The **Tiger**

at East Dean (The Green, 01323 423209) is an ancient favourite looking out over a village cricket pitch. The **George Inn** (High Street, 01323 870319) and the **Star Inn** at nearby Alfriston (High Street, 01323 870495) offer oak-beamed charm aplenty.

Circa

145 High Street, Lewes, BN7 1XT (01273 471777/ www.circacirca.com). **Food served** noon-2.30pm, 6-10pm Tue-Fri, Sun; noon-2pm, 7-10pm Sat. **Main courses** £16.50. **Set lunch** £11.75 2 courses. **Set dinner** £23 2 courses, £27.50 3 courses. **Credit** AmEx, DC, MC, V.

The space is simple, with crowded tables and neutral colours, and for those who prefer to linger over their meal, the restaurant is not short of entertainment. The striking semicircular frontage, its plate glass windows overlooking the High Street, provides plenty of opportunity for people-watching. The menu is nothing if not eclectic. Smoked tangerine tofu, steamed shiitake dumplings, stella butter and yuzu soy is an attractive mixture of texture and flavour. But pan-fried brill with a parmesan maize crust, young green coconut sambal and Moroccan balls is too complex, demonstrating a fusion-for-the-sake-of-it approach rather than sound culinary judgement. The stand-out here, however, is an indulgent bitter chocolate parfait with salted popcorn cookie dough and passion fruit lassia.

Jolly Sportsman

Chapel Lane, East Chiltington, BN7 3BA (01273 890400). **Food served** 12.30-2pm, 7-9pm Tue-Thur; 12.30-2pm, 7-10pm Fri, Sat; 12.30-3pm Sun. **Main courses** £11.95-£19.85. **Set lunch** £11 2 courses, £14.75 3 courses Tue-Sat. **Credit** MC, V.

Once a country local, this is now as close as you can find to a gastropub in rural Sussex. Forget a pint and dominoes by the fire, this place is wooden tables, candlelight, pastel shades and Kandinsky-style wall hangings. It attracts a crowd who've done well in the City, sold up, moved out and don't mind you overhearing all about it. But any nostalgia for the pub's past is put aside once you try the brilliant food, much of it locally produced. On a recent visit, Sussex lamb spiced with chilli and garlic was beautifully tender and came with melt-in-the-mouth grilled aubergines. Other positive effects of modernity include a huge wine list, a fine vegetarian menu and attentive service. The garden overlooking the Downs is a delight on summer evenings – so long as you can find room to park among the Range Rovers.

Rose Cottage

Alciston, nr Lewes, BN26 6UW (01323 870377). **Food served** *Restaurant* noon-2pm, 7-9pm daily. *Bar* noon-2pm, 7-9.30pm daily. **Main courses** £7.25-£13.95. **Credit** MC, V.

At the foot of the Downs in sleepy Alciston, this tiny old pub sticks firmly with the traditions of the English country boozer. The bar is all beamed ceilings, historical maps of local farmland and agricultural ironmongery. There's even a nod to 'English eccentricity', with a resident squawking parrot and a slightly erratic landlord. As you'd expect, there's always a bevy of locals by the bar, but they're used to squads of hikers and local families on summer weekends. For such a small outfit,

Sussex & Surrey

the range of food is huge. Alongside the standard 'chips with everything' bar menu, there are robust daily specials such as bacon and rabbit pie or lamb casserole that are loyal to local ingredients. Eat by the fire in winter or on the quiet terrace overlooking farmland in summer, and accompany your meal with a pint of Harveys.

Silletts Cottage Restaurant

Church Farm, Selmeston, nr Polegate, BN26 6TZ (01323 811343/fax 01323 811743/www.silletts cottage-restaurant.co.uk). **Food served** 7-9.30pm Mon; noon-2pm, 7-10pm Tue-Sun. **Main courses** (lunch only) £8.35-£15.25. **Set dinner** £27.95 4 courses. **Credit** AmEx, DC, MC, V.

Set in a cutesy old pile amid an elaborately floral garden, this restaurant plays up appealingly to the theme of the country idyll. Homely charms begin in the bar where the disarmingly polite proprietor invites you for a drink while you check the menu. The open fire, easy chairs, floral patterns and ubiquitous trinkets place the decor strictly in the chocolate box category. Move through to the even frillier dining area where patrons – a reserved but not unfriendly cross-section of the local older generation – enjoy a fairly traditional menu. Starters might include the likes of Caesar salad with fresh marinated anchovies, or sliced roast quail served on toast with cranberry jelly. Mains are mostly superior versions of the roast, served with plenty of veg and drenched in gravy, or other trad dishes like grilled Dover sole, or sautéd tenderloin of pork in a marsala sauce. All in all, a pleasantly nostalgic experience; just don't bring any stag parties along.

Snowdrop

119 South Street, Lewes, BN7 2BU (01273 471018). **Food served** noon-3pm, 5-9pm Mon-Thur; noon-9pm Fri-Sun. **Main courses** £6-£10. **Credit** AmEx, MC, V.

It's worth a trip to the edge of town for the food, drink and music at this wonderfully quirky pub. First impressions are of a chaotic place: there's a patio cluttered with antique bric-a-brac, and the fun continues inside. Upstairs, the town's trendily attired teenagers jostle for attention by the pool table, most of them pie-eyed. Downstairs, in a bar resembling an old ship and bedecked with murals of local characters, Lewes's finest are out in force. Liberal mums and dads choose from an enterprising vegetarian and seafood menu, including pizzas and veggieburgers, while they reminisce about the '60s. There's a good selection of wines and Harveys beer from the brewery down the road. The ageing hippie undercurrent is let loose on Monday nights when Herbie Flowers, of Lou Reed's *Transformer* fame, and his jazz band are in residence.

For Fawkes' sake, burn it

Burning effigies, sectarian slogans and kinky vicars – Lewes does Guy Fawkes Night like nowhere else. One night in 1554 the Sheriff of Sussex was ordered by Bloody Mary to hunt out Protestants. He entered the Brighton home of brewer Deryk Carver and found him 'engaged in prayer, saying the service in English as set forth in the time of Edward VI'. Carver was promptly whisked off to Lewes and burned alive, along with 16 others. Over the centuries the town, many of whose denizens tended towards the hellfire end of the religious spectrum, never forgot these martyrs.

Understandably, Guy Fawkes's attempt to blow up Parliament on 5 November 1605 didn't go down well either, but it was not until the 19th century that anti-Catholic feeling in Lewes got militant. In 1850 Pope Pius IX (look carefully in today's celebrations and he's the guy kebabed by a burning stake) restored the Catholic hierarchy in England. For God-fearing locals and young lads up for fisticuffs, this was too much. The anniversary of the Gunpowder Plot soon became an excuse for 'No Popery' and 'Death to Rome' banners amid a rising tide of violence. By the end of the century it was not uncommon for people to die in the 'celebrations', and the reading of the Riot Act became a matter of course.

These days it's a more civilised affair. The anti-Catholic banners remain but they're just a little joke, honest. Sectarian hatred has now mellowed into a rivalry between the town's five bonfire societies, each of which strives to outdo each other in the fancy-dress torch-lit processions and firework displays. The Cliffe Society regards itself as the very hardest, racing blazing tar barrels down a cobbled street, while the other four march around the town dressed as anything from Red Indians to kinky vicars. It's all very Village People.

When the marching is over, each society decamps to its own site. Brave members dress up as Catholic cardinals and stand on a makeshift altar so that a beery public can hurl bangers and abuse at them. Then it's on with the business of blowing up the Pope, Guy Fawkes and 'Enemies of Bonfire' – massive tableaux of topical hate figures stuffed full of rockets and incendiary devices. Recent victims of the Bonfire Boys' wrath have been Messrs Blair, Bush and Bin Laden. It's just a little joke after all.

Brighton

So much more than London by the sea.

The city of Brighton and Hove has been called 'London-on-Sea' so often that the phrase ought to be granted official cliché status; nevertheless, it's not hard to see why this mischievous and flirtatious city attracts the label. This is where the capital's job-jaded workforce come to let their hair down; a place of colour, temptation and opportunities for misbehaviour – with a sea view. Brighton looks after its visitors well, whether they're party conference delegates, dirty weekenders or an opportunistic hybrid of the two. Close connections to London mean that a wealth of hotels, guesthouses and restaurants, labyrinths of shops, and a vibrant, sophisticated cultural scene and nightlife are able to prosper.

However, Brighton has a character all its own and is of a more laid-back and notoriously liberal persuasion than London. With all the kitsch fun of a British seaside resort (even if the beach consists of pebbles rather than sand), there's a constant influx of coach parties and daytrippers intent on downing a few ales, buying sticks of inedible rock and thumbing their noses at malignant melanoma as they sprawl in deckchairs, turning beetroot-red.

But others are drawn to Brighton too: those relocating there in order to tune in, turn on and drop out find that the city greets outsiders with open arms and a warm heart, whether they're students, artists, families or Chris Eubank. Universities and language schools have helped make this a multicultural urban stew. With more than 60 per cent of the population under the age of 45, the 'vegetarian capital of Europe' can be a culture shock to those arriving from elderly Eastbourne (*see p67*).

A perennially thriving gay and lesbian scene has also put Brighton on the map, with local authorities and businesses acknowledging (and exploiting) the pink pound. August's Brighton Pride festival sees tens of thousands of revellers ostentatiously celebrating their sexual orientation without fear of harassment.

The seaside starts here

Brighton wasn't always such a maelstrom of profligacy and abandonment. It began life as Bristmestune (later Brighthelmstone), a small fishing village that augmented its income by encouraging smuggling, and remained relatively obscure until 1750, when Dr Richard Russell invented the seaside. Russell, whose curative preparations included cuttlefish bones, crab's eyes and tar, proclaimed that sea water had restorative benefits, which encouraged fashionable London to rush down to the coast in an 18th-century version of Fatboy Slim's 2002 beach party. Brighton become a cool holiday destination, with booming industries in hotels and 'bathing machines' – beach huts on wheels that allowed bathers to get changed and enter the sea without exposure. But the best was yet to come; in 1783 Prince George (later George IV) rented a farmhouse in Brighton, where he became the centre of a hip and happening court-in-waiting. As time went by and his mad old dad George III grew ever more deranged (but refused to die), the Prince Regent kept himself busy by converting his modest abode into an extraordinary faux-oriental pleasure palace in a makeover that would make Laurence Llewellyn-Bowen blush, and inviting the country's creative, beautiful and ambitious young things to join him for a life of drinking, womanising and gambling. This is the **Royal Pavilion**. Suddenly fashionable, the town's population expanded from 3,500 in 1780 to 40,500 in 1831.

Victorian Brighton saw a profusion of eccentric engineering projects including three piers, two of which are still standing today. **Brighton** (née Palace) **Pier** is a messy clutter of hotdog stands, karaoke, candyfloss and fairground rides, whereas the West Pier, closed since 1975, is a sorry shell of its former self, having suffered from storm damage and suspected arson. It's still standing – just. While Brighton Pier is the destination of thousands of video-gaming, chip-chomping, rollercoaster-riding funsters, it's the latter that is far more interesting (*see p82* **Funeral pier**).

By train from London

The fastest train to **Brighton** leaves **Victoria** every half-hour (journey time 50mins). There are also trains from **King's Cross Thameslink** that leave about every hour and pass through **Farringdon**, **Blackfriars**, **London Bridge** and **East Croydon** (journey time 1hr 15mins). Info: www.thameslink.co.uk.

That's entertainment

With seven miles of uninterrupted coastline, Brighton remains a seaside resort first and foremost, but there's plenty to do away from the front. Perhaps reflecting its singular character, the town has plenty of independent, non-chain shops. There's a high concentration of clothes, record and gift shops in and around North Laine (*see p80* **Life in the fast Laine**), and in the network of narrow cobbled alleyways known as the Lanes, which contain a plethora of jewellery and antiques shops. Then there are all those pubs and bars (more than there are days of the year), numerous restaurants and cafés, not to mention the clubs. With its hyperactive nightlife and a constant flow of hedonists, you can be sure that in Brighton entertainment is just around the corner.

What to see & do

Tourist Information Centre

10 Bartholomew Square, BN1 1JS (0906 711 2255/ www.visitbrighton.com). Open July, Aug 9am-5.30pm Mon-Fri; 10am-6pm Sat; 10am-4pm Sun. *Sept, Oct, Jan-June* 9am-5pm Mon-Fri; 10am-5pm Sat; 10am-4pm Sun; *Nov, Dec* 9am-5pm Mon-Fri; 10am-5pm Sat.

Bike hire

Sunrise Cycle Hire *West Pier, King's Road, BN1 2FL (01273 748881).*
About a mile from the station.

Booth Museum of Natural History

194 Dyke Road, BN1 5AA (01273 292777/www. virtualmuseum.info). Open 10am-5pm Mon-Wed, Fri, Sat; 2-5pm Sun. **Admission** free.
You'll find more than half a million natural history specimens here, including a whale, dinosaur bones and a display of British birds collected by Victorian E T Booth. In fact, you couldn't hope to find a better representation of the Victorian drive to collect, collate and display. The museum has made sterling efforts at modern presentation of this group of stuffed, mounted and skeletonised fauna and flora, with interactive galleries, temporary exhibitions and events.

Brighton Fishing Museum

201 King's Road Arches, on the lower prom between the piers, BN1 1NB (01273 723064). Open 10am-5pm daily. **Admission** free.
While you're on the seafront, it's worth a quick trip to this little museum to get an idea of Brighton's lengthy maritime history. Display cases surrounding the centrepiece, a clinker-built Sussex beach fishing boat, describe the local fishing industry and include a TV screen showing a fisherman's reminiscences, model boats and 19th-century seafaring souvenirs.

Brighton Marina

01273 693636/www.brightonmarina.co.uk.
A walk down the concrete breakwater arm of Brighton Marina (closed in rough weather) shows off the sea's elemental power to great effect. Nautical types gaze longingly at the beautiful, expensive (and occasionally historic) boats that are moored in the UK's largest yacht harbour. Call Southern Marine Services (01273 585000/www.girlgray.com) to inquire about fishing or diving trips; for sailing, try Marina Watersports (01273 818237). If actually taking to the water doesn't appeal, the marina also offers the delights of ten-pin bowling, an eight-screen cinema, and a clutch of bars, restaurants and shops. To find the marina, just walk east along the beach or promenade, past Sussex Square, passing the naked wrinklies on the nudist beach.

Brighton Museum & Art Gallery

Royal Pavilion Gardens, BN1 1EE (01273 290900/ www.virtualmuseum.info). Open 10am-7pm Tue; 10am-5pm Wed-Sat; 2-5pm Sun. **Admission** free.
Housed in an impressive building where the domed hallways are as much of a feature as the collections, this delightful museum with informative galleries is a joy to explore. A strong display of 20th-century design (majoring in art nouveau and art deco) graces the ground floor, alongside world art (Burmese textiles, Yoruba masks, an Egyptian mummy) and exhibits about the working and leisure lives of Brightonians from 1700 to the present day. The first floor includes galleries on global public performance (Burmese marionettes, Punch & Judy booths), fashion (from Georgian foppery to punk), body art (corsets to piercings) and fine art.

British Engineerium

off Nevill Road, BN3 7QA (01273 559583/ www.britishengineerium.com). Open 10am-5pm daily. **Admission** £4; £3 concessions. **No credit cards**.
The Museum of Steam and Mechanical Antiquities, to use its full title, was originally Goldstone Pumping Station, opened in 1866 to supply water for Brighton and Hove. It is still home to the huge working beam engine that powered the pumps and to immense underground boilers. There are also traction engines, locomotive models, vintage motorbikes and a horse-drawn fire engine, plus hands-on educational exhibits explaining the scientific principles at work. 'Steam Up Sundays' (first Sunday in the month, bank holiday Sundays and Mondays) see everything fired up in full steam.

Hove Museum & Art Gallery

19 New Church Road, BN3 4AB (01273 290200/ www.virtualmuseum.info). Open 10am-5pm Tue-Sat; 2-5pm Sun. **Admission** free.
Reopened in February 2003 after major redevelopment, the collections of crafts, paintings and local history artefacts have been redisplayed in much improved new galleries. The interactive toy gallery is engaging and amusing, and the film gallery's exploration of Hove's role in the birth of cinema in the 1890s and 1900s includes original early film footage that not only buff's will find fascinating. The gallery also hosts changing exhibitions: recent ones have focused on children's writers from Beatrix Potter to J K Rowling.

Mechanical Memories

250C King's Road Arches, Lower Esplanade, opposite the end of East Street (enquiries 01273 608620). Open Easter-June noon-6pm Sat, Sun, school hols. *July-Sept* noon-6pm daily. *Oct-Easter* noon-6pm Sun (weather permitting). Last entry 5.30pm. **Admission** free.

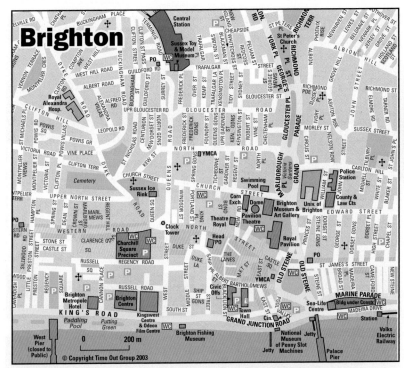

A charming diversion from the mass of seafront tack in the vicinity, this collection features finely crafted wood and brass slot machines dating from 1904 to the 1960s. Many are still in working order, and visitors can buy old pennies to operate them.

Preston Manor

Preston Park, BN1 6SB (01273 290900/www. virtualmuseum.info). **Open** 1-5pm Mon; 10am-5pm Tue-Sat; 2-5pm Sun. **Admission** £3.70; £2.15-£3 concessions. Joint ticket with Royal Pavilion £8.20. **No credit cards**.

Originally built around 1600, the manor now provides a fascinating example of the 'upstairs downstairs' nature of Edwardian life. More than 20 rooms on four floors are open to the public, containing a wealth of family heirlooms, furniture and paintings. Start at the attic nursery and basic maids' quarters, move on to grand bedrooms and drawing rooms, then head down to the basement kitchen and scullery. Adjacent to Preston Park and the disused 13th-century St Peter's Church (for entry, ask for the key from the Crown & Anchor pub on Preston Road), the manor also comprises walled gardens and a pet cemetery.

The Royal Pavilion

Brighton, BN1 1EE (01273 292820/www.royal pavilion.org.uk). **Open** *Apr-Sept* 9.30am-5.45pm daily. *Oct-Mar* 10am-5.15pm daily. **Admission**

£5.80; £3.40-£4 concessions. Joint ticket with Preston Manor £8.20. **Guided tours** (£1.25 extra) 11.30am, 2.30pm daily. **Credit** AmEx, MC, V

Once a simple rented farmhouse, now a spectacular palace, the final transformation of this Brighton landmark came about when George IV became Prince Regent in 1811. John Nash created this no-expense-spared oriental fantasy for the party prince to indulge his love of pleasure. Opulent and enormously camp, the rooms and collections are largely Chinese-themed, from the dramatic banqueting room with spectacular dragon chandelier to saloons, the magnificent dancing and concert room, and the king's apartments. Even if historic buildings aren't your thing, you'll find plenty here to amuse and astonish. The guided tours are recommended: staff bring the rooms alive by including all manner of quirky facts.

Sea-Life Centre

Marine Parade, BN2 1TB (01273 604234/www. sealife.co.uk). **Open** 10am-6pm daily. Last entry 5pm. **Admission** £7.50; £4.75-£6.50 concessions.

Opened in 1872 and now part of a Europe-wide chain of Sea-Life Centres (whose prime concern is supposedly environmental protection), this is the world's oldest still-functioning aquarium. Some have slated the centre as tatty, perhaps because it retains its elaborate Victorian columns and domes. Actually, the galleries are all the more interesting and charming for them. The 60ft-long underwater tunnel, which allows you to observe sharks,

rays and turtles swimming overhead, is a big hit. On a much smaller scale, but equally fascinating, are the sea-horse tank and Curious Creatures tank (filled with pufferfish, splendidly named wobbegongs, tiny sea ponies, prehistoric-looking shoe crabs), among tanks and rockpools of piranha, terrapins, whiskery catfish and other colourful exotic specimens.

Volks Electric Railway

285 Madeira Drive, BN2 1EN (01273 292718). **Open** *Easter-mid Sept* 11am-5pm Mon-Fri; 11am-6pm Sat, Sun. **Tickets** (single fare) £1.50; 70p-£1.20 concessions; £3.50 family (maximum 2 adults, 3 children). **No credit cards.**

Built in 1883, this is the oldest electric railway in the world in operation. Kids love the 1.25-mile, 12-minute ride along the beach, running between Black Rock near the Marina and the Sea-Life Centre.

Where to stay

When it comes to places to stay, Brighton certainly has the quantity but could be said to lack the quality. Nevertheless, it's still a good idea to book ahead all year round (there are many conferences). The Tourist Information Centre (*see p75*) operates a reservation service.

There are two main areas for hotels. On the New Steine in Kemptown there are average three-star hotels and guesthouses. Around Regency Square, opposite the West Pier, there is more variety, the best of which are the **Adelaide Hotel** (51 Regency Square, 01273 205286, doubles £68-£92) and the **Regency Hotel** (28 Regency Square, 01273 202690/www.regencybrighton.co.uk, doubles £85-£110). Russell Square also has a host of guesthouses. For a clean, cheap and central chain option try **Brighton Premier Lodge** (144 North Street, 0870 700 1334/www.premierlodge.com, doubles £52). **Brighton Backpackers** (75-76 Middle Street, 01273 777717/www.brightonbackpackers.com, £12 per person in dorms, doubles £30) is good for budget travellers. For luxury try the **Grand** (King's Road, 01273 321188/www.grandbrighton.co.uk, doubles £210-£330).

Alias Hotel Seattle

Brighton Marina, BN2 5WA (01273 679799/fax 01273 679899/www.aliashotels.com). **Rates** £95-£115 double; £100-£120 twin; £105-£125 king size; £115-£145 deluxe/family. **Rooms** (all en suite) 37 double; 4 twin; 25 king size; 5 deluxe/family. **Credit** AmEx, DC, MC, V.

Welcome aboard the Alias Seattle, a liner-inspired hip hotel in Brighton Marina and the latest addition to the quirky Alias chain. Bedrooms are funky, with white leather headboards, monsoon showers, CD players and sea views. For breakfast, order the Bento in Bed and indulge yourself with a box packed with blueberry muffins and smoked salmon bagels. Seafood dominates the menu in the Mediterranean-inspired Café Paradiso

and cocktails rule in the 'secret' Black and White bar (only open to hotel residents and their guests). Cruising has never been so cool. Children and dogs welcome.

Blanch House

17 Atlingworth Street, BN2 1PL (01273 603504/www.blanchhouse.co.uk). **Rates** £125 double/single occupancy; £150 deluxe double; £220 suite. **Rooms** (all en suite) 4 double; 5 deluxe double; 3 suites. **Credit** AmEx, MC, V.

An unassuming Kemptown terrace on the outside, Blanch House's interior is chic and style-magazine perfect, the atmosphere is laid-back and staff are friendly. As far as the rooms go, it's theme city: they zip across eras, continents and design styles – from rococo to renaissance, from India to Morocco via Acacia Avenue (1970s suburbia) and Snowstorm (silvery 1960s look). Each is beautifully done. Appearance aside, the super-comfy beds, sound systems, TV/videos, power showers, Molton Brown toiletries, slippers, robes and Belgian chocs help make rooms comfortable. There's also a sleek cocktail bar and an appealing Modern European restaurant. Children are welcome during the week.

Granville Hotel OFFER

124 King's Road, BN1 2FA (01273 326302/fax 01273 728294/www.granvillehotel.co.uk). **Rates** £55-£65 single; £85-£185 double/suite. **Rooms** (all en suite) 2 single; 22 double/suites. **Credit** AmEx, DC, MC, V.

Ideal if you're after a sea view but want something with more personality than the Grand or Metropole. The spacious front rooms have unrivalled views of what remains of the West Pier and are surprisingly quiet. If you're feeling extravagant, opt for an elaborately carved four-poster with en suite jacuzzi; other themed rooms include the art deco Noel Coward Room and the romantic Brighton Rock Room, with muslin-draped Victorian four-poster. A Pacific Rim menu is offered in the basement restaurant, DaDu. Staff are friendly and helpful. Children and pets welcome. All bedrooms are no-smoking.

Hotel du Vin

Ship Street, BN1 1AD (01273 718588/fax 01273 718599/www.hotelduvin.com). **Rates** £130 double; £225-£350 suite. **Rooms** (all en suite) 34 double; 3 suites. **Credit** AmEx, DC, MC, V.

This contender for the title of Brighton's best hotel is centrally placed – next to the shopping action but almost on the sea front. Like the other hotels in this small chain, the place has a relaxed atmosphere but it runs like clockwork. The bedrooms are modern and beautifully appointed – fans argue over whether the bathrooms or the beds are the best feature. The restaurant is worth visiting even if you're staying elsewhere (breakfast is £9 for the works); the high-ceilinged bar encourages lingering (great sofas, fabulous drinks list, billiard table, first floor terrace). Staff are welcoming and very competent. Book well in advance.

Hotel Pelirocco

10 Regency Square, BN1 2FG (01273 327055/fax 01273 733845/www.hotelpelirocco.co.uk). **Rates** £50-£55 single; £85-£125 double; £85-£100 twin; £185-£235 suite. **Rooms** (all en suite) 5 single; 9 double; 4 twin; 1 suite. **Credit** MC, V.

The Pelirocco is trendy and funky, with full-on (often kitsch) themed decor in the bedrooms. Most rooms have some kind of popular culture theme: target bedspreads and scooter wing-mirrors adorn the Modrophenia room, while Betty Page's Boudoir features fetish art (and peepholes on the bathroom door). This is a place dedicated to pleasure, so the bar is open until 4am at weekends; and, for post-clubbing insomniacs, PlayStation consoles come as standard in all rooms. Children are welcome during the week and no-smoking rooms are available.

Hotel Twenty One

21 Charlotte Street, BN2 1AG (01273 686450/ fax 01273 695560/www.smoothhound.co.uk). **Rates** £35 single; £60-£95 double; £75 twin; £75 four-poster. **Rooms** (all en suite) 1 single; 3 double; 1 four-poster; 2 twin. **Credit** MC, V.
Located in the quiet Kemptown conservation area, this is a well-run and easygoing B&B a few minutes' walk from the Palace Pier and town centre. The finest rooms have period Victorian furniture and all are cosy and comfortable, with reassuringly chintzy furnishing. All rooms have a TV, phone and en suite shower, and the large basement room also has its own small patio.

Nineteen

19 Broad Street, BN2 1TJ (01273 675529/fax 01273 675531/www.hotelnineteen.co.uk). **Rates** £95-£160 double. Minimum 2-night stay at weekends. **Rooms** (all en suite) 7 double. **Credit** MC, V.
Just seven rooms feature in this stylish townhouse hotel that successfully mixes period features with contemporary works by local artists. Thanks to minimalist decor and light colours, even the smaller rooms feel bright and airy. Beds sit on bases of illuminated coloured glass bricks, the linen and walls are fresh and white, and rooms have CD and video facilities and fresh flowers. Guests may help themselves to drinks and snacks from the kitchen, and borrow videos, CDs and magazines. Breakfast (everything is organic or free-range where possible) is served in a basement with small decked area, and there are plans for a rooftop suite and basement bar. No-smoking rooms available. No children.

Oriental Hotel

9 Oriental Place, BN1 2LJ (01273 205050/fax 01273 821096/www.orientalhotel.co.uk). **Rates** £35-£40 single; £70-£140 double. **Rooms** 1 single; 6 double (en suite); 1 suite. **Credit** MC, V.
Reasonably inexpensive, comfortably bohemian and centrally located, the Oriental can be found just off the seafront in a street full of attractive ammonite-topped columns on once-grand, now rather battered Regency architecture. The Oriental has a nicely relaxed feel about it, featuring plain-filled, brightly coloured and simply furnished rooms with lots of wood and wallhangings. Staff are welcoming and helpful, contributing to the all-round homely feel. Breakfast is served in the stylish lounge bar. Children and pets welcome.

Where to eat & drink

Unsurprisingly for a seaside town, fish and chip shops abound, and traditional no-frills fishy fare is perhaps best sampled at the **Regency** (131 King's Road, 01273 325014).

Vegetarians are well catered for at **Food for Friends** (18 Prince Albert Street, 01273 202310), **Infinity** (50 Gardner Street, 01273 670743), **Wai Kika Moo Kau** (11A Kensington Gardens, 01273 671117; 42 Meeting House Lane, 01273 323824) and the **George** (5 Trafalgar Street, 01273 681055), a veggie/vegan pub. The **Sanctuary Café** (51-5 Brunswick Street East, 01273 770002) is a popular Hove hangout, with a nicely rustic area upstairs and bands. And **Red Veg** (21 Gardner Street, 01273 679910) does the best burgers in town.

Preston Street consists entirely of restaurants, cafés and pubs, none of them particularly exciting, though **Spaghetti Junction** (60 Preston Street, 01273 737082) does decent takeaway salads and pasta. A fun caff with decent nosh is the **RockOla Coffee Bar** (29 Tidy Street, no phone), complete with 1950s freeplay jukebox and bright formica furniture.

Other places worth a visit include **Moshi Moshi Sushi** (Opticon, Bartholomew Square, 01273 719195), a conveyor belt affair; **Blind Lemon Alley** (41 Middle Street, 01273 205151) for great burgers and American diner fare; **Casa Don Carlos** (5 Union Street, 01273 327177) for tapas; **Saucy** (8 Church Road, 01273 324080), an increasingly popular Hove establishment; and chainer **Loch Fyne** (95-9 Western Road, 01273 716160) for seafood and oysters.

The best places for caffeine in a city full of coffee shops are **Nia Café Bar** (87-8 Trafalgar Street, 01273 671371), which has good grub too; **Alfresco** (Milkmaid Pavilion, King's Road Arches) for beach views; or **Kensington's Café** (1 Kensington Gardens) – the balcony is great for North Laine people-watching.

The **Hop Poles** (13 Middle Street, 01273 710444) does hands-down the cheapest and best pub grub in town; it's difficult to get a seat, though. Failing that try the **Basketmakers Arms** (12 Gloucester Road, 01273 689006) or **Great Eastern** (103 Trafalgar Street, 01273 685681) for good Sunday grub.

Pubs and bars are in abundance. Of the traditional pubs, the **Cricketers** (15 Black Lion Street), **Druid's Head** (9 Brighton Place) and **Battle of Trafalgar** (34 Guildford Road) have the most charm. Another classic Brighton boozer, the **Prince Albert** (48 Trafalgar Street), has theme nights. For a trendier watering hole, nip along to **St James** (16 Madeira Place), a good pre-club bar with DJs, or **Sidewinder** (65 Upper St James Street), both in Kemptown, and the **Hampton** (57 Upper North Street) or **Riki-Tik** (18A Bond Street) in town.

Of the gay bars, the most fun (and alfresco drinking) is to be had at the **Amsterdam Hotel** (11-12 Marine Parade); **Doctor**

Life in the fast Laine

North Laine is a destination no serious shopper should miss. While Churchill Square offers three-storey chain store action (the same chain stores that can be found in any and every town in Britain) and the Lanes provides a cobbled alleyway and antique theme park, North Laine – an area roughly bounded by Trafalgar Street, Queens Road and North Street – does what Brighton does best: showing off its colourful, free-spirited self and flogging its wares while it's about it. Gift shops galore entice with goodies you never knew you needed – Wizard of Oz Monopoly, how did you manage without it? You'll soon find your wallet emptying as all retail reasoning leaves you.

Tsena (6 Bond Street, 01273 328402) is great for original limited edition gifts by British designers – baby items and jewellery are especially appealing. **Pen to Paper** (4 Sydney Street, 01273 676670) is a snailmailer's dream shop, featuring handmade papers, waxes and inks among its stationery staples. **Tucan** (29 Bond Street, 01273 326351) provides a touch of South American exotica, with everything from chunky inlaid wood furniture to delicate silver bracelets on display. In Gardner Street, **Rapid Eye** (No.23, 01273 694323) stocks stylish kitchenware – citrus juicers and the like. Gadgets of an

entirely different nature can be found a few doors down at **Tickled** (No.15, 01273 628725); check out the basement for sex toys and 'gifts for women' at this fun store. **Pussy** (No.3A, 01273 604861) is the place to go for stylish Orla Kiely lampshades and Paul Frank bags – oh, and Hello Kitty vibrators. **Cissy Mo** (38 Sydney Street, 01273 607777), a long-time Brighton favourite, crams in kitsch and brightly coloured plastic items, from Wonderwoman mousemats to flowery Hawaiian beaded curtains. Next door is **Brighton Designers & Makers** (39 Sydney Street, 01273 671212), which sells original glass, framed pictures and jewellery by local artists. **Appendage** (36 Kensington Gardens, 01273 605901) also features arts crafts and ceramics. For striking silver, stone-encrusted jewellery, head for **Curiouser & Curiouser** (2 Sydney Street, 01273 673120).

Green and ethical shoppers will find plenty to please at **Neal's Yard Remedies** (2A Kensington Gardens, 01273 601464), **Green Buddha** (15 Bond Street, 01273 324488), **The Hemp Shop** (22 Gardner Street, 01273 818047) and, a few doors further down, **Vegetarian Shoes** (No.12, 01273 691913).

Dance music lovers will enjoy a rummage through the wares on sale at

Brighton's (16 King's Road) on the seafront features DJs playing house and techno. If you fancy camping it up large (you'll never outdo the staff), beeline it to the **Regency Tavern** (32-4 Russell Square). **Candy Bar** (33 St James Street) is a women-only lesbian hangout.

As for clubbing, Brighton has more nightclubs than you can shake a stick of rock at. To get hip with what's going down, stroll down Gardner Street or Kensington Gardens on a Saturday afternoon, and you'll leave armed with club flyers aplenty. Or simply check out one of the Brighton listings mags such as *The Latest* or *The Brighton Source*.

Black Chapati
12 Circus Parade, New England Road, BN1 4GW (01273 699011). **Food served** 7-10pm Tue-Sat. **Main courses** £11.90-£15.50. **Credit** AmEx, MC, V.
Black Chapati's drab exterior and simple café-like interior are at odds with the quality of pan-Asian cuisine on offer. The short but well co-ordinated menu features

starters such as Sri Lankan fish patties with fresh chutneys – deliciously zingy, although the flavour of the fish was somewhat lost to the heat. Mains include grilled five-spice duck breast, Chinese sausage and potato cake with rice wine sauce or succulent roast cod, dried shrimp and fresh lime salad with rice. Desserts include a wonderful ginger meringue with green tea ice-cream. Palate-pleasing and imaginative dining, although service can be disappointing, ranging from inattentive to dour.

The Epicurean
33 Western Street, BN1 2PT (01273 776618/ www.epicurean-brighton.com). **Food served** noon-2pm, 7-10pm Tue-Sat. **Main courses** (dinner) £9.90-£18.90. **Set lunch** £8.50 2 courses; £12.50 3 courses. **Credit** AmEx, MC, V.
Bruno and Theresa Pruvost made a wise choice of location when opening the Epicurean – if perhaps not of venue, a tightly converted fisherman's cottage in reasonably fashionable Western Street. There may only be half a dozen tables filling each of the two floors, but dining doesn't feel uncomfortable. The menu features eight starters and nine mains. Although served with grace on stylishly curvy tableware, neither the glazed medley of

Urban Records (24 Gardner Street, 01273 320567). For alternative music and vinyl, try **Across the Tracks** (110 Gloucester Road, 01273 677906).

Browse for bargain reading material at **Oxfam** (30 Kensington Gardens, 01273 698093) and **Sandpiper** (a couple of doors down, at No.34, 01273 605422), where remaindered books go for as little as £1. **Two Way Books** (54 Gardner Street, 01273 687729) also sells vintage magazines and children's books.

A good range of traditional and interesting toys are stocked at **Daisy**

Daisy (33 North Road, 01273 689108), and trendy designer gear is sold for label lovin' kids at **Cat & Mouse** (17 Sydney Street, 01273 600145). Alternatively, create that dippy-hippie Brighton parent-and-child look by customising with retro clobber and accessories from **Starfish** (25 Gardner Street, 01273 680068), **To Be Worn Again** (51 Providence Street, 01273 624500) and **Rokit** (23 Kensington Gardens, 01273 672053). Mod mums (the Lambretta baby seat is optional) can pick up target T-shirts and parkas (many in the original 1950s and 1960s boxes) from **Jump the Gun** (36 Gardner Street, 01273 626333). **Snoopers Paradise** (7-8 Kensington Gardens, 01273 602558) is great for the clothes and homewares of yesteryear. **North Laine Antiques & Flea Market** (5A Upper Gardner Street) is also great for eagle-eyed bargain-baggers.

Streetwear shops abound. Try **Moda Soda** (7 Gardner Street, 01273 682994) for the funkiest tops and accessories in town. Trendy Brightonians also make a beeline for very cool, urban outfits at **Minky** (32 Sydney Street, 01273 604490) and **Cutie** (33 Kensington Gardens, 01273 693968). Gola bags, trainers and combats are a speciality at **Mau Mau** (40 Gardner Street, 01273 607807) and the his 'n' hers **Badger** shops (25-6 Bond Street, 01273 325421) stock hip labels such as Duffer and Evisu.

Dover sole fillet nor the pan-fried king scallops warranted their £18.90 price tag, the modest portions not compensating with maximum flavour. The two-course and three-course lunch deals are great, though, and the desserts are exquisite.

Gingerman

21A Norfolk Square, BN1 2PD (01273 326688). **Food served** 12.30-2pm, 7-10pm Tue-Sat. **Set lunch** £9.95 1 course; £12.95 2 courses; £14.95 3 courses. **Set dinner** £22 2 courses; £25 3 courses. **Credit** AmEx, DC, MC, V.
This cracking little place is a favourite of Brighton foodies. Its buttermilk and burnt ochre decor (plus incongruous glitterball), modest dimensions (around 30 covers) and out-of-the-way location (in a residential street west of the centre) don't augur culinary fireworks, but there are impressively assured hands at work. Start with a peppery mackerel fillet encrusted with a subtle Goan spice mix and served with a cucumber raita, before heading back into more trad territory with a melting fillet of Buchan beef with potato rösti, peas, carrots and spinach. Finish off with a creamy blood orange and grapefruit gratin.

La Fourchette

101 Western Road, BN1 2AA (01273 722556). **Food served** noon-3pm, 7-10.30pm Tue-Sun. **Set lunch** £7.50 2 courses; £10 3 courses. **Set dinner** £19 2 courses; £23 3 courses. **Credit** AmEx, DC, MC, V.
The unremarkable pseudo-rustic interior of this small, crowded restaurant belies a menu of beautifully presented, authentic French fare. Heavily fish-oriented (there's a blackboard of 12 daily specials), the menu also features meaty, saucy dishes such as pheasant terrine, veal fillet or pan-roasted rack of lamb. The token vegetarian options – roast baby vegetable tartlet or croustillant of wild mushrooms and spinach – are good but it's the seafood dishes that really shine, though: roast monkfish, sea scallops in butter sauce, Mediterranean fish soup flavoured with gruyère – it's all wonderful. The largely French wine list ranges from £9.75 to £25.50.

One Paston Place

1 Paston Place, BN2 1HA (01273 606933/ www.onepastonplace.co.uk). **Food served** 12.30-1.45pm, 7.30-9.30pm Tue-Sat. **Main courses** £21-£23. **Set lunch** £16.50 2 courses; £19 3 courses. **Credit** AmEx, DC, MC, V.

Funeral pier

Brighton's oldest surviving pier – and we use the word 'surviving' loosely – was designed by Victorian civil engineering maestro Eugenius Birch (also responsible for Brighton Aquarium and 13 other piers around the country). Located opposite Regency Square, it opened in 1866, and was added to over the next 50 years until the completion of its grand concert hall in 1916. The stately edifice enjoyed great popularity for the next couple of decades, hosting plays, pantomimes and classical recitals by its resident orchestra. On the outbreak of World War II, the pier's central span was removed lest Jerry try to use it as a landing stage. Although reopened and repaired after the war, inadequate public funds for renovation and maintenance eventually led to real degeneration. Despite its use as a magnificent backdrop to films such as *Brighton Rock* and *Oh What a Lovely War!* it was finally closed in 1975. In 1987 the Great Storm not only destroyed the pier's central span but decimated the local tree population, whereupon the West Pier was adopted by homeless starlings as their roost, leading to the sight of thousands of birds flocking together at sunset above the pier. Would-be residents include boxer Chris Eubank, who wanted to buy the pier for his home, and 30 squatters who invaded it in August 1995 as a protest at government housing policy.

Sadly, a series of further misfortunes means that the pier may now be on its last piles. Firstly, more storm damage in December 2002 and January 2003 caused the still-standing concert hall to begin its slow collapse into the sea, and then incidents of suspected arson in March and May 2003 reduced this still impressive structure to a charred, partly melted frame of blackened ironwork, slumped against Brighton's pebbles as if it were the beached skeleton of some prehistoric beast.

Local reactions to these disasters have been strong but surprisingly diverse with some folk wishing the 'eyesore' good riddance even as others stood vigil on the beach watching the pier burn, as if at some loved relative's deathbed. Recent Hove immigrant Paul McCartney has voiced his support for the planned restoration, whereas local punk and poet Attila the Stockbroker (poet in residence for Brighton & Hove Albion FC) declared that residents would be better off putting their energies into campaigning for a new football stadium. The West Pier Trust, the charity that is the pier's current owner, is still confident that reconstruction plans will go ahead. Until then, in its current tormented state, the West Pier is an intriguing – if eerie – attraction to the city, and offers a complete contrast to its tawdry rival half a mile east.

In deepest residential Kemptown, this upmarket restaurant is one of Brighton's classiest. Expect assured Gallic cooking and high prices. However, the set lunch is excellent value. Start with roasted scallops with aubergine coulis, followed by loin of rabbit with roasted garlic mash, and finish with figs in red wine. Vegetarians should give notice so that a no-choice meal can be prepared: butternut squash velouté, goat's cheese and chestnut tortellini impressed. The wine is Francophile.

Terre à Terre

71 East Street, BN1 1HQ (01273 729051). **Food served** 6-10.30pm Mon; noon-11pm Tue-Sun. **Main courses** £11.50-£12.50. **Credit** AmEx, DC, MC, V.
Terre à Terre's reputation as one of the country's most celebrated vegetarian restaurants is well deserved, and the innovative menu treats diners to unusual combinations of ingredients and flavours. Mains might include deep-fried chickpea and sesame socca, drenched in saffron, thyme and orange zest, and served with smoky griddled artichoke, aubergine and peppers. Bricks of minty cracked wheat with pressed sheep cheese and preserved lemon, saffron-scented fennel, apricots and tiger nut pesto is another tastebud tickler. Desserts include cherry cioccolata churros; a wickedly calorific mix of doughnut straws, dipping chocolate and cherries sozzled in organic vodka. Organic drinks also feature. A pleasant venue for gourmet vegetarian food.

Seven Dials

1 Buckingham Place, BN1 3TD (01273 885555/ www.sevendialsrestaurant.co.uk). **Food served** 10.30am-3pm, 3.30-10.30pm Tue-Sat. **Set lunch** (Tue-Sat) £10 2 courses; £12.50 3 courses. **Set dinner** £19.50 2 courses; £23.50 3 courses. **Credit** AmEx, MC, V.
Nothing seems too much trouble for the staff here; on one visit they found the time to discuss the menu with a small child. Food-wise, praise goes to the foie gras terrine, although suckling pig and grilled tuna, and a chocolate fudge pot pudding also proved popular. The decor benefits from a high ceiling and dark wood interior enlivened by splashes of colour. One of Brighton's best restaurants, completely without pretence.

South-west Sussex

Home to Romans, racehorses and Rolling Stones.

Thatched cottages, enchanting forest walks, rolling downs, quiet creeks, castles and cathedral spires make this part of the country seem like a bygone dream of rural England. But don't be fooled by the air of tranquillity that permeates these little villages; it was here in 1967, at Redlands, a pretty moated farmhouse in East Wittering, that the drugs squad launched a dawn raid on Keith Richards and his fellow Stones, which, with its wild rumours of naked women, fur rugs and Mars Bars, became a benchmark of bad behaviour to which most rock 'n' roll wannabes can only aspire.

West Sussex is one of the most heavily wooded counties in England and more than half of it, including Chichester Harbour, the Sussex Downs and the High Weald, is designated an Area of Outstanding Natural Beauty. With more than 2,500 miles of public footpaths, including part of the South Downs Way, it is also a walker's paradise. The area around Chichester Harbour and Bosham is great for sailing, while further south the sea at Selsey is a popular place for divers – under the waves here you can explore a submerged Roman road, a World War II landing craft and a jagged outcrop of limestone that is rich in marine life.

Arundel

Seen from across the river, **Arundel**, with its castle and church at the top of the hill and river at the bottom, is more like a stage set than a real town. Despite the tourists, it has a pleasing sense of being very much at ease with itself, with tiny streets lined with antiques shops, tea shops and homely places selling country jams and the like. It's hard to imagine that as late as the 1920s it was still a working port, with big ships coming up the river.

Arundel Castle, built in the 11th century by Roger de Montgomery and now the seat of the Dukes of Norfolk and Earls of Arundel, is well worth exploring for its fine paintings, tapestries and furniture, and the gorgeous **Fitzalan Chapel**. The town's other main cultural attraction is **Arundel Cathedral** – this beautiful, imposing building is the 19th-century version of French Gothic.

When you have had enough history, mess around in a rowing boat or take a cruise on the river up to **Amberley** (Arun Cruises, Arundel Boat Yard or The Town Quay, 01903 882609).

Chichester

Chichester has all the qualities of a classic English market town but still retains a sense of being a living city.

Despite being very much a country town, the mournful cry of seagulls reminds you that the sea is not far away. The town was founded in AD 70 by the Romans, who laid out the main street plan and built the original city walls, subsequently rebuilt in flint in medieval times. The main streets of the city (called logically North, South, East and West streets) slice it neatly into four areas – the cathedral dominates the south-west sector, while the finest of the Georgian buildings are in the south-east in the streets called the Pallants. The town is at its most lively in the summer during the excellent music-oriented **Chichester Festival** in July (01243 785718/www.chifest.org.uk). There are two small museums: **Chichester District Museum** (29 Little London, 01243 784683/ www.chichester.gov.uk/museum) focuses on the district's geology, archaeology and social history; the **Guildhall Museum** (Priory Park, 01243 784683) is where William Blake was tried for sedition during its days as a courthouse. It contains some medieval frescoes.

The **cathedral** is still the centre of the city. Visible from miles away and immortalised by Turner in his painting of the Chichester Canal, it is a stunning structure, best known for its spire and a Marc Chagall stained-glass window.

Village Sussex

The pretty village of **Bosham** (pronounced 'Bozzum'), two miles west of Chichester, extends right down to the water's edge (the road here is only passable at low tide) and many of the houses have a high stoop at the front door, evidence of past floods. Well

By train from London

Trains to **Chichester** leave **Victoria** about every 15-30mins (journey time about 1hr 40mins). This train passes through **Arundel** (1hr 30mins). Info: www.connex.co.uk. (Services will be taken over by South Easern Trains in 2004; timetables should not be affected.)

The pretty port of **Bosham**. *See p83*.

known as a sailing village and with a history as a fishing port that dates back to Roman times (the Emperor Vespasian allegedly had a residence here), Bosham is one of the most attractive of all the villages on the shores of the **Chichester Harbour** estuary. The exquisitely simple Saxon church (which includes stones from the original Roman basilica) has a truly beautiful arched chapel in the crypt, lit only by a shaft of natural light from a small window. A stone coffin discovered in the church in the 19th century contained a child's body, thought to be a daughter of Canute. This, legend dictates, is the spot where he tried to turn back the tide.

From Bosham you can walk around the coast to **Bosham Hoe** where a short ferry ride has, for centuries, saved travellers a 13-mile walk around the coast to the pretty village of **West Itchenor**. As the flat coastal plain rises gently into the South Downs, numerous attractions reveal themselves. But the main attraction is the countryside. The 100-mile **South Downs Way**, the oldest long-distance footpath in Britain, passes through the area as it runs from Winchester to Seven Sisters near Dover. As most of this ancient trading route is also a bridleway it is accessible to horse and mountain bike riders. The 30-mile section that passes through West Sussex from South Harting to south of Storrington might be a bit much for a weekend but there are plenty of shorter walks that give a taste of its sweeping views and enchanted woodlands. Hardy types can stay at National Trust camping barns along the way.

What to see & do

Tourist Information Centres

61 High Street, Arundel, BN18 9AJ (01903 882268/ fax 01903 882419/www.sussexbythesea.com). **Open** *Easter-Oct* 10am-6pm Mon-Sat; 10am-4pm Sun. *Nov-Easter* 10am-3pm daily.

29A South Street, Chichester, PO19 1AH (01243 775888/fax 01243 539449/www.chichester.gov.uk). **Open** *Apr-Oct* 9.15am-5.15pm Mon-Sat; 10am-4pm Sun. *Nov-Mar* 9.15am-5.15pm Mon-Sat.

Bike hire

The Cycle Shop, *4b Azara Parade, Bracklesham Lane, Bracklesham, PO20 8HP (01243 672601).*

Chain Reaction *1 Royal Parade, Central Avenue, North Bersted, nr Chichester, PO21 5AJ (01243 841114).*

Horse riding

Northcommon Farm, Golf Links Lane, Selsey, PO20 9DP (01243 602725). **Open** *Easter-Sept* by appointment. **No credit cards.**
Trekking over the South Downs.

Arundel Castle

Arundel, BN18 9AB (01903 882173/www.arundel castle.org). **Open** *Apr-Oct* 11am-5pm Mon-Fri, Sun. Closed *Nov-Mar.* **Admission** £9; £5.50-£7 concessions; free under 5s. **Credit** MC, V.
This wonderful, imposing pile has its origins in the 11th century, although the original castle was heavily damaged during the Civil War and then extensively remodelled in the 18th and 19th centuries. Inside is a fine collection of 16th-century furniture and paintings by Van Dyck, Gainsborough, Reynolds and Mytens among others. Don't miss the 4th-century Fitzalan Chapel, a Roman Catholic chapel tucked inside an Anglican

Pet the ponies at **Fishers Farm**.

church, so that the dukes and their families could worship according to Catholic rites. It is home to a clutch of tombs of Dukes of Norfolk past, and mercifully shows no signs of the time when Cromwell used it as a stable.

Arundel Cathedral
London Road, Arundel, BN18 9AY (01903 882297 www.arundelcathedral.org). **Open** 9am-6pm/dusk Mon-Sat; 7.45am-6pm/dusk Sun. **Admission** free; donations welcome.
When he wasn't designing cabs, Joseph Hansom liked to turn his hand to architecture. This Catholic cathedral, which opened in 1873, was his take on French Gothic; its exterior is best viewed from a distance. There's a fine rose window over the west door and, inside, the shrine of St Philip Howard. Howard's father, the fourth Duke of Norfolk, was beheaded by Elizabeth I for his part in Mary Queen of Scots' intrigues. Howard converted to Catholicism and, in the anti-papist hysteria following the defeat of the Armada, was sentenced to death in 1589, although he finally died in the Tower six years later.

Arundel Wildfowl & Wetlands Trust
Mill Road, Arundel, BN18 9PB (01903 883355/ www.wwt.org.uk/visit/arundel). **Open** Apr-Oct 9.30am-5.30pm daily. *Nov-Mar* 9.30am-4.30pm daily. **Admission** £5.50; £3.50-£4.50 concessions. **Credit** MC, V.
Arundel WWT extends over 60 acres of parkland and lakes and is visited by thousands of migratory birds, including Bewick's swans, which can be observed from the hides dotted around the site. This is a lovely place for a wander.

Boxgrove Priory
Church Lane, Boxgrove, PO18 0ED (01243 774045). **Open** 7.30am-dusk daily. **Admission** free; donations welcome.

This beautiful early English church has a 16th-century painted ceiling by Lambert Barnard, a plethora of Victorian stained glass and the ruins of an 11th-century Benedictine monastery nearby.

Denmans Garden
Fontwell, nr Arundel, BN18 0SU (01243 542808/ www.denmans-garden.co.uk). **Open** Mar-Oct 9am-5pm daily. Closed Nov-Feb. **Admission** £2.95; £1.75-£2.65 concessions. **Credit** MC, V.
Created by author and garden designer John Brookes, this unique 20th-century garden is a delightfully relaxing place to stroll around. Plant sales and garden design seminars and courses available. There's also a café (open 11am-4pm).

Fishers Farm
New Pound Lane, Wisborough Green, RH14 0EG (01403 700063/www.fishersfarmpark.co.uk). **Open** 10am-5pm daily. **Admission** £7; £3.25-£6.50 concessions; free under-2s. *School summer holidays* £8; £4.25-£7.50 concessions; free under-2s. **Credit** MC, V.
A treat for kids, this farm offers more than the usual farmhouse pursuits. For starters, the Fishers Farm Players regularly perform children's productions in the Farm Theatre and magicians often pop in for special performances. There are also plenty of animals to prod, along with opportunities for pony trekking, wall climbing and bouncy castle bouncing.

Goodwood Circuit
Goodwood Estate, Chichester, PO18 0PH (01243 755055/www.goodwood.co.uk) **Dates** *Festival of Speed* July. **Revival meet** 1st week Sept. **Tickets** £13-£35 day ticket. **Credit** AmEx, MC, V.
The Festival of Speed is a major draw every year. You can also drive the circuit yourself on special trail days.

Goodwood House

Goodwood, Chichester, PO18 0PX (01243 755048/recorded info 01243 755040/www.goodwood.co.uk). **Open** *Mar-July, Sept, Oct* 1-5pm Mon, Sun. *Aug* 1-5pm Mon-Thur, Sun. Closed Nov-Feb. **Admission** £7; £3-£6 concessions. **Credit** MC, V.

A beautifully restored Regency mansion that is home to Gobelin tapestries, Sèvres porcelain and paintings by Canaletto, Stubbs and Van Dyck, as well as Napoleon Bonaparte's campaign chair. Goodwood also hosts interesting temporary exhibitions.

Goodwood Racecourse

Goodwood Estate, Chichester, PO18 0PH (0800 018 8191/01243 755022/www.goodwood.co.uk). **Admission** day tickets £6-£24 (phone for details). **Credit** MC, V.

A couple of miles north-east of Chichester lies Goodwood, one of the loveliest racecourses in Britain. The season lasts from May to September, with the five days in July, known as Glorious Goodwood, an essential part of the sporting set's social calendar.

Pallant House Gallery

9 North Pallant, Chichester, PO19 1TJ (01243 774557/www.pallant.org.uk). **Open** 10am-5pm Tue-Sat; 12.30-5pm Sun. **Admission** £4; £2.50-£3 concessions. **No credit cards.**

Housed in a lovely Queen Anne townhouse, this is an outstanding selection of 20th-century British art including works by Henry Moore, Peter Blake, Bridget Riley, Lucian Freud and Hepworth, as well as interesting temporary exhibitions. The house is closed until 2004 while a new wing is being added.

Parham House & Gardens

Nr Pulborough, RH20 4HS (01903 742021/info line 01903 744888/www.parhaminsussex.co.uk). **Open** *House* Easter-July, Sept 2-6pm Wed, Thur, Sun. Aug 2-6pm Tue-Fri, Sun. Last admission 5pm. *Gardens* Easter-July, Sept noon-6pm Wed, Thur, Sun. Aug noon-6pm Tue-Fri, Sun. Last admission 5pm. *Both* Closed Oct-Easter. **Admission** *House & gardens* £6; £2-£5.50 concessions. *Gardens only* £4; £1-£4 concessions. **Credit** MC, V.

A rare example of mid 20th-century restoration ideas in a large Elizabethan manor. The result is wonderfully harmonious and includes the fine panelled Long Gallery and Great Hall plus 11 acres of exquisite gardens.

Sculpture at Goodwood

Goodwood, nr Chichester, PO18 0QP (01243 538449/www.sculpture.org.uk). **Open** *Mar-Oct* 10.30am-4.30pm Thur-Sat. Closed Nov-Feb. **Admission** £10; free under-10s. **Credit** MC, V.

A wonderful outdoor setting for this growing collection of contemporary sculpture, including works by Elizabeth Frink, Andy Goldsworthy, Anthony Caro and David Mach displayed in 20 acres of woodland.

Uppark House

South Harting, Petersfield, GU31 5QR (01730 825415/www.nationaltrust.org.uk/uppark). **Open** *Apr-Oct* Grounds & exhibition 11am-5.30pm Mon-Thur, Sun. House 1-5pm Mon-Thur, Sun. Last admission 4.15pm. Closed Nov-Mar. **Admission** (NT) £5.50; £2.75 concessions. **Credit** AmEx, MC, V.

Uppark House was the home of novelist H G Wells, whose mother worked below stairs as a housekeeper. The lovely 17th-century house was gutted by fire in 1989 but has been lovingly restored by skilled craftsmen. An exhibition charts the history and restoration. Don't miss the famous dolls' house, magnificent views of the sea and lovely gardens. There's also an open-air theatre and flower shows in the summer.

Weald & Downland Open Air Museum

Singleton, nr Chichester, PO18 0EU (info line 01243 811348/811363/www.wealddown.co.uk). **Open** *Mar-Oct* 10.30am-6pm daily. *Nov-Feb* 10.30am-4pm Sat, Sun. Last admission 2hrs before closing. **Admission** £7; £4-£6.50 concessions. **Credit** MC, V.

One of the area's most interesting museums, this unusual collection features around 40 historic buildings that have been rescued, rebuilt and restored, and scattered over a 50-acre site to offer a fascinating historical journey through the region's architecture over the past 500 years. They include a Tudor farmstead, a 17th-century water mill and Victorian labourers' cottages. The museum is also open in the last week of December and half-term week in February.

West Dean Gardens

The Edward James Foundation, West Dean, nr Chichester, PO18 0QZ (01243 818210/www.westdean.org.uk/gardens). **Open** *Mar, Apr, Oct* 11am-5pm daily. *May-Sept* 10.30am-5pm daily. Last admission 4.30pm. Closed Nov-Feb. **Admission** £5; £2-£4.50 concessions. **Credit** MC, V.

An inspirational place to visit if you love things horticultural (though you'll find it hard to emulate unless you can also employ nine full-time gardeners). The outstanding working kitchen garden includes Victorian greenhouses with fig and peach trees and grape vines. There's also a 300ft pergola, and 35 acres of ornamental grounds with walks around an arboretum. The visitors' centre houses a licensed restaurant and a very upmarket gift shop. Summer events include a garden show, outdoor theatre and a celebration of the 170 varieties of chillies grown in the greenhouses.

Where to stay

The area has a wide range of accommodation, from humble B&Bs to grand castles and country houses. Local tourist offices have an excellent free brochure of places to stay and are happy to check availability and make bookings. Prices throughout the area rise significantly during the Festival of Speed (June) and Glorious Goodwood races (July), so either book early or avoid these weekends entirely if you don't want to get stung.

Amberley Castle

Amberley, BN18 9ND (01798 831992/fax 01798 831998/www.amberleycastle.co.uk). **Rates** £145-£170 double/twin; £195-£325 four-poster; £275-£325 suite. Breakfast £16.50 (Eng); £10 (cont). **Rooms** (all en suite) 4 double; 2 twin; 8 four-poster; 6 suites. **Credit** AmEx, DC, MC, V.

Winner of a Condé Naste award for Excellence and Innovation, this castle celebrates its 900th birthday in 2003. This is a seriously over-the-top experience. Don't even think about turning up if you haven't pre-booked and there's a strict dress code: no denim, and lounge suits for men in the evening. Expect full-on luxury: bedrooms are plush, furnished with antiques, heavy drapes and panelling. The gardens have ponds stocked with koi carp, and are also home to white peacocks, Shetland ponies and a colony of jackdaws. An 18-hole golf course opens June 2003. Don't stray too far in the evenings – the portcullis comes down at midnight. Children over 12 welcome.
B2139 SW from Storrington; first turning on right after Amberley. Alternatively, use the helicoptor pad in the grounds.

Bailiffscourt Hotel

Climping Street, Climping, nr Littlehampton, BN17 5RW (01903 723511/fax 01903 723107/www. hshotels.co.uk). **Rates** £130 single occupancy; £150-£185 double; £295-£320 deluxe double/twin; £295-£450 four-poster; £345-£450 suite. **Rooms** (all en suite) 8 double/twin; 11 deluxe double/twin; 13 four-poster; 7 suites. **Credit** AmEx, DC, MC, V.
Bailiffscourt is an extraordinary faux medieval house (it was actually built in 1927) that is perfect for an indulgent summer sojourn. The place is packed with stone flagging, tapestry-hung walls, oak beams, carved doors and Gothic mullioned windows; it also has walled gardens, and is set in 22 acres of pastureland – and it's only 200 yards from Climping beach. There are plenty of facilities, including a heated outdoor swimming pool, tennis court, croquet lawn and even a helipad. Eight new bedrooms and a health spa with indoor and outdoor pools, hot tub, steam room, sauna and gym opens in summer 2003. Children and dogs welcome.
Signposted off the A259 between Bognor and Littlehampton.

Burpham Country House Hotel

Burpham, nr Arundel, BN1 89RJ (01903 882160/ fax 01903 884627). **Rates** £58.50-£60 single; £87-£130 double; £105-£110 four-poster. **Rooms** (all en suite) 1 single; 5 double; 3 twin; 1 four-poster. **Credit** MC, V.
At the end of a two-and-a-half mile lane is this hidden gem. The 18th-century shooting lodge has a great reputation for peace and quiet and excellent service. With a conservatory with views over the South Downs and a croquet lawn, it is the perfect place to relax. You won't need to trek miles for dinner as it has a restaurant with an enviable reputation. All bedrooms are no-smoking.

Forge Hotel

Chilgrove, Chichester, PO18 9HX (01243 535333/ 537352/fax 01243 535363/www.forgehotel.com). **Rates** £55-£69 single occupancy; £110-£140 double/twin. **Rooms** (all en suite) 1 single; 4 double/twin. **Credit** AmEx, MC, V.
Fancy a house party? This wonderful B&B offers special deals on bookings for up to nine people, so you can have the run of the place. With fresh flowers, Sky TV and gourmet dinners prepared from local ingredients by the chef-owner (formerly of the White Horse next door) it might be hard to summon up the energy or inclination to explore the nearby South Downs Way. Dogs accepted by arrangement. All bedrooms are no-smoking.
From A286 N of Chichester, take B2141 towards Petersfield; turn right to Chilgrove.

Millstream Hotel & Restaurant

Bosham, Chichester, PO18 8HL (01243 573234/ fax 01243 573459/www.millstream-hotel.co.uk). **Rates** £79-£89 single; £129-£139 double/twin; £149-£159 four-poster; £169-£189 cottage/garden suite. Children £15 per night. **Rooms** (all en suite) 5 single; 27 double/twin; 2 four-poster; 3 suites. **Credit** AmEx, DC, MC, V.
This hotel is set in the idyllic waterside village of Bosham, in a converted 18th-century malthouse cottage. It's a warm and welcoming place, although the bedrooms in the modern extension lack character. Bosham is a popular destination so it's best to book well in advance; request a room with a view over the gardens. Children and dogs welcome. All bedrooms no-smoking.
Take A259 from Chichester W to Bosham; turn left at Bosham roundabout and follow signs to Bosham church and Millstream Hotel.

Spire Cottage

Church Lane, Hunston, Chichester, PO20 1AJ (01243 778937/www.spirecottage.co.uk). **Rates** £35-£45 single occupancy; £52-£70 double/twin; £55-£70 four-poster. **Rooms** 2 double/twin (1 en suite); 1 four-poster (en suite). **No credit cards**.
This Grade II-listed cottage surrounded by open fields (but only a couple of miles from Chichester) is so-named because it was built from the stones of the cathedral spire, which collapsed in 1861. It's now a peaceful B&B with restful pale decor, bare stone walls and nice touches such as log fires in winter, roll-top baths and king-sized beds. It's handy for walking, and boaters should note that the Chichester Canal runs right through the village. Children over ten welcome; dogs accepted by arrangement. No smoking throughout.
Take B2145 from Chichester bypass for 1.5 miles to Hunston. Take first left after the Spotted Cow pub into Church Lane.

Swan Inn

Lower Street, Fittleworth, RH20 1EN (01798 865429/fax 01798 865721/www.swaninn.com). **Rates** £30 single; £60 double/twin; £75 four-poster. **Rooms** (all en suite) 3 single; 8 double; 4 twin; 2 four-poster. **Credit** AmEx, DC, MC, V.
This 14th-century coaching inn offers the traditional pleasures of log fires, oak beams and four-posters. Meals can be taken in a gallery lined with Victorian oil paintings. The hotel is well placed for visiting Goodwood as well as for local fishing, horse riding, walking and golf. Children welcome. All bedrooms are no-smoking.
A3 to Guildford bypass, then Milford and Petworth, then A283 to Fittleworth.

Todhurst Farm

Lake Lane, Barnham, PO22 0AL (01243 551959). **Rates** £40-£45 single; £80-£95 double. **Rooms** 2 double (1 en suite); 1 twin. **No credit cards**.
A peaceful B&B with a friendly host, located in an excellent spot for walking or exploring Arundel. The swimming pool is open to guests, and dinner and packed lunches are available on request. Not all rooms are en suite so check when booking. Children welcome. No smoking throughout.
From Chichester A27 east (or west from Arundel). Turn south on B2132 signposted for Yapton; turn right on Lake Lane just after level crossing. House is 0.5 miles on right.

What the Romans did for us

When the Romans invaded southern Britain in AD 43 during the reign of Emperor Claudius, it is likely they landed somewhere near Chichester. It is certain that an army base was set up in the Fishbourne area a few years later, and that the region was put under the control of a Briton, Togidubnus, who was set up as client king. He was responsible for establishing the city of Noviomagus, now Chichester, roads were constructed, and many large villas, including the one at Fishbourne, were built in the surrounding countryside.

Discovered in the 1960s, the site at Fishbourne boasts the most extensive remains of a Roman palace in existence in Britain and is particularly famed for its beautiful mosaic floors, including one picturing Cupid riding a dolphin. It is likely that the original building contained around 100 rooms, although so far only the north wing has actually been excavated.

When Togidubnus died, West Sussex became part of the Roman province of Brittania. This was a time of peace and prosperity in southern Britain, with more villas being built and the iron industry in the Weald expanded. But by the end of AD 300 many of the villas near the coast had fallen into decline, perhaps because of their vulnerability to raids from overseas barbarians. Conversely, those further inland such as the one at Bignor were enlarged and improved. The Bignor villa, uncovered in 1811, has wonderful mosaic floors, one of which, at 80 feet, is the longest stretch of mosaic on display in Britain.

As the coast became increasingly inhospitable, the city of Noviomagus, with its public baths and ampitheatre, progressively declined until the collapse of Roman rule in the early fifth century. Both villas were eventually abandoned, and remained undiscovered for centuries.

Fishbourne Roman Palace

Salthill Road, Fishbourne, Chichester, PO19 3QR (01243 785859/www. sussexpast.co.uk). **Open** *Dec, Jan* 10am-4pm Sat, Sun. *Nov, Feb* 10am-4pm daily. *Mar-July, Sept, Oct* 10am-5pm daily. *Aug* 10am-6pm daily. **Admission** £5.20; £2.70-£4.50 concessions. **Credit** AmEx, MC, V.

Bignor Roman Villa

Bignor, nr Pulborough, RH20 1PH (01798 869259/www.romansinsussex.co.uk). **Open** *Mar, Apr* 10am-5pm Tue-Sun. *May, Oct* 10am-5pm daily. *June-Sept* 10am-6pm daily. Closed Nov-Feb. **Admission** £3.80; £1.60-£2.70 concessions. **Credit** MC, V.

Woodstock House Hotel

Charlton, nr Chichester, PO18 OHU (tel/fax 01243 811666/www.woodstockhousehotel.co.uk). **Rates** £45-£52 single; £60-£92 double/twin; £75-£112 family room. **Rooms** (all en suite) 2 single; 5 double; 4 twin; 1 family. **Credit** AmEx, MC, V.

A friendly and welcoming B&B, where a tray of tea appears on arrival and a dinner reservation at the pub next door, the Fox Goes Free (*see p89*), is offered when booking (take up the offer, the food is great). Breakfast is served in the pretty conservatory overlooking the flower- and bird-filled garden. Children and dogs welcome. All bedrooms are no smoking.

Where to eat & drink

Arundel and Chichester both have a decent spread of pubs and restaurants but the best food is to be had out in the country. Five miles west of Chichester is the bustling little harbour of **Emsworth**, where you can sample Ramon Farthing's classically influenced yet inventive cooking at **Restaurant 36** on the Quay (01243 375592). Just a few steps away, **Spencers** (36-8 North Street, 01243 372744) serves Modern British food and has a separate fish menu. **Burpham Country House** (Burpham, nr Arundel, 01903 882160) has a well-respected restaurant where the Swiss owner adds a flavour of her homeland to some dishes.

You can eat well at several of the traditional country pubs in the area. The **Crown & Anchor** (Dell Quay Road, 01243 781712) at Dell Quay, near Bosham, is the perfect place for a pint or a meal watching the comings and goings of the little boats and the sun setting over Chichester Harbour. Real ale aficionados should seek out the **Black Horse** (High Street, 01798 831700) at Amberley, which is handy for the South Downs Way and walks along the banks of the River Arun. Also recommended are the **Old House at Home** in Chidham

(Cots Lane, 01243 572477), Donnington's **Blacksmiths Arms** (Selsey Road, 01243 783999), the 16th-century **Woodmans Arms** in Hammerpot (01903 871240), where the landlord will provide a map of a local walk, or the **Spotted Cow** (1 High Street, 01903 783919) in Angmering, a former meeting place for smugglers, with a boules pitch and an obscure wheel game mounted on the ceiling. The pretty **Gribble Inn** (Gribble Lane, 01243 786893), east of Chichester in Oving, brews its own ales including Fursty Ferret, Plucking Pheasant and Pig's Ear.

Amberley Castle
Amberley, nr Arundel, BN18 9ND (01798 831992/ www.amberleycastle.co.uk). **Food served** 12.30-2pm, 7-9pm daily. **Set lunch** (Mon-Sat) £15 2 courses, (Sun) £25.50 3 courses. **Set dinner** £38 2 courses, £45 3 courses. **Credit** AmEx, DC, MC, V.
Dine like royalty in the 12th-century Queen's Room, which has thick stone walls, arched doors and windows, and a beautiful barrelled ceiling; or try the Great Room with oak floors, suits of armour, tapestries and some very nasty-looking weapons. Surroundings might be aged, but the food is undeniably modern. For starters, if terrine of chicken, baby leek, truffle and wild mushroom wrapped in prosciuto with spiced orange reduction sounds a tad rich, then simple smoked trout mousse with a cucumber salad, pink peppercorn dressing and tossed mixed leaves is also on offer. Mains might be seared calf's liver, red onion confit, foie gras and mashed potatoes with port and mushroom reduction, or a simple roasted tuna with sweet and sour vegetables and tomato butter sauce. This is a theatrical experience so dress up: jacket and tie are compulsory for male diners. No denim. Booking essential.

Comme Ça
67 Broyle Road, Chichester, PO19 6BD (01243 788724/www.commeca.co.uk). **Food served** noon-2pm, 6-10.30pm Tue-Sun. **Set meal** (noon-2pm, 6-7.30pm, 10-10.30pm) £15.25 2 courses, £19.95 3 courses. **Credit** AmEx, DC, MC, V.
This converted Georgian inn is an oasis of French savoir faire, with just the right degree of formality, not to mention a canopied and heated courtyard. Its popularity is down to a combination of assured, interesting food such as pan-fried local pheasant breast, baked camembert with avocado with a cabernet sauvignon dressing and Scottish moules. The wine list is well chosen with a good house wine at under a tenner. It gets packed, especially at Sunday lunchtimes, so it's a good idea to book.

Fleur de Sel
Manleys Hill, Storrington, RH20 4BT (01903 742331). **Food served** noon-2pm, 7-9pm Tue-Sat. **Set lunches** (Tue-Fri) £15.50 2 courses, £19.50 3 courses. **Set dinners** (Tue-Thur) £19.50 2 courses, £23.50 3 courses. **Credit** AmEx, MC, V.
Michel Perraud's Michelin-starred restaurant is a wonderful combination of classical French with a contemporary touch and friendly, informed service. The moment a plate of *amuse-bouche* magically appears as you sip aperitifs in the tiny bar you know you are in

good hands. The quality of the fresh ingredients is apparent in starters such as a pasta parcel of Dublin Bay prawns and a poached egg on a bed of locally grown asparagus. Mains might include perfectly judged fillets of John Dory on a wild mushroom and sorrel sauce or breast of duck in a honey and ginger sauce. Desserts such as coconut milk crème brûlée display an interesting take on classic dishes.

Fox Goes Free
Charlton, PO18 0HU (01243 811461). **Food served** noon-2.30pm, 6.30-10pm Mon-Fri; noon-10pm Sat, Sun. **Main courses** £7.50-£16.50. **Credit** MC, V.
This 300-year-old country village pub has been famed for hunting since William III used it as a retreat from London. There's a lovely garden with views over surrounding countryside, and low beams, an inglenook fireplaces and a bread oven inside. Starters include field mushrooms stuffed with garlic and goat's cheese; mains might be venison steak in port and redcurrant, or whole sea bass in lemon and olive oil. Service is friendly and helpful (these Aussies get everywhere) and wines start at £10 (including Concha y Tora merlot from Chile). Real ales on draught include Ballards Best, Bass and the pub's own Fox Goes Free bitter.

George & Dragon
Burpham, nr Arundel, BN18 9RR (01903 883131). *Bar* **Food served** noon-1.45pm, 7-9.30pm Mon-Sat; noon-2.30pm Sun. *Restaurant* **Food served** 7-9.30pm Tue-Sat. **Set dinners** £19.95 2 courses, £24.95 3 courses. **Main courses** £7.95-£15.95. **Credit** AmEx, DC, MC, V.
This rustic pub is set beside the cricket pitch in the hamlet of Burpham. Its gourmet credentials are most in evidence in the evenings, when the dining room is opened for an array of well-cooked dishes such as pavé of sea bass on a bed of leeks, goat's cheese tartlets and baked quail with foie gras, compôte of puy lentils, juniper and game sauce. At lunchtime it tends to get packed with walkers.

White Horse Inn
1 High Street, Chilgrove, PO18 9HX (01243 535219). **Food served** noon-2pm, 7-10pm Mon-Sat; noon-2pm Sun. **Main courses** £10.95-£16.95. **Credit** AmEx, MC, V.
The White Horse looks traditional enough but once inside it is light, airy and surprisingly modern. The menu in both the dining room and the less formal bar makes good use of fresh local ingredients such as Selsey crab, pheasant and wild rabbit, and menus change regularly to reflect availability. Typical starters might be char-grilled pigeon breast on a bed of green lentils or breaded lamb sweetbreads on a nest of mixed salad. This robust, traditional approach continues with mains such as wild rabbit casserole with muscat wine and grape sauce, and braised oxtail off the bone served with a purée of potatoes. There is always a fresh fish dish of the day included on the menu. The staff are well informed and friendly, and there's an award-winning list of 600 wines from France and the New World. The White Horse is just a mile and a half off the South Downs Way and walkers are welcome, but are requested to leave their muddy boots outside – padding around in socks is quite acceptable.

North Surrey Downs

Too good to be left to commuters.

'Commuter belt' isn't the most flattering term for this pretty chunk of Surrey. It's not inaccurate, but neither does it give the whole picture. Situated less than an hour by train from London, just outside the M25 and criss-crossed with major roads and two motorways, the area is home to many well-heeled commuters. However, it's also a place of rolling countryside, with attractions such as Box Hill and Leith Hill, and picturesque villages.

Around these villages are large, thriving but rather dull commuter towns such as **Reigate**, just west of the M23 intersection. Even here, though, there are reminders of a history that dates back to the Norman conquest, such as the castle (of which nothing remains but an arch) and the 18th-century market hall on the high street. But you'd be advised to head south and west to sample a clutch of infinitely more rewarding villages in the Mole Valley.

Betchworth's claim to fame is the appearance of its church in *Four Weddings and a Funeral*; St Michael's is an impressively large building, parts of which date back to Saxon times. Further west, **Brockham** has won the 'Best Kept Village in Surrey' award on several occasions. South-west of Reigate is the village of **Leigh** (pronounced 'Lye'). Its church dates back to about 1200 and has a fine east window designed at the end of the 19th century. East of Reigate, towards Redhill, **Outwood** boasts Britain's oldest working windmill. It dates from 1665 and is surrounded by acres of National Trust-owned common land – ideal for picnics and nature walks. **Godstone**, with its splendid village green, and **Oxted** have their attractions but are essentially commuter towns. South of **Westerham**, just over the border in Kent, lies Churchill's old house, **Chartwell**. **Lingfield**, the country's busiest racecourse (01342 834800/www.lingfield-racecourse.co.uk) is worth stopping at if you fancy a flutter, or visit **Epsom Downs** for Derby Day (June).

West of Reigate lies **Dorking**, a rather uninspiring town but close to some of the most beautiful parts of Surrey. Nearby **Box Hill** (*see p93* **Hill stories**) has been a favourite spot since Victorian times, with 1,200 acres of woodland and spectacular views. Further west is the splendour of **Polesden Lacey**. South is well-groomed **Coldharbour**, which is a convenient base camp for visiting **Leith Hill**.

To the west of the Downs sits the pretty town of **Guildford**. Look beyond the standard cinemas and shopping centre and you'll find the cathedral, a museum and the stone keep of Surrey's only royal castle (Castle Street, 01483 444718; closed for refurbishment until 2004). While you are here, take a boat trip along the Wey, from **Guildford Boat House** (01483 504494/www.guildfordboats.co.uk).

Further east, on the A248, are manor houses, gardens and a couple of picturesque villages, including the wonderful **Shere**, which is home to a 12th-century church with a Norman spire. The lychgate and other buildings in Shere were designed by Lutyens. Nearby **Clandon** boasts two National Trust properties: Hatchlands Park, and Clandon Park, which houses the Queens' Royal Surrey Regiment Museum (01483 223419). North of Clandon lies **RHS Wisley**, a 240-acre garden that includes a stunning springtime Alpine meadow.

What to see & do

Tourist Information Centres

Surrey Tourism, Room 404, County Hall, Kingston-upon-Thames, KT1 2DY (020 85418092/www. visitsurrey.com). **Open** 9am-5pm Mon Fri.

14 Tunsgate, Guildford, GU1 3QT (01483 444333/www.guildford.gov.uk). **Open** *Mar-Sept* 9am-5.30pm Mon-Sat; 10am-4.30pm Sun. *Oct-Feb* 9am-5pm Mon-Sat.

By train from London

Trains to **Dorking** leave **Waterloo** every half-hour (journey time 40mins). There's an hourly service to **Reigate** from **Victoria**, with a change at Redhill (total journey time 45-50mins). Fast trains to **Guildford** leave **Waterloo** every 15mins (journey time 35mins); the slower service leaves every 20mins and takes 55mins. Info: www.southwesttrains.co.uk, www.thamestrains.co.uk and www.connex.co.uk. (In 2004 Connex's services will be taken over by South Eastern Trains; timetables should not be affected.)

Beautiful **Box Hil**. *See p93.*

Clandon Park.

Town Hall, Castlefield Road, Reigate, RH2 OSH (01737 276045/www.reigate-banstead.gov.uk). **Open** 9am-5pm Mon-Fri.

Bike hire

Nirvana Cycles *2 The Green, Guildford Road, Westcott, RH4 3NH, (01306 740300/www.nirvana cycles.com).*

Chartwell

Nr Westerham, YN16 1PS (01732 868381/ www.nationaltrust.org.uk/chartwell). **Open** *Mid Mar-June, Sept, Oct* 11am-5pm Wed-Sun. *July, Aug* 11am-5pm Tue-Sun. Last admission 4.15pm. Closed Nov-mid Mar. **Admission** (NT) *House & garden* £7; £3.50 concessions; free under-5s. *Garden only* £3.50; £1.75 concessions. **Guided tours** Mid Mar-June, Sept, Oct by arrangement on Wed. **Credit** AmEx, MC, V.
The family home of Sir Winston Churchill from 1924 until his death, this peaceful, unpretentious Victorian country house overlooks the Kent Weald and is the place where Churchill wrote *A History of the English Speaking Peoples* and *The Second World War*. Churchill was also a keen painter and his works on canvas adorn the walls of the well-preserved interior (preserved right down to the books, maps and personal mementoes, in fact). The terraced gardens include Lady Churchill's rose garden.

Clandon Park

West Clandon, Guildford, GU4 7RQ (01483 222482/ www.nationaltrust.org.uk/clandonpark). **Open** *House & gardens* Apr-Oct 11am-5pm Tue-Thur, Sun. Last entry 4.30pm. Closed Nov-Mar. **Admission** (NT) *House & gardens* £6; £3 concessions; free under-5s. *Combined ticket with Hatchlands Park* £9; £4.50 concessions; free under-5s. **Credit** MC, V.
Owned by the Onslow family from 1651 until 1956, this originally Elizabethan house was rebuilt by Venetian architect Giacomo Leoni in 1793. Most of the contents were sold off in 1781, but National Trust ownership has seen it restored to 18th-century style, a restoration that has been helped by the donation of a superb collection

of 18th-century furniture and English, continental and oriental porcelain. Other must-sees are the magnificent two-storey Marble Hall and, in the grounds, the Maori House, brought back from New Zealand.

Denbies Wine Estate

London Road, Dorking, RH5 6AA (01306 742002/ 01306 876616/www.denbiesvineyard.co.uk). **Open** 10am-5.30pm Mon-Sat; 11.30am-5.30pm Sun. *Tours & tastings* 11am-4pm Mon-Sat; noon-4pm Sun. **Admission** free. *Tours & tastings* £7.25; £3-£6.50 concessions; free under-5s. *Vineyard train tours* £4; £3-£3.50 concessions; free under 5s. *Double ticket* £10.25; £5-£9.25 concessions; free under-5s. **Credit** MC, V.
Denbies is England's biggest wine estate. There are tours and tastings all year round and a Vineyard Train tour up the North Downs Way between April and October only. There's also a picture gallery, wine bar, restaurant, shop and (probably for enthusiasts) a B&B.

Guildford Cathedral

Stag Hill, Guildford, GU2 7UP (01483 547860/www. guildford-cathedral.org). **Open** 8.30am-5.30pm daily. **Admission** free; donations welcome.
Guildford's cathedral is the only one in the south of England to have been built on a new site during the 20th century. Designed by Sir Edward Maufe, its foundation stone was laid in 1936. Work stopped during World War II and its later completion was partly due to the Buy a Brick campaign, with Surrey locals paying for and signing bricks made from the clay of the hill. Look out for Irene Charleston's beautifully embroidered banner in memory of her brother, who was killed at Ypres.

Hatchlands Park

East Clandon, Guildford, GU4 7RT (01483 222482/ www.nationaltrust.org.uk). **Open** *House & garden* Apr-July, Sept, Oct 2-5.30pm Tue-Thur, Sun. Aug 2-5.30pm Tue-Fri, Sun. Last entry 5pm. Closed Nov-Mar. *Park walks* Late Mar-mid Nov 11am-6pm daily. Closed mid Nov-Mar. **Admission** (NT) *House & garden* £6; £3 concessions; free under-5s. *Park walks* £2.50; £1.25 concessions; free under-5s. *Combined ticket with Clandon Park* £9; £4.50 concessions; free under-5s. **Credit** MC, V.
Set in a 430-acre park, the Hatchlands estate was bought in 1750 by naval hero Edward Boscawen. He then had a house built, designed and decorated by Robert Adam to a nautical theme. After several owners, Adam's designs remain, and the house now also contains a fine collection of paintings and musical instruments.

Leith Hill & Tower

Off A24 SW of Dorking, 1 mile from Coldharbour (01306 711777/www.nationaltrust.org.uk). **Open** *Tower & servery* Late Mar-Oct 10am-5pm Wed, Fri, Sat, Sun. Nov-late Mar 10am-3.30pm Sat, Sun. **Admission** (NT) *Tower & servery* £1; 50p concessions; free under-5s.
Not quite as popular as Box Hill, but still the highest point in the South-east at 965ft, Leith Hill pulls in the crowds for its views (on a clear day you can see as far as the English Channel), abundance of rhododendrons during May and June, and the 18th-century Gothic tower (now blessed with a new telescope) that graces the top.

Polesden Lacey

Great Bookham, nr Dorking, RH5 6BD (01372 452048/info 01372 458203/www.nationaltrust. org.uk/polesdenlacey). **Open** *House* Mid Mar-early Nov 11am-4.30pm Wed-Sun. Closed early-Nov-mid Mar. *Garden, grounds & walks* 11am-6pm/dusk daily. **Admission** (NT) *House & garden* £7; £3.50 concessions; free under-5s. *Garden, grounds & walks* £4; £2 concessions; free under-5s. **Credit** MC, V.

This 1,400-acre estate – the present Regency-style house was completed in 1824 – saw its heyday under Edwardian society hostess the Hon Mrs Greville (the late Queen Mother and King George VI spent part of their honeymoon here in 1923). The interior, extensively remodelled by Mrs Greville, contains her collections of paintings, furniture, porcelain and silver. There are landscaped walks and gardens in the grounds.

Where to stay

Bulmer Farm

Holmbury St Mary, Dorking, RH5 6LG (01306 730210). **Rates** £38-£40 single occupancy; £54-£58 double/twin. **Rooms** (all en suite) 3 double ; 2 twin. **No credit cards**.

This peaceful 17th-century farmhouse B&B – situated at the south end of a quiet village and only eight minutes to the local pub – has comfortable, private rooms in an old barn adjoining the house. All rooms are no-smoking. Children over 12 welcome.

Burford Bridge Hotel

Foot of Box Hill, Dorking, RH5 6BX (0870 400 8283/fax 01306 887821/www.macdonaldhotels. co.uk) **Rates** £125-£145 double/twin. **Rooms** (all en suite) 57 double/twin. **Credit** AmEx, DC, MC, V.

Visitors who arrive at Box Hill by car won't miss this place, which nestles at its base. Rooms are smart, and the building dates to 1500. The hotel has fine views, and was final meeting place between Lord Nelson and Lady Hamilton before the Battle of Trafalgar, *and* the place where Keats finished *Endymion*). Children welcome.

Herons Head Farm

Mynthurst, Leigh, RH2 8QD (01293 862475/www. heronshead.co.uk). **Rates** £45-£55 single occupancy; £55-£65 double/twin; £75 family room (sleeps 3, £10 per additional child). **Rooms** (all en suite) 3 double/twin; 1 family room. **No credit cards**.

This 16th-century coaching inn in an idyllic setting has a number of period rooms – some with a whirlpool, or with great views over the garden, pond and 1,000 acres of pastureland. The owners are welcoming, and the pool and tennis courts can be used (bring your own racquets). Fine gastropub food can be had at the Seven Stars down the road. Children welcome. No smoking throughout.

Langshott Manor

Ladbroke Road, Langshott, nr Horley, RH6 9LN (01293 786680/www.langshottmanor.com). **Rates** £145-£185 single occupancy; £185 £225 double/twin; £225-£290 four-poster/suite. **Rooms** (all en suite) 17 double/twin; 4 four-poster; 1 suite. **Credit** AmEx, DC, MC, V.

Hill stories

For all the ramblers and other visitors who hit the North Downs, **Box Hill** is the big draw. Named for the small, evergreen box trees that thrive on its chalk soil, Box Hill is now looked after by the National Trust. Its pulling power lies in the spectacular views over the Kent Weald and the South Downs. Those who make it to the summit will find an information centre, shop, café and a fort, too, dating from the 1890s (there's no access to the interior).

Box Hill has many claims to fame. It was the scene of a memorable picnic in Jane Austen's *Emma*, and the place where Keats finished *Endymion* (he stayed in the Burford Bridge Hotel at the foot of the hill). In addition, the flint cottage near the summit, known as the Swiss Cottage, was where John Logie Baird conducted some of his early television experiments.

To the west of the Swiss Cottage is the hill's only burial plot – favourite spot and final resting place of loopy marine major

Peter Labilliere, who was buried here in 1800. A pal of the then Duke of Devonshire, Peter Labilliere based himself in Dorking after he left military service. As the years drew on, his eccentricities grew more apparent; among them was a conviction that the world was topsy-turvy. At his own request, he was buried upside down so that he would arrive in heaven the right way up.

Information Centre

The Old Fort, Boxhill Road, Box Hill Tadworth, KT20 7LB. Off A24, N of Dorking. (Shop & information Centre 01306 888793/office 01372 220642/www.nationaltrust.org.uk/ northdowns). **Open** *Shop & information centre* 11am-4pm daily. Credit AmEx, DC, MC, V.

Free access to the hill. Car parking £2. Box Hill has its own station – Box Hill and Westhumble – a short walk away.

This luxurious, recently expanded country hotel offers 22 rooms, some in the main manor (which was originally constructed back in 1590), and some in adjacent coach houses. Each room is individually designed and decorated (the Henry VIII room is almost worth losing your head over). All rooms are no-smoking.

Nutfield Priory

Nutfield, Redhill, RH1 4EL (01737 824400/www. nutfield-priory.com). **Rates** £115 single; £125-£165 double/twin; £185 junior suite/four-poster; £245 master suite. Breakfast £12.50 (Eng), £9.50 (cont). **Rooms** (all en suite) 8 single; 2 twin; 36 double; 7 junior suites/four-poster; 4 master suites. **Credit** AmEx, DC, MC, V.

This dramatic building was built in 1872 as an extravagant folly for MP Joshua Fielden. Inside, the stained glass and cloisters are reminiscent of the Palace of Westminster, but rooms are designed to specific themes (doffing a cap to Wordsworth and Stevenson, among others). It has embraced modernity, though, and facilities include a health and leisure club. Book well in advance. Children and dogs welcome.

Park House Farm

Hollow Lane, Abinger Common, Dorking, RH5 6LW (01306 730101/fax 01306 730643/www.smooth hound.co.uk/hotels/parkhouse). **Rates** £40-£50 single occupancy; £50-£65 double/twin. **Rooms** 2 double (both en suite); 1 twin (with private bath). **Credit** MC, V.

Situated in rural Abinger Common (between Guildford and Dorking), this B&B is set in 25 acres of countryside. The location is good for those who like country walks, and Leith Hill is nearby. No smoking throughout.

Where to eat & drink

Chapel at Hautboy

Ockham Lane, Ockham, GU23 6NP (01483 225355). **Food served** noon-2.30pm, 6.30-9.30pm Mon Sat; noon-4pm Sun. **Main courses** £7.95-£16.95. **Credit** AmEx, MC, V.

This striking Gothic building, well off the beaten track, offers an array of dishes from around the globe – duck à l'orange, Mediterranean vegetable and cheese wellington, Thai vegetable curry and steak and kidney pud among them. Service is friendly, though it can be slow. But the decent-enough nosh and fantastically eccentric Gothic dining area (feel free to talk to the parrot in the doorway) more than make up for any lack of speed.

The Dining Room

59A High Street, Reigate, RH2 9AE (01737 226650/www.tonytobinrestaurants.co.uk). **Food served** noon-2pm, 7-10pm Mon-Fri; 7-10pm Sat; 12.30-2.30pm Sun. **Set lunches** (Mon-Fri) £19.50-£22.50 2 courses; (Sun) £28.50 3 courses. **Set dinners** (Mon-Thur) £22.50 2 courses; (Fri, Sat) £28.50 2 courses. **Credit** AmEx, MC, V.

The Dining Room is announced by a first-floor sign and discreet menu by a blink-and-you'll-miss-it door. However, this is a serious restaurant – executive chef Tony Tobin's former years were spent at Chez Nico and the award-winning South Lodge in Lower Beding. This place is – if you ignore the kangaroo burger – very Modern British. A tender hunk of peppered lamb came with minted pearl barley, braised celery and super-smooth mash. Black pudding was stuffed inside rolls of succulent roast chicken and accompanied by apple chutney and mash. Top marks for presentation and further points for likeable staff and impeccable service.

Kingham's

Gomshall Lane, Shere, GU5 9HE (01483 202168/ www.kinghams-restaurant.co.uk). **Food served** 12.15-2.15pm, 7-9.15pm Tue-Sat; 12.15-2.15pm Sun. **Main courses** £10.95-£16.95. **Set lunches** (Tue-Sat) £13.95 2 courses; (Sun) £15.95 2 courses, £19.95 3 courses. **Set dinners** (Tue-Thur) £15.95 2 courses. **Credit** AmEx, DC, MC, V.

This squat, 400-year-old building was once the cottage of the local hangman; it is now, according to a waitress, also home to a resident ghost (a cat). Good use has been made of the cosy, low-lit space, packing in enough punters to make a convivial atmosphere. The menu is predominantly British, listing dishes such as Gressingham duck, roast partridge and veal escalope. Roast rib of beef with Yorkshire pud, veg and red wine jus proved there's no skimping. Chicken liver, bacon and mushroom in a puff pastry parcel, with a redcurrant and walnut salad, followed by a salmon fillet, made for a satisfying meal. Service was charming but not polished. A lengthy wine list includes a good selection of half bottles.

The Stephan Langton

Friday Street, Abinger Common, RH5 6JR (01306 730775). **Food served** 12.30-3pm, 7-10pm Tue-Sat; 12.30-3pm Sun. **Main courses** £10.25-£12.50. **Credit** MC, V.

Getting to the Stephan Langton – named after the celebrated 12th-century Archbishop of Canterbury – requires skilful negotiation of what must be the narrowest roads in Surrey. But despite being fairly casual – order at the bar – the food is classy stuff. The choices were few, just three light dishes and eight mains, and included sardines, ham hock, sausage and mash, tuna niçoise and roasts. Here, keeping things simple seems to yield great results. Roast pork came with a tasty mix of peas, diced bacon and fresh Jersey Royals, while char-grilled yellowfin tuna niçoise was tender as can be. Wines are chalked on a blackboard; 12 of each, costing between £11 and £30.

Zinfandel

4-5 Chapel Street, Guildford, GU1 3UH (01483 455150/www.zinfandel.org.uk). **Food served** noon-3pm, 6-10pm Mon-Sat; noon-4pm Sun. **Main courses** £7.95-£13.95. **Credit** AmEx, MC, V.

An alleyway off Guildford's main street is the location for Zinfandel, a minimalist chrome homage to the cuisine of California's Napa Valley. There are salad, pizza, rotisserie and char-grill options. Typical dishes might include calamares 'popcorn' with three salsas: roast garlic aïoli, key-lime guacamole and tomato-chilli jam; or a 10oz char-grilled ribeye with jalapeno slaw. A generously topped pizza of barbecued chicken, smoked gouda and mozzarella went down very nicely. If the golden nashi pear on a stem ginger rice pudding fritter feels like a step too far for pudding, then settle for the fail-safe pecan pie with maple syrup. Unsurprisingly, the wine list stays largely in California. It isn't going to win any awards for atmosphere, but it is child-friendly.

The Three Counties

Great pubs and wonderful walks.

The countryside around this area – where Hampshire, Surrey and West Sussex meet – is stunning in an unassuming way, combining rolling downs with heath and woodland. It's a great place for walking or cycling.

The land between and around Frensham Common and Hindhead (containing both heath and woodland) includes trails to the scenic Devil's Punch Bowl; sections of the North and South Downs top and tail the area; and there are wonderful gardens, ranging from the vast **Winkworth Arboretum** to the smaller **Ramster** (20 acres of woodland garden, Petworth Road, Chiddingfold, 01428 654167) and **Bohunt Manor** near Liphook (more wooded gardens, Portsmouth Road, 01428 722208). Much of the land is owned by the National Trust; its heathland management work is explained at **Witley Common Information Centre** (Haslemere Road, Witley, nr Godalming, 01428 683207), where there are also two nature trails.

The area isn't over endowed with stately homes (although there's a wealth of interesting domestic architecture), but one gem is the late 17th-century mansion at **Petworth**. Also notable, especially if you have kids in tow, is **Loseley Park**, home of Loseley ice-cream. Homes that are worth visiting for their literary associations are **Gilbert White**'s house in the engaging village of **Selborne**, and **Jane Austen**'s in Chawton.

Exploring the by-ways

In addition to the (well-signposted) sights, the towns and villages of the Three Counties reward investigation. The village of **Petworth** is stuffed with antiques shops (parking is difficult, but persevere). **Petworth Cottage**

Museum (346 High Street, 01798 342100), a restored estate worker's cottage, provides a fascinating insight into the lives of the rural working classes around the turn of the last century. The village also hosts an arts festival each summer (information from Petworth Tourist Information Centre).

A few miles west is **Midhurst**, a picturesque town that boasts a decent variety of cafés and restaurants, and the ruins of **Cowdray House** (a Tudor mansion that partly burned down in the late 18th century); it's also handy for polo at Cowdray Park (01730 813257) – if you like that sort of thing . Directly north is **Haslemere**, another very attractive town, with a decent bookshop, an idiosyncratic museum, a great cheese shop, a teashop and good restaurants. Much of the surrounding countryside is owned by the National Trust. **Blackdown** (more than 900 feet above sea level, the highest point in Sussex) offers wonderful views – Tennyson had a house on the slopes. Near to Haslemere is **Hindhead**, notable as the birthplace of **Arthur Conan Doyle** and home of **Drummonds Architectural Antiques** (25 London Road, 01428 609444/www.drummonds-arch.co.uk), a splendid architectural salvage yard.

Further north, **Farnham** has many Georgian buildings, a castle, a museum of local history with a walled garden, a range of places to eat and some interesting shops. It also claims to have more ghosts than any other town in England. Just outside Farnham is **Bentley** – worth visiting for the garden and teashop at **Bury Court** (01420 23202, open only on National Garden Scheme Days). Also near Farnham, on the B3001, is **Waverley Abbey**. These English Heritage-owned Cistercian monastery ruins can be reached by a short lakeside walk.

West of Farnham is **Godalming**, a nice-enough town, worth visiting if you're interested in the Arts and Crafts movement (which was very active in Surrey). In the town museum there's a room devoted to the Gertrude Jekyll/ Edwin Lutyens collaboration and a courtyard garden reconstructed to a Jekyll design; behind the parish church is a memorial cloister and Jekyll garden dedicated to local man Jack Phillips, the wireless operator on the *Titanic*.

Outside Godalming, at **Hambledon**, is the National Trust-owned 16th-century **Oakhurst**

By train from London

Trains to **Farnham** leave **Waterloo** every half an hour (journey time 50mins). Trains to **Petersfield** also leave **Waterloo** half-hourly (journey time about 1hr); services also pass through **Haslemere** (journey time 45mins). Trains to **Godalming** leave **Waterloo** every half an hour (journey time 40mins). Info: www.southwesttrains.co.uk.

Hannah Peschar Sculpture Garden.

Cottage, which is furnished with items from the Gertrude Jekyll collection (open by appointment only, 01428 684090/www.nationaltrust.org.uk).

What to see & do

Tourist Information Centres

Council Offices, South Street, Farnham, Surrey GU9 7RN (01252 715109/www.waverley.gov.uk). **Open** 9.30am-5.15pm Mon-Thur; 9.30am-4.45pm Fri; 9am-noon Sat.

North Street, Midhurst, West Sussex GU29 9DW (01730 817322/www.chichester.gov.uk). **Open** *Mar, Oct* 9.15am-5.15pm Mon-Sat. *Apr-Sept* 9.15am-5.15pm Mon-Sat; 11am-4pm Sun. *Nov-Feb* 9.15am-4.15pm Mon-Sat.

Market Square, Petworth, West Sussex GU28 0AF (01798 343523). **Open** *Mar, Oct* 10am-4pm Mon-Sat; *Apr-Sept* 10am-5pm Mon-Sat; 11am-4pm Sun. *Nov, Dec* 10am-3pm Wed-Sat; *Jan, Feb* 10am-2pm Fri, Sat.

Birdworld

Holt Pound, Farnham, Surrey GU10 4LD (01420 22992/www.birdworld.co.uk). **Open** *Mid Feb-Oct* 10am-6pm daily. *Nov-mid Dec, early Jan-mid Feb* 10am-4.30pm Sat, Sun. *Mid Dec-early Jan* 10am-4.30pm daily. **Admission** £9.75; £6.95-£7.50 concessions. **Credit** MC, V.
The largest bird park in the UK, apparently. There's certainly enough room for birds galore, plus attractive gardens, a children's farm, an aquarium, play areas and picnic sites, a restaurant and a gift shop.

Gilbert White's House & Oates Museum

High Street, Selborne, nr Alton, Hampshire GU34 3JH (01420 511275). **Open** 11am-5pm daily. **Admission** £4; £1-£3.50 concessions. **Credit** MC, V.
England's first ecologist, Reverend Gilbert White (1720-93), lived here for most of his life: the original manuscript of his *A Natural History of Selborne* is on show. The restoration of the beautiful garden to its 18th-century form is almost complete – there are always unusual plants for sale, and every June there's an unusual plants fair (phone for details). The Oates Museum commemorates Captain Oates (of Captain Scott, 'going out for a while' fame) and his uncle Frank Oates, a Victorian explorer. From the village, there is attractive walking on Selborne Hill, 250 acres of which are National Trust-owned.

Hannah Peschar Sculpture Garden

Black & White Cottage, Standon Lane, Ockley, Surrey RH5 5QR (01306 627269/www.hannah pescharsculpture.com). **Open** *May-Oct* 11am-6pm Fri, Sat; 2-5pm Sun; Tue-Thur by appointment. *Nov-Apr* by appointment. **Admission** £8; £5 concessions. **Credit** MC, V.
Not as well known as Sculpture at Goodwood (*see p83*) but certainly worth a visit to see a collection of contemporary sculpture in a landscaped garden setting.

Jane Austen's House

Chawton, nr Alton, Hampshire GU34 1SD (01420 83262/www.janeaustensmuseum.org.uk). **Open** *Mar-Nov* 11am-4pm daily. *Dec-Feb* 11am-4pm Sat, Sun. **Admission** £4.50; 50p-£3.50 concessions; free under-8s. **Credit** MC, V.
The author lived here with her mother and sister from 1809 until 1817. *Mansfield Park, Emma* and *Persuasion* were written in this red-brick 17th-century house. Looking round won't take long, though the collection of letters and memorabilia may detain enthusiasts. Steam train enthusiasts note that Alton, north of Chawton, is the starting point for the Mid-Hants Watercress Line.

Loseley Park

Nr Guildford, Surrey GU3 1HS (01483 304440/www.loseley-park.com). **Open** *House* June-Aug 1-5pm Wed-Sun. Closed Sept-May. *Garden, shop & tearoom/restaurant* May-Sept 11am-5pm Wed-Sun. Closed Oct-Apr. **Admission** *House & gardens* £6; £3-£5 concessions. *Gardens only* £3; £1.50-£2.50 concessions. **Credit** MC, V.
An attractive Elizabethan mansion that's home to the Loseley Jersey herd. Although the business has since moved, the house, park and even the cows remain and yoghurts, ice-creams and cream are all available from the gift shop. The grounds feature fountains and rose, herb and flower gardens. There's also a children's play area and tearoom, making the park a pleasant day out.

Lurgashall Winery

Windfallwood, Lurgashall, West Sussex GU28 9HA (01428 707292/www.lurgashall.co.uk). **Open** 9am-5pm Mon-Sat; 11am-5pm Sun. **Admission** free.
An award-winning producer, selling fruit and flower wines, meads and liqueurs, plus honey, mead mustard and chocolates. There's also a herb garden.

Peter's Barn Gallery

Beck House, South Ambersham, nr Midhurst, West Sussex GU29 0BX (01798 861388/www.petersbarn gallery.co.uk). **Open** *Apr-Oct* 2-6pm Tue-Fri; 11am-6pm Sat, Sun. Closed Nov-March. **Admission** free.
Peter's Barn is a 'garden gallery', showing work by known and up-and-coming artists. Artworks are displayed in a small barn and are also dotted around the pond, under trees and shrubs and across the lawn. Two (lovely) dogs make sure there's no funny business.

Petworth House & Park

Petworth, West Sussex GU28 0AE (01798 342207/ www.nationaltrust.org.uk/petworth). **Open** *House* Apr-Oct 11am-5.30pm Mon-Wed, Sat, Sun. Last entry 5pm. Nov-mid Dec 11am-3.30pm Wed-Sat. Closed mid Dec-Mar. *Park* 8am-dusk daily. **Admission** (NT) £7; £4 concessions; free under 5s. **Credit** AmEx, DC, MC, V.
An underrated National Treasure and home to various historical novelties: the oldest English globe (with an unusually shaped America and warnings of intriguing 'Sea Beasties'); a 15th-century manuscript by Chaucer; and the last grandfather clock made by Thomas Tompion. It is packed with works by, among others, Van Dyck, Reynolds, Titian, Blake and Turner, plus furniture, sculpture and limewood carving by Grinling Gibbons. It is also home to the largest herd of fallow deer in Europe. Not only are children welcomed, they are positively encouraged, with a Tracker Pack full of educational quizzes and activities in the seven main rooms.

Rural Life Centre

Old Kiln Museum, Reeds Road, Tilford, Surrey GU10 2DL (01252 795571/www.rural-life.org.uk). **Open** *Mar-Sept* 11am-6pm Wed-Sun. *Oct-Feb* 11am-4pm Wed, Sun. **Admission** £5; £3-£4 concessions; free under-5s. **Credit** MC, V.
A social history of rural life: agricultural implements, ploughs, crafts and buildings covering all aspects of farming and village life are displayed over ten acres of field, woodland and barns. There's a café and train rides on a Sunday.

Watts Gallery

Down Lane, Compton, Surrey GU3 1DQ (01483 810235/www.wattsgallery.org.uk). **Open** *Apr-Sept* 2-6pm Mon-Wed, Fri-Sun. *Oct-Mar* 2-4pm Mon, Tue, Fri, Sun; 11am-1pm, 2-4pm Wed, Sat. **Admission** free.
An idiosyncratic and utterly charming gallery containing the work of George Frederick Watts (1817-1904): landscapes, social comment pieces, allegories, portraits, drawings and sculptures. His wife Mary was responsible for the nearby Watts Chapel (off Down Lane, open 9am-dusk daily), a riot of symbolism and a blend of styles that demands to be seen. A visit to the hut-like tearoom rounds off a trip nicely.

Winkworth Arboretum

Hascombe Road, nr Godalming, Surrey, GU8 4AD (01483 208477/www.nationaltrust.org.uk/ winkwortharboretum). **Open** dawn-dusk daily.
Admission (NT) £4; £2 concessions. **Credit** MC, V.
National Trust-owned, this is a glorious display of more than 1,000 different shrubs and trees. In spring there are bluebell and azalea displays; in the autumn there's a fine blaze of colour. There's always plenty of wildlife (dogs must be kept on a lead) and a tearoom in the woods.

Angel Hotel

North Street, Midhurst, West Sussex GU29 9DN (01730 812421/fax 01730 815928/www.theangel midhurst.co.uk). **Rates** £80-£115 single/single occupancy; £110 double/twin; £130 superior double; £150 four-poster. **Rooms** (all en suite) 4 single; 9 double/twin; 10 superior double; 5 four-poster. **Credit** AmEx, DC, MC, V.
Now under new ownership, the Angel was undergoing its most serious makeover since a Georgian façade was added in the 16th century at the time of writing. The hotel is attempting to shed its scones and woodbeams image and attract a younger clientele. Central to this plan is the Halo bar/brasserie, which opened this May. If live music and late drinking aren't your thing, maybe one of the four-poster rooms with views of Cowdray House will satisfy. Children and dogs (£5 per night) welcome.
A3 to Hindhead; A286 to Midhurst; hotel is on main street.

Crown Inn

The Green, Petworth Road, Chiddingfold, Surrey GU8 4TX (01428 682255/fax 01428 685786). **Rates** £49.95 single occupancy; £67 double; £67-£90 four-poster; £67-£110 suite. **Rooms** (all en suite) 3 double/twin; 3 four-poster; 1 suite. **Credit** AmEx, MC, V.
A laid-back hostelry that doesn't overdo the olde worlde aspect, despite having more than its fair share of wood beams, fires, four-posters and royal visitors (back to Edward VI in 1552). Best of all is the upholstered phone booth in the hall. Bar meals are taken in a rug-strewn lounge; there's also a pleasant restaurant area spread across several rooms. The pub has a fine selection of ales from the Kings and Barnes brewery. Children welcome.
Chiddingfold is on A283; inn is on right.

Old Railway Station

Coultershaw Bridge, nr Petworth, West Sussex GU28 0JF (tel/fax 01798 342346/www.old-station.co.uk). **Rates** £50-£80 single occupancy; £72-£136 double. **Rooms** (all en suite) 8 double. **Credit** MC, V.
What was once Petworth station has been transformed into what must be one of the most striking and romantic B&Bs in England. Six of the eight rooms are in beautifully refurbished Pullman coaches that sit on the rails behind the station building. Stroll across to the Badgers (01798 342651) for dinner and a drink, or have champagne brought to your room and pretend that you are crossing Russia on the Trans-Siberian Express. You can also enjoy traditional afternoon tea on the station platform. Book well ahead (there's a minimum two-night stay at weekends). Children over ten welcome. All bedrooms are no-smoking.
On A285 1 mile S of Petworth; pull into front of Badgers pub; take slip road leading to hotel.

Park House Hotel

Bepton, nr Midhurst, West Sussex GU29 0JB (01730 819000/fax 01730 819099/www.parkhouse hotel.com). **Rates** £90-£140 single occupancy; £125-£175 double/twin. **Rooms** 17 double (all en suite); 2 twin. **Credit** AmEx, DC, MC, V.
At the end of the first phase of a massive refurbishment, Park House Hotel still manages to combine gentrified charm with 21st-century chic. Not many hotels offer a

Sussex & Surrey

Winkworth Arboretum. See p97.

room with wood beams on one side and a DVD player and flat screen TV on the other. Not to mention grounds with a putting course, tennis courts and swimming pool. The dining room and drawing rooms exude a relaxed opulence. Children and dogs welcome.
On B2226, 2 miles S of Midhurst.

Spread Eagle Hotel & Health Spa

South Street, Midhurst, West Sussex GU29 9NH (01730 816911/fax 01730 815668). **Rates** £85-£190 single occupancy; £99-£165 double/twin; £225 four-poster/suite. **Rooms** (all en suite) 32 double/twin; 5 four-poster; 2 suites. **Credit** AmEx, DC, MC, V.
Part of the Historic Sussex Hotels group, this traditional inn has been tastefully updated and extended to include a health spa complete with pool, gym, hot tub, sauna, steam room and beauty centre. Some of the pleasantly decorated bedrooms have four-poster beds, and all have satellite television. The attractive dining room offers formal dining; lighter meals can be eaten in the conservatory, terrace or courtyard, weather permitting. Children and dogs are welcome.

Swan Inn

Lower Street, Fittleworth, West Sussex RH20 1EN (01798 865429/fax 01798 865721/www.swan inn.com). **Rates** £30 single; £60-£75 double/twin; £75 four-poster. **Rooms** (all en suite) 3 single; 6 double; 4 twin; 2 four-poster. **Credit** AmEx, MC, V.
A genuinely old inn (its credentials go back to the 14th century) and, to judge by the framed endorsement by Rudyard Kipling, one that has kept visitors well fed and rested for centuries. Check out the oak-panelled restaurant-bar decorated with Victorian oil paintings provided by struggling artists 'in lieu of board and lodging', which might make you feel you are staying inside the cover illustration of a Penguin Classic. With good special break deals, this is affordable antiquity. And if your wallet is feeling extra full, go for the the luxury four-poster in a newly converted barn.
On B2138 between Pulborough and Petworth.

Where to eat & drink

The countryside around these parts is riddled with homely country pubs, in any one of which you could merrily while away a Sunday afternoon – or longer. The following are some of the beauties this area has to offer, but it's by no means an exhaustive selection: every bend of every B-road conceals a country pub and each has its own distinctive character. Try any of these or discover your own.

The **Noah's Ark** (The Green, Lurgashall, 01428 707346) is an attractive pub serving good food – the sandwiches are particularly fine. The **Red Lion** (Shamley Green, 01483 892202) has plenty of outdoor tables. The pretty **Hollist Arms** (Lodsworth, 01798 861310) serves real ale, good food and has a beautiful garden and seats under a chestnut tree at the front. An equally lovely garden can be found at the **Red Lion** (8 The Green, Fernhurst, 01428 653304), which also boasts real ale, above-average food and attractive low-slung rooms. Also in Fernhurst, the **King's Arms** (Midhurst Road, 01428 652005) serves a sophisticated menu with a French twist. Children will appreciate the outdoor play area at the red-brick **Prince of Wales** in Hammer Vale (Hammer Lane, 01428 652600), just outside Haslemere, and their parents will like the Gales ales. There's a grassy garden with a big wooden climbing frame at the **Hawkley Inn** in Hawkley (Pococks Lane, 01730 827205), a pub with real ales and a slightly left-field feel. The **White Horse** in Hascombe (The Street, 01483 208258) is a handsome inn adorned with beautiful tiles and biblical scripts; also good-looking is the

Chequers Inn in Well (White Hill, 01256 862605) where you can drink outside on a vine-covered terrace. The Tilford village green hosts the **Barley Mow** (01252 792205/www.thebar leymowtilford.com), with an admirable choice of real ales, solid ploughman's lunches and a large garden complete with waterfall and stream.

If you're looking for something less rural, Farnham has numerous bars and pubs. Remarkable among the mass is the **Coach & Horses** (1-2 Castle Street, 01252 724520), with paellas, speciality sausages and 100 per cent steak burgers. The **Queen's Head** (9 The Borne, 01252 726524) has most of the essential qualities of an English town pub: an unnecessarily comprehensive range of locally brewed bitters (George Gales Hampshire Brewery); various inexpensive meat-based bar meals; a history of being a public place of intoxication spanning several centuries (since circa 1691); and a well-documented ghost (a cavalier who must have had a dull 40 years between the Civil War and the establishment of the pub). In complete contrast, **Borelli's** (Borelli Yard, 01252 735254) is a sleek, modern bar/restaurant serving a globe-trotting menu.

Charlie's Bar & Restaurant

Knock Hundred House, Knock Hundred Row, Midhurst, West Sussex GU29 9DQ (01730 817732). **Food served** noon-2.30pm, 6-10.30pm Tue-Sat; 6-10.30pm Mon, Sun. **Main courses** £7.25-£13.95. **Credit** AmEx, MC, V.

A haunt for Midhurst youth that gets packed at weekends, the real strength here is the food. The menu spans the globe, with dishes ranging from the local (Midhurst Royal sausages) to the international (Thai green curry), by way of carefully prepared Modern European dishes (poached breast of chicken with asparagus mousse was good on a recent visit). Portions are generous.

Duke of Cumberland Arms

Henley, West Sussex GU27 3HQ (01428 652280). **Food served** noon-2.30pm, 7-9.30pm Mon-Sat; noon-2.30pm Sun. **Main courses** £9.95-£15.75. **Credit** MC, V.

The Duke of Cumberland pub has been around since the 15th century. The cosy wood-panelled bar seems barely altered by the ages (except for the numerous mobile phones nailed to the walls as a warning to punters). The three and a half acres of stepped garden, ponds, streams and view over the Weald to the North Downs are a dictionary definition of picturesque. Those trout ponds are also nature's refrigerator; the food isn't just fresh, it's still alive. Fish and seafood are specialities, but there are plenty of other options, such as pepper stuffed with mushroom risotto. In winter, it's a bit of a squeeze in the bar, where pride of place goes to an impressive log fire. Children – who will love the garden – are made welcome.

Gaudi's

Church Hill, Midhurst, West Sussex, GU29 9NX (01730 812990). **Food served** 7-10.30pm Tue; noon-2.30pm, 7-10.30pm Wed-Sun. **Main courses**

£8.50-£15.95. **Set lunches** (Wed-Sat) £14.95 2 courses, £16.95 3 courses; (Sun) £15.95 2 courses, £17.95 3 courses. **Credit** AmEx, DC, MC, V.

Fina and Jack Jurado have transformed an olde worlde inn into a unique and glittering piece of Gaudiana. The main restaurant area is fairly conservatively decorated with geckos, figurines and a print of the Sagrada Familia, while the informal bar area is adorned with customised furniture and fittings. The atmosphere is relaxed but lively; the menu is pretty traditional: oyster soup, loin of fat-free lamb with mint, châteaubriand and crêpes suzettes (flambéd at the table) are typical dishes. Upstairs is a guest room that just screams Gaudí, down to the multicoloured tiles in the bathroom.

Lickfold Inn

Lickfold, nr Lodsworth, GU28 9EY West Sussex (01798 861285). **Food served** noon-2.30pm, 7-9.30pm daily. **Main courses** £8.50-£17.95. **Credit** AmEx, MC, V.

Adjacent to a babbling brook, in a secluded leafy lane location with a roaring fire in winter and a capacious garden for the summer, the Lickfold Inn has it all. Staff make everyone welcome at this wood-beamed, herringbone brick-built pub and restaurant. There's always a good selection of local ales at the bar and a variety of wines. Starters include the likes of foie gras boudin with Madeira jelly and toast, crab soup or pan-fried chorizo in a spicy sauce. Steak au poivre needed a sharper knife the day we called in; better was pan-seared salmon with sun-blushed tomato sauce and sauté potatoes, and confit of duck leg with bubble and squeak. Apple tart was served on a rather burnt puff pastry base, with a delectable honey and cinnamon ice-cream.

Saddler's Rest

Saddler's Row, Petworth, West Sussex RH13 0PU (01798 342125). **Food served** 10am-4.30pm Tue, Wed, Sun; 10am-9pm Thur-Sat. **Main courses** £5.95-£8.95. **Credit** MC, V.

This 15th-century restaurant and tearoom offers an eclectic selection of dishes that put your average tearoom to shame. Cucumber sandwiches, scones, teacakes and the like are all here, but they are joined by ploughman's, toasties, home-made soups and cakes, roasts, buck rarebit, fillet steak, tuna piri piri and potted baked crab. Perhaps the menu has been influenced by the equally varied history of the buildings: starting life as a saddlery in 1481, the premises have housed blacksmiths, barbers, bakers, wig-makers, tobacconists, confectionery shops, upholsterers and an undertakers. Children are welcomed with toys and Disney videos.

Three Horseshoes

Elsted, West Sussex GU29 0JY (01730 825746). **Food served** noon-2pm, 6.30-9pm Mon-Sat; 7-8.30pm Sun. **Main courses** £7.50-£14.95. **Credit** MC, V.

From the oak and brick interior to the rose-adorned garden with an impressive view of the South Downs, the Three Horseshoes more than fulfils all the essential criteria for a first-class country pub. The menu changes regularly and includes various ploughman's (stilton, brie, ham), as well as the likes of gravadlax, chicken breast with bacon and mushroom sauce, and a particular favourite – a robust steak and kidney pie made with Murphys. All dishes are best accompanied by a pint of Ballards, a local brew.

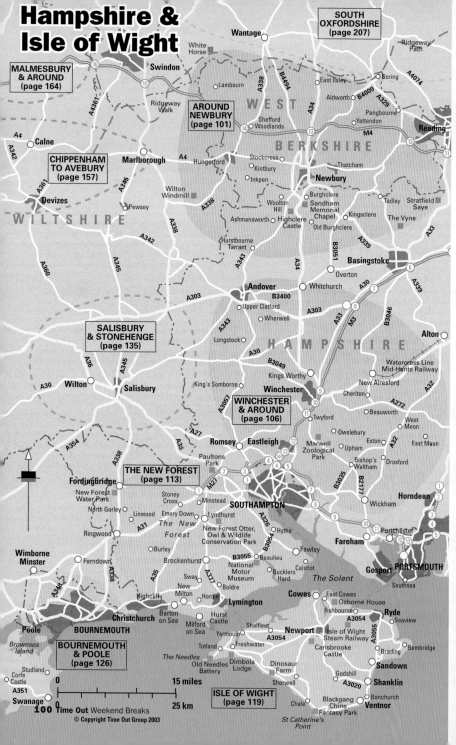

Around Newbury

Home to horses and some fine countryside.

'Around Newbury' doesn't exactly conjure up the charming rural idyll suggested by the Cotswolds, the Upper Stour Valley or the New Forest; and for good reason, since the immediate area around the town isn't blessed with rolling hills, picture-postcard villages, big skies or dense medieval forest. Indeed, **Newbury** itself sits just below the M4 and was, until recently, bisected by the A34. Not surprisingly, therefore, the town itself – with its industrial estates and business parks – is not particularly attractive. Nevertheless, hidden from the hum of constant traffic and the bustle of business, there are patches of truly pretty, unspoiled countryside here with some beautiful sleepy villages and bold country houses, and plenty of opportunities for bracing walks and hearty meals in small, unassuming pubs. This is also horse-racing country, so an early riser may see horses out with their trainers silhouetted against the skyline. It's rabbit country, too: the hillsides just south of the town have been immortalised in Richard Adams' *Watership Down*. And while Newbury is unlikely to stir the heart, just west lies **Hungerford**, a pleasant town set around a wide high street lined with Georgian townhouses, many of which are now antiques shops and tearooms.

Racing certainty

The centre of Newbury is dominated by the Kennet shopping centre, and although some buildings from earlier eras remain, the overall effect is not compelling. Those with an interest in English history, however, might wish to visit the **West Berkshire Museum** (The Wharf, 01635 30511/www.westberks.gov.uk; the tourist office is here too), which gives a detailed account of the area's role in the Civil War. Newbury is home to **Newbury Racecourse** (01635 40015/www.newbury-racecourse.co.uk), one of the best racetracks in the country. This is where the Hennessy Cognac Gold Cup is run and the racing world's community of bookmakers, stable lads, jockeys and professional gamblers can be found drowning their sorrows or celebrating their triumphs in the pubs hereabouts. Many will live in and around **Lambourn** to the north of Newbury. Here, stables are everywhere, white rails line the Downs, there are many more Irish accents

By train from London

Trains to **Newbury** leave **Paddington** hourly; journey time is about 1hr 10mins. Info: www.thamestrains.co.uk.

than you would expect for Berkshire, and horses trot home along the roads.

Early evidence of equine fascination is marked by an enormous chalk **White Horse**, carved into the hillside near Uffington. Along the crest of the Lambourn Downs runs the **Ridgeway**, the ancient wayfare held by some historians to be the oldest road in Britain. En route to Lambourn from Newbury, stop off in **Eastbury**. Quaint cottages line the stream that runs through the village, but it is the parish church of St James the Greater that is worth the stopover. Here you will find an enchanting window engraved by Laurence Whistler in celebration of the lives of the poet Edward Thomas, who was killed in action in Arras in 1917, and his wife Helen, who lived her last years in the village and is buried at the top of the churchyard. Some miles to the east lies **Aldworth**, a quiet lost-in-time village with a friendly pub and an intriguing church, inside which lie nine huge stone effigies on top of their respective tombs. Known as the **Aldworth Giants**, they represent five generations of a Norman family dating from the 14th century. Further south, the wooded lanes around **Bucklebury** and **Frilsham** lead to the soaring acoustics of **Douai Abbey** (Upper Woolhampton, 01189 715300), with its gloriously light and airy modern interior.

South of Newbury

On the south side of Newbury the villages are prosperous and genteel. One of the most rewarding to visit is **Inkpen**, home to some of the most zealous ramblers in the country. These fearless defenders of the common person's right to stroll have for 25 years run the Inkpen Rights of Way Committee, which ensures not only that the area's rights of way are kept public, but also that they are clearly signposted. As a result, two of the best walks in Berkshire originate from this village; leaflets are available from the Swan and Crown & Garter pubs.

Also good for a hearty stroll is the village of **Ashmansworth**, which is made up of little more than two working farms and a church, but is imbued with a plethora of public bridleways. The village is close to the stunning **Sandham Memorial Chapel** (*see* p103 '**What ho, Giotto!**'). Painter Stanley Spencer was a medical orderly during World War I and his experiences inspired the murals that fill the chapel's walls. Nearby is **Highclere Castle**, the stately family home of Lord and Lady Carnarvon, and, most importantly, an excellent pub called the Yew Tree in Highclere village (Andover Road, 01635 253360), with two log fires and a more than decent restaurant.

Stray further east towards Basingstoke, amid a tangle of country lanes and villages with 'Bramley' or 'Mortimer' in their names, and you will find two more country houses: **Stratfield Saye** (01256 882882/www.stratfield-saye.co.uk), which opens only occasionally, and the **Vyne**.

Tourist Information Centre

The Wharf, Newbury, Berkshire RG14 5AS (01635 30267/fax 01635 519562/www.westberks.gov.uk). **Open** *Apr-Sept* 10am-5pm Mon-Fri; 10am-4.30pm Sat. *Oct-Mar* 10am-4pm Mon-Sat.

Barge cruising

Rose of Hungerford *from Canal Walk, Hungerford (01488 683389/www.katrust.org).* **Tickets** £5; £3-£4 concessions Wed, Sat, Sun. **Credit** MC, V.

Kennet Horseboat Company *(01635 44154).* **Avon** *from Newbury*; **Kennet Valley** *from Kintbury.* **Tickets** £5.20-£6.70; £4.20-£5.70 concessions. **No** credit cards.

Highclere Castle

Highclere, Newbury, Berkshire RG20 9RN (01635 253210/www.highclerecastle.co.uk). **Open** *July, Aug* 11am-5pm Mon-Fri, Sun. Also open Easter & May bank hols. Phone to check. Closed Sept-June. **Admission** *Castle & grounds* £7; £3.50-£5.50 concessions; free under-5s. *Grounds only* £4; £1.50 concessions. **Credit** MC, V.

Home to the earls of Carnarvon (the fifth earl funded Howard Carter's Tutankhamen dig), this isn't the turreted castle of children's dreams, but more of a stately home. However, those interested in Victorian architecture will be impressed. It was built by Sir Charles Barry, architect of the Houses of Parliament, and is quite similar in style, albeit much squarer and smaller. Inside, there are Egyptian relics brought over by the fifth earl in the 1920s, and the walled garden contains a Greek-style folly and a miniature temple.

Living Rainforest

Hampstead Norreys, nr Newbury, Berkshire RG18 0TN (01635 202444/www.livingrainforest.org). **Open** 10am-5.15pm daily. Last admission 4.30pm. **Admission** £4.95; £1.95-£4.25 concessions; free under-3s. **Credit** MC, V.

A warm, wild jungle environment crammed full of plants and ponds. In among the foliage are hidden spiders, crocodiles, chameleons, fish, butterflies and birds. There's also a small shop and café.

The Vyne

Vyne Road, Sherborne St John, Basingstoke, Hampshire RG24 9HL (01256 881337/www. nationaltrust.org.uk/thevyne). **Open** *House* Apr-Oct 1-4.30pm Mon-Wed; 11am-4.30pm Sat, Sun. Closed Nov-Mar. *Grounds* Feb, Mar 11am-4.30pm Sat, Sun. Apr-Oct 11am-5pm Mon-Wed, Sat, Sun. Closed Nov-Jan. **Admission** (NT) *House & grounds* £6.60; £3.25 concessions. *Grounds only* £3.50; £1.75 concessions. **Credit** MC, V.

'What ho, Giotto!'

Set back from the road and partially hidden behind a small orchard is a work of art that stands alone in British 20th-century painting. The approach is not very inspiring. A plain brick path leads through a refreshingly ragged orchard to a plain red-brick building. Step through the plain brown door, however, and you enter the brilliant world of Stanley Spencer, and his artistic reflections on his time as a medical orderly in the Great War. He was commissioned to do the work by a Mr and Mrs Behrends in memory of Henry Willoughby Sandham, Mrs Behrends' brother, who died as a result of an illness contracted during the Macedonian campaign. The chapel was built expressly for Spencer to decorate, and when the patrons told Spencer of their proposal, his enthusiastic response was 'What ho, Giotto!'. (Giotto, one of his influences, decorated a memorial chapel in Padua.)

The chapel interior is one small, rectangular room, perhaps 16 feet wide and 26 feet long and tall. The north and south walls are covered with Spencer's murals depicting aspects of his life in the army, both in barracks at home and when he was posted to Salonica in Macedonia – 'a mixture', as he put it, 'of real and spiritual fact'. Both walls consist of several panels and cover a multitude of mundane activities. They were all painted on to canvas, some back in Hampstead, others in situ. Titles such as *Scrubbing the Floor, Sorting and Moving Kit-Bags, Sorting the Laundry, Filling Tea Urns, Map-Reading, Bedmaking* or *Washing Lockers* aren't the most alluring of subjects, but the figures are wonderfully arranged in the space, and painted with such rich colours and enchanting simplicity that you can see that for Spencer, even mundane activities held an almost spiritual fascination: 'When I was fully equipped for scrubbing – bucket, apron and "prayer mat" in hand – I used to feel much as if I was going to church.'

Spencer himself appears in several of the panels. 'I'm putting myself in places and circumstances in which I want to be,' he explained. The centrepiece, which rises over you on the east wall above the simple, small altar, is called *Resurrection of the Soldiers*. This superbly constructed design depicts a jumble of white crosses with resurrected soldiers and other detritus from a military campaign in the foreground, while in the centre two white mules turn to look back at Christ, who is receiving crosses from the dying soldiers. Although the subject matter is war, and the colours are mainly browns and greys, the overall effect is still uplifting, and endlessly intriguing. A visit here is as it was intended – truly memorable.

Sandham Memorial Chapel

Harts Lane, Burghclere, Berkshire RG20 9JT (01635 278394/www.national trust.org.uk/sandham). **Open** Apr-Oct 11am-5pm Wed-Sun. *Mar, Nov* 11am-4pm Sat, Sun. Last admission 30mins before closing. Dec-Feb open by arrangement only. **Admission** (NT) £3; £1.50 concessions. **No credit cards**.

Architectural students can get their fill of styles at the Vyne. Started in the early 16th century for Henry VIII's lord chamberlain, Lord Sandys, it was given a pioneering classical portico in the mid 17th century. The Vyne's interior is in a wonderful state of preservation, with much original oak panelling and bucketloads of antiques. Don't miss the Tudor chapel containing Renaissance stained glass or the lovely walks in the grounds.

Wilton Windmill

Wilton, nr Great Bedwyn, Marlborough, Wiltshire SN8 3SP (01672 870266/www.wiltonwindmill.co.uk). **Open** *Easter-Sept* 2-5pm Sun. Closed Oct-Easter. **Admission** £2.50; 50p-£1.50 concessions. **No credit cards.**

This brick windmill, built in 1821 for local millers, has not been used since 1920, but was restored to its former state in 1980 and is now fully operational. Floodlit at night and standing on a chalk ridge 550ft above sea level, it is a fun, low-key place to visit, and is within walking distance of the Kennet & Avon Canal.

Where to stay

This is a well-to-do area and accommodation isn't cheap; it may also be difficult to come by if a race is on at Newbury. **Langley Hall Farm** (01635 248222, doubles £55) at World's End, Beedon, has acres of walkable land; **Rookwood Farm House** (01488 608676, doubles £70) in Stockcross has a heated outdoor pool, a gorgeous garden and a kitchen for use by those preferring self-catering. For plain rooms a pillow's throw from the canal and with fine pub food to boot, try

Highclere Castle.
See p102.

the **Dundas Arms** (53 Station Road, Kintbury, 01488 658263/www.dundasarms.co.uk, doubles £80). For the full five-star treatment, there's the **Vineyard** (Stockcross, 01635 528770/www.the-vineyard.co.uk, doubles £188-£705).

Esseborne Manor OFFER

Hurstbourne Tarrant, Andover, Hampshire SP11 0ER (01264 736444/fax 01264 736725/ www.essebornemanor.com). **Rates** £95-£105 single occupancy; £100-£150 double/twin; £150 four-poster; £150-£180 deluxe double. **Rooms** (all en suite) 3 double; 6 deluxe double; 5 twin; 1 four-poster. **Credit** AmEx, DC, MC, V.
Relatively isolated on the crown of a hill, this country house hotel is good value. It has all the trappings of a luxury hotel – tennis court, croquet lawn, herb garden, an abundance of fluffy towelling robes – but its prices are not astronomical and, unlike many hotels of this size, it has more of a family than corporate atmosphere. While the rooms inside the house are grandly upholstered, the converted stable rooms are less flashy and more relaxed, with simple pine furniture and cream walls. The restaurant is worth sampling, although the Yew Tree (*see p102*) is also just down the road. Children and dogs are welcome. *A343 from Newbury; turn right at Highclere; house is on the left after 7 miles.*

Fishers Farm

Ermin Street, Shefford Woodlands, nr Hungerford, Berkshire RG17 7AB (01488 648466/fax 01488 648706/www.fishersfarm.co.uk). **Rates** £45-£50 single occupancy; £58 double/twin. **Rooms** 2 double (1 en suite); 1 twin (en suite). **No credit cards.**
This 16th-century farmhouse is part of a working arable farm. Located a long way down a dirt track, it offers a secluded home where you can lounge around in the large garden, stretch out before a log fire in the sitting room or stride purposefully across its 600 acres. The bedrooms are splendidly simple, with beamed ceilings, cream walls and pine furniture, and no TVs. This is a good place to take kids: miles away from a road, awash with cats and dogs, and surrounded by fields and woodland. No smoking throughout. *J14 M4; A338 N for 2 miles; left to B4000; farm is on right 500yds after Pheasant pub.*

Newbury Manor Hotel OFFER

London Road, Newbury, Berkshire RG14 2BY (01635 528838/fax 01635 523406/www.newbury-manor-hotel.co.uk). **Rates** £115-£265 single occupancy; £125-£200 double/twin; £215-£275 suite. **Rooms** (all en suite) 22 double; 6 twin; 5 suites. **Credit** AmEx, MC, V.
This Georgian manor house is set in nine acres of woodland and water meadows, with the Kennet and Lambourn rivers running through its grounds, a large lawn on which children can frolic and jogging paths laid through its woodland. Large and comfortable rooms have all mod cons and more (jacuzzi spa baths, white bathrobes), and some come with river-view balconies. The idyll is somewhat spoilt by the A4 a few hundred yards away, not to mention the distinctly corporate feel. Nevertheless, the River Bar creates a pleasant setting, there's an airy conservatory and the restaurant's bold decor is matched by the imaginative and high-quality dishes. Children and dogs are welcome. *J13 M4; A34 and A339 towards Newbury; at Robin Hood roundabout follow the A4 towards Thatcham and Reading. The hotel is on the right after the business park.*

Wilton House

33 High Street, Hungerford, Berkshire RG17 0NF (01488 684228/fax 01488 685037/www.wiltonhouse. freeserve.co.uk). **Rates** £40 single occupancy; £60 double. **Rooms** (both en suite) 2 double. **No credit cards.**
Described by Pevsner as 'the most ambitious house in Hungerford', this place dates back to the 15th century. The front, however, is 18th-century – but once inside, everything is creaks, slopes and bulges. The rooms, both at the front of the house, are charming: tastefully decorated in duck-egg blue or yellow. The owner, Deborah Welfare, uses organic produce in the fine breakfasts, and there is an elegant garden. With the friendly welcome and antiques shops on your doorstep, this is a real treat. Children over eight welcome. No smoking throughout.

Where to eat & drink

The best places to eat in this area are country pub/restaurants, and a handful of very smart and very expensive destination dining spots.

The **Café Blue Cobra** restaurant in Theale (20 High Street, 0118 930 4040) serves both Bengali and Thai food. The restaurant at **Esseborne Manor** (*see p104*) is also good, with a reasonably priced, traditional British menu. The pubs are at the heart of the horse-racing community. The **Crown & Horns** in East Ilsley (Compton Road, 01635 281205) is home to all things equine, from stable lads at the bar to copies of the *Racing Post* lying on the tables. The menu is extensive and is just about the only facet of the establishment without a hint of horse. Then there's the **Hare & Hounds** in Lambourn Woodlands (01488 71386), where you'll be hard-pressed to find a regular who isn't in some way connected to the racing world. Close to the Ridgeway is the 14th-century **Bell** at Aldworth (Bell Lane, 01635 578272), a great place to end a walk with superb-value rolls and soup. The **Pot Kiln** in Frilsham, Yattendon (on the Yattendon to Bucklebury Road, 01635 201366/www.wbbrew.co.uk), stands out for its location: in the middle of rambling countryside, it's a lovely place for a drink.

The Dew Pond Restaurant

Old Burghclere, Newbury, Berkshire RG20 9LH (01635 278408/www.dewpond.co.uk). **Food served** 7-10pm Tue-Sat. **Set dinner** £28 3 courses. **Credit** MC, V.

In the middle of nowhere, up a country lane and surrounded by hills, the Dew Pond looks like a rather pretty private house, not least because that's what it is. The views across the fields are charming, particularly when the cattle pass by under the window (so eat your fillet of beef with due respect). The starters won't disappoint: warm caramelised onion tart with shavings of parma ham and vine tomatoes; white crab meat and avocado with gazpacho, or twice-baked soufflé with gruyère and asparagus. Mains include the likes of free-range chicken filled with soft cheese with tagliatelle, and honey-roasted Gressingham duck breast in port wine sauce – cooked to perfection on a recent visit. With a (not so) 'miniature assortment' of gorgeous puddings to follow, the Dew Pond richly deserves its popularity.

The Harrow

West Ilsley, nr Newbury, Berkshire RG20 7AR (01635 281260). **Food served** 11am-2pm, 6.30-9pm daily. **Main courses** £10-£15. **Credit** MC, V.

Nestling in the rolling hills just south of the Ridgeway, with a view overlooking the green baize of a village cricket pitch, the Harrow is a real treat. The pews and country kitchen furniture inside are surrounded by equine art, while outside in Laura's Corner, children can enjoy a range of playground treats while their parents are scoffing faces at tables nearby. Half a dozen starters and mains include simply grilled langoustines, warm goat's cheese risotto, lamb's liver, smoked haddock with peas and pancetta risotto, or Aberdeen Angus steak. The cuts of meat were particularly tender and portions were ample but not excessive. Although service was slow, it was worth the wait.

Royal Oak

The Square, Yattendon, Berkshire RG18 0UG (01635 201325/www.chorushotel.co.uk). **Food served** noon-2pm, 7-9.30pm Mon-Thur; noon-2.30pm, 7-9.30pm Fri-Sun. **Main courses** £13.50-£19.50. **Set lunch** (Sun) £19.50 2 courses, £23.50 3 courses. **Credit** AmEx, DC, MC, V.

There's the smart end and the pub end at this pretty, 18th-century establishment in the heart of a well-to-do village just outside Newbury. Opt for the smart end, and you'll find yourself in an intimate dining room. The bar is more rustic, but still comfortable. Either way, the food is modern – don't expect homely country fare here. Starters such as watercress soup with bacon pancakes, or an artichoke, feta, chicory, pine and cherry tomato salad set the tone, followed by roast chicken with wild mushroom risotto and asparagus and leek cream sauce, or fillet of beef with wilted greens, topped by seared foie gras and pomme fondant.

The Vineyard

Stockcross, Newbury, Berkshire RG20 8JU (01635 528770/www.the-vineyard.co.uk). **Food served** noon-2pm, 7-9.30pm daily. **Set lunch** (Mon-Sat) £17 2 courses, (Sun) £26 3 courses. **Set dinner** £45 2 courses, £55 3 courses, (Fri, Sat) £70 8 courses. **Credit** AmEx, DC, MC, V.

As you approach this hotel, restaurant and spa, you could be forgiven for thinking you had turned into the sumptuous home of one of James Bond's power-hungry enemies. A valet offers to park your car and efficient staff whisking guests to and fro sets you looking for the piranhas and the white cat. Be reassured, however, that all you can expect here is a quite wonderful meal, conceived and created under the expert eye of chef John Campbell. The combinations are imaginative and original. On a recent visit, starters included roast Anjou squab with black treacle and celeriac, red mullet with fennel and honey purée, or ham hock and foie gras terrine with a lentil dressing. Mains could be corn-fed poussin tarte and truffled eggs, turbot with braised oxtail, or saddle of lamb with red cabbage and Venezuelan chocolate – beautifully presented and a real treat for the palate. The wine list extends to two spiral-bound volumes. A chocolate fondant with basil ice-cream capped a memorable meal.

Swan Inn

Craven Road, Lower Green, Inkpen, Berkshire RG17 9DX (01488 668326). **Food served** noon-2pm, 7-9pm Mon-Thur; noon-2pm, 7-9.30pm Fri; noon-2.30pm, 7-9.30pm Sat; noon-2.30pm, 7-9pm Sun. **Main courses** £14-£21. **Credit** MC, V.

Allow plenty of time to find the Swan, whose signpost may unhelpfully be pointing in the wrong direction. This is a no-frills pub serving traditional food and local ales such as Berkshire-brewed Butts Bitter and Hook Norton Mild (it was CAMRA's West Berks pub of the year in 2002). A sign over the bar reads 'safe food home-made using local organic beef and organic produce wherever possible'; wine is organic too. Dishes such as beef stroganoff, leek and bacon gratin or cod in beer batter with excellent chips can be ordered at the bar; for the likes of halibut with sesame seed crust, canon of lamb with frenchified sauces and desserts, try the attached Cygnet restaurant.

Hampshire & Isle of Wight

Winchester & Around

It's old school.

Hampshire & Isle of Wight

Winchester, the ancient capital of Wessex, may have lost its royal favour, but not its medieval majesty. The town has a long history. In about 450 BC, an Iron Age settlement was established on St Catherine's Hill, just to the east. The Romans moved the town to its present site west of the River Itchen in around AD 70, when they created the city of Venta Belgarum. After a couple of centuries it became a centre for the newly arrived Saxons, and the first cathedral was begun in 648. In 871 Alfred the Great made Winchester capital of Wessex and it challenged Norwich as the country's second city. From 1250, however, it began a steady decline. The bishops of Winchester remained wealthy and important figures, but Winchester itself became a quiet, minor country town.

And so you'll find it today. As a result of its history, though, Winchester can sometimes seem to have its head in the past more than almost any other city in Britain. Its medieval core is still the heart of town – neat, compact and very easy to wander around. Within it there is a range of ancient buildings – from one of the oldest and grandest of English cathedrals to hole-in-the-wall churches, fortified gates, the great hall of a royal palace and a 15th-century watermill. In 1382 Winchester acquired the last of its major medieval institutions when Bishop William of Wykeham founded **Winchester College**. This public school remains peculiarly prominent in the life of the town, especially south of the Cathedral Close.

After centuries in the economic doldrums, Winchester recently stirred into life. As a greenfield city of the 1980s it became attractive to small, clean, prosperous high-tech industries. At the same time, the city's ancient tranquillity and the prettiness of the surrounding villages made them magnets for commuters and second-home buyers. Consequently, Winchester and the surrounding area is now frequently cited as having the highest standard of living in Britain. This would explain the top-of-the-range four-wheel-drives, the influx of fine-dining restaurants and the increased number of barns renovated to luxurious homes.

Test Valley

Some 16 miles to the north-west is **Andover**, unloved ever since it was earmarked in the 1960s as a destination for 'London overspill'. Around it, though, are villages that seem lost in the countryside, especially in the valley of the **Test**, which runs due south. This is one of the most renowned trout-fishing rivers in Britain; it also has a beautiful footpath, the Test Way, which runs alongside, passing characterful villages with character-filled pubs, including **Wherwell**, **Longstock** and **King's Somborne**, from where another path (the Clarendon Way) leads to Winchester or Salisbury.

Shortly before the Test enters Southampton it passes through the old market town of **Romsey**, the prime attractions of which (apart from some rather twee teashops) are the 12th-century **Romsey Abbey**, one of the finest intact examples of Norman architecture in England; **King John's House**, which, despite the name, is a non-royal but remarkably complete medieval house; and **Broadlands**, family home to Lord Mountbatten.

East of Winchester, beyond the M3, the A31 runs up to the valley of the Itchen. A turn south on to the A272 Petersfield road, three miles from the city, will take you to the wonderfully named **Cheesefoot Head**, a giant ridge where the road crosses the South Downs Way. The views are spectacular, and it makes a good point for a shortish walk along the footpath.

After seven miles, the main road runs into **New Alresford**. A classically pretty old country town (the 'New' dates to the 13th century), it has a wide main street (to house a medieval sheep market), a riverside walk, a quirky range of shops and a disproportionate number of pubs. Many of its visitors are railway buffs, drawn by the Watercress Line.

South of Winchester, beyond the **Marwell Zoological Park**, the main point of interest is **Bishop's Waltham**, a likeable, unprettified, mostly Georgian town. For nearly 1,000 years it was the property of the bishops of Winchester, who built one of their many residences there, **Bishop's Waltham Palace**.

A little further south is **Wickham**, birthplace of William of Wykeham, founder of Winchester College. Although only a big village (or small town), it has a peculiarly large main square, created in 1268 to fit a market fair. Surrounded by buildings dating from medieval times and the Georgian and Victorian periods, it gives Wickham an oddly grand, urban look. It stands at the southern end of the valley of the River Meon, another trout stream. The valley contains some of the prettiest riverbank-and-hollyhocks villages in Hampshire, such as **Droxford**, **Exton** and **West Meon**. A long-distance path, the Wayfarers' Walk, runs through Exton north to New Alresford and south to the coast. Just north of Exton, the A32 valley road crosses the South Downs Way, which you can use to climb Old Winchester Hill, a massive down with the remains of an Iron Age fort at its top.

Instead of seeking out a specific destination, it can be just as enjoyable to wander between villages with no particular plan. Places such as **Upham**, **Owslebury**, **Beauworth** (just off the South Downs Way) and **Cheriton** make particularly pleasant spots to lose a few hours.

Winchester hosts several festivals, most in July: the **Hat Fair Street Theatre Festival** occupies the first weekend, followed by the all-the-arts **Winchester Festival**; at the end of July there is the **Southern Cathedrals Festival**, with lashings of choral music in the cathedral. In late September Winchester also hosts a **Literature Festival**.

Winchester is also a junction of long-distance footpaths. It is the westernmost point of the South Downs Way, which runs to Eastbourne, and the Pilgrim's Way, to Canterbury. The Itchen Way runs south to join the Solent Way, which goes to Southampton and Portsmouth, and the Clarendon Way goes west to Salisbury.

What to see & do

Tourist Information Centres

Town Mill House, 20 Bridge Street, Andover, SP10 1BL (01264 324320/www.visit-testvalley.org.uk). **Open** *Apr-Sept* 9.30am-5pm Mon-Sat. *Oct-Mar* 10am-4pm Mon-Sat.

By train from London

Trains to **Winchester** and **Portsmouth & Southsea** leave **Waterloo** every 15mins. Journey time to **Winchester** is between 55mins and 1hr 5mins, and 1hr 30mins to **Portsmouth**. Info: www.swtrains.co.uk.

Clarence Esplanade, Southsea, Portsmouth, PO5 3PB (023 9282 6722/www.visitportsmouth.co.uk). **Open** *Apr-Oct* 9.30am-5.45pm daily. *Nov-Mar* 9.30am-5.15pm daily.

13 Church Street, Romsey, SO51 8BT (01794 512987/www.visit-testvalley.org.uk). **Open** *Apr-July, Sept* 9.30am-5pm Mon-Sat. *Aug* 9.30am-5pm Mon-Sat; 2-5pm Sun. *Oct-Mar* 10am-4pm Mon-Sat.

The Guildhall, The Broadway, Winchester, SO23 9LJ (01962 840500/www.visitwinchester.co.uk). **Open** *May-Sept* 9.30am-5.30pm Mon-Sat; 11am-4pm Sun. *Oct-Apr* 10am-5pm Mon-Sat.

Bishop's Waltham Palace

Bishop's Waltham, Southampton, SO32 1DH (01489 892460/www.english-heritage.org.uk). **Open** *Apr-Sept* 10am-6pm daily. Last entry 5.30pm. *Oct* 10am-5pm daily. Last entry 4.30pm. Closed Nov-Mar. **Admission** (EH) £2.50; £1.30-£1.90 concessions; free under-5s. **Credit** MC, V.

This once-lavish residence of Winchester's medieval bishops was begun in the 1130s and has since been extended many times. However, the whole caboodle was destroyed in 1644 by Parliamentarians during the Civil War after it had been used as a Royalist stronghold. Much of the remaining palace can now only be traced in the foundations that remain, but the surviving flint walls, looming up in the middle of the town, are impressively atmospheric.

Charles Dickens' Birthplace Museum

393 Old Commercial Road, Portsmouth, PO1 4QL (02392 827261/www.charlesdickensbirthplace.co.uk). **Open** *Apr-Sept* 10am-5.30pm daily. *Oct* 10am-5pm daily. Closed Nov-Feb except 7 Feb (10am-5pm). Last entry 30mins before closing. **Admission** £2.50; £1.50-£1.80 concessions; free under-13s with full-paying adult. **No credit cards**.

Bishop's Waltham Palace.

Hampshire & Isle of Wight

Portsmouth Historic Dockyard features a collection of famous and fascinating flagships.

The great novelist actually had few memories of this house as his father, a navy clerk, moved the family on not long after Charles was born in 1812. It is, however, a charmingly preserved replica of the first home lived in by John and Elizabeth Dickens after their marriage in 1809 and it also holds several relics of the writer's later life. Normally closed in winter, it opens specially on 7 February, Dickens' birthday.

Hospital of St Cross
St Cross Road, Winchester, SO23 9SD (01962 851375). **Open** *Apr-Oct* 9.30am-5pm Mon-Sat. *Nov-Mar* 10.30am-3.30pm Mon-Sat. **Admission** £2; 50p-£1.25 concessions. **Credit** MC, V.
The medieval almshouse of St Cross, about a mile south of Winchester town centre, is the oldest still-functioning house of charity in the country (founded in 1136). The towering Norman church is 12th century; most of the other buildings were added in the 1440s. They have a marvellous tranquillity. St Cross still houses a religious community and hungry visitors can ask at the porter's lodge for the 'Wayfarer's Dole' of free bread and ale.

Marwell Zoological Park
Colden Common, Winchester, SO21 1JH (07626 943163/01962 777407/www.marwell.org.uk). **Open** *Apr-Oct* 10am-6pm daily. Last entry 4.30pm. *Nov-Mar* 10am-4pm daily. Last entry 2.30pm. **Admission** £11; £7.50-£9 concessions. **Credit** MC, V.
A family favourite, with some 1,000 animals living in 100 acres of parkland. The breeding and sustaining of endangered species is a park speciality, but there's also a kid's zoo, picnic areas, miniature railway and so on. Among the most popular attractions are World of Lemurs and Penguin World. It's off the B2177 road to Bishop's Waltham, seven miles south of Winchester. Phone for details of the special events.

Portsmouth Historic Dockyard (Flagship Portsmouth)
Porter's Lodge, 1-7 College Road, HM Naval Base, Portsmouth, PO1 3LJ (info line 02392 861512/ visitors' centre 02392 722562/861512/www.historic

dockyard.co.uk). **Open** *Apr-Oct* 10am-5.30pm daily. *Nov-Mar* 10am-5pm daily. Last entry 1hr before closing. **Admission** (each attraction) *HMS Victory & Royal Naval Museum, HMS Warrior, Mary Rose Museum, Action Stations* £9.50; £8 concessions. *Royal Naval Museum only* £4.50; £3.50 concessions. *Harbour Tour* £4 £3.50 concessions. *All inclusive ticket* (all attractions; 1 entry per attraction; unlimited life) £14.85; £11.90 concessions. *Season ticket* (all attractions; unlimited entry for 2 years; special benefits) £27; £22.70 concessions. *All attractions* free under-5s. **Credit** MC, V.
Portsmouth's star historic attraction contains four main elements: Nelson's flagship HMS *Victory*; the world's first all-iron warship, HMS *Warrior*; the remains of Henry VIII's *Mary Rose*, preserved in a fascinating visitors' centre; and the Royal Navy Museum. The old dockyard buildings are of interest in themselves, and with the 'all ships' ticket you can return any time within a year to catch up on parts you have missed. Fans of the nautical and/or military naturally have many other places to choose from around Portsmouth, such as the D-Day Museum, the Royal Marines Museum, the Royal Navy Submarine Museum and more. Information from Portsmouth Tourist Information Centre, *see p107.*

Spinnaker Tower
Gunwharf Quays, Portsmouth Harbour.
Set to open in July 2004, Spinnaker Tower is the centrepiece of a massive Portsmouth Harbour rejuvenation project. Towering 541ft high with an observation gallery at the top and the choice of high-speed or panoramic glass lift, the tower will offer spectacular views over more than 23 miles. Information from Portsmouth Tourist Information Centre, *see p107.*

Watercress Line – Mid-Hants Railway
The Station, New Alresford, SO24 9JG (01962 733810/www.watercressline.co.uk). **Timetable** phone for details. **Tickets** *Unlimited travel for 1 day* £9; £4-£8 concessions. *Single tickets* £5; £2-£4.50 concessions; free under-3s. **Credit** MC, V.

The ten-mile rural rail line between Alresford and Alton was cast aside by British Rail in 1973, but has been kept going by determined local volunteers. It boasts an all-steam fleet, with trains every Sunday and most Saturdays from February to October, and almost daily from June to August and during December. The line also offers special trips such as silver-service dining-car lunches and cream teas, Thomas the Tank Engine tours, and so on. The line has played parts in umpteen period television programmes.

Winchester Cathedral & Close

The Close, Winchester, SO23 9LS (01962 857200/ www.winchester-cathedral.org.uk). **Open** *Cathedral* 8.30am-6pm Mon-Sat; 8.30am-5pm Sun. *Triforium & library* Easter-Oct 2-4.30pm Mon; 11am-4.30pm Tue-Fri; 10.30am-4.30pm Sat. Nov, Dec, Mar 11am-3.30pm Wed, Sat. Jan, Feb 11am-3.30pm Sat. *Visitors' centre* 9.30am-5.30pm daily. **Admission** *Cathedral* free; recommended donation £3.50. *Triforium & library* £1; 50p concessions. **Credit** AmEx, MC, V.

Winchester's majestic Norman cathedral was begun in 1079. To build it, the Norman conquerors swept aside the old Saxon cathedral, the outline of which can still be seen in the Close. This cathedral contained the first tomb of St Swithun, Bishop of Winchester 837-61; as every book on Winchester has to remind you, if it rains on his feast day (15 July), it's due to pour down for 40 days thereafter. In the present cathedral, the beautifully simple transepts are those of the 11th-century building; the huge Gothic nave was added in the 14th century and is the longest in Europe. Inside, the cathedral has too many treasures to detail here, among them 12th-century wall paintings in the Chapel of the Holy Sepulchre, and the grave of Jane Austen. Don't miss the climb up to the Triforium, which gives a spectacular view of the transepts and contains a remarkable collection of carvings in stone and wood; in the 17th-century library the centrepiece is the Winchester Bible, a dazzling illuminated manuscript that was begun in 1160. Informative guided tours of the cathedral are available; ask at the information desk.

The other buildings around the Close are almost as historic. The Deanery dates from the 13th century; next to it, Dean Garnier's Garden contains the remains of a Gothic cloister. The huge half-timbered Cheyney Court, by the southern gate of the Close, was originally the bishops' courthouse. As a change from the medieval, around the Close there is also now an interesting collection of entirely modern sculpture. Ask at the cathedral information desk about tours of the Close buildings, most of which are not normally open to visitors.

Winchester City Mill

Bridge Street, Winchester, SO23 8EJ (01962 870057/www.nationaltrust.org.uk/winchestercitymill). **Open** *Mar* 11am-5pm Sat, Sun. *Apr-June, Sept-Dec* 11am-5pm Wed-Sun. *July, Aug* 11am-5pm daily. Last entry 4.30pm. Closed Jan, Feb. **Admission** (NT) £2; £1 concessions. **Credit** MC, V.

Established in the 15th century and last rebuilt in 1744, this grand watermill is a very impressive example of early technology, with spectacular timbering and a riverside garden behind it. Run by the National Trust, it also houses a video exhibition on the working of the mill, a shop and Winchester's youth hostel.

Winchester Great Hall & Westgate

Great Hall *Castle Avenue, Winchester, SO23 8UL (01962 846476/www.hants.gov.uk/discover/places/ great-hall.html).* **Open** 9am-5pm daily. **Admission** free; donations welcome.
Westgate *High Street, Winchester, SO23 8UL (01962 869864/www.winchester.gov.uk).* **Open** *Feb-Mar* 10am-4pm Tue-Sat; noon-4pm Sun. *Apr-Oct* 10am-5pm Mon-Sat; noon-5pm Sun. Closed Nov-Jan. **Admission** free; donations welcome.

One of Winchester's lesser-known gems, Henry III's spectacular Great Hall (1222-35) is the last remaining part of what was for 500 years one of England's principal royal palaces. Its most famous feature is the 'Round Table' hanging on one wall, believed to have been made in the 13th century and repainted for Henry VIII in 1522. In the small museum in the Westgate there's a 16th-century painted ceiling from Winchester College, but all eyes are drawn to the 17th-century graffiti, carved by prisoners locked up in the gate.

Winchester Military Museums

Peninsula Barracks, Romsey Road, Winchester, SO23 8TS.
Gurkha Museum *01962 828536/www.thegurkha museum.co.uk.* **Admission** £1.50; 50p-75p concessions.
Light Infantry Museum *01962 828550.* **Admission** free.
King's Royal Hussars Museum *01962 828541/www.hants.gov.uk/discover/places/royal-hussars.html.* **Admission** free.
Royal Green Jackets Museum *01962 828549/ www.royalgreenjackets.co.uk.* **Admission** £2; £1 concessions.
Royal Hampshire Regiment Museum *01962 863658.* **Admission** free.
Military buffs can spend the whole day in Winchester going round the Peninsula Barracks. Admission times vary; phone the individual sights for details. None of the museums accepts credit cards.

Wolvesey Castle (Old Bishop's Palace)

College Street, Winchester, SO23 9NB (01962 854766/www.english-heritage.org.uk). **Open** *Apr-Sept* 10am-6pm daily. *Oct* 10am-5pm daily. Closed Nov-Mar. **Admission** (EH) £2.20; £1.10-£1.70 concessions. **Credit** MC, V.

The 12th-century main residence of the bishops of Winchester was one of the largest medieval palaces in England. Like Bishop's Waltham it was mostly destroyed in the 1640s and is now a rambling ruin.

Where to stay

Enmill Barn

Enmill Lane, Pitt, Winchester, SO22 5QR (01962 856740/www.enmill-barn.co.uk). **Rates** £30-£35 single; £40 single occupancy; £55-£60 double/twin. **Rooms** 1 single; 1 double (en suite); 1 twin (en suite). **No credit cards.**
Top end in B&B quality, but accessibly priced and very welcoming, this huge converted barn just two miles outside Winchester has been designed specifically for

guests. Ideally placed for walking in the South Downs, it comes complete with proper pool table, brick fireplace, big sofas and an ornamental cider press. The family lives in an adjoining barn in the 'east wing' (guests occupy the 'west wing'). Each of the three rooms (double, twin and single) are spacious, clean and interesting, equipped with fridges filled with nibbles, fresh milk and beverages (put 50p in a jar). Breakfast includes duck eggs from the neighbouring farm in the full English, as well as a choice of yoghurts and fresh fruit. Guests also have access to the on-site tennis courts. Children over five welcome. All bedrooms are no-smoking.

5 Clifton Terrace

Winchester, SO22 5BJ (01962 890053/fax 01962 626566/www.s-h-systems.co.uk/hotels/cliftonterrace). **Rates** £50 single occupancy; £60 double; £60-£80 family room. **Rooms** 1 double; 1 family. **No credit cards.**

A friendly, professional townhouse B&B, minutes from the train station, Clifton Terrace has two immaculate, self-contained bedrooms on the lower floors, one with its own entrance. Both are large, white and elegantly decorated with stylish bathrooms. The house is bright and airy with large windows and white shutters. Breakfast is served in the dining room upstairs, with views down the hill over central Winchester. Lovely. Children over five welcome. No smoking throughout.

Fortitude Cottage

51 Broad Street, Old Portsmouth, PO1 2JD (tel/fax 02392 823748/www.fortitudecottage.co.uk). **Rates** £30-£35 single occupancy; £50 double/twin. **Rooms** 2 double (en suite); 2 twin (1 en suite). **Credit** MC, V.

The Isle of Wight ferry looms large over the breakfast room of this cosy little B&B, positioned on the main quayside street of Spice Island. Fortitude Cottage is a white-painted terraced house unsurprisingly adorned with ornamental sailors, yachts and suspended wooden fish. The four bedrooms (two double, two twin) are spotlessly clean and white. For the most space, best views and an outside terrace, request the en suite top-floor double (room No.4). No smoking throughout.

Hotel du Vin

14 Southgate Street, Winchester, SO23 9EF (01962 841414/fax 01962 842458/www.hotelduvin.com). **Rates** £109-£120 double; £119-£175 superior double; £135-£160 garden double/twin; £185-£225 four-poster/suite. Breakfast £13.50 (Eng), £9.50 (cont). **Rooms** (all en suite) 5 double; 13 superior double/twin; 4 garden double/twin; 1 four-poster/suite. **Credit** AmEx, DC, MC, V.

Hotel du Vin is not about superfluous frills, just sober luxury in the form of simple fabrics and comforting linens. Each of the 23 subtly dressed rooms is sponsored by well-known champagne, cognac or wine houses such as Veuve Cliquot (don't worry, its room's not orange) and Laroche. Towels are huge, beds wide and baths deep. Breakfast is not included in the room rate, but the artistically arranged array of hot croissants, pain au chocolat and full English breakfast in the eclectically dressed, sunshine-filled bistro is worth getting up for. Staff, mainly French, are young and friendly, the atmosphere casual (dress as you please) and the clientele a mix of tourists and locals up for a quality bite. Children welcome. For bistro, *see p112*.

Priory Inn

Winchester Road, Bishop's Waltham, SO32 1BE (01489 891313/fax 01489 896370). **Rates** £30 single occupancy; £55 double/twin. **Rooms** (both en suite) 1 double; 1 twin. **Credit** MC, V.

An unfussy, friendly locals' pub on the north-west road out of Bishop's Waltham, the Priory has two spotless, light and comfortable rooms with good-sized bathrooms, TVs and tea-making facilities. It might lack the character and charm of other B&Bs in the area, but it's more reasonably priced. Breakfast is served in the bar. At lunchtime and in the evenings there is a wide choice of grub, with a steaming Thai buffet every other Saturday night. Children welcome. All bedrooms are no-smoking.

M3 J12; follow signs to Marwell Zoological Park; turn left on to B2117; inn is on the left on the way into Bishop's Waltham.

Westgate Hotel

2 Romsey Road, Winchester, SO23 8TP (tel/fax 01962 820222). **Rates** £65-£80 single occupancy/double/twin. **Rooms** 8 double/twin (6 en suite). **Credit** MC, V.

A cheerful, family-run pub/hotel located in a prime position overlooking the Great Hall and town centre. Tatty from the outside, a tad dingy in the pub below, the Westgate has eight rooms, each named after famous Winchester-ites, some with wrought iron balconies or curved French doors, high ceilings and thick carpets. Don't expect luxury but do expect a threadbare elegance, heavy drapes and brass chandeliers. Breakfast is in a sunny dining room on the first floor. Lunch and evenings, high-quality, local gastro-nosh is served in the pub, along with real ales (Flowers IPA, Ansells Bitter). A popular drinking spot for barristers from the courts next door.

Wykeham Arms

75 Kingsgate Street, Winchester, SO23 9PE (01962 853834/fax 01962 854411/www.gales.co.uk). **Rates** £50 single; £80-£99 single occupancy; £90-£95 double/twin; £120 suite. **Rooms** (all en suite) 2 single; 3 twin; 8 double; 1 suite. **Credit** AmEx, DC, MC, V.

One of Winchester's most historic inns, open since 1755, the Wykeham Arms is so steeped in character you could bottle it for export. Every inch of wall and rickety beam is crammed with memorabilia: hanging tankards, mortar boards, a mitre once belonging to Bishop Pike and plenty more. There are fourteen rooms in total, seven upstairs, seven more in St George's Annexe, an 18th-century house across the narrow street. All have been modernised (leaving the quirks), bar the opulently rouge Hamilton Room, which, by popular demand, has been left as is. Best rooms are the Nelson, with a four-poster bed and the secluded two-storey Bakehouse Suite, overlooking the leafy courtyard. All bedrooms are no-smoking.

M3 J9; follow signs to Winchester over 3 roundabouts into Garnier Road; right at the T junction into Kingsgate; pub is on the left.

Where to eat & drink

Winchester has a big choice of eating places, some of them of a very high class indeed. For good-value breakfasts, lunches or snacks, the **Cathedral Refectory** (01962 857200) in the Visitors' Centre is a good bet; it's licensed, with

Wonder Walker

Nine hundred years ago, Winchester Cathedral was constructed on top of a quagmire. For hundreds of years this went unnoticed until, in 1905, large cracks started appearing on the east and south sides of the cathedral and the outside walls developed a 2.5-degree lean. Brought in to investigate, John Colson, the consulting cathedral architect, warned: 'Little or no attention has been paid to the really serious condition of some portions of the fabric, which if not somewhat immediately taken in hand, may lead to disaster.'

It was discovered that the cathedral had been built on timber foundations. These were rotting, and just 16 feet below the peat and chalky marl was a water-charged gravel bed. Civil engineer Francis Fox, responsible for constructing the London Underground, was brought in to fix the problem. After several attempts at the drawing board, he realised that the only option was to employ a diver. William Walker, six feet tall and 14 stone, was considered the 'best man for the task'.

Walker's job was to dig out the rotting timbers and replace them with bags of cement and concrete blocks. Every day, six hours a day, for six years, Walker worked in the pitch-black murky water until 25,800 bags of concrete and 114,900 concrete blocks had been laid, £113,000 spent and the cathedral was secured.

George V honoured Walker with a Royal Victoria Medal as 'the man who saved the cathedral with his two hands'. In 1964, in celebration of the 50th anniversary of Walker's achievements, the lord lieutenant of Hampshire offered to finance the construction of a statue of the diver, commissioning Sir Charles Wheeler, president of the Royal Academy.

When the statue was unveiled, Walker's relatives were astonished to see not the broad, moustachioed face of Walker but the sharp features of civil engineer Fox. A group photo had been given to Sir Charles Wheeler and he had sculpted the wrong man. Despite not actually being William Walker, the bronze sculpture was erected in the cathedral with the inscription: 'In honour of William Walker, the diver who saved the cathedral with his two hands.' It remained on show for 37 years.

In 2001, after much campaigning by the Historical Diving Society, a brand new statue was unveiled, this time of the correct William Walker. It now stands in the cathedral.

plenty of choice for vegetarians. The **Forte Tea Rooms** (78 Parchment Street, 01962 856840) offers a varied, well-priced menu including pasta dishes and home-made cakes. For those seeking a stiffer tipple, the **Moloko Bar** (31B The Square, 01962 849236) serves warm, filling paninis until 5pm, and thereafter reinvents itself as a lively bar.

Of the many pubs, the tiny **Eclipse Inn** (23 The Square, 01962 865676), once the rectory of St Lawrence's church, has reliable pub nosh, but the **Old Vine**, also on the Square (01962 854616), is bigger and has a wider choice. Near the river, the **Mash Tun** on Eastgate Street (01962 861440) is a student favourite. In the Test Valley, the **Peat Spade** in Longstock (01264 810612) has excellent organic fare. Among the most enjoyable places to visit south and east of Winchester are the **White Horse** in Droxford (South Hill, 01489 877490), which also has accommodation; the historic and ancient **Brushmakers' Arms** in Upham (Shoe Lane, 01489 860231); the even more

ancient 250-year-old **Milbury's** in Beauworth (01962 771248); and the **Globe on the Lake** in Alresford (The Soke, 01962 732294).

Wickham has a great local caff, the **Wickham Tea House** (The Square, 01329 835017) open for breakfast and lunch every day, with tables on the Square. Portsmouth, true to form, has a clutch of high-quality (well-priced) fish and seafood restaurants. For fine dining try **Les Copains d'Abord** in Leckford (01264 810738) or the **Greyhound** in Stockbridge (31 The High Street, 01264 810833). For barbecued buffalo burgers or roasted hog, visit one of Hampshire's weekly farmers' markets (01962 845135/www.hampshirefarmers markets.co.uk). The UK's largest is hosted by Winchester on the last Sunday of every month.

American Bar Restaurant

58 White Hart Road, Portsmouth, PO1 2JA (023 9281 1585/www.americanbar.co.uk). **Food served** noon-10pm Mon-Thur, Sun; noon-10.30pm Fri, Sat. **Main courses** £8.95-£16.50. **Credit** AmEx, DC, MC, V.

The **Wykeham Arms** is a local institution.

The only evidence of America in this garishly painted seafood restaurant is a spiel on the menu purporting that the building was once a prison for convicts en route to the colonies. Besides that, it's a Gallic/Anglo blend right down to the daytrippers from Cherbourg and the fish and chips. Service might be lacking in smiles, but yellow walls and nautical knick-knacks cheer up the smoky bar with dining off to one side. It's directly opposite a fish market, so there need be no quibbles about freshness. Starters include hot garlic prawns or French fish soup, with fisherman's pie or meltingly tender salmon among the mains. A large range of non-fishy dishes is also included, as is a list of more than 135 wines.

Chesil Rectory

1 Chesil Street, Winchester, SO23 0HU (01962 851555). **Food served** 7-9.30pm Tue-Fri; noon-2pm, 7-9.30pm Sat. **Set lunch** £35 3 courses. **Set dinner** £45 6 courses. **Credit** AmEx, DC, MC, V.
If you manage to avoid concussion from one of the antique beams, then expect an evening in this 15th-century building to be a glorious experience. The decor is minimalist – white walls and black beams – and the clientele casual. Each new six-course menu designed by chef-proprietor Philip Storey spends three months in development. Every course is small enough to whet the appetite for the next. Pork and black pudding with mustard mash was artistically stacked and drizzled with apple butter sauce. The 'refresher' was a green tea and lime mousse served through a straw. The finale a (very) rich chocolate fondant with peanut butter ice-cream.

Hotel du Vin Bistro

14 Southgate Street, Winchester, SO23 9EF (01962 841414/www.hotelduvin.com). **Food served** noon-1.45pm, 7-9.45pm daily. **Main courses** £14.50. **Credit** AmEx, DC, MC, V.
One of Winchester's best places to eat and drink. Every inch of the distressed gold walls is filled with photos, prints or paintings linked to food, drink and drunken-ness. Unsurprisingly, then, by night the mood is lively, the air filled with the smell of wine, cigars and firewood. The menu blends the contemporary – pavé of salmon with wilted pak choi and red peppers – with the classics – corned beef hash with fried egg and HP sauce. Service is relaxed but efficient and the sommelier's suggested wines were a helpful guide for manoeuvring through the extensive list.

Lemon Sole

123 High Street, Portsmouth, PO1 2HW (023 9281 1303/www.lemonsole.co.uk). **Food served** noon-2pm, 6-9.45pm Mon-Sat. **Main courses** prices vary according to availability. **Set lunch** £8.95 2 courses. **Credit** AmEx, DC, MC, V.
Choose your fish from the ice cabinet, your wine from the rack and your bread from the basket, then kick back and tuck in. This winning formula for fishophiles features a vast choice: bream, skate, tuna, blue spotted grouper, anything special caught that day or a medley of all. Fish can be char-grilled, poached, steamed or 'as you like'. Starters include whitebait served in a conch, moules or soup, with main dishes accompanied by a choice of chips, mash or new potatoes. Non-fishy folk are catered for but it's less fun. Decor is clean and simple, with (guess what) a fishy theme.

Loch Fyne

18 Jewry Street, Winchester, SO23 8RZ (01962 872930/fax 01962 872931/www.loch-fyne.com). **Food served** 9am-10pm Mon-Thur; 9am-11pm Fri, Sat; 10am-10pm Sun. **Main courses** £7.95-£39.95. **Set lunch** (Mon-Fri) £11.95 2 courses. **Credit** AmEx, MC, V.
In contrast to the 15th-century façade, Loch Fyne's interior is a stylishly modern set-up with chunky wooden tables and floor-to-ceiling windows overlooking an elegantly lit, leafy garden. Service is expert and speedy as you'd expect from a small chain that's garnered a decent reputation. Fish is the thing, of course (though there are steak and sausages too). On a recent visit, clam, pea and crab chowder was a good combo – creamy, with a generous amount of shellfish. To follow, poached smoked haddock with creamed spinach was meltingly tender. French wines dominate the menu with a keen focus on the organic and eco-friendly.

Wykeham Arms

75 Kingsgate Street, Winchester, SO23 9PE (01962 853834/www.gales.co.uk). **Food served** noon-2.30pm, 6.30-8.45pm Mon-Sat; noon-1.45pm Sun. **Main courses** £10.75-£15.50. **Set lunches** £14.50 2 courses, £18.50 3 courses. **Credit** AmEx, DC, MC, V.
The kooky Wykeham Arms is more institution than pub, frequented by the upper echelons of Winchester society: dons from Winchester College, judges and clergy at lunch and anyone else lucky enough to get a table for dinner. Most gather in Nelson's Bar for local ales (Gales). Dining, which could be in the Watchmakers Shop, Bishops Bar or V&A dining room, is a contemporary affair, with a daily changing menu that's big on local produc: roasted rack of Hampshire Down lamb with bacon and rosemary new potatoes or char-grilled 10oz ribeye steak on horseradish mash. Fish is also a popular feature. The wine list is vast and staff are young and laid-back.

The New Forest

Wonderful woods and water – but mind the horses.

Cross the border (and miserable traffic bottleneck) at Lyndhurst and you enter an enchanted forest where stocky ponies roam wild, grazing in leisurely fashion along unspoilt heathland roads, calmly oblivious to the cars queuing in their wake.

One of the most individual stretches of countryside in the south of England, the New Forest even retains its own government, the ancient Verderers' Court, which meets on the third Monday of every month at the Queen's

House in **Lyndhurst** to safeguard the sacred commoners' rights to pasture, cut firewood and let their pigs eat acorns.

Neither new nor really a forest, much of the area could more aptly be described as open heath, although the wooded parts do contain a notable variety of trees in their 145 or so square miles; among them are holly, yew, birch, Scots pine, oak and beech. Deer also abound, although it's the ponies who are the real kings of the road and give the area its character.

The historic towns and villages in the area throng with visitors, but it's always possible to get away from them all by taking a walk in the woods. Park the car and head off with a map; the **Forestry Commission** (023 8028 3141/www.forestry.gov.uk) provides details of walks, camping and disabled facilities within the forest. Cycling is another popular way to make the most of the scenery; there are plenty of traffic-free routes – and plenty of pubs to stop off at and recover from your exertions.

If you want to know more about the history of the area, or get up to date on forest issues, visit the **New Forest Museum and Visitor Centre** (023 8028 3914/www.newforest museum.org.uk) in Lyndhurst.

By train from London

To explore the New Forest properly you'll need your own transport, but a healthy alternative to driving is to take the train and hire bikes. Trains to **Ashurst New Forest** leave **Waterloo** every other hour (journey time 1hr 45mins to 2hrs). Trains to **Brockenhurst** leave **Waterloo** about every 20mins (journey time 1hr 30mins); change here for **Lymington** (which takes an additional 9mins). Info: www.southwestrains.co.uk.

Shipping news

Woodland isn't the area's only attraction. The nearby Solent makes it a popular sailing destination too, and hundreds of boats are moored on the Lymington river. **Lymington** itself is an ancient port that is famous for its saltworkings. From the always very busy main street you can walk down the pretty cobbled passageway to the quay and watch the nautical comings and goings. The tiny passageway is lined with twee little shops selling locally made ice-cream and knick-knacks, but the High Street has a good weekend market.

Wild things

If you're looking for a little more seclusion, the village of **Sway** nestles in the wide open heathland section of the forest, where you can drive, walk or cycle through beautiful open stretches of land teeming with plant and animal life (including darling foals that you'll want to take home). In fact, if flowers and furry friends are your thing, you're definitely in the right place. Gardens are a local mania – many hotels and guesthouses take as much pride in their grounds as their rooms and there are a number of open gardens to visit (**Spinners Garden**, Boldre, Lymington, 01590 673347; **Furzey Gardens**, Minstead, nr Lyndhurst, 023 8081 2464; **Exbury Gardens**, nr Beaulieu, 023 8089 1203; **Braxton Gardens**, Lymore Lane, Milford-on-Sea, 01590 642008), as well as the fab **New Forest Otter, Owl & Wildlife Conservation Park** (*see right*).

If the beach is more your bag, **Milford-on-Sea** in Christchurch Bay has a good beach for swimming and windsurfing, while the village is quieter and less yacht-ridden than Lymington. Georgian-fronted buildings, shops and pubs crowd around the tiny village green.

Montagus and corvettes

In the south-east corner of the forest, **Beaulieu** (pronounced 'Bewley') is home to the Montagu family, who have managed to stave off selling their ancestral home by creating a popular and unpretentious motoring museum. The village itself is gorgeous, with thatched and red-roofed dwellings clustered around the Beaulieu river. It's a lovely stroll from here along the river to **Buckler's Hard**, the single-street village where many of the ships in Nelson's fleet were cobbled together. The **Maritime Museum** (01590 616203) charts the history of this unique riverside community, and one cottage has been reconstructed to show how life would have been for those working for Nelson in 1793. Other cottages have been incorporated into the rebuilt **Master Builder's House Hotel** (*see p116*), which serves good lunches and drinks out in the garden overlooking the river.

Further east, a string of little villages known as the Waterside lines Southampton Water, the biggest being **Hythe**, from where the *Titanic* first sailed. **Fawley** and **Calshot** are also extremely pretty, with good walking and sailing areas, and **Lepe** has a great sandy beach, with views across the Solent.

What to see & do

Tourist Information Centre

New Forest Museum & Visitors' Centre, Main Car Park, Lyndhurst, SO43 7NY (023 8028 2269/www.thenewforest.co.uk). **Open** *July-Sept* 10am-5pm daily. *Aug* 10am-6pm daily. *Oct-June* 10am-5pm daily.

Bike hire

AA Bike Hire *Fern Glen, Gosport Lane, Lyndhurst, SO43 7BL (023 8028 3349/www. aabikehirenewforest.co.uk).*

Forest Leisure Cycling *Burley Village Centre, Burley, BH24 4AB (01425 403584/www. forestleisurecycling.co.uk).*

Forest Leisure Cycling *at the National Motor Museum, Beaulieu, SO42 7ZN (01590 611029).* **Open** 9am-5pm daily.

New Forest Cycle Experience *2-4 Brookley Road, Brockenhurst, SO42 7RR (01590 624204/ www.cyclex.co.uk).*

National Motor Museum

John Montagu Building, Beaulieu, SO42 7ZN (info 01590 612345/www.beaulieu.co.uk). **Open** 10am-5pm daily. Last entry 4.20pm. **Admission** £13.50; £6.50-£12.50 concessions. **Credit** MC, V.

The famous Palace House at Beaulieu has been in the Montagu family since 1538, and to keep it that way the current Lord Montagu has had to come up with a few visitor-friendly ideas to attract the tourists. The result is an odd mix of social and transport history, with lots to see and do. There are more than 250 vehicles on display here, and you can also wander down a 1930s street or motor through time in a space-age pod. In the house itself, you can chat to Victorian characters about the price of fish (literally). Or you can check out the exhibition of monastic life at the Domus of Beaulieu Abbey, dating from 1204, before switching centuries once again for a ride on the monorail.

New Forest Otter, Owl & Wildlife Park

Deerleap Lane, Longdown, Ashurst, SO40 4UH (023 8029 2408/www.ottersandowls.co.uk). **Open** *Jan, Feb* 10am-5.30pm Sat, Sun. *Mar-Dec* 10am-5pm daily (open until 6pm during school summer holidays). **Admission** £6.50; £4.50 concessions; free under-4s. **Credit** MC, V.

Set in 25 acres of ancient woodland right on the eastern edge of the New Forest, this excellent conservation park is home to Europe's largest collection of otters, owls and other indigenous wildlife. The lovely tree-lined walks make the most of the park's location, and there's also a tearoom to relax in afterwards.

Milford-on-Sea. *See p114.*

New Forest Water Park

Hucklesbrook Lakes, Ringwood Road, Fordingbridge, SP6 2EY (01425 656868/www.newforestwater park.co.uk). **Open** *Easter, Oct-mid Nov* 10am-9pm/dusk Sat, Sun. *May* 10am-9pm Wed-Sun. *June-Sept* 10am-9pm daily. Closed mid Nov-Easter. **Rates** Waterskiing (per tow) from £15. Aquarides £6. **Credit** DC, MC, V.

Get wet 'n' wild with all sorts of activities: waterskiing gives you four laps around the lake; aquarides are on inflatable bananas or tyres. Tuition is available; booking is advisable.

Paultons Park

Ower, nr Romsey, SO51 6AL (023 8081 4442/ www.paultonspark.co.uk). **Open** *Mid Mar-Oct* 10am-6.30pm daily. Last admission 4.30pm. *Nov, Dec* times vary; phone to check. Closed Jan-mid Mar. **Admission** £12.50; £11.50 concessions; free children under 1m. **Credit** MC, V.

It's hardly Disneyworld, but there's plenty to keep children amused here, with attractions such as the Runaway Train, Dinosaurland and, for younger kids, Tiny Tots Town. Restaurants, shops and a picnic area complete the picture. The park is located off Junction 2 of the M27.

Rockbourne Roman Villa

Rockbourne, Fordingbridge, SP6 3PG (01725 518541/www.hants.gov.uk/museum/rockbourne). **Open** *Apr-Sept* 10.30am-6pm daily. Last admission 5.30pm. Closed Oct-Mar. **Admission** £1.95; £1.10 concessions. **No credit cards.**

West of Fordingbridge is one of the largest Roman villas ever excavated in Britain. There's an informative display on Roman life here, followed by a well-signposted look around the site itself, highlights being the exposed underfloor heating of the bath houses built around AD 150 and the mosaic on the dining room floor.

Where to stay

Restaurants and pubs often have a few rooms to let in this very tourist-oriented area. The **Montagu Arms** in Beaulieu (01590 612324/ www.newforest-hotels.co.uk) and the **Nurse's Cottage** (*see p118*, rates £75 per person including dinner) are good examples. Contact the Tourist Information Centre for a full list.

Alderholt Mill

Sandleheath Road, Fordingbridge, SP6 1PU (01425 653130/fax 01425 652868/www.alderholtmill. co.uk). **Rates** £25 single; £25-£35 per person double/twin. **Rooms** (all en suite) 1 single; 3 double. **Credit** MC, V.

On a tributary of the Hampshire Avon just outside the pretty riverside town of Fordingbridge, Alderholt is a working watermill that dates back to the early 18th century. Sandra and Richard Harte's delightful B&B is situated in the Victorian workers' cottages on Monkey Island next door. Here you can fall asleep to the comforting distant sound of rushing water, and wake up to an excellent breakfast featuring bread freshly baked with home-ground flour. Rooms are plain, with decent showers and pleasant outlooks. In summer, barbecues

are sometimes held in the sweet back garden overlooking water-meadows. The mill is open to the public (weekends only) and cream teas are served on the front patio. There are also two basic but comfortable self-catering flats for two. All in all, a secluded treasure and very good value. Children over eight and dogs are welcome but there is no smoking throughout.
Follow signs to Sandleheath from Fordingbridge; beyond the post office in Sandleheath, turn left at crossroads; downhill in the direction of the brown sign for the mill.

Chewton Glen

Christchurch Road, New Milton, BH25 6QS (01425 275341/fax 01425 272310/www.chewtonglen.com). **Rates** £250-£275 double; £340-£365 superior double; £480-£695 suite. **Rooms** (all en suite) 16 double/twin; 16 superior double; 31 suites. Breakfast £20 (Eng); £15.50 (cont). **Credit** AmEx, DC, MC, V.

Despite the undeniably no-holds-barred luxury of Chewton Glen – the deep pile carpets, heavy drapes, new 17m swimming pool, three tennis courts, croquet lawn, golf course and numerous luxurious touches in each well-appointed room – the overall vibe is one of bland corporate comfort. Out and out pampering is guaranteed (it's what you pay for), but somehow it's all less than joyful – the kind of place where Alan Partridge would come to die. Children over six welcome. For the restaurant, *see p118*.
M3/M27 towards Bournemouth; turn left (3 miles after J1) to Emery Down; at T-junction take A35 towards Christchurch; after 8 miles turn left at staggered junction; take second left after Walkford into Chewton Farm Road.

Master Builder's House Hotel

Buckler's Hard, Beaulieu, SO42 7XB (01590 616253/fax 01590 616297/www.themasterbuilders. co.uk). **Rates** £125 single occupancy; £125-£265 double/twin. **Rooms** (all en suite) 25 double. **Credit** MC, V.

Probably the best-located hotel in the area, the refurbished Master Builder's House occupies an absurdly picturesque spot on the banks of the Beaulieu river at the end of the single grassy street that is Buckler's Hard. Once the day trippers have left, guests and yachters from the nearby marina have this peaceful haven pretty much to themselves. Inside, the hotel is decked out in the Best Western version of country house style and there are six particularly 'superior rooms' with splendid views of the river. There's a formal Riverview Restaurant as well as a cheaper, popular pub/bar and pleasant outside terrace. There's also a little thatched self-catering or fully serviced cottage at the bottom of the garden. Children welcome. Pets by arrangement.
M3/M27 towards Bournemouth; at Junction 1 take A337 to Lyndhurst from where the B3056 goes to Beaulieu; follow signs from here to Buckler's Hard.

Stanwell House Hotel

14 High Street, Lymington, SO41 9AA (01590 677123/fax 01590 677756/www.stanwellhouse hotel.co.uk). **Rates** £85 single occupancy; £110 double/twin; £130 four-poster; £150-£160 suites. **Rooms** (all en suite) 7 twin; 12 double; 2 four-posters; 6 suites. **Credit** AmEx, DC, MC, V.

In a prime position on Lymington's High Street, this is a rambling coaching inn offering decent bedrooms, idiosyncratic decoration and lively public areas. There's a bistro/restaurant serving Modern European dishes

Hurst Castle

Occupying the very tip of a shingle spit that extends almost two miles into the Solent from Milford-on-Sea, **Hurst Castle** has spectacular views and a warren of atmospheric rooms to explore. The forbidding-looking fortress was built by Henry VIII in 1544 as one of a chain of coastal defences. It guards the narrow entrance to the Solent at a point where the ebb and flow of tides create strong currents, putting would-be invaders at the castle's mercy and protecting the important ports of Southampton and Portsmouth. During the Civil War, Charles I was held prisoner here and later the castle was extensively modernised by the Victorians. During World War II it was manned with coastal gun batteries and searchlights. Today, its lighthouse continues to guide vessels through the hazardous western approaches of the Solent through the Needles Channel. Back on land, it's an enjoyably blustery, muscle-toning walk along the spit out to the castle, but you can also take a boat through the salt marsh nature reserve to the castle from Keyhaven.

Hurst Castle
Nr Milford-on-Sea, SO41 0QU (01590 642344/www.hurst-castle.co.uk/ www.english-heritage.org.uk). **Open** *Apr-Sept* 10am-5.30pm daily. *Oct* 10am-4pm daily. Closed Nov-Mar. **Admission** £2.80; £1.60-£2.50 concessions. **No credit cards**.

Ferry times
Apr-Oct departs Keyhaven Quay on the hr from 10am daily; returns from Hurst Castle on the half hr until 5.30pm daily. Closed Nov-Mar. **Tickets** (EH) £3.60 return; £2.20-£3.30 concessions. **No credit cards**.

such as corn-fed chicken with puy lentils, or rump of lamb with goat's cheese and olives, a street-front bar and a relaxed, flagstoned conservatory filled with plants and velvet cushions in lurid shades. There's even a pretty garden at the back. Staff are pleasant and helpful. Children and pets are welcome.
M3/M27 towards Bournemouth; at Junction 1 take A337 via Lyndhurst for Lymington.

Westover Hall
Park Lane, Milford-on-Sea, SO41 0PT (01590 643044/fax 01590 644490/www.westoverhall hotel.com). **Rates** £90 single; £145 double/twin; £200 half-tester/superior double; £200-£250 family room. **Rooms** (all en suite) 1 single; 8 double/twin; 3 superior double; 1 half-tester; 1 family. **Credit** AmEx, DC, MC, V.
Worth a visit for its commanding view of the Needles alone, Westover Hall also offers bags of character and a very pleasant atmosphere. It's a family-run business where the family takes great pains to make guests feel at home with the minimum of fuss or pretence. There's a bright, sunny bar and restaurant, a comfortable sitting room with giant sofas to sprawl on and a panelled, galleried hall that acts as a hub. Decor pays sympathetic rather than slavish homage to the 19th-century surroundings, with many modern flourishes. Rooms (the Needles, the Wight Room or the Crow's Nest) are comfortably kitted out with hairdryers, ironing boards, modern bathrooms and Molton Brown toiletries. Breakfasts run to fresh fruit and cracking croissants as well as a superior cooked variety. Children and pets welcome (pets at £10 per night). All bedrooms are no-smoking. For the restaurant, *see p118*.
J1 off M27; take A337 to Lymington; after Lymington follow signs to Milford-on-Sea and B3058; hotel is on clifftop after Milford-on-Sea.

Where to eat & drink

A good place to stop if you're cycling through the forest, the **Red Lion** (01590 673177) in Boldre is an archetypal country pub with a nice garden. Also worth seeking out is the pretty **George** (Bridge Street, Fordingbridge, 01425 652040), which has a terrace overlooking the river. In Lymington, **Egan's** (24 Gosport Street, 01590 676165) is a friendly bistro that's very popular among locals.

Chequers
Lower Woodside, Lymington, SO41 8AH (01590 673415/www.chequersinn.com). **Food served** noon-2pm, 7-9.30pm Sat; noon-9pm Sun. **Main courses** £5.50-£12.90. **Credit** MC V.
This hard-to-find pub is absurdly popular. On the edge of town, towards one of Lymington's marinas, the small place gets packed with sailing types who come to eat the above-average grub served in the restaurant and marquee at the back. In summer, tables spill out into an alfresco bar and courtyard strung with lights that has heaters to stave off the chill. Roast lamb with redcurrant and rosemary, venison steak with port and stilton sauce or fresh fish are typical choices, and there's also steak sandwiches, New Forest sausages, beans and chips, and cajun chicken and chips to keep the crowds happy. Book in advance, bring a hearty appetite and tuck in.

East End Arms
Main Road, East End, SO41 5SY (01590 626223/ www.eastendarms.co.uk). **Lunch served** noon-2pm Tue-Sun. **Dinner served** 7-9pm Tue-Sat. **Main courses** £12. **Credit** MC, V.

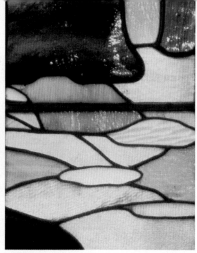

Westover Hall: perfect views of the Solent and Victorian stained glass.

Well worth beating a path to, this likeable pub tucked down a country lane a few miles from Beaulieu has a tiny garden, a green and whitewashed exterior and a cream and panelled restaurant at the back. The surroundings are low key, but the food is simple, fresh and very good value – home cooking at its best. Fresh fish is a forte and there's ribeye steak and chips, sausage and egg pie and a range of salads or baguettes, as well as chocolate tart, bread and butter pudding, rhubarb fool or apple pie to finish. If only more pubs were like this.

Marryat Restaurant
Chewton Glen, Christchurch Road, New Milton (01425 275341/www.chewtonglen.com). **Food served** 12.30-1.45pm, 7.30-9.30pm daily. **Main courses** (lunch only) £13.50-£26.50. **Set dinner** £55 3 courses. **Set lunch** £20 3 courses. **Credit** AmEx, DC, MC, V.

Michael Winner voted this his favourite restaurant but despite that its reputation is certainly impressive. Perhaps it was the conservative air of corporate comfort and the gentlemen's club decor that won his vote. Or the serried ranks of unsmiling but efficient staff. Or just the helipad. Despite the well-turned-out classical menu (grilled lemon sole with tomato-infused béarnaise, perfect Sunday roast chicken with bread sauce and buttery vegetables, beef tournedos with horseradish sauce) and the 400-strong wine list, the Marryat lacks one essential ingredient of good dining: *joie de vivre*.

Nurse's Cottage
Station Road, Sway, SO41 6BA (tel/fax 01590 683402/www.nursescottage.co.uk). **Food served** 6.30-8pm Mon-Sat; 12.30-2pm, 6.30-8pm Sun. **Set lunch** £15.85 3 courses. **Set dinner** £20.95 3 courses. **Credit** AmEx, MC, V.

Run by enthusiastic chef-proprietor Tony Barnfield, this tiny white pebbledashed cottage was once home to Sway's successive district nurses (hence the name). Now a restaurant with rooms, the place has been recently extensively refurbished and doubled in size. Decor retains a touch of the clinical, but the seasonally changing classic British menu is just what the doctor ordered.

Ingredients are locally sourced where possible, some from the cottage's own herb and vegetable garden. Specialities include avocado, orange and prawn salad; breast of guinea fowl flavoured with tarragon and white wine; salmon with Cointreau; and, to finish, a gloriously nostalgic bananas flambée. The wine list contains more than 60 choices from around the world, with many half bottles. Children over ten and pets welcome. No smoking throughout.

Royal Oak
Old Ringwood Road, North Gorley, Fordingbridge, SP6 2PB (01425 652244). **Food served** noon-2pm, 6-9pm daily. **Main courses** £2.75-£31 (lobster). **Credit** MC, V.

The very chocolate box image of a thatched country pub, the Royal Oak is in a pretty village on the western edge of the forest. You can sit out front and talk to the flapping, quacking ducks while watching the local gang of Morris dancers perform as you sip your pint from the Ringwood Brewery, or you could cosy up inside with a generous plateful of roast chicken or sea bass. There's also a good children's play area to tire out tiny, and a secluded garden for mummy and daddy at the back.

Westover Hall `OFFER`
Park Lane, Milford-on-Sea, SO41 0PT (01590 643044/www.westoverhallhotel.com). **Food served** noon-1.45pm, 7-8.45pm daily. **Set lunch** £25 3 courses. **Set dinner** £32.50 3 courses. **Credit** AmEx, DC, MC, V.

The bright and sunny restaurant in Westover Hall offers picture-postcard views of the Solent and the Isle of White and shares the hotel's agreeable, friendly, welcoming atmosphere. Drop in for a quick mid-morning coffee or afternoon tea, or linger longer over lunch or dinner to sample the more sophisticated fare produced by the busy kitchen. There's ham hock and foie gras terrine with pea purée or wild mushroom risotto to start, with brill with mousseline sauce or roasted partridge and root veg to follow. Coffee or tea comes with petits fours and at £32.50 for three courses at dinner, the price is more than reasonable. For the hotel, *see p117*.

Isle of Wight

Over the sea but not far away.

Mention the Isle of Wight to almost anyone and they'll say: 'I went there once on a geography field trip.' With its crumbling chalk cliffs, downs, creeks, groynes and landslips it's a geography teacher's dream come true. From **Tennyson Down**, named in honour of the poet who lived nearby and described the air as being 'worth sixpence a pint', the Isle of Wight lies before you like a child's drawing of an island. Shaped like a pair of bee-stung lips, to the north-west the River Yar flows out to the Solent past the castle guarding Yarmouth harbour; at the far western tip of the island, the jagged chalk line of the **Needles**, jutting from the sea, ends with a red-and-white lighthouse; to the south is the great crumbling sweep of **Compton Bay**, while further south the sheer cliffs of **Blackgang Chine** fall dramatically (and literally) into the Channel.

Often described as encompassing the whole of southern England in miniature, the island's 147 square miles contain rolling farmland, marshy estuaries, castles, cliffs, vineyards, beaches, steam trains, Roman villas, dinosaur fossils, red squirrels and a whole clutch of manor houses. During the 1800s visitors poured in from all over Europe to enjoy the water, the sea air and the balmy climate. As well as Tennyson – whose home, **Farringford**, at

Freshwater, is now a hotel – the poet Swinburne was born (and buried) in **Bonchurch**, where Dickens wrote *David Copperfield*; and the Russian writer Turgenev conceived his most famous novel, *Fathers and Sons*, while visiting **Ventnor** for the bathing. Meanwhile at Dimbola Lodge, Tennyson's neighbour, the Victorian photographer Julia Cameron, was taking pictures of whoever she could persuade to sit still long enough and developing the results in the coal shed (*see p122* **Flash photography**). And, of course, Queen Victoria herself spent summers with her family at **Osborne House** in East Cowes.

In the 20th century the island's star waned. In his novel *England, England* – in which the Isle of Wight has become a giant heritage theme park – Julian Barnes describes it as 'a mixture of rolling chalk downland of considerable beauty and bungaloid dystopia'. Many of today's tourists stick to **Sandown** and **Shanklin**, taking in the thatched tearooms of **Godshill**, **Blackgang Chine Fantasy Park**, the **Pearl Centre** and the **Needles Pleasure Park**. All the better for the rest of us, as it leaves most of the island blissfully free of visitors even at the height of summer. There is one drawback, though. The south-west of the island is disappearing into the sea, not inch by inch, but acre by acre. Every winter more cliffs collapse like a soufflé on to the beaches below, leaving fences and steps suspended precariously in mid-air.

The free pocket guide (available on ferries and at tourist offices) is crammed with ideas of 'attractions', but unless it's raining stair rods and blowing a gale, give them a miss and explore the cliff paths, downs, woods, creeks and beaches on foot instead. This is the best way to discover the island, a paradise for walkers, cyclists and horse riders. It boasts more footpaths per square mile than anywhere else in Britain – all meticulously signposted and maintained. The 77-mile coastal path around the island might be a bit much for a weekend, but to get a flavour of it take the train to Shanklin. Here you can join the path as it climbs up from the sea, before descending again through the mysterious ferny depths of the **Landslip** (so-called because much of it fell into the sea in 1810) to the pretty beach at Bonchurch. From there you can walk around

By train from London

Trains from **Waterloo** to **Portsmouth** leave about every 20mins (journey time approximately 1hr 30mins), from where there's a ferry crossing to **Ryde**, and from **Waterloo** to **Lymington** (2hrs 15mins), with a ferry crossing to **Yarmouth**. **Wightlink** (0870 582 7744) runs car and passenger ferries from **Portsmouth Harbour** to **Fishbourne** (crossing time 35mins) and from **Lymington** to **Yarmouth** (30mins), while a catamaran runs from **Portsmouth** to **Ryde** (15mins). Info: www.southwesttrains.co.uk and www.wightlink.co.uk. Passengers can also travel by hydrofoil: Red Funnel (01703 334010) from **Southampton** to **Cowes**, Hovertravel (01983 811000) from **Southsea** to **Ryde**.

Newport's **Carisbroke Castle**. See p121.

Ventnor, and if you still have the energy, on to **Steephill Cove** and the **Botanical Gardens**. Another lovely walk is along the north-west coast from **Shalfleet** to **Yarmouth**.

For beach fans, Sandown, Shanklin and **Ryde** offer all the traditional delights of miniature golf, amusement arcades and fish and chips. If that is your idea of hell, head for **Compton Bay**, a beautiful sweep of sand beneath collapsing cliffs (mind your head!), all without a kiss-me-quick hat in sight. **Totland Bay**, with good sand, clean water and views across to **Hurst Castle**, is a lovely place to watch the sun go down. At high tide the beach all but disappears and becomes a playground for the island's many surfers.

Surfers also brave the waves at **Compton Bay**, where fossil hunters admire the casts of dinosaurs' footprints at low tide, paragliders hurl themselves off the cliffs and kite-surfers leap and soar across the sea. Meanwhile, sailors weigh anchor in the natural harbours of Yarmouth, **Cowes** and **Bembridge**.

Many attractions are closed between the end of October and Easter, so phone ahead to check what's open when planning a visit. There are many seasonal events, including Britain's biggest walking festival in May, an international kite festival in July, a cycling season in September and White Air, a festival of extreme sports, at the end of October. For information on cycling and walking, call Rights of Way (01983 823741/www.iwight.com) or get a map from a Tourist Information Centre (*see below*).

For boat fans there is the Yarmouth Old Gaffers Classic Boat Festival during the May bank holiday weekend, the Round the Island Yacht Race in June and, of course, the famous Cowes Week in August. Indeed, for this very reason, those looking for a quiet weekend away might want to avoid Cowes in August as the place gets rammed with yacht lovers. Also worth noting is the Isle of Wight Music Festival, which takes place in Newport in June each year (www.isleofwightfestival.com).

What to see & do

Tourist Information Centres

Isle of Wight tourist information line (01983 813818/www.islandbreaks.co.uk).

Western Esplanade, Ryde, PO33 2LW. **Open** *Mar-Oct* 9am-5.30pm Mon-Sat; 10am-4pm Sun. *Nov-Feb* 9.30am-4.30pm daily.

Fountain Quay, Cowes, PO31 3AR. **Open** *June-Sept* 9.30am-5.30pm Mon-Sat; 10am-4pm Sun. *Oct-Apr* 9.30am-5.30pm Tue-Sat.

8 High Street, Sandown, PO36 0DG. **Open** *Mar-Oct* 9am-5.30pm Mon-Sat; 9am-4.30pm Sun. *Nov-Feb* 10am-4pm Mon-Sat.

67 High Street, Shanklin, PO37 6JJ. **Open** *Apr-Sept* 9am-5.30pm Mon-Sat; 9am-4.30pm Sun. *Oct-Mar* 10am-4pm Mon-Sat.

Salisbury Gardens, Dudley Road, Ventnor, PO38 1EJ. **Open** 9.30am-4.30pm Mon-Sat.

The Quay, Yarmouth, PO41 4PQ. **Open** *Apr-June, Sept, Oct* 9.30am-5.30pm Mon-Sat; 10am-4pm Sun. *July, Aug* 9.30am-4.30pm daily. *Nov-Mar* 9.30am-4.30pm Mon-Sun.

Coastal Path Visitors' Centre, Dudley Road, Ventnor, PO38 1EJ (www.coastalwight.gov.uk). **Open** 9.30am-5pm Mon-Sat.

Bike hire
Autovogue *140 High Street, Ryde, PO33 2RE (01983 812989).*
Ten-minute walk from the ferry terminal.

Blackgang Chine Fantasy Park
Blackgang Chine, Chale, PO38 2HN (01983 730330/www.blackgangchine.com). **Open** *Apr-June, Sept, Oct* 10am-5.30pm daily. *July, Aug* 10am-10pm daily. Closed Nov-Mar. Times vary during half-term; phone for details. **Admission** £7.50; £5.50 concessions. **Credit** MC, V.
One of the oldest in the country, it's a wonder that this low-key theme park is still clinging to the side of the cliff. Locals mourn favourite rides that have slid into the Channel below. The current highlight is Wild West Town, where for the price of a pistol and some caps (from the shop), kids can charge around the saloon blasting the living daylights out of total strangers. Blissfully non-PC. The most exciting ride is the waterslide, with rubber boats that hurtle down from the top of the cliff.

Boat trips
Boat trips are available from Yarmouth pier around the Needles or across the Solent to Hurst Castle through Puffin Cruises (07850 947618). Fishing trips are available daily from Bembridge harbour (01983 872828).

Botanical Gardens & Museum of Smuggling History
Botanical Gardens, Ventnor, PO38 1UL (01983 853677). **Open** *Apr-Sept* 10am-5pm daily. **Admission** *Museum* £2.80; £1.40 concessions. *Gardens* free. **No credit cards**.
Housed in the underground vaults of the lovely botanical gardens, this museum recounts the ingenious methods used by smugglers over the last 700 years.

Brading Roman Villa
Morton Old Road, Brading, PO36 0EN (01983 406223). **Open** *June-Oct* 9.30am-5pm daily. **Admission** £2.95; £1.55 concessions. **No credit cards**.
There are fine mosaic floors to admire in this villa just north of Sandown. Look out for the figure representing winter, whose British hooded cloak became a wardrobe must-have for expat Romans in these chilly climes. (The villa will be closed from October 2003 while a new building is erected, so call to check it's open before your visit.)

Carisbroke Castle
Carisbroke, nr Newport, PO30 1XY (01983 522107/www.english-heritage.org.uk). **Open** *Apr-Sept* 10am-6pm daily. *Oct-Mar* 10am-4pm daily. **Admission** (EH) £5; £2.50-£3.80 concessions. **Credit** MC, V.
Charles I was held in this hilltop Norman castle before being taken back to London to be executed. The museum inside tells the story of his incarceration, as well as that of other royal residents. There are wonderful views of the island from the battlements, plus jousting, fayres and ghost walks in the summer months (tickets available from Tourist Information Centres).

High Adventure Paragliding
Sandpipers, Freshwater Bay, PO40 9QX (01983 752322/www.high-adventure.uk.com). **Open** 9am-5pm daily. Phone or see website for details of courses and prices. **Credit** MC, V.
Despite its sleepy image, in recent years the island has become a centre for all kinds of high adrenaline sports. Its climate and geography make it particularly ideal for paragliders, and there are one-day courses for beginners. For groups of six or more, sister company Island Activities (01983 753839/www.islandactivities.co.uk) can arrange energetic pursuits such as powerboating, jet biking, sailing, watersports, clay pigeon shooting, horse riding, laser paintball, gliding and mountain biking.

Isle of Wight Steam Railway
The Railway Station, Havenstreet, PO33 4DS (01983 884343/882204/www.iwsteamrailway.co.uk). **Open** *mid Mar-Oct* 9.30am-5pm daily. Closed Nov-mid Mar. **Tickets** £7.50; £4-£7 concessions. **Credit** MC, V.
This five-mile line connects with electric trains at Ryde and features beautifully restored locomotives and a steam museum.

Museum of Island History
The Guildhall, High Street, Newport, PO30 1TY (01983 823366). **Open** 10am-5pm Mon-Sat; 11am-3.30pm Sun. **Admission** £1.80; £1 concessions. **No credit cards**.
A delightful hands-on history of the island, housed in the old town clock tower.

Needles Old Battery
West High Down, Totland Bay, PO39 0JH (01983 754772/www.nationaltrust.org.uk). **Open** *May, June, Sept, Oct* 10.30am-4.30pm Mon-Thur, Sat, Sun. *July, Aug* 10.30am-4.30pm daily. Closed Nov-Apr. **Admission** (NT) £3.50; free under-5s. **Credit** MC, V.
This Victorian fort was built to guard the entrance to the Solent against invasion by Napoleon and was also used during both World Wars. Don't miss the underground tunnel that leads to the searchlight emplacement. Just above was the launch site for Britain's atomic missile and space rocket programme between 1955 and 1971. The site offers spectacular views over the Needles, the Solent and the Channel. It makes a good conclusion to a bracing walk over Tennyson Down from Freshwater, or from the Needles Pleasure Park if you're feeling less energetic.

Osborne House
York Avenue, East Cowes, PO32 6JY (01983 200022/www.english-heritage.org.uk). **Open** *House* Apr-Oct 10am-5pm daily. Nov-Mar check website for opening times. *Grounds* Apr-Sept 10am-6pm daily. Oct 10am-5pm daily. Closed Nov-Mar. **Admission** (EH) £8; £4-£6 concessions. **Credit** MC, V.
Built in the style of an Italian villa by Thomas Cubitt, this was the much-loved country retreat of Queen Victoria and has been maintained as it was at her death here in 1901. Don't miss the lovely gardens and the Swiss Cottage, built as a playhouse in the garden for the royal children and larger than many modern flats. Pre-booking for guided tours (spring and autumn only) is essential. There is a garden show in June and an outdoor concert of popular classical music with fireworks in July.

Where to stay

George Hotel

Quay Street, Yarmouth, PO41 0PE (01983 760331/ fax 01983 760425/www.thegeorge.co.uk). **Rates** £90-£145 single; £175-£225 double/twin; £225 four-poster/balcony. **Rooms** (all en suite) 2 single; 12 double/twin; 2 balcony; 1 four-poster. **Credit** MC, V.

The perfect hotel for a car-free weekend: disembark from the Lymington–Yarmouth ferry and the hotel is less than a minute's stroll away. The George is housed in the 17th-century former home of the island's governor, hard up against the wall of the castle. Some rooms retain their original panelling, but try to avoid those at the back as they can be noisy. The hotel has easy access to the shops and restaurants of this tiny port and also boasts a restaurant and brasserie of its own (*see p125*). If you're flush or feeling reckless, a private motor launch is available for charter. Children and dogs welcome.

Lisle Combe

Undercliffe Drive, St Lawrence, PO38 1UW (01983 852582/www.lislecombe.co.uk). **Rates** £27.50 per person. Closed Nov-Mar. **Rooms** 1 single; 2 twin/ double. **No credit cards.**

This Elizabethan-style early 19th-century house (check out the barley sugar twist chimneys) was once the home of the poet Alfred Noyes. Walk through the gardens with their pools and palm trees to find a delightful sandy beach below. This quiet, comfortable B&B is a great location for walks along the south coast of the island. Children welcome. No smoking throughout.
Take A3055 from Ventnor.

Newnham Farm

Newnham Lane, Binstead, Ryde, PO33 4ED (01983 882423/ www.newnhamfarm.co.uk). **Rates** £32-£45 single occupancy; £64-£80 double/twin; £76-£104 family room. **Rooms** (both en suite) 1 double/twin; 1 double/twin/family. **No credit cards.**

An award-winning B&B on a working farm in idyllic surroundings a stone's throw from Quarr Abbey and Fishbourne car ferry terminal. Sunny bedrooms, lovely gardens and a great breakfast that includes honey from the farm's own hives make this a wonderful place to stay. Wellies can be borrowed from the farm owners so residents can enjoy the many excellent local walks through the area. Children are welcome; note that this is a no-smoking house throughout.

Northcourt

Shorwell, PO30 3JG (01983 740415/fax 01983 740409/www.wightfarmholidays.co.uk). **Rates** £26-£32 per person. **Rooms** (all en suite) 6 double/twin. **No credit cards.**

As you round the bend in the drive and see this imposing Jacobean pile rear up before you, you'd be forgiven for thinking you've come to the wrong place. Set among 15 acres of gardens with brooks (babbling, natch), terraces, shady woodland, exotic flowers and an Italian garden, Northcourt seems more like a country house than a B&B. Five miles south-west of Newport, it is an ideal stopping-off point if you're walking across the island. If you're looking for less frenetic exercise, a full-sized snooker table has been installed in the library, while table tennis, croquet and lawn tennis are also

available for guests. Stroll through the gardens to the Crown Inn (*see p125*) for supper. The house is no smoking throughout. Children are welcome by arrangement.
5 miles SW of Newport on Newport–Brightstone Road; B&B is in middle of Shorwell village.

Old House

Gotten Manor, Gotten Lane, Chale, PO38 2HQ (01983 551368/www.gottenmanor.co.uk). **Rates** *Rooms* £30-£40 per person. Self-catering cottages £300-£1,000 per wk. **Rooms** (both en suite) 2 double; 2 converted barns sleep 4-6; 1 converted barn sleeps 6-10. **No credit cards.**

You'll definitely need transport if you plan to stay here; Gotten Manor is right at the end of a long lane at the southern end of the island. The bedrooms, all based in the limewashed 14th-century annexe, have wooden floors, Persian rugs and antique cast-iron baths in the rooms, making it the perfect choice for a romantic weekend. To add to the charm, delicious home-made jams and other locally sourced products are served at breakfast. Self-catering accommodation is available in three converted barns. No children under 12 can stay in the B&B, and there is no smoking throughout.
On B3399 2 miles S of Chale Green; after village, turn left at Gotten Lane; Old House is at end of lane.

Priory Bay Hotel

Priory Drive, Seaview, PO34 5BU (01983 613146/ fax 01983 616539/www.priorybay.co.uk). **Rates** £55-£129 per person. **Rooms** (all en suite) 9 double/ twin; 7 deluxe double/twin; 2 family suites; 7 cottage suites. **Credit** AmEx, MC, V.

Opened by the genial Andrew Palmer in 1998, Priory Bay has established itself as the choicest and most individual of the island's luxury hotels. It is a thoroughly relaxed place, boasting a nine-hole golf course and an unheated outdoor pool among its facilities. The elevated position, surrounded by trees and overlooking the sea, is stunning; walking down through the woods, past the Oyster Seafood Café to the wide sweep of sandy beach, you'd swear you were in the Mediterranean. All bedrooms are individually decorated with panache. Self-catering accommodation, with limited room service, is available in 16 cottages in the grounds. The hotel has two restaurants: the Priory Bay restaurant and, in high season, the beautifully situated Oyster Seafood Café. Both are very good. Children and dogs are welcome.
From Fishbourne ferry terminal follow signs to Ryde, then Nettlestone and St Helen's; pass through Nettlestone; after 2 miles turn left at sign to Priory Bay Hotel.

Redway Farm

East Lane, Merstone, PO30 3DJ (01983 865228/ www.redway-farm.co.uk). **Rates** £30-£35 per person. **Rooms** (all en suite) 2 double; 1 twin. **No credit cards.**

This 17th-century farmhouse is set in spacious grounds with its own fishing lake. A working farm for more than three generations, it is situated on the walking and cycling path through the Arreton Valley. The master bedroom features an antique half-tester 17th-century double bed – so no bouncing. All rooms have tea- and coffee-making facilities, TV, hairdryers and radios. Children welcome by arrangement.
Turn off Newport to Sandown road for Merstone; in Merstone, turn left down Bury Lane and go over the small crossroads at the top of the lane; Redway Farm is at the end.

Dine at the **George Hotel**. *See p125*.

Royal Hotel

*Belgrave Road, Ventnor, PO38 1JJ (01983 852186/
fax 01983 855395/www.royalhoteliow.co.uk).* **Rates**
£70-£95 single occupancy; £115-£135 double/twin;
family room rates on application. **Rooms** (all en
suite) 5 single; 43 double/twin; 7 family. **Credit**
AmEx, DC, MC, V.

A short stroll from the town centre and the beach (but
not so close that it's likely to go the way of a rival establishment that slipped into the sea), this stately stone
building has been refurbished to a high standard. The
rooms are light and comfortable – in a grandish but not
overly heavy country house style – with views over the
garden, where there is a heated swimming pool. Children
are catered for with early suppers, high chairs and baby-
listening devices, so parents can enjoy the restaurant
(*see p126*) in peace. Dogs accepted by arrangement.
*Follow one-way system in Ventnor; turn left at traffic lights;
follow road up hill and bear left into Belgrave Road; hotel is
at end of road on right.*

Seaview Hotel

*High Street, Seaview, PO34 5EX (01983 612711/fax
01983 613729/www.seaviewhotel.co.uk).* **Rates** £55-
£95 single; £70-£130 single occupancy; £95-£165
double/twin; £180-£235 family room; £320-£700 per
wk self-catering cottage (2 bedrooms); £600-£2,000
per week self-catering cottage (sleeps 10). **Rooms**
(all en suite) 2 single; 13 double/twin; 2 self-catering
cottages. **Credit** AmEx, DC, MC, V.

Described by its many regular guests as the perfect seaside hotel, the award-winning Seaview caters equally
happily to families, romantic couples and old salts. A
couple of steps from the beach, it's the social centre of
the village. The hotel is very child-friendly, with high
chairs and baby-listening devices; even dogs are welcome in the hotel (although not in the cottages). For
restaurant, *see p126.*

Where to eat & drink

Fish is everywhere on the Isle of Wight and that
is what most of the restaurants listed below
specialise in. Most pubs also serve local lobster
and crab in some form or another, though it's
often let down by the limited accompaniments
(sachets of malt vinegar and salad cream).

Real ale fans should check out the local
beers from **Goddard's** and the **Ventnor
Brewery**. You can eat and drink right by the
sea at the **Waterfront Bar and Bay View
Restaurant** (01983 756969) and the **Totland
Pier Café** (01983 756677), both of which are
on the promenade at Totland Bay. Also by the
sea is the **Boathouse** (Westhill Lane, 01983
760935), at Fort Victoria near Yarmouth. The
Beach House Café (01983 856488) and the
Horseshoe Bay Restaurant (01983 856800),
both at Bonchurch, have tables outside with
views over the Channel. Beach cafés are often
only open at lunchtime – except during high
season – so it's a good idea to phone beforehand.
For afternoon tea in peaceful surroundings visit
the gardens of one of the many manor houses or
vineyards, or better still try **Quarr Abbey** at
Binstead, Ryde (01983 882420).

Country inns serving good pub grub include
the **Chequers** (Niton Road, Rookley, 01983
840314) and the **Crown Inn** (Walkers Lane,
Shorwell, 01983 740293). Both have playgrounds
and children's menus. The **Spy Glass Inn**,
perched above the beach at Ventnor is the
perfect place for a pint and a plate of seafood.

Flash photography

Julia Margaret Cameron has been described as 'the greatest photographer of the 19th century'. Her haunting photos, whether of Victorian celebrities or housemaids and local fishermen dressed up as romantic heroines and heroes, have an eerie beauty. It was at her home, **Dimbola Lodge** in Freshwater, that her most famous photos were produced.

Born into an unconventional family in India in 1815, she took up the new craze of photography at 49, when her daughter Julia gave her a camera as a present. A celebrated and eccentric Victorian society hostess with few practical skills, she learned her craft by trial and error, cajoling and bribing her subjects, who were often young children, to sit completely still for as long as ten minutes at a time. She turned a henhouse into a darkroom and an old greenhouse into a studio, blanketing out panes to direct the available light.

Cameron learnt to develop her pictures from large glass plates using dangerous chemicals and acids. She scoured the island looking for interesting faces and hired her maids more for their soulful looks than their housekeeping skills.

In Freshwater, Cameron was at the centre of an artistic and cultural community; her first visit to the island in 1855 had been to stay with Alfred Lord Tennyson. Dimbola Lodge, named after the family's plantation in India, was originally two houses that she had joined together with a fashionable Gothic tower. It lies halfway between Tennyson's home and the sea. The poet laureate was such a celebrity in his day and so avidly pursued by fans that Cameron had a special gate built for him in the back garden so that he would not be bothered by autograph hunters.

Always keen to preserve his privacy, he had a tall tree in his garden chopped

Baywatch on the Beach Restaurant

The Duver, St Helen's, PO33 1RP (01983 873259/ www.bay-watch.co.uk). **Food served** *Mar-Sept* 10am-3pm, 6.15-9pm daily. Closed Nov-Apr (phone to confirm winter closing times). **Main courses** £6.90-£14.95. **Credit** MC, V.

Bembridge harbour, overlooking St Helen's Fort, is the gorgeous setting for this airy beach restaurant. Starters include crab soup or smoked mackerel and shrimp salad; moules and plenty of fish (specials change daily) – as well as pasta, steak and burgers – comprise the mains selection. We've found the portions generally large: a fearsome-looking whole-baked strawberry grouper came with salad (you'll have to ask for dressing) and was delicious, although its bed of samphire was stingy; a whole lobster and king prawn salad was huge.

George Hotel

Quay Street, Yarmouth, PO41 0PE (01983 760331/ www.thegeorge.co.uk). **Food served** *Restaurant* 7.15-9pm Tue-Sat. *Brasserie* 8-10am, noon-3pm, 7-10pm daily. **Set dinner** (Restaurant) £45 3 courses. **Main courses** (Brasserie only) £11.95-£29.95. **Credit** AmEx, MC, V.

The waterside garden of the George Hotel's brasserie is a beautiful setting for a meal. Inside, the sunshine yellow room, with its dressers of china and brassware works less well on a dark evening. Chef Kevin Mangeolles creates Modern British dishes with French and Californian touches, with lots of fish and locally sourced ingredients. The dishes can be a bit hit and miss, though the emphasis on fish means that everything is very fresh; vegetables are organic. Service is helpful.

The Net

Sherbourne Street, Bembridge, PO35 5RZ (01983 875800/www.bembridge.net). **Food served** noon-2.15pm, 7-9.30pm Mon-Sat. **Main courses** £12.95-£13.95. **Credit** MC, V.

With a name like that they can only serve fish, and so it's no surprise that there's lots of it on the menu in this modern, light, airy restaurant. Choose from dishes such as seared salmon with spicy noodles or sea bass with lime Caesar salad, but don't expect a sea view as the restaurant is in the town. Booking is strongly advised.

New Inn

Mill Road, Shalfleet, PO3 4NS (01983 531314/ www.thenew-inn.co.uk). **Food served** noon-2.30pm, 6-9.30pm daily. **Main courses** £6.95-£17.95. **Credit** AmEx, DC, MC, V.

This 17th-century inn with oak beams, huge fireplaces and a sunny garden has won a slew of awards and a well-deserved reputation for excellent food, which includes steaks, local crab and lobster, and a 'seafood royale' platter (£50 for two). The wine list is well chosen and refreshingly informative. The garden gets very crowded in summer but there are lots of tables inside, with high chairs for children. It's a perfect spot for lunch if you're exploring the lovely paths around Newtown and Shalfleet Creek, between Newport and Yarmouth.

Red Lion

Church Place, Freshwater, PO40 9BP (01983 754925/www.redlion-wight.co.uk). **Food served** noon-2pm, 6.30-9pm Mon-Sat; noon-2pm, 7-9pm Sun. **Main courses** £7.50-£12. **Credit** MC, V.

down when he noticed a fan peering into his study window from its branches. On another occasion he legged it smartly to avoid a flock of sheep that he had mistaken for a group of literary tourists (he was rather short-sighted). However, Tennyson was delighted with Cameron's portrait of him – he thought it made him look like 'a dirty monk'.

As well as Tennyson, the great and the good of the Victorian age – including the esteemed likes of Robert Browning, Thomas Carlyle, Henry Longfellow, Charles Darwin and Anthony Trollope – were all ushered into Cameron's glasshouse to sit for her.

At the peak of her fame, after ten years of work in which her reputation as a photographer was established, Cameron and her husband packed their belongings into their coffins (why not?) and went to live in Sri Lanka (or Ceylon, as it was still known then).

When she died in 1879 she hadn't lost her photographer's eye; the last word she uttered looking up at the starry sky from her deathbed was 'beautiful'.

Over the years the house fell into a state of disrepair: the glass photographic plates were used to protect vegetables from frost in local gardens, the studio was torn down and a bungalow was built over the coalshed darkroom.

Then, in 1993, the house was bought, restored and preserved as the present museum. Dimbola Lodge now hosts contemporary exhibitions, a camera museum, an antiquarian bookshop and a vegetarian café.

Dimbola Lodge Museum
Terrace Lane, Freshwater Bay, PO40 9QE (01983 756814/www.dimbola.co.uk). **Open** 10am-5pm Tue-Sun. Open Mon during school summer holidays & bank hols. **Admission** £3.50; free under-16s. **Credit** AmEx, DC, MC, V.

A traditional pub popular with locals, walkers and the dinghy sailors who come down the river from Yarmouth for lunch when the tide is right. This is also a good place to stop if you're cycling or walking along the estuary towards Freshwater. Switch off your mobile phone – if it rings you'll pay a £5 fine to the local lifeboat. Daily specials on the blackboard might include herring roe on toast, local pork cutlets with brandy and mushroom sauce or steak and kidney pie. Delicious traditional puddings are hard to resist.

Royal Hotel
Belgrave Road, Ventnor, PO38 1JJ (01983 852186/www.royalhoteliow.co.uk). **Food served** *Restaurant* 7-9.15pm daily. *Bar* noon-2pm daily. **Set dinner** £29.50 3 courses. **Credit** AmEx, DC, MC, V.
Chef Alan Staley has been awarded two AA rosettes for his reliably classy cooking at this hotel restaurant close to the sea. His qualities are best seen in dishes such as Mediterranean fish soup flavoured with fennel, served with rouille and toasted garlic croûtes, or mains such as medallions of beef fillet with pan-fried potato and horseradish rösti, sauté of wild mushrooms and a truffle-scented jus. For a less formal setting, light lunches such as salads and omelettes are served in the bar and conservatory. Early suppers are available for children.

Seaview Hotel
High Street, Seaview, PO34 5EX (01983 612711/www.seaviewhotel.co.uk). **Food served** noon-1.30pm, 7.15-9.30pm Mon-Sat. **Set lunch** (Sun) £16.95 3 courses. **Main courses** £13.95-£17.95. **Credit** AmEx, DC, MC, V.

One of the best places to eat on the island. There are two relaxed and pretty dining rooms (smoking and no smoking) in this charming and child-friendly hotel, and food is imaginative and modern. Typical starters might be sautéd soft herring roe on brioche with capers, butter and lemon or baked goat's cheese with rocket and beetroot salad. Mains make excellent use of local produce, with dishes such as breast of free-range chicken with oak-smoked garlic and rosemary risotto or fillet of local beef with Perigord hollandaise and fondant potato. Puddings are Minghella's ice-cream and English cheeses served with chutney from the Garlic Farm. If you don't want a full meal, you can have a superior bar snack sitting under the umbrellas at the front, looking at the lovely harbour below.

Sian-Elins
Quay Street, Yarmouth, PO41 0NT (01983 760054). **Food served** *Nov, Dec, Feb* 8.30-11.30am, noon-2.30pm, 6-9.30pm Thur-Sun (subject to weather). *Mar-June* 8.30-11.30am, noon-2.30pm, 6-9.30pm Wed-Sun. *July-Oct* 8.30-11.30am, noon-2.30pm, 6-9.30pm daily. Closed Jan. **Main courses** £6-£14. **Credit** MC, V.
The large deck overlooking the ferry terminal is a terrific place to sit and watch the boats come in. A full English breakfast is served to hungry sailors between 8am and 10am, just after they've finished work. The lunch menu is served until 2pm and includes crayfish Caesar salad, local crab sandwiches, and fish cakes, as well as steaks and burgers. In the evening there are specials such as baked whole sea bass and grilled sardines. Coffee and cakes are available all day.

Bournemouth & Poole

So – is this the new Brighton?

Hampshire & Isle of Wight

Mention Bournemouth and you'll invariably get one of two responses: 'that's where old people go to die', or, more recently: 'they say Bournemouth is the new Brighton'. There's an element of truth to both stereotypes. You certainly do come across your fair share of the blue-rinse brigade. But, in recent years, Help the Aged shops have had to compete with slick new bars, clubs and gay-friendly watering holes – all very Brightonesque. In fact, Bournemouth's beaches – seven miles of white sand set against a backdrop of grassy cliffs – are far superior to Brighton's, both in terms of cleanliness and aesthetics. Several of the beaches are reached via steep wooded pathways called 'chines': try Flaghead, Middle, Branksome or Alum Chine for a romantic approach to the sea. **Sandbanks** is the region's most famous beach: midway between Bournemouth and Poole, it has won several Blue Flag awards. Unfortunately, Sandbanks' reputation means it is plagued by crowds in summer. A short ferry journey from Sandbanks is **Studland**, a nature reserve with miles of white sand and grassy dunes. It also has a nudist beach, which is popular with gay men. For more family-oriented beach fun, the town of **Swanage**, half an hour's drive south of Studland, has a stunning harbour, a lovely beach and clifftop walks. But kids might prefer to head back north to Bournemouth Pier with its arcades, junk food and IMAX cinema.

Compared to its beaches, Bournemouth town is a bit of a disappointment: post-war urban planners stuck major roads and roundabouts right through the middle. The shopping, too, is mostly high-street stuff. Still, the town centre has lovely subtropical gardens meandering through it, a couple of the main streets are pedestrianised and, away from the main drag, the manicured, tree-lined neighbourhoods are worthy of the fancified English Riviera title.

If you find the relentless trendiness of the bars and clubs begin to grate, the nearby town of **Christchurch** offers respite. Its marketplace hasn't changed much since medieval times, and its quaint streets are dotted with old pubs and smart shops. The Priory church is notable for its fine medieval carvings and 'miraculous' beam – apparently fitted by the hand of God himself. The restored water mill and Georgian Red House Museum and Gardens (Quay Road, 01202 482860), with its walled herb garden and dolls' house collection, are also worth a look. For church aficionados, Wimborne Minster, in the nearby town of **Wimborne**, is another gem.

Take a dip into Poole

Poole, in contrast to its younger, trendier neighbour, is steeped in history. Blessed with an enormous sheltered harbour, it has been a bustling port since the Middle Ages. It was particularly prosperous during Georgian times, with the development of fishing grounds on the Grand Banks off Newfoundland. During this period, local fishing fleets brought back huge quantities of salted cod from across the Atlantic. Poole became a boom town, and many magnificent merchant houses and quayside warehouses from the period still stand. To soak up the ancient atmosphere, follow the signposted Cockle Trail, a one-hour walk around the old town (leaflets are available from the tourist office, otherwise just look for the bronze cockles on the pavement). Along the way, you'll pass the vast **Poole Pottery** (*see p129*), housed in an old wharf building.

The main waterfront drag is **Poole Quay**, where you can drool at the gorgeous yachts (dream on). There's no beach in the main town, but the white sands of Sandbanks and Studland are not far away, and there's a lovely waterfront park from which to take in a couple of Poole's

By train from London

Trains run from **Waterloo** to **Bournemouth** about every 20mins. The fast train takes 1hr 45mins, slow trains take 2hrs 15mins. The station is about a mile east of the town centre, but there are frequent buses from opposite the train station into town. Trains arrive in **Poole** about 10mins after **Bournemouth**, on certain routes. Info: www.swtrains.co.uk.

greatest assets: **Poole Harbour**, the second largest harbour in the world after Sydney, and **Brownsea Island**, a woodland sanctuary owned by the National Trust.

What to see & do

You could have a lovely break in Bournemouth and Poole if you did nothing else but lie on the beach. Beach huts (01202 261306), deckchairs and parasols can be hired during the summer. For board and yacht sailing, waterskiing, jetskiing, canoes and speedboat rides, contact the tourist office in Poole (*see below*). Gorgeous as the beaches are, however, this is England and the elements could wreak havoc with your plans. So here are some other attractions.

Tourist Information Centres

Westover Road, Bournemouth, BH1 2BU (0906 802 0234/fax 01202 451799/www.bournemouth.co.uk). **Open** *mid July-Aug* 9.30am-7pm Mon-Sat; 10.30am-5.30pm Sun. *Sept-mid July* 9.30am-5.30pm Mon-Sat.

4 High Street, Poole, BH15 1BW (01202 253253/ www.pooletourism.com). **Open** *Apr, May* 10am-5pm Mon-Fri; 10am-4.30pm Sat, Sun. *June, July, Sept* 10am-5.30pm Mon-Fri; 10am-5pm Sat, Sun. *Aug* 10am-6pm daily. *Oct-Mar* 10am-5pm Mon-Fri; 10am-3pm Sat; noon-3pm Sun.

23 High Street, Christchurch, BH23 1AB (01202 471780/www.resort-guide.co.uk/christchurch). **Open** *July, Aug* 9.30am-5.30pm Mon-Fri; 9.30am-5pm Sat; 10am-2pm Sun. *Sept-June* 9.30am-5pm Mon-Fri; 9.30am-4.30pm Sat.

Bike hire

Rent a Bike *88 Charminster Road, Bournemouth, BH8 8UE (01202 315855).*
About 15 minutes' walk from the station.

Action Bikes *Link Mall, Dolphin Centre, Poole, BH15 1TF (01202 680123).*
In the mall, five minutes' walk from the station.

Alice in Wonderland Family Park

Merritown Lane (opposite Bournemouth International Airport), Hurn, Christchurch, BH23 6BA (01202 483444/www.aliceinwonderland park.co.uk). **Open** 10am-6pm daily (last entry 4pm). **Admission** £6.50; free under-3s. **Credit** DC, MC, V.
Bouncy castles, anyone? This seven-acre park has them, as well as Alice-themed rides, Europe's largest maze, farmyard animals and a restaurant called the Mad Hatter.

Brownsea Island

Poole Harbour, BH13 7EE (01202 707744/www. nationaltrust.org.uk/brownsea). **Open** *Mar* 10am-4pm daily. *Apr-June* 10am-5pm daily. *July, Aug* 10am-6pm daily. *Sept* 10am-5pm daily. Closed Oct-Feb. Last boat leaves in the last hr of opening times. **Admission** (NT) £3.70; £1.60 children. Additional ferry charge, check price with ferry companies. **No credit cards.**
You can't miss the island – it sits smack in the middle of Poole Harbour – nor should you, it's a nature lovers' paradise. Owned by the National Trust, the island is known for its forested trails, fine views and picnic spots. It's also the last English habitat of the red squirrel (for more information contact the Dorset Wildlife Trust Warden on 01202 079445). The striking Brownsea Castle adds to the mysterious air. But the only way to see inside is to get a job with John Lewis: it's a holiday home for the company's staff.

Compton Acres

Canford Cliffs Road, Canford Cliffs, Poole, BH13 7EF (01202 708036/www.comptonacres.co.uk). **Open** 9am-6pm daily (last entry 5.15pm). **Admission** £5.95; £3.95-£5.45 concessions. **Credit** MC, V.
Bournemouth's mild climate makes it a wonderful place for gardens, and there are flowers in bloom all year at Compton Acres. It features rare plants, Italian and Japanese gardens, a Roman garden and a deer sanctuary.

Oceanarium

Pier Approach, West Beach, Bournemouth, BH2 5AA (01202 311993/www.oceanarium.co.uk). **Open** 10am-6pm daily. **Admission** £6.25; £4.95 concessions; £3.95 children; free under-3s. **Credit** MC, V.

Situated on the seafront beside the pier, the aquarium is one of Bournemouth's top attractions. It's small, but comprehensive: it covers the globe, from the Amazon and the Nile to the Great Barrier Reef and the Caribbean. The best bit is the sharks' area: there's a dazzling underwater glass tunnel where the awesome creatures swim virtually on top of you. Other show-stoppers include the turtles, stingrays and piranhas. In June 2003 nine dwarf chameleons were born in the Oceanarium – the first time they've been successfully bred in the UK. When you're finished with marine life, the café boasts excellent views.

Poole Park

An attractive park near the town centre, with a lovely lake, rose garden and plenty of attractions for kids: Gus Gorilla's Jungle Playground (a ball pool), crazy golf, boat hire and a mini train. The Cygnet Continental Café Bar (01202 742842) has a children's play area.

Poole Pottery

The Quay, Poole, BH15 1RF (01202 669800). **Open** 9am-5.30pm Mon-Sat; 10.30am-4.30pm Sun. **Credit** MC, V.
Poole has long been associated with pottery, due to the rich red clay found in the area. The Poole Pottery Factory Shop sells bright, brassy crockery and assorted homewares at discount prices. There's a paint-your-own activity corner that is great for kids. Upstairs, in the fashion emporium, high-street names are sold on the cheap.

Russell-Cotes Museum & Art Gallery

East Cliff, Bournemouth, BH1 3AA (01202 451858/ www.russell-cotes.bournemouth.gov.uk). **Open** 10am-4.45pm Tue-Sun. **Admission** free.
This recently refurbished museum boasts a vast collection of Victorian and Edwardian English paintings, along with European objets d'art, furnishings and porcelain. The building is a superb example of late Victorian architecture, combining elements of Scottish baronial castle, French château and Italian villa. The interior is just as lavish, with stunning plasterwork, wallpapers and friezes. The garden, overlooking the bay, has one of the best views in Bournemouth.

Splashdown

Tower Park Leisure Complex, Poole, BH12 4NY (01202 716000). **Open** *June-mid July* 10am-9pm Mon-Fri; 10am-7pm Sat, Sun. *Mid July-Aug* 9am-10pm Mon-Fri; 9am-7pm Sat, Sun. *Sept-Dec, Feb-May* 2-9pm Mon-Fri; 10am-7pm Sat, Sun. Closed Jan. **Admission** £6.60; £2.70 under-5s. **Credit** AmEx, DC, MC, V.
This popular waterpark is sweet relief on a hot day or, for that matter, a dreary winter's day – Splashdown has indoor slides as well. Riders must be 1m tall, and for smaller kids there's a paddling pool. Adults can only watch in envy. All prices are for two-hour sessions; phone to ask about longer hours during school holidays.

Upton Country Park

3 miles N of Poole, signposted from A3049 and A35, BH17 7BJ (01202 672625). **Open** *Park* 9am-dusk daily. *Heritage Centre* 10.30am-4pm daily. **Admission** free except for special events.
A lovely way to approach the park is by bike, on a woodland path alongside Poole Harbour. Once there, you'll find a park that's suitable for picnics, ball games and cycling. It's also a twitcher's delight: there's a special birdwatching lookout point across the estuary. The Heritage Centre has recently been turned into an art gallery.

Waterfront & Scaplen's Court Museums

4 High Street, Poole, BH15 1BW (01202 262600). **Open** *Waterfront Museum* Apr-Oct 10am-5pm Mon-Sat; noon-5pm Sun. Nov-Mar 10am-3pm Mon-Sat; noon-3pm Sun. *Scaplen's Court Museum* Aug 10am-5pm Mon-Sat; noon-5pm Sun. **Admission** free.

The Waterfront Museum traces the history of the area from Roman times. It features old-fashioned street scenes and replicas of old shops, plus Poole pottery, seafaring tales and nautical watercolours. Next door is the Local History Centre where you can do serious research. Scaplen's Court Museum, currently open only in August, features more local history and a walled garden.

Where to stay

A notable new hotel, which opened too late to be reviewed for this guide, is **Harbour Heights** (Haven Road, Sandbanks, 01202 707272, doubles £115 per person), a boutique hotel in a renovated 1920s building with spectacular views over Poole Harbour.

Bournemouth Highcliffe Marriott
St Michaels Road, West Cliff, Bournemouth, BH2 5DU (01202 557702/fax 01202 293155/ www.marriotthotels.com/bohbm). **Rates** (per person) £116-£220 double/twin; £220 suite. **Rooms** (all en suite) 133 double/twin; 19 suites. **Credit** AmEx, DC, MC, V.
The grand old dame of Bournemouth hotels, this sprawling seaside mansion has period glamour: the opulent lobby, tearoom, library and restaurant are throwbacks to another era. Rooms at the Bournemouth Highcliffe Marriott (most of them no-smoking) are comfortable if a bit bland – ask for a sea view if you can afford it. Leisure facilities are top-notch – indoor and outdoor pools, tennis court and gym – as is the location: sitting proudly atop a cliff, a short walk from the beach and town centre.

Chine Hotel
25 Boscombe Spa Road, Bournemouth, BH5 1AX (01202 396234/fax 01202 391737/www.chine hotel.co.uk). **Rates** (per person) *July-Sept* £100. *Oct-June* £70. Child supplement for family rooms £2.50 for each year of child's age. **Rooms** (all en suite) 6 single; 40 double; 33 twin; 15 family; 1 four-poster. **Credit** AmEx, DC, MC, V.
The Chine is one of Bournemouth's more glamorous period hotels, with an elegant lobby, posh restaurant and Victorian caged lift. Situated in the leafy suburb of Boscombe, the Chine is far from the madding crowd, not too far – a five-minute drive will get you to the town centre. The hotel is family-friendly and the rooms are comfortable, if unspectacular. The best bits about the hotel are the spa, with its luxurious indoor pool – there's also a lovely outdoor one – and the acres of lush gardens, with shady paths leading down towards the beach.

Cumberland Hotel
East Overcliff Drive, Bournemouth, BH1 3AF (01202 290722/311394/www.arthuryoung.co.uk). **Rates** (per person) £59.50; £67 sea view. **Rooms** 12 single; 90 double/twin/family. **Credit** AmEx, DC, MC, V.
Bournemouth's first art deco building, the Cumberland Hotel could have stepped out of an Agatha Christie novel. The stylish white stucco building overlooks the sea, there's a wonderfully retro outdoor pool and a striking lobby. Truth be told, the rest of the hotel is a bit dowdy, but it's steps from the sea, a short walk from town and is a refreshing change from the endless stream of Victorian hotels.

Haven Hotel
Sandbanks, Poole, BH13 7QL (01202 707333/ www.fjbhotels.co.uk). **Rates** (per person) *Winter* from £100; *Summer* from £115. **Rooms** 6 single; 73 double. **Credit** AmEx, DC, MC, V.
This modern, luxury hotel has a lot going for it: a gourmet restaurant, state-of-the-art leisure facilities and a gorgeous indoor-outdoor pool. But the hotel's biggest asset is its location; it's situated at the southern tip of the Sandbanks peninsula and there are miles of beaches at your doorstep. The pristine sands of the Studland nature reserve and Brownsea Island are only a short ferry ride away.

Inverness Hotel
26 Tregonwell Road, Bournemouth, BH2 5NS (01202 554968/fax 01202 294197). **Rates** £21-£36 per person. **Rooms** (all en suite) 1 single; 6 double; 1 twin; 2 family. **Credit** MC, V.
Within walking distance of the beach, this Edwardian hotel is also a stone's throw from Bournemouth's other big draw: the bars and clubs. It's a gay-friendly place (the posters of Bette Davis and Joan Crawford are a dead giveaway). The rooms are comfy and, given the bargain price, surprisingly tasteful. There's also a homely lounge, but perhaps the best feature is the friendly staff. The hotel is no-smoking throughout.

Langtry Manor Hotel
26 Derby Road, Bournemouth, BH1 3QB (01202 553887/fax 01202 290115/www.langtrymanor.com). **Rates** (per person) £59.75-£64.75 double/twin; £69.75 four-poster or jacuzzi; £89.75 suite; £104.75 King's Room. £10 supplement for children. **Rooms** (all en suite) 13 double/twin; 5 four-poster; 4 suites; 2 double with jacuzzi; 2 four-poster with jacuzzi. **Credit** AmEx, DC, MC, V.
They don't get more atmospheric than this. King Edward VII built this gable-roofed, half-timbered mansion for his mistress, Lillie Langtry, in 1877, and it hasn't changed much since. The decor is wonderfully over the top – red velvet and huge sparkling chandeliers – and the ambience delightfully quaint: creaky passages, antique furniture and chambermaids dressed in Edwardian uniforms. Suites are named after famous guests: Oscar Wilde, Disraeli and Edward VII; Lillie's boudoir even has its own heart-shaped jacuzzi. The rooms are floral and feminine, as are the adorable squeaky-voiced ladies who keep the place ticking over. For a nostalgic treat, try the six-course banquet held every Saturday night in the magnificent dining room (smart dress required). Children and pets are welcome.

Mansion House
Thames Street, Poole, BH15 1JN (01202 685666/ fax 01202 665709/www.themansionhouse.co.uk). **Rates** (per person) £70-£90 single; £125 double/twin. **Rooms** (all en suite) 9 single; 21 double/twin; 2 deluxe double/twin; 2 family. **Credit** AmEx, DC, MC, V.
Once the home of a wealthy merchant family, this Georgian mansion is Poole's most elegant hotel. The lobby is graced by a sweeping staircase and grand Corinthian columns, there's a tasteful residents' lounge, a swish bar and acclaimed restaurant. The plush bedrooms are filled with antiques, without scrimping on the modern creature comforts. Poole Harbour is just steps away. Children are not admitted to the restaurant.

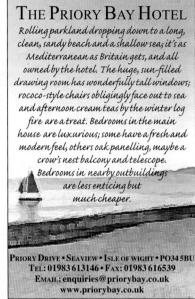

Menzies East Cliff Court

*East Overcliff Drive, Bournemouth, BH1 3AN
(www.bookmenzies.com/0870 600 3013/fax 01332
511144/01202 552011).* **Rates** £70 double; £92.50
sea view; £100 suite. **Rooms** 7 single; 40 double; 17
twin; 3 four-poster. **Credit** AmEx, DC, MC, V.
Getting turned down was the best thing that ever happened to this beautiful hotel. Following a £5m restoration, the Menzies East Cliff Court is a contender for
Bournemouth's most stylish address. The stucco building is painted in striking green pastels and the interior
is just as eye-catching, with polished wood floors, cream
walls and lots of art deco touches. The minimalist bedrooms are modern and luxurious, with crisp white linens,
smart wood furniture and gleaming new bathrooms. If
this is the new Bournemouth, things are looking up.
Children and pets are welcome.

Royal Bath Hotel

*Bath Road, Bournemouth, BH1 2EW (01202 555555/
fax 01202 554158/www.deveroyalbath.co.uk).* **Rates**
£135 single occupancy; £170-£215 double; £315-£365
suite. **Rooms** (all en suite) 22 single; 109 double;
9 suites. **Credit** AmEx, DC, MC, V.
On our visit to the Royal Bath, the most spectacular of
Bournemouth's Victorian palaces, one of the guests
arrived by helicopter. The public rooms are dazzlingly
ornate but the bedrooms pale by comparison. There's a
lovely indoor pool, though, and the glitzy restaurants
are straight out of an old movie. Even if you can't afford
to stay here, pop in for afternoon tea and soak up the
romance. Children are welcome but leave pets at home.

The Tudor Grange Hotel

*31 Gervis Road, Bournemouth, BH1 3EE (01202
291472/fax 01202 311503/www.tudorgrangehotel.
co.uk).* **Rates** (per person) £30-£35. **Rooms** 11.
Credit AmEx, DC, MC, V.
The Tudor Grange is a slice of village England just ten
minutes' walk from Bournemouth town centre. The half-
timbered cottage is cosy and atmospheric. With its oak
panelling and dark passageways, it could be straight
out of a murder mystery weekend. Bedrooms are small
and traditionally decorated. There's a cute little bar, and
guests have use of the indoor pool at a neighbouring
hotel. Children and dogs are admitted.

Where to eat & drink

Once, if you wanted to get a decent meal in
Poole or Bournemouth, hotel restaurants were
your best bet. The **Chine Hotel** (*see p130*) and
the **Langtry Manor Hotel** (*see p131*) still
have stellar reputations. But, in recent years, a
thriving restaurant scene has been taking shape
beyond hotel dining rooms. In Poole, the
Warehouse Brasserie (Poole Quay, 01202
677238) is a pleasant fish restaurant. **Café
Shore** (10-14 Banks Road, 01202 707271) in
Sandbanks has a Modern British/fusion menu.
Style restaurants have also arrived: **Klute &
Bree's** (20 Exeter Road, 01202 252511), the
city's fashionable new bar, has an attractive,
Kon-Tiki-style restaurant with an ambitious

menu and romantic views. For a break from
yuppie food, **Retro** (79-81 Charminster Road,
01202 315865) is Bournemouth's only Lebanese
restaurant and a perennial favourite. **Bistro on
the Bridge** (3-5 Bridge Street, Christchurch,
01202 482522) is a modern brasserie, and sister
restaurant to the **Bistro on the Beach** (*see
below*). **Salad Centre** (667 Christchurch Road,
01202 393673) does what it says on the tin. For
something a little different, one of the hottest
tickets in town is **Rubyz** (103 Commercial Road,
01202 780255) where drag queens perform
cabaret while you eat. It's popular, so book.

Poole is full of olde worlde nautical-style
pubs: the **King Charles** (Thames Street), the
Antelope (8 High Street) and the **Jolly Sailor**,
Lord Nelson and **Poole Arms** (all at Poole
Quay) are some of the best. But the beautiful
young things need somewhere to pose, too:
enter the **Oyster Quay Bar and Grill**
(Poole Quay, 01202 668669), a stunning new
space with a futuristic design and a huge
aquarium behind the bar.

These days, you can't move for stylish
new bars in Bournemouth. **Fruit** (219 Old
Christchurch Road, 01202 551927), **Klute
& Bree's** (*see above*) and **Casa** (Richmond
Hill, 01202 317686) are a few of the hipper
destinations, while **Slam Bar** (Fir Vale Road,
01202 555129) and **Consortium** (3 Richmond
Hill, 01202 555155), the city's best-known DJ
bars, stay open late and attract big-name jocks.
For proper clubbing, try **Elements** (Fir
Vale Road, 01202 311178) or Bournemouth's
most famous club, the **Opera House** (570
Christchurch Road, Boscombe, 01202 399922).

The most positive sign that Bournemouth
may one day be a cool city is its burgeoning
gay scene. Unlike the splintered London scene,
gays and lesbians party together in this town.
The **Branksome** is Bournemouth's most
popular gay pub (Commercial Road, 01202
552544) and the shiny, sparkling **Rubyz**
(30 The Triangle, 01202 297607), around the
corner from the restaurant of the same name,
is the best gay nightclub.

Bistro on the Beach

*Solent Promenade, Southbourne Coast Road,
Bournemouth, BH6 4BE (01202 431473).*
Food served Beach café 9am-4pm daily. Dinner
6-10pm Wed-Sat. **Main courses** £9.95-£16.95.
Set dinner £15.95 2 courses, £17.95 3 courses.
Credit AmEx, MC, V.
The name doesn't lie: this famous Bournemouth restaurant is perched precariously at the edge of the sea – at
high tide the waves almost lap at your feet. Fittingly,
the interior has been decked out in aquamarine tones
and the blackboard menu is heavy on fish. Some dishes
have a modish twist, such as a smoked eel starter, served
with asparagus, pecorino and garlic croustades. Others
– a perfect whole grilled Dover sole with parsley butter,

Call of the Five

Everyone knows that Dorset is Thomas Hardy country. But the countryside around Poole and Bournemouth could be more familiar to some through the books of another famous author, albeit one not so highly regarded in literary circles: Enid Blyton. Damned by contemporary critics for being politically incorrect and formulaic, Blyton's books have been getting a bad rap of late. But there's no question her jolly children's adventure stories and nostalgic vision of England turned millions of children around the world on to reading. And much of the imagery that pervades series such as the Famous Five was inspired by Blyton's annual summer holidays to coastal Dorset.

Corfe Castle, a striking ruin half an hour's drive from Poole, was the inspiration for Kirrin Castle, where the Five enjoyed several adventures during their preternaturally exciting school holidays. Other castles in the area, such as Durlston Castle, Lulworth Castle and the old water tower at Swanage, were also said to be inspirational to Blyton.

A couple of miles from Corfe Castle lies Hartland Moor. With its abandoned railway lines, swirling mists and abundance of heather and gorse, it was an ideal setting for *Five Go to Mystery Moor*. Nearby is the Isle of Purbeck Golf Club, once owned by Blyton. Here, the author lazed about on summer afternoons dreaming up ideas for new stories.

Brownsea Island, in the middle of Poole Harbour, with its handsome medieval castle and dense woodland, was the mysterious Whispering Island in *Five Have a Mystery to Solve*. Experts also think that Blyton's first full-length novel, *The Secret Island*, was inspired by one of the many wild islands in Poole Harbour.

Children who read the Mallory Towers boarding school series are often dazzled by the girls' saltwater swimming pool, carved out of rocks and constantly replenished by the incoming tide. For a glimpse of the pool that inspired Blyton, go to Dancing Ledge, a three-mile walk along the coastal path from Swanage. Blown out of the rocks by a headmaster of nearby Durnford Prep School at Langton Matravers (who made his boys bathe naked here every morning), the pool is now open for visitors to take a dip.

Other Blyton landmarks: Noddy fans might want to catch a glimpse of the Old Police House in Studland, where Mr Plod did his rounds. Some Blyton devotees believe that the village of Studland was the model for Kirrin village in the Five series. Then there's the Grand Hotel in Swanage (Burlington Road, 01929 423353), where Blyton spent several holidays. Further afield, near Sherborne, lies Manor Farm in Stourton Caundle. Blyton owned this farm and set *Five Go to Finniston Farm* here.

For information on Enid Blyton short breaks in Dorset, contact Ginger Pop (01202 620660/www.gingerpop.co.uk).

for example – are more traditional. There are vegetarian dishes too, such as roasted cherry tomato risotto with parmesan crisps and balsamic dressing. Puddings sounded delectable: the likes of rhubarb and grenadine crumble with ginger crème anglaise.

Chef Hong Kong

150-152 Old Christchurch Road, Bournemouth, BH1 1NL (01202 316996). **Food served** noon-3.30pm, 6-11.30pm Mon-Sat; noon-11.30pm Sun. **Main courses** £4.25-£25. **Set lunch** (Mon-Fri) £5.95 2 courses. **Set dinner** £15.50-£23 3 courses. **Credit** AmEx, DC, MC, V.

Bournemouth's numerous British oldies head up the road to the posh Mandarin when they want a decent Chinese meal, but this cheeky young upstart is generally crammed with Chinese people – a good sign as any connoisseur of Chinatown will be happy to tell you. The decor is simple and smart, with wood floors, cheerful yellow walls and a bit of oriental art, and the naff Chinese pop music is adorable (if you like that sort of thing). But the main attraction is the dim sum menu, full of authentic surprises such as grilled turnip paste, Vietnamese pancake rolls, egg custard tarts, minced prawn in bean curd pastry, savoury meat croquettes and juicy dumplings.

CH2

37 Exeter Road, Bournemouth, BH2 5AF (01202 296296). **Food served** noon-2.30pm, 6-10.30pm Tue-Sat. **Main courses** £5.50-£19. **Credit** AmEx, MC, V.
They say the new Bournemouth is young, hip and happening, and the trendy CH2 has clearly been created with such a market in mind: there are purple formica tables plus weird pop art and lots of industrial-chic flourishes. The menu is just as up to date, although the food doesn't always live up to expectations. On our visit, starters included fanned melon served with Italian cured ham and paw paw dressing, or spinach, red onion and ricotta tartlet. Mains range from steaks to pasta dishes, but you're probably best sticking to the thin-crust pizzas, which come with fashionable topping combinations such as goat's cheese, chicken, mango, pine nuts and pesto. Puddings were disappointing, but we've been assured the menu is being revamped.

Coriander

22 Richmond Hill, Bournemouth, BH2 6EJ (01202 552202/www.coriander-restaurant.co.uk). **Food served** noon-10.30pm Mon-Thur, Sun; noon-11pm Fri, Sat. **Main courses** £7.75-£9.95. **Credit** AmEx, DC, MC, V.
This friendly, funky Mexican favourite is a refreshing alternative to Bournemouth's deluge of wannabe-style restaurants. The interior is rustic and playful, with sombreros and Mexican blankets hanging from the walls, colourful tiles and cacti in the corner. The food is just as fun: well-prepared enchiladas, quesadillas, burritos and tacos, raspberry pavlovas and lime cheesecake for dessert, plus, of course, jugs of Margarita.

Custom House

Poole Quay, Poole, BH15 1HP (01202 676767). **Food served** 10am-2.30pm, 6.30-9.30pm daily. **Main courses** (café only) £5.95-£12.25. **Set lunch** (restaurant) £14.95 3 courses. **Set dinner** (restaurant) £19.95 2 courses, £24.95 3 courses. **Credit** AmEx, DC, MC, V.
This elegant, waterfront Georgian building seems to be featured on every Poole postcard, and now it houses a restaurant that is just as famous. The minimalist, first-floor space is the epitome of good taste, with blond wood floors, Rennie Mackintosh-style chairs and art on the walls. By and large, the food lives up to the stylish surroundings. Starters include the likes of gravadlax with dill mustard and horseradish sauce on a salad of beetroot, or steamed local mussels in a Thai curry sauce. Mains, such as Dorset shank of lamb with caramelised shallots and rosemary jus or fillet steak with a lime butter and prawns, were generous in portion and well prepared. Romantic views of Poole Harbour and candlelight made the meal all the more palatable.

Mansion House

7-11 Thames Street, Poole, BH15 1JN (01202 685666/www.themansionhouse.co.uk). **Food served** noon-2.30pm, 7-9.30pm Tue-Fri; 7-9.30pm Sat; noon-2.30pm Sun. **Main courses** £8.75 (lunch). **Set lunch** £15.95 3 courses. **Set dinner** £18.95 2 courses. **Credit** AmEx, DC, MC, V.
Poole's classiest hotel also houses what is widely thought to be its best restaurant. The swish main restaurant is a supremely elegant space, with cherry wood panelling, palm trees and a grand piano, while the romantic bistro – open to hotel residents only – is a cosy spot with brick walls, wood-beamed ceilings and a huge copper hearth. Both spaces share the same award-winning kitchen, serving modern European food with a skilled touch. Our celeriac and apple soup was, well, sublime. A main course piece of salmon served with sweet onions, mushroom and red wine sauce was pretty faultless. A sinfully good crème brûlée rounded off an excellent meal.

La Roche Restaurant

Haven Hotel, 116 Banks Road, Sandbanks, Poole, BH13 7QL (01202 707333/www.havenhotel.co.uk/ restaurants.htm). **Food served** noon-2.30pm, 7-9pm daily. **Main courses** (restaurant only) £14.25-£18.25. **Set lunch** (main dining room only) £17.50 3 courses Mon-Sat, £19.50 3 courses Sun. **Set dinner** (main dining room) £24.50 3 courses. **Credit** AmEx, DC, MC, V.
The Haven has a sterling reputation. The dining room has won several awards, but it's a bit starchy: for a more stylish experience, try the adjoining brasserie, a long art deco room with views of Poole Bay. Starters might include home-cured gravadlax served with a julienne of pickled cucumber and mint, or diver-caught scallops on spinach with lime and coriander jus. Mains such as pan-fried strips of corn-fed, lemon- and lime-marinated chicken or Pacific halibut pavé topped with goat's cheese, black olives and chorizo are expertly prepared.

Salterns Restaurant at Salterns Harbourside Hotel

38 Salterns Way, Lilliput, Poole, BH14 8JR (01202 707321/www.salterns.co.uk). **Food served** *Bar* noon-9pm daily. *Restaurant* 7.30-9.30pm daily. **Main courses** (restaurant) £12-£18.50. **Credit** AmEx, DC, MC, V.
This bright and breezy restaurant boasts one of Poole's best dining locations: overlooking the Salterns Marina, with plenty of outdoor seating during summer. The cooking is decent too. You can choose from fresh local seafood – such as steamed mussels in a white wine garlic sauce to start or a main course of pan-fried sea bass with spring vegetables, lemon and vanilla butter and cherry tomatoes. There are also traditional meat dishes such as prime fillet steak or pork loin in Somerset cider sauce. For more casual fare – pasta, curries, bangers and mash – try the light and airy bar next door.

Storm Restaurant

16 High Street, Poole, BH15 1BP (01202 674970/ www.stormfish.co.uk). **Food served** *Nov, Jan-Apr* 7-9.30pm Wed-Sat. *Dec* 7-9.30pm Tue-Sun. *May-Oct* 7-10pm daily (phone to confirm times). **Set dinner** £20.95 2 courses; £26.95 3 courses. **Credit** AmEx, MC, V.
Poole's newest fish restaurant is a romantic spot, with rough wood floors, candlelight and David Gray playing softly in the background. The chef is a fisherman, and the food is fresh and simply prepared. Starters include cracked Dorset coast crab with saffron aïoli, and a pleasantly peppery vegetable and fish soup with crème fraîche. For mains, roast cod was cooked with a Welsh rarebit crust on sweet potato mash, while the char-grilled royal bream was tender and delicate. By the time we finished the wonderful own-made herbed bread – served with olive oil – we had no room for Cointreau and walnut truffle mousse or rich chocolate pots. We'll be back.

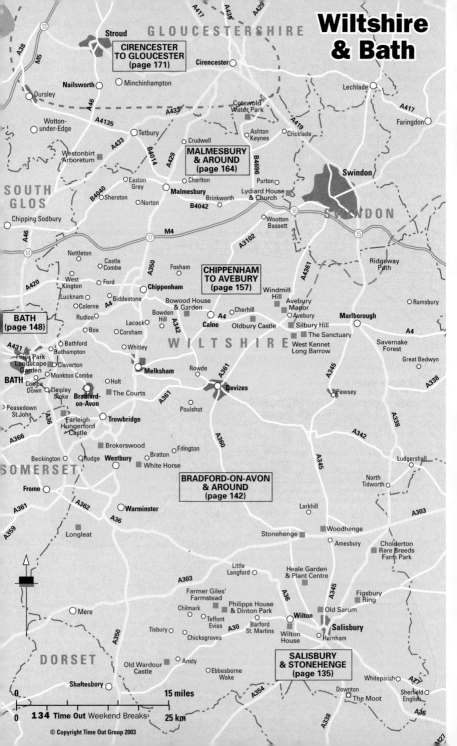

Wiltshire & Bath

CIRENCESTER TO GLOUCESTER (page 171)

MALMESBURY & AROUND (page 164)

CHIPPENHAM TO AVEBURY (page 157)

BATH (page 148)

BRADFORD-ON-AVON & AROUND (page 142)

SALISBURY & STONEHENGE (page 135)

GLOUCESTERSHIRE

Stroud

Nailsworth

Dursley

Minchinhampton

Cirencester

Lechlade

Cotswold Water Park

Wotton-under-Edge

Tetbury

Crudwell

Ashton Keynes

Cricklade

Faringdon

Westonbirt Arboretum

Charlton

Purton

Swindon

SOUTH GLOS

Easton Grey

Sherston

Malmesbury

Norton

Brinkworth

Lydiard House & Church

SWINDON

Chipping Sodbury

Wootton Bassett

Nettleton

Castle Combe

Foxham

Ridgeway Path

West Kington

Ford

Chippenham

Windmill Hill

Avebury Manor

Ramsbury

Lucknam

Colerne

Biddestone

Bowood House & Garden

Cherhill

Avebury

Marlborough

BATH (page 148)

Rudloe

Box

Bowden Hill

Lacock

Calne

Oldbury Castle

Silbury Hill

The Sanctuary

West Kennet Long Barrow

Savernake Forest

A4

Corsham

Whitley

WILTSHIRE

Great Bedwyn

Bathford

Bathampton

Prior Park Landscape Garden

Claverton

Monkton Combe

Holt

Melksham

Rowde

Pewsey

BATH

Combe Down

Limpley Stoke

The Courts

Devizes

Bradford-on-Avon

Poulshot

Peasedown St. John

Farleigh Hungerford Castle

Trowbridge

Brokerswood

Edington

Beckington

Rudge

Westbury

Bratton

White Horse

Ludgershall

SOMERSET

Frome

North Tidworth

BRADFORD-ON-AVON & AROUND (page 142)

Larkhill

Warminster

Longleat

Stonehenge

Woodhenge

Amesbury

Cholderton Rare Breeds Farm Park

Little Langford

Heale Garden & Plant Centre

Figsbury Ring

Mere

Farmer Giles' Farmstead

Chilmark

Philipps House & Dinton Park

Old Sarum

Tisbury

Teffont Evias

Barford St. Martins

Wilton

Salisbury

Chicksgroves

Wilton House

Harnham

DORSET

Old Wardour Castle

Ansty

Ebbesborne Wake

SALISBURY & STONEHENGE (page 135)

Whiteparish

Shaftesbury

Downton

The Moot

Sherfield English

0   15 miles

0   25 km

Salisbury & Stonehenge

Spectacular stones and a stunning spire.

Monuments to paganism and Christianity are the main attractions in this part of the world. The impressive stone circle of **Stonehenge** on windswept Salisbury Plain was heaved into place 4,000 or so years ago, while the equally inspiring **Salisbury Cathedral** was erected in the 13th century: two of the most famous buildings in the world within a few miles of each other – not bad for a small market town. And there's more. Eminently walkable and quintessentially English, Salisbury can be explored for its illustrious history, narrow lanes, busy market and profusion of tearooms. Outside the town, Wiltshire has the largest collection of neolithic and Bronze Age remains to be found anywhere in Britain, and the picturesque rolling countryside is remarkably unspoilt, with plenty of pretty villages built in knapped flint and local stone (there's a reason stone constructions are a big deal round here). The West Country also has a long tradition of pub-going and beer-brewing.

As far as the history of the town goes, **Salisbury** is a relocation of nearby Old Sarum. In the days before Sarum was 'Old', it was to this neck of the woods what 'new' Salisbury is now: the provincial capital. Then someone had the bright idea of moving the whole shooting match, lock, stock and masonry, about one mile down the road. Salisbury therefore occupies an attractive little valley nailed to the landscape by the second highest steeple in Europe. Around the cathedral's steeple is the famous walled Close, home to Edward Heath and where motor cars give way to the human traffic of camera-laden tourists. So dominant is the marvellous cathedral that the other items of interest in the town are necessarily eclipsed. However, this

doesn't mean they don't exist and history anoraks in need of a fuller historical briefing can seek satisfaction at the **Salisbury & South Wiltshire Museum**, **Mompesson House**, the **Wardrobe**, the **Medieval Hall** and the Tourist Information Centre in the Guildhall on the main square. This is not to mention the wealth of historical information to be found in the cathedral and its **chapter house**, which stores one of the few original copies of the Magna Carta of 1215.

For those restless modern souls unmoved by history, the market on Saturday and Tuesday offers good-value local agricultural produce, including both fish and fowl – the latter creatures' sacrifice to our dining tables being movingly commemorated by the stone stilted **Poultry Cross**. The **Market Square**, moreover, is an architecturally attractive space good for lounging about and fist-fighting on a Saturday night. The other thing that no market town can be without in this day and age is an annoying one-way system. Luckily, however, Salisbury is not only small enough to walk around, it is also small enough to walk out of altogether. One particularly popular walk takes you through the elegant **Queen Elizabeth Gardens**, across the water-meadows on the south side of the city where Constable parked his easel to paint his famous picture of the spire. Those who cannot live on architectural nostalgia alone can make the prettily located Old Mill pub and restaurant in **Harnham** their destination.

Outside Salisbury

Three miles west of Salisbury lies **Wilton**, the ancient capital of Wessex and home of Wilton carpets, the stately grandeur of **Wilton House** and more antiques shops than you can shake a Louis XIV brocaded stick at. This is classy idling country, with its startling Italianate church, ruined abbey and river walks along the Wylye. Further afield, six miles south of Salisbury, **Downton** is a chocolate-box, thatched village on the Avon, replete with village greens, Cuckoo Fair (first bank holiday Saturday in May) and the Moot monument. In the other direction, six miles north, next to the

By train from London

Trains to **Salisbury** leave from **Waterloo** approximately every hour, passing through Clapham Junction; journey time is 1hr 30mins. Info: www.swtrains.co.uk.

Wiltshire & Bath

Rock of ages

Perhaps the most famous pile of rocks on the planet, Stonehenge has attracted and mystified visitors for 5,000 years. Although much is now known about how it was built, we still don't know why or what for, with archaeologists, scientists, Druids, New Agers and the just plain curious all having their own pet theories; it's been variously described as an astronomical observatory, site of ritual human sacrifice, war memorial, neolithic computer – some even think Merlin was involved, transporting the ring of stones from Ireland by magic.

What you see today is a ruin of the final construction built between 4,500

MOD's razor-wired expanses of Salisbury Plain, the quiet market town of **Amesbury** offers B&Bs and inns galore, but none of Salisbury's grander distractions.

Unquestionably, the big draw outside the cathedral city is **Stonehenge** (*see above* **Rock of ages**). The site is complemented by the prototype **Woodhenge** nearby, although the **Moot**, several miles south in Downton, is a lesser known, more stimulating ancient monument. It is reputed to be a Saxon parliament, but also has a medieval 'bailie' mound and amphitheatre set in Grade I-listed 18th-century ornamental gardens.

What to see & do

Tourist Information Centres
In addition to the offices listed below, the website at www.salisburycity.co.uk is also worth a look.

Fish Row, Salisbury, SP1 1EJ (01722 334956/ www.visitsalisbury.com). **Open** *May* 9.30am-5pm Mon-Sat; 10.30am-4.30pm Sun. *June-Sept* 9.30am-6pm Mon-Sat; 10.30am-4.30pm Sun. *Oct-Apr* 9.30am-5pm Mon-Sat.

Redworth House, Flower Lane, Amesbury, SP4 7HG (01980 622833/www.visitsalisbury.com). **Open** *June-Aug* 9am-5pm Mon-Fri; 10am-4pm Sat. *Sept-May* 9am-5pm Mon-Fri.

Bike hire
Hayballs *26-30 Winchester Street, Salisbury, SP1 1HG (01722 411378).*

Cholderton Rare Breeds Farm Park
Amesbury Road, Cholderton, SP4 0EW (01980 629438/www.rabbitworld.co.uk). **Open** *Mid Mar-Oct* 10am-6pm daily. Last admission 4.30pm. *Nov-mid Mar* 11am-4pm Sat, Sun. Last admission 3pm. **Admission** £5.50; £3.50-£4.50 concessions. **Credit** AmEx, DC, MC, V.

and 4,000 years ago. Originally, the site of Stonehenge was occupied by a large ceremonial earthwork, then a timber structure and, finally, a stone version, with bluestones (the smaller ones) brought from the Preseli Mountains in Wales in 2,600 BC, followed by the construction of the massive, lintel-topped stone circle with sarsens from Marlborough Downs. (The lintels, unique to Stonehenge, set it apart from other great prehistoric monuments.)

It's a huge engineering achievement; apart from the problem of transporting the stones in the first place – each sarsen weighs over 25 tons, while the bluestones had to travel 240 miles by sea and land – they then had to be shaped and erected. With very primitive tools, and a lot of human muscle, these prehistoric builders managed some sophisticated building techniques: each lintel was secured in place with mortice and tenon joints, and then linked to the next lintel with tongue and groove joints.

Of course, you can't actually see this for yourself. For reasons of preservation, Stonehenge (which, along with nearby Avebury, was designated a World Heritage Site in 1986) is now managed by English Heritage and fenced off. There's a path around the edge, but you can't get very close, let alone touch anything. It can still be an atmospheric spot (and a windswept one, so dress warm), but the current arrangement is a mess, with facilities completely inadequate for the number of visitors. There's not enough parking, and the toilets, money-spinning souvenir shop and tea stall ('megalithic' rock cakes, anyone?) are housed in ugly pre-fab huts – no way to treat a world-famous monument.

If current plans – much argued over – go ahead, this will all change by 2008. The intention is to return the whole World Heritage Site to a more 'natural' setting, removing traffic (by closing the A344 and putting part of the A303 in a tunnel) and building a new visitors' centre a couple of miles away, with shuttle buses dropping visitors within walking distance of the monument.

But you still won't be able to get in among the stones; some say Stonehenge will end up as some kind of prehistoric theme park – and you're better off visiting lesser-known, and left-alone, Avebury.

Stonehenge
By junction of A303 & A344, west of Amesbury, SP4 7DE (info line 01980 624715/www.english-heritage.org.uk). **Open** *Mid Mar-May, Sept-mid Oct* 9.30am-6pm daily. *June-Aug* 9am-7pm daily. *Mid Oct-mid Mar* 9.30am-4pm daily. **Admission** (EH & NT) £5; £2.50-£3.80 concessions. **Credit** MC, V.

Get a preview of genetic engineering in years to come: lop-eared bunnies, spotty percy pigs and seaweed-eating sheep (really). Plus tractor rides, pig-racing, an adventure playground and animals for sale.

Farmer Giles' Farmstead
Teffont Magna, Salisbury, SP3 5QY (01722 716338/www.farmergiles.co.uk). **Open** *Mid Mar-early Nov* 10am-5pm daily. *Early Nov-mid Mar* 10am-dusk Sat, Sun. **Admission** £3.95; £2.85-£3.50 concessions. **Credit** MC, V.
Kids can bottle-feed lambs or ride a tractor on this working dairy farm 11 miles west of Salisbury on the B3089. Furry friends include pigs, sheep, rabbits and Shetland ponies, and there's also a restaurant and gift shop.

Figsbury Ring
Just north of A30, 3 miles NE of Salisbury.
A ritual site? A settlement? Although commonly taken to be an Iron Age hillfort, there's little evidence to support this. However, this vast circular earthwork with a deep inner ditch does support a reasonable scenic view.

Heale Garden & Plant Centre
Middle Woodford, SP4 6NT (01722 782504). **Open** *Garden* 10am-5pm Tue-Sun. Last entry 4.30pm. *Plant Centre* 10am-5pm daily. **Admission** £3.75; £1.50 concessions; free under-5s. **Credit** MC, V.
The eight-acre gardens of Heale House (which is not open to the public) feature a lovely collection of roses, shrubs and plants amid clipped hedges and mellow stonework. The grounds also boast a water garden with a Japanese tea house. In addition, there are unusual plants for sale.

Medieval Hall
West Walk, Cathedral Close, Salisbury, SP1 2EY (01722 412472/www.medieval-hall.co.uk). **Open** *Apr-Sept* 11am-5pm daily. Phone to check. *Oct-Mar* open by arrangement. **Admission** £2; £1.50 concessions; free under-6s. **No credit cards**. This beamed 13th-century hall is the setting for a 40-minute audio-visual presentation on Salisbury's history.

Wiltshire & Bath

The decaying magnificence of **Old Wardour Castle**.

Mompesson House

Choristers' Green, Cathedral Close, Salisbury, SP1 2EL (01722 335659/www.nationaltrust.org.uk). **Open** *Apr-Oct* 11am-5pm Mon-Wed, Sat, Sun. Closed Nov-Mar. **Admission** (NT) *House* £3.90; £1.95 concessions. *Garden only* 80p. **No credit cards.**

An elegant 18th-century Queen Anne house, which featured in the award-winning film version of *Sense and Sensibility*. Attractions at Mompesson include the Turnbull collection of glasses, as well as period furniture and a walled garden.

New Art Centre Sculpture Park & Gallery

Roche Court, East Winterslow, Salisbury, SP5 1BG (01980 862244/www.sculpture.uk.com). **Open** 11am-4pm daily. **Admission** free.

Sculptures by Barbara Hepworth, Henry Moore, Bill Woodrow, Julian Opie and other luminaries sit amid the trees, lawns and parkland of 19th-century Roche Court (the house is not open to the public). Changing exhibitions are held in the tiny, award-winning gallery. *7 miles E of Salisbury, just south of A30 near East Winterslow.*

Old Sarum

Castle Road, Salisbury, SP1 3SD (01722 335398/ www.english-heritage.org.uk). **Open** *Apr-June, Sept* 10am-6pm daily. *July, Aug* 9am-6pm daily. *Oct* 10am-5pm daily. *Nov-Mar* 10am-4pm daily. **Admission** (EH) £2.50; £1.30-£1.90 concessions. **Credit** MC, V.

The knee-high remains of Old Salisbury – including a Norman palace, castle and cathedral – perched atop an impressive Iron Age earthwork.

Old Wardour Castle

N of A30, nr Tisbury, SP3 6RR (01747 870487/ www.english-heritage.org.uk). **Open** *Apr-Sept* 10am-6pm daily. *Oct* 10am-5pm daily. *Nov-Mar* 10am-1pm, 2-4pm Wed-Sun. **Admission** (EH) £2.60; £1.30-£2 concessions. **Credit** MC, V.

The unusual hexagonal ruins of this dreamy lakeside castle (which had a starring role in Kevin Costner's *Robin Hood: Prince of Thieves*) last saw violent action in the Civil War – disruptive picnickers aside. Landscaped grounds include a rockwork grotto.

Salisbury Cathedral

The Close, Salisbury, SP1 2EJ (01722 555120/ www.salisburycathedral.org.uk). **Open** *June-Aug* 7.15am-7.30pm Mon-Sat; 7.15am-6.15pm Sun. *Sept-May* 7.15am-6.15pm daily. **Admission** free; £3.80 suggested donation.

Stunningly located in the green heart of the Close, Salisbury Cathedral is an undoubted masterpiece, one of the most elegant and spectacular buildings in the UK, indeed the world. Finished in 1258 (after an amazingly short 38 years of construction work), it's a fantastic example of early English Gothic architecture, with the most famous spire in the country – and the tallest at 404ft. Highlights include the medieval clock, the statue-covered west front and the cloisters (the largest in the country), but it's best to just wander at will, taking in the glory of the whole – and marvelling at the skill of the anonymous craftsmen who built it. The well-preserved chapter house houses one of the four surviving original copies of the Magna Carta (1215) and a carved medieval frieze depicting scenes from Genesis and Exodus (Noah's ark is easy to spot).

Salisbury Festival

Festival Office, 75 New Street, Salisbury, SP1 2PH (01722 332241/www.salisburyfestival.co.uk). **Dates** (2004) 21 May-6 June. **Tickets** £3-£30. **Credit** AmEx, DC, MC, V.

The annual international summer festival in May and June is dominated by classical music and attracts such major players as the City of Birmingham Symphony Orchestra, the Jan Garbarek Quartet, Tenebrae and Ravi Shankar. The impressive line-up of events also features jazz, opera, theatre and dance in various venues including the Salisbury Playhouse and the cathedral itself.

Salisbury Playhouse
Malthouse Lane, Salisbury, SP2 7RA (01722 320333/www.salisburyplayhouse.com).
Performances Jan-June, Sept-Dec. **Open** *Box office* 10am-6pm Mon-Sat. **Tickets** £9.50-£18.50; £7.50-£16.50 concessions. **Credit** AmEx, DC, MC, V.

One of the real powerhouses of British regional theatre, producing its own seasons and receiving major touring companies before they move on to perform in London's West End. There's also a studio space presenting new and alternative talent.

Salisbury & South Wiltshire Museum
The King's House, 65 The Close, Salisbury, SP1 2EN (01722 332151/www.salisburymuseum.org.uk).
Open *July, Aug* 10am-5pm Mon-Sat; 2-5pm Sun. *Sept-June* 10am-5pm Mon-Sat. **Admission** £3.50; £1-£2.30 concessions; free under-5s. **Credit** MC, V.

Bill Bryson liked this friendly and idiosyncratic museum, which contains a fine Stonehenge gallery, a seminal archaeological collection (including the story of General Pitt Rivers, the founding father of modern archaeology), as well as local costumes, ceramics, stuffed birds and surprise Turner watercolours. Look out for the mummified black rat found in the skull of the Earl of Salisbury when his tomb in the cathedral was opened in 1791.

Stourhead
Stourton, Warminster, BA12 6QD (01747 841152/www.nationaltrust.org.uk). **Open** *Garden* 9am-7pm/dusk daily. *House* mid Mar-Sept 11am-5pm Mon, Tue, Fri-Sun. Oct 11am-4.30pm Mon, Tue, Fri-Sun. Last admission 30mins before closing. Closed Nov-mid Mar. *Tower* Mid Mar-Oct noon-5pm/dusk daily. Last admission 30mins before closing. Closed Nov-mid Mar. **Admission** (NT) *House & garden* (Nov-mid Mar) £9.40; £4.50 concessions; free under-5s. *House or garden* (Apr-Oct) £5.40; £3 concessions; free under-5s. *Garden only* (Nov-Mar) £3.95; £1.90 concessions; free under-5s. *Tower* £2; £1 concessions. **Credit** MC, V.

Some 27 miles west of Salisbury, Stourhead is a marvellous example of 18th-century English landscaping. Designed by Henry Hoare (of the banking family) and laid out between 1741 and 1780, it's full of magnificent mature trees, rhododendrons and azaleas (best in May), with a series of classical temples strategically located around a central lake. Climb King Alfred's Tower for a fine view over the estate. Food and five rooms (doubles £90) are available at the Spread Eagle Inn at the entrance to the gardens (01747 840587).
Stourhead is off B3092, 3 miles north of Mere on A303.

The Wardrobe
58 Cathedral Close, Salisbury, SP1 2EX (01722 419419/www.thewardrobe.org.uk). **Open** *Feb, Mar, Nov* 10am-5pm Tue-Sun. *Apr-Oct* 10am-5pm daily. Closed Dec, Jan. **Admission** £2.75; 75p-£2 concessions. *Garden only* 75p. **Credit** (over £10) AmEx, MC, V.

The local regimental museum is housed in a fine house dating from 1254, which was used by bishops in the 14th century to house clothing, hence its nickname. The

attractive garden at the back contains a glorious 300-year-old copper beech, and cream teas are on offer in the Bernières Tea Room (*see p141*).

Wilton Carpet Factory
King Street, Wilton, SP2 0AY (01722 742733/www.wiltoncarpets.com). **Open** *Shop* 9.30am-5.30pm Mon-Sat; 11am-5pm Sun. **Tours** 11am, 12.30pm, 2pm, 3.30pm Mon-Fri. **Tickets** £4; £2.50-£3.75 concessions. **No credit cards.**

Unravel the mysteries of Wilton and Axminster carpet-making, which dates back nearly 300 years. The Wilton factory outlet shop (plus fashion, sports equipment and gifts) is in the Wilton Shopping Village on Minster Street (01722 741211/www.wiltonshoppingvillage.co.uk).

Wilton House
Wilton, Salisbury, SP2 0BJ (01722 746729/www.wiltonhouse.com). **Open** *House* Easter-Oct 10.30am-5.30pm Tue-Sun. Last entry 4.30pm. *Grounds* Easter-Oct 10.30am-5.30pm daily. *Both* closed Nov-Easter. **Admission** *House & grounds* £9.75; £5.50-£8 concessions. *Grounds only* £4.50; £3.50 concessions. **Credit** MC, V.

The Earl of Pembroke's family pad, which was designed by Inigo Jones, is not so much stately as absurdly OTT (especially the Single and Double Cube Rooms). It's got a fabulous art collection (including works by Van Dyck, Reynolds, Rembrandt and Brueghel) as well as 21 acres of landscaped parkland, a Palladian bridge over the Nadder, a Tudor kitchen and an adventure playground.

Woodhenge
Off A345, just N of Amesbury.
Site of a covered wooden monument that predated Stonehenge, discovered in 1925. Concrete posts mark the many excavated postholes. Enthusiasts only.

Where to stay

Smart farmhouse B&Bs dot the countryside of south Wiltshire, while Salisbury has a number of conference-quality hotels, as well as decent guesthouses and inns with rooms, such as the **King's Arms** (St John's Street, 01722 327629/www.activehotels.com, doubles £99) and the rather garish **Red Lion** (4 Milford Street, 01722 323334/www.the-redlion.co.uk, doubles £110, breakfast extra), part of which dates from 1230. Six rooms are also available at the charming **Beckford Arms** (*see p141*, doubles £75-£85) near Fonthill Gifford.

Howard's House Hotel
Teffont Evias, SP3 5RJ (01722 716392/fax 01722 716820/www.howardshousehotel.com). **Rates** £95 single occupancy; £145 twin/double; £165 four-poster; £30 child supplement when sharing parents' room. **Rooms** (all en suite) 1 twin; 6 double; 1 four-poster; 1 family. **Credit** AmEx, DC, MC, V.

Book well ahead if you want to stay in this upmarket country hotel, a wisteria-covered, 17th-century dower house located in an absurdly pretty village ten miles west of Salisbury. Large pastel-coloured bedrooms, a classic English garden and top-class modern British cooking in the small dining room (open to non-residents for both lunch and dinner) ensure a quality time is had by all, children and dogs included. Children and dogs (£7 per night) welcome.

A303 west; 2 miles after Wylye intersection with A36, turn left towards Teffont; after a quarter of a mile turn left to Teffont Evias; turn right at sharp bend in village; follow signs to hotel.

Newton Farmhouse

Southampton Road (A36), Whiteparish, Salisbury, SP5 2QL (tel/fax 01794 884416/www.newton farmhouse.co.uk). **Rates** £35-£45 single occupancy; £50-£60 twin; £70-£80 four-poster; £10 (5-11), £15 (12-18) child supplement when sharing parents' room. **Rooms** (all en suite) 2 twin; 6 four-poster/family. **No credit cards**.

You're guaranteed a super-friendly welcome from Suzi and John Lanham, the owners of this 16th-century listed farmhouse on the fringes of the New Forest. Eight miles south of Salisbury, it once belonged to Lord Nelson's family. Attractions include four-poster beds in the floral bedrooms (each one with an individual theme – the Redouté room is the largest and nicest), the lavish breakfasts, a bougainvillea-draped conservatory and a large garden. There's an outdoor (unheated) swimming pool too. Children are welcome. No smoking throughout.

J2 M27; A36 past sign for Whiteparish; house is on left after half a mile, immediately before the turning to Downton and Redlynch.

UPSTAIRS

Salisbury Festival. *See p138.*

CUORE D'ITAL

Onion Store

Wellow Drove, Sherfield English, nr Romsey, Hampshire SO51 6DU (tel/fax 01794 323227/ www.theonionstore.co.uk). **Open** *May-early Oct* Mon-Wed, Fri-Sun. **Rates** £90-£100 single occpuancy; £110-£120 suite. **Rooms** (all en suite) 3 suites. **No credit cards**.

This wildly romantic hideaway offers three unique and idiosyncratic suites in self-contained outhouses in the gardens of thatched Wellow Mead house. The Onion Store is the largest, with an upstairs bedroom; the Apple Store has a hot tub and a silver birch tree bed; the Grain Store has a muslin-draped bed and a French cast-iron bath. The indoor swimming pool in the conservatory doubles as the breakfast room. You won't find a more charming retreat from the stresses of modern living; not surprisingly, it's a hit with honeymooners. No TVs and no smoking throughout.

Sherfield English is off the A27, W of Romsey. At the Hatchett Inn, turn on to Mill Road; after half a mile or so, turn left on to Wellow Drove; the Onion Store is on the right after 300yds.

River Barn

Fonthill Bishop, SP3 5SF (01747 820232/fax 01747 820105/www.theriverbarn.co.uk). **Rates** £28 single occupancy; £48 double/twin. **Rooms** (all en suite) 1 twin; 2 double. **No credit cards**.

B&B, café-bar, post office, art gallery, gift shop: the River Barn's got the lot. Housed in a collection of red-brick buildings next to a river in the picturesque Nadder Valley, this tranquil spot has three recently refurbished rooms (all on the ground floor) and a pretty café serving fab home-made food: cream teas, quiches, stews, fish chowder. The gallery specialises in work by local artists. Book well ahead; Children over 12 and dogs welcome. No smoking throughout.

Fonthill Bishop is 14 miles W of Salisbury, on the B3089.

White Hart

St John's Street, Salisbury, SP1 2SD (0870 400 8125/fax 01722 412761/www.macdonaldhotels. co.uk). **Rates** £60-£115 single; £110-£135 double/ twin/family; £130-£165 deluxe double/four-poster/ suite. **Rooms** (all en suite) 15 single; 18 double; 21 twin; 3 deluxe double; 6 family; 4 four-poster; 1 suite. **Credit** AmEx, DC, MC, V.

Adjacent to Cathedral Close in the centre of town, this smartly porticoed 17th-century building houses a large, 'traditional' English hotel. Reliable, comfortable and well appointed with unostentatious clean facilities, it has a slightly corporate but personable air. Head up to the second floor, where the bedrooms have been classily refurbished in muted cream, mushroom and beige colours, with old prints of Stonehenge. A dining room and capacious lounge round off the facilities. Children and dogs (£10 per stay) welcome.

Where to eat & drink

Drinking is one of the things they do best in these parts – though historic boozers are more common than sleek, modern bars. For the former, try the pink-painted **Wig & Quill** (1 New Street, 01722 335665), a fine old Wadworth's pub serving up a range of robust real ales. For the latter, there's the trendy **Moloko Bar** (5 Bridge Street, 01722 507050/ www.molokobar.com), offering a wide range of vodkas. Alternatively, the youth of today favour the **Cathedral Hotel**, a bland variation on All Bar One (7-9 Milford Street, 01722 343700) or the lively music/comedy venue, **Chicago Rock Café** (30 Fisherton Street, 01722 322998). Older folk may prefer the tranquillity of the town's many tearooms. **David Brown's** (31 Catherine Street, 01722 329363) offers wholesome, reasonably priced snacks, while other top tearooms include **Michael Snell** (8 St Thomas Square, 01722 336037) and **Mompesson House** in the Close (see p138).

If you're looking for an authentic country pub, it's best to venture out west, deeper into Hardy Country, and enjoy the rural boozing idylls of **Chilmark**, **Tisbury**, **Chicksgrove**, **Ansty** and other villages in the pretty Nadder Valley.

Angel Inn

Angel Lane, Hindon, SP3 6BJ (01747 820696/ www.theangelhindon.fslife.co.uk). **Food served** noon-2pm, 7-9pm Mon-Sat; noon-2pm Sun. **Main courses** £9.95-£14. **Credit** MC, V.
At the heart of the unspoilt Georgian village of Hindon, the Angel Inn's classic exterior is contrasted by a smart, modern interior. The two bars have pine furniture, wine-red walls and a blackboard menu listing the daily changing carte. The restaurant towards the rear is light and airy: tables with candles and flowers, black-and-white photos of local scenes on the pale walls and a look-in on the open-plan kitchen. The same menu applies throughout and is an imaginative mix: crispy fish cake with remoulade sauce; smoked ham, chips and two duck eggs; sausages, mash and onion gravy; slow-roast lamb shank with bubble and squeak and Madeira jus. To finish, try the panettone bread and butter pudding or the pineapple tarte tatin with coconut ice-cream.

Beckford Arms

Fonthill Gifford, SP3 6PX (01747 870385). **Food served** noon-2pm, 7-9pm daily. **Main courses** £8.90-£15.95. **Credit** MC, V.
Situated on the edge of the Fonthill estate that once belonged to the eccentric William Beckford, this charming 18th-century inn operates as both a B&B and a very pleasant pub/restaurant. Wooden floors, rustic tables, an open fire and an airy garden room provide a casual setting for some fine Modern European food served by friendly young staff. Starters include the likes of oak-smoked salmon with rocket, or goat's cheese, red pepper and oregano tart; some starters are also available as mains. Inventive meat, fish and pasta dishes – beef with balsamic roast onions, butterfish with prawn and caper salsa or Thai vegetable curry – make up the mains. Superior baguettes (pesto chicken and black olive tapenade, for example) are also offered at lunchtime. Well-kept beers come from Hop Back, Greene King and Timothy Taylor.

Bernières Tea Room

The Wardrobe, 58 Cathedral Close, Salisbury, SP1 2EX (01722 413666/www.thewardrobe.org.uk). **Open** Oct-Easter 10am-2pm daily. Easter-Sept 10am-4.30pm daily. **Main courses** £6.50. **No credit cards.**
This green-and-pink tearoom in a converted coach house in front of the local regimental museum is a handy spot for a cream tea (£3.95) after touring the cathedral. Here you can tuck into old-fashioned cakes or a selection of sandwiches while eavesdropping on the gossip of local matrons. Home-cooked lunches (served noon-2pm) offer the likes of steak and kidney pie and roast beef. A railway station sign from the Normandy village of Bernières hangs above the window; it was presented to British troops by the village's grateful mayor after the D-Day landings. There are a couple of tables outside for sunny days.

Haunch of Venison

1-5 Minster Street, Salisbury, SP1 1TB (01722 322024). **Food served** noon-3pm, 6-9pm Mon-Thur; noon-3pm, 6-10.30pm Fri, Sat. **Main courses** £5-£15. **Set meal** (noon-1pm, 6-7pm) £5 1 course incl glass of wine. **Credit** MC, V.
As you might expect from the name, venison is the speciality at this original Dickensian chop-house, with black-timbered walls and floors every bit as crooked as Fagin. If you don't fancy venison sausages with mash and red onion marmalade or the Haunch Platter (a selection of venison dishes plus beer or wine), fish and chicken dishes also put in an appearance. Homely puds include apple tart with vanilla ice-cream and a delicious mini summer pudding. Cooking is hearty rather than sophisticated, but the setting is marvellous. Alternatively, you can just have a pint in one of Britain's two remaining pewter bars in the tiny nobs' snug situated halfway up the cramped staircase.

Milburns Restaurant

The Refectory, Salisbury Cathedral, Salisbury, SP1 2EJ (01722 555175/www.salisburycathedral.org.uk). **Food served** 9.30am-5.30pm daily. **Main courses** £4.25-£6.95. **Credit** MC, V.
Enjoy good coffee, yummy chocolate brownies and light lunch dishes – cold parmesan-crusted salmon with salad or chicken in mustard, red wine and bacon sauce, say – in this self-service café wedged between the cathedral and chapter house. Tempting desserts include ginger and marmalade cheesecake, and a limited range of beer and wine is also available. It's a light and airy space, with a fine view of the spire through the glass roof. The cathedral shop occupies one end.

Old Mill Hotel

Town Path, Harnham, SP2 8EU (01722 327517/ www.comeoninn.co.uk/oldmill). **Food served** noon-2pm, 7-9pm Mon-Sat; noon-9pm Sun. **Main courses** £10-£15. **Credit** AmEx, MC, V.
Stroll across the water-meadows to reach this popular pub/restaurant on the banks of the River Avon; the views back to Salisbury are lovely. Simple pleasures are available in the form of pub lunches, while the plush adjoining restaurant offers more gastronomic delights (swordfish, fillet steak, mushroom casserole and the like). There are 11 bedrooms (doubles £80-£95) in case you can't face leaving.

Wiltshire & Bath

Bradford-on-Avon & Around

An industrial past gives way to a more leisurely present.

Sitting just before west Wiltshire drifts into Somerset, this former weaving town is largely built of local Cotswold stone, which gives it its characteristic honey colour. The distinctive weavers' cottages that huddle along the steep river valley certainly lend charm, but the town avoids chi-chi overload thanks to a still-visible industrial past. The large, flat-fronted mills that loom up along the River Avon as it bisects the town can make it seem quite forbidding on an overcast day.

The town dates back to prehistoric times, having sprung up around a handy crossing point across the Avon. The Iron Age settlement was developed and expanded in turn by Roman and Saxon settlers, leaving behind historical highlights such as the tiny and atmospheric Saxon **Church of St Laurence** on Church Street.

The 'broad ford' was spanned in the 13th century by a stone town bridge, which still forms the centre of the town today. During the next few centuries Bradford became a powerful centre for the wool and cloth industries, its prosperity reflected in the massive size of the 14th-century **Tithe Barn** (located half a mile south of the town bridge). Bradford's affluence reached a peak in the 17th century – huge merchants' houses surviving from that time give an idea of its wealth. Weavers' cottages (once modest, now sought-after) were built on the steep hillside north of the river – the best examples are along Tory, Middle Rank and Newtown.

With the arrival of mechanisation, the wool trade moved from individual houses to large mills, which can still be seen (in various degrees of restoration or disrepair) next to the river. By the 1840s, however, the wool trade had collapsed following a steady decline. The town managed to reinvent itself as a rubber manufacturer almost immediately afterwards, meaning that the mills could simply be retooled (*see p146* **From wool to rubber**). You can find out more about the town's history at the tiny museum, which is located above the library.

Today, Bradford-on-Avon is a small, quiet town of cramped medieval streets and 21st-century traffic. You may well exhaust its attractions after a day or so, but as **Bath** is only 15 minutes away by train or car (*see p148*), it makes an ideal base for exploring that great Georgian city and the lovely countryside around the area.

Canal town

There's nothing more relaxing than sitting at a waterside pub watching the narrowboats drift past – or, for the marginally more adventurous, renting a vessel and taking the helm yourself – and as Bradford lies on the route of the **Kennet & Avon Canal**, there is plenty of opportunity for both. The canal, opened in 1810, links Bristol with the Thames at Reading and was one of the most ambitious waterway projects ever undertaken in Britain. But by the 1840s it was all but superseded by the Great Western Railway, which runs parallel to it, as though in open mockery. The canal remained neglected until the 1980s, when its recreational potential sparked a massive, still ongoing restoration plan.

With no steep gradients – apart from a series of 22 locks at Devizes (*see p159*) – and with leisurely barges comprising the only motor traffic, the canal towpath makes a very pleasant walking route, threading through some delightful woodland, country parks and 19th-century architecture. There is one lock in the

By train from London

There are roughly three direct trains a day that run from **Waterloo** to **Bradford-on-Avon** (via Warminster), with a journey time of just under 2hrs. Trains also leave from **Paddington** half-hourly, but passengers must change at Bath Spa or Westbury, with a 15-30min wait for connections. Journey time is about 2hrs and 2hr 30mins respectively. Info: www.great-western-trains.co.uk and www.walesandwest.co.uk.

Symbol of wealth – Bradford's massive 14th-century **Tithe Barn**.

town, and it's fun to watch the levels rise and drop, the boats plunge down and the water spurt through so powerfully. You can walk to Bath along the canalside – it takes about three hours – and you will cross splendid aqueducts at **Avoncliff** and **Dundas**, and pass a Victorian water-powered pumping station at **Claverton**, not to mention plenty of waterside watering holes at Avoncliff, Limpley Stoke, Claverton and Bathampton. The towpaths are also popular with anglers and cyclists (*see below* **Bike hire**). Canoes and self-drive day boats are also available, and the nearby **Bradford-on-Avon Wharf** (01225 868683) runs 1½-hour narrowboat trips three days a week from April to October. If you'd like to stay afloat for longer, **Sally Boats** at Bradford-on-Avon Marina (A363 south of the town centre; 01225 864923/www.sallyboats.ltd.uk) hires out narrowboats for holidays.

Further afield

Scattered throughout the Mendip Hills and the valleys of the Avon and Frome rivers is a profusion of stately homes, gardens, prehistoric monoliths, medieval castles and picturesque villages. Close by are the attractive gardens of **Iford Manor** and **Courts**, while half an hour's drive south is **Longleat**, the Elizabethan home of the eccentric Marquis of Bath and his lions.

Go east from Longleat towards Salisbury Plain and carved into the chalky side of a hill overlooking the town of Westbury, and visible on a clear day from Bradford-on-Avon, is one of the oldest and largest white horses in the country. **Westbury White Horse** possibly dates back to the ninth century; it has since been re-cut and concreted. There are great views and hang-gliding from the top of the hill, if the urge should take you. In the early 1990s the fields below were the site of some of Wiltshire's most elaborate crop circles (fake or otherwise). Nearby is the Iron Age hill fort of **Bratton Castle** and the fortified 14th-century mansion

Edington Priory (01380 830010). Every August a festival of church music is held here.

The area around Westbury and Warminster is particularly pleasant countryside for walking and cycling, and includes the privately owned (but accessible) ancient forest of **Brokerswood**.

What to see & do

Tourist Information Centres

50 St Margaret's Street, Bradford-on-Avon, BA15 1JX (01225 865797/www.bradfordonavon.org.uk). **Open** *Apr-Christmas* 10am-5pm daily. *Jan-Mar* 10am-4pm daily.
Central Car Park, Warminster, BA12 9BT (01985 218548). **Open** *Apr-Oct* 9.30am-5.30pm Mon-Sat. *Nov-Mar* 9.30am-4.30pm Mon-Sat.

Bike hire

Lock Inn Cottage, Frome Road, Bradford-on-Avon, BA15 1LE (01225 867187).
A five- to ten-minute walk from the station. Also hires boats and canoes.

Courts Garden

Holt, nr Bradford-on-Avon, BA14 6RR (01225 782340/www.nationaltrust.org.uk). **Open** *Apr-Oct* 11am-5.30pm Mon-Fri, Sun. Out of season by appointment only. **Admission** (NT) £4.20; £2.10 concessions. **No credit cards.**
Seven acres of authentic English country garden run by the National Trust. Well maintained, with water features, yew hedges and unusual topiary. No tripods or easels are allowed without prior consent.

Farleigh Hungerford Castle

Farleigh Hungerford, nr Bath, BA2 7RS (01225 754026/www.english-heritage.org.uk). **Open** *Apr-Sept* 10am-6pm daily. *Oct* 10am-5pm daily. *Nov-Mar* 10am-4pm Wed-Sun. **Admission** (EH) £2.50; £1.30-£1.90 concessions. (Admission for events sometimes higher.) **Credit** MC, V.
This large, semi-ruined castle in the Frome Valley was once home to the Hungerford Lords, whose colourful deeds during the Middle Ages are explained in a free audio tour. There are battle re-enactments throughout the year (phone for details).

Iford Manor Garden

Off A36, 8 miles SE of Bath, BA15 2BA (01225 863146/www.ifordmanor.co.uk). **Open** *Apr, Oct* 2-5pm Sun. *May-Sept* 2-5pm Tue-Thur, Sat, Sun. Closed Nov-Mar. **Admission** £4; £3.50 concessions; free under-10s (weekdays only). **No credit cards.**

The residence of 19th-century architect Harold Peto is famed for its romantic, award-winning Italianate gardens. Peto plundered classical artefacts and design ideas from across Europe, combining plants and architectural features to create his vision of the perfect garden. The result is enchanting. During the summer you can enjoy a picnic, and hear baroque or medieval ensembles, chamber music, and jazz groups, Japanese drummers and gypsy violinists (June-Aug). Candlelit opera performances take place in the cloister. Call 01225 868124 or visit www.ifordarts.co.uk for details. Children under ten are not allowed in the garden at weekends.

Longleat

Nr Warminster, BA12 7NW (01985 844400/ www.longleat.co.uk). **Open** *House* Easter-Sept 10am-5.30pm daily. Oct-Easter 11am-3pm daily. *Safari park* Mar-Oct 10am-4pm Mon-Fri; 10am-5pm daily, school hols. Closed Nov-Feb. *Attractions* Mar-Oct 11am-5.30pm daily. Closed Nov-Feb. **Admission** £16; £13 concessions. **Credit** MC, V.

The Marquis of Bath's home has amassed an ever-expanding roll-call of attractions over the years: safari park, cosmic-themed hedge mazes, *Dr Who* exhibition, *Postman Pat* village. Oh yes, there's a house here, too – an exquisite manor stacked with art treasures, historic exhibits and general relics of aristocracy, not to mention his famous murals, which he started painting back in the 1960s and continues today. Themes include the *Karma Sutra* and Bluebeard, which gives some clue to the breadth of their subject matter. Where there are attractions there are crowds, however, and on a hot summer weekend you may find yourself wishing that you'd gone elsewhere. The 'Lion-Link' bus service collects visitors from Warminster.

Westwood Manor

Westwood, Bradford-on-Avon, BA15 2AF (01225 863374/www.nationaltrust.org.uk). **Open** *Apr-Sept* 2-5pm Tue, Wed, Sun; by appointment at other times. **Admission** (NT) £4.20. **No credit cards.**

Two miles from Bradford in the village of Westwood, this 15th-century manor house was built by the Horton family, the first residents of Iford Manor (*see above*). The original building was altered in the 17th century to add late Gothic and Jacobean features and fine plasterwork.

Where to stay

For a touch of luxury, try **Babington House**, at Babington, north-west of Frome (01373 812266/www.babingtonhouse.co.uk, doubles from £215). Other, more down-to-earth options include the **Tollgate Inn** in Holt (*see p147*), the **Georgian Lodge** in Bradford-on-Avon (*see p147*, 01225 862268, doubles £75), the **Woolpack** in Beckington (*see p147*, 01373 831244, doubles £85) and **Dundas Lock**

Cottage (01225 723890, doubles £55) at the intersection of two canals just off the main road to Bath. For a different kind of break, consider **Center Parcs Village** (01985 848000/08705 200300/www.centerparcs.com, prices vary on the type of villa and the time of year, call for details), a purpose-built holiday complex located in Longleat Forest.

Bishopstrow House

Off B3414, Warminster, BA12 9HH (01985 212312/fax 01985 216769/www.bishopstrow.co.uk). **Rates** £99 single without breakfast; £199 double with breakfast; £330 suite; £390 suite with breakfast and dinner. **Rooms** (all en suite) 17 standard; 9 deluxe; 5 suites. **Credit** AmEx, DC, MC, V.

Bishopstrow House is a classic country house hotel (part of a small chain), formed from a Georgian mansion, and set in vast grounds outside Warminster. There are tennis courts, a gym, a spa, hair salon, sauna, croquet, a children's playroom and two large heated pools, one indoor, one outdoor. You can access parts of the grounds by a special tunnel under the B3414 – including a stretch along the River Wylye, where you can fish for trout or wander among the gazebos. If time is tight, you can even charter a helicopter to pick you up, as the hotel is equipped with a helipad. The 31 rooms are very comfortable, and many are furnished with antiques. Children are welcome, and there is plenty for them to do. Dogs are accepted too.

Bradford Old Windmill

4 Masons Lane, Bradford-on-Avon, BA15 1QN (01225 866842/fax 01225 866648/www. bradfordoldwindmill.co.uk). **Rates** £69-£99 single occupancy; £79-£109 double. **Rooms** (all en suite) 3 double. **Credit** MC, V.

Hidden away among the trees on the hillside above the town is the stump of Bradford's one and only windmill. Its ornate Victorian spiral staircase, pointed Gothic windows, oak gallery, and stone tower with conical stone tiled roof certainly help it stand out, but its popularity can mean a longish wait for a booking in busy periods. Exposed beams, mill-related ornaments, ethnic knick-knacks and folkie decor dominate to create a cluttered but enjoyable atmosphere. The three rooms all have a character of their own: the cheapest, Damsel, features a waterbed and high conical ceiling; Great Spur has a round bed and a hanging wicker chair; and Fantail has its own lounge, plus a minstrels' gallery with a box bed for kids. Well-travelled owners Priscilla and Peter Roberts provide ethnic vegetarian evening meals (and carnivore-friendly breakfasts). No smoking throughout. Children are welcome, except at weekends.

A363 S towards Bradford-on-Avon town centre; shortly after Castle pub turn left into private drive; house is the round building immediately before first roadside house (no sign or number).

Eagle House

Church Street, Bathford, nr Bath, BA1 7RS (01225 859946/fax 01225 859430/www.eagle house.co.uk). **Rates** £44-£56 single/single occupancy; £54-£88 double; £105 suite. Breakfast £3.80 (Eng). **Rooms** (all en suite) 2 single; 4 double; 2 cottage rooms. **Credit** MC, V.

Cross the **Town Bridge**.

In an attractive conservation village a few miles closer to Bath than Bradford, you will find this beautiful, refined Georgian house designed by Bath planner John Wood the Elder. Its quintessential English atmosphere, friendly welcome and reasonable prices help make it a great base for exploring the area. The elegant but unstuffy interior includes a large octagonal drawing room with marble fireplace overlooking the terraced garden (with grass tennis court). The six bedrooms vary in size, with good views of the surrounding countryside. There is also a much sought-after self-contained two-bedroom cottage in the adjoining walled garden, which has its own kitchen and sitting room. Children and dogs welcome. No-smoking rooms available. Recommended.
A4 NE from Bath; after 3 miles turn right on to A363; after 100 yards take left fork into Bathford Hill; after 300 yards, take first right into Church Street; house on right after 200 yards.

Great Barn Maplecroft

Leigh Road West, Bradford-on-Avon, BA15 2RB (tel/fax 01225 868790/www.gbarn.co.uk). **Rates** £30-£35 single occupancy; £50-£65 double; £65 family room (sleeps 5) plus £10 per child, £15 per adult. **Rooms** (all en suite) 2 double; 1 family. **No credit cards**.

A mile or so outside the town centre, the Great Barn Maplecroft offers a peaceful setting with inspiring views of the surrounding countryside – and a viciously whistling hilltop wind at times. The friendly owners have painstakingly redeveloped a cluster of farm buildings as single-storey, modern, ultra-clean guest rooms, complete with acres of cosy pine and floral bedlinen. Arranged around a central courtyard, the rooms are quite exposed to view, but the warm welcome and great breakfasts make up for it, and kids will enjoy playing on the timber outdoor equipment or feeding the hens. No smoking throughout.
From Bradford-on-Avon town centre, take B3109 N towards Chippenham. At traffic lights turn left on B3105, going W; after about 4 miles, turn into a private drive on the right. The Great Barn is signposted.

Grey Lodge

Summer Lane, Combe Down, nr Bath, BA2 7EU (01225 832069/fax 01225 830161). **Rates** £35-£45 single occupancy; £60-£75 double/twin; £75-£110 family suite. **Rooms** (all en suite) 2 double/twin; 1 family suite. **Credit** MC, V.

This 19th-century house with well-maintained gardens feels as if it's in the middle of nowhere but it's actually less than ten minutes' drive from either Bath or Bradford-on-Avon. The house enjoys beautiful views across the valley from the steep garden and the two back bedrooms, one of which has a small adjoining room with an extra single bed. The third room overlooks the front garden and road but is just as quiet. All three rooms are very comfortable, tasteful and well equipped. Above all, the owners are genuinely warm and accommodating. Children welcome. No smoking throughout.
A36 S from Bath; after 4 miles turn right up hill at traffic lights by Viaduct Inn; take first left to Monkton Combe; 2 miles after village, first house on left.

Priory Steps

Newtown, Bradford-on-Avon, BA15 1NQ (01225 862230/fax 01225 866248/www.priorysteps.co.uk). **Rates** £64 single occupancy; £76-£84 double per person. **Rooms** (all en suite) 2 twin; 3 double. **Credit** MC, V.

Carey and Diana Chapman have converted six 17th-century weavers' cottages just outside the town to provide five tasteful guest suites, all with a relaxing own-home feel and lovely views out towards Salisbury Plain. Retreat to the library and into its squashy leather armchairs for drinks or a board game in the winter, or stroll around the enclosed private gardens overlooking the town and the Avon when it gets warmer. Children welcome. All bedrooms are no-smoking.
From centre of Bradford-on-Avon, take A363 N towards Bath; then second turning on the left signed to Turleigh; Priory Steps is third house on the left on this road.

Woolley Grange

Woolley Green, Bradford-on-Avon, BA15 1TX (01225 864705/fax 01225 864059/www.woolley grange.com). **Rates** £95-£135 small double; £195-£210 double; £200-£250 large double; £239-£285 suite; £260-£340 interconnecting rooms. 10% reduction for single occupancy. **Rooms** (all en suite) 17 double; 3 suites; 3 pairs of interconnecting rooms. **Credit**, MC, V.

For people with children and plenty of cash – think Nappy Valley and three-wheeled buggies – Woolley Grange (part of the Luxury Family Hotel group) could be the ultimate place to stay. On a quiet lane just outside the town, this gorgeous Jacobean mansion offers beautiful grounds to explore, sun-trap terraces, an

From wool to rubber

Bradford-on-Avon's history as an industrial town began with wool. The trade was born in the Middle Ages as a cottage industry and Bradford soon became a wool and weaving hub. The industry continued to flourish until the beginning of the 19th century, moving from homes into factories with the advent of mechanisation. But the arrival of superior cloth from abroad put paid to Bradford's boom-town years. In the space of around 50 years the wool trade withered and all but died. Meanwhile, the whole country was hit by recession following the Napoleonic Wars, and in 1841 the local bank failed. These were tough times for Bradford – the cloth industry was ruined and it has never recovered.

However, Bradford-on-Avon bounced back thanks to collaboration between one Charles Goodyear and Stephen Moulton, whose rubber processing plant took over the former woollen mills in the town at the end of the 19th century. The plant was eventually sold to the Avon Rubber Company. Bradford's links with rubber continue to this day. Dr Alex Moulton, Stephen Moulton's direct descendant, still lives here and continues to develop the world-renowned Moulton Bicycles (01225 865895/www.alexmoulton.co.uk). You can see an early example suspended in the lounge of the Swan Hotel in the town centre.

However Kingston Mill, which until recently was home to the Avon Rubber Company, is currently being developed into a housing complex, much to the annoyance of local conservation groups who fear that the proposed extra height of the building will destroy the town's historic centre.

outdoor heated pool, swingball, croquet and numerous other energetic activities during the warmer months. Then in winter there are snug libraries, roaring fires, cosy velvet sofas and piles of board games. It's completely geared for kids, with a crèche – the Woolley Bears' Den – staffed by at least two nannies, a games room, bikes that can be borrowed at will and an outdoor play area. Parents get spoiled too: beauty and relaxation therapies come to your room, and the babysitting and listening services mean you can go kids-free or dine until late in the excellent restaurant (see p147). Rooms are characterful and spacious; some beds are large enough to accommodate at least three people, and children can stay for free in their parents' room.

Where to eat & drink

Bradford-on-Avon is little more than a large village, but what it lacks in shops it makes up for in pubs – it can boast a feisty 20 or so, many of them serving pretty decent food. In the town centre, locals flock to the **Bunch of Grapes** (14 Silver Street, 01225 863877) and the **Dandy Lion** (35 Market Street, 01225 863433) for food, drink and a convivial atmosphere. In summer, you can sit by the canal and watch the activity around the lock at the **Barge Inn** (17 Frome Road, 01225 863403), or walk east along the towpath to the **Beehive** (263 Trowbridge Road, 01225 863620) for very adequate pub grub and a pretty garden with two climbing frames for kids. A pleasant walk in the other direction will bring you to the **Cross Guns** at Avoncliff (01225 862335), a hostelry that is hugely popular (or hideously packed) due to its enviable position right beside the aqueduct. Further afield, try the **George Inn** at Bathampton (01373 834224), the **Hop Pole** in Limpley Stoke (01225 723134) or the **Full Moon** in Rudge (01373 830936) for the best of local flavours – cuisine, ales and people. Slightly further out on the A366 is the darkly atmospheric **George** (01373 834224) in Norton St Philip, a 700-year-old pub based around a series of medieval rooms that serves up formidable, meaty food and has rooms to stay in too.

There are several run-of-the-mill restaurants in and around the town, but if these or the pub option don't appeal, you might be better off heading to nearby **Bath** (see p148). If you don't mind splashing out, luxurious dining and a grand backdrop await you at the divine **Mulberry Restaurant** in Bishopstrow House (see p147). Otherwise, **Le Mangetout** (01225 863111) is centrally located on Silver Street, and serves perfectly decent and affordable modern European food at lunchtimes and evenings, or coffee and pastries for breakfast – bring your own newspaper. For teas (nearly 30 different types), coffees and own-made cream cakes sagging with richness, don't miss the atmospheric **Bridge Tea Rooms** at 24A Bridge Street (01225 865537). Alternatively you can go eco-friendly with organic vegetarian food at the **Cottage Co-Operative** (33 Silver Street, 01225 867444).

Georgian Lodge Hotel & Restaurant

25 Bridge Street, Bradford-on-Avon, BA15 1BY (01225 862268). **Food served** noon-2pm, 6.30pm-late Tue-Sat. **Main courses** £12.50-£14.50. **Set lunch** £10 2 courses. **Set dinner** (6.30-7.45pm) £15.95 2 courses; £17.95 3 courses. **Credit** AmEx, MC, V.

Right in the centre of town next to the library, this former coaching inn is an extremely convenient place to both eat and stay, if not the most atmospheric establishment in town. At the front of the building is the bright, vaguely art deco restaurant (go further back and it morphs into a rather grim 1960s tearoom, complete with white china dogs and spindle back chairs). The food is reassuringly modern and as well presented as it is well cooked, with a menu that inclines towards the Mediterranean. Starters might include deep-fried goat's cheese beignets with fresh fig and marinated artichoke, but there's also an option of robust braised Wiltshire faggot with crispy fried onions and mustard gravy. Mains could be seared Cornish scallops and salmon with spring onion mash or aubergine and sweet pepper relish or perhaps the lamb with chorizo sausage, puy lentils and jus.

Mulberry Restaurant

Bishopstrow House Hotel, off B3414, Warminster, BA12 9HH (01985 212312/fax 01985 216769/ www.bishopstrow.co.uk). **Food served** *Lounge/ conservatory* 11am-9.30pm daily. *Restaurant* 12.30-2.15pm, 7.30-9.30pm daily. **Main courses** (lounge/conservatory only) £8-£17. **Set lunch** (restaurant) £12 2 courses. **Set dinner** (restaurant) £38 3 courses. **Credit** AmEx, DC, MC, V.

The Georgian formal grandeur of Bishopstrow House Hotel (*see p144*) is offset by the welcome and relaxed atmosphere of its connected Mulberry Restaurant, which overlooks the lovely garden and outdoor pool. Chef Chris Suter makes use of the excellent local and often organic ingredients, especially game when it is in season. For lunch or a light bite in the bar, there's an eclectic choice of flavoursome dishes, while the fixed-price dinner menu is no less imaginative: seared tiger prawns with chorizo and rocket; crispy duck confit with colcannon, wild mushrooms and peppercorn sauce; toffee and cappuccino tartlet with vanilla ice-cream. Simple snacks are served in the lounge, or the garden in fine weather, between 2pm and 6pm.

Thai Barn

24 Bridge Street, Bradford-on-Avon, BA15 1BY (01225 866443). **Food served** noon-2.30pm, 6-10.30pm Tue-Sun. **Main courses** £5.95-£8.50. **Set lunch** £7.95 2 courses. **Set dinner** £18.95 2 courses. **Credit** MC, V.

Next to the Georgian Lodge and Bridge Tea Rooms, in a 17th-century building that was once the village smithy, this cosy and popular Thai restaurant offers authentic cuisine at affordable prices – the perfect combination. Curries are especially good, as the pastes are made on the premises from fresh herbs and chillies. The restaurant's interior is a spacious converted barn (hence the name) with high ceilings and a split-level dining area. Mains won't cost you more than a tenner, there's a cheap set lunch menu and a takeaway service.

Tollgate Inn

Ham Green, Holt, nr Bradford-on-Avon, BA14 6PX (01225 782326/fax 01225 782805/ www.tollgateholt.co.uk). **Food served** noon-2pm, 7-9pm Tue-Sat; noon-2pm Sun. **Main courses** £10.50-£16.50. **Set lunch** £9.95 2 courses. **Set meal** (Tue-Sat) £11.95 3 courses. **Credit** MC, V.

Food is served downstairs in the comfortable bar area or upstairs in the cutesy, cosy, old-fashioned (and no-smoking) restaurant. The menu has a modern Mediterranean touch and uses ingredients of local provenance where possible in dishes such as lamb shank braised with an elderberry and sage sauce or steamed sea bass with ginger, herbs and fennel. There are good English farmhouse cheeses and desserts feature own-made ice-creams such as lavender with honey and rose petal. Lunchtime sees bargain set-price deals, with a tempting light-bite menu that includes a very good omelette Arnold Bennett made with natural smoked haddock. The Tollgate tends to attract a rather formal, older clientele. They're often residents, staying in one of six well-furnished rooms. Children receive a decidedly frosty reception.

Woolley Grange Hotel Restaurant

Woolley Green, Bradford-on-Avon, BA15 1TX (01225 864705). **Food served** noon-2pm, 7-9pm daily. **Main courses** £18. **Set lunches** £15.50 2 courses, £20 3 courses. **Set dinner** £34.50 3 courses. **Credit** AmEx, DC, MC, V.

The Woolley Grange restaurant certainly lives up to its grand country house setting, though diners have some say over the degree of formality, with a choice between a fairly formal main room, a smaller annexe, the more relaxed conservatory (the Orangery) or the open air in warm weather. Chef Phil Rimmer produces high quality, well-presented food (much of it from local suppliers). Vegetables come from the Grange's own garden. Typical starters include duck liver parfait with pickled pear and crispy prosciutto, or roasted sea scallops with spicy puy lentils and mango fritter. Main courses take in loin of venison with crushed sweet potatoes, mushroom relish, glazed pears and chestnuts or honey-roasted Gressingham duck breast with glazed apples and mead-scented sauce. Puddings are just as inspired. You don't have to be a guest to eat here, but you need to book well ahead if you're planning to visit at weekends or during school holidays.

Woolpack

Warminster Road, Beckington, nr Bath, BA11 6SP (01373 831244). **Food served** noon-2.30pm, 6.30-9.30pm Mon-Sat; noon-2.30pm, 7-9pm Sun. **Main courses** £10.95-£16.95. **Set dinner** £18.95 3 courses. **Credit** AmEx, MC, V.

This unassuming 16th-century coaching inn (owned by Old English Inns) offers a pleasantly high standard of cooking and service. You can order a complete meal or just a snack, and sit in the airy bar area with its flagstone floor and large open fireplace, in the cosy restaurant or the more informal garden room at the back (good for children). Food at lunchtime is simple and homemade: grilled goat's cheese salad, chicken and leek pie or home-made sausages with a sticky toffee pudding afterwards. Evening meals are along similar lines but slightly grander and more substantial.

Bath

A town with a spring in its step.

To the approaching visitor, Bath is a veritable sight for sore eyes – a fantasy in golden limestone, sprawled elegantly in a river valley and surrounded, like Rome, by seven hills. And, as if the city weren't alluring enough, it now has a state-of-the-art, restored spa – Britain's only hot one – to add to its long list of enticements.

Celtic legend has it that the city was founded by the prince-turned-leper-turned-swineherd Bladud in 863 BC, when he noticed that his pigs were cured of leprosy after a roll in the naturally hot water here. He eventually lured them out with acorns, plunged in himself, was healed, and bingo, Bath was born.

Since then, Bath's legendary ability to restore and revive – its 'holiday' vibe – has been exploited and enjoyed by successive generations. It was the arrival of the Romans in AD 43 that spelled the beginning of Bath's transformation into a major spa, but there is evidence that our Stone Age and Bronze Age ancestors also paddled their feet here. Medieval times saw swarms of pilgrims and monks transform the town into an ecclesiastical centre, while their less holy contemporaries revelled in nude mixed bathing in the hot springs. In the early 18th century Bath's reputation grew, and it became a fashionable destination for high society – all balls, bathing and banter.

A housing boom in the 18th century signalled the rise of Georgian Bath. About 7,000 new houses were built between 1714 and 1830, of which 200 were designed by the visionary architect John Wood the Elder (1704-54), who dreamed of a creating a new Rome, and his son John Wood the Younger (1728-82). Although much of the building was speculative, it created an extraordinary unity of architecture – an English Palladianism that remains the epitome of elegance. Economic imperatives meant that houses were built in terraces, with minimal external decoration. The city's famously golden stone – much of it supplied by the quarries of the Woods' patron, Ralph Allen – was only used for façades, resulting in the motley appearance of many Bath buildings from the rear.

Although Woods and Allen provided the glorious setting, the mastermind behind Bath's Golden Age was Richard 'Beau' Nash (1674-1762), the self-styled 'Uncrowned King of Bath', 'Arbiter of Elegance' and 'Dictator of the Manners of Polite Society'. A bon viveur with enormous social influence, Beau Nash was made Master of Ceremonies in the city in 1705. He ran Bath society with a rod of iron and would severely reprimand any gentleman who dared to turn up to functions wearing riding boots.

Bath's heyday lasted almost a century, until Jane Austen's time (she lived here from 1800 to 1805), when Bath began gradually to lose its air of glamour. The middle classes limped in the footsteps of Beau Nash's trendy crowd, and the city became a final resting place for retired dignitaries and their bath-chairs.

The decline continued into the 20th century, aided by wartime bombing in 1942 that destroyed much of the working-class district around the station and river. Miraculously, the **Royal Crescent**, the **Circus** and many other architectural gems survived virtually unscathed, and in 1987 the UN declared Bath a World Heritage city – the only one in Britain – for the quality of its Roman remains and Georgian splendours.

Bath can be stiflingly crowded in summer, with most of its three million annual visitors passing through at this time. Fierce debate rages in the pages of the local press and on the streets between the conflicting needs of residents and tourists. You, however, will probably find it difficult to muster the energy to adjust your sunglasses. It's just that kind of place. Tranquil, compact and with barely an unsightly square inch to be found, Bath lends itself perfectly to a short break.

Tours

Regular free guided walks, starting from the Abbey Churchyard, are offered by the **Mayor's Honorary Guides** (01225 477411/ www.thecityofbath.co.uk), unpaid volunteers who are genuinely passionate about the city. As an alternative, **Bizarre Bath** (01225 335124, www.bizarrebath.co.uk, tickets £5, £4.50 concessions) is a well-established comedy tour,

---

By train from London

Trains leave **Paddington** for **Bath Spa** approximately every half hour, taking 1hr 25mins. Info: www.great-western-trains.co.uk.

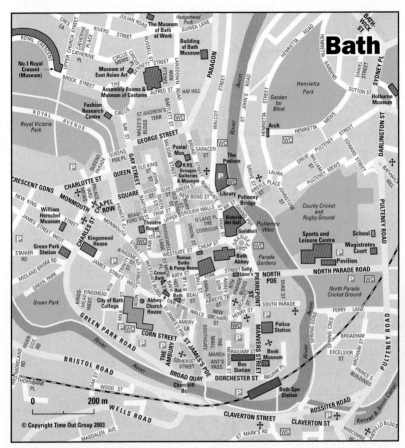

departing from outside the **Huntsman** pub, Bog Island, at 8pm daily.

For the techno-savvy visitor there's **Texting Trails** (£5.99) – a guide texted to your mobile phone. Contact the **Tourist Information Centre** (*see below*) for details.

What to see & do

Bath is packed with museums (around 20), most of them excellent. And if the weather is fine, hire a boat, punt or canoe at the **Victorian Bath Boating Station** (Forester Road, 01225 312900), or indulge in a champagne flight available with **Bath Balloon Flights** (01225 466888) for £139 per person. For cyclists, the Bristol and Bath railway path offers a flat ride through countryside between the two cities.

For details, pick up a free leaflet *Cycling in Bath and Beyond* from the Tourist Information Centre (*see below*).

Tourist Information Centre
Abbey Chambers, Abbey Churchyard, BA1 1LY (09067 112000/www.visitbath.co.uk). **Open** *Oct-Apr* 9.30am-5pm Mon-Sat; 10am-4pm Sun. *May-Sept* 9.30am-6pm Mon-Sat; 10am-4pm Sun.

American Museum in Britain
Claverton Manor, BA2 7BD (01225 460503/www. americanmuseum.org). **Open** *Late Mar-Oct* noon-5pm Tue-Sun. *Mid Nov-mid Dec* 1-4pm Tue-Sun. Closed early Nov, mid Dec-late Mar. **Admission** £6.50; £4-£6 concessions; free under-5s. **No credit cards**.
This fascinating museum is housed in an 1820 manor house that was converted into a museum in 1961 by two Americans in the noble pursuit of improving transatlantic relations. It paints a picture of the lives of the 17th- to 19th-century Americans through a series of

reconstructed rooms, including a village shop and a New Orleans bedroom. A celestial and terrestrial map exhibition, entitled Heaven Above, Earth Beneath, is due to open in March 2004. A short bus ride out of town.

Bath Abbey & Heritage Vaults

Abbey Churchyard, BA1 1LT (01225 422462/www. bathabbey.org). **Open** *Easter-Oct* 9am-6pm Mon-Sat. *Nov-Easter* 9am-4.30pm Mon-Sat. **Admission** free; donations appreciated. *Vaults* £1. **No credit cards.**
Above the great west door of the abbey is a Latin inscription that translates as: 'Behold, how good and pleasing it is.' How true. Bath Abbey dates back to the 15th century, although it incorporates parts of a once-massive Norman predecessor. It was the last Tudor church to be built before the Reformation and suffered at the hands of Henry VIII; however, Elizabeth I ensured its reconstruction and called it the 'Lantern of the West', due to its huge and plentiful stained-glass windows. Subterranean explorers can discover the site's 1,600-year history in the 18th-century cellars.

Bath Postal Museum

8 Broad Street, BA1 5LJ (01225 460333/ www.bathpostalmuseum.org). **Open** 11am-5pm Mon-Sat. Closed 2nd wk Jan. **Admission** £2.90; £1.50-£2.40 concessions; free under-5s. **No credit cards.**
The world's first postage stamp, the Penny Black, was posted here in 1840. This surprisingly interesting museum follows the history of mail from 2000 BC to the present day, with a reconstruction of a Victorian post office, a kids' activity room, film room and a special nod to local bigwig Ralph Allen, who streamlined the national mail system in the 18th century.

Building of Bath Museum

The Countess of Huntingdon's Chapel, The Vineyards, BA1 5NA (01225 333895/www.bath-preservation-trust.org.uk). **Open** *Mid Feb-Nov* 10.30am-5pm Tue-Sun. Closed Dec-mid Feb. **Admission** £4; £1.50-£3 concessions. **Credit** AmEx, MC, V.
This absorbing museum is set in a 18th-century Gothic chapel, and describes life in Georgian Bath.

Holburne Museum of Art

Great Pulteney Street, BA2 4DB (01225 466669/ www.bath.ac.uk/holburne). **Open** *Feb-mid Dec* 10am-5pm Tue-Sat; 2.30-5.30pm Sun. Closed mid Dec-Jan. **Admission** £4; £1.50-£3.50 concessions. **No credit cards.**
In Jane Austen's day (she lived opposite here between 1801 and 1804) this was a hotel for the glitterati of Georgian Bath, but today it houses the fine and decorative art collection of the 19th-century enthusiast Sir William Holburne. You will also find paintings by Turner, Gainsborough and Stubbs, plus gleaming displays of silverware, porcelain, majolica, glass and bronze.

Jane Austen Centre

40 Gay Street, BA1 2NT (01225 443000/www. janeausten.co.uk). **Open** 10am-5.30pm Mon-Sat; 10.30am-5.30pm Sun. **Walking tours** phone for details. **Admission** £4.45; £2.45-£3.95 concessions; free under-6s. **Credit** AmEx, MC, V.
The author lived for a time at 25 Gay Street, and this nearby house now houses a museum dedicated to her life. There are displays, reproduction costumes and facsimile

documents celebrating the writer's connection with the city, but the highlight for many will be the amusing talk that dispels the twee Jane of popular thought and reveals the witty woman so loved by Austenophiles.

Museum of Bath at Work

Bath Industrial Heritage Centre, Julian Road, BA1 2RH (01225 318348/www.bath-at-work.org.uk). **Open** *Apr-Oct* 10am-5pm daily. *Nov-Mar* 10am-5pm Sat, Sun. **Admission** £3.50; £2.50 concessions. **No credit cards.**
This museum explores the life of working folk through an exhibition based on the life and toil of one Mr Bowler – engineer, gas-fitter, locksmith, bell-hanger, maker of soda-water machinery and producer of fizzy drinks. His family-run business lasted 97 years and is reconstructed here in all its chaos.

Museum of Costume & Assembly Rooms

Bennett Street, BA1 2QH (01225 477789/ www.museumofcostume.co.uk). **Open** 10am-5pm daily. Last entry 4.30pm. **Admission** £5.50; £3.75-£4.50 concessions. **Credit** MC, V.
The beautifully restored Assembly Rooms are a set of public rooms designed by John Wood the Younger in 1771 as a playground for polite society to hobnob, dance, play cards and flirt. Downstairs, the Museum of Costume, dimly lit to preserve its treasures, includes more than 150 male and female outfits dating from the 16th century up to the present day. The Card Room Café is the place for a dignified cuppa.

Museum of East Asian Art

12 Bennett Street, BA1 2QJ (01225 464640). **Open** 10am-5pm Tue-Sat; noon-5pm Sun. **Admission** £3.50; £1-£3 concessions. **No credit cards.**
This discreet townhouse has 7,000 years' worth of Chinese, Japanese, Korean and South-east Asian art. Rarities include more than 100 examples of Chinese jade and bronzes created for nomadic horsemen. There are also exhibitions by contemporary Asian artists.

No.1 Royal Crescent

1 Royal Crescent, BA1 2LR (01225 428126/ www.bath-preservation-trust.org.uk). **Open** *Mid Feb-Oct* 10.30am-5pm Tue-Sun. *Nov* 10.30am-4pm Tue-Sun. *1st 2wks Dec* 10.30am-4pm. Sat, Sun. Last entry 30mins before closing. Closed mid Dec-mid Feb. **Admission** £4; £3.50 concessions; free under-5s. **No credit cards.**
The corner townhouse (nearest the centre) in John Wood's famous crescent, designated a World Heritage Building, has been lovingly restored with authentic 18th-century furniture and decoration. A team of guides – brisk, redoubtable pensioners – talk you through each room with undeniable authority.

Prior Park Landscape Garden

Ralph Allen Drive, BA2 5AH (01225 833422/ info line 09001 335242/www.nationaltrust.org.uk). **Open** *Feb-Nov* 11am-5.30pm/dusk Mon, Wed-Sun. *Dec, Jan* 11am-dusk Fri-Sun. **Admission** (NT) £4.10; £2-£3.10 concessions. **No credit cards.**
This hilltop 18th-century garden was built by one of Bath's founding fathers, Ralph Allen (with advice from 'Capability' Brown and poet Alexander Pope). The

Wiltshire & Bath

Thermae Bath Spa

'Wonderful and most excellent against... rhumes, agues, lethargies, apoplexies, the scratch, inflammation of the fits, hectic flushes, pocks, deafness, forgetfullness, shakings and weakness of any member.' Thus was the water of Bath described in Georgian times. Blue-green, hot, mineral-rich, slightly opaque and sulphur-scented, it is the result of rain that fell on the Mendip Hills thousands of years ago, filtered through the limestone and heated by volcanic strata to around 46°C before emerging into the heart of the city. Touch one of the manhole covers in the Bath Street area and you can feel the heat as the water flows under your feet.

The waters are Bath's *raison d'être*. Without them the city would be like Rome without its forum, Vienna without its waltz. However, since the closure of the Roman Baths to bathers following a public health scare in the late '70s, a million litres a day of this precious and unique resource have been gushing – unused – straight into the River Avon.

An astonishing waste? That's what the brains behind the Thermae Bath Spa thought, so they decided to build a brand new spa to tend to the rhumes and agues of modern Britain. The keenly awaited venture aims to rejuvenate spa culture in the city by harnessing Bath's hot 'n' wholesome H_2O and promoting it as the only natural thermal spa in the UK (other springs, such as Buxton, are cold).

It's to the credit of all concerned that the spa isn't a corny Roman or Georgian pastiche. Instead, the main building is a vision in glass and Bath stone created by renowned architect Nicholas Grimshaw, and its pièce de résistance is a rooftop, open-air swimming pool with views across the city.

The complex also lovingly incorporates a handful of existing spa buildings that have lain neglected for decades or more. The Cross Bath, a Grade I-listed Georgian building that was originally erected on the site of an earlier medieval bath, has now been restored as an open-air thermal pool, while the nearby Hot Bath, designed by John Wood the Younger in 1773, houses a variety of treatment rooms that offer everything from acupuncture to mud

wraps for those in need of some extra care. The 18th-century Hetling Pump Room serves as the visitors' centre.

With no membership fees and reasonable entrance prices, the aim is to create a venue that is inclusive and unpretentious – after all, pigs, beggars and royalty have all swilled their aching bodies in Bath's famous waters. A two-hour session includes use of the rooftop pool, main spa, whirlpool, steam rooms – in the shape of space-age circular glass pods – foot-baths, relaxation areas and yoga and meditation classes. Complementary treatments, massages and the solarium cost extra. The only proviso is that you bring your costume: Bath isn't quite ready for a return to public displays of nudity just yet...

Thermae Bath Spa

Hot Bath Street, BA1 1SJ (01225 477051/advance bookings 01225 331234/www.thermaebathspa.com). **Open** 9am-10pm daily. **Admission** *2hr session £17. 4hr session £23. All day £35.* **Credit** AmEx, MC, V.

house, built by John Wood the Elder, is now a school, but the grounds are open to the public and include a Palladian bridge, three lakes and plenty of wooded paths. No parking on the site.

Roman Baths
Abbey Churchyard, BA1 1LZ (01225 477785/ www.romanbaths.co.uk). **Open** *Jan, Feb, Nov, Dec* 9.30am-5.30pm daily. *Mar-June, Sept, Oct* 9am-6pm daily. *July, Aug* 9am-10pm daily. Last entry 1hr before closing. **Admission** £8.50; £4.80-£7.50 concessions; free under-6s. **Credit** MC, V.
The Baths are the most visited attraction in the city and their popularity is well deserved. Apart from the photogenic Great Bath, there are surprising complexes of indoor baths, the Minerva temple and bubbling King's Bath source, plus great collections of temple sculpture, jewellery, wishing-spa coins and curses. Admission isn't cheap, but you do get a lot of information for your cash, via a handset. Don't come expecting a dip; the waters haven't been used for bathing since 1970s. But now that the Thermae Bath Spa project (*see p152* **Thermae Bath Spa**) is up and running, you can have the full aquatic experience just a few streets away.

Sally Lunn's Refreshment House & Museum
4 North Parade Passage, BA1 1NX (01225 461634/ www.sallylunns.co.uk). **Open** *Restaurant* 10am-10pm Mon-Sat; 11am-10pm Sun. *Museum* 10am-6pm Mon-Sat; 11am-6pm Sun. **Admission** *Museum* 30p; free concessions. **No credit cards.**
This is widely considered to be the oldest house in Bath. It dates back to the 12th century when it formed part of a large monastic estate, and is said to be haunted by the ghost of a Benedictine monk. Sally Lunn baked her first Bath bun (like brioche) here in the 1680s, and they're still on sale today – along with an entire Lunn-related menu. The tiny museum occupies the basement, and shows the ancient foundations, plus Roman and medieval objects and period kitchen equipment.

Victoria Art Gallery
Bridge Street, BA2 4AT (01225 477233/www. victoriagal.org.uk). **Open** 10am-5.30pm Tue-Fri; 10am-5pm Sat; 2-5pm Sun. **Admission** free.
This excellent gallery, housed in a splendid two-floor Georgian building, has a permanent collection of British and European art dating from the 15th century right up to the present day.

William Herschel Museum
19 New King Street, BA1 2BL (01225 311342/ www.bath-preservation-trust.org.uk). **Open** *Mid Feb-Oct* 2-5pm Mon, Tue, Thur, Fri; 11am-5pm Sat, Sun. Closed Nov-mid Feb. **Admission** £3.50; £2 concessions. **No credit cards.**
Here's the very house where the astronomer discovered Uranus in 1781, complete with a replica of the telescope through which he spotted it.

Where to stay

Unlike the other towns and cities in the region, there are no pubs offering a good standard of accommodation anywhere in the centre of Bath.

The genteel evolution of the city has given rise to three options: a classy hotel near the centre; an almost as classy guesthouse perched somewhere up on the rim of the bowl enveloping the golden city – try **Haydon House** (9 Bloomfield Park, 01225 444919/ www.haydonhouse.co.uk, doubles £88-£103); or a genteel B&B a couple of miles out of town. Another option is the **Bath Priory Hotel** (Weston Road, 01225 331922/www.thebath priory.co.uk), which, at £245-£360 a night, is a place you should really stay when the weather is so appalling that you can justify staying in the (free to guests) spa and health club all day.

Albany Guest House
24 Crescent Gardens, BA1 2NB (01225 313339/ www.bath.org/public_html/hotel/albany.htm). **Rates** £35-£45 single occupancy; £40-£60 double. **Rooms** 3 double (2 en suite); 1 twin. **No credit cards.**
Not far from the Royal Crescent and the Royal Victoria Gardens, this lovely B&B offers good value for such a central location. It's on busy Crescent Gardens, but double-glazing ensures that things inside stay nice and quiet. A friendly owner, and home-made vegetarian sausages for breakfast are other attractions. Children over seven welcome. No smoking throughout.

Athole Guest House
33 Upper Oldfield Park, BA2 3JX (01225 334307/ fax 01225 320009/www.atholehouse.co.uk). **Rates** £48 single occupancy; £68-£78 double. **Rooms** (all en suite) 3 double. **Credit** AmEx, MC, V.
Athole Guest House prides itself on being one of the few Bath guesthouses to be Laura Ashley-free. Instead, the spotless, yellow bedrooms come with contemporary furniture, laptop connections, minibars and satellite TV. Modern, clean, pristine and comfortable, this is perfect for those on a budget but wanting to avoid chintz. Children welcome. No smoking throughout.

Bath Spa Hotel
Sydney Road, BA2 6JF (01225 444424/www.bath spahotel.com). **Rates** £155-£375 single occupancy; £250-£290 double/twin; £280-£320 superior double; £350-£390 four-poster; £450-£490 suite. **Rooms** (all en suite) 59 double/twin; 32 superior; 6 four-poster; 5 suites. **Credit** AmEx, DC, MC, V.
This is the place for all-out, five-star, no-expense-spared pampering – ideal for a special treat or romantic break. The hotel grounds come complete with whirlpool bath, tennis courts, fountain- and cedar-strewn grounds, and service that is thoroughly top class. The rooms themselves are more traditional than cutting-edge, with heavy curtains, marble and dark colours. Children and dogs (£25 per stay) are welcome.

Harington's Hotel
8-10 Queen Street, BA1 1HE (01225 461728/fax 01225 444804/www.haringtonshotel.co.uk). **Rates** £68-£108 single occupancy; £88-£128 double/twin; £108-£138 triple. **Rooms** (all en suite) 10 double; 2 twin; 1 triple. **Credit** AmEx, DC, MC, V.
Probably Bath's best budget hotel, Harington's is in the heart of the action on one of Bath's most-photographed streets, the famous Queen Street. This locates it about

100 yards from the main shopping street and round the corner from a handful of recommended bars and restaurants. Rooms are functional but spacious, if a little motelish, and staff are friendly. There are reserved spaces for guests in nearby Charlotte Street car park. Children are made to feel welcome. All bedrooms are no-smoking.

Laura Place Hotel

3 Laura Place, Great Pulteney Street , BA2 4BH (01225 463815/fax 01225 310222). **Rates** £60 single occupancy; £70-£95 double; £75 twin. £115 family room (4 people). **Rooms** (all en suite) 6 double; 1 twin; 1 family. **Credit** AmEx, MC, V.
A great-value gaff with huge, romantic rooms crammed full of antiques, Laura Place is a fine example of how to do traditional florals tastefully. A change of ownership is in the offing, but we have been assured that the hotel will remain largely unchanged. It overlooks the very pretty Laura Place and is handily located close to Henrietta Park. No smoking throughout.

Milsoms Hotel

24 Milsom Street, BA1 1DG (01225 750128/fax 01225 750129/www.milsomshotel.co.uk). **Rates** £75 double; £95 executive double. **Rooms** (all en suite) 6 double; 3 executive double. **Credit** AmEx, DC, MC, V.
A stylish, spanking new hotel bang in the middle of town. Browns and beiges make for a creamy, chic style, and a maritime theme ties in with the fine fish restaurant that's attached. Prices are improbably reasonable, but bear in mind that Milsoms feels more like a 'restaurant with rooms', with a day-only receptionist and an entrance that takes you temptingly through the restaurant. Children welcome. All bedrooms are no-smoking.

Paradise House Hotel

86-88 Holloway, BA2 4PX (01225 317723/fax 01225 482005/www.paradise-house.co.uk). **Rates** £65-£95 single occupancy; £75-£105 double; £85-£125 superior; £110-£160 four-poster double. **Rooms** (all en suite) 2 double; 6 superior double; 3 four-poster. **Credit** AmEx, MC, V.
The name might be a slight exaggeration but it certainly isn't an outright lie. With a sumptuous garden and pleasingly tasteful rooms to match, Paradise House is nigh-on irresistible. Ask for a room with a view and soak in the marvellous panorama of the city (it's based just outside). For all these reasons, it is very popular with honeymooners. Children welcome. No smoking throughout.

Queensberry Hotel

Russell Street, BA1 2QF (01225 447928/fax 01225 446065/www.thequeensberry.co.uk). **Rates** £100-£195 double/twin; £195-£285 four-poster. Breakfast £9.50 (Eng). **Rooms** (all en suite) 28 double/twin; 1 four-poster. **Credit** AmEx, MC, V.
This is a charming hotel made up of four Regency townhouses close to the Royal Crescent. The houses were purchased gradually over the years by owners Stephen and Penny Ross. Of the 29 rooms, the grandest are at the front (former drawing rooms in the main), but the best views are at the back. Prices and ceiling heights descend the higher up the hotel (and closer to the servants' quarters) you go. The whole place is full of cosy nooks and crannies, such as the intimate bar and the walled courtyard at the rear, while the attached Olive Tree restaurant (*see p156*) is highly acclaimed. Children welcome.

Royal Crescent

16 Royal Crescent, BA1 2LS (01225 823333/0800 980 0987/fax 01225 339401/www.royalcrescent. co.uk). **Rates** £170-£240 single occupancy/double/ twin; £245-£340 deluxe double/twin; £410-£800 suite; £590-£650 four-poster suite. Breakfast £18.50 (Eng); £16.50 (cont). **Rooms** (all en suite) 16 double/twin; 15 deluxe double/twin; 2 four-poster suites; 12 suites. **Credit** AmEx, DC, MC, V.
Without a shadow of a doubt, this is the ultimate place to stay in Bath – it's one of Britain's most sought-after addresses, after all. Due to heritage restrictions, there's no sign outside the hotel, just an open door and some foliage to add a splash of colour. Decor is in keeping with the Georgian heritage wherever possible, which makes the Royal Crescent a fine antidote to soulless chain hotels. It's dripping with history and idiosyncrasies – guests' names are hand-written on the door and televisions hidden in antique cabinets. The former stable block houses a dreamy spa complex. All this comes at a price, mind, but while you're supping your aperitif on the immaculate croquet lawn you'll be convinced it's worth every penny. Children and dogs welcome.

Bath has a formidable gourmet reputation and is said to have more restaurants per capita in the UK than any city outside London.

Although some of Bath's top pub locations have been snaffled up by the chain gang, there are still numerous authentic watering holes to experience. For unpretentious fun, the **Pig & Fiddle** (2 Saracen Street, 01225 460868) is a good bet; other central options include the intimate **Old Green Tree** (12 Green Street, 01225 448259) and the historic **Crystal Palace** (10-11 Abbey Green, 01225 482666); this pub is nearly 300 years old and Nelson once convalesced here. The **Salamander** (3 John Street, 01225 428889) is a stylish spot to sink some Bath Ales (and you can take them away in natty microcasks), or to eat in the fine restaurant upstairs. For live music and a heated garden try the **Bell Inn** (103 Walcot Street, 01225 460426), or the ramshackle **Hat & Feather** (14 London Street, 01225 425672). Wood-panelled ambience can be found at the more civilised **Curfew** (11 Cleveland Place West, 01225 424210).

Uptown, try **St James' Wine Vaults** (10 St James Street, 01225 310335), a small local covered in framed Russian posters. Those in search of a swankier tipple can strike a pose at the art deco-styled **Delfter Krug** (4 Saw Close, 01225 443352), the mellow **Raincheck Bar** (34 Monmouth Street, 01225 444770) and, particularly, the excellent **Central Wine Bar** (10 Upper Borough Walls, 01225 333939).

The **Pump Room** (Abbey Churchyard, (01225 444477) is on pretty much every tourist agenda for tea, cakes and perhaps a taste of the smelly waters, served in grand surroundings.

The curving **Circus** is one of Bath's many Georgian architectural gems. *See p148.*

Le Beaujolais

5 Chapel Row, BA1 1HN (01225 423417/www.
beaujolaisrestaurantbath.co.uk). **Food served**
6-10pm Mon; noon-2.30pm, 6-10pm Tue-Thur; noon-
2.30pm, 6-10.30pm Fri, Sat; 6-10.30pm Sun. **Main**
courses £11.80-£17.80. **Credit** AmEx, DC, MC, V.
The small, burgundy-painted shopfront opens out into a
spacious room with warm yellow walls and hand-carved
wooden lamps of a naked woman with a giant snail (you
might wish to avoid the escargots). Authentic French
bistro cuisine predominates (foie gras, coq au vin, pot au
feu and so on), with a fish of the day, and a somewhat
nannyishly healthy dessert menu. Peopled largely by
middle-aged Francophiles and well-off pensioners, it's a
great spot to take your in-laws. The portions can be
small, and it's pricey – you won't get much change out
of £20 for a modest-sized fillet steak with vegetables –
but the charming waiters, who teeter just on the
respectable side of flirtation, rapidly elicit forgiveness.

Bistro Papillon

2 Margaret's Buildings, Brock Street, BA1 2LP
(01225 310064). **Food served** noon-2.15pm, 6.30-
10pm Tue-Sat. **Main courses** £9-£13. **Set lunch**
£7.50 2 courses. **Credit** MC, V.
Miraculously, given the tiny kitchen and skeleton staff,
this charming Gallic enclave offers a hard-to-beat night
out. Recalling the kind of 'menu-touristique' vanguards
of French catering, there's no haute cuisine or snooty
service. The friendly, efficient owner (from Limoges)
treats his diners like guests at his own home – and for
a great, mid-range price. French classics from moules
frites to lamb's liver dominate, but with Edith Piaf on
the stereo, chequered tablecloths, flickering candles and
Normandy cider available by the glass, the ambience is
as strong a reason to come as the food.

Demuths

2 North Parade Passage, off Abbey Green, BA1 1NX
(01225 446059). **Food served** 10-11.30am, noon-
3.30pm, 6-9.30pm daily. **Main courses** £10-£13.
Credit MC, V.
Demuths has been dedicating itself to preparing innovative vegetarian and vegan food for some 15 years
now, and it is showing no signs of fatigue. On the contrary, its combination of bold, clashing decor and fresh,
vibrant food seems as popular among the locals as it
ever was. Gastronomic inspiration comes from far and
wide, with dishes such as southern Indian mallung and
cajun rice and beans, as well as close to home, with a
local Bath soft cheese wrap. The entirely organic wine
list is an unusual find.

The Hole in the Wall

16 George Street, BA1 2EH (01225 425242). **Food**
served noon-2pm, 6-9.30pm Mon-Thur; noon-2pm,
6-10pm Fri, Sat. **Main courses** £13-£17.50. **Set**
lunches £12.50 2 courses, £17.25 3 courses. **Credit**
AmEx, MC, V.
The Hole in the Wall's stuffy reputation is more to do
with its longevity, and the age of the average customer,
than its jolly staff or modern takes on classic Brit cuisine. It makes innovative use of seasonal produce – witness the asparagus, lemon and spinach soup. It also
neatly balances delicate and earthy flavours – as in
tuna with slow-roasted tomatoes and artichokes – and
the vegetarian options are refreshingly imaginative.
The two-course set lunch is served without the
remotest pressure to order extras and service is as
sweet as the desserts. It's a pleasant-looking place, too,
with rustic, varnished tables and Van Gogh chairs
arranged throughout flagstoned, spacious no-smoking
and smoking areas.

The Hop Pole

7 Albion Buildings, Upper Bristol Road, BA1 3AR (01225 446327). **Food served** noon-2pm, 6-9pm Tue-Sat; noon-3pm, 7-9pm Sun. **Main courses** £7.95-£15.95. **Credit** MC, V.

Recent darling of the broadsheets – to rousing hurrahs from its fans – Barry Wallace and Elaine Dennehy's pub/restaurant has long been one of Bath's best-kept secrets. Lunches and dinners are available either in the wood-panelled pub or in the airier, more relaxed basement restaurant and are executed with a gourmand's passion – unfussy, generous and hearty, with a zeal for old-fashioned dishes. Go easy on the starters, mouthwatering though piquillo peppers or crispy whitebait are – if you're aiming for a large main such as braised oxtail or pigeon breast with haggis, followed by a comfort pudding.

Moody Goose

7A Kingsmead Square, BA1 2BA (01225 466688/ www.moody-goose.com). **Food served** noon-1.30pm, 6-9.30pm Mon-Sat. **Main courses** £18-£19.50. **Set lunch** £17.50 3 courses. **Set dinner** £25 3 courses. **Credit** AmEx, DC, MC, V.

The Modern British fare served in this basement-level restaurant is widely considered to be some of the finest food in Bath. Fresh, locally sourced ingredients are used to craft aesthetically pleasing dishes, often with a whiff of France, such as Cornish lobster with truffle oil and quails' eggs or rump of lamb with pine kernel crust and ratatouille. Make sure you leave room for tantalising desserts such as vanilla and pear bavarois. The set menus are great value for money, but going à la carte for dinner can leave a sting. Waiting staff are discreet, and help to create a calm, rather sober, atmosphere.

No.5 Restaurant

5 Argyle Street, BA2 4BA (01225 444499). **Food served** noon-2.30pm, 6.30-10pm Mon-Thur, Sun; noon-2.30pm, 6.30-10.30pm Fri; noon-2.30pm, 6.30-11pm Sat. **Main courses** £12.50-£17. **Credit** AmEx, MC, V.

The paper tablecloths suggest 'quick bite', but the service and quality of the food implore you to linger over a meal at this classic French bistro. Chef Michel Lemoine trained under the Roux brothers and his delicate brushstrokes are everywhere: the perfectly tossed and dressed curly salad; the vibrant colour and gleam of the sardines stuffed with tomatoes, red onion and lemon in chive butter. The lunch menu is restrictive yet perfect for the smaller appetite (and wallet – with a glass of something it'll come in at around a tenner). The place is popular with business folk and older tourists, who are no doubt tickled by the attentive French waiters trilling 'bon appetit'.

The Olive Tree

Queensberry Hotel, Russell Street, BA1 2QF (01225 447928/www.thequeensberry.co.uk). **Lunch served** 7-10pm Mon; noon-2pm, 7-10pm Tue-Sat; 12.30-2.30pm, 7-10pm Sun. **Main courses** £12.50-£18.95. **Set lunches** (Tue-Sat) £13.50 2 courses, £15.50 3 courses, (Sun) £22.50 3 courses. **Set dinner** (Mon-Fri, Sun) £26 3 courses. **Credit** AmEx, MC, V.

Downstairs from the Queensberry Hotel (*see p154*), but quite independent, the Olive Tree has an impressive reputation. Elegant but not snooty, this is a place to really spoil your taste buds. Starters might include a Cornish seafood sausage or seared scallops, while mains could

offer up a fillet of beef with Parma ham and shallots, or pan-fried John Dory. Olive Tree ice-creams take a walk on the wild side, with unusual oat and basil flavours, but in general this is a calm, mature kind of place, where many male diners don a shirt and tie. Informed and friendly staff are on hand to answer any questions.

Pimpernel's

Royal Crescent Hotel, 16 Royal Crescent, BA1 2LS (01225 823333). **Food served** noon-2pm, 7-10pm Mon-Thur, Sun; noon-2pm, 7-10.30pm Fri, Sat. **Main courses** £25. **Set lunches** £18 2 courses, £25 3 courses. **Set dinner** £45 3 courses. **Credit** AmEx, DC, MC, V.

This place is named after the Scarlet Pimpernel, who lived at this address. Chef Stephen Blake deserves praise for his seasonal menus built around Modern British cuisine with global influences. The bald descriptions ('fried cod and dauphinoise potatoes with bacon lardons') are at odds with the fine ingredients, picturesque presentation and lavish flavours. Hand-painted wallpaper decorates the Regency-style dining room, which is softened by ochre banquettes with puffed-up cushions. Disappointingly, the waiters can verge on the frosty, displaying little knowledge or interest in the menu's offerings. However, for the set lunch deal it's worth suffering some belittlement.

The Priory

Weston Road, BA1 2XT (01225 331922). **Lunch served** noon-1.30pm, 7-9.30pm Mon-Sat; noon-1.30pm, 7-9pm Sun. **Set lunches** (Mon-Sat) £20 2 courses, £25 3 courses, (Sun) £30 3 courses. **Set dinner** £47.50 3 courses. **Credit** AmEx, DC, MC, V.

Exceptional in numerous ways, not least the fact that this beautiful country house hotel makes you feel like royalty. Allow a complimentary amuse-bouche to prime the tastebuds for some true event-dining. The menu might include ravioli of crab and ginger with langoustine sauce, honey-glazed Gressingham duck breast, or vanilla pannacotta with passion fruit sorbet. Expect to pay a little over £100 for a blowout three-course dinner with wine. The hushed drawing room-style dining room covered in contemporary art overlooks the huge garden – which also supplies vegetables and herbs to the chopping board of chef Robert Clayton (who learnt at the elbow of Nico Ladenis and bagged Michelin stars for the Priory from 1999-2001).

Rajpoot

4 Argyle Street, BA2 4BA (01225 466833). **Food served** 11am-2.30pm, 6-11pm Mon-Thur, Sun; 11am-2.30pm, 6-11.30pm Fri, Sat. **Main courses** £8-£15. **Set dinner** £18-£25 4 courses. **Credit** AmEx, DC, MC, V.

Descending the stairs into Rajpoot is a magical experience. Bowing waiters usher you into a low-ceilinged cavern, its dark atmosphere lit by candles and lanterns throwing patterns on to stone walls. Of the three dining rooms, Old India's intimate green booths are always popular with couples sampling the gourmet Bengali cuisine, with dishes such as lamb rezala and shahi murg mussalam, and the stew-like chicken jaflong. Everything shares a loving attention to detail and a masterful use of herbs and spices. Staff willingly explain dishes and at busy times the beautifully ornate bar area makes waiting a pleasure. More expensive than the average curry house but breathtakingly worth it.

Chippenham to Avebury

A neolithic neighbourhood.

The pocket of England that sits between the towns of Newbury and Bath is defined by its history. Signs of modernity here seem crass and unnecessary next to the untouched villages and rolling countryside that dominate the area; add in the presence of several neolithic sites of great import, and the 21st century seems a long way away. Two or three villages – chiefly **Lacock** and **Castle Combe** – soak up much of the area's tourist trade; most visitors are weekend breakers or daytrippers from nearby Bath (*see p148*). But beyond these landmark settlements are other towns and villages not without their charms, but without quite so many visitors.

Marlborough country and beyond

Heading west from London into Wiltshire, **Marlborough** is an understandably popular stop. Built on the slopes of the River Kennet's valley and named for the chalk mound ('marl') that's lain neglected here over the centuries, the town has a wide, attractive high street lined with coaching inns and colonnaded Georgian buildings, now largely given over to touristy pubs, shops and tearooms. Nearby sits Marlborough College, a prestigious and very traditional public school.

To the west lies the gentle skein of the Marlborough Downs and an assortment of neolithic sites that are interesting chiefly – though not exclusively – to druids and Americans. From Hackpen Hill, the A361 slices through the village and famous stone circle of **Avebury** (*see p160*). Nearby sits **Silbury Hill**, at more than 4,500 years old and 130 feet high it is one of the largest man-made prehistoric mounds in Europe (currently closed for repair by English Heritage), and **West Kennett Long Barrow**, one of Britain's biggest neolithic burial tombs. This area is so rich with sites that it's easy to succumb to barrow-, circle-, stone- and dolmen-fatigue, and take for granted the near-miracle of these remarkable landmarks, their creation and survival.

Heading west on the A4 towards Bath, the ancient gives way to the merely old: historic houses such as **Dyrham Park**, **Corsham Court** and stunning **Bowood**. Another of the area's historic phenomena are the white horses carved into the hills. Chalk sits just below the grassy surfaces, making such a practice fairly straightforward. However, though the white horse of **Uffington** (*see p101*) is some 3,000 years old, it wasn't until the late 1770s that imitators started to crop up, crudely battered into the landscape by schoolboys (as occurred at Marlborough, 1804), farmers (**Broad Town**, 1864) and local townspeople celebrating the millennium (**Devizes**, 2000).

This is pig-rearing country, centred around **Calne**, which had its day in 1864 when the former Harris bacon factory became the first to use the principle of bacon curing. Nearby **Chippenham** holds a fair amount of historical interest (King Alfred sited his hunting lodge in this market town), yet little of contemporary worth (he did so on a site that's now at the heart of a ring-road system, while the town's market stallholders now trade in mobile phone fascias and bargain batteries).

The western wedge of this area is the most attractive, and **Corsham**, founded on stone and cloth, is a historic treasure. Investigate the High Street, with houses dating back to 1540, the finest almshouses in the country on Pound Pill, and the only shaft stone mine in the world to be open to the public. The **Hare & Hounds** was once the residence of Moses Pickwick, Dickens's inspiration for *The Pickwick Papers*.

Village people

An atmosphere of unreality envelops **Castle Combe**, which wears its (chiefly self-proclaimed, but also much awarded) status as the prettiest village in Ye Merrie Olde Englande as a badge of honour. It's defined by a slew of perfectly preserved chocolate-box cottages, a

By train from London

Trains to **Chippenham** leave **Paddington** about every half an hour (journey time 1hr 13mins), passing through **Reading** and **Swindon**. Info: www.greatwesterntrains.co.uk.

Wiltshire & Bath

A bridge over untroubled waters in pretty and unspoilt **Castle Combe**. *See p157.*

tinkling river and a graceful lack of modernity; there are no TV aerials or streetlamps in the village, the only after-dark illumination coming from lights in the windows of the village's two pubs and the glowing crucifix atop the church.

However, such quaintness, when allied with a rare talent for self-promotion, has resulted in Castle Combe drawing more tourists than it knows what to do with. It's beautiful, yes, but unless you're staying here – meaning you'll be able to wander round it before the coach parties show up and after they've gone – you may be overwhelmed by the hordes. Happily, the sweet villages nearby aren't as popular with snap-happy tour groups: among them are **Nettleton**, **West Kington** and **Biddestone**, whose village green and duckpond are postcard-perfect.

A short drive to the south, the abbey village of **Lacock** (*see p161* **Picture this**) also finds itself strangely frozen in time. It's a delight to visit and the preserved-in-aspic feel – the village has served as the set for some period dramas including *Pride and Prejudice* and *Moll Flanders* – is slightly alleviated by the knowledge that people actually live here.

Devizes

Dipping south again, the countryside irons itself out towards the Vale of Pewsey, the Kennet and Avon Canal and **Devizes**. There are 500 listed buildings in Devizes, and a healthy proportion of them are Wadworth pubs fuelled by the rambling Victorian brewery that looms over the western entrance to the Market Place. Arty-crafty shops, a theatre and a private Victorian folly that would like to be known as a castle are among the attractions, but if you've any sense, you're only here for the beer.

Just outside Devizes is the famous **Caen Hill** flight of 29 locks, the longest in the country. If you're smitten by the romance of the canal, you can 'adopt' a section of it (contact the Kennet and Avon Canal Trust, 01380 721279), but boat trips and canal holidays are the most relaxing way to take in this pastoral region (White Horse Boats, 8 Southgate Close, Pans Lane, Devizes, 01380 728504).

Following the canal and the A365 west, you'll come to **Melksham**, once a centre for the weaving trade and now a town whose ability to trade on its history is only marginally compromised by the clumps of charmless modern houses that ring its centre.

By foot and by bike

Barging aside, there's good walking country all over the region. The many great pathways to latch on to include the **Macmillan Way**, the **Ridgeway** and the **Cotswold Way**. The **Savernake Forest**, just east of Marlborough,

is an ancient hunting forest now sculpted with superb beech-lined paths that emanate from a central hub. For bikers, the **Wiltshire Cycleways** have some fantastic routes, notably Corsham to Great Bedwyn (about 41 miles). If you don't fancy the exercise, take a lazy drive; there are plenty of lanes to explore: try around **Bowden Hill** from the A342 to **Lacock** (part of an old route taken by Pepys and others from London to Bath); and from the A4 at **Box**, taking in the villages of **Colerne** and **Ford**. Great hostelries pop up at every turn, and Wadworth beer is the choice tipple. Paddle, pedal, hike or drive: some people will do anything for a pint of 6X.

What to see & do

Tourist Information Centres

George Lane car park, Marlborough, SN8 1EE (01672 513989). **Open** *Apr-Oct* 10am-5pm Mon-Sat. *Nov-Mar* 10am-4.30pm Mon-Sat.

Avebury Chapel Centre, Green Street, SN8 1RE (01672 539425/www.kennet.gov.uk). **Open** 10am-5pm Tue-Sun.

Chippenham Tourist Centre, Yield Hall, Market Place, Chippenham, SN15 3HL (01249 706333). **Open** 9.30am-5pm Mon-Sat.

Cromwell House, The Market Place, Devizes, SN10 1JG (01380 729408). **Open** *Apr-Oct* 9.30am-5pm Mon-Sat. *Nov-Mar* 9.30am-4.30pm Mon-Sat. Also here is a small exhibition focusing on the history of the castle, particularly its role in Stephen and Matilda's struggle for power in the 11th century.

Church Street, Melksham, SN12 6LS (01225 707424). **Open** *Apr-Oct* 9am-5pm Mon-Fri; 9.30am-4.30pm Sat. *Nov-Mar* 9.30am-4.30pm Mon-Fri; 10am-4pm Sat.

Bike hire

Pedlers *59 Northgate Street, Devizes, SN10 1JJ (01380 722236).*

Alexander Kieller Museum

High Street, Avebury, SN8 1RF (01672 539250). **Open** *Apr-Oct* 10am-6pm daily. *Nov-Mar* 10am-4pm daily. **Admission** (NT) £4; £2 concessions; free under-5s.
Founded in the 1930s, this museum displays many of the thrilling bits and bobs from the great archaeologist Alexander Kieller's Stone Age excavations on Windmill Hill, north-west of Avebury. Note the curious curled remains of a child buried 5,000 years ago in a ditch below the hill.

Atwell Wilson Motor Museum Trust

Stockley Lane, Calne, SN11 ONF (01249 813119). **Open** *Apr-Oct* 11am-5pm Mon-Thur, Sun. *Nov-Mar* 11am-4pm Mon-Thur, Sun. **Admission** £2.50; £1 concessions.
A collection of vintage classic cars and motorcycles from 1924 to 1983, Model T Fords to Cadillacs, lovingly restored and in perfect running order.

Avebury Manor
High Street, Avebury, SN8 1RF (01672 539250).
Open *Gardens* Apr-Oct 11am-5pm. Tue, Wed, Fri-Sun. *House* Apr-Oct 2-5.30pm Tue, Wed, Fri-Sun.
Last admission 4.40pm. **Admission** (NT) *House & gardens* £4; £2 concessions; free under-5s. *Gardens only* £2.80; £1.40 concessions; free under-5s.
Dating from 1550, Avebury Manor was extended in the 17th century. Its grounds contain the formal Monk's Garden, topiary, fine borders, a wishing well and fountains. Charles II and Queen Anne stayed here.

Avebury Stones
Considered one of the greatest achievements in prehistoric Europe, Avebury's stone circles are not complete; many of the original stones were destroyed to provide stone for the village. However, they're still impressive, mystical sights. The stones aren't cordoned off, so you can wander among them or visit the Henge shop to unravel their significance.

Bowood House & Gardens
Off A4 at Derry Hill, between Calne & Chippenham (01249 812102/www.bowood-estate.co.uk). **Open** *Apr-Oct* 11am-6pm daily. **Admission** £5.90; £3.70-£4.90 concessions; free under-5s.
Bowood, begun in 1625 and home to the Earl and Countess of Shelburne, has two claims to fame: Dr Joseph Priestley discovered oxygen here in 1774, and Napoleon's death mask is on show. There are other attractions, however. 'Capability' Brown masterminded the gardens, with lawns running down to a long lake, plus grottoes and cascades. In May and June, when the rhododendrons are in bloom, hordes of visitors come to Bowood for the rhododendron walks. There's also a fabulous treehouse adventure playground, and lovely too.

Broadleas Gardens Charitable Trust
Broadleas, Devizes, SN10 5JQ (01380 722035).
Open *Apr-Oct* 2-6pm Wed, Thur, Sun. **Admission** £4.00; £1.50 concessions.
Lady Anne Cowdray's beautiful valley gardens feature a secret garden, a winter garden, a wood, a sunken rose garden and a silver border packed with tender plants rarely seen in the English open air.

Castle Combe Race Circuit
Westway House, Parcel Combe, Chippenham, SN14 7EY (01249 782417/www.castlecombecircuit.co.uk).
Open 9am-4pm daily. **Admission** varies.
Whether you're keen on spectating or participating, this racing circuit has been the home of motor, biking and karting thrills for 50 years. It's south of Castle Combe on the B4039.

Corsham Court
Off Church Street, Corsham, SN13 0BZ (01249 701610/www.corsham-court.co.uk). **Open** *Jan-Mar, Oct, Nov* 2-4pm Sat, Sun. *Apr-Sept* 2-5pm Tue-Sun.
Last entry 30mins before closing. Closed Dec.
Admission *House & garden* £5; £2.50-£4.50 concessions. *Garden only* £2; £1-£1.50 concessions.
The site of a royal manor in Saxon times, the present house dates back to 1582. It contains more than 140 paintings and statues; the 'Capability' Brown-designed grounds contain a fine Gothic bath house. The house was the backdrop for the film *The Remains of the Day*.

Dyrham Park
Nr Chippenham, SN14 8ER (01179 372501).
Open noon-4.45pm Mon, Tue, Fri-Sun.
Admission (NT) £7.90.
Built around the turn of the 18th century for William III's 'Secretary at State and at War', this National Trust property is furnished with paintings, furniture and ceramics, reflecting the Dutch style. Recently restored Victorian domestic rooms include the kitchen, bakehouse, tenants' hall, Delft-tiled dairy and larders.

Lacock Abbey & Grounds & Fox Talbot Museum
Lacock, SN15 2LG (01249 730459/www.r-cube. co.uk/fox-talbot). **Open** *Museum* Mar-Oct 11am-5.30pm daily. Nov-Feb 11am-4pm Sat, Sun. *Abbey* Apr-Oct 1-5.30pm. Mon, Wed-Sun. Closed Nov-Mar.
Admission *Museum* £4.20. *Abbey* £5.30. *Museum & abbey* £6.50.
When it was converted into a country house in 1539, the new owners of Lacock Abbey added a brewery, the Great Hall and Gothic archway, but retained the cloisters running round its centre.

Wiltshire Heritage Museum, Gallery & Library
41 Long Street, Devizes, SN10 1NS (01380 727369/ www.wiltshireheritage.org.uk). **Open** 10am-5pm Mon-Sat; noon-4pm Sun. **Admission** £1; free under-16s. Free Mon, Sun. **No credit cards.**
Owned by the Wiltshire Archaeological and Natural History Society, the museum boasts one of the finest prehistoric collections in Europe. The library is shut on the first Saturday of the month.

Where to stay

Marlborough High Street holds several perfectly fine options, among them the **Merlin** Hotel (36-9, High Street, 01672 512151, doubles £60-£70), the **Ivy House Hotel** (43 High Street, 01672 515333, doubles £65-£98) and the **Castle & Ball** (High Street, 01672 515201, doubles £95). In Chippenham, try the **Bear** Hotel (12 Market Place, 01249 658176, doubles £75). In Devizes, the **Black Swan** (Market Place, 01380 723259, doubles £75) or the **Elm Tree Inn** at the end of Long Street (01380 723834, doubles £50) are recommended.

Away from the main towns, you'll find plenty of cosy B&Bs and pubs with accommodation. Aside from Whitley's recently expanded **Pear Tree** (*see p163*), there's B&B at **Fosse Farmhouse** in Nettleton (Fosse Farmhouse Country Hotel, Nettleton Shrub, Nettleton, 01249 782286, doubles £85-£125).

If you can't stretch to the **Manor House** in Castle Combe, the nearby **Castle Inn** (01249 783030, doubles £120-£165) is a more than adequate alternative. The bedrooms are handsome and cosy, the downstairs bar agreeably peaceful (though locals tend to congregate at the earthier White Hart opposite)

Wiltshire & Bath

Picture this

It doesn't look impressive; just a dark, slightly crooked picture of a window, about the size of a postage stamp. But William Fox Talbot's photograph of a window (the very window pictured above) at his home, **Lacock Abbey** (*see p160*), is of unparalleled importance. For this

was the world's first negative, and without Fox Talbot's invention of the process that led to its creation in August 1835, photography may not have evolved in the way it has.

Fox Talbot was a Renaissance man, as skilled as a classicist as he was a scientist. However, it was his interest in art that fired his greatest discovery. After using both a camera obscura and a camera lucida (essentially, a reflecting prism) as aids to drawing, Talbot's curiosity was piqued enough that he became determined to find a way of permanently retaining the images projected by them. This he managed with the aid of drawing paper soaked in salt solution and a silver nitrate solution; the resulting technique, which reversed the hues of the image and was named a 'negative' by Fox Talbot's friend Sir John Herschel, became the basis for modern photography.

A museum in the grounds of Lacock Abbey, now owned by the National Trust but still inhabited by Fox Talbot's descendants, details the great man's research in an approachable fashion, and the abbey itself displays a copy of this original negative next to the window it details. Doubtless, Fox Talbot would be tickled to learn that his old house is still making pictorial history, albeit of a very different kind: the cloisters behind the abbey double as Hogwarts School in the Harry Potter movies.

and the full English breakfast faultless. And for Avebury aficionados, the **New Inn** (01672 539240, doubles £50) in Winterbourne Monkton, a backwater village just a couple of minutes' drive from Avebury stone circle, is a tiny and pleasant pub with rooms.

At the Sign of the Angel
6 Church Street, Lacock, SN15 2LB (01249 730230/fax 01249 730527/www.lacock.co.uk).
Rates £72 single occupancy (Mon-Fri, Sun only); £99-£149.50 double/twin. **Rooms** (all en suite) 8 standard double; 2 twin. **Credit** AmEx, DC, MC, V.
George Hardy is the welcoming angel at this ship-like 15th-century hotel in Lacock, the most handsome place to stay in Wiltshire's most handsome village. The

bedrooms in the main house have been immaculately maintained, a perfect marriage of antique furniture and modern furnishings; fires and wobbly beams contribute to the homely atmosphere. Ask for a room in this building, for while the bedrooms in the cottage across the garden are clean and tasteful, they're not quite as appealing. The dining rooms serve traditional British fare. All bedrooms are no-smoking.
M4 J17 to Chippenham and Warminster; village is 3 miles south of Chippenham on A350; hotel is at far end of village.

Castle Hotel
New Park Street, Devizes, SN10 1DS (01380 729300/fax 01380 729155/www.castledevizes.com).
Rates £55 single occupancy; £75 double/twin; £90-£120 family room. **Rooms** (all en suite) 5 single, 10 double/twin, 3 family. **Credit** MC, V.

Wiltshire & Bath

Jez and Diane Lenton took over this former coaching inn, based on a busy corner, in 2001, and immediately set about a major programme of refurbishment. Now all the bedrooms have been renovated; if the lively colour schemes aren't to everyone's taste, the rooms are at least immaculately clean and tidy. The next stage is the addition of a guests-only games room, a nice companion piece to the bar and restaurant that fronts the street. Children are welcome – there are decent-value family rooms – and all bedrooms are no smoking. Oh, and give our regards to Spike the lizard, contentedly housed in a glass-faced cupboard in one of the hotel's corridors.

Chilvester Hill House

Calne, SN11 0LP (01249 813981/fax 01249 814217/www.chilvesterhillhouse.co.uk). **Rates** £50-£60 single occupancy; £80-£90 double/twin. **Rooms** (all en suite) 3 double/twin. **Credit** AmEx, DC, MC, V.

Dr and Mrs Dilley welcome guests into their Victorian home (now part of the Wolsey Lodge group). The house has recently been refurbished in William Morris style. The Dilleys do dinner for around £23; everyone eats together. When it comes to food, Jill (army daughter and well travelled) likes to mix traditional English with Middle Eastern. Her breakfasts were given 11 out of ten by broadcaster Derek Cooper. No children under 12.
Take A4 from Calne towards Chippenham; after 1 mile turn right towards Bremhill & Ratford, then immediately right into hotel driveway.

Manor House Hotel

Castle Combe, SN14 7HR (01249 782206/fax 01249 782159/www.exclusivehotels.co.uk). **Rates** £145 single occupancy; £175 double; £285-£350 four-poster. **Rooms** (all en suite) 31 double; 18 four-poster. **Credit** MC, V.

This impressive 'heraldic' traditional hotel, dating back to the 14th century, is approached by a sweeping drive over a weir and the trout-stuffed Bybrook. It sits in 26 acres of grounds, including the romantic Italian gardens. The luxurious rooms, named after fields in the Castle Combe parish, feature bathrooms with TVs and phones. There's grand feasting in the barn-style restaurant (a full English costs £15); non-residents are welcome to drop in for Sunday lunch. Children are welcome; smoking is allowed in the lounge.
Castle Combe is off B4039.

Red Lion

High Street, Avebury, SN8 1RF (01672 539266/fax 01672 539377). **Rates** £40 single occupancy; £60 double/twin. **Rooms** 1 single (en suite); 1 double; 1 twin (en suite); 1 family room. **Credit** MC, V.

Travelling with a copy of Julian Cope's stone circle guide *The Modern Antiquarian*? Here's yer hotel. There's nowhere else in the world where you can snap open your curtains to find yourself in the middle of a stone circle, which is why the four bedrooms are in such high demand. The Red Lion's fame has spread further since it appeared on TV detailing Britain's most haunted sites: there are reputed to be three ghosts here. A recent refurb spruced things up but, happily, the 85-foot well that now doubles as a table (and down which one unfortunate villager is said to have met his demise) survived the builders. Smokers staying here must adjourn to the sprawling downstairs bar for a puff.

Red Lion

1 High Street, Lacock, SN15 2LQ (01249 730456/ fax 01249 730766). **Rates** £55 single occupancy; £75 double/twin. **Rooms** (all en suite) 1 single; 1 twin; 4 double. **Credit** AmEx, MC, V.

The bedrooms here are comfortable enough, worth investigating if At the Sign of the Angel (*see p161*) is booked up or beyond your means. But doused as it is in history and quality, the Red Lion will never lose sight of the fact that it's a pub at heart. The no-nonsense red-brick frontage belies the early 18th-century origins. The bar is appealing, all flagged or scuffed wooden floors, rough beams, amber light and well-kept Wadworth ales. The food is hearty fare, predictable but pleasant. Kids are welcome, and all bedrooms are smoke-free.

Rudloe Hall Hotel

Leafy Lane, Rudloe, SN13 0PA (01225 810555/fax 01225 811412/www.rudloehall.co.uk). **Rates** (per person) £89-£199 single occupancy; £64.50-£84.50 double; £109.50-£117.50 four-poster; £159 suite. **Rooms** (all en suite) 7 double; 4 four-poster; 1 suite. **Credit** AmEx, DC, MC, V.

An exercise in Victorian kooky Gothic, John and May Lyndsey-Walker's target audience is 'the discerning romantic'. They've hit the bullseye, too. The rooms are theatrically melodramatic, the grander variety boasting four-posters, baths on legs and screens behind which the modest can undress. The biscuit is taken by the Tower Suite, a decadent three-floored suite with its own rooftop terrace and outdoor spa. You can take dinner in your own room, but then you would miss the candlelit dining room. Wherever you choose to eat, a post-prandial walk around the lovely gardens or a nip of brandy over a game of snooker is highly recommended. Dogs are welcome (there's a £10 charge per night), children under 14 aren't, and no-smoking rooms are available.
At the top of Box Hill on A4 between Box & Corsham (6 miles east of Bath).

Where to eat & drink

Thanks to the presence of two fantastic local breweries, Moles at Melksham and Wadworth at Devizes, there are some cracking boozers in this part of Wiltshire, all serving real ale with due care and attention. Among the best are the **Rising Sun** (01249 730363) up Bowden Hill and the **Six Bells** (01225 742413) in Colerne. Both the **Quarryman's Arms** at Box (01225 743569) and the **Raven** at Poulshot (01380 828271) have fine restaurants.

For more upmarket eating, you can try the **Ivy House** (High Street, Marlborough, 01672 515333), the **Castle Hotel** (*see p161*) and the **Bybrook Restaurant** at the Manor House Hotel (*see above*), which also serves a well-regarded high tea. **Bowood House** (*see p160*) and the **Stable Tea Rooms** (01249 730585) at Lacock also do a fine tea, with the **Lacock Bakery** (01249 730457) making an excellent alternative to the latter. For light snacks, **Polly's** (01672 512146) tearoom in Marlborough offers some terrific cakes.

Circle Restaurant

Off High Street, Avebury, SN8 1RF (01672 539514). **Food served** 10am-6pm daily. **Main courses** £3.50-£6. **Credit** MC, V.

This National Trust-owned veggie canteen is the perfect place to feed your hunger after a trot around the famous and fantastic stone circles of Avebury. It's an endearingly simple place, the decor unmemorable and service buffet-style, but that's of no matter: the undeniable and unadorned excellence of the food is compensation enough. The menu here is entirely vegetarian, largely organic (some ingredients are grown right here in the garden) and subsequently subject to daily change. However, you can guarantee that there's always a soup, and the list of mains might include bean casserole with polenta, vegetarian lasagne or quiche. It's hearty food for warming the soul, and very cheap; you can have three courses – and it's a pity to miss the third, as the terrific desserts are served in brick-sized slices – for not much more than a tenner. Staff are all smiles.

George Inn

4 West Street, Lacock, SN15 2LH (01249 730263). **Food served** noon-2pm, 6-9pm daily. **Main courses** £7.50-£13.50. **Credit** MC, V.

Not even the incongruous piped music can quite ruin this handsome old pub, which dates back to the 13th century and still has a wonderful rural air about it. And for that, credit John Glass, a natural-born landlord who's happy to show the many tourists the old dogwheel that once turned a spit. Unfortunately, the food's not up to much: a smoked chicken salad was dank and watery, and an otherwise fine portion of pork fillet medallions was a little stingy for the price (£10.75). Still, if you stick to the bar – and the local Wadworth ales – you'll find that this is a fine place to while away an evening. There are also five guest bedrooms, housed in a nearby building.

George & Dragon

High Street, Rowde, SN10 2PN (01380 723053). **Food served** noon-2pm, 7-10pm Tue-Sat. **Main courses** £8.50-£16. **Set lunch** £10 2 courses, £12.50 3 courses. **Credit** MC, V.

Both the name and the decor imply that this is a pub, but don't be fooled: despite the fine ales that are found on tap behind the wood-panelled bar, drinking at Helen and Tim Withers' welcoming operation comes second to the food. The list of starters is a guaranteed appetite-whetter, taking in the likes of a rich boudin of chicken and duck with apple sauce, enjoyably simple asparagus and ham pancakes, and oak-smoked salmon tart. The restaurant has built its reputation on fresh fish, brought in directly from Cornwall. Dishes change daily and the list chalked up above the bar when we visited included a meaty skate with capers and black butter, and fillet of John Dory with a perfectly balanced crab sauce. If you're lucky, desserts will include marmalade sponge pudding with whisky sauce and custard. The wine list has also been commended for its quality and fair price.

The Healthy Life

4 Little Brittox, Devizes, SN10 1AR (01380 725558). Café **Food served** 10am-4pm Mon-Sat. **Main courses** £3.95-£6. *Bistro* **Food served** 7-11pm Tue-Sat. **Set dinner** £14.95 2 courses, £19.95 3 courses. **Credit** AmEx, MC, V.

Peter Vaughan offers what he terms 'body-friendly' foods in his natural food shop and first-floor café-cum-bistro, located in the pedestrianised town centre. A good proportion of the ethically sourced, organic and bio-dynamic ingredients used in the food preparation are taken from within the county, while others are of fair trade origin. Peter's experience in five-star hotel restaurants ensures that dishes possess a commendable degree of sophistication and innovation (and no trace of the crankiness that was once associated with the average healthfood establishment). This is imaginative and enjoyable stuff. Tasty too. The set-price three-course menu (good value at under £20 a head) could kick off with fricassée of chicken livers and apple with Somerset apple brandy flambé, followed by boiled Bromham ham with lovage and parsley broth and mashed potatoes. Ricotta and lemon cheesecake, or a selection of local cheeses might round things off.

Lucknam Park Hotel

Colerne, SN14 8AZ (01225 742777/www.lucknam park.co.uk). **Food served** 7.30-9.30pm Mon-Thur; 7-10pm Fri, Sat; 12.30-2.30pm, 7.30-9.30pm Sun. **Main courses** £18-£27. **Set lunch** £27 3 courses. **Set dinner** £48.50 3 courses. **Credit** AmEx, MC, V.

The Lucknam Park experience starts with the mile-long, tree-lined drive that takes you from the gates to the door of this Palladian mansion. Grand, certainly, but it gets still grander. You'll be ushered into an imposing drawing room, plied with *amuse-gueules* and handed chef Robin Zavou's menu, an appealing take on traditional English cooking with a few more adventurous dishes to boot. Starters may include a slightly overcomplicated tian of crab, smoked salmon and avocado; mains might run to immaculate Dover sole with wild mushroom and truffle oil sauce, or tender venison in a red wine sauce served with a deliciously poached pear. All in all, very good, but at these prices, it should be; for two people, each having a pre-dinner drink, three courses and coffee, and sharing a mid-priced bottle of wine, the bill came to £180. Adding the tip (service, the sniffy sommelier excepted, was immaculate) sent it over the £100-a-head mark. One for very special occasions.

Pear Tree

Top Lane, Whitley, SN12 8QX (01225 709131). **Food served** noon-2pm, 6.30-9.30pm Mon-Thur, Sun; noon-2pm, 6.30-10pm Fri, Sat. **Main courses** £8.50-£18. **Set lunch** £12.50 2 courses, £14.95 3 courses. **Credit** MC, V.

The front room of this bigger-than-it-looks stone farmhouse is enjoyably carefree, a cluster of comfortable seats in front of a tidy bar. But the pile of magazines give away the fact that, for many, it serves only as a waiting room for the handsome, award-winning restaurant that consumes much of the building. Mark Nacchia's menu is long and varied. It includes traditional options – a simple but impeccable plum tomato and celery soup, a perfectly tender piece of roast beef served with spuds and a Yorkshire pud – balanced by more playful concoctions such as a deceptively rich starter of warm wood pigeon salad and a most flavourful main of baked cod in parma ham. Best of the lot was the sticky apricot and walnut pudding in a toffee sauce, with which we rounded off our £15 three-course set lunch. Terrific, all told.

Wiltshire & Bath

Malmesbury & Around

A place where nothing much happens.

In 1010 a monk called Eilmer decided he could fly so he built himself some wings and jumped from the steeple of the old Minster Church in Malmesbury. He remained airborne for an estimated 200 yards before hitting the ground with a wallop, breaking both his legs. One wonders whether anything quite so exciting has happened to Malmesbury ever since. This is a town where nothing happens, slowly. As a guilt-free destination for the perennially lazy, Malmesbury and the countryside that surrounds it is an ancient, cobbled dream of excellent food, antiques, beautiful walks and idle, boozy contemplation.

Perhaps that's not entirely fair. Eilmer aside, Malmesbury has managed to rack up some other claims to fame in its 1,300-odd years. Philosopher Thomas Hobbes was born in these parts, proving that boozy contemplation brings its own rewards. The town is also the site of Malmesbury Abbey, an ancient, sprawling church that was built in the 12th century and was at the time famed as one of the largest buildings in the country. Although it has fallen into disrepair over the centuries, the enormous abbey and its garden is still the dominant feature of this pretty hilltop town and the main draw for tourists.

That such an impressive structure was built here is no real surprise. Because of its superb natural defences, the hill has been occupied since the earliest recorded period of time. It has been called Malmesbury since the seventh century. In 880 King Alfred was impressed enough to name Malmesbury a borough, making it the oldest in England. For centuries, the town was the heavily defended frontier of the kingdom of Wessex. Just five miles away

lies **Tetbury**, then in Mercia. The animosity between the two towns was considerable. These days, that rivalry is more concerned with who has the better hotels, the finer restaurants and the more interesting shops. In between and around lie many other lovely villages, most with a decent pub in which to while away the time between walks.

As far as activity goes, **Cotswald Water Park**, 132 lakes of aquatic entertainment, is sufficient to keep the younger visitor occupied. For the more mature tourist, less frenetic exercise can be found with a languorous stroll around nearby **Westonbirt Arboretum** (*see p168* **Tree trails**), or one of the handful of stately homes in the area (**Chavenage House**, **Lydiard House**). More expensively, there's the option of taking a gander at Tetbury's dozens of antiques shops. These now occupy every other site in the tiny town. There are so many that, as one resident confided, 'you can't even find anywhere that sells underwear anymore'. Tetbury's other main feature is the fixed **Market House** built on stilts in 1655 as a sheltered market. The Georgian Gothic church of St Mary the Virgin is also worth a look.

John Betjeman was among those smitten by Malmesbury. A plaque at the site of the town's Old West Gate recites some lines by the former laureate: 'You wouldn't know, driving through Malmesbury, what a surreal and peculiar place it is. You wouldn't know what gives it an atmosphere you can almost touch and see.'

What to see & do

Tourist Information Centre
Town Hall, Market Lane, Malmesbury, Wiltshire SN16 9BZ (01666 823748/www.malmesbury. gov.uk). **Open** 9am-4.50pm Mon-Thur; 9am-4.20pm Fri; 10am-4.30pm Sat.

33 Church Street, Tetbury, Gloucestershire GL8 8JG (01666 503552/www.tetbury.com). **Open** *Mar-Oct* 9.30am-4pm Mon-Sat. *Nov-Feb* 11am-2pm Mon-Sat.

Bike hire
CH White & Son, High Street, Malmesbury, Wiltshire SN16 9AG (01666 822330/www. cwhite.btinternet.co.uk).

By train from London

The nearest station is at **Kemble**, a couple of miles north of Crudwell; trains leave **Paddington** via Swindon every 15mins and take about 1hr. Info: www.firstgreatwestern.co.uk.

Malmesbury Abbey, and the Naked Gardener in the nearby **Abbey House Gardens**.

Abbey House Gardens

Market Cross, Malmesbury, Wiltshire SN16 9AS (01666 822212/www.abbeyhousegardens.co.uk). **Open** *Mar-Sept* 11am-6pm daily. Closed Nov-Feb. **Admission** £5; £2-£4.50 concessions. **No credit cards.**

Barbara and Ian Pollard have painstakingly tended these gorgeous gardens right next to the abbey. The huge variety of plants, flowers and shrubs includes hellebore, camellia and azalea, 180 fruit cordons, 30,000 tulips, 2,000 roses and almost 2,000 herbal plants. You can also see wildlife such as voles and kingfishers. Turner daubed here in 1794.

Chavenage House

Tetbury, Gloucestershire GL8 8XP (01666 502329/ fax 01453 836778/www.chavenage.com). **Open** *May-Sept* 2-5pm Thur, Sun. Closed Oct-Apr. **Admission** £4; £2 concessions. **No credit cards.**

Close to Tetbury, this Elizabethan house has tapestry rooms, furniture and relics of the Cromwellian period, plus the requisite ghost (with added headless coachman). If it looks familiar, that's because it has been used as the location for countless TV serials including *Casualty*, *House of Eliot* and *Cider with Rosie*.

Cotswold Water Park

Keynes Country Park, Spratsgate Lane, Shorncote, Gloucestershire GL7 9DF (01285 861459/www. waterpark.org). **Open** 9am-9pm daily. **Admission** *June-Sept* £3 Mon-Fri; £6 Sat, Sun; free for those on foot or bicycle. *Oct-May* £1-£2; free for those on foot or bicycle. **Credit** (shop only) MC, V.

Water lot of fun. This is a mammoth water park that is ideal for all manner of splashing about with the family. There is a ridiculous number of water-borne activities available on the 132 lakes fashioned out of gravel quarries: sailing, canoeing, windsurfing, water- and jet-skiing, sub-aqua diving, powerboating, and coarse and flyfishing. Those with a drier sensibility can hike, cycle, play golf or tennis, go horse riding or birdwatching. Children get to frolic in their own beach and play area. The less energetic can sunbathe or simply spectate from the various cafés and picnic areas. Activities should be booked in advance – prices vary, but boat hire costs £5 per half hour.

Lydiard House & Church

Lydiard Tregoze, Swindon, Wiltshire SN5 3PA (01793 770401). **Open** *Mar-Oct* 10am-5pm Mon-Sat; 2-5pm Sun. *Nov-Feb* 10am-4pm Mon-Sat; 2-4pm Sun. **Admission** £1.50; 75p concessions. **No credit cards.**

This magnificent Georgian residence, the ancestral home of the Bollingbrokes, has been rescued from dilapidation and is now beautifully restored. An adjoining parish church (get the key from the house) contains interesting 17th-century memorials. The extensive parkland includes an adventure playground.

Malmesbury Abbey

Enquiries: Malmesbury Parish Office, The Old Squash Court, Holloway, Malmesbury, Wiltshire SN16 9JF (01666 826666/www.malmesburyabbey. com). **Open** *Apr-Sept* 10am-5pm daily. *Oct-Mar* 10am-4pm daily. **Admission** free. **Tours** on request.

Although only about one third of the original structure remains intact, Malmesbury Abbey still dominates the town. Built in the 12th century, the abbey church is a fine example of Norman ecclesiastical architecture and includes a magnificent south porch carved with tales from the Bible. The first attempt at restoration took place in the 14th century, when a huge spire standing some 445ft high was added. It collapsed 100 years later. Historically, Malmesbury was a centre of monasticism: until the dissolution, the entire northern part of the town was given over to monastic buildings. The abbey now functions as a parish church.

Making a splash at the **Cotswold Water Park**, fun for water babies of all ages. *See p165.*

Trull House Gardens

Nr Tetbury, Gloucestershire GL8 8SQ (01285 841255). **Open** *Easter-May, July-Oct* 2-6pm Wed, Sat. *June* 2-6pm Wed, Sat; 6-8pm Tue, Fri. Also by appointment. Closed Nov-Easter. **Admission** £3; free children. **No credit cards**.

Eight acres including a sunken lily pond, rockery, wild garden and walled garden, as well as mature trees and shrubs. Horticulturists can make seedy purchases, and everybody else can enjoy a pot of tea in the adjacent café.

Where to stay

The area boasts a mix of high-end country house piles and good B&Bs. In addition to the places mentioned below, **Whatley Manor Hotel** (Easton Grey, Malmesbury, 01666 822888/www.whatleymanor.com, doubles £325-£420) is a massive new country house hotel that opened in July 2003. The **Snooty Fox** (Market Place, 01666 502 436/www.snooty-fox.co.uk, doubles £73-£140) in Tetbury is ideally placed opposite the market, with decent rooms and a friendly if formal ambience. The **India Suite** (01666 503 597) is run by the people behind the Central Asian-themed Artique shop. It features a Bollywood-style kitchen, Persian bathroom and lounge area with raised platform bed.

Cove House

Cove House, Ashton Keynes, nr Swindon, Wiltshire SN6 6NS (01285 861226). **Rates** £35-£36 single occupancy; £56-£58 double. **Rooms** (all en suite) 2 double. **No credit cards**.

In the delightfully English village of Ashton Keynes – all cutesy cottages, babbling brooks and popular pubs – Valerie Threlfall has created a delightfully English boarding house. The large manor house is liberally dotted with lovely personal touches – a silver mirror-and-comb set in one of the comfortable and welcoming rooms, a dressmaker's dummy in 1950s clothing in the hallway – and features a red dining room lined with William Morris wallpaper. There is a lounge room for guests to share and a magnificent 250-year-old copper beech in the garden under which you can sit and ponder life's imponderables. All rooms are no smoking and children are welcome.

A419 towards Cirencester; follow signs for Cotswold Water Park and Ashton Keynes; turn right at the White Hart pub, then left into the driveway behind a large stone wall.

Calcot Manor Hotel

Calcot Manor, nr Tetbury, Gloucestershire GL8 8YJ (01666 890391/www.calcotmanor.co.uk). **Rates** £140 single; £165-£270 double. **Rooms** (all en suite) 28 double/twin. **Credit** AmEx, DC, MC, V.

A couple of miles outside Tetbury, Calcot Manor – a farmhouse and attendant buildings clustered around charming flower-filled courtyards – oozes class. This is not a place for raised voices or, God forbid, football shirts. Calcot Manor originally housed 14th-century Cistercian monks; one wonders what they would make of the very recent addition of a health spa. This boasts a 16m indoor pool, gym, sauna, steam room, hot tub, fitness room, exercise studio and seven beauty treatment rooms. Those preferring a more relaxed approach to fitness might note the exquisite croquet lawn at the rear. The hotel also boasts two very good restaurants. Dogs are admitted by arrangement and children are welcome. *A4135 out of Tetbury; the hotel is on the right after around 3 miles.*

Close Hotel

Long Street, Tetbury, Gloucestershire GL8 8AH
(01666 502272/www.theclosehotel.co.uk). **Rates** £75-
£120 single; £100-£120 double. **Rooms** (all en suite)
15 double. **Credit** AmEx, DC, MC, V.

This townhouse, right in the heart of Tetbury, was built
in 1585 and has operated as a hotel since 1974. It's a
great place to stay, with each of the 15 large rooms taking a different theme (the Elizabethan has aged furniture and exposed beams, the Deco a lovely Art Deco
bathroom). The hotel has recently been taken over
by Greene King, but the personal touch has not been
lost, with fresh fruit placed in every room and guests
invited to take a welcoming glass of Madeira. Flash
widescreen TVs and DVD players add a modern edge.
The beautiful walled garden lends the place a sense of
serenity that can be almost disconcerting to those used
to London's hustle. Children and dogs are welcome.
From Malmesbury enter Tetbury and follow along the High
Street, over a roundabout, and take the 1st left for Dursley,
then 1st left again into Close Gardens (by library). The hotel
car park is at the end.

Kings Arms Hotel

High Street, Malmesbury, Wiltshire SN16 9AA
(01666 823383). **Rates** £40 single; £60-£75 double.
Rooms (all en suite) 11 double. **Credit** AmEx, MC, V.

Slap bang on Malmesbury High Street, the Kings Arms
is almost as well situated and certainly less expensive
than its chief rival, the Old Bell (*see below*). The bedrooms are well sized, clean and comfy, with a recent
refurbishment adding more rooms. There are also plans
to expand the conservatory dining area. The Kings
Arms has been an inn since Elizabethan times and features a cosy public bar and restaurant, the latter specialising in fresh fish. The noisier adjoining Coach House
bar is populated by Malmesbury's younger set. Children
are welcome.

Manor Farmhouse

Crudwell, Malmesbury, Wiltshire SN16 9ER
(01666 577375). **Rates** £35 single occupancy;
£30 per person. **Rooms** (all en suite) 2 double.
No credit cards.

Tucked behind Crudwell's square-turreted parish
church, Helen Carter's B&B takes on overspill from the
nearby Old Rectory (*see below*) but is a great place to
stay in its own right. Simple, clean and comfortable,
there are only two rooms, both with their own bathroom.
These are quite enough for Mrs Carter, who looks after
guests with bread baked in the Aga and vegetables from
her own organic garden. Sporty types might be
interested to learn that the Farmhouse's tennis court has
just been resurfaced. No smoking throughout. Children
admitted by arrangement only.
A429, 3 miles N of Malmesbury towards Crudwell; turn
right at the Plough Inn; immediate left after the church.

Old Bell Hotel

Abbey Row, Malmesbury, Wiltshire SN16 0AG
(01666 822344/www.oldbellhotel.com). **Rates** £85
single; £110-£200 double. **Rooms** (all en suite) 25
double; 3 single; 3 twin. **Credit** AmEx, MC, V.

The Old Bell claims to be the oldest hotel in the country, a boast resting on the fact that when it was built in
1220, its stated function was to entertain important
guests and it has been entertaining them ever since.

Old Rectory – fine food and Victorian porn.

Benefiting from a location so close to the abbey that it
could be an extension, the sturdy Old Bell is a rambling
den with individually decorated rooms, a mediocre
restaurant and a cosy lounge patrolled by hotel cat Dave.
The original building was massively expanded in 1908
when the then owner, a humble innkeeper, spent the
equivalent of £1m on renovations after claiming to find
a lost cache of gold. A faux Japanese extension is a more
recent addition. The hotel is child-friendly, with play
areas both inside and out. Pets are allowed.
A429; follow signs to the town centre and the abbey; the
hotel is next to the abbey at the top of the hill.

Old Rectory

Crudwell, Malmesbury ,Wiltshire SN16 9EP (01666
577194/www.oldrectorycrudwell.co.uk). **Rates** £75-
£95 single; £98-£105 double. **Rooms** (all en suite)
12 double. **Credit** AmEx, DC, MC, V.

If only all hotels were like this. Derek and Karen Woods
have done a spectacular job on this imposing 16th-
century rectory since they moved here three years ago.
Every room has been refurbished and handed a floral
theme (Hollyhock, Daisy, Bluebell and so on) and the
gardens, which are overlooked by every room, have been
beautifully landscaped. The bedrooms are large, with
many boasting spa baths and four-poster beds; the
largest of the lot, at the top of the building, is a very sat-
isfactory-looking suite. A downstairs lounge with
well-stocked bar is warmed by a gas fire, and the
owners go out of their way to make you feel welcome.
The Victorian pornography in the men's toilet is a
curious touch. Women have to make do with pottery
hats. All rooms are no-smoking. Children and dogs
admitted by arrangement only.
A429, 3 miles N of Malmesbury towards Crudwell; turn right
at the Plough Inn; immediate left before the church.

Where to eat & drink

The best restaurants in the area are listed below, but these are also recommended: the **Pear Tree** in Purton (01793 772100) is a quiet, luxuriously converted rectory with good food such as creamed leek and smoked haddock broth, and roast lamb with olive mash and pesto gravy. Brinkworth's **Three Crowns** (01666 510366) is a popular gastropub using not-quite-traditional ingredients such as kangaroo, venison and ostrich alongside less unusual options. **Som's Thai Café** (Stainbridge Mill, Gloucester Road, Malmesbury, 01666 822022) is a good and inexpensive Thai restaurant above a fitness centre. The restaurant at the **Old Bell** in Malmesbury (01666 822344) was once considered the very best in the area, but standards seem to have slipped, and we found the food disappointingly bland on a recent visit.

Close Hotel

Long Street, Tetbury, Gloucestershire GL8 8AH (01666 502272/www.theclosehotel.co.uk). **Food served** noon-2pm, 7-9.30pm daily. **Main courses** £22.50. **Set lunch** £16.50. **Set dinner** £28.50 3 courses. **Credit** AmEx, DC, MC, V.

The setting might be country house traditional, but the Close Hotel's kitchen is anything but. After a playful appetiser of asparagus cappuccino, it was down to business. Inventive starters set the scene. Assiette of smoked salmon starter has the fish in myriad form: tortellini, tartare and a deliciously moist bundled sausage. From the mains, study of Cotswold lamb – a medley of mini kidney pie, loin, sweetbreads and faggots – worked less well, veering towards the pretentious. Pan-fried cod with seafood foam was a treat, though, and the wonderfully witty trio of apple dessert capped everything; you'll never see an apple pie in quite the same way again. Oh, and the selection of British cheeses is not to be sniffed at (literally, in the case of the stinking bishop). Excellent service too, despite the slightly formal surroundings. For those looking to push their tastebuds to the edge, the multi-course taster menu is unmissable.

Tree trails

This is an area filled with good walks. Close by are parts of the Cotswald Way, a 100-mile trek from Chipping Campden to Bath; the Macmillan Way, a 200-mile route from Rutland to Dorest; and Monarch's Way, 610 miles from Worcester to Shoreham. The best of the lot, though, is to be found at **Westonbirt Arboretum**, an arboreal paradise of 18 miles of marked trails through 600 acres of landscaped countryside. With lots of trees.

The arboretum was founded as an extension to the Holford family estate in 1829. These days it is a carefully cultivated enclave of remarkable, towering, flowering trees as well as a home for an incredible diversity of wild flowers, fungi, birds and animals. Every season brings out a different aspect of Westonbirt. Flowering displays burst into life in the spring; autumn turns the place into a parade of flaming scarlets and golds. While an unguided wander can prove thoroughly involving, it won't teach you much about the trees around you. For that, you need a guided tour. The arboretum offers many: bat spotting, conifer identification, the dawn chorus, the gorgeous Japanese flowering cherries. There's even a Badgers' Night Out walk.

The arboretum also hosts special events. The Festival of Wood is a week of tree-carving (careful with the chainsaw

kids!), there are regular fireworks displays and musicians such as Jools Holland often perform concerts here. But if you are heading out under your own steam, just prepare a picnic and prepare to lose yourself in the wonderful, pastoral, thoroughly relaxing calm of this blissful, shady, tree-filled spot.

Westonbirt National Arboretum

Tetbury, Gloucestershire GL8 8QS (01666 880220/www.forestry.gsi.gov.uk/ westonbirt). **Open** 10am-dusk daily. **Admission** £7.50; £1-£6.50 concessions. **Credit** MC, V.

Wiltshire & Bath

The Dining Room & Le Mazot at Whatley Manor

Easton Grey, Wiltshire SN16 0RB (01666 822888/ www.whatleymanor.com). **Food served** *Le Mazot* noon-2pm, 7-10pm daily. *Dining Room* 7-10pm daily. **Main courses** *Le Mazot* £11.50-£14. *Dining Room* £15-£21. **Set dinners** *Dining Room* £60 3 courses, £75 7-course tasting menu. **Credit** AmEx, DC, MC, V.
The newly opened somewhat exclusive Whatley Manor just outside Tetbury is more beautiful private home than rigidly formal hotel. Martin Burge heads the kitchen and his time with the likes of John Burton-Race and Raymond Blanc has enabled him to introduce a menu of very appealing modern, classically based dishes. In the elegant Dining Room the carte is supplemented by a gourmand menu. The food is simpler, but no less enjoyable, in the brasserie-style Le Mazot, named and themed in the style of an original wooden Swiss chalet. Here, chicken liver parfait with a walnut salad and crusty bread might be followed by sea bream steamed with cockles and mussels, served with fresh pasta and a lightly creamed sauce.

Gumstool Inn & Conservatory at Calcot Manor

Calcot Manor, nr Tetbury, Gloucestershire GL8 8YJ (01666 890391/www.calcotmanor.co.uk). **Food served** noon-2pm, 7-9.30pm daily. **Main courses** £7.75-£12. **Credit** AmEx, DC, MC, V.
The Gumstool Inn, Calcot Manor's more laid-back dining area, is smart but very relaxed. The menu offers a choice of 'ample' or 'generous' portions of moderately priced dishes such as Cornish fish pasties and crispy roast pork belly. There are also decent vegetarian options (the asparagus, leek and mushroom pancake with gruyère was delicious) and good, filling pasta dishes. Its unusual name comes from a style of ducking stool that wives and other petty miscreants were tied to. Cooking in the Conservatory is more sophisticated: wonderfully melting griddled scallops with sweet chilli sauce, for instance, or peppered breast of Gressingham duck with creamed spinach and candied shallots. The caramelised banana shortbread with candied pineapple and rum and raisin ice-cream is not to be missed.

Old Rectory

Crudwell, Malmesbury , Wiltshire SN16 9EP (01666 577194/www.oldrectorycrudwell.co.uk). **Food served** noon-1.45pm, 7-9pm daily. **Set lunch** £15.95 2 courses, £18.95 3 courses. **Set dinner** £26.50 3 courses. **Credit** AmEx, DC, MC, V.
Chef Peter Fairclough has earned this excellent hotel restaurant much acclaim with a Modern British style that places an emphasis on fresh seasonal ingredients that are organic wherever possible. Meals are served in a lovely dining area, informal but smart and looking out to an impeccable garden – a planned conservatory extension will improve things still further. A clever cappuccino of wild mushroom appetiser set the tone, followed by lovely roast chump of lamb with dauphinoise potato, spinach and rosemary and baby caper jus. There's a good cheeseboard to follow but leave room for dessert (the iced banana parfait with glazed banana and dark chocolate sauce is a must). Take heart that when owners Derek and Karen Woods do the rounds to ask if you've had a good time, you won't be telling any porkies.

Rattlebone

Church Street, Shearston, Wiltshire SN16 (01666 840871). **Food served** noon-3pm, 6pm-10pm daily. **Main courses** £6.95-£12.95. **Credit** MC, V.
Locals felt standards were slipping at this old village inn, something that new managers Emma and John Williams have worked hard to rectify. It's a Young's house, so the beer's quality can be taken as read, and the food is classic and satisfying (chicken and leek pie, seafood pie, grilled sardines) and generally priced at under a tenner. Active minds will appreciate the countless games on offer (Connect Four, shove-ha'penny, cribbage). Come for the second Saturday of July to watch the pub's annual boules tournament.

Smoking Dog

62 High Street, Malmesbury, Wiltshire SN16 9AT (01666 825823). **Food served** noon-2pm, 5.30-9.30pm daily. **Main courses** £3.25-£17. **Credit** MC, V.
Perennially rammed, the Smoking Dog is a good, simple, chatty pub at the bottom end of Malmesbury's not exactly massive High Street. As well as a fairly standard snacks menu of ciabattas and pastas, there is a dinner menu that includes supreme red snapper with stem ginger, duck kebabs, grilled open mussels and smoked salmon and watercress salad. The beers are good and, if you time your visit correctly, you could arrive for the annual sausage and ale festival – the ideal marriage of meat and mead. A back garden offers lovely views over the picturesque town.

Trouble House

Nr Tetbury, Gloucestershire GL8 8SG (01666 502206/www.troublehouse.co.uk). **Food served** noon-2pm, 7-9.30pm Tue-Sat; 7-9pm Sun. **Main courses** £11.75-£14.50. **Credit** AmEx, DC, MC, V.
The whitewashed exterior may not promise much, and even inside the decor has been kept simple and rustic, but chef-proprietor Michael Bedford, who was Gary Rhodes's head chef, offers food that is a cut well above the average. As might be expected, the style is Modern British and may include fried smoked haddock dumpling with parsley sauce or cauliflower cheese soufflé to begin, followed by own-made faggots with mash and onion gravy or braised pork belly with sweet and sour red cabbage and spiced fruits. Warm pistachio frangipane with a soft chocolate centre or nougat glacé with pineapple are further fine examples of how sophisticated some pub food has become of late. The wines, like the food, are well balanced and kindly priced.

Vine Tree

Foxley Road, Norton, nr Malmesbury, Wiltshire SN16 0JP (01666 837654). **Food served** noon-2pm, 7pm-9.30pm Mon-Fri; noon-2.30pm, 7-9.30pm Sat; noon-3pm, 7-9.30pm Sun. **Main courses** £8.95-£15.50. **Credit** AmEx, DC, MC, V.
This pretty and remote 18th-century mill house has a kitchen that relies on seasonal ingredients and a bar that offers some very decent ales. The menu includes such treats as pork cutlet with honey and apple gravy and black pudding mash, and roasted baby fennel and vodka risotto. Young royal scallywags are sometimes seen here, showing surprisingly good taste as they seek refuge from the nearby stately piles of Prince Charles, Princess Anne and Prince and Princess Michael of Kent.

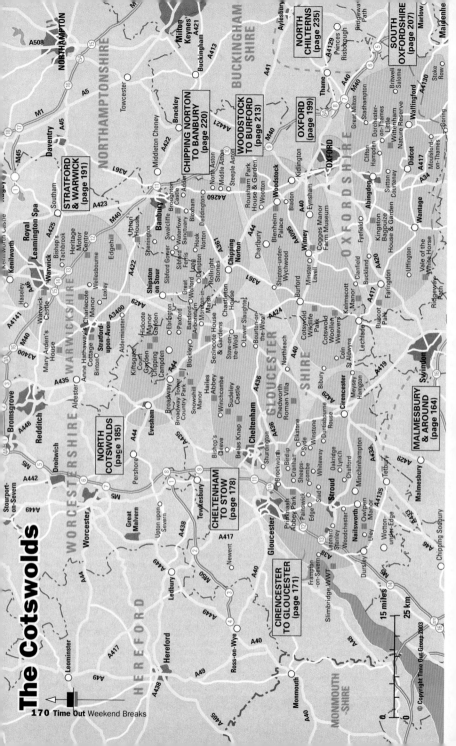

The Cotswolds

© Copyright Time Out Group 2003

STRATFORD & WARWICK (page 191)

CHIPPING NORTON TO BANBURY (page 220)

WOODSTOCK TO BURFORD (page 213)

OXFORD (page 199)

NORTH CHILTERNS (page 235)

SOUTH OXFORDSHIRE (page 207)

NORTH COTSWOLDS (page 185)

CHELTENHAM TO STOW (page 178)

MALMESBURY & AROUND (page 164)

CIRENCESTER TO GLOUCESTER (page 171)

15 miles

25 km

Cirencester to Gloucester

Where Romans meet royalty.

Stony-faced in the churchyard at **St Bartholomew's** in **Winstone**. *See p172.*

See p172.

By train from London

There are four direct trains a day from
Paddington to **Gloucester** (journey time
is 1hr 50mins) and to **Stroud** (journey
time 1hr 30mins), although you can also
take the hourly train to **Swindon** and
change, which takes about 2hrs (1hr
40mins to **Stroud**). Direct trains from
Paddington (four a day) to **Kemble** take
1hr 10mins to 1hr 30mins; an hourly
linking coach service (01242 522021)
runs to **Cirencester**, four miles away.
Info: www.firstgreatwestern.co.uk and
www.stagecoachgroup.co.uk.

Covering an area that is roughly 40 miles
long and 20 miles broad, one cannot
pinpoint exactly where the Cotswolds actually
begins or ends. Its devotees hold vigorous
opinions on the subject, but most agree that
the main part is contained in the area around
Gloucestershire. Between the Roman towns of
Cirencester (Corinium) and Gloucester (Glevum)
lies a world of historic homes, gastronomic
delights, luscious countryside and ancient sites.

The area is anything but isolated: the M4 and
M5 aren't far away, there are major towns in
abundance and a significant rural population.
Yet there's a beguiling intimacy to this historic
corner of the country, perched on the doorstep
of Wales and the South-west. The **Cotswold**

Way bisects the region, meandering along woodland-clad ridges overlooking sheltered valleys, which are at their most seductive in the area around **Painswick**. This gem of a town (aka 'Queen of the Cotswolds'), tumbling down the valley, is hardly undiscovered, yet has valiantly resisted the onslaught of the tearooms. The town centres around the **Church of St Mary** and its extraordinary churchyard, famed for its altar tombs and 99 yew trees (the oldest dating back to 1792). Standing sentinel, they are trimmed into rather eerie shapes and, according to legend, are impossible to count (although that does beg a question).

Close by is Dennis French's wonderful shop **Painswick Woodcrafts** (3 New Street, 01452 814195). French has been working in wood for more than 50 years, and his expertise shows in beautiful domestic pieces such as bowls and cheeseboards. Another must-see is the unique **Painswick Rococo Garden**. A tour of the easygoing neighbouring villages of **Edge**, **Sheepscombe** and **Slad** is rewarding. If you've heard of the latter, chances are it is through the childhood recollections of Laurie Lee's *Cider with Rosie*. Lee grew up in Slad and was a long-time regular at the Woolpack. It's still a likeable, down-to-earth (and tiny) pub. Lee is buried in Slad churchyard, a short stumble from the pub. **Prinknash Abbey Park**, between Slad and Gloucester, offers the delights of birds, tame deer, fine walks and monk-made pottery. **Gloucester** was described by Dickens as 'a wonderful and misleading city'. In some strange way, and despite what locals might say, it still is. It's actually a rather downmarket working town, but this is a refreshing contrast to the tweeness of nearby Cheltenham (*see p178*) and most of the Cotswolds. Much of the centre is blighted by characterless modern development, and strolling the streets is hardly a joy. Yet there are interesting sights to discover, the most rewarding of which is the wonderful cathedral.

The restored Victorian docks are also well worth a look. Within the buildings are the **National Waterways Museum** and the **Gloucester Antiques Centre**, home to 90 dealers. The **Gloucester City Museum and Art Gallery** is also worth a visit.

Cirencester and around

Around 20 miles south-east of Gloucester lies the agreeable small town of **Cirencester**. A considerable leap of imagination is required to picture this gentle local centre as the one-time capital city of the Dobunni tribe and then the strategically vital Roman town of Corinium, commanding the juncture of the Fosse Way, Ermine Street and Akeman Street. It was once the second-largest Roman city in the country after London; the population today is little more than 15,000, but there is plenty of evidence of Cirencester's heyday. The **Corinium Museum** is the best source of Roman relics. To the west of the town are the remains of the 2 BC Roman amphitheatre. The other main sight in town is the wonderful 'wool' church, **St John the Baptist**, on Market Place, with its elaborate perpendicular-style porch (c1500). Church lovers shouldn't miss a tour of the **Dunt Valley**, just north-west of Cirencester off the A417, where there are some lovely villages (**Elkstone**, **Syde**) and also the superb church of **St Bartholomew's** in tiny **Winstone**.

Go west

From Cirencester heading west towards Stroud, you pass through royal country (Prince Charles's Highgrove and Princess Anne's Gatcombe Park are nearby) down into the **Golden Valley** of the River Frome, the Thames and Severn Canal.

The grand project for a canal joining the Severn and the Thames was completed in 1789 and immodestly described by its builders as 'an elaborate and stupendous work of art'. Its high point (literally) is the **Sapperton Tunnel**, running for more than two miles through the Cotswold limestone. Stop at **Chalford**; pick up the old towpath and walk east up a delightful wooded valley to the tunnel portal. It's always been short of water, and the last boat went through in 1911, so don't expect much activity on what water remains, but there's plenty of wildlife and a pub at the halfway point.

Stroud is a working town, with a large 'alternative' community into all things green. The centre isn't particularly attractive, but is largely pedestrianised and has some good shops and cafés. There's a regular farmers' market and, on the High Street, **Woodruffs Organic Café** (01453 759195) and **Bishopston Trading Company** (01453 766355), which sells Indian-made fair-trade clothes.

The region to the south is the more densely populated, but still worth exploring. The huge wind-tossed expanse of **Minchinhampton Common** is a wonderful spot to fly a kite, and there's bags of history and culture to be discovered in these parts. Sights range from the remnants of an Iron Age hill fort at **Uley** and the nearby long barrow (the magnificently named **Hetty Pegler's Tump**), both off the B4066, through the Tudor **Owlpen Manor** to the spooky unfinished Victorian masterpiece of **Woodchester Mansion**.

West of here the country flattens towards the Severn – ideal for twitchers at the **Slimbridge Wildfowl and Wetlands Trust**.

Woodchester Mansion. See p175.

What to see & do

Tourist Information Centres

*Corn Hall, Market Place, Cirencester, GL7 2NW
(01285 654180/www.cotswold.gov.uk/tourism).*
Open *Apr-Dec* 9.30am-5.30pm Mon-Sat. *Jan-Mar*
9.30am-5pm Mon-Sat.

*28 Southgate Street, Gloucester, GL1 2DP (01452
421188/www.visit-glos.org.uk).* **Open** *Sept-June*
10am-5pm Mon-Sat. *July, Aug* 10am-5pm Mon-Sat;
11am-3pm Sun.

*Subscription Rooms, George Street, Stroud, GL5
1AE (01453 760960/www.visitthecotswolds.org.uk).*
Open 10am-5pm Mon-Sat.

Corinium Museum

*Park Street, Cirencester, GL7 2BX (01285 655611/
www.cotswold.gov.uk/museum).*
This award-winning museum concentrates on the
Roman history of Cirencester. It is closed for refurbishment until June/July 2004.

Gloucester Cathedral

*College Green, Gloucester, GL1 2LR (01452 528095/
www.gloucestercathedral.uk.com).* **Open** 7.30am-6pm
Mon-Fri; 7.30am-5pm Sat; 7.30am-4pm Sun.
Admission free; donations welcome.
With much of old Gloucester gone, it's surprising and
refreshing to find its massive cathedral (or the Cathedral
Church of St Peter and the Holy and Indivisible Trinity,
to use its official title) in such a fine state of preservation.
A Saxon abbey first stood on this site, but the building
that is here now was begun by Benedictine monks in the

11th century. When Gloucester agreed to take the body
of Edward II (remember that red-hot poker?) in 1327,
after the cathedrals at Bristol and Malmesbury had
refused it, the cathedral became a place of pilgrimage;
the revenue earned was used to finance its 14th- and
15th-century development into the greatest example of
the Perpendicular style in the country. The huge
expanse of the Great East Window (1350) is a magnificent sight, as is the fan vaulting in the cloisters (the first
example of such vaulting in Britain).

Gloucester City Museum & Art Gallery

*Brunswick Road, Gloucester, GL1 1HP (01452
524131/www.gloucester.gov.uk).* **Open** 10am-
5pm Tue-Sat. **Admission** £2; £1 concessions;
free children & Gloucester city residents.
Credit MC, V.
An entertaining and informative city museum that
focuses on Gloucestershire's history and prehistory, and
includes dinosaur bones and the re-creation of the
appearance of the 2,000-year-old 'Birdlip Lady', a skull
from a Celtic grave discovered in the area. There's also
some fine 18th-century furniture and paintings by the
likes of Rembrandt, Gainsborough and Turner, plus
enough hands-on stuff to keep the kids amused.

National Waterways Museum

*Llanthony Warehouse, Gloucester Docks, Gloucester,
GL1 2EH (01452 318200/www.nwm.org.uk).* **Open**
10am-5pm daily. **Admission** £5; £4 concessions;
free under-5s. *Boat trip* Easter-Oct £3; £2.50
concessions. **Credit** AmEx, MC, V.

Hall Garth Golf Hotel, Darlington

Leisure times

Corus hotels have a range of welcoming hotels throughout the UK, where you can escape from just £29 per person per night.

Our hotels are bright and stylish with an enthusiastic approach to service and a commitment to getting the simple things right . . . every time.

Each of our full service hotels have a unique character, and offer a variety of bars, bistros and restaurants, many with extensive leisure facilities.

contact For a brochure please call 0870 2400 111.
To book please call 0845 300 2000.
Or e-mail reservations@corushotels.com

www.corushotels.com

A must for bargees, this great museum tells the 200-year story of Britain's extensive network of canals, using working models, engines, archive film, hands-on and interactive exhibits to explain the history of these wonderful feats of Victorian engineering.

Owlpen Manor Uley

Nr Dursley, GL11 5BZ (01453 860261/www. owlpen.com). **Open** *Apr-Sept* 2-5pm Tue-Sun. Closed Oct-Mar. **Admission** £4.80; £2 concessions. *Gardens only* £2.80. **Credit** DC, MC, V.

Formal terraced yew gardens and bluebell woods surround this lovely Tudor manor (1450-1616), currently home to the Mander family. The interior contains some fine Arts and Crafts furniture and 17th-century wall hangings. Teas are served in the Tithe Barn. The house feels wonderfully remote – 'Owlpen – ah, what a dream is there!' as Vita Sackville-West was moved to say. There are some lovely holiday cottages scattered around the house (www.owlpen.com/cottages.htm).

Painswick Rococo Garden

Painswick, GL6 7TH (01452 813204/www. rococogarden.co.uk). **Open** *Mid Jan-Oct* 11am-5pm daily. Closed Nov-mid Jan. **Admission** £4; £2-£3.50 concessions. **Credit** MC, V.

Charles Hyett built Painswick House in the 1730s and in the following decade his son Benjamin created a flamboyant rococo garden. Restored in the 1980s, Painswick is England's only remaining example of the rococo genre. The result is wonderful – a combination of the formal (geometric patterns, long vistas, architectural features) and the informal (winding paths, off-centre designs, woodland walks). There's also a maze and a snowdrop meadow that is simply stunning.

Prinknash Abbey Visitors Centre & Bird Park

Cranham, GL4 8EX (shop 01452 812066/bird park 01452 812727/www.prinknashabbey.org.uk). **Open** *Visitors' centre* Apr-Sept 9am-5.30pm Mon-Sat; 10am-5.30pm Sun. Oct-Mar 9am-4.30pm daily. *Bird park* Apr-Oct 10am-5pm daily. Nov-Mar 10am-4pm daily. **Admission** *Bird park* £3.90; £2-£3 concessions. *Visitors' centre* free. **No credit cards**.

The Benedictine Abbey of Prinknash (the 'k' is silent) combines a (remarkably ugly) working abbey with a pottery (where the monks' creations can be bought), a bird park (packed with peacocks and waterfowl, most of which will take food from your hand) and a deer park (many of the deer can be petted and fed). There's also the Tudor Wendy House, the Monks' Fish Pond, a lake, tearoom, gift shop and the 13th-century Old Grange building. A definite hit with kids.

Slimbridge Wildfowl & Wetlands Trust

Slimbridge, GL2 7BT (01453 890333/www.wwt. org.uk). **Open** *Apr-Oct* 9.30am-5pm daily. *Nov-Mar* 9.30am-4.30pm daily. **Admission** £6.40; £3.90-£5.10 concessions. **Credit** DC, MC, V.

The Wildfowl & Wetlands Trust was set up by naturalist Sir Peter Scott in 1946 to promote his belief in the interaction between people and wildlife. A wide range of birdlife can be seen, including six types of flamingo and the world's largest collection of ducks, geese and swans.

Woodchester Mansion

Nympsfield, Stonehouse, GL10 3TS (01453 750455/ www.woodchestermansion.org.uk). **Open** *Apr-Sept* 11am-5.30pm most Sat, Sun, bank hols (last admission 4pm). Phone or see website to check. **Admission** (guided tours) £5; £4 concessions; free under-14s. **Credit** MC, V.

This extravagant exercise in Victorian Gothic is one of the most unusual and enigmatic country houses in Britain, not least because it was never finished. The over-optimistic vision of Catholic zealot Edward Leigh, it is a unique example of a Victorian work-in-progress and has been described as 'one of the great achievements of 19th-century domestic architecture'. It is almost entirely constructed from golden limestone and original wooden scaffolding still supports unfinished walls. The only access to the mansion is from a car park close to the Coaley Peak picnic site and viewpoint on the B4066 Stroud to Dursley road. From here it's a pleasant one-mile walk to the house, or a trip in the shuttle bus.

Where to stay

The **Village Pub** in Barnsley has rooms (*see p177*, doubles £70-£125), as has the **Bathurst Arms** in North Cerney (*see p177*, doubles £65-£70) – both serve notable food. There are also good B&Bs in Meysey Hampton, east of Cirencester – **Hampton Fields** (01285 850070, doubles £64-£70) and the rectory of **Winstone Glebe** (01285 821451/www.winstoneglebe.com, doubles £60-£72) in Winstone, located just off the A417. The **Old Passage Inn** (01452 740547/www.fishattheoldpassageinn.co.uk, doubles £80-£90) has rooms above a fish restaurant right on the banks of the Severn.

Cardynham House

The Cross, Painswick, GL6 6XX (01452 814006/ fax 01452 812321/www.cardynham.co.uk). **Rates** £47-£75 single; £69-£280 double/four-poster. **Rooms** (all en suite) 1 double; 7 four-poster; 1 family (sleeps 4). **Credit** AmEx, MC, V.

Too twee for some, but you can't deny that this B&B is a stunner. Californian Carol Keyes has decorated every room with a dash that most hotels can only envy. There are four-posters in every room bar one (and even that has a half-tester), and if you thought that theming was naff, just wait until you see Old Tuscany or Palm Springs. The huge room at the top, Dovecote, is suitable for families, and, amazingly, the Pool Room actually contains a small swimming pool. Prepare for an American-sized breakfast with hash browns, pancakes and maple syrup, as well as English dishes. Warmer service would be nice, though. Book in advance. Children welcome.

A46 N of Stroud; once in Painswick pass churchyard on right; take first right into Victoria Street; turn left at end of road; house is next to March Hare restaurant.

Frampton Court

The Green, Frampton-on-Severn, GL2 7EU (01452 740267/fax 01452 740698/www.framptoncourt estate.uk.com). **Rates** £45 per person. **Rooms** 2 single (1 en suite); 1 double (en suite); 1 twin (en suite); 1 four-poster; 1 self-catering house. **No credit cards**.

The Cotswolds

Even if you don't intend to stay, this incredible mansion is worth a visit. The Clifford family have been living in Frampton since the 11th century and their phenomenal early 18th-century Grade I-listed mansion gives up four bedrooms for B&B. The Cliffords also let out the orangery for self-caterers (sleeps eight; phone for prices). The B&B rooms are large – the double is hung with a Flemish tapestry and equipped with a double-tester bed; the twin has some lovely wood panelling and enjoys wonderful views. At first a little austere, this historic building is warmed by the charming woman in charge, who takes pride in recounting the history of the Clifford family and will light a log fire for you in winter. Frampton Court is surrounded by extensive parkland. The lake, which can be seen from the Court, is home to water fowls and swans. Frampton itself is an intriguing village, close to the Severn estuary. Children and dogs are welcome in the orangery. All bedrooms are no-smoking.
Take B4071 off A38; turn left and go through village green; house is on left (no signpost; entrance between the first set of chestnut trees).

Mason's Arms

28 High Street, Meysey Hampton, GL7 5JT (tel/fax 01285 850164/www.smoothhound. co.uk/hotels/mason.html). **Rates** £45-£55 single; £65 £85 double; £85-£130 family room. **Rooms** (all en suite) 9 double/twin/family room. **Credit** MC, V.
The 17th-century Mason's Arms is the focal point of the dozy village of Meysey Hampton. It's a deservedly popular pub, with a good range of rooms to rent with all mod cons; some also have beams and exposed brickwork to give you that feeling of authenticity. Less refined than some places in the area, this is a no-nonsense sort of place with first-rate ales at the bar and decent grub. Children and dogs (£5 per night) are welcome.
A419 towards Cirencester; take the Fairford turning; then signs for Latton; turn right through Down Ampney; into Meysey Hampton, pub is on village green.

The Old Rectory

Church Street, Meysey Hampton, nr Cirencester, GL7 5JX (01285 851200/fax 01285 850452). **Rates** £43 single occupancy; £66-£75 double. **Rooms** (both en suite) 1 twin; 1 double. **No credit cards**.
This superb B&B in lovely Meysey Hampton is ideal if you're looking for a rural experience. Set back from the road, the house sits in seven acres of grounds; there is also a tennis court and an outdoor pool. Flagstone floors, fireplaces, a friendly dog and the charming owner Caroline Cerne and her husband make the Old Rectory a truly relaxing place to stay. Home-made jam and local eggs are served for breakfast, and the Old Rectory is just a stone's throw away from the Mason's Arms (*see above*) and not too far from the Village Pub (*see p177*). Children are welcome.

Painswick Hotel

Kemps Lane, Painswick, GL6 6YB (01452 812160/ fax 01452 814059/www.painswickhotel.com). **Rates** £75-£135 single; £125-£180 double/twin; £200 four-poster; £125-£140 family room. **Rooms** (all en suite) 2 single; 4 twin; 9 double; 2 four-poster; 2 family. **Credit** AmEx, MC, V.
Painswick's grandest accommodation option clings to the hillside just down from the town's wonderful yew-filled churchyard. It's a friendly hotel with beautiful views from many of the well-proportioned and -decorated rooms (some with four-posters). The hotel manages to bridge the gap between grand sophistication and rustic charm, with an open fireplace, home-made biscuits and comfy interior complementing its grand five-star feel. Relaxing gardens and a good restaurant serving upmarket dishes or light lunches are further attractions. Children and pets welcome.
A46 N of Stroud; once in Painswick pass churchyard on right, and turn right into Victoria Street; right at March Hare; hotel is on right down hill.

Where to eat & drink

The **Crown of Crucis** in Ampney Crucis (east of Cirencester) is an ambitious pub/restaurant/hotel (01285 851806). South of Cirencester; the comfy **Wild Duck** in Ewen (01285 770310) does good grub; and the **Eliot Arms** in South Cerney (01285 860215) is another popular haunt. South of Stroud, there's food, bedrooms and working waterwheels at the **Egypt Mill** in Nailsworth (01453 833449). In Cranham, north-east of Painswick, try the lovely but tiny 17th-century **Black Horse** (01452 812217) for above-average food and beer.

For fine fish and delicacies in a picturesque location take a trip to the **Old Passage Inn** in Arlingham (01452 740547/www.fishattheold passageinn.co.uk) on the banks of the River Severn. Another pub that successfully melds fine cuisine with a good selection of real ales is the **Royal Oak** in North Woodchester (Church Road, 01453 872735). An unusual setting for authentic, top-quality Thai is Cardynham House (*see p175*), home to the excellent **Ban Thai at the March Hare**.

Bathurst Arms

North Cerney, nr Cirencester, GL7 7BZ (01285 831281). **Food served** noon-2pm, 7-9pm Mon-Thur, Sun; noon-2.30pm, 7-9.30pm Fri, Sat. **Main courses** £6.95-£12.25. **Credit** AmEx, MC, V.

This unpretentious, welcoming inn combines good food and rustic charm with a proper pub atmosphere: there's a fire for winter and a garden for summer. The gregarious new owners intend to capitalise on its stone floors and fireplaces by making them a feature of a more extensive dining room. Food is bistro standards: salmon, steak, fish cakes in nicely presented, good-sized portions. There is also a children's menu. The pub also lets out clean, ample rooms with lovely views at fair prices.

Bell at Sapperton

Sapperton, GL7 6LE (01285 760298/www.foodathe bell.co.uk). **Food served** noon-2pm, 7-9.30pm daily. **Main courses** £9.50-£16. **Credit** MC, V.

This 300-year-old pub is popular with ramblers and horse riders as well as locals. Renovated in 2000, the building retains a civilised air, with polished flagstones and wooden furniture. You can eat on the terraces, in the courtyard or inside by the fire. The food is varied and imaginative, with fresh fish from Cornwall and the likes of risotto of wild garlic and jumbo prawns or chicken stuffed with bresaola and smoked mozzarella. There are good wines by the glass, plus a 'fine wine' list.

Butchers' Arms

Oakridge Lynch, nr Stroud, GL6 7NZ (01285 760371). **Food served** noon-2pm, 6.30-9.30pm Tue-Sat; noon-2pm Sun. **Main courses** £5.75-£16.95. **Credit** MC, V.

Amid the cuteness of much of the Cotswolds, the Butcher's Arms comes as a stark relief: the place isn't especially attractive. However, it does stock a fine selection of ales, and behind the pleasant, stripped-wood Stable Room, ideal for low-key lunches and snacks. The garden is perfect for kids, and its location among the hills of Oakridge Lynch makes it a haven for hikers.

Hare & Hounds

Fosse Cross, nr Chedworth, GL54 4NN (01285 720288/fax 01285 720488). **Food served** noon-2.30pm, 7-9.30pm Mon-Sat; noon-3pm, 7-9pm Sun. **Main courses** £5.50-£17. **Credit** MC, V.

It's a pity this pub is stranded on a main road because it is the kind of place where you want to wine and dine until late and then stumble home. Stripped floors, an open fire, a conservatory at the back and stylish country-home touches are reflected in refined cuisine. The menu includes dishes such as seafood spaghetti, breast of pigeon and wild mushroom stroganoff. Puddings are a strong suit so leave room for Italian chocolate and coffee liqueur cheesecake. A children's menu is available.

Mad Hatters

3 Cossack Square, Nailsworth, GL6 0DB (01453 832615). **Food served** 12.30-2pm, 7.30-9pm Wed-Sat; 1pm Sun by appointment only. **Main courses** £14.50-£17.50. **Set lunch** (Sun) £15 3 courses. **Credit** AmEx, MC, V.

Mike and Caroline Findlay's passion for honest, wholesome food has resulted in this little peach of a restaurant, where organic and free-range are the bywords. The pretty Georgian bow-fronted exterior hides a delightfully cosy interior. Good quality local produce features heavily among the unpretentious dishes. Try a fabulous fish soup, or pork and venison terrine starter, then rabbit dijonnaise or monkfish basquaise. The dinner menu extends the simpler lunchtime choice.

Royal Oak

Church Road, North Woodchester, GL5 5PQ (01453 872735). **Food served** 6.30-9.30pm Mon, Tue; 12.15-2.30pm, 6.30-9.30pm Wed-Sun. **Main courses** £6.95-£14.95. **Credit** AmEx, MC, V.

Squashed up a hillside, this cosy, modest-looking pub achieve quality cuisine and talent for presentation. Few pubs achieve the refined balance between modernism and olde worlde charm, but this one does. You can eat in the plain but classy dining room with wonderful country views or the bright conservatory. Food is excellent: choose from lamb shank, sea bass, breast of woodpigeon or seared king scallops or go for a hearty ploughman's with an assortment of cheeses. The jolly locals indulging in the fine ales give the place a bustly warmth.

Village Pub

High Street, Barnsley, GL7 5EF (01285 740421/ www.thevillagepub.co.uk). **Food served** noon-2.30pm, 7-9.30pm Mon-Thur; noon-3pm, 7-10pm Fri, Sat; noon-3pm, 7-9.30pm Sun. **Main courses** £10.50-£16. **Credit** MC, V.

Deep terracotta and exposed brick line the walls of one room here, while mahogany bookcases stand against pea green paint in another. The food is equally stylish but unpretentious, though portions could be bigger. Expect dishes such as chicken livers and foie gras parfait with fig chutney followed by baked haddock with chive mash, mustard shallots and french beans. Desserts weren't as exquisite as the chocolates that came with coffee. Given the exclusive feel of the place, the atmosphere is surprisingly laid-back and welcoming.

The Cotswolds

Cheltenham to Stow

Did somebody say Regency?

The image of Cheltenham as a gateway to the Cotswolds is surpassed only by its reputation as the epicentre of conservative Middle England, replete with parks, tree-lined avenues, picturesque Regency houses – and retired colonels. Start your journey in its frighteningly ordinary high street, however, and you could feel like you've stumbled into the wrong town.

Cheltenham's better half lies to the south, connected by the Promenade – which is as famous for its seasonal flowerbeds as its imposing stone façades – and consisting of the area roughly framed by Montpellier's delightful gardens. Cheltenham's spa was discovered in 1716, turning a previously unknown Cotswold settlement into an immensely popular resort. Its healing properties were promoted by various nobles and literary figures, among them the Duke of Wellington and Charles Dickens. It also attracted the royal patronage of George III, upon whose coat-tails the middle classes descended en masse.

Illustrious history and class-bound image aside, there is another side to Cheltenham, which is reflected in a series of **festivals**, covering everything from folk music to science and literature, that bring real colour to the town (visit www.cheltenhamfestivals.co.uk for more information or phone 01242 237377 for a brochure).

Two Slaughters are better than one

Cheltenham really is the gateway to the Cotswolds; being here is a great opportunity to explore the surrounding countryside. The less tentative the steps taken into Cheltenham's outlying landscape, the greater the rewards: the rural expanse stretching towards Stow is a grand vista of hills and fields, peppered with villages worth hunting down if only for their terrific collection of local pubs and restaurants. This part of the Cotswolds, as a rule, hasn't 'enjoyed' quite as large an influx of Ferrari-driving gin-swilling types as some other areas. It means that pubs such as the **Mount** in Stanton and the **Plough** in Ford have retained not only their aesthetic beauty, but also their essentially rural character.

Other villages worth a visit are **Bourton-on-the-Water**, for its beautiful network of low-lying streams, **Northleach** for its 15th-century church and the pleasantly unthreatening **Slaughters** (don't be scared, now) – Upper and Lower – the latter of which is particularly stunning. Several historic landmarks in the area, including **Hailes Abbey** and **Sudeley Castle**, merit a visit too. This is also a great area for walking so take to your heels and enjoy some spectacular strolling .

Lastly, don't miss the opportunity to indulge in a little window-shopping in the tranquil market town of **Stow-on-the-Wold**. Its name literally translated means 'meeting place on the uplands', and with eight separate roads converging on somewhere this small, it's easy to see why. Stow is a pretty town of honey-coloured stone houses and cottages, with a fine central marketplace flanked on all sides by antique and bric-a-brac shops and tearooms. Hordes of day trippers pass through the town on summer days, but stay on into the evening and the pace settles down.

By train from London

There are four trains a day that run directly from **Paddington** to **Cheltenham Spa**. Journey time is **2hrs 10mins**. Note that the station is about a mile from the town centre. Info: www.firstgreatwestern.co.uk.

What to see & do

Tourist Information Centres

77 Promenade, Cheltenham, GL50 1PJ (01242 226554/www.visitcheltenham.info). **Open** 9.30am-5.15pm Mon-Sat.

Cotswold Visitor Information Centre, Hollis House, The Square, Stow-on-the-Wold, GL54 1AF (01451 831082). **Open** *Easter-Sept* 9.30am-5.30pm Mon-Sat. *Oct-Easter* 9.30am-4.30pm Mon-Sat.

The Cotswolds

Hailes Abbey
– or what's left of it.

Bike hire

Compass Holidays *Cheltenham Spa rail station, Queens Road, Cheltenham, GL51 8NT (01242 250642/www.compass-holidays.com).* **Open** 8.45am-5.45pm Mon-Sat; 9am-5pm Sun. Rental costs start at £8 a day.

Birdland Park & Gardens

Bourton-on-the-Water, GL54 2BN (01451 820480). **Open** *Apr-Oct* 10am-6pm daily. *Nov-Mar* 10am-4pm daily (last admission 1hr before closing). **Admission** £4.75; £2.65-£3.57 concessions; free under-4s. **Credit** MC, V.

Fans of our feathered friends will find many rare creatures at Birdland: there are 500 species in all, inhabiting more than seven acres. A lively community of parrots, macaws and cockatoos fly around, descending as they please to charm and delight visitors.

Chedworth Roman Villa

Yanworth, on A429 nr Northleach, GL54 3LJ (01242 890256/www.nationaltrust.org.uk). **Open** *Late Feb-late Mar, late Oct-mid Nov* 11am-4pm Tue-Sun. *Late Mar-late Oct* 10am-5pm Tue-Sun, bank hols. **Admission** (NT) £3.90; £2 concessions.

In the mid 19th century, fate smiled on a local gamekeeper looking for his ferret. His hunt led him to uncover some small ceramic fragments, which eventually led to a full excavation of one of the largest, best-preserved Romano-British villas in the country. There's no record of what happened to the ferret. Dating from around AD 2, the site serves as proof that rich people have had it easy since the year dot. It houses the remains of various rooms, some of which had underfloor heating, as well as two bath houses, a shrine and several ornate mosaics.

Cheltenham Art Gallery & Museum

Clarence Street, Cheltenham, GL50 3JT (01242 237431/www.cheltenhammuseum.org.uk). **Open** 10am-5.20pm Mon-Sat; 2-4.20pm Sun. **Admission** free; donations welcome.

Although home to exhibits from across the world, the collections here tend to be interwoven with local history, whether it's an in-depth archaeological survey of the surrounding countryside or a single room dedicated to Edward Wilson, the Cheltenham-born explorer who followed Scott to the Antarctic. The large gallery devoted to work from the Arts and Crafts movement is a highlight. The museum doesn't open until 11am on the first Thursday of every month.

Cheltenham Racecourse

Prestbury Park, Cheltenham, GL50 4SH (01242 513014/www.cheltenham.co.uk). **Admission** varies. **Credit** AmEx, MC, V.

The beating heart of a town whose name is synonymous with horse racing. During its 15 days of racing the course attracts around 275,000 people – more than the total number who visit Cheltenham throughout the rest of the year. The course is home to the prestigious Cheltenham Gold Cup steeplechase event.

Hailes Abbey

Off B4632 nr Winchcombe, GL54 5PB (01242 602398/www.english-heritage.org.uk). **Open** *Apr-Sept* 10am-6pm daily. *Oct* 10am-5pm daily. Closed Nov-Mar. **Admission** £3.60; £2.30 concessions. **Credit** MC, V.

Founded in 1246, this Cistercian abbey was the focus of feverish pilgrimage throughout the Middle Ages thanks to its boasting a small phial of the blood of Christ.

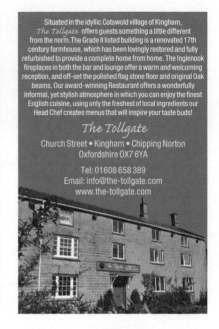

You'll not find such improbable relics here today – the abbey became derelict after the dissolution of the monasteries in 1539 – but the sight of these ancient ruins, surrounded by lush and untamed woodland, makes the journey worthwhile.

Holst Birthplace Museum

4 Clarence Road, Cheltenham, GL52 2AY (01242 524846/www.holstmuseum.org.uk). **Open** 10am-4pm Tue-Sat. **Admission** £2.50; £2 concessions. **No credit cards**.

Gustav Holst was a great lover of the quintessentially English way of life, with a fascination for folk songs. The elegant Regency terrace house where he was born in 1874 is now faithfully reconstructed as a museum and includes both the bedroom he was born in and his music room. In the latter sits the original piano on which much of his most famous work was composed.

Model Village

High Street, Bourton-on-the-Water, GL54 2AF (01451 820467/fax 01451 810236). **Open** Apr-Oct 9am-5.45pm daily. Nov-Mar 10am-4pm daily. **Admission** £2.75; £2-£2.50 concessions; free under-4s. **Credit** MC, V.

This is a miniature reproduction of picturesque Bourton-on-the-Water. The 1:9 scale model is composed entirely of the same honey-coloured Cotswold stone as the originals. The whole site takes up roughly half an acre and is completed by tiny trees, downsized shrubbery and a replica of the wonderful network of running rivers that has led Bourton-on-the-Water to be dubbed the Venice of the Cotswolds.

Sudeley Castle & Gardens

Winchcombe, nr Cheltenham, GL54 5JD (01242 602308/www.stratford.co.uk/sudeley). **Open** Gardens Mar-Oct 10.30am-5.30pm daily. Castle Apr-Oct 11am-5pm daily. Last entry 4.30pm. **Admission** Castle & gardens £6.70; £5.70 concessions. Gardens only £5; £2.50-£4.70 concessions. **Credit** MC, V.

The history of Sudeley spans more than 1,000 years, touching many famous lives. Lady Jane Grey lived here and the chapel houses the tomb of Henry VIII's sixth wife, Katherine Parr. After Henry's death in 1547, Katherine married her former lover, Lord Seymour of Sudeley, but died in childbirth here only a year later. The castle was also Charles I's headquarters during the Civil War. In addition to the castle itself, there are nine stunning gardens and an art collection containing works by Constable, Rubens and Turner.

Where to stay

Cheltenham has decidedly fewer good hotels than it has places to eat. The **Queen's Hotel** (0870 400 8107, £149-£209), a crowned and pillared Regency building looming over Imperial Square, is the most obvious choice for those seeking grandeur. The **Hotel on the Park** (38 Evesham Road, 01242 518898, from £108) is another beautifully restored Regency number.

Outside Cheltenham, **Buckland Manor** (01386 852626, from £225) is a 13th-century house near Broadway, complete with sprawling gardens, private putting green and a luxurious heated swimming pool. Equally suitable for luxury-seekers is the appropriately titled **Lords of the Manor** (01451 820243, from £155) in Lower Slaughter. Here, all rooms are individually designed and decked out with antiques and period furniture. In Stow, the **Unicorn** (01451 830257, weekend £105) on Sheep Street provides comfortable accommodation, while the lavish **Wyck Hill House** (01451 831936, www.wyckhill.com, from £85), on the A44 between Stow and Burford, offers a good base for exploring the surrounding countryside.

Finally, some of the better pub/restaurants mentioned, including the **King's Arms** in Stow (*see p184*) and the **Fox** in Oddington (*see p184*), also have rooms.

Dial House Hotel

The Chestnuts, High Street, Bourton-on-the-Water, GL54 2AN (01451 822244/fax 01451 810126/ www.dialhousehotel.com). **Rates** (per person) £55-£60 double; £75 four-poster. **Rooms** (all en suite) 11 double; 3 four-poster. **Credit** MC, V.

The 14 bedrooms in this 17th-century building have each been decorated differently, but all are cosy and comfortable in English country-house style. Not that there's anything conventional about Adrian and Jane Campbell's fresh, modern take on old world refinement – as anyone who dines in their award-winning restaurant will discover. Children are admitted during the week only. Smoking is permitted in the bar and lounge.

The Greenway

Shurdington, nr Cheltenham, GL51 4UG (01242 862352/fax 01242 862780). **Rates** £79-£139 single occupancy; £165 double; £260 four-poster. **Rooms** (all en suite) 1 single; 20 double/twin; 1 four-poster. **Credit** AmEx, DC, MC, V.

The Greenway is an ivy-covered 16th-century manor house, a maze of balustrades and high windows, which backs on to extensive grounds with a summer croquet lawn and several smaller gardens separated by topiary. It's welcoming and luxurious, but manages to avoid too much formality. The opulent hotel dining room – all crisp linen and fresh-cut flowers – serves elaborate and well-executed dishes. Children and pets are welcome, as are smokers – the latter only in the lounge and bar.

Lower Slaughter Manor

Lower Slaughter, GL54 2HP (01451 820456/ fax 01451 822150/www.lowerslaughter.co.uk). **Rates** £175 single occupancy; £200 double; £260-£325 deluxe double/twin; £350 four-poster; £350-£400 suite. **Rooms** (all en suite) 2 double; 9 deluxe double/twin; 2 four-poster; 3 suites. **Credit** AmEx, DC, MC, V.

Home to a heated indoor pool, outdoor tennis court and croquet lawn, this Grade II listed building boasts a beautiful two-storey dovecote dating back to its days as a 15th-century convent. Indoors, space and elegance reign supreme, and rooms tend towards the extravagant, with lots of antiques. You'll have to indulge without the little ones, though, as children are not allowed.

Letting off steam

Perhaps the most amazing thing about the Gloucestershire Warwickshire Railway is that you get to ride it at all. Twenty years ago this track was completely torn up after the route – opened in 1900 to connect Birmingham with Cheltenham – was closed. Station masters blew their final whistles, moss started to creep into disused waiting rooms, weeds choked the platforms and the rest, as they say, is history.

Or, rather, it would have been were it not for a dedicated group of railway enthusiasts who purchased the trackbeds in 1981, and who by 1984 had laid sufficient line to allow the first locomotive to run a journey of a quarter of a mile. From these humble beginnings, bridges have been rebuilt, signs repainted and polished and, one by one, stations along the way have been refurbished until – in April 2003 – the reopened terminus at Cheltenham Spa finally marked the dawn of a second steam age.

The 20-mile stretch of steam line between Toddington and Cheltenham is now open. Immediately after leaving Toddington, the sky is framed by the fabulous Cotswolds, and the surrounding countryside becomes a quilt of patchwork fields criss-crossed with country lanes. After pulling out of Winchcombe, the engine enters the 693-yard long tunnel at Greet – always a high point for kids – before emerging into a vista that reaches across the Vale of Evesham to the Malvern Hills. Once you get beyond Gotherington, the panorama stretches to the Brecon Beacons in Wales.

Day passes cost a reasonable £9, giving unlimited access to the line. Santa Specials run each December, while Thomas the Tank Engine turns up twice annually – once in April and again in August – to whisk kids to Winchcombe and back. Several vintage conventions and nostalgia days take place throughout the year (phone for details), and luxury dining is available on board special Elegant Excursions, which run on selected Saturday evenings and most Sunday lunchtimes throughout the year (call for details). At Toddington, an on-site shop selling locomotive bits and bobs is run alongside a snack bar, ice-cream stand and the Flag and Whistle café.

GWR
01242 621405/www.gwsr.plc.uk.

The Royalist

Digbeth Street, Stow-on-the-Wold, GL54 1BN
(01451 830670/www.theroyalisthotel.co.uk).
Rates £50-£90 single; £70-£180 double. **Rooms**
(all en suite) 2 twin; 4 double; 1 four-poster; 1 suite.
Credit AmEx, DC, MC, V.
Owned by Alan and Georgina Thompson, formerly of
755 in Fulham, the Royalist is England's oldest inn
(authenticated by the *Guinness Book of Records*). It has
12 stunning rooms, access to the adjacent Eagle & Child
pub and a restaurant, 947AD, where Alan cooks modern
European food with flair. An atmosphere of unfussy
elegance prevails: the restaurant is open to visitors,
while the Eagle serves brilliant food all day. Children
are accepted and some dogs (but phone to check).

Wesley House

High Street, Winchcombe, GL54 5LJ (01242
602366/fax 01242 609046/www.wesleyhouse.co.uk).
Rates £40-£55 single; £37.50-£40 per person
double/twin. **Rooms** (all en suite) 1 single; 2 twin;
3 double. **Credit** AmEx, MC, V.
Set among Winchcombe's delightful clutter of Cotswold
cottages, a half-timbered building houses Wesley House
restaurant and B&B. Most of the smallish bedrooms
are directly above the restaurant and are reached via a
rickety little staircase. The place is clean, crisp and very
pleasant. Staff are friendly and informal. The elegant
and popular restaurant has stunning terrace views.
Smoking is allowed in the bar only. Children welcome.

Where to eat & drink

Cheltenham's high street is no gold mine of
gastronomic delights – the one exception being
Orange Tree (01242 234232), Shai Patel's
inspired vegetarian oasis. **Scena Bistro**
(01242 238134), on Rodney Road, is an intimate
spot to fill up on good Gallic grub, while
Pirandello (01242 234599) is a popular Italian
on the Promenade. **New Land** (01242 525346),
virtually next door, offers Vietnamese food in a
stylish underground setting, while the **Athens
Greek Taverna** (01242 237200), on Clarence
Parade, is a great place to party.

Good boozers are less easy to find. You're
most likely to end up in a faceless wine bar or
some sanitised chain pub. If it's pints you're
after, head out into the country (there's some
good food to be had there too). Winchcombe
has several fine pubs, the best of which, the
White Lion (37 North Street, 01242 603300),
is also home to **Oysters Restaurant**, while its
near neighbour, the recently opened **5 North
Street** (01242 604566), is an understated
restaurant that's already packing in the
customers. There is also the **Mount** in Stanton
(01386 584316), with superb, commanding
views over the surrounding landscape, and
| both the **Halfway House** (01242 525654) in
Tineton and the deservedly popular **Plough**
(01386 584215) in Ford are delightful rough
village diamonds. The **Craven Arms** in

Brockhampton (01242 820410) has been one
of the best pub restaurants in the country for
more than 15 years (it's sadly up for sale,
so hurry), and the recently refurbished
Royal Oak in Gretton (01242 604999) is
well worth a visit, as is the **Horse & Groom**
(01451 830584) in Oddington.

It's also worth noting that several of the
hotels listed in the previous section have first-
class restaurants: **Wesley House**, **Hotel on
the Park**, the **Greenway**, the **Dial House
Hotel** and the **Royalist** are all known for their
dining as well as their accommodation.

The Beehive

1-3 Montpellier Villas, Cheltenham, GL50 TXE
(01242 579443/fax 01242 269330/www.slak.co.uk).
Food served *Restaurant* 7-10pm Mon-Sat; noon-
3pm, 6-9pm Sun. *Pub* noon-2pm Mon, Tue; noon-2pm,
6-11pm Wed-Sat; 6-9pm Sun. **Main courses** £7.95-
£12. **Credit** MC, V.
The Beehive exudes a gloriously thrown-together
charm, with newspapers piled haphazardly on a crum-
pled piano and the large, crowded bar cluttered with a
random collection of wooden chairs and chequerboard
chess tables. Check the blackboard, however, and you'll
see that this delightful little boozer is also a brilliant
place to eat, with an upstairs restaurant (blue this time,
and dominated by a central candelabra, but equally fun
and informal), where starters such as spiced squid salad
with caper relish precede reasonably priced main courses
such as aubergine and red onion tart with broccoli and
gorgonzola. What with simultaneously being the best
pub in town and offering some of the finest food, it's no
wonder the Beehive hums sweetly all day.

Le Champignon Sauvage

24-26 Suffolk Road, Cheltenham, GL50 2AQ (01242
573449/www.lechampignonsauvage.com). **Food
served** noon-1.30pm, 7.30-9pm Tue-Sat. **Set lunch**
£21 3 courses, £42 3 courses. **Set dinner** £22
3 courses, £42 3 courses. **Credit** AmEx, DC, MC, V.
Le Champignon looks fairly modest for a temple of
gastronomy (run-of-the-mill Middle England decor with
cheery yellow walls, blue velvet seating, art on the
walls). However, the cooking is pretty flawless. David
Everitt-Matthias is in the kitchen; his wife, Helen, does
front of house with quiet charm. He makes some brave
and bold combinations, but everything we tried worked
– and then some – from an appetiser of velouté of
smoked eel to an unfeasibly light lemon mousse served
with a ball of melon sorbet and sticks of rhubarb, not to
mention the fabulous petits fours. Further skill was
revealed by a starter of roe deer tortellini matched by
the sharper tang of apple purée and turnip segments that
had been soaked in red wine. A main of cod with a confit of pig's trotter and tomato was an unlikely but fine
combination. Great own-made bread and a huge board
of English and French cheeses are other pluses. One
quibble: we were late (but still within the serving times)
because, like the other diners, we were stuck in traffic.
Despite having phoned to let them know, noises from
the kitchen made it pretty clear that we were causing a
major inconvenience. However, such was the sheer
seductiveness of the food, we were won over anyway.

The Cotswolds

Chelsea Square

60 St George's Place, Cheltenham, GL50 3PN
(01242 269926). **Food served** noon-2.30pm,
6-10.30pm Mon-Sat. **Main courses** £7.95-£12.95.
Credit MC, V.

A relatively small front facing on to a quiet street leads
via a smart bar area into a long room where, during the
day, the conservatory roof lets in plenty of natural light.
This is just as well as the walls are blue and purple –
colours that come into their own late at night when the
lights are dimmed. With regular light entertainment and
a fashionably contemporary menu that's very reasonably priced and changes quarterly, Chelsea Square
attracts a trendy local clientele. Dishes include grilled
goat's cheese on parmesan polenta, and overnight slow-
cooked lamb with potato and parsnip mash, while hot
chocolate moelleux with Madagascan vanilla ice-cream
is justifiably one of the most popular pudding choices.
There's a commendable list of cocktails to relish and
wines that aren't greedily priced.

The Daffodil

18-20 Suffolk Parade, Cheltenham, GL50 2AE
(01242 700055/fax 01242 700088). **Food served**
noon-2.30pm, 6-10pm Mon-Sat. **Main courses**
£11.75-£19.50. **Set lunch** £10 2 courses, £12.50
3 courses. **Credit** AmEx, MC, V.

Its name isn't the only thing the Daffodil has retained
from its original incarnation as a picture house: seating
is staggered across the auditorium, with drinks mixed
in the gallery and a kitchen plonked where the silver
screen used to be. Food tends to taste as good as it looks.
A starter of scallops was perfectly soft and presented in
glorious technicolour with avocado, chilli and ginger,
while a loin of lamb en croûte came with a rich feta
cheese mash and red wine onions. But it's the interior
design that really makes the Daffodil bloom – with its
low lighting, long-leaf plants and original art deco
furnishings, dining here is a treat from the opening titles
right up to the final curtain.

The Fox Inn

Lower Oddington, nr Moreton-in-Marsh, GL56 0UR
(01451 870555/www.foxinn.net). **Food served**
noon-2pm, 6.30-10pm Mon-Sat; 6.30-9.30pm Sun.
Main courses £7.95-£12.25. **Credit** MC, V.

No guide to the county would be complete without at
least mentioning the Fox. With an exterior swathed in
virginia creeper and a cosy and inestimably snug interior, this old hostelry (it dates back to the 11th century)
remains very much a local. Food is imaginative but
uncomplicated. Mains could include gorgeous cold
poached salmon with pesto dressing, or a lively baked
sea trout with creamed leeks and saffron. Sticky toffee
pudding provides a lovely rich finale. Few dishes cost
more than a tenner and little on the extensive wine list
will break the £20 barrier.

Hollow Bottom

Winchcombe Road, Guiting Power, GL54 5UX
(01451 850392/www.hollowbottom.com). **Open**
11am-11pm Mon-Sat; noon-10.30pm Sun. **Food
served** noon-2pm, 6-9pm daily. **Main courses**
£8.95-£14. **Credit** MC, V.

Sparsely decorated with racing memorabilia and
warmed by a large open fire, the Hollow Bottom is a real
local, but one that is also welcoming to strangers. Food

comes courtesy of Charlie Pettigrew, a former Young
Scottish Chef of the Year and advocate of such out-
landish delicacies as rattlesnake in sherry, tomato and
mushroom sauce. It's not all bison and wild boar, however: the menu changes daily and there's always plenty
of more traditional food chalked up on the board, including fresh seafood dishes at around £8 and a delightful
range of own-made desserts.

King's Arms

Market Square, Stow-on-the-Wold, GL54 1AF
(01451 830364/www.kingsarms-stowonthewold.
co.uk). **Open** 11am-11pm Mon-Sat; noon-10.30pm
Sun. **Food served** noon-2pm, 6-9.30pm Mon-
Sat; 7-9pm Sun. **Main courses** £8-£15.
Credit AmEx, MC, V.

Neither self-consciously pubby nor pretentious, the
King's Arms is the perfect spot for a quiet pint, with
original stone walls and windows overlooking Stow's
peaceful town square. Food here is exceptional, as you
might expect from Pete Robinson. He and his wife
Louise took over this 500-year-old former coaching inn
in 2002, after a stint at the Tresanton Hotel in Cornwall.
The upstairs restaurant is brilliantly unfussy, and
shares its thoroughly modern menu with the ground-
floor bar. Typical dishes are duck confit cleverly part-
nered with balsamic figs, perhaps followed by sea bream
with salsa rossa or porcini mushroom risotto; then perhaps round off with British cheeses or panna cotta and
fresh fruit. Wines are unusually featured, wine merchant
style, in racks along a wall.

Lumiere

Clarence Parade, Cheltenham, GL50 3PA (01242
222200). **Food served** 7-8.30pm Tue-Sat. **Set
dinner** £32 3 courses. **Credit** AmEx, MC, V.

Local epicureans tend to lose their composure when
they're talking about Lumiere, an understated jewel in
Cheltenham's culinary crown that they quite reasonably
want to keep for themselves. Lin and Geoff Chapman's
eclectic modern menu mixes starters such as goat's
cheese filo parcels with pan-fried potato and caramelised
apple with mains as striking as chicken breast with
Thai wild boar stuffing in a red pepper and peanut
sauce. Three courses cost £32, and although the menu
changes regularly, the atmosphere – bathed in soft white
light and as intimate as it is intoxicating – remains
a wonderfully tranquil and strangely tactile place to
indulge the senses all year round.

Vanilla

9-10 Cambray Place, Cheltenham, GL50 1JS
(01242 228228). **Food served** 7-9.30pm Mon, Sat;
noon-2pm, 7-9.30pm Tue-Fri. **Main courses** £9-£16.
Credit AmEx, MC, V.

This intimate dining space, accessed by an almost
unmarked door and doubling up as a hairdressing salon,
is one of Cheltenham's most stylish places to eat: candles
send shadows dancing over polished wood floors and
the whole scene is artfully captured in a large fisheye
mirror at one end of the hall. The menu, however, is the
real scene-stealer with regularly changing à la carte
starters, such as carpaccio of tuna with horseradish
coleslaw, main courses including supreme of salmon,
lime and coriander butter sauce and various daily
specials. It gets very busy in the evening, and that is
when staff tend to be at their least affable.

North Cotswolds

Seductive charm and mysterious disappearances.

The moneyed countryside of the North Cotswolds looks like someone's cliché of an idealised England – John Major's perhaps. Pristine villages with beautiful honey-toned cottages and perfect lawns are sprinkled around an area spotted by handsome churches, fine mansions and rows of pretty almshouses, all paid for by the vast fortunes of beneficent wool merchants. Things have not always been so rosy, however: following the decline of the wool industry in the 18th century, the area suffered terrible hardship. Ironically, poverty meant that few new buildings were put up, accounting for the area's 'unspoiled' appearance today.

Easy does it

The North Cotswolds are not a well-kept secret. Accessibility and immense popularity mean that during the summer months you could, without careful planning, end up sharing your rural escape with thousands of others. It's also worth pointing out that most of the discreet charms of this area are adult-oriented: village-hopping, walking, visiting gardens, antiques browsing, eating and drinking; there are few attractions specifically aimed at energetic young children (or the just plain energetic).

When the sun is shining and the road is clear, however, the North Cotswolds are a gloriously seductive spot – slow-paced, sensuous and visually stunning. Whether idling through the architecturally distinctive towns and villages, strolling along country footpaths or grazing in the area's top-class pubs and restaurants, the North Cotswolds offer a tonic for weary metropolitan senses. After a short stay, even the most hardcore urbanite will struggle to suppress those subversive *Good Life* fantasies about giving it all up and moving out here to take life more slowly and while away the long summer evenings tending a cottage garden.

By train from London

Trains from **Paddington** to **Moreton-in-Marsh** leave half-hourly. Journey time is between 1hr 20mins and 1hr 50mins. Info: www.thamestrains.co.uk.

Broadway Tower.
See p187.

The lie of the land

The lively market town of **Moreton-in-Marsh** – its wide main street lined with 17th- and 18th-century coaching inns and pubs – has for centuries been a stop-off point for Londoners on their way north (it is on the old London–Worcester road, now the A44). It is worth a stroll down the main drag (a section of the Roman Fosse Way) to admire the buildings, some of which claim diverting historical trivia of the 'King Charles I sheltered here during the Civil War' variety (that man sure got around). You can restock your hamper and wallet here (cashpoints are thin on the ground elsewhere). Weekenders will miss the vast market held in the town centre on Tuesdays.

Broadway, another former staging post on the road from Worcester to London, claims to be the Cotswolds' most-visited village. Broadway's role as a coaching stop has bequeathed it an array of inns and hotels, pubs and tearooms. These are accompanied by numerous shops of varying degrees of frivolity and tweeness. Here you will find purveyors of all manner of souvenirs and handicrafts – some ghastly, some desirable, all expensive. A five-minute walk up the main street to the east takes you away from the madding crowds, however, and reminds you why the village was a magnet for William Morris and the Pre-Raphaelite artists. Gorgeous limestone cottages are everywhere, picturesquely covered by wisteria, clematis and climbing roses.

South of Broadway are the idyllic villages of **Stanton** and **Stanway**. The 17th-century **Stanway House** (Stanway, 01386 584469) is open to the public and boasts an elaborate gatehouse where Stanway beer is still brewed in copper vats over log fires. Also worth seeing is the thatched cricket pavilion, perched on staddle stones to keep out the damp. Stanton is arguably the loveliest Cotswold village of all, the warm golden stone appearing sundrenched year round.

Chipping Campden, east of Broadway, centres on its gently curving main street and 17th-century market hall. Wealthy wool merchants bankrolled the towering church of **St James**; brasses on the floor of the church pay tribute to their wisdom and munificence. Sadly, the church, like so many in this area, was 'restored' in the 19th century – in other words medieval wall paintings were whitewashed and ornately carved pews with candelabras at either end were torn out – but it's still worth seeing for the wonderful stained glass windows, marble effigies of local benefactors and 15th-century altar hangings. Like the rest of the area, the town's fortunes crashed with the end of the wool trade, rising again when C R Ashbee made

it the base for his bold Guild of Handicraft experiment in 1902. He moved here from the East End of London with a group of cockney craftsmen intent on protecting and promoting traditional craft skills against the mass production techniques of modern industry. Although his Arts and Crafts project ultimately failed (mass production rivals imitated the Guild's goods and then sold them more cheaply), the town has remained a centre for silversmiths, jewellers, wood carvers, cabinet makers and enamellers, as well as a mecca for Arts and Crafts movement devotees from all over the world.

The town's rustic and unspoilt ambience is actually the product of rigidly enforced modern planning strictures. The Campden Trust, formed by craftsmen and architects in 1929, restored many of the town's old buildings and set exacting conservation standards. Telegraph wires and power cables are buried underground or tucked away out of sight, while shops, pubs and restaurants are forced to maintain a discreet presence.

Chipping Campden is a convenient base for ramblers: the 100-mile **Cotswold Way** starts here en route to Bath, and there are countless local walks. A strenuous one-mile hike up **Dover's Hill** to the north of the town offers impressive views over the Vale of Evesham.

A number of delightful villages lie within a five-mile radius of Chipping Campden, as well as stately homes and magnificent gardens. Immediately south lies **Broad Campden**, where you can catch a glimpse of C R Ashbee's former abode, a converted Norman chapel. **Blockley**, with its gently flowing brook, was the thriving centre of the silk industry in the 18th and 19th centuries. The old silk mills are now converted into sumptuous houses. You may be lucky enough to catch a languorous afternoon's village cricket match at **Ebrington**, with its dinky pitch in the shadow of a fine old church. Look out, too, for the clever millennium sundial on the diminutive village green.

What to see & do

Tourist Information Centres

1 Cotswold Court, Broadway, Worcestershire WR12 7AA (01386 852937). **Open** *10am-1pm, 2-5pm Mon-Sat.*

The Old Police Station, High Street, Chipping Campden, Gloucestershire GL55 6HB (01386 841206/www.chippingcampden.co.uk). **Open** *Apr-Oct 10am-5.30pm daily. Nov-Mar 10am-5pm daily.*

Cotswold District Council, Moreton Area Centre, High Street, Moreton-in-Marsh, Gloucestershire GL56 0AZ (01608 650881/www.cotswold.gov.uk).

Open *Apr-Sept* 8.45am-4pm Mon; 8.45am-5.15pm Tue, Wed; 8.45am-7.30pm Thur; 8.45am-4.45pm Fri; 9.30am-1pm Sat. *Oct-Mar* 8.45am-4pm Mon; 8.45am-5.15pm Tue-Thur; 8.45am-4.45pm Fri; 9.30am-1pm Sat.

Bike hire
The Toy Shop, *High Street, Moreton-in-Marsh, Gloucestershire GL56 0AD (01608 650756).*
Cotswold Country Cycles *Longlands Farm Cottage, Chipping Campden, Gloucestershire GL55 6LJ (01386 438706/www.cotswoldcountrycycles.com).*

Broadway Tower Country Park
Just off A44, Broadway, Worcestershire WR12 7LB (01386 852390/www.broadway-cotswolds.co.uk/ tower.html). **Open** *Tower* Apr-Oct 10.30am-5pm daily. Nov-Mar 11am-3pm Sat, Sun. *Park* closed until further notice. **Admission** £3; £1.50-£2.50 concessions. **Credit** MC, V.
The tower is an 18th-century folly, housing exhibitions on its one-time occupant, William Morris.

Cotswold Falconry Centre & Batsford Arboretum
Batsford Park, off A44, nr Moreton-in-Marsh, Gloucestershire GL56 9QB (01386 701043/www. cotswold-falconry.co.uk). **Open** mid Feb-mid Nov 10.30am-5.30pm daily. Last admission 3.30pm in Oct, Nov. Closed mid Nov-mid Feb. **Admission** £5; £2.50-£4 concessions. **Credit** AmEx, MC, V.
Falconry demonstrations. The arboretum next door contains more than 1,500 species of tree and shrub.

Gloucester Warwickshire Steam Railway
The Railway Station, Toddington, Gloucestershire GL54 5DT (info line & 01242 621405). **Fares** (unlimited travel) £9; £5.50-£7.50 concessions; free under-5s. **Credit** MC, V.

A bird in the hand at **Cotswold Falconry.**

Take a pleasant 13-mile round trip to Gretton on a wonderful steam train. The journey boasts great views over the Cotswold hills.

Hidcote Manor Garden
Hidcote Bartrim, nr Chipping Campden, Gloucestershire GL55 6LA (01386 438333/www. nationaltrust.org.uk/hidcote). **Open** *Apr-Sept* 10.30am-5pm Mon-Wed, Sat, Sun. *Oct* 10.30am-4pm Mon-Wed, Sat, Sun. Closed Nov-Mar. **Admission** (NT) phone for prices. **No credit cards.**
Magnificent, highly influential formal gardens designed by Major Lawrence Johnston in the early 20th century. He travelled the globe to find specimens for the different 'rooms', each separated by walls and hedges. Liable to serious overcrowding on Sundays and bank holidays.

Kiftsgate Court Gardens
Nr Hidcote, 4 miles NE of Chipping Campden, Gloucestershire GL55 6LN (01386 438777/www. kiftsgate.co.uk). **Open** *Apr, May, Aug, Sept* 2-6pm Wed, Thur, Sun. *June, July* noon-6pm Mon, Wed, Thur, Sat, Sun. Closed Oct-Mar. **Admission** £5; £1 concessions. **No credit cards.**
This magical garden designed by three generations of women lies a few minutes from Hidcote. Set on the edge of the Cotswold escarpment, with heart-stopping views over the Vale of Evesham, this is a space to treasure. Look out for the splendid swimming pool, the famous Kiftsgate rose, which grows up to 60ft high, and a recently added water garden.

The Magic Experience – Broadway Teddy Bear Museum
76 High Street, Broadway, Worcestershire WR12 7AJ (01386 858323). **Open** 10am-4pm Tue-Sun. **Admission** £2.50; £1.75 concessions. **Credit** MC, V.
Kids will adore this charming pint-sized museum with buttons to press, and teddies gathered from around the world. Adults, meanwhile, can moon nostalgically over Big Ted. There's also a hospital for ailing bears and dolls that are in need of stitches or have had the stuffing knocked out of them.

Sezincote House & Gardens
Moreton-in-Marsh, Gloucestershire GL56 9AW (01386 700444). **Open** *House* May-July, Sept 2.30-5.30pm Thur, Fri. Closed Aug, Oct-Apr. *Garden* Jan-Nov 2-6pm/dusk Thur, Fri, bank hols. Closed Dec. **Admission** *House & garden* £5. *Garden only* £3.50; £1 concessions; free under-5s. **No credit cards.**
An exotic place, with Asian influences everywhere, from the Hindu statues hidden among the bamboo and Japanese maples to the house itself, which was inspired by Indian temples and fortresses, and was the model for Brighton Pavilion. Children under 16 are not admitted to the house.
2 miles SW of Moreton-in-Marsh, off A44.

Snowshill Manor
Snowshill, nr Broadway, Worcestershire WR12 7JU (01386 852410/www.nationaltrust.org.uk). **Open** *Grounds* Apr-Oct 11am-5.30pm Wed-Sun. Closed Nov-Mar. *House* currently closed, due to reopen Mar 2005. **Admission** (NT) *Grounds* £3.80; £1.90 concessions. **Credit** AmEx, MC, V.

The Cotswolds

The Campden Wonder

It's not all peace and quiet around here; in fact, things are not quite what they seem. Beneath the façade of honey-toned cottages and rolling hills lies an unsolved mystery of death and deception with a dash of 17th-century witchcraft thrown in for good measure.

The story begins with the strange disappearance of one William Harrison on 16 August 1660. The steward of Lady Juliana Hicks, Harrison lived in the lodge of Campden House in Chipping Campden (only the East and West Banqueting Houses and Gate Lodge remain today, restored and rented out by the Landmark Trust). That evening he went out to collect rent from Lady Hicks's estate two miles away in Charingworth. When he hadn't returned by dusk, his wife sent out John Perry, their servant, to find him.

Having failed in his search that evening, Perry tried again the following morning, this time accompanied by Harrison's son Edward. The pair soon discovered William Harrison's battered comb and bloodied shirt collar on the road to Ebrington. Despite no sign of a body, murder was assumed, with Perry the main suspect. In protesting his innocence Perry – a man with a reputation for storytelling – implicated his brother Richard and mother Joan (who locals believed to be a witch) in the murder.

Richard and Joan were arrested, and despite their pleas of innocence, were executed – along with Perry. John Perry's contradictory stories lasted until his final seconds, when he confessed he had no idea what had happened to William Harrison, nor who had murdered him,

Eccentric owner Charles Wade was forced to live in a simple cottage in the lovely terraced gardens of this 15th- and 16th-century manor after he had filled the main house's rooms with breathtaking collections of toys, clocks, musical instruments, spinning wheels, bicycles and more. The house is closed for refurbishment until March 2005 but the small, pretty garden and Wade's cottage are worth a visit, if for no other reason than to try to learn more about this strange man. Expect big crowds at weekends.

Where to stay

This area boasts a phenomenal range of accommodation options. It is essential to book in advance, and don't even think of trying for a room during the Cheltenham National Hunt Festival in March (see p178), when the North Cotswolds get swamped by race-goers. Expect a similar rush for accommodation during Cheltenham's music and literature festivals in July and October respectively. The following are just a sample; the Tourist Information Centres provide lists of more basic B&Bs.

Cotswold House

The Square, Chipping Campden, Gloucestershire GL55 6AN (01386 840330/fax 01386 840310/ www.cotswoldhouse.com). **Rates** £110-£300 single occupancy; £115-£250 double/twin; £250-£275 four-poster; £275-£350 cottage rooms; £325-£550 suite. **Rooms** (all en suite) 14 double/twin; 1 four-poster; 4 cottage; 2 suites. **Credit** AmEx, MC, V.
Since taking over this stately building three years ago Ian Taylor has succeeded in creating the area's most luxurious hotel. Refurbishment of the entrance and

hallways of the main Georgian building will continue until January 2004. Meanwhile, all the bedrooms have been decorated in an understated modern style. No expense has been spared: each is individually styled, with tasteful furnishings and Bang & Olufsen televisions. If you're looking for the ultimate in luxury and relaxation this is the place. The most trying decision will be choosing goose down or duck down from the pillow menu (yes, there's a pillow menu). The hotel even claims to have rooms overlooking the 'most beautiful street in England'. The Garden Restaurant and Hick's Brasserie (see p190) provide excellent dining to match the high level of living. Children and dogs are welcome and all bedrooms are no-smoking.
A44 W of Moreton-in-Marsh; hotel is in square on main street in Chipping Campden, on B4081.

Holly House

Ebrington, nr Chipping Campden, Gloucestershire GL55 6NL (01386 593213/fax 01386 593181/ www.hollyhousebandb.co.uk). **Rates** £35-£55 single occupancy; £50-£60 double (£12 extra per child). **Rooms** (all en suite) 3 double/twin/family. **No credit cards.**
After nine years as the owners of Holly House, Jeffrey and Candida Hutsby have perfected the art of being welcoming yet unobtrusive hosts. All the rooms have a private entrance and although basic they are clean and have en suite facilities. Breakfast is served in a lounge and the same room can be used in the evening, should the charms of the nearby Ebrington Arms not appeal. Without, perhaps, the character of some of its more expensive rivals, it is perfectly situated within walking distance of Hidcote, Kiftsgate and Chipping Campden while being far enough away to escape the crowds. Children welcome. No smoking throughout.
B4035 E from Chipping Campden; follow signs to Ebrington on left; house is in village after Ebrington Arms pub.

The Cotswolds

but rather cryptically suggested that all would soon be revealed.

The twist in the tale came two years later when William Harrison walked back into the village claiming his absence was due to the fact that he had been abducted by Turkish slave traders (although at 70 years of age William Harrison was an unlikely target for even the most myopic slave trader). A little later Harrison's wife committed suicide, adding another dimension to the intrigue.

The 'Wonder' was first documented by local magistrate Sir Thomas Overbury. Since then, many solutions have been put forward – from the theory that Harrison's son Edward had packed him off in order to get his inheritance early, to the notion that William Harrison was a Restoration-era 007.

Joan Perry and Harrison's wife have both been implicated in theories based around black magic and witchcraft – a commonplace accusation in the heavily austere, repressive and paranoid atmosphere of post-Cromwellian England. Did Joan Perry bewitch her sons so they couldn't tell the truth? Or were William Harrison and his wife cursed by Joan Perry after hatching an elaborate scheme to do away with her?

Poet and children's author John Masefield was inspired to write two novels on the subject, while Sir George Clark provided the authoritative report *The Campden Wonder* in 1959.

It's an undeniably intriguing tale and aspiring amateur detectives can visit the website www.campdenwonder.plus.com for more in-depth sleuthing.

Lower Brook House
Lower Street, Blockley, Gloucestershire GL56 9DS (tel/fax 01386 700286/www.lowerbrookhouse.co.uk). **Rates** £65 single occupancy (weekdays only); £80-£125 double; £135-£145 four-poster. **Rooms** (all en suite) 3 double; 2 double/twin; 2 four-poster. **Credit** MC, V.

This lovely hotel sits on the edge of Blockley and reflects the character of owner Marie Mosedale-Cooper. A brook runs through a verdant front garden that is almost as charming as the front room, filled with interesting antiques. The personal touch is carried through to the rooms, with decorative furnishings and bric-a-brac collected by the family. The restaurant uses vegetables from the hotel's garden. Children welcome. All rooms are no-smoking.
Off A44 between Moreton-in-Marsh and Broadway; at Bourton-on-the-Hill take turning to Blockley; head into valley, straight into hotel drive.

Lygon Arms Hotel `OFFER`
High Street, Broadway, Worcestershire WR12 7DU (01386 852255/fax 01386 858611/www.thelygon arms.com). **Rates** £119-£159 single occupancy; £179-£240 double; £239-£355 four-poster; £279-£495 suite. **Rooms** (all en suite) 52 double/twin; 11 four-poster/suites. **Credit** AmEx, DC, MC, V.

Recently sold to the Furlong Hotel group, the Lygon Arms is an impressive 16th-century building. In an area with plenty of buildings rich in history, this one is unparalleled – you can stay in the oak-panelled Charles I suite, complete with secret tunnel. The best rooms are in the original building, although the incongruous '60s extension isn't as bad as it looks. A popular choice for show-biz royalty. Children and dogs welcome.
Off A44 between Moreton-in-Marsh and Evesham; on High Street in Broadway village centre.

Malt House Hotel
Broad Campden, nr Chipping Campden, Gloucestershire GL55 6UU (01386 840295/fax 01386 841334/www.malt-house.co.uk). **Rates** £91.50 single occupancy; £118.50-£124.50 double; £139.50 suite. **Rooms** (all en suite) 2 double; 4 double/twin; 1 suite. **Credit** AmEx, MC, V.

This long, low house built of golden stone perfectly captures the charms of the tranquil Cotswold countryside. Follow resident cat Dizzy's lead and relax in a plush fireside armchair in one of the low-ceilinged sitting rooms. This inviting and cosy mood is carried through to the individually decorated rooms, named after local rivers, all of which have divine views over the croquet lawn (with summerhouse for a G&T when the weather is warm) and hotel orchard. Suites for families have been created in the converted stables next to the main building. Children welcome. No smoking throughout.
A44 towards Evesham; take B4081 towards Chipping Campden; signs to Broad Campden; hotel in village centre.

Broadway village. See p186.

Old Bakery

*High Street, Blockley, Gloucestershire GL56 9EU
(tel/fax 01386 700408).* **Rates** (bed, breakfast,
dinner) £95-£125 single occupancy; £140-£170
double/twin. **Rooms** (all en suite) 3 double/twin.
Credit AmEx, MC, V.

Winner of the 2003 Gold Award for Best B&B in
England in the British Tourist Board's Excellence in
England Awards, Linda Helme should have no trouble
filling her beautiful house with guests. Comfort takes
precedence over luxury, and nothing in the well-
proportioned rooms (given the age and size of the
property) detracts from the refined, homely feel. The
French restaurant is Linda Helme's first love and is an
extra bonus to this great B&B. No smoking throughout.

Where to eat & drink

Beams, log fires, real ale and decent food come
as standard in most of the village pubs around
here. One of the joys of the area is happening
upon a village pub. The larger towns of
Moreton-in-Marsh and Evesham don't offer
much, with the **Bell Inn** (01608 651688) and
Redesdale Arms Hotel (01608 650308) on
the main drag in Moreton and the **Royal Oak**
(01386 442465) on Vine Street, Evesham the
pick of the bunch. A better idea is to head out
to the friendly area's villages. You can't go wrong with
the friendly **Baker's Arms** (01386 840515)
in Broad Campden, where there's often a game
of darts in progress, or the **Ebrington Arms**
(Ebrington, nr Chipping Campden, 01386
593223), which has recently spruced up its
menu while still retaining its cosy, well-worn
pub atmosphere.

Thanks to planning restrictions, there is a
limited number of interesting dining choices
in Broadway. **Tisane's Tea Shop** (Cotswold
House, 21 The Green, 01386 852112) and
Garford's (47 High Street, 01386 858522)
offer different options for afternoon tea, but
if you fancy sampling a curry in traditional
16th-century English surroundings, head to
Sheik's Tandoori (The Coach House, The
Green, 01386 858137). Among the excellent
options in Chipping Campden is a good Italian,
Caminetto (High Street, 01386 840934).

Churchill Arms

*Paxford, nr Chipping Campden, Gloucestershire
GL55 6XH (01386 594000/www.thechurchill
arms.com).* **Food served** noon-2pm, 7-9pm daily.
Main courses £9-£14. **Credit** MC, V.

Culinary wizard Sonya Kidney produces innovative
dishes at this much fêted Paxford pub. Visitors to the
area are advised to take an early lunch or dinner as the
no-booking policy means the place is often jam-packed
with locals enjoying well-prepared dishes such as black
bream with fennel or delicately flavoured lemon sole.
Despite the breadth of choice on the blackboard menu,
the undemonstrative staff remain busiest serving traditional fare of roast beef or steak and ale pies. Any flair

is left to the cooking: the L-shaped interior is free of over
twee country pub *objets*, and is just as conducive to sink-
ing a few ales by the bar as it is to sampling excellent
starters such as pan-fried scallops with cucumber and
sweet chilli, or pigeon breast with roasted red peppers.
Puddings include a great gooey toffee pudding and the
wine list also has some excellent choices.

Eight Bells Inn

*Church Street, Chipping Campden, Gloucestershire
GL55 6GJ (01386 840371/www.eightbellsinn.co.uk).*
Food served noon-2pm, 6.30-9.30pm Mon-Thur;
noon-2.30pm, 7-10pm Fri, Sat; noon-2.30pm, 7-9pm
Sun. **Main courses** £8.50-£14.75. **Credit** MC, V.

The dark and cosy charms of this favoured boozer are
matched by numerous dishes designed to warm the
heart as well as the stomach. Starters such as deep-fried
brie or black pudding with creamy mash go better with
a pint of local ale than a packet of pork scratchings. The
rest of the no-nonsense dishes lean towards the roast
beef and pie variety, although there are also inspired
offerings such as warm salad of lamb kidneys with crou-
tons and pine kernels and baked trout with champ. The
wine list is decent enough, but it's the fresh cask ales
that really get the place swaying.

Hicks' Brasserie Bar

*Cotswold House Hotel, The Square, Chipping
Campden, Gloucestershire GL55 6AN (01386
840330/www.cotswoldhouse.com).* **Food served**
noon-2.30pm, 6-9.45pm daily. **Main courses**
£10-£15. **Credit** AmEx, MC, V.

Adding some welcome modern flash to the olde worlde
charms of Chipping Campden, Hicks' manages to retain
a restrained sophistication despite the slick, shininess
of its decor and incongruous background house music.
The superb cooking by Michel Roux scholarship-
winning chef Alan Dann provides the substance that
more than matches the style. On a recent visit, starters
of squid with chilli had a pleasing kick, while seared
scallops and rhubarb were an interesting counterpoint.
Caesar salad with smoked chicken was a simple, well-
executed main as was the more hearty roast guinea fowl
and fresh tagliatelle. With a heated terrace and a new
menu featuring ten vegetarian dishes, Hicks' is setting
the standard for classy yet comfortable dining in the
Cotswolds. For the hotel, *see p188.*

Howard Arms

*Lower Green, Ilmington, Warwickshire CV36 4LT
(tel/fax 01608 682226/www.howardarms.com).*
Food served noon-2pm, 7-9pm Mon-Thur; noon-
2pm, 7-9.30pm Fri, Sat; noon-2.30pm, 6.30-8.30pm
Sun. **Main courses** £9-£20. **Set lunch** £17.50
3 courses. **Credit** MC, V.

This sturdy freehouse is the centre of life in Ilmington
and follows a similar culinary path to the Churchill
Arms (*see above*) in presenting a mixture of bold, inventive dishes while not frightening away less adventurous
palates. Appealing country pub requirements are all
present: exposed beams, stone floors and a roaring open
fire. But it's dishes – poached sea trout in a mousseline
sauce, for example, and duck with sweet red cabbage
– that really leave a mark. The placid, generally older
clientele indulge in the interesting New World wines
(this is posh countryside after all), although the
excellent local Genesis ale is available too.

The Cotswolds

Stratford, Warwick & Leamington Spa

For Shakespeare, castles and the best balti outside Birmingham.

The heart of England is a classic destination for a weekend break – it's got culture by the spadeload, hustle and bustle, peaceful green countryside, easy-on-the-eye industrial history and major heritage sites. Whether you want to potter about on a river, hunt antiques or find more contemporary bargains, immerse yourself in food and drink or 400-year-old drama, you'll find opportunities aplenty clustered handily around the Avon. Warwickshire's three main towns are so different, so geographically close by and so complementary, that they offer a rich and varied break. Don't be put off by the ubiquitous marketing of Shakespeare Country – although do maybe consider a trip off-season if you're hoping to avoid crowds at the main attractions. Stratford is England's second-biggest tourist draw outside London.

The American wit Margaret Halsey famously noted, 'All of Stratford suggests powdered history – add hot water and stir and you have a delicious, nourishing Shakespeare.' The irony of her words is not always readily appreciated in these parts, but the fact is, it's easy to come down a little too hard on Will's home town: you often see it described grudgingly in guides as little more than 'a tourist trap', or 'an otherwise unremarkable place'.

Clearly, local proprietors aren't shy when it comes to milking Shakespeare's connection with the town – look out for names such as Thespian's (a restaurant), Will's Place (a hotel bar), Much Ado About Toys, and so on. Sheep Street, in particular, has fallen prey to pricey boutiques, restaurants and souvenir shops. If this all sounds a little too touristy, the key may be to find somewhere to stay in one of the farms or guesthouses in the surrounding villages, and just dive into town for a pleasantly antiquated sherbert, a meal and a play at one of the three very different theatres that are based down by the waterside.

When in Stratford, you really must take advantage of the river. The Stratford-upon-Avon Canal meets the River Avon at the Bancroft Basin and lock in front of the **Royal Shakespeare Theatre**. This stretch of waterway is one of Stratford's greatest attractions, providing visitors with the chance to cruise, row, canoe, punt or just stroll and laze under willows on the grassy banks. The **Countess of Evesham** (Bancroft Basin, 01789 293477/www.countessofevesham. mistral.co.uk) offers lunch and dinner cruises along the River Avon. Alternatively, there's **Prince Regent II** (Radford Semele, nr Leamington Spa, 01608 662216), a luxury cruising restaurant. For a regular hour-long cruise, head for **Bancroft Cruises**, at the Moat House Hotel landing stage next to Stratford Marina (Moat House, Bridgefoot, 01789 269669). And for something totally different, try **Avon Boating** (Swan's Nest Lane, 01789 267073/www.avon-boating.co.uk), which rents out an Edwardian craft or genuine Venetian gondolas for short cruises, along with more standard rowing boats, punts and electric launches. For further information on activities, including boat hire companies, leaflets, walks and education packs, phone or send an SAE to British Waterways,Brome Hall Lane, Lapworth, Solihull, B94 5RB (01564 784634/ www.britishwaterways.co.uk).

Wonderful Warwick

The county town of **Warwick**, an appealingly small and low-key place, is famed for its quite magnificent castle, whose grounds virtually equal the rest of the town centre in size. A 17th-century fire destroyed much of the original market town that had grown up outside the

By train from London

Trains to **Warwick** and **Stratford-upon-Avon** leave **Paddington** every 2hrs. Journey time to Warwick is 1hr 50mins; it is an additional 25mins to Stratford. Trains to **Royal Leamington Spa** leave **Marylebone** half-hourly; the journey time is 1hr 40mins. Info: www.thamestrains.co.uk and www.chilternrailways.co.uk.

Striking **Warwick Castle**. *See p193*

walls of the castle; the Saturday produce market still thrives amid the extensive rebuilding. Warwick is one of the most complete Georgian centres in the country – an ideal setting for a Saturday afternoon potter through the many antiques shops that have sprung up over the years. Only on the outskirts do older buildings survive. The **Lord Leycester Hospital**, built in the 14th century and established as a hospital for war veterans in 1571, is one of Britain's finest examples of medieval architecture. Those interested in the area's local history can visit the excellent **Warwickshire Museum** (Market Place, Warwick, 01926 412500).

Lovely Leamington Spa

Where Warwick has its castle and Stratford has its bard, **Royal Leamington Spa** once had its health-giving waters to draw visitors to town. Now, sadly, it just has its shopping centre. However, Leamington's strict grid-pattern of streets, combination of grand Regency and Victorian architecture, wide tree-lined avenues and elegant squares still retain something of the air of an English seaside town fallen on quiet times. The park-strewn area around the **Pump Rooms** (now reinvented as a gallery, tearooms and public space) and the magnificent old town hall readily bring to mind the days when Leamington was a playground for the rich and famous. Nowadays, the attractive Parade and Royal Priors shopping centre have a good selection of high street and speciality outlets.

Although the healing waters have run dry and the imposing Regent Hotel is boarded up, Leamington is still a arty little backwater – and you can get a very decent curry in the old town area over the River Leam.

If these tourist-heavy towns get too much, take heart in the fact that there are many lesser-known (and less crowded) places of interest that are well worth seeing. Visit **Charlecote House**, with its terrific gardens landscaped by 'Capability' Brown, or the old watermill at **Wellesbourne** (Kineton Road, 01789 470237/www.wellesbournemill.co.uk, phone for opening times); alternatively, take a brisk walk up **Edgehill**, site of the first battle in the Civil War in 1642, for views of Warwickshire, with the Cotswolds on the horizon.

What to see & do

Tourist Information Centres

Royal Pump Rooms, The Parade, Royal Leamington Spa, CV32 4AB (01926 742762/www.shakespeare-country.co.uk). **Open** *Easter-Oct* 9.30am-5pm Mon-Sat; 11am-4pm Sun. *Nov-Easter* 9.30am-5pm Mon-Fri; 9.30am-4pm Sat; 11am-3pm Sun.

Bridgefoot, Stratford-upon-Avon, CV37 6GW (01789 293127/www.shakespeare-country.co.uk). **Open** *Easter-Oct* 9.30am-5.30pm Mon-Sat; 10.30am-4.30pm Sun. *Nov-Easter* 9am-5pm Mon-Sat; 10am-3pm Sun.

The Court House, Jury Street, Warwick, CV34 4EW (01926 492212/www.warwick-uk.co.uk). **Open** 9.30am-4.30pm daily.

Charlecote Park

Charlecote, CV35 9ER, 5 miles E of Stratford-upon-Avon (01789 470277/www.nationaltrust.org.uk). **Open** *House* early Mar-June, Sept, Oct noon-5pm Mon, Tue, Fri-Sun. *July, Aug* noon-5pm Mon-Wed, Fri-Sun. Closed Nov-early Mar. *Grounds* early Mar-June, Sept, Oct 10.30am-6pm Mon,Tue, Fri-Sun. July, Aug 10.30am-6pm Mon-Wed, Fri-Sun. Closed Nov-Easter. **Admission** (NT) *House, park & gardens* £6.40; £3.20 concessions; free under-5s. *Park & gardens* £3; £1.50. **Credit** MC, V.
Though the present house dates from the mid 16th century, the interior is early Victorian. Shakespeare is said to have been caught poaching in the fine deer park, which was later landscaped by 'Capability' Brown.

Hatton Country World & Shopping Village

Dark Lane, Hatton, Warwick, CV35 8XA (01926 843411/www.hattonworld.com). **Open** 10am-5pm daily. **Admission** £7.95; £6.95 concessions. **Credit** MC, V.
It's great value for the young ones; you pay five quid and they get to spend an unlimited amount of time on the bouncy castles, see-saws and slides. They can cuddle and stroke a wide variety of barnyard and domestic animals too. And while they're doing that, you can spend money at the adjoining American-style outlet centre – there's everything from jewellery and fashion to fancy metalwork and wood-turned goodies.

Heritage Motor Centre

Banbury Road, Gaydon, CV35 0BJ, 10 miles SE of Warwick (01926 641188/www.heritage-motor-centre. co.uk). **Open** 10am-5pm daily. **Admission** £8; £6-£7 concessions; free under-5s. **Credit** AmEx, MC, V.
Holding the largest collection of historic British cars in the world – there are 200 classic vehicles on display, charting the progress of the British car industry from the turn of the last century to the present day – the Heritage Motor Centre also offers a programme of demonstrations and activities in its 63 acres of grounds (call for details).

Kenilworth Castle

Kenilworth, CV8 1ME (01926 852078/www. english-heritage.org.uk). **Open** *Apr-Sept* 10am-6pm daily. *Oct* 10am-5pm daily. *Nov-Mar* 10am-4pm daily. **Admission** (EH) £4.50; £2.30-£3.40 concessions; free under-5s. **Credit** MC, V.
The impressive red sandstone ruins are all that is left of 12th-century Kenilworth Castle. Visitors can see the Norman keep, great hall and the wonderful reconstructed Tudor gardens. Audio tours available.

Lord Leycester Hospital

High Street, Warwick, CV34 4BH (01926 491422). **Open** *Hospital* Easter-Sept 10am-5pm Tue-Sun. Oct-Easter 10am-4pm Tue-Sun. *Garden* Easter-Sept 10am-4.30pm Tue-Sun. Closed Oct-Easter. **Admission** *Hospital* £3.20; £2.20-£2.70 concessions. *Garden* £1.50; free children. **No credit cards**.
Built in the 14th century, the hospital was acquired by Robert Dudley, Earl of Leicester in 1571. The chapel, great hall, guild hall, galleried courtyard and restored garden (nearly 600 years old) are all open to the public.

Art Gallery & Museum at the Royal Pump Rooms

The Parade, Royal Leamington Spa, CV32 4AB (01926 742700/742762/www.royal-pump-rooms. co.uk). **Open** 10.30am-5pm Tue, Wed, Fri, Sat; 1.30-8pm Thur; 11am-4pm Sun. **Admission** free.
Next to Jephson Gardens, the Pump Rooms are where people once came to take the health-giving Leamington waters. A major restoration programme has created a complex containing the Assembly Room, the Royal Pump Rooms, an art gallery/museum, library, Tourist Information Centre and café.

Royal Shakespeare Company

Waterside, Stratford-upon-Avon, CV37 6BB (box office 01789 403403/tours 01789 403405/ www.rsc.org.uk). **Backstage tours** times vary; phone to check. **Tickets** *Tour* £4; £3 concessions. *Performances* prices vary. **Credit** MC, V.
See a production of one of Shakespeare's plays or take a backstage tour at the Royal Shakespeare Theatre, The Swan or the Other Place. The RST seats 1,500, and produces six or so Shakespeares each season. The Swan is a re-creation of an Elizabethan playhouse, holding an audience of 430 seated on three sides of the stage, while the Other Place, just a little further down the Avon, opened in the '90s as a showcase for more experimental drama. Tickets cost anything between £5 and £50, dependent on venue and performance.

St John's House Museum

St John's, Warwick, CV34 4NF (01926 412132). **Open** *May-Sept* 10am-5pm Tue-Sat; 2.30-5pm Sun. *Oct-Apr* 10am-5pm Tue-Sat. **Admission** free; donations welcome.
This beautiful Jacobean mansion contains displays relating to the social history of Warwickshire, including costumes and a 19th-century kitchen, parlour and schoolroom. It also houses the Royal Warwickshire Regimental Museum.

Stratford-upon-Avon Butterfly Farm

Swans Nest Lane, Stratford-upon-Avon, CV37 7LS (01789 299288/www.butterflyfarm.co.uk). **Open** *Apr-Sept* 10am-6pm daily. *Oct-Mar* 10am-5pm/dusk daily. **Admission** £4.25; £3.25-£3.75 concessions. **Credit** AmEx, MC, V.
Situated just over the river from the RSC, these connected greenhouses cum miniature rain forest provide a very different kind of drama – namely, wildly exotic butterflies with six-inch wingspans flapping around in thick, humid air, often alighting for a rest on your head or to take a swig at your drink can. There are iguanas, hatching pupae, fat carp and creepy-crawlies too. Recommended.

Warwick Castle

Warwick, CV34 4QU (01926 406600/info line 0870 442200/www.warwick-castle.co.uk). **Open** *Apr-Oct* 10am-6pm daily. *Nov-Mar* 10am-5pm daily. **Admission** (seasonal prices) £11.25-£13.50 adult; £6.95-£10 concessions; free under-4s. **Credit** MC, V.
Warwick Castle began life in 914, when the mound of earth upon which it sits was claimed by Ethelfleda. The motte and bailey were further fortified by William the

Seeking Shakespeare

As one of the greatest men born to this sceptred isle, and surely the finest inventor and entertainer ever to work with the Queen's English, surprisingly little is known about the real William Shakespeare. The true extent of the vacuum only becomes apparent when you realise that no likeness of the man survives that was actually created during his lifetime.

It isn't just his face that's nebulous, but also his life and times. Nowadays, it's almost unimaginable that a master of language should sign his name at least half a dozen different ways – Shakeshank, Shaksper, what's in a name? – adding a further cognitive chasm between us and him, now and 400 years ago.

Ignoring the countless assumptions and the hearsay, the complete biography of Shakespeare is sketchy: he was born in Stratford, worked for his father and had three children with Anne Hathaway before heading for London with a theatre troupe. He wrote 38 hugely popular plays, staging them at the Globe, then retired early to Stratford before shuffling off this mortal coil, and vanishing into thin air.

Shakespeare's impact on us all is immense: he has permeated our culture, language and consciousness far more than we generally realise. A trip to Stratford can only heighten our appreciation to a limited degree; after all, his legacy springs from his words and their universality, rather than specifics of the houses he or his relatives may have lived in as viewed from behind a guide-rope. Nevertheless, Stratford's status as England's second-greatest tourist draw outside London is founded entirely on visitors from all corners of the world hoping to inhabit Shakespeare's space, to breathe the air he breathed and see the sights that were familiar to him.

So, is the Stratford Shakespeare industry such stuff as dreams are made on, or a fool's paradise that beggars description? Don't they rather lay it on with a trowel? Is there method amid the madness, or too much of a good thing? Will your hair stand on end? Has Stratford seen better days? Is it a sorry sight?

Neither here nor there? Much ado about nothing? As dead as a doornail? Or a dish fit for the gods?

There's really only one way to find out for yourself: visit the so-called Shakespeare houses, which represent key scenes from the playwright's life.

Shakespeare's Birthplace

Henley Street, Stratford-upon-Avon, CV37 6QW (01789 204016/ www.shakespeare.org.uk). **Open** *Apr-May, Sept Oct* 10am-5pm Mon-Sat; 10.30am-5pm Sun. *June-Aug* 9am-5pm Mon-Sat; 9.30am-5pm Sun. *Nov-Mar* 10am-4pm Mon-Sat; 10.30am-4pm Sun. **Admission** £6.50; £2.50-£5.50 concessions; free under-5s. **Credit** AmEx, MC, V.

The half-timbered house where Shakespeare spent his early years, and which he inherited from his father, who worked here either as a glover, a butcher or a wool merchant. Indeed, it isn't even actually certain that the poet was even born here, or on what date. The rooms are all decked out in 16th-century style – including the glovers' workshop. Handles on reality include a first edition of Shakespeare's collected plays, dating from seven years after he died, plus the scrawlings on a window of 19th-century culture pilgrims.

Anne Hathaway's Cottage

Cottage Lane, Shottery, Stratford-upon-Avon, CV37 9HH (01789 292100/ www.shakespeare.org.uk). **Open** *Apr-Oct* 9am-5pm Mon-Sat; 9.30am-5pm Sun. *Nov-Mar* 9.30am-4pm Mon-Sat; 10am-4pm Sun. **Admission** £5; £2-£4 concessions. **Credit** AmEx, MC, V.

This thatched cottage, parts of which date back to the 1460s, was the home of Shakespeare's wife before they married in 1582, when he was 18 and she 25. It's surrounded by beautiful gardens, complete with Elizabethan-style maze and Elizabethan-inspired sculptures, and many pleasant walks lead from the property. There are furnishings and country artefacts that date back to the poet's day – and you can also visit 'the room where Shakespeare is thought to have wooed Anne'.

2 miles W of Stratford-upon-Avon.

Mary Arden's House & Shakespeare Countryside Museum

Station Road, Wilmcote, CV37 9UN (01789 293455/www.shakespeare. org.uk). **Open** *June-Aug 9.30am-5pm Mon-Sat; 10am-5pm Sun. Apr, May, Sept, Oct 10am-5pm Mon-Sat; 10.30am-5pm Sun. Nov-Mar 10am-4pm Mon-Sat; 10.30am-4pm Sun.* **Admission** £5.50; £2.50-£5 concessions; free under-5s. **Credit** AmEx, MC, V.

From the 18th century until just recently, it was thought that Mary Arden, William Shakespeare's mum, had lived in the imaginatively named Mary Arden's House, in the village of Wilmcote. Three years ago, however, research unearthed the fact that she actually lived in the rather more downmarket cottage next door, hitherto known as Glebe Farm. As a result, Glebe Farm has now been renamed Mary Arden's House. The former Mary Arden's House is now called Palmer's Farm, after its 16th-century owner. Because of the difficulty involved in returning the house to its 16th-century condition, it was decided to keep the eclectic Edwardian furnishings of its last occupant, who died in 1978. The falconry exhibit is great, but the rare breeds and barnyard attractions at the Countryside Museum are a bit thin on the ground. *4 miles NW of Stratford-upon-Avon.*

Hall's Croft

Old Town, Stratford-upon-Avon, CV37 6BG (01789 292107/www.shakespeare. org.uk). **Open** *Apr, May, Sept, Oct 11am-5pm daily. June-Aug 9.30am-5pm Mon-Sat; 10am-5pm Sun. Nov-Mar 11am-4pm daily.* **Admission** £3.50; £1.70-£3 concessions. **Credit** AmEx, MC, V.

This grand 16th-century house was the home of John Hall, the doctor husband of Shakespeare's eldest daughter, Susanna. The period furniture, decent artworks and beautiful gardens are all very fine, and it's more than possible to 'learn what it was like to be both doctor and patient in Shakespeare's day'. Pretty gruesome, as it happens.

Nash's House & New Place

22 Chapel Street, Stratford-upon-Avon, CV37 6EP (01789 292325/www.shake speare.org.uk). **Open** *Apr, May, Sept, Oct 11am-5pm daily. June-Aug 9.30am-5pm Mon-Sat; 10am-5pm Sun. Nov-Mar 11am-4pm daily.* **Admission** £3.50; £1.70-£3 concessions; free under-5s. **Credit** AmEx, MC, V.

This house was once owned by Thomas Nash, who married Shakespeare's granddaughter. Now a minor museum, it features an exhibition on the history of Stratford, which is unfortunately rather dull. You can see 'the kind of' furniture, pottery, paintings and tapestries that might once have adorned the house. Outside, in the Elizabethan-style garden, are plants that feature in Shakespeare's writings, and also the remaining foundations of New Place, the house that Shakespeare bought in 1597 for around £120, and where he later retired and died in 1616.

Holy Trinity Church

Old Town, Stratford-upon-Avon, CV37 6BG (01789 266316/www.stratford- upon-avon.org). **Open** *Mar, Oct 9am- 5pm Mon-Sat; noon-5pm Sun. Apr-Sept 8.30am-6pm Mon-Sat; noon-5pm Sun. Nov-Feb 9am-4pm Mon-Sat; noon-5pm Sun.* **Admission** £1; 50p concessions; free under-5s. **No credit cards**.

Set on the banks of the River Avon, this beautiful parish church is the site of Shakespeare's grave and contains records of the playwright's baptism and death exhibited in a case. The plaster effigy on a modest wall-mounted memorial was at least put up during the lifetime of Shakespeare's widow, so it can be safely assumed it's a reasonable likeness. Comfortingly, it looks a lot like Shakespeare.

The Cotswolds

Conqueror. Among the highlights of the present-day building are the Ghost Tower – said to be haunted by the ghost of the impressively named Sir Fulke Greville, who owned the castle in the 17th century – the great hall, restored to its former glory after a devastating fire in 1871, the elegant state rooms and the 17th-century chapel. The castle is impressive enough, but if you're expecting to be educated, you'll be disappointed. Visitors are shuffled from one room to the next, and there's little in the way of explanations about the exhibits. Phone for details of special events.

Where to stay

Should you take the plunge and stay right in the centre of Stratford, or opt for somewhere more relaxing and countrified?

If it's peace and quiet you're after, **Loxley Farm** (Loxley, Warwick, 01789 840265, doubles £64-£70) has two bedrooms in a converted barn, and breakfast is served in the late 13th-century cottage where Charles I is said to have stayed after his defeat at the Battle of Edgehill.

The Falcon Hotel

Chapel Street, Stratford-upon-Avon, CV37 6HA (0870 609 6122/www.corushotels.com/thefalcon). **Rates** £59-£89 single; £130-£160 double/twin/family room/four-poster. **Rooms** (all en suite) 4 single; 80 double/twin/family/four-poster. **Credit** AmEx, DC, MC, V.

At least 20 of the 84 en suite bedrooms at the Falcon are situated in the original 16th-century inn, which is one of the best olde worlde ratios for a hotel in the centre of town, where many rooms are often in modern annexes. Book early and you'll increase your chances of landing a room in the three-storey black-and-white timbered frontage, with a four-poster bed and views out over New Place and the Guild Chapel. Otherwise, the rooms in the large extension at the rear are a shade groovier than the average, decked out in bold colour schemes and a polite version of modernist style. There's a decent restaurant, a bistro, two bars and (a rare commodity in these parts) a garden in which to relax. Children and dogs welcome.

The Royal Leamington Hotel

64 Upper Holly Walk, Royal Leamington Spa CV32 4JL (01926 883777/fax 01926 330467/www.merid ianleisure.com). **Rates** £50-£80 single; £60-£90 double/twin; £70-£90 four-poster. Breakfast £5.95 (Eng). **Rooms** (all en suite) 1 single; 29 double/twin; 2 four-poster. **Credit** AmEx, DC, MC, V.

Blending in well with the rest of Leamington's grand architecture, the Leamington Hotel & Bistro does a roaring trade. Though it's big, and now owned by the Best Western chain, the staff have managed to keep a personal, down-to-earth feel to the place. Rooms vary in size and decor, but furnishings are all good quality, if a little corporate. The Bistro menu won't win any awards for adventurousness but prices are good. Children and dogs (£10 per night) are welcome.

Mallory Court

Harbury Lane, Bishop's Tachbrook, CV33 9QB (01926 330214/fax 01926 451714/www.mallory. co.uk). **Rates** £175-£275 single occupancy; £185-

£320 double/twin. Breakfast £10 (Eng). **Rooms** 18 double/twin (16 en suite). **Credit** AmEx, DC, MC, V.

The self-styled 'most beautiful hotel in Warwickshire' is an oasis of expensive calm, created in a superb Lutyens-style manor house in the countryside outside Leamington. Sitting in a cool ten acres of manicured grounds, Mallory Court has recently been expanded with the addition of a wing of eight additional suites that are expertly blended into the rest of the building. Personal touches are evident throughout, and bedrooms are beautifully and individually furnished. In warmer weather guests can sit out on the terrace overlooking the gardens and outdoor swimming pool. Absolute luxury and all-round quality are evidenced in every detail: the restaurant has recently been awarded a Michelin star. An additional 11 rooms are to be added in 2004.

Shrewley Pools Farm

Haseley, nr Warwick, CV35 7HB (01926 484315/ www.bbgl.co.uk/lodgings). **Rates** £30 single occupancy; £45-£60 double/twin/family; child supplement. **Rooms** (both en suite) 1 twin; 1 double/family. **No credit cards.**

If it's a farm experience you're after, you've come to the right place: this is no ex-farmhouse converted into a B&B; the barns here are used for hay rather than extra bedrooms. This 17th-century house retains many of its original features – exposed beams, uneven floors, leaded windows and mind-your-head doorways. The rooms are comfy, owner Cathy Dodd is friendly and generous. Guests are welcome to stroll around the rambling garden, with its rhododendrons and herbaceous borders. Children welcome. No smoking throughout.

Victoria Spa Lodge

Bishopton Lane, Bishopton, Stratford-upon-Avon, CV37 9QY (01789 267985/fax 01789 204728/ www.stratford-upon-avon.co.uk/victoriaspa.htm). **Rates** £50 single occupancy; £65 double/twin; £80-£100 family room. **Rooms** (all en suite) 3 double; 1 twin; 3 family. **Credit** MC, V.

Twenty minutes from Stratford if you choose to take a rural gambol (and considerably less by car, obviously), Victoria Spa Lodge has the feel of a grand country house. Originally built as a spa house, the Georgian property has been restored by Paul and Dreen Tozer to a state of genuine elegance, with a characterful dining room and floral decor in the seven bedrooms. Princess Victoria stayed here for the waters before ascending the throne in 1837, and her coat of arms is built into the gables. Children welcome. No smoking throughout.

Where to eat & drink

Most Stratford restaurants open early and close late, and offer good value pre- and post-theatre meals. If you're after a quick bite rather than a lengthy gastronomic experience, try the **Black Swan** (Waterside, 01789 297312), more commonly known as the Dirty Duck, where you may find yourself brushing shoulders with members of the RSC. Over the road at the RSC, **Quarto's** (Waterside, 01789 403415) is a new modern restaurant with views out over the

Everybody's an actor in **Stratford-upon-Avon**, where Shakespeare's memory dominates.

Avon, serving contemporary European food; the redesigned **1564** café/bar on the ground floor is altogether less formal. **Opposition** at 13 Sheep Street (01789 269980) is highly rated. **Russon's** (8 Church Street, 01789 268822) specialises in fish – it does a great haddock in beer batter with chips and pea mint purée.

For a snack in Stratford town centre check out the **Vintner** (4-5 Sheep Street, 01789 297259) or the **Deli Café** (13-14 Meer Street, 01789 295705); alternatively, get into the spirit of the place with a dollop of clotted cream, jam and a scone to balance it on, washed down with a cuppa. **Hathaway's Tea Rooms** (19 High Street, 01789 292404) set in the eaves above its own bakery, serves a good cream tea.

In Kenilworth, the **Coconut Lagoon** (149 Warwick Road, 01926 864500) serves the southern Indian fare of Kerala, Goa, Karnataka and Andhra Pradesh.

There are plenty of good boozers in the area, though you'll be hard-pressed to find one more quaintly pokey than the brilliantly dark and deliciously secret 16th-century **Garrick Inn** on Stratford High Street (01789 292186). The **King's Head** at Aston Cantlow (21 Bearley Road, 01789 488242) is worth a visit for its quality Italian and Mediterranean food. For good pub grub and a fruity pint of real ale, try the **Fox** at Loxley (High Street, 01789 840991), the **Bell** at Shottery (Bell Lane, 01789 269645), or watch the world go by at the **Tilted Wig** in Warwick's Market Place (01926 410466). For

something posher, try the highly rated **Restaurant Bosquet** in Kenilworth (97A Warwick Road, 01926 852463), which produces regional French cooking of the south-west.

Callands

13-14 Meer Street, Stratford-upon-Avon, CV37 6QB (01789 269304/www.desports.co.uk). **Food served** noon-2pm, 6-9.30pm Tue-Sat; noon-2pm Sun. **Set lunches** £5.95 2 courses, £7.95 3 courses. **Set dinners** £19.95 2 courses, £23.95 3 courses. **Credit** AmEx, DC, MC, V.
Set above the deli of the same name, the original features of the 16th-century building, including the wooden beams, are effectively combined with contemporary bright colours. The menu is short and eclectic, though the dishes stop short of being over-elaborate: the quality of the cooking is indisputably high – as in the excellent pheasant roasted in its own juices with honey-glazed parsnips, pickled red cabbage and game chips. A three-course £24 deal includes a priceless warm coconut and rum tart with mango ice-cream. Service is friendly and agreeably unhurried – let's not say slow.

Findon's

7 Old Square, Warwick, CV34 4TT (01926 411755/ www.findons-restaurant.co.uk). **Food served** 6.30-9.30pm Mon-Sat. **Main courses** £12.95-£18.95. **Credit** MC, V.
Occupying an early Georgian townhouse and serving French-influenced food in an environment of swish curtains and chandeliers, there's no denying the pedigree of the modern cooking at Findon's. Typical starters are a salad of pigeon breast with wild mushrooms in a Madeira jus, or crispy fillet of sea bass with tomato oil and a balsamic dressing. Main courses

The Cotswolds

might include pavé of new season lamb with a herb crust, pea and roasted shallot sauce; imaginative vegetarian dishes include the likes of warm salad of goat's cheese, portobello mushrooms, rocket, basil and walnut pesto with spiced polenta cake. The standard of cooking is very high throughout.

Fox & Goose Inn

Armscote, off A3400, Stratford-upon-Avon, CV37 8DD (01608 682293/www.foxandgoose.co.uk). **Food served** noon-2.30pm, 7-9.30pm daily. **Main courses** £8.95-£14.95. **Credit** AmEx, MC, V.
The interior of the reinvented, renovated Fox & Goose is inviting and sumptuous – dark red walls and velvet cushions. The inventive food from the daily changing menu is a major attraction. A warm salad starter of black pudding, bacon, chorizo, sausage and sesame works alchemical magic, likewise pumpkin and chilli soup. Next, try seared razor clams and linguine, or home-made cep mushroom and goat's cheese tagliatelle. The wine list is also first class, with champagne available by the glass, and beers and ales including the pub's own Fox & Goose Bitter by Brakspear. You can stay here too. The self-described 'slightly eccentric' Cluedo-themed bedrooms are true to their name, but are nonetheless luxurious (doubles £80). Diners can sit out on the deck in the lovely garden (where barbecues are held in the summer).

Howard Arms

Lower Green, Ilmington, CV36 4LT (01608 682226/www.howardarms.com). **Food served** noon-2pm, 7-9pm Mon-Thur; noon-2pm, 7-9.30pm Fri, Sat; 12.30-2.30pm, 6.30-8.30pm Sun. **Set lunches** (Sun) £17.50 3 courses. **Credit** MC, V.
The vibe is definitely pub at the Howard Arms – although there is a separate dining room, you choose from the chalked-up menu and order from the bar. The weekly changing menu incorporates seasonal produce, and dishes are imaginative but not overfussy – a sauté of lamb's kidneys, spinach, grain mustard and cream to start, perhaps; prime lamb steak with roast garlic sauce and aubergine purée, or char-grilled tuna, garlic and thyme potato cake with anchovy cream sauce to follow. As it's a free house, there's a good choice of cask ales and keg beers, including Everard's Tiger and North Cotswold Brewery's Genesis. If you've overdone it, repair to one of the cosy bedrooms upstairs (doubles £74-£84), look out on to the village green and dream of moving to the country.

King Baba

58 Bath Street, Royal Leamington Spa, CV31 3AE (01926 888869). **Food served** 6pm-midnight Tue-Thur, Sun; 6pm-2.30am Fri, Sat. **Main courses** £4.75-£6.50. **Credit** AmEx, MC, V.
Leamington is close enough to Birmingham to rightfully claim a share of the second city's glory as home of the authentic balti dish. If you've never had the pleasure, prepare for a sizzling iron skillet of fresh-cooked mix-and-match ingredients. For example, you might go for a balti chicken, sag and chana, cooked madras-hot with sizzling tomatoes and onions, or a coconut lamb korma balti, mopped up with a large, sweet, buttery tandoori nan. Balti options are around six quid, plus rice and bread and side dishes. Staff are smart, helpful, child-doting and chatty, if you're in the mood.

Lamb's of Sheep Street

12 Sheep Street, Stratford-upon-Avon, CV37 6EF (01789 292554/www.lambsrestaurant.co.uk). **Food served** noon-1.45pm, 5-9.30pm Mon-Fri; noon-1.45pm, 5-10pm Sat; noon-3pm Sun. **Main courses** £7.25-£15.95. **Set meals** (lunch, 5-7pm) £11.50 2 courses, £14 3 courses. **Credit** MC, V.
Olde worlde is overplayed in Stratford, but Lamb's – which really was here when the Bard was a boy – combines a fresh, modern feel with its ancient oak beams. The menu offers a bistro-style selection. When we visited, one of the day's specials, tuna with shiitake mushrooms, was exceptional and a more traditional platter of devilled whitebait featured lots of juicy fish. Of the mains, roast cod with chorizo cassoulet was a fine mix, though pork escalopes pan-fried with sage, Italian ham, spinach and mash wasn't quite so impressive. Desserts brought invention – pannacotta with espresso poured over it. Our solitary grouch would be the practice of charging for absolutely everything (including chocolate truffles with the coffee). The staff are young, bright and helpful.

Love's

15 Dormer Place, Royal Leamington Spa, CV32 5AA (01926 315522). **Food served** noon-2pm, 7-9.30pm Tue-Sat. **Set lunches** (menu rapide) £13.50 3 courses. **Set dinners** £23.50 2 courses, £27.50 3 courses, £25 3 courses Tue-Thur, £37.50 6 courses. **Credit** AmEx, DC, MC, V.
After studying under the Roux brothers and Alain Ducasse in Paris, local chef Steve Love set up shop independently at the end of 2001. His menus offer notably intricate dishes: on a recent visit, a starter of beetroot risotto with goat's cheese crêpinette and garlic broth had a smooth, satisfying mix of flavours. To follow, an assiete de vinades was a bravura demonstration of Love's skill with meats, featuring a pork and black pudding crêpinette, pan-fried pork fillet and braised shoulder of lamb. Dessert was another opulent combination, a 'trio of lemon' with glazed tartlet, a sorbet and a deliciously fresh mousse. Almost as memorable were the many complementary little bits and pieces that punctuated a leisurely meal: appetisers of braised lentils, Toulouse sausages and cumin broth, a black cheery sorbet between starter and main and a 'pre-dessert' of rhubarb jelly with cinnamon cream. Prices remain extremely reasonable and there's a well-chosen wine list to match.

Simpson's Restaurant

101-3 Warwick Road, Kenilworth, CV8 1HL (01926 864567/www.simpsons-restaurant.co.uk). **Food served** 12.30-1.45pm, 7-9.30pm Tue-Sat. **Main courses** £9.95-£13.25. **Set meals** £30 3 courses, £45 5 courses. **Credit** AmEx, DC, MC, V.
Contrasting starkly with its less-than-glamourous location on the traffic-heavy Warwick Road, Simpson's is an arresting sight – perfectly manicured miniature trees outside, blonde wood and crisp linen tablecloths inside. House specialities include a torte of Salcombe crab, Loch Fyne smoked salmon and creamed guacamole, followed by honey-glazed shank of lamb with Swiss chard and chickpea gremolata. Andreas Antona's restaurant is deservedly Michelin-starred, and accordingly pricey – but the three-course £30 set meal deal represents real value.

Oxford

Education, education, education.

Try as you might, it is impossible to separate Oxford from its colleges. They have defined the town since the middle of the 12th century. The remarkable architecture of Oxford is the architecture of the university, and it is to the university that the tourists flock in such massive numbers. Just about everything else – the quirky and interesting galleries and museums, the good restaurants, the expansive greenery – stem from the colleges and the money they generate.

It wasn't always this way. Oxford arose as a Saxon burg built to defend Wessex from the dastardly Danes – the 11th-century **St Michael's Tower** in Cornmarket Street is the only surviving building of this period. The first written evidence, not only of the existence of Oxford but also of its importance, comes from the Anglo-Saxon *Chronicle* (begun in the ninth century and continued until 1154), where it is stated that Edward (the Elder), took control of 'London and Oxford and the lands obedient to

those cities'. Oxford had naturally developed as an important town due to its strategic location. A location important both politically, because it marked the border of the two kingdoms of Mercia and Wessex, and commercially, because it lay at the confluence of two rivers. Its position at the meeting place of these two rivers, the **Cherwell** and **Isis** (a river that everybody else is content to call the Thames), also made it easy to defend. Charles I concurred and made the city his Royalist capital during the Civil War after the Battle of Edgehill in 1642. A store of stones was kept in the tower at Magdalen (pronounced 'maudlin', another Oxford affectation, and there are many, many more) to hurl at the approaching enemy. They were not required as the town was never attacked by Cromwell's army.

Prior to this, as a consequence of the reorganisation of the Church in England, Henry VIII created the new diocese of Oxford and in 1542 Oxford was granted the status of a city

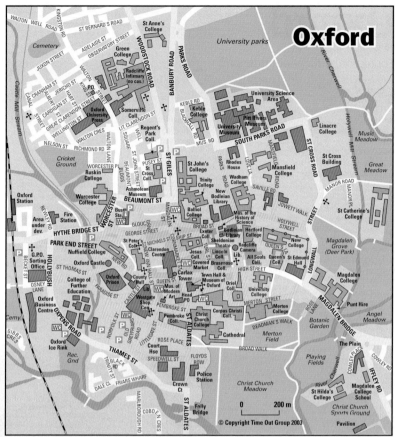

Oxford

University parks

Cemetery

© Copyright Time Out Group 2003

with its cathedral at **Christ Church**. By now the university was well established (*see p204* **Oxford revisited**). These were dangerous times. Although the dissolution of the monasteries meant that much of Oxford's land and money passed from the Church to the colleges, it also meant that as most of the scholars and lecturers were clerics, there was a serious disruption of academic activities and a subsequent decline in the number of students. It was also becoming increasingly dangerous to hold radical ideas and these factors were enough to deter many from attending the university. There was bloodshed too. In 1555-6 the Protestant martyrs **Cranmer**, **Ridley** and **Latimer** were burnt at the stake in Broad Street (an X marks the spot, literally). The reign of Elizabeth, with its demand for clerics, lawyers and teachers, restored life to the city.

From then on, town and college prospered together, but the relationship has not always been a happy one. There is a long history of trouble between the town and its students (the gown). A largely class-based feud, these days it manifests itself in the odd nasty look at the city centre kebab vans. In the past things were a lot more serious. In 1355 more than 60 students were killed in a vicious battle that started in the Swyndlestock Tavern (now the Abbey National at Carfax crossroads). For their part in the fight, the city's representatives were forced to attend a pentitential mass. Every year. For 500 years. Be warned, the colleges have long memories.

Leave the car at home
Despite the city's links with the car (the Morris plant at Cowley is one of the area's main employers), its main streets have long

The Forest Fire by Piero di Cosimo at the **Ashmolean Museum**.

been pedestrianised, with access restricted for the roads that remain open to traffic. A park and ride service operates from the outskirts of town; the easiest way to get around the town centre is on foot or by bicycle. This helps make Oxford an excellent place to visit.

Although the centre can get uncomfortably clogged with tourists at weekends, there are always the distinct neighbourhoods of **Jericho**, **Summertown** and **Cowley** to explore. Oxford is also a very open, airy city, and when you've seen the sights, you'll find plenty of places to rest your feet. Most of the colleges have grassy quads, while **Christ Church** and **Madgalen** also have meadows. The **University Botanic Garden** are another marvellous spot of tranquillity and well worth the entrance fee in summer. There are also the University Parks slightly further afield and beyond Jericho is **Port Meadow**, one of the largest expanses of common land in the country, where wild horses roam and houseboats are moored.

What to see and do

Oxford Information Centre
15-16 Broad Street, OX1 3AS (01865 726871/fax 01865 240261/www.visitoxford.org). **Open** *Easter-Oct* 9.30am-5pm Mon-Sat; 10am-3.30pm Sun. *Nov-Easter* 9.30am-5.30pm Mon-Sat. Closed between Christmas & New Year.

Bike hire
Bike Zone *Market Street, OX1 3EQ (01865 728877).*

Alice Shop
83 St Aldate's, OX1 1RA (01865 723793). **Open** 11am-5pm daily. **Credit** AmEx, DC, MC, V.
The author of *Alice's Adventures in Wonderland*, Lewis Carroll, was a tutor at Christ Church. Alice Lidell, the inspiration for his books, was the daughter of the college dean. Christ Church itself is not frightened of playing on that history to appeal to tourists, and this independent shop is also devoted to the Alice tales.

Ashmolean Museum
Beaumont Street, OX1 2PH (01865 278000/www.ashmol.ox.ac.uk). **Open** 10am-5pm Tue-Sat; 2-5pm Sun. **Admission** free.
A gem of a museum, the Ashmolean hit the headlines on New Year's Day 2000 when it was the subject of an audacious burglary that lifted a Cézanne from its walls. The museum is perfectly sized to explore in a morning or afternoon and has a striking array of collections, ranging from Greek coins and Roman busts to works by Michelangelo, Titian, Picasso and Van Gogh.

Bate Collection of Musical Instruments
St Aldate's, OX1 1DB (01865 276139). **Open** *Term-time only* 2-5pm Mon-Fri. **Admission** free.
Selection of musical instruments that date back several hundred years.

Bodleian Library
Broad Street, OX1 3BG (01865 277000/www.bodley.ox.ac.uk). **Open** 9am-4.45pm Mon-Fri; 9am-12.30pm Sat. **Guided tours** *Mid Mar-Oct* 10.30am, 11.30am, 2pm, 3pm Mon-Fri; 10.30am, 11.30am Sat. *Nov-mid Mar* 2pm, 3pm Mon-Fri; 10.30am, 11.30am Sat. **Admission** *Tour* £4. **No credit cards**.
The university's huge, reference-only library is a spectacular building, with the oldest part, the Divinity School, dating back to 1488. It contains every book published in the United Kingdom and Ireland since 1709 and there are more than seven million of them stored in its 110 miles of underground shelving. Of the reading rooms, Duke Humfrey's Library is still in use today and down the years 25 prime ministers, 40 Nobel prize winners and five kings have poured over the pages there. In 1602 the library was refounded by Thomas Bodley, which led to the construction of the Jacobean Old Schools Quadrangle. Another later construction is the James Gibbs' reading rotunda, known as the Radcliffe Camera (1749). Guided tours of one and a half hours take you to all the key areas. Children under 14 are not admitted on tours.

Carfax Tower
Carfax, OX1 4AF (01865 792653). **Open** *Apr-Oct* 10am-5.30pm (last entry 5.10pm). *Nov-Mar* 10am-3.30pm (last entry 3.10pm). **Admission** £1.40; 70p concessions. **No credit cards**.

Pondlife at the **University Botanic Garden**.

All that remains of St Martin's Church – demolished to make room for traffic in 1896 – this 13th-century tower offers spectacular views of the city and the hills beyond.

Christ Church Picture Gallery
Oriel Square, OX1 1DP (01865 276172/www.chch. ox.ac.uk). **Open** *Apr-Sept* 10.30am-5pm Mon-Sat; 2-5pm Sun. *Oct-Mar* 10.30am-1pm, 2-4.30pm Mon-Sat; 2-4.30pm Sun. **Admission** £2; £1 concessions; free under-12s. **No credit cards**.
The college has its own gallery, which includes work by Leonardo, Titian, Tintoretto, Van Dyk and Frans Hals. Note: the admission charge is on top of that paid for entry to Christ Church College.

Martyrs' Memorial
St Giles'.
George Gilbert Scott's 1841 Gothic spire commemorates the Protestant martyrs Cranmer, Latimer and Ridley, who were burnt on the orders of Queen Mary around the corner in Broad Street, opposite Balliol College.

Modern Art Oxford
30 Pembroke Street, OX1 1BP (01865 722733/www. modernartoxford.org.uk). **Open** 10am-5pm Tue-Sat; noon-5pm Sun (closed between exhibitions so phone to check). **Admission** free.

A rather swanky converted brewery with all the hard lines and exposed concrete you would expect of a contemporary art gallery. There is no permanent exhibition, so it's a popular space for touring works by the biggest names on the contemporary art scene (the likes of Jack and Dinos Chapman have exhibited here). If you're in Oxford on a day when there is no exhibition at the gallery, you can still visit the decent basement café for filling if basic grub.

Museum of the History of Science
Broad Street, OX1 3AZ (01865 277280/www.mhs. ox.ac.uk). **Open** noon-4pm Tue-Sat; 2-5pm Sun. **Admission** free; donations welcome.
The original premises of the Ashmolean, this 17th-century building is crammed with a fascinating collection of timepieces, astrolabes, microscopes and other scientific ephemera, including Einstein's blackboard (he was a Christ Church man).

Museum of Oxford
St Aldate's, OX1 1DZ (01865 252761/www.oxford. gov.uk/museum). **Open** 10am-4.30pm Tue-Fri; 10am-5pm Sat; noon-4pm Sun. **Admission** £2; 50p-£1.50 concessions. **No credit cards**.
This museum provides an informative history of the city and university and the land on which it stands. The story begins in prehistoric time, and a number of the exhibits are showing their age.

Official Walking Tours
Meet at Oxford Information Centre, Broad Street, OX1 3AS (01865 726871/www.visitoxford.org). **Tours** 11am, 2pm daily. **Tickets** (limited to 19 places) £6.50; £3.50 concessions. **Credit** MC, V.
Pushed for time? Experienced guides take you round the colleges and historic buildings on these guided tours that last around two hours. The company also runs occasional Inspector Morse tours (the grumpy fictional detective called Oxford his home) and ghost tours; other tours can be arranged and pre-booked on request.

The Oxford Story
6 Broad Street, OX1 3AJ (01865 790055/www. oxfordstory.co.uk). **Open** *Sept-June* 10am-5pm daily. *July, Aug* 9.30am-5.30pm daily. **Admission** £6.75; £5.25-£5.75 concessions; family ticket £22. **Credit** DC, MC, V.
Tacky touristy history of the university, in which visitors sit behind mobile desks that trundle past a series of lame exhibits. Popular with Americans and teachers seeking a break. Lasts 25 minutes but seems longer.

Oxford University Botanic Garden
Rose Lane, OX1 4AZ (01865 286690). **Open** 9am-4.15pm (last admission) daily. **Admission** £2.50; free under-12s. **No credit cards**.
In a city not short of pretty sights, this is one of the most attractive. The botanic garden is the oldest in Great Britain and has occupied this idyllic spot by the Cherwell for more than 375 years. Originally intended to grow medicinal plants, its five acres now contain a huge and diverse collection of plants, amid tended lawns, rock gardens, water features and glasshouses. Those obsessed by all things green and oxygen-oozing will adore it; non-horticulturists will just think it's a lovely place to have a picnic.

Pitt Rivers Museum

Parks Road, OX1 3PP (01865 270927/www.prm. ox.ac.uk). **Open** noon-4.30pm Mon-Sat; 2-4.30pm Sun. **Admission** free; donations welcome.

Quirky anthropological annexe of the University Museum (*see below*) that is chock-a-block with such arcane delights as voodoo dolls, shrunken heads and a totem poll. Spectacular in a donnish way, and a real winner with children.

Punting

The quintessential Oxbridge pastime, punting has developed from a form of freight transportation to a lazy summer pursuit – the punter propels the boat with a long pole from the hollow of the stern. There are two principal departure points on the Cherwell: Magdalen Bridge Boathouse (01865 202643; punt hire £10 per hour weekdays, £12 per hour weekends) or the Cherwell Boathouse on Bardwell Road (01865 515978; punt hire £10 per hr weekdays, £12 per hr weekends). Teddy bear not included. Queues can get silly in the summer.

Sheldonian Theatre

Broad Street, OX1 3AZ (01865 277299/www.sheld on.ox.ac.uk). **Open** *Mar-Oct* 10am-12.30pm, 2-4.30pm Mon-Sat. *Nov-Feb* 10am-12.30pm, 2-3.30pm Mon-Sat. Closed for ceremonies, phone to check. **Admission** £1.50; £1 concessions. **No credit cards.**

This Restoration theatre was built by Christopher Wren, a Wadham College old boy. It was intended to be used purely for degree ceremonies, although these days the grimacing cherubs painted on the ceiling also look down on concerts. The hirsute busts outside, sometimes referred to as emperors, are actually stylised versions of non-specific, off-the-shelf Romans.

Turrill Sculpture Garden

Behind the library, South Parade, Summertown (01865 310587/www.summertown2000.org.uk). **Open** (library) 9.30am-5pm Mon, Thur, Fri; 9.30am-7pm Tue; 9.30am-1pm Sat. **Admission** free.

A sculpture garden created in 2000 that shows the work of local sculptors in a little oasis behind Summertown Library. All work is for sale.

University Museum

Parks Road, OX1 3PW (01865 272950/www. oum.ox.ax.uk). **Open** noon-5pm daily. **Admission** free; donations welcome.

A taxidermist's dream, this natural history museum is stuffed with numerous beasties and dinosaurs. It's worth visiting purely for its Victorian Gothic architecture and the vaulted glass-and-iron roof. Hidden at the back is the Pitt Rivers Museum (*see above*).

Where to stay

Oxford is not blessed with the world's greatest accommodation, and what there is available tends to be expensive due to the town's year-round popularity with tourists, businessmen and parents of students. The places listed below are recommended, but you could also try the following: **Oxford Spires** (Abingdon Road, 01865 324324/www.fourpillars.co.uk,

doubles £169), which has 115 en suite rooms; **St Thomas' Mews** (58 St Thomas Street, 01865 254000/www.oxstay.co.uk, doubles £130), which offers luxury short-stay central apartments; or **Eastgate** (High Street, 0870 4008201/www.heritage-hotels.co.uk, doubles £95-£145), a secluded 17th-century coaching inn. **Parklands Hotel** (Linton Road, 01865 554374/www.oxfordcity.co.uk/hotels/parkland, doubles £89) is a cheaper option, 15 minutes' walk down Banbury Road.

Bath Place Hotel

4 & 5 Bath Place, OX1 3SQ (01865 791812/www. bathplace.co.uk). **Rates** £95-£130 single occupancy; £105-£160 double; £140-£185 suite. **Rooms** (all en suite) 10 double; 2 twin; 2 suites. **Credit** AmEx, DC, MC, V.

Smack in the centre of town, down a little alleyway enlivened by the presence of the popular, studenty Turf Tavern (with enclosed beer garden), this hotel is housed in converted 16th-century Jacobean weavers' cottages. The rooms carry the authentic stamp of age, with low exposed bonce-threatening beams, wonky floors and whitewashed walls. Sections of the old city wall can be seen in the restaurant area. Children and small dogs accepted. No smoking throughout.

Burlington House

374 Banbury Road, OX2 7PP (01865 513513/www. burlington-house.co.uk). **Rates** £40 single; £58 single en suite; £75 double; £80 queen-size; £85 king-size. **Rooms** 6 single (3 en suite); 6 twin/double (all en suite). **Credit** AmEx, MC, V.

Like the Victorian house has avoided the fussy chintz of most B&Bs and is a stylish, small hotel with big rooms and contemporary designs and furnishings. The hearty, *almost* healthy breakfasts are highly recommended, with own-made bread and biscuits to go alongside the locally sourced ingredients. Two rooms in a converted garage have disabled access. No smoking throughout.

Gables Guesthouse

6 Cumnor Hill, OX2 9HA (01865 862153/www. oxfordcity.co.uk/accom/gables). **Rates** £38 single; £60 double/twin. **Rooms** (all en suite) 2 single; 2 double; 2 twin. **Credit** MC, V.

Again, this B&B is a hike out of town, down the Botley Road. Landlady Sally Tompkins is rightly proud of her AA Landlady of the Year award from 1998; be assured that standards has not slipped in the meantime. The guesthouse is situated in lovely, large gardens, and the bedrooms are clean and well sized. No smoking throughout. Children welcome.

Galaxie Hotel

180 Banbury Road, OX2 7DT (01865 515688/www. galaxie.co.uk). **Rates** £49 single standard; £60 single en suite; £85 double/twin standard; £88 double/twin en suite; £115 executive. **Rooms** 6 single (4 en suite); 28 double/twin/family (24 en suite). **Credit** MC, V.

The Galaxie is a large, ivy-clad building in Summertown that strikes a mid-point both in price and location

Oxford revisited

When you first see the majestic colleges of Oxford, something will probably catch in the back of your throat. Whether that something is pride or envy probably depends upon how you feel about the stranglehold this smallish provincial town has had on the British establishment for the past 800 years. A roll call of the alumni from even the smallest of the 40 or so separate and self-sufficient colleges would shame almost any other seat of learning in the country. Christ Church alone can count 13 prime ministers who have passed through its ancient doors.

The French are to blame, apparently. One account of the university's origins is that the first students were English exiles from the University of Paris, which expelled all foreigners in 1167. Another myth says that King Alfred (he of cake-burning fame) was the first patron of the university. The third and most likely story is that the first students came into the town from local monasteries and the education industry expanded from there. Whatever the truth, Oxford has been an academic centre since the 12th century. Its ten oldest colleges all date from before 1438. History is everywhere.

While the origins of the university are in question, and the colleges can't yet decide between themselves which is the oldest (University and Merton have been slugging that one out for centuries), the beauty of the town's architecture is undeniable. There are many outstanding features to seek out, whether it be Hertford's bridge, Christ Church's Wren-designed Tom Quad, the Hawksmoor-designed fellows-only All Souls, the gardens of Magdalen (where deer run free) or the greenery of Trinity; even the much-maligned modernist St Catherine's is an outstanding example of its era and

between the city centre hotels and peripheral B&Bs. Breakfast is taken in a large, light conservatory that looks out on to fabulous gardens, complete with a pond filled with koi carp. Rooms are nice and clean, with the one most recently converted from offices boasting a splendid fireplace and ornaments brought back by the owner from his honeymoon. Smoking allowed in the lounge only. Children and dogs welcome.

Old Bank Hotel

92-4 High Street, OX1 4BN (01865 799599/www. oldbank-hotel.co.uk). **Rates** £140 single occupancy; £160-£235 double; £265-£320 suite. Breakfast £12 (Eng); £9 (cont). **Rooms** (all en suite) 4 single; 35 double; 2 suites. **Credit** AmEx, DC, MC, V.
The über-stylish Old Bank sits proudly on the High Street in a converted bank (you might have guessed that for yourself). It's all very tasteful, in a sleek and modern – if slightly flash and antiseptic – way, with impeccable furnishings, marble bathrooms, digital CD players and original art in every room (check the Stanley Spencer sketches that practically wallpaper the bar area). Views are splendid, among the best in the city. Breakfast is served at the neighbouring Quod restaurant (both are owned by Jeremy Mogford, the Oxford hotelier and restaurateur also responsible for the Old Parsonage Hotel (*see below*) and Gee's restaurant (*see p206*). Children welcome.

Old Parsonage Hotel

1 Banbury Road, OX2 6NN (01865 310210/www. oxford-hotels-restaurants.co.uk). **Rates** £124 single; £153 double. Breakfast £12 (Eng); £9 (cont). **Rooms** (all en suite) 26 double; 4 deluxe. **Credit** AmEx, DC, MC, V.

Built in 1308, the Old Parsonage – an ivy-clad landmark next to St Giles' – is as old a building as almost any in Oxford. Oscar Wilde stayed here as an undergraduate, and before being pressed into service as a hotel it had served as a nunnery and a leper colony. Given it's age and history, the rumours of various ghosts should not come as a great surprise. These days the comfortable, if slightly farmhousey, rooms have an authentic creakiness; some lead to a delightful secluded garden where you can sip your aperitif in isolation, others to a secret roof terrace where you can worship the sun. The bar serves breakfast, lunch, afternoon tea and dinner, and there is 24-hour room service. Service is excellent throughout. No children, but dogs are accepted.

The Randolph

Beaumont Street, OX1 2LN (0870 400 8200/www. heritage-hotels.com). **Rates** £120 single; £140-£160 double; £180 half-tester; £200 four-poster; £300-£500 suite. Breakfast £14.95 (Eng); £7 (cont). **Rooms** (all en suite) 20 single; 15 twin; 51 double; 13 half-tester; 2 four-poster; 10 suites. **Credit** AmEx, DC, MC, V.
The most prestigious hotel in Oxford occupies a dominant city centre site right opposite the Ashmolean Museum and next to the Martyrs' Monument. The central staircase next to the check-in desk sets the scene – massive, grand and humbling. There are seven classes of room, though all come with CD players and large bathrooms. The Morse bar is popular with tourists, while the new Oyster bar has made good use of the old restaurant area. There are also plenty of function rooms of varying size, and plans are under way to build a health spa and to add a further 40 rooms to the 100 or so already in use. Children are welcome, as are dogs (as long as they stay out of the bar).

boasts more Grade I-listed features than the much-photographed Christ Church.

The colleges still like to pride themselves on their perceived differences to each other. So Merton and St John's (the richest college and Tony Blair's alma mater) are regarded as the most stuffy and academic, Christ Church is full of snobs, Balliol people are left-leaning, Jesus is for the Welsh and St Edmund Hall (Teddy Hall) is home to rugger buggers. These differences are kept alive by the university's traditions, such as the wearing of gowns (sub fusc) for all exams (plus different coloured buttonholes depending on which year the student is from). At matriculation first-year students are made full members of the university by donning the sub fusc and marching crocodile fashion through town to the Sheldonian Theatre for a ceremony instituted in 1420. May Day is another

big event in Oxford's calendar, as the choirboys of Magdalen sing a Latin hymn at dawn and everybody else gets drunk and jumps in the river.

You can find out much about these various traditions by joining the tourists trailing around the largest colleges, most of which charge a small fee for the privilege. Christ Church and Magdalen colleges are particularly worthy of a look and the former also has its own gallery (*see p202*). However, some of the smaller colleges, such as Somerville (Margaret Thatcher's old college, with a hall named after her to prove it) can be just as interesting purely because they are not so geared towards tourists and so provide a much better idea of what it must be like to study in them. For all, opening times are subject to private events and exams. Details of these are displayed at the porter's lodges by the gates.

Royal Oxford Hotel

Park End Street, OX1 1HR (01865 248432/www. royaloxfordhotel.co.uk). **Rates** £109 single; £129 twin/double; £140 family room. **Rooms** (all en suite) 1 single; 2 family; 10 twin; 13 double. **Credit** AmEx, MC, V.

Next to the station, the Royal Oxford has worked hard to lose that clinical Travelodge look and offers perfectly clean and comfortable rooms at rates that are reasonable for the centre of Oxford. Each one has a luxury shower, Sky TV and tea- and coffee-making facilities. Popular with a business clientele due to its location next to the station. Children and dogs welcome.

Where to eat & drink

While Oxford has a lot of good-quality restaurants, there are not that many in the city centre. Cafés are a better bet here: there's the **Grand Café** (84 High Street, 01865 204463) on the site of the first coffee house in England (opened in 1641) and the **Rose** (51 High Street, 01865 244429), which does traditional English breakfasts and classic cream teas. **Edamame** (15 Holywell Street, 01865 246916) is a tiny and much-loved hole-in-the-wall place serving excellent Japanese food. Close to the station, newcomer **Savannah** (17 Park End Street; 01865 793793), a minimalist accompaniment to the Royal Oxford Hotel (*see above*), has decent basics and an innovative wine list (you can try before you buy). **Quod** (92-4 High Street, 01865 202505) is attached to the sleek and modern Old

Bank Hotel (*see p204*). It serves a stylish take on Italian classics, and while the food is fine it is probably the central location and trendy surroundings that attract the customers. The lack of vegetarian dishes is a disappointment.

Jericho is a groovy place to hang out and eat. **Freud Arts Café** (119 Walton Street, 01865 311171) is a café in a neo-classical former church, complete with pews and stained glass windows; it serves pizzas, coffee and cocktails. **Le Petit Blanc** (71-2 Walton Street, 01865 324930) is a popular, fun brasserie from Raymond Blanc.

Down the vaguely bohemian Cowley Road are a large number of curry houses and Chinese takeaways, as well as **Mario** (No.103, 01865 722955), an excellent pizzeria, and the **Hi-Lo Jamaican Eating House** (No.70, 01865 725984), a Caribbean restaurant with a menu that changes daily. **Kazbar** (No.25-7, 01865 202920) offers Spanish and North African tapas-style food in a Moorish interior. **Aziz Indian Cuisine** (No.228-230, 01865 794945) has good Indian food in a smart and light restaurant. **Café Coco** (No.23, 01865 200232) is a perennially popular pizza place that serves a famous 'breakfast pizza'.

In Headington, Iranian restaurant the **Flame** (1 The Parade, Windmill Road, 01865 760309) serves great kebabs and fruity Persian stews, while **Bar Meze** (146 London Road, 01865 761106) is a modish Turkish meze joint.

The Cotswolds

Oxford pubs are plentiful, but neither cheap nor quiet. Among the more studenty choices are the **King's Arms** at the corner of Holywell Street, the **Bear** on Blue Boar Street (low ceilings and a 'fascinating' collection of ties), and the **Turf Tavern**, Oxford's oldest inn, between Hertford and New colleges. They must put something in the beer at the **Eagle & Child** (St Giles') – it was the pub of choice of both J R R Tolkien and C S Lewis. The part-thatched **Perch** on Binsey Lane has a big garden and children's play area. The **Trout Inn** at Lower Wolvercote (01865 302071) is a beauty; it's just beside a weir and serves good pub food, but is very popular with students and so can get royally packed.

Branca Bar Italian Brasserie

111 Walton Street, OX2 6AJ (01865 556111/www. branca-restaurants.com). **Food served** noon-11pm Mon-Thur, Sun; noon-11.30pm Fri, Sat. **Main courses** £8.25-£16.95. **Set lunch** (noon-5pm Mon-Fri) £5 1 course. **Set dinner** (5-7pm Mon-Fri) £10 2 courses. **Credit** AmEx, MC, V.

Bright, confident, bustling: the three-year-old Branca is well suited to Jericho. This large, trend-conscious bar-brasserie offers a well-sourced collection of modern Italian dishes: char-grilled squid salad, say, or a creamy, parsley-speckled smoked haddock risotto topped with a perfect poached egg. The menu also has room for stone-baked pizzas, a clutch of pastas and more substantial mains, such as roast monkfish with smoked Italian ham and braised lentils. Breezy young women in white tops and jeans provide the service. Cocktails, an interesting Italian wine choice and a well-thought-out children's menu also augur well.

Cherwell Boathouse Restaurant

Bardwell Road, OX2 6ST (01865 552746). **Food served** 12.15-2pm; 6.30-9pm daily. **Main courses** £12-£14.50. **Set lunch** (Mon-Fri £19.50 3 courses, (Sat, Sun) £20.50 3 courses. **Set dinner** £18 2 courses, £22.50 3 courses. **Credit** AmEx, DC, MC, V.

Based at one of the city's major punting termini, diners at the Cherwell Boathouse Restaurant might find it difficult to shake off the suspicion that an evening there is more about the exquisite waterside location than the quality of food on offer. The menu features the likes of sweetcorn and spring onion risotto or grilled fillet of salmon with mustard and basil butter. The standard isn't great, but the wine list is exceptional. And it really is a beautiful place for a meal.

Chiang Mai Kitchen

Kemp Hall Passage, 130A High Street, OX1 4DH (01865 202233/www.chiangmaikitchen.co.uk). **Food served** noon-2.30pm, 6-10.15pm Mon-Thur; noon-2.30pm, 6-10.30pm Fri, Sat; noon-2.30pm, 6-11pm Sun. **Main courses** £7-£10. **Credit** AmEx, DC, MC, V.

Like much of Oxford, it is the surroundings that make this popular, upmarket Thai so memorable. The beautiful 14th-century building that houses the restaurant is hidden down a dinky side street off the High Street opposite the covered market. The main dining room upstairs is more reminiscent of an Edwardian gentlemen's club

than a modern Thai restaurant. The food is generally excellent – the starter of rice dumplings stuffed with pork had delightful little nuggets of water chestnut hidden in the mix. The stir-fried beef with garlic was a tad chewy, but all fish dishes proved successful and satisfying. There is a high turnaround of customers here, for proof of that look no further than the paper tablecloths, so service can sometimes seem slightly abrupt if attentive. Excellent value, though, and a lovely setting.

Gee's

61A Banbury Road, OX2 6PE (01865 553540/www. gees-restaurant.co.uk). **Food served** noon-2.30pm, 6-10.30pm Mon-Thur; noon-2.30pm, 6-11pm Fri, Sat; noon-3.30pm Sun. **Main courses** £10.50-£18.95. **Set lunches** (Mon-Fri) £12.50 2 courses, £16 3 courses. **Set dinners** £24.95 2 courses. **Credit** AmEx, MC, V.

A capacious Victorian conservatory with wrought-iron candelabras and bamboo chairs makes an impressive dining venue. Gee's offers a menu suffused with Mediterranean modishness, plus seasonal 'star dishes' (pan-fried sea bass with tagliatelle and samphire, say) and some modern takes on standards (marinated pork steak with black pudding and apple slices). Standards can slip occasionally, but on the whole Gee's deserves its popularity.

Liaison

29 Castle Street, OX1 1LJ (01865 242944/251481). **Food served** 6.30-11.30pm Mon-Thur; 6.30pm-12.30am Fri, Sat; 7-11pm Sun. **Main courses** £1.80-£28. **Set dinner** £14.95-£18 3 courses. **Credit** AmEx, MC, V.

To find Liaison in a quaint building in Oxford is astonishing, for this is a real Chinese restaurant attracting real Chinese diners. Come at lunchtime for dim sum that's on a par with many in London's Chinatown (if occasionally of indelicate construction). On a recent visit, a moutain of gelatinous pig's skin paired with tender squid testicles was a textural treat, grilled pork dumplings were nicely scorched, and king prawn cheung fun featured slithery fresh pasta. The full menu, too, contains food rarely seen outside Chinatowns: hot-pots such as belly pork wth preserved vegetables and textural juxtapositions such as fried aubergine with minced prawns. Service is abundant.

The Old Parsonage

1 Banbury Road, OX2 6NN (01865 310210). **Food served** 7-10.30am, noon-2.30pm, 3-5.30pm, 6-10.30pm daily. **Main courses** £10-£15. **Credit** AmEx, DC, MC, V.

For a fairly posh hotel in the centre of Oxford, the main dining space of the Old Parsonage is wonderfully informal – more like a pub lounge than a restaurant, with comfy armchairs, low tables and walls plastered with Oxford-themed prints and photographs. Food is MOR Modern European: seared tuna; salmon and dill fish cakes; rump of Welsh lamb with roast peppers and raspberry jus. The excellent twice-baked spinach and parmesan soufflé hinted at the heights the kitchen can hit. Most starters are also available as main courses, which isn't a bad option. There is a pretty sunken front garden to eat in on sunny days and the restaurant is also open for breakfast, lunch and highly recommended scone and cream-crammed afternoon teas.

South Oxfordshire

Historic market towns on the Thames overlooked by the Chilterns and the Downs.

The area south of Oxford presents a mixed landscape. To the south-east is gentle, unspectacular countryside, well cultivated and packed with carefully groomed commuter villages and rich farmland. The River Thames wends its way northwards through the university town and then west towards its source in Gloucestershire. Further south, the ancient Ridgeway path crosses the Berkshire Downs, and as it works west, the land becomes altogether more undulating. Beyond Wantage there's a pagan dash of the primitive, as the impressionistic slash of the chalk White Horse fuels countless local legends and gives its name to the adjacent valley, the Vale of the White Horse.

Abingdon, painted by Turner and admired by Ruskin, is the oldest continuously occupied town in England and the largest in the Vale. Sadly choked by traffic at the weekends, but with a good Thames-side setting and pleasant river walks, it contains the remains of an abbey that was founded in the late seventh century, a row of 15th-century almshouses still in use (the Long Alley Almshouses) and the magnificent English Baroque County Hall (now a museum), built by a protégé of Christopher Wren. River trips to Oxford by steamer leave from Nags Head Island between May and September (**Salter Brothers**, 01865 243421/www. salterssteamers.co.uk) and there are boats and bicycles for hire to help you explore the surrounding countryside (enquire at the Tourist Information Centre on Bridge Street, or *see* *p208* **Bike hire**). Just south of Abingdon is the village of **Sutton Courtenay**. The churchyard there contains the grave of one Eric Arthur Blair, better known as George Orwell.

The other main towns in the area are **Faringdon**, to the west, off the A420, which was besieged by Cromwell's troops during the Civil War and is now particularly noteworthy for Lord Berners' 140-foot-tall brick folly, built on the outskirts in the 1930s, and some charming 16th-century tombs in the church that overlooks the town. Further south and east, the town of **Wantage** was the birthplace, in 848, of Alfred the Great, warrior, statesman, cake burner and educational pioneer. His statue is the centrepiece of the pretty town square, which is also the site of a twice-weekly market (Wednesdays and Saturdays). Behind the large town church lies a small garden park with a set of stones commemorating the fact that the poet laureate John Betjeman once lived in the town.

At **Wallingford**, a town that strategically straddles the Thames to the east, there are the disappointingly meagre remains of Wallingford Castle (one of the largest in the country until it was dismantled by Oliver Cromwell), Saxon earthworks and a fine medieval bridge, as well as antiques shops galore. South of Wallingford, the stretch of the Thames occupied by the Beetle & Wedge (*see p209*) was immortalised by Kenneth Graham in *The Wind in the Willows*, and by Jerome K Jerome. The hotel is one of several that claim he was in residence when he wrote *Three Men in a Boat*.

Among the many pretty villages in the area are the thatched and half-timbered **Blewbury**, off the A417 south of Didcot, and **Buscot** (off the A417 beyond Faringdon to the west, whose church of St Mary contains a superb set of stained-glass windows by Edward Burne-Jones, manufactured by Morris & Company. The chancel dates from around 1200. **Buscot Park** is the home to impressive gardens and the magnificent paintings of the Faringdon Collection.

Nearby are two small churches worth a visit. In **Compton Beauchamp** is a quirky little white church dating from the 15th century, but with plenty of 20th-century craftsmanship inside, including an entrancing vine mural in the chancel. To the east is **Uffington**'s 13th-century early Gothic church, with an 18th-century octagonal tower – a church so admired by John Betjeman that he became churchwarden here.

By train from London

Trains for **Didcot Parkway** leave **Paddington** up to five times an hour (twice an hour on Sundays). The journey takes between 45mins and 1hr 20mins. Info: www.greatwesterntrains.co.uk or www.thamestrains.co.uk.

An altogether grander affair is the splendid
abbey at **Dorchester-on-Thames**. Built
on the site of a Saxon cathedral, it has been
a centre of Christianity for nearly 14 centuries.
The present building was begun during the
12th century and still contains a Norman font,
medieval floor tiles, an intriguing Tree of
Jesse window and the 13th-century effigy
of an unknown knight in the act of drawing
his sword, said to have influenced Henry
Moore. Take a wander around the village along
the (Roman) Watling Lane and past the grand
antiques shops. Sleepy **Ewelme**, a few miles
south-east of Dorchester and on the edge of the
Chiltern Hills, boasts a picturesque 15th-
century church with almshouses and school
(founded by Alice Chaucer, granddaughter of
the poet Geoffrey Chaucer). The church is in
demand as a location for TV dramas; the school
is now a state primary. A brook (Ewelme means
'spring source' in old English) runs the length
of the village, alongside the main street.

Alice Chaucer's **Ewelme primary school**.

What to see & do

Tourist Information Centres

*25 Bridge Street, Abingdon, OX14 3HN (01235
522711/www.whitehorsedc.gov.uk/tourism).* **Open**
Apr-Oct 10am-5pm Mon-Sat; 1.30-4.15pm Sun.
Nov-Mar 10am-4pm Mon-Fri; 9.30am-2.30pm Sat.
*7A Market Place, Faringdon, SN7 7HL (01367
242191/www.faringdon.org).* **Open** *Apr-Oct* 10am-
5pm Mon-Fri; 10am-1pm Sat. *Nov-Mar* 10am-1pm
Mon-Sat.

Bike hire

*Pedal Power, 92 The Vineyard, Oxford Road,
Abingdon, OX14 3PB (01235 525123).*
If you're coming from Oxford, you'll need to catch a bus
or taxi to Abingdon as there's no train station here.

Buscot Park

*Faringdon, SN7 8BU (01367 240786/www.national
trust.org.uk/www.buscot-park.com).* **Open** *House*
Apr-Sept 2-6pm Wed-Fri, 2-6pm 2nd & 4th Sat, Sun
of mth. Closed Oct-Mar. *Grounds* Apr-Sept 2-6pm
Mon-Fri, 2nd & 4th Sat, Sun of mth. Closed Oct-Mar.
Admission (NT) *House & grounds* £6.50; £3.75
concessions; free under-5s. *Grounds only* £4.50; £2.25
concessions; free under-5s. **Credit** MC, V.
An imposing 18th-century monument to the lucrative
rewards of City finance and Empire trade, Buscot Park
also played a fascinating role in mid 20th-century left-
wing politics and cultural life. Under the second Lord
Faringdon, the flamboyant socialist Gavin Henderson,
Buscot epitomised the peculiarly 1930s intermingling of
aestheticism, connoisseurship, radical politics and country-house decadence. These days, it is better known for
an astonishing Peto water garden, and a large and
impressive art collection. Rembrandt rubs shoulders
with Rubens and Rossetti, while the highlight is probably Edward Burne-Jones's vast pre-Raphaelite mural,
the *Legend of the Briar Rose*. A gem.

Didcot Rail Centre

*Entrance through Didcot Parkway station, Didcot,
OX11 7NJ (01235 817200/www.didcotrailway
centre.org.uk).* **Open** *End May-early Sept* 10am-5pm
daily. *Early Sept-end May* 10am-4pm Sat, Sun &
school hols. **Admission** £4; £3-£3.50 concessions.
Steam days £8; £5-£6.50 concessions. **Credit** MC, V.
A homage to Isambard Kingdom Brunel's Great
Western Railway and a trainspotters' paradise. It
contains a collection of steam locomotives, either
lovingly restored or in the process of being renovated,
and a variety of GWR passenger coaches and freight
wagons. There's a level crossing and signalbox, a
travelling post office and mail exchange, and, for the
really besotted, special Railway Experience Days when
punters can drive a steam engine.

Kingston Bagpuize
House & Garden

*Kingston Bagpuize, nr Abingdon, OX13 5AX (01865
820259/www.kingstonbagpuizehouse.org.uk).* **Open**
Feb-Nov selected dates only; phone for details.
Closed Dec, Jan. **Admission** *House & garden* £4.50;
£2.50 concessions (no under-5s). *Garden only* £2; free
under-16s. **No credit cards.**
A handsome red-brick and wood-panelled baroque
house set in mature parkland containing an early
Georgian gazebo.

Little Wittenham Nature Reserve

*Information 01865 407792/www.northmoor
trust.co.uk.*
The reserve incorporates Little Wittenham Wood and
Wittenham Clumps. Comfrey and teasel grow along the
woodland paths and more than 30 different species of
butterfly have been spotted in the area (so bring your
net), although it is better known for its amphibians and
dragonflies. Climb to the top of Round Hill for expansive views over Oxfordshire, the Cotswolds and the

Chilterns, while on Castle Hill you can find the site of the remains of an Iron Age hill fort. A riverside walk from here leads to Dorchester Abbey.

Wellplace Zoo

Ipsden, OX10 6QZ (01491 680473/www.wellplace zoo.fsnet.co.uk). Open Apr-Sept 10am-5pm daily. Oct-Mar 10am-5pm Sat, Sun. Admission £2.50; £1 concessions. No credit cards.

A modest, idiosyncratic collection of real farmyard animals, exotic and domestic birds, and life-size replica dinosaurs. There seems to be a rather ramshackle air about the place, but the animals are undoubtedly spirited and remain fairly happy. No surprises, then, but terrific fun for younger kids, who can feed and pet the goats and donkeys, and attempt to converse with the talking parrot.

White Horse & Ridgeway

The oldest and possibly most famous of the 17 white horses in England, this one isn't etched into the hillside like the others, but made from several 10-foot wide, chalk-filled trenches that have to be weeded and refilled from time to time – a service performed by locals for generations, but now carried out by the National Trust. The figure has been dated back nearly 3,000 years to the late Bronze or early Iron Age, and may have acted as a banner for the inhabitants of Uffington Castle, the hill fort whose remains lie just above the horse's head. The distinctive, flat-topped hill below the horse is Dragon Hill, where St George reputedly slew the beast – the grass never grows on the top on account of all the blood spilt there. Below the horse are the glacial terraces known as the Giants Steps, that in turn lead to a deep combe known as the Manger, where the horse reputedly feeds. And about a mile to the west along the ancient Ridgeway path is the prehistoric chambered tomb known as Wayland's Smithy, where legend has it that horses left overnight would be shod by Wayland, the Anglo-Saxon smith god. The White Horse and Ridgeway path are accessible up a narrow path leading off the B4507; although the approach is spectacular, the horse is best seen from a distance, near Fernham (south of Faringdon) or from the Highworth to Shrivenham road. The Ridgeway is popular with horse-riders and cyclists as well as walkers, and can get very muddy.

Where to stay

There is no shortage of unremarkable wayside inns, basic B&Bs or rooms above pubs in the area, though their proximity to London and Oxford tends to be reflected in their prices. For instance, the **Plough** in Clifton Hampden has eight rooms (01865 407811, doubles £82.50), the nicest of which are the ones in the separate barn; since the pub changed hands as we went to press, changes may be afoot. Here are a few other noteworthy options.

Beetle & Wedge Hotel

Ferry Lane, Moulsford-on-Thames, OX10 9JF (01491 651381/fax 01491 651376/www. beetleandwedge.co.uk). Rates £99-£135 single

occupancy; £175-£250 double/twin. Extra bed for child £25. **Rooms** (all en suite) 10 double/twin. **Credit** AmEx, DC, MC, V.

This splendid hotel overlooking the Thames has fabulous views and beautiful gardens unfolding down to the riverbank. Rooms are generally spacious and comfortable, some have wonderful bathrooms, and it's worth paying extra for one with a clear river view. There are two restaurants: a formal dining room and the more relaxed Boathouse restaurant (*see p210*), but the river is the star, and the prospect of a cool glass of wine by the water's edge on a sunny summer's afternoon is what it's all about. It's popular with weddings and Henley Regatta goers, and the owners suggest booking at least three months ahead for the summer. Children and dogs welcome. All bedrooms are no-smoking.

From M4, take J12 towards Reading; take A4 S; at second roundabout take A340 towards Pangbourne; then A329 towards Streatley and Moulsford; turn down Ferry Lane in the village; hotel is at end of lane.

The Craven

Fernham Road, Uffington, SN7 7RD (01367 820449/www.thecraven.co.uk). Rates £30 single; £40-£60 single occupancy; £55-£85 double/four-poster/family room. Rooms 1 single; 1 double; 2 double (en suite, half-testers); 1 four-poster (en suite); 1 family room. Credit AmEx, MC, V.

This is a wonderful 300-year-old thatched cottage in pretty Uffington village, near the White Horse and the Ridgeway. Carol Wadsworth treats her guests as part of the family, so breakfast is shared by guests at a large table in the kitchen, with french windows opening on to the terrace and a free and friendly atmosphere. One of the best rooms, the Elizabethan double, with chintz-hung four-poster, is on the ground floor; the others are up the crooked stairs and down winding passageways stocked with faded family photos and antiques. Children welcome by arrangement. No smoking throughout.

Turn off the B4057 for Kingston Lisle. Go through Kingston Lisle; after about 2 miles you are in Uffington; take first right out of village after the church; after about 3 mile the Craven is on the left hand side.

Crazy Bear Hotel

Bear Lane, Stadhampton, OX44 7UR (01865 890714/fax 01865 400481/www.crazybearhotel. co.uk). Rates £60-£110 single occupancy; £100-£150 double; £250-£280 suite; £160-£340 cottage. Rooms (all en suite) 5 double; 4 suites; 2 cottages (sleep 5 or 6). Credit AmEx, MC, V.

A 16th-century building refurbished in the mid 1990s, the Crazy Bear pursues a robustly individual approach based on the simple but sound proposition that a hotel should be nothing at all like home. Hence, bright colours and bold looks for each one of the individually designed, themed rooms. Crazy, yes, but fun, and infused with a passionate, idiosyncratic spirit; this will soon be further demonstrated by the plan to relocate the reception to an old Routemaster double-decker that is currently parked in the car park. It's not all frivolity: there are also two excellent restaurants (one a very popular Thai restaurant), a garden terrace, and a cosy bar offering champagne on draught. Children welcome.

J7 off M40 towards Birmingham; left at end of the slip road; follow A329 for 4 miles; straight across mini-roundabout; turn immediately left after petrol station; turn sharp left down Bear Lane.

The Cotswolds

George Hotel

High Street, Dorchester-on-Thames, OX10 7HH (01865 340404/fax 01865 341620/www.thegeorge dorchester.com). **Rates** £70 single; £80 single occupancy; £95 double/twin; £120 four-poster/ family room. **Rooms** (all en suite) 2 single; 13 double/twin; 2 four-poster; 1 family room. **Credit** AmEx, MC, V.

This 15th-century whitewashed coaching inn is a useful stopover in the heart of a beautiful historic village. The en suite rooms in the main building (there are more modern rooms in the courtyard annexe) are large and low-beamed, if a little gloomy, with some charming period furniture and the occasional beamed bathroom. There's a pleasant bar downstairs and a gorgeous high-roofed drawing room next to the restaurant. There's also a large garden at the back, and Dorchester Abbey and the village antiques shops are seconds away. Children and dogs welcome (guests' bedrooms only).

Le Manoir aux Quat' Saisons Relais Château

Church Road, Great Milton, OX44 7PD (01844 278881/fax 01844 278847/www.manoir.com). **Rates** £295-£470 double/twin; £525-£850 suite; £1,200 superior suite. **Rooms** (all en suite) 6 double/twin; 12 superior double; 14 suites. **Credit** AmEx, DC, MC, V.

The delights of chef Raymond Blanc's famous two-Michelin-starred restaurant need no introduction *(see p212)*. But Le Manoir also offers serious luxury as a hotel – not to mention being 'a hymn to contemporary style', according to Sir Terence Conran. There are 32 individually and extravagantly themed rooms, from traditional English to French farmhouse to Oriental, almost all with their own sitting-room and small garden terrace. You'll find music to welcome you into your room, and individually designed bathrooms, many of which seem to be sculpted from marble. Clearly, prices aren't what one would call 'competitive', so it's a good idea to preview the rooms on the website before booking, as it would be a shame to choose the wrong one at these prices. Children and dogs welcome (there are kennels in the grounds).
In Great Milton village centre, past the church.

Where to eat & drink

The area is peppered with good pubs. Among those recommended for eating as well as drinking are the **Red Lion** in Chalgrove (115 High Street, 01865 890625), which has been owned by the local church for several hundred years, and the **Pot Boys** bar in the George Hotel at Dorchester *(see above)*. The **Barley Mow** (01865 407847) in Clifton Hampden has a good garden, and is an ideal place to refuel after a Thameside walk, although the grub is pretty standard fare. The **Lamb** at Buckland (Lamb Lane, 01367 870484/www.thelambatbuckland. co.uk) takes food seriously, with a menu featuring robust, meat-based dishes.

Further south, the **Bear & Ragged Staff** in Cumnor has roaring log fires in winter and

sofas to slump in, while the **Star** at Sparsholt, near Wantage, is a simple, low-ceilinged inn featuring eccentric locals with one eye on the horse racing on the TV in the corner. The **White Hart** in Fyfield (Main Road, 01865 390585) boasts several rambling rooms, a high-ceilinged, beamed main hall filled with refectory tables and an extensive blackboard bar menu.

Beetle & Wedge

Ferry Lane, Moulsford, OX10 9JF (01491 651381/ www.beetleandwedge.co.uk). **Food served** *Brasserie* noon-2pm, 7-10pm daily. *Restaurant* 7-10pm Thur-Sat; noon-2pm Sun. **Main courses** *Brasserie* £12-£20. *Restaurant* £15-£21.50. **Set lunch** (restaurant) £37.50 3 courses. **Credit** AmEx, DC, MC, V.

This is the place to bring your parents for that special meal, or for a romantic getaway from the city, although best to come in a Range Rover if you don't want to feel out of place. The impeccably decorated dining room feels more like a sumptuous drawing room, and a grand conservatory overlooks the Thames as it glides idly by. The old boat house offers a large, more down-to-earth dining area. Whichever you choose, expect an enticing menu (vegetarians excepted). The dining room begins with an emphasis on fish – avocado and Cornish crab salad, gravadlax, or saffron risotto with parmesan shavings, asparagus, mussels, tiger prawns and langoustines. Monkfish or Dover sole are also available for mains, but this is when the meat muscles in – Gressingham duck, saddle of venison with chestnuts, beef with shallots or veal cutlets and liver. Cuts are tender and juicy, sauces sweet and subtle. There's a wider choice in the boathouse brasserie, but it's not much cheaper. All in all, though, it's well worth a mooring fee. For hotel, *see p209.*

Boar's Head

Church Street, Ardington, OX12 8QA (01235 833254). **Food served** 7-9pm Mon; noon-2pm, 7-9pm Tue-Thur; noon-2pm, 7-10pm Fri, Sat; noon-2.30pm Sun. **Main courses** £13.95-£16.95. **Credit** AmEx, MC, V.

Ardington is a pretty estate village just outside Wantage, and the Boar's Head is believed to have been an inn since the 18th century. These days, there is an eating area beyond the bar, in a couple of rooms opened up and lightened with the strategic use of simple blocks of colour. The Modern British food is equally bright and breezy. On a recent visit, a terrine of foie gras came with a drizzle of quince syrup and balsamic jelly, while roast tomato tatin was filled out with melted goat's cheese and a rather anonymous avocado salsa. The salsa was the weakest link in a fine selection of flavoured sauces – breast of duck came with a flighty elderflower sauce; steamed turbot with scallop mousse was sweetened by a rich chive butter sauce; and Dover sole with a truffle hollandaise. While the Boar's Head is not premier league, we've never left disappointed.

Crooked Billet

Newland Lane, Stoke Row, RG9 5PU (01491 681048/www.thecrookedbillet.co.uk). **Food served** noon-2.30pm, 7-10pm Mon-Fri; noon-10pm Sat, Sun.

Great Coxwell Barn

In a country dotted with grand castles, opulent country homes and beautifully crafted town houses, it might come as a surprise to learn that William Morris, that great aesthete and style guru (how he would hate that label) of the 19th century, considered the 'finest piece of architecture in England' to be a barn. Not a barn conversion, mind, but a plain stone barn on the outskirts of a pleasant but unremarkable Cotswold village.

Morris, who lived nearby at Kelmscott (see p213), describes this early 14th-century tithe barn as 'unapproachable in its dignity, as beautiful as a cathedral, yet with no ostentation of the builder's art'. Built between 1300 and 1310 from Cotswold stone-walling and supporting a colossal Cotswold slate roof, it served as a storage barn for the Cistercian grange based here, which was part of Beaulieu Abbey, far away near the New Forest. The walls are some four feet thick, with 28 buttresses supporting the monolith, and huge doorways at either end.

The barn is in cruciform, shape with several slit windows, although more noticeable are the numerous small square holes that would have held the masons' scaffold poles when it was built. The interior is 140 feet long and 40 feet wide, with a series of pillars reaching up from the dirt floor to the wooden rafters above. Some might be excited by the small, plain dovecote above the east door; others might itch to climb the rafters to drool over the pegged mortice-and-tenon joints and marvel at the lobed and keeled internal corbels of the doors. But you don't have to be an expert in craftsmanship to appreciate this building: you cannot fail to be impressed by its sheer scale, elegant simplicity and quiet dignity.

Great Coxwell Barn

Great Coxwell, nr Faringdon (01793 762209/www.nationaltrust.co.uk). **Open** free access. **Admission** free, donations welcome.

Main courses £10.75-£19.50. **Set lunches** (Mon-Sat) £11.95 2 courses, £14.95 3 courses, (Sun) £16.95 3 courses. **Credit** MC, V.

Although it calls itself a pub, the Crooked Billet is in reality more of a restaurant, with a busy sideline in weddings. Ironically, perhaps, for an institution so keen to launch couples into wedded bliss, children are not so welcome – a notice on the door demands that they behave themselves. As a result, even the small front garden is a relatively child-free zone. The food is excellent: grilled local asparagus cooked just the right side of al dente, served with hollandaise; moreish ham hock with crisp salad and a puy lentil vinaigrette. There were four different fish on the mains menu when we last ate here – haddock, halibut, sea bass and monkfish – but we opted for a hefty roast rump of lamb with Tuscan country vegetables. Service was quick and efficient.

Greyhound

Gallowstree Lane, Rotherfield Peppard, RG9 5HT (01189 722227). **Food served** noon-3pm, 7-9.30pm daily. **Main courses** £12-£16. **Credit** AmEx, DC, MC, V.

This charming period building is a local favourite, drawing well-heeled inhabitants from their leafy retreats in and around Henley. The huge vaulted dining room is not quite as Elizabethan as its impressive beamed interior suggests; it is, in point of fact, only about 20 years old. Nevertheless, with portraits and grand oil paintings gracing the walls, the Greyhound succeeds in presenting an aged image. The menu, however, is anything but old. On a recent visit, a creamy smooth haddock and mushy pea fish cake was a beautifully presented blend of flavours, and two generous slices of calf's liver on a bed of mash was sweetened by a red wine jus and caramelised onion. Gruyère and spinach soufflé, and fillet steak in a rich peppercorn and garlic sauce were equally successful.

Leatherne Bottel

The Bridleway, Goring-on-Thames, RG8 0HS (01491 872667/www.leathernebottel.co.uk) **Food served** noon-2pm, 7-9pm Mon-Thur; noon-2pm, 7-9.30pm Fri; noon-2.30pm, 7-9.30pm Sat; noon-3.30pm Sun. **Main courses** £17-£20. **Set dinner** (Mon-Fri) £23.50 3 courses. **Credit** AmEx, MC, V.

If you can't decide on a river or countryside setting, this one's for you. Pick a sunny day, relax and drink in the peace and champers – there's plenty of both and the first one is free. The two-part sunshine yellow dining room is decorated with sleek bronze nudes and jolly oil paintings of Cuba (both for sale). Cigars, caviar and fine wines advertise their presence rather pompously and the menu isn't exactly a bargain, with vegetarian main courses running at £18, but you can have a piece of riverside paradise for as long as you like once you've ordered. Garden crosses into kitchen often, such as in an own-grown herb salad with at least a dozen different leaves, and in an elderflower and lemon meringue roulade. Otherwise, roast vegetable and goat's cheese lasagne is light and punchily flavoured, and Thai fish curry is another extrovert dish. Children are not encouraged.

Le Manoir aux Quat' Saisons

Church Road, Great Milton, OX44 7PD (01844 278881/www.manoir.com). **Food served** 11.15am-2.45pm, 6.45-9.30pm daily. **Main courses** £36-£38. **Set lunch** (Mon-Fri) £45 3 courses. **Set meal** £95 7 courses. **Credit** AmEx, DC, MC, V.

It's hard to imagine having a better meal anywhere. Raymond Blanc's winning formula is simple: you pay serious money for seriously good food in a beautiful setting. While the house and gardens are wonderfully maintained, they're comfortable rather than pretentious. In fact, while the Manoir is undoubtedly smart and expensive, it really isn't stuffy. You'll be waited on hand and foot by a young, all-smiling, all-French assortment of staff as you enjoy drinks and a plate of appetisers (mini soufflés, smoked salmon blinis, tapenade on toastlets) in the drawing room, and from there it's to your table and a bonne-bouche (in our case a tiny cup of gazpacho) and a wonderful choice of ten or so breads. Hors d'oeuvres could include pan-seared scallops and langoustines or baby garden vegetable risotto, Sicilian tomatoes and mascarpone cream. Then on to roast breast of Trelough duck, gratin dauphinois and foie gras sauce, perhaps, or pan-fried veal kidneys, Burgundy snails, red wine jus with green chartreuse and purée of shallots (and there's always at least one vegetarian and three fish dishes). Puddings such as raspberry soufflé and its own sorbet and crème brûlée with Tahiti vanilla make a fine finish. You'll need to book four to six weeks in advance to be sure of a table.

Thyme & Plaice

8 Newbury Street, Wantage, OX12 8BS (01235 760568). **Food served** noon-2pm, 7-9pm Tue-Fri; 7-9pm Sat. **Main courses** £15. **Set lunch** £10 2 courses. **Set dinner** (Tue-Thur) £18.50 3 courses. **Credit** AmEx, MC, V.

In an 18th-century townhouse, Thyme & Plaice comprises two rooms either side of the hallway, with red-backed chairs adding colour to a simple decor. A small bar fronts the kitchen, where the owner, Duncan, conjures up a choice selection of Modern British fare. Begin with crab with sweet and sour cucumber and mango salsa, or a smoked duck, pepper and mango salad, and move on to a lamb leg steak on braised lettuce, shallots and minted peas with lemon thyme rösti or a pavé of lightly smoked salmon steak on warm pasta. Mains also include the likes of barbary duck, roast pork fillet and grilled sea bass, but vegetarians are only catered for by request.

Trout

Tadpole Bridge, Buckland Marsh, Buckland, SN7 8RF (01367 870382/www.trout-inn.co.uk). **Food served** noon-2pm, 7-9pm Mon-Sat; noon-2pm Sun. **Main courses** £7.95-£15.95. **Credit** MC, V.

The Trout can cater for both the hearty drinker at the bar at the front, or for parties of diners at the tables round the side and in the garden. Formalities are kept to a minimum – on our visit the maitre d' (too grand a title) wore shorts, while the bar is a reminder that there is no point in standing on ceremony. The menu is original: a pork terrine starter comes with a prune compote and a poached pear; the trout gravadlax with marinated cucumber and drop scones. Mains are equally inspiring. Try rack of lamb with haggis sauce, almond-crusted loin of venison with vanilla risotto and chocolate sauce or pan-fried loin of pork with apple tatin and black pudding. Combinations were very successful, and reflect a refreshing appetite for experimentation in the kitchen.

Woodstock to Burford

Where an Englishman's home is his castle and his rolling Cotswold land green and pleasant.

This southern tranche of the Cotswolds lives up to the idyllic image the name evokes. Clusters of fairytale stone cottages with thatched or lichened roofs and smoking chimneys give each village a beauty that's very civilised and terribly, terribly English. Pheasants waddle through glowing fields of rape, rabbits leap in hedgerows, birds sing and blossom falls: the Cotswolds exemplify rural England. It's all fecundity, fresh air and four-wheel drives. But it is only occasionally precious: even the cutest towns and villages have a life beyond their photogenic façades, even if it is part-fuelled by commuter and retirement culture; and there are plenty that are a soft centre away from chocolate box, relatively unvisited, and a pleasure to stumble upon.

The Romans are ultimately responsible for the area's wealth; they introduced the long-woolled breed of sheep, the 'Cotswold Lion', to these parts. Cotswold wool quickly gained an international reputation, flourishing between 1300 and 1500, and the wealth it brought to the area paid for the churches and grand houses that still dominate the villages. In the Middle Ages, grazing sheep took priority over human residents, occupying great tracts of land; in some cases, villagers were even evacuated from villages to give the sheep more room.

Nowadays, and especially post foot and mouth, the Cotswolds' main industry is tourism, a fact that's reflected in some steep prices and a slew of themed attractions. Yet the main attractions are free. Planted deep in the rich countryside are ancient ruins and historical country piles. There are attractive walks between most of the small villages – and pubs en route to ease the effort. The Thames Path (www.thames-path.co.uk) passes this way prettily, in the river's buoyant adolescence. It becomes navigable at Lechlade, and there are plenty of tour boats around to prove it.

Eight miles north of Oxford lies the historic market town of **Woodstock**, gateway to the country seat of the Duke of Marlborough, **Blenheim Palace**. The birthplace of Sir Winston Churchill (who was buried in St Martin's churchyard in nearby Bladon), Blenheim is one of the most extraordinary buildings in the country: its sheer size will stop first-time visitors in their tracks, while the luxury and splendour of Sir John Vanbrugh's design is simply breathtaking.

Woodstock itself was known for many centuries for two main crafts – glove-making and decorative steel work – and supplied royalty with both. You can follow the area's heritage at the new **Oxfordshire Museum** (Fletcher's House, Park Street, 01993 811456/ 01993 813276, www.oxfordshire.gov.uk/ the_oxfordshire_museum), but you won't see many signs of an artisan existence in the streets, which are filled with cars bearing custom for the classy pubs and restaurants attracting Oxonians (often embarrassed student-parent pairings) on evenings out of town. There are also antiques shops and a farmers' market on the first Saturday morning of the month.

Within reach of Woodstock are **Rousham House**, a rather stern-looking Tudor Gothic pile with exquisite landscaped gardens, and **Bicester Village** (50 Pingle Drive, 01869 323200), a giant discount shopping outlet offering some impressive brands.

Heading west towards Burford, **Minster Lovell** is worth a stop and a stroll. One of the quietest and most unspoilt villages in the area, it boasts not only a gorgeous 15th-century

By train from London

The nearest station to **Woodstock** is **Hanborough**, 2½ miles away. The journey from **Paddington** takes 1hr 20mins and trains run every 2hrs. Buses from **Hanborough** to **Woodstock** are scarce, so you're better off getting a taxi (Pejay Taxis 01993 881103). For Burford, your best bet is to get a train to **Oxford** (see p197), then get a bus to **Burford**. Info: www.thamestrains.co.uk.

The Cotswolds

The lovely village of **Minster Lovell** and its 15th-century church. *See p213.*

church but also the dramatic ruins of Minster Lovell Hall. Dating from the 1440s, the Hall and its well-restored medieval dovecote make an imposing sight on the banks of the River Windrush, and the thatched cottages are some of the prettiest around. **Swinbrook**, where writer Nancy Mitford is buried, and **Asthall** are also worth continuing the detour for.

Burford, an elegant and historic coaching town, makes a good, if pricey, base from which to explore the surrounding area. The broad main street comprises a welter of pretty buildings clinging to the slope down to the River Windrush, and is smattered with all manner of middle England gift and antiques shops. For much of the year, the entire town is chockful of traffic; aim to visit in early spring or winter.

Burford's Norman church, remodelled in the 1400s, is proud of its graffiti, inflicted during the 17th century by some of the 400 Leveller mutineers imprisoned here by Cromwell. Insights into Burford's history are found in the **Tolsey Museum** (126 High Street, 01993 823196).

There are plenty of good riverside walks nearby; try the path to Taynton via the Barringtons or east to Swinbrook. To the north, there are paintings and fragments of Roman mosaics in the tiny church at **Widford**. A few miles north of Burford, the petite village of **Shipton-under-Wychwood** boasts a pretty church, which has a stained-glass window designed by the William Morris company and some pre-Raphaelite archangels.

England's prettiest village?

It's worth continuing about ten miles to the west of Burford to see the village described by William Morris as the most beautiful in England. It seems that the rest of England flocks to **Bibury** each year to check the truth of this statement. Based around a wetland nature reserve, the Rack Isle, and the trout-filled River Colne, Bibury has a certain tweeness and no real centre, but is undeniably pretty. Indeed, when Henry Ford visited in the 1920s he liked it so much he tried to take part of it (a row of weavers' cottages called Arlington Row) back to the States with him. Fortunately, he was stopped. Off the main drag, the Saxon church of St Mary's, rebuilt by the Normans in 1156, is awesomely peaceful. There's a lovely walk from Bibury along the River Coln to Coln St Aldwyns.

What to see & do

Tourist information centres

The Brewery, Sheep Street, Burford, Oxfordshire OX18 4LP (01993 823558/www.oxfordshirecots wolds.org). Open Mar-Oct 9.30am-5.30pm Mon-Sat; 10.30am-3pm Sun. Nov-Feb 10am-4.30pm Mon-Sat.

The Oxfordshire Museum, Fletcher's House, Park Street, Woodstock, Oxfordshire OX20 1SP (01993 813276/www.oxfordshirecotswolds.org). Open Mar-Oct 9.30am-5.30pm Mon-Sat; 1-5pm Sun. Nov-Feb 10am-5pm Mon-Sat; 1-5pm Sun.

Bike hire

Burford Bike Hire *Woollands, Barns Lane, Burford, Oxfordshire OX18 4NE (01993 823326/07713 444519).*
Phone ahead to book, Monday to Friday. The shop is a one-minute walk from the bus stop.

Blenheim Palace

Woodstock, Oxfordshire OX20 1PX (24hr info line 01993 811325/www.blenheimpalace.com). Open Palace & Gardens Mid Feb-Oct 10.30am-5.30pm daily. Nov-mid Dec 10.30am-5.30pm Wed-Sun. Last entry 4.45pm. Closed mid Dec-mid Feb. Park 9am-5.30pm daily. Last entry 4.45pm. Admission Peak (Easter weekend, June-mid Sept) Palace, Park & Gardens £12.50; £7-£10 concessions. Park & Gardens £7.50; £3.50-£5.50. Off peak (mid Feb-May, mid Sept-mid Dec) Palace, Park and Gardens £11; £5.50-£8.50 concessions. Park & Gardens £6; £2-£4 concessions. Park only £2; £1 concessions. Peak & off-peak free under-5s. Credit AmEx, DC, MC, V.
Blenheim Palace was the lavish reward bestowed on John Churchill, first Duke of Marlborough, by Queen Anne for defeating the French at the crucial Battle of Blenheim in 1704. Designed by Sir John Vanbrugh with the assistance of Nicholas Hawksmoor and set in 2,100 acres of grounds landscaped by 'Capability' Brown, Blenheim is the only non-royal residence in the country that's grand enough to be given the title 'palace'. Outside and in, it's awe-inspiring. Only part of the palace is open to the public, and at weekends crowds ensure it's a bit of a production-line trudge. But it's worth it to see the remarkable long library, gilded state rooms, some distinguished paintings and tapestry and a Churchiliana exhibition (Sir Winston was born here, and buried at nearby Bladon) – and to gain an insight into the power and self-importance of the nobility. The park too is a sumptuous manifestation of ego, with its artificial bridged lake, waterfall and temple: there are marked walks, boats to rent and plenty of idyllic picnic spots. The Pleasure Gardens, linked to the house by a mini railway and containing the world's largest maze, plus an adventure playground, putting green, butterfly house and model village, is a modern addition designed to keep family visitors – and ticket revenues – rolling in. In fine weather, plan to spend most of the day here.

Cogges Manor Farm Museum

Church Lane, Cogges, Witney, Oxfordshire OX28 3LA (01993 772602/www.cogges.org). Open Apr-Oct 10.30am-5.30pm Tue-Fri; noon-5.30pm Sat, Sun. Closed Nov-Mar (phone to confirm). Admission £4.40; £2.30-£2.85 concessions; free under-3s. Credit MC, V.
Featuring costumed guides and a working farm, this charming museum aims to recreate rural Oxfordshire in Victorian times. Covering 20 acres, the farm is stocked with traditional Victorian breeds of livestock, and has displays of implements and machinery. In the manor house, you can chat to the maids in the kitchen about the history of the house, sample fresh baking from the range, and explore a variety of period displays

including a Victorian bedroom and nursery. Outdoors, you can stroll in the gardens or to the River Windrush or picnic at tables in the orchard. Special events, such as falconry displays, take place throughout the year.

Cotswold Wildlife Park

Burford, Oxfordshire OX18 4JW (01993 823006/www.cotswoldwildlifepark.co.uk). **Open** *Mar-Sept* 10am-6pm daily. Last entry 4.30pm. *Oct-Feb* 10am-4.30pm daily. Last entry 3.30pm. **Admission** £7.50; £5 concessions; free under-3s. **Credit** MC, V.
Set in 160 acres of gardens and parkland around a listed Victorian manor house, the Cotswold Wildlife Park is one of the Oxfordshire Cotswolds' most popular attractions. There are rhinos, zebras, lions and ostriches roaming in spacious paddocks. Among the many endangered species that the park helps to conserve are red pandas and giant tortoises. Penguins, tropical birds, monkeys, meerkats and otters live in the walled gardens, and there are houses for insects and reptiles and an aquarium. A mini-railway runs between April and October, and there's a children's farmyard and adventure playground.

Cotswold Woollen Weavers

Filkins, nr Lechlade, Gloucestershire GL7 3JJ (01367 860491/www.naturalbest.co.uk). **Open** 10am-6pm Mon-Sat; 2-6pm Sun. **Admission** free.
At this working woollen mill you can discover more about the history of the wool trade and watch fleece being woven into woollen fabric using age-old skills. The museum shop has a wide range of knitwear and rugs and there's also a coffee shop, free parking.

Rousham Park House & Garden

Nr Steeple Aston, Bicester, Oxfordshire OX25 4QX (01869 347110/www.rousham.org). **Open** *House* Apr-Sept 2-4.30pm Wed, Sun, bank hol Mon. Closed Oct-Mar. *Garden* 10am-4.30pm daily. **Admission** *House* £3. *Garden* £3. **No credit cards.**
This rather gloomy, imposing Jacobean mansion was remodelled in Tudor Gothic style by William Kent, a predecessor of 'Capability' Brown, in the 18th century. But the real point here is his outstanding garden, inspired by Italian landscape painting, with grouped trees, winding paths, glades, and waterfalls dotted with statues and temples – which has remained pretty much unchanged. Inside, Rousham is determinedly uncommercialised, with no shop or tearoom; you're encouraged to bring a picnic and stay for the day wandering the grounds. Children under 15 and dogs are not welcome.

Where to stay

Several of the pubs and restaurants we recommend also have pleasant accommodation. They include: the **Village Pub**, **Jonathan's at the Angel** and the two **Lamb** inns (Burford and Shipton-under-Wychwood).

Bay Tree Hotel

Sheep Street, Burford, Oxfordshire OX18 4LW (01993 822791/fax 01993 823008/www.cotswold-inns-hotels.co.uk). **Rates** £119 single occupancy; £155 double/twin; £165-£185 garden double; £205 junior suite; £230 master suite. **Rooms** (all en suite) 10 double/twin; 4 garden double; 3 junior suites; 4 master suites. **Credit** AmEx, MC, V.

The Bay Tree has a slightly institutional feel, emphasised by its consistent popularity for weddings and conferences. But the rooms are pleasantly individual in feel and nicely kept, resolutely traditional in decor but charmingly unstuffy, and the staff are friendly. The attractive wooden-floored restaurant offers quality modern British cuisine in a pleasant, candlelit dining room overlooking the lovely split-level herb garden. Children and dogs (£10 per night) welcome.

Bibury Court Hotel

Bibury, Cirencester, Gloucestershire GL7 5NT (01285 740337/fax 01285 740660/www.bibury court.com). **Rates** £115 single occupancy; £130 double/twin; £150-£170 four-poster; £200 suite. Breakfast £5.25-£7.25 (Eng). **Rooms** 11 double/twin (all en suite); 6 four-poster (5 en suite); 1 suite (en suite). **Credit** AmEx, DC, MC, V.
The 17th-century builders of lovely Bibury Court knew a prime piece of real estate when they saw one. They set their mansion next to Bibury's Saxon church and backed it up to the River Coln, which today marks the southern boundary of the hotel's six-acre grounds. A highlight here is taking tea on the patio or in the conservatory and looking across the lawn to the river. Indoors, a genteel feeling pervades, emanating from kindly, professional staff. Rooms have four-posters, panelling and antiques of haphazard quality. They also have a slightly institutional feel, as do the public areas. There's a sofa-filled drawing room and a tartan-carpeted dining room where very decent food is served. Children and dogs welcome.
A40 W of Oxford; take left on to B4425 to Bibury; hotel is in the village centre in front of church.

Burford House Hotel

99 High Street, Burford, Oxfordshire OX18 4QA (01993 823151/fax 01993 823240/www.burford house.co.uk). **Rates** £80-£140 single occupancy; £105-£140 double/twin/four-poster. **Rooms** (all en suite) 3 double; 2 twin; 3 four-poster. **Credit** AmEx, MC, V.
No one could fail to fall in love with this effortlessly charming and comfortable 17th-centry townhouse hotel, whose owners take a fierce pride in providing a warm and welcome ambience, lovely rooms and cooking of the highest standard. This is the epitome of the non-institutional instituion and homely touches abound. Bedrooms are decorated in country-house style with a nice eye and comforting items such as quality quilts and tub baths. Only breakfast, lunch and afternoon tea are served (residents only Sunday and Monday); staff bake daily. You're on your own for dinner, but that's hardly a trial around here, and if you fancy an evening in you can dip into the honour bar and sit in front of the sitting room fire or out in the flower-filled courtyard garden, depending on the time of year. Children welcome. All bedrooms are no-smoking.

Feathers Hotel

Market Street, Woodstock, Oxfordshire OX20 1SX (01993 812291/fax 01993 813158/www.feathers. co.uk). **Rates** £90-£135 single occupancy; £135-£185 double/twin; £200-£225 suite. **Rooms** (all en suite) 15 double/twin; 5 suites. **Credit** AmEx, DC, MC, V.
With a prime location and august reputation, the classy Feathers sets the pace in Woodstock as both hotel and restaurant (*see p218*). It's a large and pleasantly warren-like building, made up at some point in its history of five

Kelmscott Manor

In 1871, William Morris, father of the Arts and Crafts movement, went looking for a summer home for his family. His wife, Janey, and daughters May and Jenny needed to escape the unhealthy London air, and he found pleasure and artistic inspiration in the countryside and its traditional architecture. However a less conventional motive lurked in the background: the need to hide from prying eyes the intense relationship that was burgeoning between his younger and beautiful wife and the pre-Raphaelite poet and artist Dante Gabriel Rossetti. When Morris found Kelmscott Manor – 'a heaven on earth; an old stone Elizabethan house... and such a garden!' – Rossetti co-signed the lease.

A visit to the house today is an extraordinary experience. It is primarily a showcase for the works of Morris – magnificent tapestries, fabrics and wallpapers, examples of his printing, painting and writing – and his wife, who helped revive traditional embroidery techniques. In this domestic context, they are witness to his philosophy of making the functional beautiful in a way that no museum could be. The personalities of the family inhabit the house through their renovations of it, the displays of their so evidently time-consuming work and their repeated images, many of Janey by Rossetti (it is not known if their relationship was more than platonic, and it was certainly discreet, but the married couple kept separate bedrooms, lending the idyllic family home a certain plangency). Their affection for the place is evident in their work: Morris and Rossetti both idealise it in their writings. A gabled

Tudor farmhouse made of the local limestone, extended in the 17th century (and wrongly renamed a manor by a later occupant), Kelmscott is substantial but not ostentatious. It doesn't take too much imagination to summon thoughts of its occupants stitching and drawing in the afternoon light by a mullioned window, playing hide and seek in the attic or running through the meadow to push a punt out on to the Thames.

Morris has many devotees, so a visit here is unlike the factory tours of some stately homes (though you may be allocated a time slot and asked to return). People make a day of it, picnic by the river, argue points of Morris lore and technique with the attendants and sunbathe in the garden that's gradually – absent elm trees notwithstanding – being returned to the plantings shown in Morris-era photographs. On a dead end road, with a small church that's worth a look (Morris is buried in the graveyard, with a stone designed by friend and architect Philip Webb), the village is almost preternaturally quiet and doubtless little changed since Morris's day, bar perhaps the introduction of lager at the Plough Inn (with food and rooms).

Kelmscott Manor

Kelmscott, nr Lechlade, GL7 3HJ (01367 252486/www.kelmscottmanor.co.uk). **Open** *Apr-June, Sept* 11am-1pm, 2-5pm Wed; 2-5pm 3rd Sat of mth. *July, Aug* 11am-1pm, 2-5pm Wed; 2-5pm 1st, 3rd Sat of mth. Last entry 30mins before closing. Closed Oct-Mar. **Admission** £7; £3.50 concessions; free under-8s. **Credit** MC, V.

separate houses. The management work hard to stay ahead of the game, with a rolling programme of renovations: the bar area has had the most recent refurb (classy traditional with some modern art) and the bedrooms are following suit. Ask for one of the renovated rooms. They're nice and smart, decorated with a pleasant range of fabrics in country-house vernacular, with the TV tucked away in a cabinet. Children and dogs welcome.

King's Arms Hotel OFFER

19 Market Street, Woodstock, Oxfordshire OX20 1SU (01993 813636/fax 01993 813737). **Rates** £70 single occupancy; £110-£150 double/twin. **Rooms** (all en suite) 14 double; 1 twin. **Credit** AmEx, MC, V.

Directly opposite the historic Feathers Hotel (*see p216*), the King's Arms wisely decides not to compete in the heritage stakes. Instead, it provides the area's only contemporary hotel experience, and provides it very well indeed. The newly furnished rooms are smartly designed with slick off-whites, black and white prints and striking bedspreads; bathrooms are modern, with admirably large heated towel rails and Molton Brown products. The breakfast area downstairs doubles as a bar and brasserie, again in modern style (large pot plants and prints, couches, black and white tiled floor). It's popular with the local youth, so at weekends you might get a bit of noise on your way to bed. All bedrooms are no-smoking.

Mill & Old Swan Inn

Minster Lovell, Oxfordshire OX29 0RN (01993 774441/fax 01993 702002/www.millandoldswanisc.co.uk). **Rates** *Swan* £55 single; £100 double/twin; £120 poster-four. *Mill* £45 single; £60-£80 double/twin. **Rooms** (all en suite) *Swan* 2 single; 4 twin; 7 double; 3 four-poster. *Mill* 2 single; 16 twin; 29 double. **Credit** AmEx, DC, MC, V.

The Mill & Old Swan complex, on the banks of the River Windrush, is primarily a conference and training venue, but don't let that put you off. It means you get the place pretty much to yourself at weekends, with good rates and little competition for a wide range of facilities: a tennis court, trout fishing, putting green and driving nets, gym, croquet lawn and, not insignificantly around here, parking. The accommodation is a little secondary, it's true: the rooms are nice enough but not designed to detain you from your duties, particularly at the Mill. At the Swan just down the road where breakfast is taken, they're a little more characterful (and pricier): many feature exposed beams, several have four-posters, and one even has a ghost. Children and dogs (£10 per night) welcome.
A40 W of Oxford; after 14 miles take the sliproad on right signposted 'Carterton, Minster Lovell'; right at junction; through Minster Lovell; right at T-junction; immediate left into valley; left over stone bridge; hotel reception is on the left.

New Inn at Coln

Coln St Aldwyns, Gloucestershire GL7 5AN (01285 750651/fax 01285 750657/www.new-inn.co.uk). **Rates** £85 single; £115-£148 double/twin. **Rooms** (all en suite) 1 single; 3 twin; 9 double. **Credit** AmEx, MC, V.

Very well known in the area, the creeper-clad New Inn offers pub, restaurant and hotel in one slick, well-run package, selling Cotswold charm and country values to local Land-Rovered devotees and a mixed bunch of guests. The smart, individually decorated bedrooms are divided between the main building and the Dovecote, and feature notably comfy beds and plenty of chintz and floral motifs (perhaps to a fault). The popular restaurant serves modern versions of pub classics, with a brasserie twist. Children and dogs welcome.
A40 W towards Cheltenham; turn left on to B4425 towards Bibury 1 mile after passing Burford; continue for 5 miles; turn left shortly after Oldsworth; take signs to Coln St Aldwyns.

The Old Post Office

Southrop, nr Lechlade, Gloucestershire GL7 3NY (01367 850231/www.theoldpostoffice.org). **Rates** £22-£40 single occupancy; £42-£54 double/twin. **Rooms** 2 double (1 en suite); 1 twin. **No credit cards.**

You're a bit out of the tourist mainstream in Southrop, even though it's well situated and very pretty, with an ace pub restaurant in the Swan across the road. Which probably helps account for the reasonable rates. It's an above-average B&B (with a cottage to rent, as well), in a handsome old post office, with a pleasant country-cottage breakfast room and comfortable bedrooms. Children are very welcome. No smoking throughout.

Shaven Crown Hotel

High Street, Shipton-under-Wychwood, Oxfordshire OX7 6BA (01993 830330/fax 01993 832136/www.shavencrown.co.uk). **Rates** £65 single

occupancy; £85-£95 double/twin; £130 four-poster. **Rooms** (all en suite) 8 double/twin; 1 four-poster. **Credit** AmEx, MC, V.

This fabulously historic hotel, dating back to the 14th century and used as a hunting lodge by Queen Elizabeth I, derives its rather unusual name from the fact that it once housed a monk's hospice. Today, while the pub part of the operation remains in fine fettle, the hotel side is a little neglected, but it nonetheless offers good value for a quirky stay. Reception and lounge are in a galleried medieval hall and there is also a beamed dining room, albeit rather in need of a refurb. Likewise the rooms: reasonably comfortable but decorated in a generic, and slightly dated, country-house style. The hotel has the use of two tennis courts and a bowling green. Children and dogs welcome.
A40 W of Oxford past Witney; turn right at Burford on to A361 to Shipton-under-Wychwood.

Where to eat & drink

In general, the area cashes in on its appeal to tourists: prices and standards are high and menus often conservative. We recommend you book ahead and change out of walking clothes; even in pubs, dining rooms can be quite formal.

On Burford High Street, the **Golden Pheasant** (01993 823223) and the **Old Bull** (01993 822220) both serve reasonable food at reasonable prices, and **Huffkins** (01993 822126) bakery serves a mean cream tea. Off the main drag, the tankard-bedecked **Royal Oak** (26 Witney Street, 01993 823278) is popular for its pies and other home-cooked staples.

Meanwhile, away from the Burford hordes, the **Swan Inn** (01993 822165) in Swinbrook is an unspoiled, down-to-earth old bar by the river serving decent pub-style food. In Bibury, indulge in a proper afternoon tea at **Bibury Court** (*see p216*). In Woodstock there is a highly regarded Chinese restaurant, **Chef Imperial** (22 High Street, 01993 813591).

In easy reach of the Wildlife Park and other southern area attractions, the **Swan** at Southrop (01367 850205) is a 16th-century inn appreciated for both its food and drink.

Feathers Hotel

Market Street, Woodstock, Oxfordshire OX20 1SX (01993 812291/www.feathers.co.uk). **Food served** *Restaurant* 12.30-2pm, 7-9pm Mon-Fri; 12.30-2pm, 7-9pm Sat, Sun. *Bar* 12.30-2.30pm, 3.30-5.30pm (afternoon tea), 6.30-9pm Mon-Fri, Sun; 12.30-2.30pm, 3.30-5.30pm (afternoon tea) Sat. **Set lunches** *Restaurant* £15.50 2 courses, £19.50 3 courses; (Sun) £23.95 3 courses. **Set dinners** £28 2 courses, £35 3 courses. **Main courses** *Restaurant* £18-£22. *Bar* £6.95-£12. **Credit** AmEx, DC, MC, V.

In keeping with the luxurious accommodation of the hotel, the award-winning restaurant at the Feathers is a seriously swanky affair. Dinner in the beautiful oak-panelled dining room (no smoking) includes starters

Blenheim Palace. *See p215.*

than the brasserie setting might suggest: try monkfish roasted in smoked bacon with a citrus salsa, followed by fig and frangipane tart with pecan and maple syrup ice-cream. There's often game too. In summer there's the back terrace, with awning, if the very pine-heavy dining room doesn't appeal.

Lamb Inn & Restaurant
Sheep Street, Burford, Oxfordshire OX18 4LR (01993 823155). **Lunch served** *Bar* noon-2.30pm daily. *Restaurant* noon-2pm daily. **Dinner served** *Bar* 7-9pm daily. *Restaurant* 7-9.30pm daily. **Main courses** £14.95-£19.50. **Set lunches** (Sun) £15 2 courses, £22.50 3 courses. **Credit** MC, V.
An upmarket pub that's kept its wooden bar settles and a proper drinking area (admittedly gentrified), it has a lovely dining room and candlelit courtyard terrace, all smartly kept and staffed. The restaurant is formal without being oppressive: simple white nappery and paintwork, botanical prints, rich curtains and well-designed modern cutlery. The menu is short and uses luxury and seasonal ingredients in dishes firmly in the modern vernacular. When we visited, cooking varied from the good (pancetta-wrapped monkfish with sesame seed rice) to the excellent (foie gras and guinea fowl ravioli), though we're not sure where on that continuum to place a strawberry cake whose tired fruit was unsubtly overlaid with fresh cream.

Lamb Inn
Simons Lane, Shipton-under-Wychwood, Oxfordshire OX7 6DQ (01993 830465/www.traditionalvillageinn. co.uk). **Food served** noon-2.45pm, 6.30-9.45pm daily. **Main courses** £8-£15. **Credit** AmEx, MC, V.
This lovely Cotswold stone inn dates back to the 16th century but its current tenants have given both menu and interior a sleek 21st-century update: it's charming, but not chocolate-box. Sit in the tiny restaurant area, the larger low-lit bar or on tree-shaded or sunny terraces, drink a glass of ale and choose boldly flavoured dishes from an internationally influenced menu: perhaps grilled scallops with cucumber noodles and tomato and herb consommé; a herb-suffused haddock and saffron risotto; or sirloin steak with chorizo and garlic jus. Seasonal fruit dishes aside, puddings know little restraint (just try the banana tarte tatin) and the Bailey's bottle rather well. The young staff are friendly and very professional.

Red Lion
South Side, Steeple Aston, Oxfordshire OX25 4RY (01869 340225/www.leorufus.co.uk). **Food served** noon-2pm, 7-9pm Tue-Sat; noon-2pm Sun. **Main courses** £7.50-£14.95. **Set lunches** (Sun) £12.95 2 courses, £14.95 3 courses. **Credit** MC, V.
Not to be confused with the White Lion in the same village, the red version is a small, handsome country pub with jovial bar staff. The tiny, wonky-walled dining room makes you realise how Alice in Wonderland felt when she took that magic pill. Don't be put off by the predictable menu – it's the way they cook that counts. Pâté-stuffed mushrooms are nothing to write home about, but chicken liver terrine is. The local steak is dry-aged and has a gamey tang, and beef bourguignon is a rich, sticky mass. Chocolate truffle torte is a perfect cylinder of wickedness and its crowning white chocolate truffle is the booziest we've tasted. Even the house wines are good.

such as risotto of wild mushrooms and duck confit, generous mains like roast fillet of sea bass served with crushed potatoes, sauce vierge and caviar aubergine, and luxurious desserts such as hazelnut parfait with fresh strawberries and red fruits. A more informal menu is available in the hotel bar. Non-residents can enjoy lunch, tea or a drink in the pretty garden. For hotel, *see p216.*

King's Head
Chapel Hill, Wootton, Oxfordshire OX20 1DX (01993 811340/www.kings-head.co.uk). **Food served** noon-2pm, 7-8.30pm Mon-Sat; noon-2pm Sun. **Main courses** £9.95-£16.50. **Credit** MC, V.
An unpretentious and very personal pub/restaurant. A meal here is like being cooked for by severely talented, somewhat genteel friends and attended to in their own dining room. Though the decor may not appeal (a few too many Jocasta Innes wall splashes and flowery sofas, perhaps), it's comfortable, low-lit and relaxing. And it's what's on the plate that counts: quality ingredients, exquisitely prepared and elaborately presented. Very good on our visit were an olive pâté with artichoke hearts and bramble dressing, pork medallions with onion confit and plump juniper berries, and a warm fish salad with fir apple potatoes, the latter from a blackboard menu changed according to availability. Special mention should also go to a lovingly made sticky toffee pudding. The wine list is well put together, by taste category.

Jonathan's at the Angel
14 Witney Street, Burford, Oxfordshire OX18 4SN (01993 822714/www.theangeluk.com). **Food served** noon-2pm, 7-9.30pm Tue-Sat; noon-2pm Sun. **Main courses** £13.95-£18.50. **Set lunches** £14.50 2 courses, £18.50 3 courses. **Credit** MC, V.
This country-kitchen brasserie, housed in a 16th-century coaching inn, comes as something of a relief after all the formal pub dining rooms in the area. It has a mellow, welcoming feel and unmistakeably personal tone – perhaps because chef/patron Jonathan Lewis is very hands-on. Dishes are Modern British/European, more complex

The Cotswolds

Chipping Norton to Banbury

Ride a cock-horse to honeypot villages and pints of 'Hooky'.

The trouble with country idylls is they tend to get overrun with weekenders trying to find their own piece of bucolic tranquillity away from the hordes in the tearooms and souvenir shops. Such can be the case with the better-known Cotswold villages. If you want real peace and quiet in the Cotswolds it might be better to head to the north Oxfordshire/south Warwickshire border between Oxford and Stratford – an area that has its fair share of honeypot villages and fine country pubs, plus peaceful cow-parsley lanes, undulating meadows and wooded hills, without the crowds.

Stone has always been cheap around here, so builders used glorious red-brown ironstone – now speckled with orange lichen – or sun-soaking, golden Cotswold limestone. Wool money paid for handsome churches, with local stone-cutting skills evident in fine tracery and detailing. The medieval vocabulary of mullioned windows and gables is also much in evidence in the striking Jacobean cottages, farmhouses and manor houses that seem to appear at every turn.

Antique shops and a wool church

Chipping Norton itself is a small market town, pretty but not overwhelmingly touristy. There are plenty of traditional teashops, inns and pubs; all are peopled with locals, and the place has an affluent, relaxed feel.

Terraced into the hillside, it's the highest town in Oxfordshire, and you get glimpses of rolling countryside between the rooftops, as well as the bizarre and now defunct **Bliss Tweed Mill**, designed to resemble a great stately home with a giant chimney rising from the centre, and now turned into luxury flats. In addition to a small museum, there are lots of antiques shops in Chipping Norton, with far keener prices than those of the northern Cotswolds. The **Station Mill Antique Centre** (Station Road, 01608 644563) is a great place to browse for an hour or so, and has a small café. The tourist office's new brochure, *Antiques Trail*, lists a wealth of antiques shops around town, along with those in **Woodstock**,

Burford and **Witney** as well as mapping other attractions along the trail.

Also worth a visit, if only to see the Graham Rust murals in the bar and wonderful theatrical cartoons in the lavatories, is the highly regarded **Chipping Norton Theatre** on Spring Street. Just down from there, on **Church Lane**, are pretty 17th-century almshouses and the imposing wool church of **St Mary**, which has one of the finest 15th-century interiors in the county.

Just like a Rollright stone

North and north-west of Chipping Norton are the pretty villages of **Great Rollright** – grey stone cottages on a breezy hillside – and **Little Rollright**, an unspoiled hamlet set among meadows. Between them lie the **Rollright Stones**, a group of prehistoric stones said to be third in the stone-circle pecking order after Stonehenge and Avebury. There are beautiful walks to be had around this area, and it's not far to **Hook Norton**, a large ironstone village where the wonderful beer of the same name – known locally as 'Hooky' – is brewed. West of Chipping Norton, the A44 takes you further into the Cotswolds and to **Chastleton House**, one of the best-preserved Jacobean houses in the country, set in a cosy hillside nook. Continue on the A44 and you'll get to Moreton-in-Marsh; taking the A429 will take you to **Stow-on-the-Wold** (*see p178*).

The sleepy villages roll on; high on the hilltops above Hook Norton are the **Sibfords**

By train from London

Trains from **Marylebone** to **Banbury** leave every half-hour (journey time approximately **1hr 20mins**). There is no station for Chipping Norton – the nearest is at **Kingham**, five miles away. Trains leave **Paddington** every 2hrs; journey time is **1hr 30mins**. Info: www.chilternrailways.co.uk and www.thamestrains.co.uk.

The Cotswolds

– **Gower** and **Ferris** – **Swalcliffe** and **Shenington**, and across the border into Warwickshire, the upper and lower **Brailes** and **Compton Wynyates**, an elegant Tudor country house no longer open to the public but surrounded by lovely walks. From the nearby village of **Tysoe**, there's great hillwalking along **Edgehill**, and spectacular views across to **Stratford-upon-Avon** (*see p192*). Nearby is the 17th-century **Upton House**, with a staggering art collection and beautiful gardens descending to pools in the valley below.

Ride a cock-horse

To the east is **Banbury**, a market town known for its cakes and its cross, immortalised in the nursery rhyme 'Ride a cock-horse to Banbury Cross'. After the demise of its world-famous cattle market there was little to attract the visitor, until the recent development of **Castle Quay** (*see p223* **Mall with a difference**), a shopping complex that also houses the new Banbury Museum, a working boatyard and canalside café. Just south-west of the town is the romantic **Broughton Castle** and, to the south, three pretty villages known for their imposing church spires: 'Bloxham for length, **Adderbury** for strength, **Kings Sutton** for beauty' – as the local saying goes.

Further south, down the A4260, is the historic market town of **Deddington**, now a centre for antiques. Then, on the banks of the winding Cherwell river, the **Astons**: **North**, **Middle** and **Steeple**, with more fine walking and some excellent pubs. The Arcadian landscape of wooded hills and small villages continues from here back to Chipping Norton, by way of the Bartons, Kiddington, the Enstones, Glympton and the Tews.

The jewel in the crown is the fabulously picturesque **Great Tew**, a village with perfect thatched cottages nestling in a lushly wooded dell. The way it looks is no accident: in Victorian times the village's owners planned the effect carefully, planting great clumps of trees and adding Gothic porches to all the cottages, so the village would complement the rest of their estate.

What to see & do

This area is best for gentle meandering on foot, by bicycle or by car. The tourist information centres (*see below*) have leaflets outlining circular walks and bike rides throughout the area. In general, Oxfordshire's paths and bridleways seem to be very well signposted.

Tourist Information Centres

The Guildhall, Goddards Lane, Chipping Norton, OX7 5NJ (tel/fax 01608 644379/ www.oxfordshirecotswolds.org). **Open** *Mar-Oct* 9.30am-1pm, 1.30-5.30pm Mon-Sat. *Nov-Feb* 10am-1pm, 1.30-3pm Mon-Sat.

Castle Quay Shopping Centre, Spiceball Park Road, Banbury, OX16 2PQ (01295 259855/fax 01295 269469/www.visit-northoxfordshire.co.uk). **Open** 9.30am-5pm Mon-Sat; 10.30am-4.30pm Sun.

Broughton Castle

SW of Banbury, OX15 5EB (01295 276070/ www.broughtoncastle.demon.co.uk). **Open** *Mid May-mid Sept* 2-5pm Wed, Sun, bank hols. *July, Aug* 2-5pm Wed, Thur, Sun, bank hols. Closed Oct-mid May. **Admission** £5.50; £2-£4.50 concessions. **No credit cards**.
More of a moated manor house, really, Broughton Castle is perhaps best known as a location for *Shakespeare in Love*. Bought by William of Wykeham in the 14th century, it has been in the same family ever since. Their

Broughton Castle.

surname changed to Fiennes through marriage in the 15th century, and Ralph, Joseph and Ranulph are all cousins of the present owner, Nathaniel. The house has some impressive plasterwork ceilings and atmospheric vaulted passages, as well as heirlooms connected with the many colourful episodes in the family's history – not least as a hotbed of anti-monarchical intrigue during the Civil War.

Chastleton House
Chastleton, off A44 NW of Chipping Norton, GL56 OSU (01608 674355/advance booking 01494 755585/www.nationaltrust.org.uk/regions/ thameschilterns). **Open** *Apr-Sept* 1-5pm Wed-Sat. *Oct* 1-4pm Wed-Sat. Closed Nov-Mar. **Admission** (NT) £5.60; £2.80 concessions. **No credit cards.**
A Jacobean manor house with a dramatic five-gabled front. Inside there is a great collection of original panelling, furniture, tapestries and embroideries. The gardens display some fine and imaginative topiary. It's now in the care of the National Trust and you have to pre-book to visit.

Hook Norton Brewery
Brewery Lane, Hook Norton, OX15 5NY (01608 737210/www.hooknortonbrewery.co.uk). **Open** *Museum & shop* 9am-5pm Mon-Fri. **Admission** *Museum* £2; £1 concessions. *Tours* phone for details. **Credit** MC, V.
Tours of this haunted house-like building – one of the last tower breweries in the country – are very popular; you'll need to book a long way in advance. The visitors' centre and shop next door sells various bottled brews and paraphernalia, plus a range of country wines. Upstairs the museum charts the company's history, including the time when the brewery dropped its prices in response to government restrictions forcing brewers to cut alcohol levels. What decent souls they were.

Rollright Stones
S of A3400 NW of Chipping Norton (contact PO Box 444, Bicester, OX25 4AT/www.rollrightstones.co.uk). **Open** sunrise-sunset daily. **Admission** 25p-50p. **No credit cards.**
A mysterious collection of prehistoric stones in three distinct groupings. The most impressive is the ceremonial stone circle of 77 weather-beaten rocks overlooking Long Compton, which, legend has it, was populated by witches. Fifty yards away, technically in Warwickshire, is the King Stone monolith. A few hundred yards from him are the five Whispering Knights – upright stones so named because of their conspiratorial huddle – part of a 5,000-year-old burial chamber.

Upton House
Off A422 S of Edgehill, nr Banbury, OX15 6HT (01295 670266/www.nationaltrust.org.uk). **Open** *House* Apr-Oct 1-5pm Mon-Wed, Sat, Sun. Last admission 4.30pm. *Garden & restaurant* Apr-Oct noon-5pm Mon-Wed; 11am-5pm Sat, Sun. *Both* Closed Nov-Mar. **Admission** (NT) *House & garden* £6.50; £3.50 concessions. *Garden only* £3.50; £1.50 concessions. **Credit** MC,V.
A late 17th-century house that is famous for its extensive art collection, with work by artists including Stubbs, Canaletto, Hogarth and El Greco, as well as Sèvres porcelain, Brussels tapestries and 18th-century

furniture. The gardens at Upton House are pretty spectacular, too, containing ornamental pools and all kinds of colourful surprises.

Water Fowl Sanctuary & Children's Animal Centre
Wiggington Heath, nr Bloxham, OX15 4LQ (01608 730252). **Open** *Summer* 10.30am-5.30pm daily. *Winter* 10.30am-dusk daily. **Admission** £3.50; £2.50-£3 concessions. **No credit cards.**
An unlikely home for ostriches, emus, parrots, chipmunks and a glorious snowy white peacock. This is an eccentric, tumbledown place owned by a creature-crazy family who provide shelter for unwanted pets. There are lots of farmyard friends and an inordinate number of ducks in a series of ponds criss-crossed by pathways. Kids will love the petting room, where they can pick up fluffy rabbits, chicks and duncklings. Wellies advisable.

Castle Inn
Edgehill, nr Banbury, OX15 6DJ (01295 670255/ fax 01295 670521/www.thecastle-edgehill.co.uk). **Rates** £57.50 double; £67.50 four-poster. **Rooms** (all en suite) 1 double; 1 twin; 1 four-poster. **Credit** AmEx, DC, MC, V.
Built on the summit of Edgehill in the 18th century, this extraordinary folly marks the spot where Charles I's army gathered before the first major battle of the Civil War. There are two towers, each containing two bedrooms – those in the main tower are the ones to go for, with sweeping views over the erstwhile battlefield below. Rooms are comfortable if unimaginatively decorated, but the pub downstairs has nooks and crannies, decent food and a large garden. All rooms are no-smoking.

College Farmhouse
Kings Sutton, nr Banbury, OX17 3PS (01295 811473/fax 01295 812505/www.banburytown. co.uk/accom/collegefarm/index). **Rates** £40 single occupancy; £64 double/twin. **Rooms** (all en suite) 3 double/twin. **Credit** MC, V.
Once you've tracked down the unnamed house at the end of an unmarked road, things pick up considerably. This wonderfully relaxed 18th-century house has a beautiful, secluded garden, tennis court and even a lake. Inside, there's a large, beamed sitting room with an inglenook fireplace; an airy kitchen with jolly, painted units; bedrooms that feel more like a friend's rather nice spare rooms, and piles of books for visitors to peruse. You're very much a guest in a family house – and delicious organic breakfasts are taken *en famille*. Loners should opt for the larger Barn Room, in a separate outbuilding with its own kitchen. Dinner costs £20 (three courses) and is served by arrangement only. Children welcome. All bedrooms no-smoking.
B4100 towards Adderbury; after 5 miles turn right to Kings Sutton; at crossroads in centre of village turn right down Astrop Road; after 500 yards take last turning right before leaving village down a lane towards College Farmhouse.

Crown & Cushion Hotel
High Street, Chipping Norton, OX7 5AD (01608 642533/fax 01608 642926/www.thecrown andcushion.com). **Rates** £64-£85 single occupancy;

£78-£120 double; £120-£150 four-poster. **Rooms** (all en suite) 5 single; 10 double; 12 four-poster. **Credit** AmEx, DC, MC, V.

The rooms in this 15th-century former coaching inn are nothing fancy and indeed could use a refurb, but they are comfortable, with good-sized bathrooms (which come in two styles: floral or blue and white, the latter infinitely preferable). Those overlooking the high street are best value. It's hard to believe from the rambling layout, dusty beams and laid-back staff that this is a 'conference and leisure centre', or that it was once owned by Keith Moon, although you could well imagine him propping up the hotel bar. Hidden away at the back is a small fitness centre and indoor pool (*sans* Rolls Royce). Some cheap deals can be had from the surprisingly extensive menu in the hotel's country cottage-style dining room. Children and pets are welcome and no-smoking rooms are available.

Mall with a difference

Banbury boasts the biggest shopping mall in Oxfordshire, looming beside the Oxford Canal. This may not be particularly remarkable in itself, but trot up the stairs at the back of the new Tourist Information Centre, tucked inside the complex, and you'll find yourself in a glass walkway that marks the start of the new Banbury Museum. Fittingly, this bridge, spanning the canal and the moored boats beneath, is the **Waterways Gallery**, a hands-on foray through the history of the Oxford Canal, with models demonstrating such skills as how to load cargo without capsizing your boat and how to work a lock.

At the end of the walkway, the **Discoveries Gallery** introduces the town, its famous currant cakes, Cross and nursery rhyme. Upstairs, the **Treasures Gallery** charts Banbury's history from the 1600s to the present day. Exhibits illustrate the town's role in the Civil War and World War II, there's a hangman's gibbet, a time capsule and even a Vivienne Westwood corset. There's also a changing and unrelated exhibition in another room.

Downstairs at water level is **Café Quay**, with glass frontage and outside seats, weather permitting. It's run by the owners of **Rosamund the Fair**, a pretty narrowboat moored close by, offering haute cuisine dining and a two-hour cruise (£52 per head, book well in advance on 01295 278690/www.rosamundthefair.co.uk). Despite the informal, utilitarian look, Café Quay has waiter service and dishes include classy sandwiches and snacks, and delicious home-made cakes.

Next door is **Tooley's Historic Boatyard**. It has the oldest working dry dock in Britain, in operation since 1790 when the canal system was at its height. Since roads and rail took over business has slowed, but there's still a steady trickle of mainly recreational boats coming in for a service. The tour, which should be booked in advance, includes trips round the restored 1930s workshops and the fabulous 200-year-old forge, where you can watch the resident blacksmith ply his fiery trade.

Tooley's Historic Boatyard
Castle Quay Shopping Centre, Spiceball Park Road, Banbury, OX16 2PQ (01295 272917). **Open** 9am-5.30pm Mon-Sat. *Guided tours* 2.30pm Fri, Sat. **Admission** £5.50; £3.50-£4.95 concessions.

Banbury Museum
Spiceball Park Road, Banbury, OX16 2PQ (01295 259855/www.cherwell-dc.gov.uk/banburymuseum). **Open** 9.30am-5pm Mon-Sat; 10.30am-4.30pm Sun. **Admission** free.

Café Quay
Spiceball Park Road, Banbury, OX16 2PQ (01295 270444/www.rosamundthefair.co.uk). **Open** 9.30am-6pm Mon-Sat; 10.30am-4.30pm Sun. **Credit** MC, V.

The Cotswolds

Fine ales, fine food and plenty of Cotswold charm at the **Blue Boar** in Chipping Norton.

Falkland Arms

Great Tew, nr Chipping Norton, OX7 4DB (01608 683653/fax 01608 683656/www.falklandarms. org.uk). **Rates** £40 single; £65-£80 double; £75 four-poster. **Rooms** (all en suite) 3 double; 1 single; 2 four-poster. **Credit** AmEx, MC, V.

How this creeper-clad, thatched pub in Great Tew retains its olde worlde feel while thronged with weekending Londoners is something of a mystery, but policies such as a ban on mobile phones help. Old mugs, jugs, pipes and snuffboxes line every inch of shelf and beam, a fire blazes in an inglenook, and outside a large garden looks out over rolling hills. The same view can be had from the spacious attic room, which is pricier but worth it as the others can be cramped and chintzy. Location is what you're paying for – not just the great pub stairs, but one of the most beautiful villages in the country. Lunch and dinner are available and booking is essential, even for guests. Forget Friday or Saturday evening as the diminutive dining room books up months in advance. No children under 14. All bedrooms are no-smoking.

A361 SW from Banbury; follow signs to Great Tew; on outskirts of the village, bear right towards the post office; Falkland Arms is three houses down from the post office.

Heythrop Park

Enstone, Chipping Norton, OX7 5UE (01608 673333/ fax 01608 673799/www.heythroppark.co.uk). **Rates** *Main house* £185 double; £285 deluxe room; £450 suite. *Falcon & Archer* £99 single occupancy; £119 double; £149 suite. **Rooms** (all en suite) 14 double in main house; 270 double in conference wings. **Credit** AmEx, DC, MC, V.

Once home to the Earl of Shrewsbury and (more recently) a Natwest training centre, this stately pile has now been restored to something like its original glory, and is open for business as a country house hotel. The rooms in the main house are impressive, particularly those upstairs, which command sweeping views of the extensive grounds. Each is different, but all have high ceilings, elegant decor and fabulous bathrooms with monsoon showers, roll-top baths and fluffy robes. Breakfast is buffet style – excellent pastries – in the grand dining room overlooking an Italian garden. If money's no object, go for the Fern suite, which is bigger than most London flats. For a last-minute place to crash, try the cheaper modern wings. They're basic conference-block style, with small, shower-only bathrooms. The

Falcon wing is the newest. There's a pool and gym in a separate block and a nine-hole golf course. Plans are afoot to turn Heythrop into a premier spa resort and to bump up the golf course to a championship-standard 18 holes. Children welcome.

A361 NE of Chipping Norton towards Oxford, through Bloxham & South Newington. Ignore sign to Heythrop Park & continue to roundabout. Take first exit on to A3400, signposted to Enstone & Woodstock. After five miles just before a sharp right-hand bend & Harrow Inn take left turn on to B4030. Entrance is 250 yards along on the left.

King's Head

The Green, Bledington, nr Kingham, OX7 6XQ (01608 658365/fax 01608 658902/www.kingshead inn.net). **Rates** £50 single occupancy (Mon-Thur, Sun only); £65-85 double/twin; £90 four-poster. **Rooms** (all en suite) 10 double/twin; 1 four-poster. **Credit** AmEx, MC, V.

Overlooking a classic village green – complete with ducks known by name locally – and within walking distance of Kingham station, the King's Head is a popular gaff, and deservedly so. Bedrooms are either old (but with modern, classy bathrooms), beamed, haunted and above the 15th-century inn or new, slightly bigger (presumably ghost-free) and across the courtyard. The room with the half-tester has a good view. Whichever you favour, all are pale, restful and charming. The lovely old low-beamed bar has an inglenook fireplace. Locals are carefully looked after with guest beers and their own room to escape the visiting masses. The restaurant is pale and interesting like the rooms and serves good food. Children welcome. All bedrooms are no-smoking.

B4450 from Chipping Norton towards Stow; turn off left for Bledington; the King's Head is on the Green.

The Mill House

North Newington, nr Banbury, OX15 6AA (01295 730212/fax 01295 730363/www.themillhouse banbury.com). **Rates** £49-£69 single occupancy; £69-£89 double; £105 four-poster; £89-£99 family room. **Rooms** (all en suite) 3 double/twin; 1 four-poster; 2 family. **Credit** AmEx, DC, MC, V.

The new owner has restored the old name to this 17th-century Jacobean mill house, idyllically situated in a beautiful garden with a stream, stunning views and a swimming pool tucked out of sight for use in the summer months. Guest rooms are low-ceilinged and beamed with fading floral patterns. The china wheelbarrows filled with dried flowers are gone but the rooms could

use a paintbrush. (And, apparently, that's exactly what they're going to get.) The exception is the lovely four-poster room, with huge bathroom and modern decor. To enjoy great views, ask for a room at the front of the house and throw open the windows. Friendly staff serve up excellent breakfasts in a pretty dining room. Children welcome. All bedrooms are no-smoking.
B4035 SW of Banbury; follow the signs to North Newington, the house is on the right before the village.

Where to eat & drink

There are surprisingly few top-notch restaurants for such a well-heeled area, but **Bowlers** (Market Place, Deddington, 01869 338813), which has replaced Chav Brasserie in Chipping Norton, is a pricey eaterie with flash ingredients and a more casual brasserie below. Also in town is the **Devil's Kitchen** (7 Horsefair, Chipping Norton, 01608 644666), a new arrival with more than a few hearty offerings. Luckily, there are an increasing number of pubs that have raised the bar food-wise. Aside from those reviewed below, others worthy of note include the newly refurbished **Great Western Arms** at Aynho (01869 338288), the **King's Head** in Bledington (*see p224*) and the tiny thatched **Stag's Head** at Swalcliffe (01295 780232).

Other cosy hostelries serving good ales and decent food include the beamed **Blue Boar** in Chipping Norton (01608 643525), the **Mason's Arms** in nearby Swerford (01608 683212), the **Duke of Cumberland's Head** in Clifton (01869 338534), the friendly **Blinking Owl** in North Newington (01295 730650) and the **North Arms** in Wroxton (01295 730318). The **Falkland Arms** (*see p224*) has an extensive range of real ales, English country wines and real cider; it also serves decent lunches in the garden. For out and out drinking, the **Pear Tree** (01608 737482) or the **Sun** (01608 737570) in Hook Norton are both popular, as is the **Cherington Arms** (01608 686233) in Cherington, where there's a lovely garden.

Fox & Hounds Inn
Great Wolford, CV36 5NQ (01608 674220). **Food served** noon-2pm, 7-9pm Tue-Sat; noon-2.30pm Sun. **Main courses** £8.95-£13. **Credit** MC, V.
A pair of beady foxy eyes watches your approach to this wisteria-clad 16th-century pub. The bar, with nearly 200 bottles of alphabetically arranged malt whiskies, is a lovely place to linger and the pub food is very good, so book ahead. Modern British dishes made with quality produce are well executed and beautifully presented. On a recent visit, creamy chicken liver parfait came with crisp toasted brioche and contrasted well with a citrussy Oxford sauce. Delicately smoked haddock was grilled to perfection, retaining its moist, yielding texture. It was paired with sautéed potatoes and a sassy bacon and chorizo combo. Puddings, such as bread and butter or sticky toffee, are belt looseners.

Joiner's Arms
Old Bridge Road, Bloxham, OX15 4LY (01295 720223). **Food served** noon-2pm, 6-10pm Mon-Sat; noon-9pm Sun. **Main courses** £6.95-£15.25. **Credit** MC, V.
Conveniently located on the A631 between Banbury and Chipping Norton, the Joiner's is a bright, attractive pub with stripped-pine interior, plenty of tables and a largish garden running down to a stream. It's a handy refuelling stop for a range of hearty sandwiches and jacket potatoes or even more substantial steak and mushroom pie. Other robust dishes include home-made sausages with coriander mash and redcurrant and thyme gravy. This is a family-friendly place, with a kids' menu at lunch, but steer toddlers away from the stream.

Red Lion
South Side, Steeple Aston, OX25 4RY (01869 340225). **Food served** noon-2pm, 7-9pm Tue-Sat; noon-3pm Sun. **Main courses** £7.50-£14.95. **Set lunch** (Sun) £12.95 2 courses, £14.95 3 courses. **Credit** MC, V.
Not to be confused with the White Lion in the village, the red version is a small, handsome country pub with jovial bar staff. The tiny, wonky-walled dining room makes you realise how Alice in Wonderland felt when she took that magic pill. Don't be put off by the predictable menu – it's the way they cook 'em that counts. Fair enough, pâté-stuffed mushrooms are nothing to write home about, but the chicken liver terrine is. The local steak is dry aged and has a lovely gamey tang, and beef bourguignon is a rich, sticky mass. Chocolate truffle torte is a perfect cylinder of wickedness and its crowning white chocolate truffle is the booziest we've tasted.

Whistlers
9 Middle Row, Chipping Norton, OX7 5NH (01608 643363). **Food served** noon-2.45pm, 6-10pm daily. **Main courses** £6.95-£12. **Set dinner** (Mon-Thur) £11.95 3 courses. **Credit** MC, V.
Whistlers' ground floor seems a perfectly decent local brasserie. The basement, however, is an art nouveau theme park, with posters of cavorting Parisian showgirls pasted all over the theatrically red walls. The menu offers standard brasserie fare (lamb cutlets with Lyonnaise potatoes, sea bass with lemon beurre blanc), with the odd twist (watermelon and feta salad), plus pizzas and a prix fixe menu. Afters are few and include syrup sponge pudding and crème brûlée. Service tends to be breezy.

White Horse
The Square, Kings Sutton, OX17 3RF (01295 810843). **Food served** noon-2pm, 6-9pm Mon-Sat; 12.30-4pm Sun. **Main courses** £6.95-£13.95. **Credit** AmEx, MC, V.
A refurb has turned this sports bar into the chic local dining destination. The look is stripped pine mis-matched chairs and tables, softened with warm tones on the walls, pillar candles and arty lamps. Starters are under a fiver and include the likes of black pudding salad with lardons and a poached egg. We tried beer-battered cod – a chunky piece of fish with a crisp batter. The accompanying hand-cut chips were a refreshing change from reconstituted starch. Coffee crème brûlée with macaroon biscuits was extremely good, too, with a perfect caramel crust. The dark chocolate tart, though, was tired and the chocolate measly.

The Cotswolds

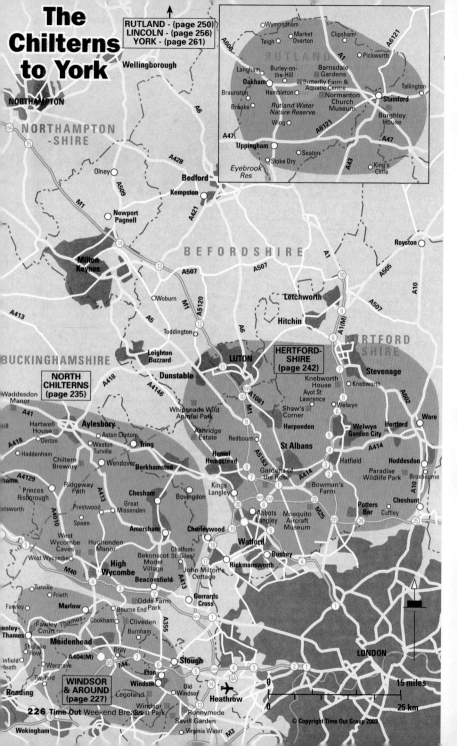

Windsor & Around

A place so rich the royals named themselves after it.

The beating heart of Windsor, its **castle**, is rich in history and aesthetically astonishing. It's also a well-baited tourist trap that in high season becomes a hell of crowds and snapping cameras. This is not to say that it should be avoided: if you don't fancy the full-on tourist experience, there are fantastic views of the exterior from the Long Walk in Windsor Great Park or from a boat along the river.

The castle was originally built by William the Conqueror and has since experienced countless rambling extensions, plus the odd fire (the last in 1992). Royals have always liked the castle and town of Windsor, so much so that during World War I the ruling family of Saxe-Coburg-Gothas decided to adopt it as their surname. The cobbled precinct round the castle is known as Guildhall Island, named after the Guildhall that stands within it, which was built by Sir Christopher Wren in the late 17th century. Today you can take tea in the curious lopsided timber building, imaginatively called the Crooked House Tea Rooms (01753 857534). Inside you'll notice that the pillars don't quite reach the ceiling – this was Wren's way of cocking a snook at the town planners, who insisted that there be columns inside the building in the interests of safety.

Eton College is another of Windsor's famous landmarks, and one equally worth visiting: the approach to the college via Eton Bridge is sepia postcard stuff. Eton is linked to Windsor by a footbridge at the foot of Thames Street and the college sits at the end of a street lined with antiques shops, Edwardian uniform outfitters, 'heritage' pubs and the Cockpit restaurant, which still has the original

cock-fighting area from the 17th century. The college was founded in 1440 by Henry VI for just 70 pupils and now has about 1,300 on the roster. Arrange a guided tour to see the Perpendicular chapel and the famous playing fields where the Battle of Waterloo was won, according to Wellington.

If you're pining for some greenery after these historic buildings, there are several parks and gardens within easy reach of Windsor, chief among them the ancient Windsor Great Park. One seasonal attraction of the area is the relatively low-key spectacle of Swan Upping, the marking of the Queen's swans by the official Monarch's Swan Marker, accompanied by brave members of the Royal Vintners and Dyers livery companies in suitably medieval attire. The small flotilla of rowing skiffs sets out from Windsor on the third week of July, embarking on a five-day journey upstream.

But if it's real tranquillity you're after, you'll need to look further afield. Some of the villages in the countryside around Windsor are so peaceable that they make the metropolis recede to little more than a smog-tinged memory. This is footballers' wives turf, so watch the prices: **Bray** may boast some of the best pubs and restaurants in the country, but food and lodgings don't come cheap, especially if you choose to dine in either of Heston Blumenthal's local garrisons of gastronomic fantasy, the **Fat Duck** and its gosling accomplice, the **Riverside Brasserie**.

At least it costs next to nothing to explore the expansive and sedate countryside. From Bray, follow the A4094 to **Cookham**, birthplace of eccentric and outstanding painter Sir Stanley Spencer. A short drive or cycle up the hill brings you to idyllic **Cookham Dean**, a picture of picnic spots and country lanes.

If it's walking you are after, head for **Marlow**. The town itself is big on links though small on sights. Jerome K Jerome penned much of *Three Men in a Boat* in the **Two Brewers**, a tidy little boozer on St Peter's Street, while Mary Shelley wrote *Frankenstein* in Albion House on West Street. Even the lofty T S Eliot descended from his cloud long enough to live at No.31, just down the road. While Marlow's popularity is due to its riverside location, you'll find more overwhelming natural beauty north-west of the town. This area is a rambler's

By train from London

Direct trains from **Waterloo** to **Windsor & Eton Riverside** depart every half hour, and take 50mins. Trains to **Henley-on-Thames** leave hourly from **Paddington**; with a change at **Twyford**, the journey takes just under 1hr. Hourly trains to **Marlow** leave from **Paddington** (change at **Maidenhead**); journey time is about 1hr. Info: www.thamestrains.co.uk and www.southwesttrains.co.uk

paradise, with refreshments available in the villages of **Frieth** and **Turville**, the latter of which is home to both *The Vicar of Dibley* and the smart modern dining of the **Bull and Butcher** (01491 638283). Also worth a visit is **Runnymede**, where King John sealed the Magna Carta and home of a secluded JFK memorial. Also nearby is **Cliveden**, where that quintessentially '60s scandal – John Profumo and Christine Keeler – had its beginnings.

What to see & do

Tourist Information Centres

King's Arms Barn, Kings Road, Henley-on-Thames, RG9 2DG (01491 578034/fax 01491 411766/www. henley-on-thames.org.uk). **Open** *Apr-Sept* 9.30am-6pm daily. *Oct-Mar* 9.30am-4pm daily.

24 High Street, Windsor, SL4 1LH (01753 743900/ accommodation 01753 743907/fax 01753 743904/ www.windsor.gov.uk). **Open** *mid Apr-June* 10am-4pm Mon-Fri; 10am-5.30pm Sat; 10am-4.30pm Sun. *July, Aug* 10am-6pm daily. *Sept-mid Apr* 10am-4pm daily.

Bike hire

Windsor Roller Rink & Cycle Hire *Alexandra Gardens, Alma Road, Windsor, SL4 5HZ (01753 830220/www.extrememotion.com).*

Ascot Racecourse

Ascot, SL5 7JN (01344 876876/www.ascot.co.uk). **Admission** £13-£33 (not incl Royal Ascot). **Credit** AmEx, DC, MC, V.

Home to horses to shameless hats and plenty of short men in silk tights. Highlights of the annual racing calendar include Royal Ascot (June), the Shergar Cup (August) and the Ascot Festival (September).

Cliveden

Off B476, Taplow, nr Maidenhead, SL6 0JA (01628 605069/hotel 01628 668561/www.national trust.org.uk). **Open** *Grounds* Mar-Oct 11am-6pm daily. Nov-Dec 11am-4pm daily. Closed Jan, Feb. *House & Octagon Temple* Apr-Oct 3-6pm Thur, Sun. Closed Nov-Mar. **Admission** (NT) *Grounds* £6; £3 concessions. *House, Octagon Temple & grounds* £1 extra; 50p extra. **Credit** MC, V.

With 375 acres of gardens, woodland cliffs overlooking the Thames and Roman remains scattered liberally around, it can be quite easy to forget that you're still in the UK, let alone 30 miles from London. Owned for three decades by the illustrious Astor family – during which time one John Profumo met a certain Christine Keeler in the pool – this imposing Italianate mansion (construction began in the 17th century) is now a hotel, where one night's stay in a standard double will cost you £345. It is also a National Trust property and admits visitors to the gardens and, between April and October, to the Octagon Temple and a few rooms in the house.

Dorney Court

Dorney, Windsor, SL4 6QP (01628 604638/fax 01628 665772/www.dorneycourt.co.uk). **Open** *May* 1.30-4.30pm bank hols & preceding Sun. *Aug* 1.30-4.30pm Mon-Fri, Sun. **Admission** £5.50; £3.50 concessions. **No credit cards**.

An impeccably preserved Tudor mansion in a Domesday village. Lunches are available and pick-your-own fruit and veg afternoons take place every summer.

Eton College

Eton High Street, Eton, SL4 6DW (01753 671177/ www.etoncollege.com). **Open** *Term-time* 2-4.30pm daily. *Holidays* 10.30am-4.30pm daily. *Guided tour* Apr-Sept 2.15pm, 3.15pm daily. **Admission** £3.70; £2.50 under-15s. *Guided tour* £4.70; £3.50 under-15s. **No credit cards**.

Hat's life at **Windsor Castle**. *See p231.*

Britain's most famous public school is worth a visit for its staggering 15th-century architecture and distinguished history: the college was founded in 1440 by Henry VI to provide a free education for just 70 pupils; it now has a roll of around 1,300 (and charges fees of more than £6,000 a term), and has produced 18 prime ministers. Tours include the elaborate chapel, extensive gardens and gabled school courts, culminating at the Museum of Eton Life beneath College Hall.

Fawley Court
Marlow Road, Henley-on-Thames, RG9 3AE (01491 574917). **Open** *May-Oct* (except Easter & Whitsun weekends) 2-5.30pm Wed, Thur, Sun. Closed Nov-Apr. **Admission** £4; £1.50-£3 concessions. **No credit cards**.
The grounds at Fawley date back more than 1,000 years, although the house wasn't built until the end of the 17th century. The architect is unknown – some attribute the work to local luminary Christopher Wren – but regardless of its maker, this red-brick manor house is worth a trip for 'Capability' Brown's landscaped gardens alone.

Frogmore House
Home Park, Windsor, SL4 1NJ (0207 321 2233/ www.royalresidences.com). **Open** *May* dates vary; usually weekend in mid May. *Aug* bank holiday weekend. **Admission** £5.20; £3.20-£4.20 concessions. **Credit** AmEx, MC, V.
Queen Victoria found Frogmore so calming that she decided to spend eternity here: her remains are interred alongside Albert's in a mausoleum in the grounds. The interior of the house – which dates from 1680 – is furnished with works of art by several generations of royalty, while the garden is a botanist's dream; it was developed by the green-fingered Queen Charlotte, wife of George III, who in the 18th century raised countless rare plants and flowers here, many of which remain.

Legoland Windsor
Winkfield Road, Windsor, SL5 4AY (01753 626111/www.legoland.co.uk). **Open** *mid Mar-July, Sept, Oct* 10am-6pm daily. *July, Aug* 10am-7pm daily. Closed Nov-mid Mar. **Admission** £19; £13-£16 concessions. **Credit** MV, V.
Those with reservations about crossing the M25 and leaving behind the familiar sights and sounds of London need have no fear: with scaled-down Lego versions of the Millennium Eye, Tower of London, and Buckingham Palace recently installed in this popular theme park's new attraction, Miniland London, you'll feel right at home. Alternatively, those who can't get far enough away from the capital might prefer to take a wild trip on the Lego safari, or encounter crocodiles, snakes and Chinese dragons on the Orient Expedition. Children will love you forever (or for a couple of hours at least) if you bring them here. The only problem lies in the enormous appeal of the world's favourite building blocks: queues are huge, and admission prices are high.

River & Rowing Museum
Mill Meadows, Henley-on-Thames, RG9 1BF (01491 415600/www.rrm.co.uk). **Open** *May-Aug* 10am-5.30pm daily. *Sept-Apr* 10am-5pm daily. **Admission** £4.95; £3.75 concessions.
The structure housing this museum is an architectural award-winner built of exposed concrete and glass and raised on columns above water meadows. There are three galleries; the first deals with rowing (from the ancient Greeks to the Sydney Olympics and beyond), the second with the history of the Thames and the third with the development of the town of Henley.

Royal Windsor Horse Show
Royal Mews, Windsor Castle, Windsor, SL4 1NG (01753 860633/www.royal-windsor-horse-show.co.uk).
Set in Windsor Castle's own Home Park, the royal residence makes a stunning backdrop for the country's largest equestrian event, which takes place over five days each May. Appropriately enough, the show attracts not only regal company, but also royal competition, with the Queen regularly entering many of her own horses and ponies.

Royal Windsor Racecourse
Maidenhead Road, Windsor, SL4 5JJ (01753 498400/www.windsor-racecourse.co.uk).
A regular programme of race days takes place throughout the year. The annual summer festival (end of May, beginning of June) has both a Family Day, with bands and rides, and a Ladies Night.

Stanley Spencer Gallery
King's Hall, High Street, Cookham, SL6 9DE (01628 471885/www.stanleyspencer.org.uk). **Open** *Easter-Oct* 10.30am-5.30pm daily. *Nov-Easter* 11am-5pm Sat, Sun, bank hols. **Admission** £1; 50p concessions; free children.
If Stanley Spencer was Windsor's William Blake, then Cookham is his Peckham Rye, a place of heavenly visitations and religious visions that informed his work until the day he died. This small, stand-alone gallery – a stone's throw from the cottage where Spencer was born and raised – offers an excellent introduction to this enigmatic artist, combining a permanent exhibition of his paintings with letters and memorabilia from his life.

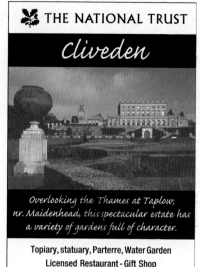

Windsor Castle

Windsor, SL4 1NJ (0207 766 7304/www.royal.gov.uk). **Open** *Mar-Oct* 9.45am-4pm (last entry) daily. *Nov-Feb* 9.45am-3pm (last entry) daily. **Changing of the Guard** (weather permitting) *Apr-June* 11am Mon-Sat. *July-Mar* check information line. **Admission** £11.50; £6-£9.50 concessions. **Credit** AmEx, MC, V.

As it's one of the Queen's official residences, it's hardly surprising that this, the largest and oldest occupied castle in the world, seems more formal than most. Admission to the castle usually includes entry to the state apartments, St George's Chapel, Queen Mary's dolls' house, the Albert Memorial Chapel, the castle precincts and the gallery. The state rooms include the opulent Waterloo Chamber, built to celebrate the victory over Napoleon in 1815. The gorgeous 15th-century St George's Chapel is the burial place of ten monarchs, including Henry VIII. The Queen Mother also lies there, since her death in 2002. The chapel is closed to visitors on Sunday, though worshippers are welcome. Edward Lutyens's amazing dolls' house (complete with flushing loos and electricity) involved the work of 1,500 men and took three years to complete.

Windsor Great Park

A 5,000-acre hunting ground dating back to the 13th century, the central feature of the park is the Long Walk, which begins at the gates of the castle and stretches as far as the artificial lake and associated curios of Virginia Water at the south end of the park; the Valley Gardens, on the northern shores of the lake; a 100ft, 12-ton totem pole; the artificial waterfall and grotto; the obelisk raised by George II; and the Roman ruins imported from Tripoli and erected here by the Prince Regent. En route the Long Walk also takes in the statue of the copper horse on Snow Hill, the huge expanse of Savill Gardens – one of the finest landscaped woodland gardens in temperate climes – and an excess of grass, woodland and fresh air. The manned gateway near Bishop's Gate is the entrance to the Royal Lodge, which was the Queen Mother's Windsor residence. Indeed, the hiding away of so much private land within the park boundaries adds to its mystery. Elsewhere within its 14-mile circumference the park houses Cumberland Lodge college, Smiths Lawn (home of the Guards Polo Club), a village for the people who work here and a school for their children.

Where to stay

Windsor is full of large, vaguely impersonal hotels, while the surrounding villages are peppered with places of real character. The **Holmwood** in Binfield Heath (01189 478747) offers comfortable B&B lodgings in a beautiful Georgian building, while the **Red Lion** on Hart Street (01491 572161) has the smartest digs in Henley. **Martens House** in Wargrave (01189 403707) occupies a tranquil riverside setting, and the **Runnymede Hotel** (Runnymede, 01784 436171) might not look like much from the outside, but it's perfect for large families, and boasts one of the best health spas in the area if you're looking for relaxation.

Restaurants with rooms include the **Walnut Tree** (01491 638360, Fawley Green, Henley-on-Thames), Bray's **Waterside Inn** on Ferry Road (01628 620691) and the **Cottage Inn** in Maidens Green (01344 882242), while the Georgian **Taplow House Hotel** on Berry Hill, Taplow (01628 670056), set in secluded grounds, may suit those not quite up to the hefty prices at neighbouring **Cliveden** (01628 668561). Finally, the **Little Parmoor** in Frieth (01494 881600) offers homely, family-run accommodation that won't break the bank.

Inn on the Green

The Old Cricket Common, Cookham Dean, SL6 9NZ (01628 482638/fax 01628 487474/www.theinnonthegreen.com). **Rate**s £100-£110 single; £130-£150 double. **Rooms** (all en suite) 9 double. **Credit** AmEx, MC, V.

A recent refurbishment has lent each of the Inn's nine chambers its own distinct character. They include a deluxe double in a striking marine blue, and an oversized room supported by heavy wooden timbers and awash with natural light. Perhaps the most impressive contrast, however, is between the rural idyll of the immediate surroundings (the Inn faces Cookham Dean's old cricket ground), and the truly cosmopolitan magic cooked up by Michelin-starred chef Gary Hollihead. Pets accepted by arrangement. Children welcome.

Monkey Island Hotel

Old Mill Lane, Bray-on-Thames, SL6 2EE (01628 623400/fax 01628 784732/www.monkeyisland.co.uk). **Rates** £130 single; £190-£205 double/twin; £235-£295 suite. **Rooms** (all en suite) 2 single; 10 double; 2 suites. **Credit** AmEx, DC, MC, V.

Monkey Island is a miniature Elysium, an island surrounded by the lapping Thames, accessed by a single bridge. It is a haven for local wildlife – although the only monkeys you'll find are painted on the ceiling of the former banqueting hall of the hotel building, originally a hunting lodge built by the third Duke of Marlborough in 1723. Accommodation is functional but fun, and the charm of wandering the periphery of your secluded piece of paradise is just too good to pass up. Children welcome. All rooms are no-smoking.

Oakley Court Hotel

Windsor Road, Water Oakley, SL4 5UR (01753 609988/fax 01628 637011/www.moathousehotels.com). **Rates** £165-£192 single occupancy; £140-£229 double/twin; £165-£269 family room; £200-£320 four-poster/suite. **Rooms** 20 twin; 71 double; 12 four-poster/suite; 20 family. **Credit** AmEx, DC, MC, V.

If Oakley Court is the Bentley of the hotel world, then it's one built in Dr Frankenstein's private garage. A looming Gothic mansion guarded by a legion of lofty gargoyles, the building has played a lead role in several Hammer horror classics (Hammer's studios are nearby in Bray). These days, the house is more Jekyll than Hyde, with superb accommodation, excellent service and a first-class restaurant (breakfast clocks in at £14.95 extra) overlooking riverside gardens. Combine this with the thrill of creeping around the creaking staircases after

Messing about on the river

The Thames at Windsor has an altogether different, more gentle quality from the river in London. And a summer boat trip here is a great way to seek refuge from the rigours of the tourist trail.

John Logie (The Promenade, Barry Avenue, Windsor, 07774 983809) hires small motorboats for up to six people (£18 for half an hour, £34 for an hour), as well as traditional rowing boats (£8 for half an hour, £14 for an hour). The company operates between Easter and September. The views of the castle from this part of the river are superb.

In an hour, however, you aren't going to get too far, and more adventurous boaters may be better off a stone's throw down the promenade at **French Brother's Ltd** (The Clewer Boathouse, Clewer Court Road, Windsor, SL4 5JH, 01753 851900/www.boat-trips.co.uk). Two-hour tours leave twice daily, and cruise all the way to Bray and back (£6.60 adults, £3.30 children, £18 family). Sights include Bray Studios (birthplace of *Thunderbirds* and the special effects in *Star Wars*), the miniature church at Boveney (seats 12, open twice a year) and Clewer Point, the sharpest corner on the Thames (rock aficionados may be more interested in peering throught the windows of neighbouring Clewer House, home to one Jimmy Page).

dark, bumping into the occasional suit of armour, Scooby-style, along the way, and you'll find yourself wishing that you could haunt these halls forever. Children welcome.

Sir Christopher Wren House Hotel `OFFER`

Thames Street, Windsor, SL4 1PX (01753 861354/ fax 01753 860172/www.wrensgroup.com). **Rates** (breakfast incl weekend only) £120-£150 single; £150-£200 double/twin; £170-£225 deluxe double/ twin/four-poster; £200-£275 suite. **Rooms** (all en suite) 11 single; 24 double; 8 twin; 16 deluxe double; 2 deluxe twin; 3 four-poster; 1 triple; 5 suites. **Credit** AmEx, DC, MC, V.
Once the family home of Sir Christopher Wren, the House Hotel offers some of the smartest accommodation in Windsor. The building is perched on the Thames beside Eton Bridge, with the option of several riverside balcony rooms. Cheaper rooms are available in several annexes along the High Street. Children welcome.

Where to eat & drink

Windsor has its fair share of traditional English restaurants, but for something a little different, grab a quality Turkish grill at the **Antalya**

Restaurant (64 Peascod Street, 01753 831300), fill up on hearty, home-made pasta (and some of the best cheesecake around) at **Claudio's** (83-4 Peascod Street, 01753 621818), or enjoy a pad Thai among palatial surroundings in the recently opened **Thai Square** (01753 868900, 29 Thames Street). The best pub grub in Windsor is found in the broom-closet sized **Two Brewers** (34 Park Street, 01753 855426) – be sure to book in advance.

The real gems are to be found outside the city, however, in smaller villages such as Bray and Cookham: Bray High Street is home to the delightful **Hind's Head** (01628 626151). Meanwhile, Cookham is the place to go for a top-notch curry, with **Malik's** (High Street, 01628 520085) and the **Cookham Tandoori** (High Street, 01628 522584) on opposite sides of the road, while the **Peking Inn** (High Street, 01628 520900) offers an adequate Chinese in more than adequate surroundings.

Hotels that offer a dining room worth cancelling the cab for include **Oakley Court Hotel** (*see p231*) and the **Taplow House Hotel** (Berry Hill, Taplow, 01628

Alternatively, **Kris Cruisers** (Southlea Road, Datchet, Slough, SL3 9BU, 01753 543930/www.kriscruisers.co.uk) rents self-drive holiday boats out of Datchet. One week on an eight-person cruiser costs from £574, and with a little elbow grease (six to seven hours sailing a day) you can make it to Oxford and be back in time for Sunday lunch. Mooring is permitted anywhere along the river unless otherwise indicated.

The area is perhaps best known for the **Henley Regatta** (01491 572153/ www.hrr.co.uk): Ascot with boats. This celebration of rowing draws competitors from across the world (the 2004 Regatta will be held between 30 June and 4 July). Small children may be more interested in the altogether less strenuous **Puppet Barge** (020 7249 6876/www.puppet barge.com), which moors at both Henley Bridge and Marlow during the summer.

670056), while the **Walnut Tree** at Fawley (Henley-on-Thames, 01491 638360) and the **White Hart** in Shiplake Row (01189 403673) are all pubs that are well worth tracking down.

Al Fassia

27 St Leonards Road, Windsor, SL4 3BP (01753 855370). **Food served** noon-2.30pm, 6.30-11pm daily. **Main courses** £8.95-£12.95. **Credit** AmEx, DC, MC, V.

Al Fassia calls itself a 'Restaurant Gastronomique Marocaine' but after that mouthful it's a model of unpretentiousness and welcomes you with Moroccan friendliness. The long, slim den of a room is filled with filigree brass lamps, embroidered horse ornaments and well-fed people. The scent of tagines and mint tea is beguiling: this is Moroccan dining at its most attractive and hospitable. Briwats are deep-fried crunchy filo parcels filled with gently spiced vegetables, minced pork (an adaptation for the British market, we presume) or sardines, while zaalouk – a smoky aubergine and garlic paste – is served at room temperature with own-made bread. In another break from tradition, tagines are served with featherweight couscous (not done in Morocco, but it's a good combination). Long spears of grilled meat and veggie options, such as Sahara-style white bean stew, are other popular dishes. Desserts are of the honeyed pastry and nut variety. Fabulous.

Bel and the Dragon

High Street, Cookham, SL6 9SQ (01628 521263/ www.belandthedragon.co.uk). **Food served** noon-2.30pm, 7-10pm Mon-Sat; noon-3pm, 7-9.30pm Sun. **Main courses** £11-£20. **Credit** AmEx, MC, V.

Dan McDonald's Dragon is now turning out some of the best food in central Windsor, but the original Cookham branch is still the best. It looks like a golden oldie from the outside, but inside it opens cavernously into a red-painted, church-chaired, many-staffed eating hall. Efficiency is the watchword, with orders rapidly taken and thereafter dizzying waves of bread, oil, relishes, wine and other paraphernalia are rushed to the table. Spot-on sandwiches, served with the sort of chips you could build a small house with, are joined by an eclectic selection of other dishes: seafood hotpot with summer vegetables and lime; gnocchi tossed with roast peppers, sunblushed tomatoes, fennel and rosemary; or roast rib of beef, capped by a pudding the size of Yorkshire.

Cottage Inn

Winkfield Street, Maidens Green, Winkfield, SL4 4SW (01344 882242/www.cottage-inn.co.uk). **Food served** noon-2.30pm, 7-9.30pm daily. **Main courses** £11.55-£44. **Credit** AmEx, DC, MC, V.

Owners John and Bobby have been drawing crowds to their unimposing little pub, framed by rolling fields and farmland, for 15 years now. Game is a popular choice

The Chilterns to York

with many of the regulars, with grouse and pheasant served with lashings of bacon, gravy and a traditional bread sauce. Specials include plenty of fresh fish, with dishes such as grilled salmon in saffron beurre blanc sauce and sea bass fillet with lime and mango salsa chalked up daily on the blackboard.

Crown Inn

High Street, Bray, SL6 2AH (01628 621936). **Food served** noon-2pm, 7-9.30pm daily. **Main courses** £6.75-£14.80 lunch; £13.95-£18.50 dinner. **Credit** AmEx, MC, V.

In an area where style (but what style!) so often wins over content, the Crown Inn, thankfully, remains true to its roots as a local that just happens to serve outstanding food at reasonable prices. Park yourself somewhere near the open fire and ponder the menu of traditional English and Mediterranean options, ranging from the likes of home-made chicken and tarragon pie to succulent breast of Barbary duck in a port and fig sauce. Desserts are decent but it's the prices that will really put a smile on your face.

Fat Duck

High Street, Bray, SL6 2AQ (01628 580333/ www.thefatduck.co.uk). **Food served** noon-2pm, 7-9.30pm daily. **Set lunch** £27.95 3 courses; £60 8 courses, £75 12-course tasting menu. **Set dinner** £60 8 courses; £75 12-course tasting menu. **Credit** AmEx, DC, MC, V.

The spiky metalwork has been replaced by a suave collection of softer furnishings, the front of house staff have lost their sometimes disdainful airs and the food has never been better – it seems the Fat Duck team is maturing with the years. Legendary chef Heston Blumenthal is a culinary witchdoctor, wilfully ignoring convention and abstractedly combining the mundane and mad to powerful and extraordinary effect. Concoctions could be something like cuttlefish and duck cannelloni, layered quail, langoustine and pea mousse, or a cauliflower and chocolate risotto. Colours are always wild, flavours intricate and interwoven, and presentation toe-curlingly good. Push the boat out and go for the 12-course tasting menu to get the full benefit of the Blumenthal experience. This is a posh frock restaurant with serious prices and a satisfying wow factor.

Riverside Brasserie

Bray Marina, Monkey Island Lane, Bray, SL6 2AQ (01628 780553/www.riversidebrasserie.co.uk). **Food served** noon-3pm, 6-10pm Tue-Sun. **Main courses** £13-£16. **Credit** AmEx, DC, MC, V.

Set amid a forest of masts and sails at Bray Marina, the Riverside Brasserie is an intimate space, with a tranquil waterside terrace. It is the sister restaurant to the Fat Duck (*see above*), so diners should know what to expect from mad scientist-cum-chef Heston Blumenthal: bright, bizarre and bold dishes, characterised by strange colours and stranger combinations. Prices can seem on the high side: a fish soup starter was flavoursome, but at £8.25 for roughly ten spoonfuls, rather unsatisfying. Peppers stuffed with mackerel were rather tasteless. Things improved with the mains, however: a soft square of pork belly was imaginatively complemented by a sharp celeriac puree, and poached salmon was beautifully accompanied by a textured white bean sauce. Service is intimate and unhurried.

Spice Route

18A Thames Street, Boots Passage, Windsor, SL4 1PL (01753 860720/www.mridula.co.uk). **Food served** noon-2.30pm, 6-11pm daily. **Set lunch** £5. **Set dinner** £12.95 (early evening). **Main courses** £6.95-£14.50. **Credit** AmEx, MC, V.

Not your usual Indian restaurant this, with its noisily stark interior and a more than decent wine list (gasp!). The proprietor is Indian cookery writer and sometime TV chef Mridula Baljekar, a polite and petite woman who can be seen at customers' tables quietly mopping up praise, while her head chef beavers away behind closed doors coming up with some superb flavours. Instead of jarringly Anglicised versions of nowhere-near-Indian dishes found in even many of the better Indian restaurants in this country, this team turns out cracklingly authentic food such as pomegranate and spinach soup, venison tikka, clay oven-cooked potatoes and Himalayan wok-cooked chicken. Rice and bread are super-fresh, fragrant and sublime; you can see the bread come out of the heat-shimmered tandoor.

Waterside Inn

Ferry Road, Bray, SL6 2AT (01628 620691/ www.waterside-inn.co.uk). **Food served** Feb-May, Sept-Dec noon-2pm, 7-10pm Wed-Sat; noon-2.30pm, 7-10pm Sun. *June-Aug* 7-10pm Tue; noon-2pm, 7-10pm Wed-Sat; noon-2.30pm, 7-10pm Sun. Closed Jan. **Main courses** £34-£44. **Set lunch** (Mon-Sat) £36 2 courses, (Sun) £52 3 courses. **Set dinner** £78 5 courses. **Credit** AmEx, DC, MC, V.

Outside there's little indication that this is hallowed ground for gourmets (the only other establishment in Great Britain or Ireland to have earned a complement of three Michelin stars is Gordon Ramsay in London). Within, a small plush lounge leads to a dining room that might be considered dated and gaudy. Mirrors interspersed with wall panels painted with floral scenes are set behind green banquettes. Yet the view of the Thames is glorious and an expanse of French windows shows it off to grand effect. Michel Roux and his son Alain's haute French cooking is similarly spectacular. The seasonal 'menu extraordinaire' enables you to sample five courses taken from the carte: in smaller portions, and without ingredients such as sturgeon, foie gras and truffles in such abundance. It will tether the bill to around £100 a head if you opt for one of the half-dozen wines costing under £25 (from a vast French-only list). Choice is limited, but heavenly extras ensure the gamut of gastronomic fireworks is experienced – from *amuse-bouches* such as asparagus quiches, via delectable pre-starters such as lobster morsels in a gelée under a creamy fennel mousse topped with sevruga caviar, to luxurious petits fours with coffee. Imagination yet restraint, clarity of flavour and lightness of touch characterise such dishes as an inspiring fish course of steamed salmon fillet flavoured with grapefruit (a successfully bitter counterfoil), served with sliced asparagus, red lentils and an asparagus nage. The only faintly questionable dish was a rose petal sorbet that perfectly captured the floral essence but seemed too sweet a palate-cleanser. Yet rolled loin of lamb with grain mustard, pancetta, soft white beans and girolle mushrooms made a divine, full-flavoured main course, the meat rare and tender. Paunchy power-brokers dine here, but so do couples celebrating life-shaping events.

North Chilterns

Find paradise in Milton country.

In 1965 the Chiltern Hills were designated an Area of Outstanding Beauty, a recognition of the fact that the countryside here is some of the finest in England. Close to London, yet without a real urban centre of its own, it's a great place for cycling and walking – twice the national average of footpaths cross the Chilterns, there are plenty of quiet lanes, and the area is studded with characterful pubs.

There are many fine houses here too. **Waddesdon Manor**, for example, is a grand 19th-century palace built by Baron Ferdinand de Rothschild in the style of a 16th-century French château, housing a stunning collection of art and boasting magnificent gardens. **Hughenden Manor** is a former home of Benjamin Disraeli, while the 90-acre grounds of **Hartwell House**, a residence of Louis XVIII while in exile and now a first-class hotel, are worth the trip even if all you can afford to do there is put your feet up and sip coffee fit for a king.

If putting your feet up is the last thing on your mind, slip on your hiking boots and head for the Chiltern Way. The **Chiltern Society** (The White Hill Centre, White Hill, Chesham, 01494 771250) recently launched this 134-mile walk, which takes in four counties as it weaves a loose circle in the landscape.

The Vale of Aylesbury provides the perfect location for cyclists as it's at the heart of the National Cycle Network. You can choose between quiet country lanes through gently

By train from London

Direct trains from **Marylebone** to **Aylesbury** leave about every 20mins and take just under 1hr. Some services stop at **Wendover**, **Great Missenden** and **Amersham**. There are three trains an hour from **Marylebone** to **High Wycombe**, which take between 30mins and 40mins; some stop at **Beaconsfield**. Info: www.chilterntrains.co.uk.

hilly countryside, or rougher trails that allow you to explore the woodland environment at close quarters. For those seeking a challenge, Wendover Woods has a specially designated mountain bike course at **Aston Hill**.

If you're not quite so energetic, there are plenty of less exacting ways to enjoy the great outdoors. **Tring** is a good starting point for those seeking beauty without the blisters; its riverside rambles along the Grand Union Canal are splendid, while the Ridgeway Path leads from the town to **Ivinghoe Beacon**, megalithic portal to the Chilterns. From here you can wander 85 miles into Wiltshire on one of the oldest pathway in England, the Icknield Way (dating back 3,000 years). Refurbished steam trains – operating between **Chinnor** and **Princes Risborough** – follow much of the same route on the restored Icknield Line.

Milton's Cottage. *See p237.*

The village of **Lacey Green** lies along the top of another Chiltern ridge, above the main Princes Risborough to High Wycombe road. It's windmill is the oldest surviving mill of its type in the country. Two miles south-east of Lacey Green is the village of **Speen**, embraced on three sides by the arms of an Iron Age earthwork, Grims Ditch, giving rise to the theory that the village marks the site of an ancient settlement.

Amersham has a 12th-century Norman church in the old half of the town, as well as some of the finest food in the Chilterns. **Thame** is also worth a visit, if only to tour the fine 13th-century parish church, modelled on Lincoln Cathedral and housing a memorial to one Geoffrey Dormer, who fathered no fewer than 25 children with only two wives.

After a look at **Rycote Chapel**'s ornate wooden carvings, travel north-west from Thame to **Brill**, a village of superb views with neolithic ruins. Nearby is **Ludgershall Church** – where John Wycliffe began his translation of the scriptures into English in 1378. A far less upstanding history, spiritually speaking, is attached to **West Wycombe Caves**, once home of the black rituals of the infamous and appropriately named Hellfire Club.

For literary connections, head to **Great Missenden**, to pay homage to one-time resident Roald Dahl. The troubled Robert Louis Stevenson was also a local, although if it's genuinely disturbed genius you're after, John Milton's cottage, in **Chalfont St Giles**, offers a unique insight into one of the most revolutionary imaginations of all time.

Things to see & do

Tourist Information Centres

8 Bourbon Street, Aylesbury, Buckinghamshire HP20 2RR (01296 330559/www.visitbuckinghamshire. org/www.aylesburyvale.net). Open Apr-Oct 9.30am-5pm Mon-Sat. Nov-Mar 10am-4.30pm Mon-Sat.

Market House, North Street, Thame, Oxfordshire OX9 3HH (01844 212834). Open Jan-July, Sept-Dec 9.30am-5pm Mon-Fri; 10am-4pm Sat. Aug 9.30am-5pm Mon-Fri; 10am-4pm Sat; 10am-3pm Sun.

The Clock Tower, High Street, Wendover, Buckinghamshire HP22 6DU (01296 696759/ www.chilternweb.co.uk/wendover). Open 10am-4pm Mon-Sat.

Paul's Row, High Wycombe, HP11 2HQ (01494 421892/www.wycombe.gov.uk). Open 9.30am-5pm Mon-Thur; 9.30am-4.30pm Fri; 9.30am-4pm Sat.

Bekonscot Model Village

Warwick Road, Beaconsfield, Buckinghamshire HP9 2PL (01494 672919/www.bekonscot.com). Open Mid Feb-Oct 10am-5pm daily. Closed Nov-mid Feb. **Admission** *£4.80; £3-£4 concessions; free under-3s.* **Credit** MC, V.

Stretching over more than an acre, Bekonscot Model Village is devoted to faithfully reproducing 1930s village life. The streets are teeming with model villagers frozen in the details of their daily routines: chatting in the street, strolling the public zoo or just lazily soaking up the cricket, while a Gauge One model railway weaves its way over downsized hills and dales.

Chenies Manor House

Chenies, Buckinghamshire WD3 6ER (01494 762888). Open Apr-Oct 2-5pm Wed, Thur. Closed Nov-Mar. **Admission** *House & gardens £5; £3 concessions. Gardens only £3; £1.50 concessions.* **No credit cards.**

This picturesque manor house, built by Sir John Cheyne in the first half of the 17th century, is a fortress fit for royalty. Both Henry VIII and Elizabeth I were entertained here, and the house is suitably attired with contemporary furniture, antique tapestries and a network of underground passages, crypts and a medieval well. It's Chenies' splendid gardens, however, that garner most attention.

Chiltern Brewery

Nash Lee Road (on B4009), Terrick, nr Aylesbury, Buckinghamshire HP17 0TQ (01296 613647/ www.chilternbrewery.co.uk). Open Museum 9am-5pm Mon-Sat. Guided tours phone for details. **Admission** *Museum free. Guided tours £3.50; £3 concessions.* **Credit** MC, V.

Tours of one of Britain's oldest and best-loved working breweries can be booked in advance, and may include a meal as well as plenty of unavoidable and utterly legitimate beer tasting. It's all in the name of education, after all. And as if to prove it, there's a small on-site museum, as well as a Chilterns Brewery store where your new friends can be picked up by the bottle or in cases.

Chiltern Open Air Museum

Newlands Park, Gorelands Lane, Chalfont St Giles, Buckinghamshire HP8 4AB (01494 871117/ 24hr info 01494 872163/www.coam.org.uk). Open Apr-Oct 10am-5pm daily. Closed Nov-Mar. **Admission** *£6; £3.50-£5 concessions; free under-5s.* **Credit** MC, V.

Over the years, more than 30 historically significant buildings have been spared demolition, transported and reassembled here. These include a 16th-century Arborfield barn, a 100-year-old public toilet from Caversham and even a primitive Iron Age dwelling. A working Victorian farm offers horse and cart rides alongside the chance to pet some genuinely playful animals.

Hughenden Manor

Valley Road, High Wycombe, Buckinghamshire HP14 4LA (01494 755573/info line 01494 755565/ www.nationaltrust.org.uk). Open House Mar 1-5pm Sat, Sun. Apr-Oct 1-5pm Wed-Sun. Garden Mar noon-5pm Sat, Sun. Apr-Oct noon-5pm Wed-Sun. Both Closed Nov-Feb. **Admission** *(NT) House & garden £4.70; £2.30 concessions. Garden £1.70; 80p concessions.* **No credit cards.**

Hughenden was once the home of Britain's first and only Jewish prime minister, the accomplished Victorian author, debater and all-round dandy Benjamin Disraeli. On display are many of Disraeli's original pictures and books, including an autographed copy of Queen Victoria's only published work. The gardens have been

Bekonscot Model Village. *See p236.*

Rothschild Zoological Museum. *See p240.*

re-created according to designs by Mary Anne, his wife, and there are plenty of attractive walks to be had in the surrounding woodland.

Milton's Cottage

Deanway, Chalfont St Giles, Buckinghamshire HP8 4JH (01494 872313/www.miltonscottage.org). **Open** *Mar-Oct* 10am-1pm, 2-6pm Tue-Sun. Closed Nov-Feb. **Admission** £3; £1 concessions. **No credit cards**.

In 1665, as plague raged in London, Milton asked his friend and secretary Thomas Ellwood to search for lodgings in the country; he found this 'pretty box' in the village of 'Giles Chalfont'. It was here that he is said to have finished his epic *Paradise Lost*, begun 20 years earlier. As well as being England's greatest poet, Milton was a renowned political activist and staunch anti-royalist. He eventually curtailed his writings to follow the Parliamentary cause, becoming Latin Secretary to Oliver Cromwell. An on-site museum sheds light on one of the most tortured and significant minds in literary history.

Rycote Chapel

Off A329, nr Thame, Oxfordshire (01483 252000). **Open** *Apr-Sept* 2-6pm Fri-Sun. Closed Oct-Mar. **Admission** (EH) £1.70; £1.30-90p concessions. **No credit cards**.

An original 15th-century chapel with intricate carved fittings, ceilings painted with stars, and a musicians' gallery precariously balanced on the north pew. Built by one-time High Sheriff of Oxfordshire Richard Quatermain, the chapel was used by many Tudor and Stewart monarchs during trips to nearby Rycote Palace, only part of which now remains, privately owned.

Steam Trains

Talking timetable/info line 01844 353535/www. cprra.co.uk. **Tickets** £6; £3-£5 concessions. **Credit** MC, V.

Lovingly restored by buffs, Chinnor station is the scene of hissing carriages and blowing whistles. Chinnor is the perfect place to jump on one of many locomotives chasing the Icknield Line all the way to Princes Risborough through glorious countryside. Teas are available, and Thomas the Tank Engine makes occasional appearances to appease his fans (phone for more information).

Waddesdon Manor

Waddesdon, nr Aylesbury, Buckinghamshire HP18 0JH (01296 653226/www.waddesdon.org.uk). **Open** *House* (including wine cellars) Apr-Oct 11am-4pm Wed-Sun. Closed Nov-Mar. *Grounds* Mar-Dec 10am-5pm Wed-Sun. Closed Jan, Feb. **Admission** (NT) *House & grounds* £11; £8 concessions; free under-5s. *Grounds* £4; £2 concessions; free under-5s. **Credit** AmEx, MC, V.

Originally built by Baron Ferdinand de Rothschild to house and display his stunning collection of European art and antique furniture, and set in sumptuous grounds, Waddesdon remains an essential stop for art lovers, gardeners, and anyone who likes amazing, opulent buildings. An annual programme of events includes lectures, walks and regular wine tasting sessions: phone for a brochure.

West Wycombe Caves

West Wycombe Hill Road, West Wycombe, Buckinghamshire HP14 3AJ (01494 533739/www.hell firecaves.co.uk). **Open** *Mar-Oct* 11am-5.30pm daily. *Nov-Feb* 11am-5.30pm Sat, Sun. **Admission** £3.75; £2.50-£3 concessions. **Credit** AmEx, DC, MC, V.

Sir Francis Dashwood excavated this ancient quarry in the mid 18th century. His purpose was altruistic: to find work for unemployed farm hands after a string of bad harvests. No sooner were the caves uncovered, however, than Dashwood and his mates were dressing as monks and conducting black masses in their darkest recesses, with plenty of mock nuns – drawn from London's legion of prostitutes – helping distribute the booze and wafers. The Hellfire Club was born. Oh, if these walls could talk.

Where to stay

You aren't quite so spoiled for choice when it comes to finding a bed in the North Chilterns as you are for eating and knocking back pints, but there are still plenty of charming inns and hotels. In addition to those listed below, a pleasant stay can be had at the **Three Horse Shoes** in Bennett End, Radnage (Horse Shoe Road, 01494 483273) and the **King's Arms** in Stokenchurch (Oxford Road, 01494 609090).

Of the restaurants we list, both the **Angel** (*see p241*) and the **Old Trout** (*see p241*) have rooms. **Champneys** at Wiggington near Tring (01442 291000/08703 300300/www.champneys. com) is a sprawling health resort where you can relax and recharge the batteries in style.

There are numerous farmhouses in the area that offer unfussy accommodation in idyllic surroundings: **Poletrees Farm** in Brill (Ludgershall Road, 01844 238276) and **Hallbottom Farm** near Chinnor (Park Lane, Stokenchurch, 01494 482520/www.hall bottomfarm.co.uk) are two of the best.

Hartwell House

Oxford Road, nr Aylesbury, Buckinghamshire HP17 8NL (01296 747444/fax 01296 747450/www. hartwell-house.com). **Rates** £145-£195 single; £240 double/twin; £355-£425 four-poster; £345-£700 suites. Breakfast £17.50 (Eng); £13.50 (cont). **Rooms** (all en suite) 7 single; 22 double/twin; 5 four-poster; 12 suites. **Credit** AmEx, MC, V.

Extensively restored in recent years, this magnificent stately home – a five-year sanctuary for the exiled French King Louis XVIII – retains an atmosphere of almost overwhelming grandeur. From fireside couches in the ornate drawing rooms, to the intricately carved Gothic warriors standing vigil over the winding staircase, Hartwell House allows anyone to play king for a day (if you have the funds). Rooms are suitably furnished with antiques, while some of the grander, first-floor suites offer superb views over 90 acres of sprawling grounds, complete with cedar trees and ruined chapel. Children over eight welcome; dogs welcome in the Hartwell Court annexe.

The George & Dragon

High Street, West Wycombe, Buckinghamshire HP14 3AB (01494 464414/fax 01494 462432/ www.george-and-dragon.co.uk). **Rates** £75-£80 double/twin; £75 family room (sleeps 3; £10 for extra person); £80 four-poster. **Rooms** (all en suite) 7 double; 1 twin; 1 family room; 2 four-poster. **Credit** AmEx, DC, MC, V.

The George & Dragon is an old timbered coaching inn, physically buckling under more than 300 years of history. Eleven en suite rooms are inventively adapted to make best use of the building's uneven floors and sloping walls: one straddles a brick archway separating the stone courtyard from West Wycombe's tranquil High Street. The hotel's quintessential Chiltern charm gives a little during dinner, with Mediterranean and Eastern meals served in the bar alongside more traditional steaks, pies and sticky puds. Children and dogs welcome.

The Five Arrows Hotel

High Street, Waddesdon, Buckinghamshire HP18 0JE (01296 651727/fax 01296 658596/www. waddesdon.org.uk). **Rates** £65 single; £70-£85 single occupancy; £85-£95 double; £150 suite. **Rooms** (all en suite) 1 single; 8 double; 2 suites. **Credit** AmEx, MC, V.

Baron Ferdinand de Rothschild built Waddesdon Manor in the second half of the 19th century to house his outstanding collection of European art. He bestowed upon his chosen villagers a schoolhouse, village hall and – although he himself never touched the hard stuff – a public house, the Five Arrows. This ivy-covered inn is less formal than you might imagine, dressed in a bric-a-brac of copper bells, brass horns and the like. The 11 rooms are similarly homely and unpretentious, although two suites have four-poster beds, sitting room furniture and an open fire. All bedrooms are no-smoking.

The Crazy Bear

Bear Lane, Stadhampton, Oxfordshire OX44 7UR (01865 890714/fax 01865 400481/www.crazybear hotel.co.uk). **Rates** £85-£110 single occupancy (Sun-Thur only); £120-£150 double; £250-£280 suite. **Rooms** (all en suite) 7 double; 4 suite; 1 cottage. **Credit** AmEx, MC, V.

If you're unamused by the decorative mainstay of traditional country inns – ornamental plough blades and horseshoes nailed to the hearth – then beat a retreat to the Crazy Bear, where bold, modern decor dominates. Rooms are all individually designed in suitably stark shapes, arrangements and colours: the bath in the airy peppermint suite, for example, is at the foot of the bed. The restaurant offers Thai food alongside an inventive à la carte menu, and the bar has draught champagne on tap. If it sounds strange, then that's because it is – garishly, gloriously so. A Japanese water garden babbles merrily out back and the grizzly in question – stuffed and manacled – overlooks everything with a roar that is almost audible. Children welcome.

Where to eat & drink

The North Chilterns has more than its fair share of fine dining: along with the places listed below, the restaurant at the **Swan Hotel** in Thame (Upper High Street, 01844 261211) is worth a visit, as is the **Rose & Crown** at Saunderton (Wycombe Road, 01844 345299), although the stark contours of its duo-tone interior might ward off traditionalists.

The real charm of the Chilterns, however, is its pubs: the place has a seemingly endless supply of real gems, many serving quality food to boot. The **Chequers** in Watlington (58 Love Lane, 01491 612874) is a good example, lush and intimately lit, while the ever-popular **Shepherd's Crook** in Crowell (The Green, 01844 351431) offers fine and fresh fish specials. The **Mole & Chicken** at Easington (01844 208387) is a slightly more upbeat watering hole, with hearty meals at reasonable prices, and both the **Olde Leathern Bottel** at Lewknor (1 High Street, 01844 351482) and the **Bell** in Chearsley (The Green, 01844 208077) are picturesque little pubs worth making a detour for. The **Fox & Hounds** (Christmas Common, nr Watlington, 01491 612599) combines rural flagstone aesthetics in the cosy bar with a modern restaurant in an annexe, while the **Green Dragon** at Haddenham (8 Churchway, 01844 291403) serves award-winning local ale along with modern food, prepared with flair.

Animal magic

Wildlife watchers and animal lovers of all kinds will find plenty of interest in the North Chilterns.

This area is renowned as a birdwatchers' paradise where rare breeds, from barn owls and buzzards to curlews and plovers, can be seen in beautiful surroundings. The **Hawk & Owl Trust** (01494 876262/ www.hawkandowl.org), which operates out of a restored 19th-century barn at the excellent Chiltern Open Air Museum (*see p236*), organises an annual programme of birdwatching events, from weekend workshops to 'owl prowls' and dawn chorus walks.

Odds Farm Park is a very popular venue with younger animal lovers; it's a perfect spot for children to get up close and personal with a host of kids (the goat kind), calves and chicks. Other regular activities include shearing and feeding, with a host of other events (bottle-feeding spring lambs, for example) dependent on the time of year: check the website for a calendar.

The **St Tiggywinkles Wildlife Hospital** Trust began life in the Stocker family's garden shed. It has expanded over the past two decades to include x-ray rooms, intensive care units and state of the art nurseries. The emphasis on improvisation remains unchanged, however: staff still use shopping trollies to transport tetchy swans, while splints for birds are cut from cereal boxes. The hospital itself is off-limits to the public, but there's an informative visitors' centre where more long-term disabled residents live, including Ruffty the blind badger and Snowflake the albino hedgehog.

Horses in need of some good old TLC are catered for at the **Home of Rest for Horses** (Westcroft Stables, Speen Farm, Slad Lane, Princes Risborough, 01494 488464/www.homeofrestforhorses.co.uk). Equine residents can be afflicted by anything from show jumping injuries to some horrible cases of owner neglect.

It's a colourful community, home to real characters such as 30-year-old Echo, a resident here ever since he was caught in the IRA's 1982 Hyde Park bombing, or Kettledrum and Janus, who both served in the Household Cavalry for more than 15 years.

Finally, for those who prefer their animals less, er, alive, there is the **Rothschild Zoological Museum**. In this monument to 19th-century taxidermy you'll find more than 4,000 species of dangerous animals, including crocs, tigers and giant snakes.

Odds Farm Park
Woburn Common, High Wycombe, Buckinghamshire HP10 0IX (01628 520188/www.oddsfarm.co.uk). **Open** *Mid Feb-June, Sept, Oct 10am-5.30pm daily. July, Aug 10am-6pm daily. Nov-mid Feb 10am-4.30pm daily. Last admission 1hr before closing. Closed 2wks Christmas & New Year.* **Admission** £5.50; £3.50-£5 concessions. **Credit** MC, V.

St Tiggywinkles Wildlife Hospital
Aston Road, Haddenham, Buckinghamshire HP17 8AF (01844 292292/www.sttiggywinkles.org.uk). **Open** *Easter-Sept 10am-4pm daily. Oct-Easter 10am-4pm Mon-Fri.* **Admission** £3.80; £2.80 concessions; free under-5s. **Credit** MC, V.

Home Of Rest For Horses
Westcroft Stables, Speen Farm, Slad Lane, Princes Risborough, Buckinghamshire HP27 0PP (01494 488464/www.homeofrestforhorses. co.uk). **Open** 2-4pm daily. **Admission** free, donations welcome.

Rothschild Zoological Museum
Akeman Street, Tring, Hertfordshire, HP23 6AP (020 7942 6171/www.nhm. ac.uk/museum/tring). **Open** 10am-5pm Mon-Sat, 2-5pm Sun. **Admission** free, donations welcome.

Amersham, in particular, has an abundance of good places to eat, including the **King's Arms** (30 High Street, 01494 726333), a decent pub, and **La Zucca** (18 High Street, 01494 728667), as well as **Gilbey's** (1 Market Square, 01494 723216) and the **Famous Fish Company** (11 Market Square, 01494 728665), which serves fantastically fresh fish.

Finally, don't miss the **Frog** in Skermit (geddit?), if only to scoff a king-sized sandwich surrounded by its stunning 'middle of nowhere' garden views.

The Angel

47 Bicester Road, Long Crendon, Buckinghamshire HP18 9EE (01844 208268). **Food served** noon-2.30pm Mon-Sat; 7-9.30pm Sun. **Main courses** £12.95-£19.75. **Set lunches** £11.75 1 course, £14.75 2 courses, £17.50 3 courses. **Credit** MC, V.

With leather couches framing the laid-back bar and a conservatory dining room bathed in natural light, the Angel's interior is a treat. It's the food, however, that is genuinely heaven sent. Starters include original delights such as salad of roast quail, black pudding and pancetta with mustard butter, while mains tend to be as extravagant but impeccably executed: breast of guinea fowl, for example, comes wrapped in parma ham and accompanied with a vegetable, saffron and barley broth. Fresh fish is imported daily from Billingsgate market, and three bedrooms are available for those who, quite understandably, refuse to leave.

Annie Baileys

Chesham Road, Great Missenden, Buckinghamshire HP16 0QT (01494 865625). **Food served** noon-2.30pm, 7-9.45pm Mon-Sat; noon-8pm Sun. **Main courses** £9.50-£15.95. **Set lunches** £15 2 courses, £18.50 3 courses. **Credit** AmEx, MC, V.

Any restaurant whose front door opens on to rows and rows of Taittinger has its priorities sorted. And punters are kept in high spirits from the moment they arrive at this restaurant and bar, bubbling with ambience, until the replete moment of departure. Expect starters such as baked plum tomatoes on toast with crème fraîche or fresh crab risotto, mains of Gressingham duck with red wine and lentils or fabulous black bream with tomatoes, olives and buttery baked potato slices. Desserts are less predictable than usual, panettone pudding with cinnamon baked pears, perhaps. Quite a find.

La Chouette

Westlington Green, Westlington, nr Dinton, Aylesbury, Buckinghamshire HP17 8UW (01296 747422). **Food served** noon-2pm, 7-9pm Mon-Fri; 7-9pm Sat. **Main courses** £13-£17. **Set lunch** £11 3 courses. **Set dinners** £29.50 4 courses, £36.50 5 courses. **Credit** MC, V.

Labyrinthine lanes winding through fields dotted with country houses are the only landmark en route to this tucked-away Belgian restaurant. Look for a lone faded sign pointing vaguely to Westlington Green and La Chouette, one of a number of 300-year-old buildings in this tiny village. While the building may be typically English, the chef is typically Belgian. It's not an obvious partnership, but Frederic Desmette knows his onions. Food is hearty but polished and includes Belgian dishes such as asparagus spears with butter and barley scrambled egg, or roast salmon with crispy onions and lardons. The wine list will capture imaginations with its breadth. Book ahead as it doesn't open if it's not busy.

Old Trout

29-30 Lower High Street, Thame, Oxfordshire OX9 2AA (01844 212146/www.theoldtrouthotel.co.uk). **Food served** noon-3pm, 6.30-9.30pm daily. **Main courses** £9.50-£16.95. **Set Lunch** (Mon-Sat) £12 2 courses, (Sun) £16 3 courses. **Credit** AmEx, MC, V.

This 500-year-old curiosity, teeming with nooks, crannies and tangled corridors, is bursting with character. As is the food: whoever whipped up the frighteningly

moreish starter of stilton and walnut cheesecake deserves a medal. Mains were no less impressive. Brill came baked en papillote with chanterelle mushrooms and a champagne sauce, while lamb shank was complemented by a spiced sausage and lentil cassoulet. Staff are good fun and the atmosphere is laid-back if occasionally chaotic.

La Petite Auberge

107 High Street, Great Missenden, Buckinghamshire HP16 0BB (01494 865370). **Food served** 7.30-10pm Mon-Sat. **Main courses** £15.60-£16.90. **Credit** MC, V.

This French restaurant is petite even by the bijoux standards of Great Missenden. Its interior is like granny's front room: spotlessly clean with too much furniture and pictures from a lost era. Though the menu changes little, the food is very good, and the front of house staff, including the wife of the chef, Mrs Martel, are crisply efficient, if distant. Locals love this place, so booking is essential if you want to sample the likes of crab in a courgette flower, scallops and salsify, tender pan-fried venison with cranberries, pinkly roasted lamb and crème brûlée. All are cooked with aplomb. The atmosphere can be curiously muted and melancholic, however.

Sir Charles Napier

Spriggs Alley, nr Chinnor, Oxfordshire OX39 4BX (01494 483011/www.sircharlesnapier.co.uk). **Food served** noon-2.30pm, 7-9.30pm Tue-Fri; noon-2.30pm, 7-10pm Sat; 12.30-3.30pm Sun. **Main courses** £11.50-£17.50. **Set meal** (Tue-Fri) £16.50 2 courses. **Credit** AmEx, DC, MC, V.

There's something simultaneously formal and unfussy about the Napier: throughout the building, ornate mirrors and artful, modern furnishings compete for space with a glorious jumble of wicker baskets and raffia placemats. There's nothing haphazard about the menu, however, which is subtle and superb from the start. On a recent visit, a starter of tomato risotto with squid and parmesan was a masterpiece of complementary colours and flavours, as was a main course of baked red mullet with orange ratatouille. In winter there might be pumpkin and garlic soup followed by roast woodcock, braised endive and rösti. This is fun food to be taken very seriously indeed.

The Swan

5 High Street, Tetsworth, Oxfordshire OX9 7AB (01844 281182/www.theswan.co.uk). **Food served** noon-2.15pm Mon; noon-2.15pm, 7-9.30pm Tue-Sat; noon-1.30pm Sun. **Main courses** £10.50-£16.75. **Credit** MC, V.

A local institution, the Swan has been refreshing travellers for over 500 years. In the late 1980s, however, it fell into disrepair and a fire saw it close altogether. In 1995 it reopened as the novel pairing of restaurant and antiques centre. It was presumably the source for many of the collectable furnishings within the small and delightfully rickety restaurant. Restaurant staff are young and unassuming and the first-class menu offers unpretentious, well-prepared food, such as scallop and bacon salad, crispy duck salad with red pepper and chilli dressing, sea bass fillets with citrus vanilla vinaigrette, and calf's liver and colcannon imaginatively paired with lime and sage oil.

Hertfordshire

Rural bliss just a step from the city.

Jump on a train or in the car, head due north and you can exchange the Smoke for surprisingly pretty, rolling countryside in around half an hour. Hertfordshire is not the most high-profile home county, but if you're not after thrills and spills it's as good – and accessible – a short break as any other. The area is served by several motorways (A1, M25 and M1) and speedy train services laid on for the commutobots, so it's possible to be in the thick of meadows, glistening fairways and leafy lanes very quickly.

Aside from the area's numerous excellent golfing greens, there are several fine stately homes, such as **Knebworth House**, which has extensive grounds and diverse programmes of activities throughout the year. The gentle gradient of the countryside around here makes for easy walking, and there are enough well-marked footpaths (and cycle routes), decent pubs and pretty villages to make a good walking or cycling weekend. And off the beaten track, it's as attractive as anywhere in the south-east of England.

But Hertfordshire goes from the sublime to the ridiculous: Luton and Stansted airports provide a steady flow of low-flying air traffic, while the same busy motorways that make the county so accessible also chop the county into pieces. Letchworth Garden City (the first in the country) and Welwyn Garden City are not quite as elysian as their names might suggest; these days there's more of the city and less of the garden about them. **Bushey**, on the other hand, does live up to its name, with plenty of fields, a golf course, an animal encounter centre and riding stables. **Watford**, the butt of many a joke, has been undergoing trendification and now sports a recent crop of bars and cafés.

Up the A1

Just into Hertfordshire is **Hatfield**, home to the Galleria shopping centre that looms over the motorway, but also to delightful **Hatfield House** and **Mill Green Museum** (Mill Green, 01707 271362), a working watermill that produces organic flour. Due north is the hip yet ultra-quaint little town of **Hitchin**. The town has several historic buildings, from **St Mary's Church** to the **Skynners' Almshouses**, dating from 1670. Pick up a leaflet from **Hitchin Library** (Paynes Park, 01438 737333)

with suggestions for tours. The **Market Place** is good for refreshments and shopping. Then head for Bridge Street, just off Sun Street, for bookshop browsing, fine art, beauty treatments and dinner. East of here is **Cromer Windmill** (on the B1037, between Cromer and Walkern, 01279 843301). The windmill dates from 1679 and was in use until 1923. After many years of restoration work, it is now open to the public at weekends, but phone to check opening times.

Market towns

The deep south of Herts is made up of small villages and market towns, which have expanded to such an extent that the boundaries between them are unclear. In the far west of the county, before you even hit the M25, **Bushey** lies cheek by jowl with **Oxhey**, which in turn is within walking distance of Watford. Bushey (apart from being home to George Michael) is also famous for the **Herkomer School of Art**, which flourished between 1883 and 1912. Sadly, all that's left of the school is the rose garden and small park area over the road from Bushey Golf Course. Nearby, on Melbourne Road, stands one of Europe's oldest remaining daylight film studios. The founder of the school and the studio, Sir Hubert von Herkomer, also had his home on Melbourne Road, called 'Lululand'. Only the frontage remains, now cunningly reworked into the porch of the British Legion Club. The home of another famous former resident, painter Lucy Kemp-Welch, is here as well 'Kingsley', at 20 High Street.

Following the canal (and train route) westwards you come to **Berkhamsted**, once home to luminaries as diverse as Graham Greene, Michael Meacher and Robin Knox-Johnston. J M Barrie often stayed at the Rectory here, and the children who lived in it were the inspiration for *Peter Pan*. Just behind the train station are the remains of a Norman castle.

By train from London

Probably the only Hertfordshire town with enough to do to warrant a visit by train is **St Albans**. It is a mere 19mins from **King's Cross Thameslink** by the quarter-hourly fast trains. Info: www.thameslink.co.uk.

In fine weather, the very helpful guide will present an impromptu re-enactment of Norman life (call Mr Stevens on 01442 871737). The castle looks quite spectacular after a torrent, when the moat fills and cuts it off like an island. Berkhamsted town centre sports the usual chain shops, Café Rouge and Pizza Express. Behind these is the canal, which has fine views and is a good place for a leisurely walk.

A Roman first

Slightly further east, sandwiched between the A1 and M25 motorways and usually choked with traffic, the attractive market town of **St Albans** clings on to its Roman past. In AD 43 the first Roman fort was built to the north-east of the settlement of Verlamion. All that remains of this stage in the town's history are sections of the city walls and hypocaust (Roman heating system) in Verulamium Park at the foot of the town, and the famous thoroughfare of Watling Street. However, the Verulamium Museum (*see p245*) is full of well-preserved artefacts.

Other attractions include the market, which still bustles away on St Peter's Street on Wednesdays and Saturdays; the cathedral, which has some magnificent 13th-century wall paintings and Fishpool Street's coaching houses and mix of Elizabethan and Georgian architectural styles.

What to see & do

Tourist Information Centres

Dacorum Information Centre, Marlowes, Hemel Hempstead, HP1 1DT (01442 234222/www. dacorum.gov.uk). **Open** 9.30am-5pm Mon-Fri; 9.30am-1pm Sat.

Town Hall, Market Place, St Albans, AL3 5DJ (01727 864511/www.stalbans.gov.uk). **Open** *Easter-mid July* 9.30am-5.30pm Mon-Sat. *Mid July-mid Sept* 9.30am-5.30pm Mon-Sat; 10am-4pm Sun. *Mid Sept-Easter* 10am-4pm Mon-Sat.

Useful websites

Confusingly, Hertfordshire is divided into different regions. Local authority-run websites include: www.hertsdirect.org general, which has links to other local authorities and tourist organisations; www.east-herts.gov.uk (east); www.nhdc.gov.uk (north); www.da corum.gov.uk (west); www.hertsmuseums.org.uk, which has information about museums in Hertfordshire; www.hertsheritage.org, with details of modern heritage, including film studios, transport and industry.

Aklowa Centre

Brewers End, Takeley, Bishop's Stortford, CM22 6QJ (01279 871062). **Open** by appointment only 10am-noon, 1-3pm Mon-Sat. **Admission** £4; £3 concessions. **No credit cards.**
A 'West African village' offering visitors the chance to join in dance, games, cooking, arts and crafts and general discussion. You need to book for a two-hour session.

Ashridge Estate

Ringshall, Berkhamsted, HP4 1LX (01442 851227/ information 01494 755557/www.nationaltrust. org.uk). **Open** *Monument* noon-5pm Sat, Sun. *Estate* free access. *Visitors' centre* 1-5pm Mon-Fri; noon-5pm Sat, Sun. **Admission** (NT) *Monument* £1.20; 60p concessions; free under-5s. **No credit cards.**
This splendid estate runs across the borders of Herts and Bucks, along the main ridge of the Chiltern Hills. There are woodlands and commons supporting a rich variety of wildlife and offering lovely, scenic walks. The focal point of the area is the Monument, erected in 1832 to the Duke of Bridgewater. There are also great views from Ivinghoe Beacon, accessible from Steps Hill.

Hatfield House

Just off A1, Hatfield, AL9 5NQ (01707 287010/ www.hatfield-house.co.uk). **Open** *House* Easter-Sept noon-4pm daily. *Park & West Gardens* Easter-Sept 11am-5.30pm daily. *East Gardens* Easter-Sept 11am-5.30pm Fri. *All* Closed Oct-Easter. **Guided tours** noon-4pm Mon-Fri. **Admission** *House, park & gardens* £7.50; £4 concessions. *Park & gardens* £4.50; £3.50 concessions. *Park only* £2; £1 concessions. **Credit** MC, V.
Built by Robert Cecil, Earl of Salisbury, in 1611, this superb Jacobean mansion oozes history. In the grounds stands the remaining wing of the Royal Palace of Hatfield, the childhood home of Elizabeth I, where in 1558 she held her first Council of State. The 42 acres of gardens include herb terraces, orchards and fountains restored to their former glory by the present marchioness, as well as a woodland timber playground for children. Special events such as craft fairs run throughout the year.

The Henry Moore Foundation

Dane Tree House, Perry Green, Much Hadham, SG10 6EE (01279 843333/www.henry-moore-fdn.co.uk). **Open** *Apr-Sept* Mon-Fri, Sun by appointment only. Closed Nov-Mar. **Admission** £7; £3 concessions; free under-18s. **No credit cards.**
The 70-acre estate at Perry Green is home to the studios, barns and galleries gifted to the Foundation by Henry Moore. Many of the buildings are still as they were in his lifetime. The spacious sculpture gardens and adjoining fields house an awe-inspiring and ever-changing exhibition of Moore's monumental sculptures. The park is open by appointment only.

Knebworth House, Park & Gardens

Knebworth, nr Stevenage, SG3 6PY (01438 812661/ www.knebworthhouse.com). **Open** *House* Easter-early July noon-5pm Sat, Sun. Early July-Aug noon-5pm daily. Sept noon-5pm Sat, Sun. *Park* Easter-early July 11am-5.30pm Sat, Sun. Early July-Aug 11am-5.30pm daily. Sept 11am-5.30pm Sat, Sun. *Both* Closed Oct-Easter. **Admission** *House, park & playground* £7.50; £7 concessions; free under-4s. *Park & playground* £5.50; free under-4s. **Credit** MC, V.
Home to the Lyttons since 1490, this Gothic-embellished Tudor house is still the family residence. The 250-acre park contains gardens and woodland, a maze, the 'Fort Knebworth' adventure playground and a miniature railway. Major rock concerts have been added to the attractions since 1974; Led Zep played a legendary show and a performance by Robbie Williams in summer 2003 was

Heavy metallist **Henry Moore**. *See p243.*

modestly billed as the 'biggest music event in British history'. Car shows, craft fairs, flower festivals and classical concerts also take place here. Knebworth opens daily during school holidays outside the summer season; phone or check the website for information.

Museum of St Albans
Hatfield Road, St Albans, AL1 3RR (01727 819340/ www.stalbansmuseums.org.uk). **Open** 10am-5pm Mon-Sat; 2-5pm Sun. **Admission** free.
Impressive display of local history with plenty of medieval and Roman artefacts. Downstairs there's a collection of tools used in carpentry and agriculture, plus a gallery to the rear on two levels.

Paradise Wildlife Park
White Stubbs Lane, Broxbourne, EN10 7QA (01992 470490/www.pwpark.com). **Open** *Apr-Oct* 9.30am-6pm daily. *Nov-Mar* 10am-5pm daily. **Admission** £9; £7 concessions. **Credit** MC, V.
Despite its popularity, this wildlife park never seems to get horribly busy, and there's enough here to keep the kids entertained for a whole day virtually all year round. As well as animals and birds, there is an adventure playground, a small funfair, a miniature train, talks and shows, a soft play area and small farmyard where you can pet and feed donkeys, goats and rabbits. More exotic species include reptiles, wolves, monkeys, big cats, camels and birds of prey. Refreshments for visitors and feed for the animals are available.

Redbournbury Watermill
Redbournbury Lane, Redbourn Road, St Albans, AL3 6RS (01582 792874/www.redbournmill.co.uk). **Open** *Apr-Oct* 2.30-5pm Sun, bank hols, open days (phone for details). Closed Nov-Mar. **Admission** £1.50; 80p concessions. Free sun. **No credit cards**.

This 18th-century working watermill is at the end of a massive rebuilding and restoration project, which took more than ten years to complete. It is now established as a museum and as the only working mill on the River Ver. You can buy certified organic flour, and there are craft displays, folk dancing, jazz and poetry events throughout the year, plus open days such as New Year's Day – check the website or phone for details. Cream teas are served from 2.30pm until 5pm on Sundays.

Scott's Grotto
Scott's Road, Ware, SG12 9JQ (01920 464131/www. scotts-grotto.org). **Open** *Apr-Sept* 2-4.30pm Sat, bank hols (other times by appointment). Closed Oct-Mar. **Admission** by donation. **No credit cards**.
A series of quirky subterranean passages built by poet John Scott of Amwell House (now part of Ware College). Dating back to around 1760, and fronted by a flint-encrusted portico, the tunnels extend 67ft into the hillside, with seven chambers decorated with shells from around the world, plus local flints and minerals. Visitors are requested to bring a torch with them.

Shaw's Corner
Ayot St Lawrence, nr Welwyn, AL6 9BX (01438 820307/NT information 01494 755567/www. nationaltrust.org.uk/shawscorner). **Open** *House* Apr-Oct 1-5pm Wed-Sun. *Garden* Apr-Oct noon-5pm Wed-Sun. Last entry 4.30pm. *Both* Closed Nov-Mar. **Admission** (NT) £3.60; £1.80 concessions; free under-5s. **No credit cards**.
Writer George Bernard Shaw lived in this large, red-brick house from 1906 to 1950. Many of the rooms are as the great man left them, including his restored revolving writing hut at the bottom of the garden. Shaw wrote *Pygmalion* and *St Joan* here, and his plays are performed in the grounds during the summer.

Brocket Hall

Welwyn, AL8 7XG (01707 335241/fax 01707 375166/www.brocket-hall.co.uk). **Rates** (Melbourne Lodge) £150 single; £170 double. **Rooms** (all en suite) 4 single; 12 double. **Credit** AmEx, DC, MC, V.
Brocket Hall was home to the cuckolded first Lord Melbourne, whose spouse cavorted with George IV, while the second Lord Melbourne married Lady Caroline Lamb, whose love for Lord Byron was anything but discreet. Wild times. These days life at Brocket Hall is altogether more pedestrian: the house proper is mainly used for conferences, although there are parties (wedding and similar) here too. Melbourne Lodge, a golf buggy's journey away from the hall, manages to maintain an air of opulence and even romance, with lashings of taffeta drapery and brocade, and wooded vistas. Golf and country sports are a big deal here, and since much of the parkland is given over to the golf course there are few places to take a stroll without fear of flying balls. Clay pigeon shooting, coarse and game fishing, croquet, tennis and archery are also available. Note that jeans, trainers and baseball caps are banned. Children welcome. No-smoking rooms available.
A1 J4; follow signs to Wheathampstead & B653; once on Brocket Road, turn into entrance to golf club & restaurant for Melbourne Lodge.

Homewood

Old Knebworth, SG3 6PP (01438 812105/fax 01438 812572/www.homewood-bb.co.uk). **Rates** £45 single occupancy; £70 double; £15 supplement per child. **Rooms** (all en suite) 1 double; 1 family/suite. **No credit cards.**
You get a real flavour of eccentric English gentility in this Lutyens-designed house, indeed a 'bit of friendly, gracious living', as its brochure promises. It's a very attractive, informal old place, with spacious grounds to stroll around, a terrace where breakfast can be taken and a pretty woodland setting – the only shame is the visible motorway just a few hundred yards away. The rooms are light and airy, accessed off a lovely, wood-floored landing whose walls are painted with old maps of London. You can get a location map from the website. Children welcome. Dogs by arrangement. No smoking throughout.
B197 into Knebworth; turn into Station Road (which becomes Park Lane), 300 yards after crossing motorway bridge, left into public footpath; after 300 yards bear left through lodge gates, house is at end.

Lord Lister Hotel

1 Park Street, Hitchin, SG4 9AH (01462 432712/459451/fax 01462 438506/www.lordlisterhotel.co.uk). **Rates** £60 single; £70 double/twin; £85 four-poster; £75 family room. **Rooms** (all en suite) 4 single; 10 double; 3 family; 2 twin; 1 four-poster. **Credit** AmEx, DC, MC, V.
A very friendly family-run hotel (you'll run into a few of the owners' offspring in the lounge) with a creaky winding staircase and immaculately clean rooms. There's a small bar downstairs, a TV lounge and a large, bright breakfast room. The history of the hotel is intriguing. It was once a Quaker school, where the young Joseph Lister (father of antiseptics) received his formative education. During the late 1800s the building became a home for 'weak-minded and deficient girls'. Children welcome. No-smoking rooms available.

Verulamium Museum

St Michael's, St Albans, AL3 4SW (01727 751810/www.stalbansmuseums.org.uk). **Open** 10am-5.30pm Mon-Sat; 2-5.30pm Sun. Last entry 5pm. **Admission** £3.30; £2 concessions; free under-5s. **Credit** MC, V.
This modern, well-designed museum right by the Roman ruins in Verulamium Park is testament to St Albans' past, and features recreated Roman rooms, hands-on discovery areas, video touch-screen databases and some of the finest Roman mosaics and wall plasters outside the Mediterranean. Visitors should be prepared for invasion every second weekend in the month, when Roman soldiers arrive to demonstrate the tactics and equipment of the Imperial Army.

Victorian Chemist Shop & Physic Garden

Hitchin Museum, Paynes Park, Hitchin, SG5 1EH (01462 434476/www.nhdc.gov.uk). **Open** 10am-5pm Mon, Tue, Thur-Sat. **Admission** free.
Joseph Lister's medical memorabilia and pharmaceutical artefacts are on display. The physic garden reveals the importance of medicinal herbs through the years.

Where to stay

Hertfordshire has plenty of grand hotels, converted from illustrious but ill-fated country estates, plus some unique and remote guesthouses, and pub accommodation in most major towns. At the corporate end of the hotel trade, the **Watford Hilton** (01923 235881, www.hilton.com, doubles £99-£145) is the largest hotel in the Bushey area. Some of the choicest places to stay are listed below.

The Chilterns to York

St Michael's Manor

Fishpool Street, St Albans, AL3 4RY (01727 864444/fax 01727 848909/www.stmichaels manor.com). **Rates** £140-£175 single; £175-£240 double/twin; £225 four-poster single; £300 four-poster double; £225 single suite; £300 double suite. **Rooms** (all en suite) 2 single; 3 twin; 15 double; 1 double four-poster; 1 suite. **Credit** AmEx, DC, MC, V.
This attractive, independently owned hotel (just a couple of minutes' walk from the cathedral and Verulamium Park right at the bottom of the town) has been added to numerous times since it was first built in the 16th century, but the overall effect is still gracious and peaceful. The 23 rooms are all different, many have nice antique furniture and come with so many 'extras' – from bathrobes to magazines and games – that luggage can be kept to a minimum. The higher up the creaky staircase you go the more quirky the rooms are, with sunken baths, and shower cubicles built in under the roof beams. If your budget can stand it, opt for the suite with a balcony for a fine view of the garden. There are trays of strawberries and nuts in the lobby and lounges, and the grounds are beautifully designed with fountains and wildfowl in abundance. Saturdays are popular for weddings. Children welcome. No-smoking rooms available.

Where to eat & drink

In Bushey, the **Swan** (Park Road, 020 8950 2256) is a lovely backstreet real ale pub. Rolls and toasties are available at lunchtime and there's a sizeable garden to the rear. The **Three Crowns** (High Road, Bushey Heath, 020 8950 2851) does a mean Sunday lunch and has a selection of good wines.

If you're around Knebworth, it's worth dropping in to the friendly, unpretentious **Lytton Arms** (Park Lane, 01438 812312) – named after the family who have owned Knebworth House for generations – for its excellent real ale, good pub food and large patio garden.

Watford has been given a new lease of life courtesy of several modern bars. Among them are the delightfully laid-back **Aura** (77-9 The Parade, 01923 253335), with waitress service and comfy sofas, and **Øl Bier Grill** (9 Market Street, 01923 256601), a Danish establishment with an elegant steak restaurant below. The **Green Man** in Great Offley (High Street, 01462 768256) is a good bet if you're heading north towards Letchworth and Hitchin; it offers a fantastic range of high-quality dishes, good beers and brilliant views over the countryside. In Hitchin itself, the **Sun Hotel** (Sun Street, 01462 436411) dates back to 1575 and was the most important coaching inn of its time. It now serves fairly decent food in its brasserie. The **Rose & Crown** in Hemel Hempstead (19 Old High Street, 01442 395054) is a popular pub that is very accommodating to children, and has a fine Thai restaurant.

There are numerous real ale pubs in St Albans, including the oldest, the **Lower Red Lion** at 36 Fishpool Street (01727 855669), which serves cask bitter (including changing guest beers), country wines and cheap eats, and has a pretty enclosed garden at the back. It also offers accommodation (doubles from £45). For entertainment, the **Horn** (01727 853143) on Victoria Street has jazz at weekends. The owners of St Michael's Manor (*see above*) have recently opened **Darcy's** (2 Hatfield Road, 01727 730777), a restaurant with international leanings, thanks to its Australian chef.

In Watton at Stone, the **George & Dragon** (High Street, 01920 830285) has a civilised atmosphere (provided by antiques, modern prints, newspapers, inglenook fireplace) and highly regarded local food – it's been voted Dining Pub of the Year several times. The **White Lion** in Walkern, just east of Stevenage (31 High Street, 01438 861251) is ideal for children, with an excellent play area.

The small village of Ayot St Lawrence, as well as being home to Shaw's Corner (*see p244*), also has the **Brocket Arms** (01438 820250), a delightful 14th-century inn that has a cosy inglenook fireplace to huddle round in the winter, a large, enclosed garden and very decent food. The Brocket was originally monastic quarters attached to the now-ruined Norman church down the road – ask the landlord for the key if you want to look round. The **Sow of Pigs** at Thundridge (Cambridge Road, 01920 463281) is good for families, with a spacious garden and large rustic tables in the dining area. If you feel like dressing up and splashing out, the **Zodiac** in the Marriot Hanbury Manor, Ware (01920 487722) is grand indeed; its sister establishment, **Vardon's**, is more relaxed and family-friendly.

Alford Arms

Frithsden, HP1 3DD (01442 864480). **Lunch served** noon-2.30pm, 7-10pm Mon-Sat; noon-3pm, 7-10pm Sun. **Main courses** £9.25-£13. **Credit** AmEx, MC, V.
Set in an absurdly picturesque hamlet set in a pastoral valley, the Alford Arms is one of those secrets that everyone seems to know about. Inside, it's simply decorated with pale colours and plain wood giving it a Shaker-ish quality; outside there's a small patio that heaves when the temperature rises. Despite the numbers, the staff seem to cope well, taking orders at the bar or from the dining area with good humour. Food is competently cooked and presented. 'Small plates' such as rustic breads with roast garlic, balsamic vinegar and olive oil or seared scallops on mixed leaves with yellow pepper dressing kick the tastebuds into action. The dozen or so main dishes incline towards the hearty: roast leg of lamb with redcurrant and rosemary jus; pork, oregano and basil sausages with mash and roast red onion gravy; or cajun chicken on mash with crushed

Visit **Knebworth**, the stately home where they know how to hold a party. *See p243.*

black pepper sauce. You have to pay extra for vegetables or salad. In some ways, the Alford is a victim of its own popularity: at weekends its fans clog up the pretty lanes nearby and make impulsive visits a no-no; book well in advance to get a table.

Auberge du Lac

Brocket Hall, Welwyn, AL8 7XG (01707 368888/ www.brocket-hall.co.uk). **Food served** noon-2.15pm, 7-10.30pm Tue-Sat; noon-2.15pm Sun. **Main courses** £14.50-£30. **Set lunches** £28 3 courses Tue-Fri, £35 3 courses Sat, Sun. **Credit** AmEx, DC, MC, V.
Talented, high-profile chef Jean-Christophe Novelli has risen phoenix-like from the charred remains of his former London venture to set up the Auberge du Lac. A pretty, green-shuttered 18th-century hunting lodge in a handsome parkland setting, it overlooks the lake across from Brocket Hall (*see p245*). It's furnished in a rather opulent English country-house style that just escapes being naff, but the food is extravagantly French, with no apologies to vegetarians. Mains tend towards the robust, but are so highly crafted you are never in danger of overkill. Popular choices include braised pig's trotter or 'selection of the day butcher plate', chosen 'according to Jean-Christophe's versatile mood'. Lighter but no less accomplished concoctions include a crab, avocado and Norwegian prawn salad with lemon, poached quail's egg, caviar and anchovy dressing, exquisitely flavoured. Desserts revolve around fresh fruit, cream and spirals of spun sugar; the wine list, as you'd expect, is extensive and with a strong French presence. Guests are well looked after by a young and enthusiastic (if occasionally supercilious) staff, and you may be graced with a visit from the great man himself.

The Chilterns to York

Walking by water

If you're heading out of London for a couple of days, you could conceivably walk all the way through Hertfordshire along waterside paths, thanks to various footpaths that cut through the county.

One such is the **Lee Valley Walk**, a 50-mile path along the River Lee, which stretches from Islington as far as Luton, through the countryside of Hertfordshire. Visit www.leevalley-online.co.uk for details of walks, watery activities and recommended pubs along the way.

If 50 miles is pushing it, you could try the stretch from **Hertford to Broxbourne**. This eight-mile section takes you from the pleasant old market town of Hertford and neighbouring town of Ware to Broxbourne. From **Hertford Lock** you walk along the river to **New Guage**, a Victorian brick building that is the starting point for the New River. This man-made water course was built in 1613 as a means to transport fresh water from Hertfordshire to London. More than 20 million gallons per day travel along this course. (The New River Path has been recently restored. You can now follow the water from New Guage to Stoke Newington and on to the head of the New River in Islington.)

If you carry on alongside the River Lee from New Guage, you pass through the largest area of grazed riverside flood meadow left in Hertfordshire. Known as the **Meads**, it is home to bats, dragonflies and many ducks, gulls and waders. It is managed by the Wildlife Trust. Visit www.wildlifetrust.org.uk/herts for details of species to look out for.

Approaching **Ware**, the river starts to turn south and flows through the centre of the town, which has a few good shops, pubs and a small local museum. Signposts point you towards **Amwell Quarry Nature Reserve** (there is no public access to the reserve, but there are excellent viewing facilities from around the perimeter), then on to the village of **Stanstead Abbotts**, home to a thriving malting industry and the popular riverside Jolly Fisherman pub.

After a quiet stretch of riverbank you may hear the sound of go-karts emanating from around **Rye House**, thanks to the greyhound/stockcar/athletics stadium and kart circuit there. Rye House itself dates from 1443 and is most famous as the place where the Rye House Plot to assassinate Charles II was hatched in 1683. The surviving part of the house, the brickwork gatehouse, is open in summer (phone 01992 702200 for information). The Riverside pub (the best along this stretch) and nearby **RSPB reserve** are both well worth a visit.

From here the walk takes you past **Nazeing Glass Works** (Nazeing New Road, Broxbourne, 01992 708250), where glass is still blown and pressed by hand. You can then continue along a towpath and footpath to Broxbourne station.

La Casetta

18 High Street, Kings Langley, WD4 8BH (01923 263823/www.lacasetta.co.uk). **Food served** noon-2.30pm, 7-10.30pm Tue-Fri; 7-10.30pm Sat; 12.30-3pm 1st Sun of mth. **Main courses** £10.25-£15.95. **Set lunch** £11.95 2 courses. **Set dinner** £18.95 2 courses, £22.50 3 courses Fri, Sat. **Credit** MC, V.

You have to virtually crawl up the steep, creaky old staircase to the series of tiny olde worlde dining rooms in this former 16th-century cottage, but of course that's part of the charm for the blazer-and-blouse brigade who habitually dine here. It's an incredibly popular venue – book well ahead – thanks to rustic charm, extremely diligent service and well-executed modern-ish Italian food. The set menus offer good value. On our visit a pretty standard selection of antipasti was lifted by the inclusion of smoked salmon and spiced mussels; carpaccio of smoked duck breast, red currant and port sauce with rocket salad was a successful blend of sweet, peppery and smoky. Roasted chicken breast, spinach and roast potatoes with fresh grapes and Vin Santo jus was tasty but unspectacular and a tad dry. Roast salmon with pesto butter crust and niçoise-style vegetables was succulent and flavoursome. The wine list is mainly Italian, but broadened out with a few New World options.

The Conservatory

St Michael's Manor Hotel, Fishpool Street, St Albans, AL3 4RY (01727 864444/www.stmichaelsmanor. com). **Food served** 12.30-2pm, 7-9.30pm Mon-Sat; 12.30-2pm, 7-9pm Sun. **Set lunch** £21.50 2 courses, £25 3 courses. **Set dinner** £36 3 courses. **Credit** AmEx, MC, V.

The dining room and adjoining conservatory of this stately old ivy-clad hotel are very much in a grand period style – though the exact era is unclear – with an abundance of gilt mirrors, sombre prints, potted palms, chandeliers and fleur-de-lys wallpaper. During the week it tends to host corporate meetings, with families (children are welcome) couples and wedding parties more prevalent at weekends. The food is modern and eclectic, and combines beautiful presentation with an imaginative and light-handed blend of ingredients. Fish is especially good. Starters include langoustine and papaya salad with tamarind dressing, and crab and avocado salad with a lemon- and orange-scented hollandaise. Main courses could be rack of lamb en croûte on a bed of celeriac purée; baby aubergines filled with wild mushrooms, topped with basil breadcrumbs and tarragon cream; or carpaccio of beef with rocket, fresh figs and balsamic dressing. Puddings are light and fragrant, with plenty of ice-cream and fresh fruit. The extensive wine list is updated every six months. Sit in the spacious, sunny conservatory if you can; the view over the award-winning gardens and lake is lovely.

Fornovivo

69 High Street, Tring, HP23 4AB (01442 890005/ www.fornovivo.com). **Food served** noon-3pm, 6-10.30pm Mon-Fri; noon-10.30pm Sat; noon-10pm Sun. **Main courses** £5.75-£10.95. **Credit** MC, V.

Housed imaginatively in a former post office is this well-designed, spacious pizzeria. The minimalist wood-and-concrete setting looks great, although the acoustics challenge your vocal and aural organs, especially with naff Italian music playing at full blast. But let's not be churlish. The pizzas (around £5-£8) are slim, crispy and loaded with all of the best toppings, and cooked in front of you in an enormous stone oven. There are standard but well-presented starters such as a generous platter of cold meats, cheese and char-grilled vegetables, and traditional pasta and meat mains (£5.50-£12). Service is swift and efficient, the management friendly and the whole operation thoroughly spick and span. Kids are welcome, and there's a special menu featuring mini portions for £3-£4.

Lemon Tree

14-16 Water Lane, Bishop's Stortford, CM23 2LB (01279 757788/www.lemontree.co.uk). **Food served** noon-2.30pm, 7-9.30pm Tue-Sat; 1-4pm Sun. **Main courses** £10-£16. **Set lunch** (Tue-Sat) £7 1 course, £11 2 courses, £15 3 courses. **Set dinner** £15.50 2 courses, £19.95 3 courses. **Credit** MC, V.

Like Bishop's Stortford, the Lemon Tree is a quiet, respectable concern. There can't be anywhere for miles around that offers such well-considered, elegant and imaginative cooking. The lunch set menu is flexible and good value, enabling you to have a quick snack or the full works – the popular £7 '7lt' menu is one course (from a choice of seven) with a glass of wine and filter coffee. Starters include poached egg with black pudding, parma ham and Worcestershire sauce, or roast red pepper and goat's cheese crostini with tapenade and salad. Mains might be seared tuna with borlotti beans, fennel and tapenade; or oven-roast skate with puy lentils, savoy cabbage and mustard sauce. Meaty options include confit of duck with thyme-baked new potatoes, black olives and garlic; and grilled calf's liver with bacon, caramelised onions and creamed potatoes. Veggies are well catered for, too, with dishes such as fricassé of wild mushrooms, parmesan and asparagus. The wine list travels round the world, with plenty of bottles available by the glass. The restaurant is split into small rooms, which should make it welcoming, though we found the atmosphere a tad austere for a Saturday lunchtime. Service was sprightly at first but soon tailed off.

St James Restaurant

30 High Street, Bushey, WD23 3HL (020 8950 2480). **Food served** noon-2pm, 6.30-9.30pm Mon-Sat. **Main courses** £10.95-£19.95. **Set meal** £13.95 2 courses. **Credit** AmEx, MC, V.

Overlooking its namesake church, St James is a smart but relaxed venue where business lunchers sit alongside casual diners. The largely European menu features classic fish and meat dishes, well presented and served by discreet yet attentive staff. Starters might include grilled calamares, mussel and chorizo salad, or pan-fried beef fillet patty with quail's egg. For mains, there's sautéed calf's liver with crispy bacon, dauphinoise potatoes and pea purée, or roast pork fillet with pommery mash. Fish dishes include grilled swordfish with Waldorf salad, with seared salmon, spiced Thai green curry and crispy wun tuns providing an oriental touch. Four vegetarian options (available as either starter or main) include marinated vegetable kebabs with houmous, and couscous with field mushrooms topped with melted goat's cheese and pesto dressing – well executed, if rather unimaginative. Dessert selections, while similarly standard, include a voluptuous lemon posset with fresh berries.

The Chilterns to York

Rutland

Small is beautiful.

The work of the BBC's late Geoff Hamilton lives on at **Barnsdale Gardens**. *See p251.*

'I am the only person I have ever known who has been to Rutland. I admit that I have known men who have passed through Rutland in search of a fox, but I have never met a man who has deliberately set out to go to Rutland; and I do not suppose you have.'

Back in the 1920s Rutland made an uncharacteristically big impression on the travel writer H V Morton, when he was writing his classic *In Search of England*. He could hardly believe England's smallest county's absence of industry, and that Oakham, the county town, 'looks like a village'.

The tranquillity that so spurred H V's enthusiasm is still much in evidence today. Sixteen miles square in the middle of nowhere, Rutland offers a complete antidote to the noise and fumes of London. A weekend break here shouldn't be planned around a manic itinerary of places to visit and sights to hoover up; best take it easy and enjoy the glorious absence of crowds and traffic and pressure. The county motto is, after all, 'Multum In Parvo' – much in little.

In the 30 years since the picturesque Gwash Valley was dammed and flooded to create Britain's largest man-made lake, the county has

become far more geared up for visitors. There's plenty to do on and around **Rutland Water** – cycling, bird-watching, cruising – but the real glory still resides in the countryside, the quiet roads and still-life honey-stone villages that recall the timeless atmosphere of Agatha Christie or Enid Blyton. You can potter through unspoiled pasturelands; but just in case you weaken and grow twitchy for urban life, the attractive medieval town of **Stamford** lies on Rutland's doorstep, in Lincolnshire to the east.

The political unrest that surrounded the creation of Rutland Water – locals feared Rutland would become 'a footpath around

By train from London

Trains for **Stamford** and **Oakham** leave **King's Cross** hourly. There is a change at **Peterborough**; total journey time is between 1hr and 1hr 30mins. Oakham is the stop 12mins after Stamford. Info: www.gner.co.uk and www.centraltrains.co.uk.

the lake' – is now committed to history along with the county's long and savage war of independence against the faceless oppressors of Leicestershire. Rutland is free, and the great horseshoe lake has become a natural centre for pleasure cruising, sailing, watersports, fishing and birdwatching, as well as cycling and hiking around the 23-mile perimeter.

The picture-book quality of **Oakham**, the county town, has been a little compromised by progress, but it is still has some delightful Victorian streets, Georgian villas and older jewels. The public school is 16th century, nestling between the one-time castle's **Great Hall** (famous for its horseshoe collection, a tax on passing nobs) and a superb little market square (market days are Wednesday and Saturday), centred around the octagonal **Butter Cross** and old public stocks. The **Rutland County Museum** (Catmos Street, 01572 758440/www.rutnet.co.uk) has plenty on rural life and agriculture.

Better still is **Uppingham**, a few miles south – a tiny market town (market on Friday) dominated by another 16th-century public school whose clock tower, cupolas and lawns are hidden away behind a towering stone façade better suited to a prison. The high street is quintessential film-set England, but agreeably unselfconscious of the fact, and it is a beautiful place to wake up on a bustly Saturday morning. Look out for the three good bookshops, all open on Sundays: there's the 12-foot square, three-storey Rutland Bookshop, the Tardis-like Forest Books and Goldmark Books on Orange Street.

Stamford's stock has risen sharply since it starred in the BBC's *Middlemarch* series. Barely a single building fails to conform to the symphony of weathered-yellow Lincolnshire stone, still with its medieval street pattern, clinging to the River Welland. It has been helped in maintaining its historical integrity by being designated as the first conservation area in the country in 1967. Historically a wealthy textile town and staging post, Stamford was also once home to William Cecil, chief minister of Elizabeth I, who built his splendid **Burghley House** close by. Charles I spent his last days as a free man in Stamford before riding to Southwell where he was betrayed and handed over to Parliament. A few miles north-east of Stamford is **Tallington Lakes** (01778 347000/www. tallington.com), a watersports centre with eight spring-fed lakes covering 160 acres.

Back out in the open countryside, the Viking Way walking trail passes through on its journey from the Humber to Oakham, heading through villages, hamlets and superb woodland

along the way. It is marked by a distinctive Viking Helmet. The Jurassic Way (look for the shell sign) runs between Stamford and Banbury, cutting through Stamford's meadows and continuing on via the horseshoe entrance of Tinwell forge to the picturesque Easton-on-the-Hill. The Rutland Round is a 65-mile path, circular from Oakham, linking up beauty spots along its route.

Elsewhere in Rutland, there's an 82-arch viaduct near **Harringworth**; John Betjeman's favourite church is at **Brooke**; and the old smithy at **Burley-on-the-Hill** was the inspiration for Longfellow's 'Underneath the Spreading Chestnut Tree'. See the stocks on the green at **Market Overton**, where Sir Isaac Newton played as a child. Explore the ancient turf maze at **Wing** (*see p255* **Sites, rites and local legends**), the strange yew-tree avenue in **Clipsham** and Geoff Hamilton's beautiful **Barnsdale Gardens**.

What to see & do

Tourist Information Centres

The Arts Centre, 27 St Mary's Street, Stamford, PE9 2DL (01780 755611/www.southwestlincs.com). **Open** *Easter-Oct* 9.30am-5pm Mon-Sat; 10am-4pm Sun, bank hols. *Nov-Easter* 9.30am-5pm Mon-Fri; 9.30am-4pm Sat; 11am-4pm bank hols.

The Victoria Hall, 39 High Street, Oakham, LE15 6AH (01572 724329/www.rutnet.co.uk). **Open** 11am-3pm Tue-Sat.

Barnsdale Gardens

The Avenue, Exton, Oakham LE15 8AH (01572 813200/www.barnsdalegardens.co.uk). **Open** *Mar-May, Sept, Oct* 9am-5pm daily. *June-Aug* 9am-7pm daily. *Nov-Feb* 10am-4pm daily. Last entry 2hrs before closing. **Admission** £5; free under-16s. **Credit** AmEx, DC, MC, V.

In tribute to the work of Geoff Hamilton, who died in 1996, Barnsdale Garden, familiar to viewers of BBC2's *Gardeners' World* as 'the garden that Geoff built', is now open to the public. Choice and unusual plants are for sale at the adjoining nursery.

Belvoir Castle

Grantham, Leicestershire, NG32 1PE (01476 871002/www.belvoircastle.com). **Open** *Mar, Oct* 11am-5pm Sun. *Apr-June, Sept* 11am-5pm Tue-Thur, Sat. *July, Aug* 11am-5pm daily. Closed Nov-Feb. **Admission** *Castle, grounds & Duchess's garden* £12; £9-£11 concessions. *Castle & grounds* £8; £5-£7 concessions. *Grounds only* (Mon-Fri) £3; £1 concessions. **Credit** MC, V.

To drop in on the Duke and Duchess of Rutland, it's necessary to cross a few miles into the land of the Coritanian oppressors (people from Leicester, that is). The castle is the fourth to have stood on the site since Norman times – previous structures suffered total or partial destruction in the War of the Roses, the Civil War and in a fire in 1816. The current building dates from the early 19th century, and has some stunning interiors. It houses collections of furniture, porcelain, silk, tapestries, sculpture and painting, with work by Gainsborough, Reynolds, Holbein and Poussin. The castle is also home to the Queen's Royal Lancers Museum. Guides wear period costume and there are frequent events: falconry, theatre, battle re-enactments, and so on.

Browne's Hospital
Broad Street, Stamford, PE9 1PF (01780 763153/ 763756/www.pennhenry.co.uk). **Open** *May-Sept* 11am-4pm Sat, Sun. Other times by arrangement. **Admisson** £2.50; £1-£2 concessions. **No credit cards.**
Ancient almshouses founded in 1482, and still in use today. There's a chapel with original stained glass and woodwork and a museum of almshouse life, with documents, uniforms and furniture.

Burghley House
1 mile E of Stamford on B1443, PE9 3JY (01780 752451/www.burghley.co.uk). **Open** *House* Apr-Oct 11am-5pm daily. Last admission 4.30pm. Closed Nov-Mar. *Parkland* Mar-Oct 8am-8pm daily. Nov-Apr 8am-6pm daily. **Admission** *House* £7.50; £3.70-£6.80 concessions; free 5-12s (one per full-paying adult). *Parkland* free. **Credit** MC, V.
One of the grandest Elizabethan houses in England, constructed from finely carved local limestone on the remains of a 12th-century monastery. Commissioned by William Cecil, the first Lord Burghley, the house was later used as a Royalist refuge in the Civil War and came under siege by Cromwell, who never carried out his threat to raze the place to the ground. Of the 18 state rooms, those decorated with Antonio Verrio's lavish 17th-century frescoes are the most famous, the finest examples being his Heaven and Hell Rooms. The art, sculpture and porcelain on display comprise one of the most important private collections in the world. There's also a deer park, a 1932 Olympic silver medal, courtesy of Lord *'Chariots of Fire'* Burghley, the annual horse trials every September, and Queen Victoria's hard, lumpy bed.

Clipsham Yew Tree Avenue
Half mile east of Clipsham; follow brown signs from village (01780 444394). **Open** free access. **Admission** free.
An amazing half-mile avenue of 150-year-old yews, clipped into fantastical shapes. Some commemorate historic events while others are cut into chair shapes or shaved into elephants and astronauts.

Lyddington Bede House
Blue Coat Lane, Lyddington, LE15 9LZ (01572 8224380/www.english-heritage.co.uk). **Open** *Apr-Sept* 10am-6pm daily. *Oct* 10am-5pm daily. Closed Nov-Mar. **Admission** (EH) £3.20; £1.60-£2.40 concessions. **Credit** MC, V.
A medieval palace originally built for the sporting Bishops of Lincoln, later converted into almshouses after the Reformation. It's a lovely, rambling house with 16th-century interiors and events throughout the summer.

Normanton Church Museum
Normanton, Rutland Water (01572 6530267). **Open** *Easter-Sept* 11am-4pm Mon-Fri; 11am-5pm Sat, Sun. *Oct* 11am-5pm Sat, Sun. Closed Nov-Easter. **Admission** £1; 50p concessions. **Credit** MC, V.

Rutland's best-known landmark is this Italianate Georgian church that was rescued from the submerged Normanton estate. Now standing on a promontory on the edge of the reservoir, it houses a museum with a display dedicated to the history of the Anglian Water reservoir and surrounding area.
Off A606 between Oakham and Stamford; from Empingham follow brown and white boards for Normanton South Shore.

Oakham Castle
Off Market Place, Oakham, LE15 6DT (01572 758440/www.rutnet.co.uk/rcccastle). **Open** 10.30am-1pm, 1.30-5pm Mon-Sat; 2-4pm Sun. **Admission** free; donations welcome.
The marvellous arched Great Hall is all that's left of 12th-century Oakham Castle these days. It houses a collection of horseshoes, presented by peers and royalty to Lords of the Manor. The building is still in use as a court and is licensed for weddings.

Rockingham Castle
Rockingham, Market Harborough, Lincolnshire LE16 8TH (01536 770240/www.rockinghamcastle.com). **Open** *Castle* Apr-June, Sept 1-5pm Sun. July Aug 1-5pm Tue, Thur, Sun. *Grounds* Apr-June, Sept noon-5pm Sun. July, Aug noon-5pm Tue, Thur, Sun. Closed Oct-Mar. **Admission** *Castle & grounds* £6; £4-£5.50 concessions; free under-5s. *Grounds only* £4. **Credit** MC, V.
A couple of hundred yards outside Rutland, this hilltop castle offers a view over the whole of England's smallest county from high battlements. It was commissioned by William the Conqueror and hosted monarchs including Richard the Lionheart and Henry VIII before being commandeered by the Roundheads during the Civil War. The interior is open to the public, with room sets reflecting its millennium of history, right through to the current owners' 20th-century art.

Rutland Belle Cruises
Rutland Water Cruises, The Harbour, Whitwell, Rutland Water North Shore, off A606 (01572 787630/www.rutlandwatercruises.com). **Cruises** *Apr, Oct* 1pm, 2pm, 3pm Sat, Sun. *May-Sept* 1pm, 2pm, 3pm daily (phone to confirm). Closed Nov-Mar. **Tickets** £5; £3.50 concessions. **No credit cards.**
Take an afternoon trip around Rutland Water, embarking either from Whitwell harbour (on the north shore; vehicular access) or Normanton Church (on the south shore). There's a 20-minute trip each way amid the anglers, sailors and waterbirds, with commentary on points of interest.

Rutland Water Butterfly Farm & Aquatic Centre
Sykes Lane car park, North Shore, Rutland Water, Oakham, LE15 8PX (01780 460515). **Open** *Apr-Oct* 10.30am-5pm daily. Last entry 4.30pm. Closed Nov-Mar. **Admission** £3.95; £2.95 concessions. **Credit** MC, V.
One of the best freshwater aquariums in the country, with waterfalls and stream and reservoir displays. There's also a heated 'free flight' butterfly house, with parrots, terrapins and iguanas in the undergrowth. The 'Twilight Zone', home to creepy-crawlies and reptiles, is for not for the fainthearted.

Lyddington Bede House. *See p253.*

Rutland Water Cycling

Whitwell Centre *Whitwell car park, nr Oakham, LE15 8BL (01780 460705/www.rutlandcycling. co.uk)* **Open** 9.15am-6pm/dusk daily. **Day hire** £12.95. **Credit** MC, V.
Normanton Centre *Normanton car park, nr Edith Weston , Oakham, LE15 8HD (01780 720888/ www.rutlandcycling.co.uk).* **Open** 9.15am-6pm/dusk daily. **Day hire** £12.95. **Credit** MC, V.
Idyllic, traffic-free lakeside cycling.

Rutland Water Nature Reserve

Anglian Water Birdwatching Centre, Egleton Reserve, LE15 8BT, 1 mile S of Oakham (01572 770651/ www.rutlandwater.org.uk); Lyndon Reserve, 1 mile E of Manton on S shore. **Open** *Egleton* Mar-Oct 9am-5pm daily. *Nov-Feb* 9am-4pm daily. *Lyndon* Mar-Oct 9am-5pm daily. Nov-Feb 9am-4pm Sat, Sun. **Admission** £4; £2-£3 concessions; free under-6s. **Credit** MC, V.
Both visitor centres feature well-stocked shops, and sell day permits for the reserve.

Sacrewell Farm & Country Centre

Thornhaugh, PE8 6HJ (01780 782254/www. sacrewell.org.uk). **Open** 9.30am-5pm daily. **Admission** £4; £2.50-£3 concessions; free under-3s. **Credit** AmEx, DC, MC, V.
Explore a working farm, meet the farm animals and investigate a watermill. There are also nature trails and hungry animals for the kids to feed.

Stamford Museum

Broad Street, Stamford, PE9 1PJ (01780 766317/ www.lincolnshire.gov.uk/stamfordmuseum). **Open** *Apr-Sept* 10am-5pm Mon-Sat; 2-5pm Sun. *Oct-Mar* 10am-5pm Mon-Sat. **Admission** free.
Two full floors on the town's history, but best cut to the chase… side by side are the legendary bad-taste life-size models of 52-stone Daniel Lambert, who died in town while visiting the races, and 3ft 4in tall General Charles Stratton, who visited it several years later.

Stamford Shakespeare Company

Tolethorpe Hall, Little Casterton, Stamford, PE9 4BH (01780 754381/box office 01780 756133/ www.stamfordshakespeare.co.uk). **Open** *June-Aug* Grounds from 5pm, performances 8pm Mon-Thur; 8.30pm Fri, Sat. **Tickets** £10-£14. **Credit** AmEx, DC, MC, V.
Only Stamford Shakespeare Company actors need pray for fine weather at this 600-seat auditorium in an idyllic woodland setting: while they perform on an uncovered stage, the audience is entirely sheltered. There's a bar, a picnic area and a restaurant. Amateur dramatics at their loveliest, with a theatre bar, picnic areas in gardens and a pre-theatre restaurant seating 90.

Melbourn Brothers, All Saints Brewery

All Saints Street, Stamford, PE9 2PA (01780 752186). **Tours** (1hr) 11am-5pm Wed-Sun. **Tickets** £3.50; £3 concessions. **Credit** AmEx, DC, MC, V.
Dating from 1825, this was Stamford's oldest surviving brewery until it closed in 1974. It's now functioning again, making fruit beers, and offers tours to the public. There are also exhibitions on the brewery's history.

Where to stay

There's an abundance of reinvented coaching inns and village pubs, plus good farmhouse B&Bs scattered throughout Rutland and the flats of south-west Lincolnshire. Small hotels are clustered in Uppingham: the **Falcon** (The Market Place, 01572 823535, doubles £80) is a 16th-century coaching inn on the market place, whose honeymoon suite features an original Elizabethan four-poster. In Oakham, check out **Lord Nelson's House** (11 Market Place, 01572 723199, doubles £80-£90). All four rooms are very groovy. In Stamford, try **Lady Anne's**

The Chilterns to York

Time Out Weekend Breaks **253**

Hotel in St Martin's High Street (01780 481184, doubles £75-£105), or the antiques-strewn **Garden House Hotel** (St Martin's High Street, 01780 763359, doubles £89).

Barnsdale Hall Hotel

nr Oakham, Rutland LE15 8AB (01572 757901/fax 01572 756235/www.barnsdalehotel.co.uk). **Rates** £70 single; £90-£110 double/twin/disabled room; £130 family; £140-£150 four poster. **Rooms** (all en suite) 10 single; 4 twin; 37 double; 9 executive/family; 3 four-poster; 2 disabled rooms. **Credit** AmEx, DC, MC, V.
Originally a 19th-century hunting lodge, Barnsdale Hall stands on the slopes leading down to Rutland Water's north shore. There's a superb array of leisure facilities on offer, including a 22-metre swimming pool, childrens' and spa pools, sauna, steam room, fitness centre, squash courts, and pool and snooker tables. Outside, there are six tennis courts, a nine-hole pitch-and-putt course, plus bowling/croquet lawns. Golf, shooting, horse-riding, sailing, windsurfing and dry slope skiing can be organised. Children welcome. No-smoking rooms available.

Barnsdale Lodge Hotel

The Avenue, Rutland Water North Shore, nr Oakham, LE15 8AH (01572 724678/fax 01572 724961/www.barnsdalelodge.co.uk). **Rates** £75 single; £99.50-£120 double/twin/four-poster/suite; family room. **Rooms** (all en suite) 8 single; 28 double/twin; 2 four-poster; 5 suites; 2 family rooms. **Credit** AmEx, DC, MC, V.
A couple of miles outside Oakham, the 17th-century Barnsdale Lodge farmhouse made a successful career-switch when its land disappeared under the waves of Rutland Water. Now extended and expanded – with the addition of bedrooms around a bright courtyard – the stone walls and flagged floors of the old building retain great character amid a cornucopia of Edwardian-chic decor. Children and dogs (£10 charge) welcome.

The Whipper-in

Market Place, Oakham, LE15 6DT (01572 756971/ fax 01572 757759/www.brook-hotels.co.uk). **Rates** £75 single; £85 double/twin; £99 executive; £104 four-poster. **Rooms** 3 single (all en suite); 15 double/ twin (14 en suite, 1 private bathroom); 4 executive (all en suite); 2 four-poster (both en suite). **Credit** AmEx, DC, MC, V.
This stuccoed 17th-century coaching inn on the tiny market square rates as one of Oakham's smartest places to stay or dine. The individual bedrooms are charmingly ancient, many with timber beams. The atmosphere and food at the George restaurant is agreeably traditional, while at No.5 a Modern British menu is imaginatively conceived and prepared. The Market Bar is popular with locals. Children welcome.

Where to eat & drink

For foodie pubs, you could do a lot worse than the **Old Plough** at Braunston, near Oakham (01572 722714), or the **Black Bull** in Market Overton (2 Teigh, 01572 767677).
More 'pubby' pubs include the **Hole in the Wall**, up narrow, crooked Cheyne Lane

in Stamford (01780 764226); the **Waggon & Horses** at 64 High Street East, Uppingham (01572 822203); the **White Horse** in Empingham (Main Street, 01780 460221); and the **Millstone Inn** on Millstone Lane, Barnack, Lincolnshire (01780 740296) – good luck finding this last one! Try the **Grainstore Brewery** on Station Approach in Oakham (01572 770065), notable for the excellent beers brewed on site by the former head brewer at the sadly missed Ruddles Brewery in Langham (note: Ruddles ales are now nothing to do with Rutland). Also enjoy a tour of the wonderful **Melbourn Brothers' Brewery** (*see p253*), and drink some apricot beer while you're there.
For fine dining, **Nick's Restaurant** at Lord Nelson's House in Oakham (01572 723199) serves Modern British food, prepared with great care. Meanwhile, balti aficionados will be pleased to hear that the management and staff of the **Voujon Balti Hut** (4 Burley Corner, High Street, Oakham, 01572 723043) make a daily trek all the way from Birmingham.

Finch's Arms

Oakham Road, Hambleton, LE15 8TL (01572 756575). **Food served** noon-2pm, 6.30-9.30pm Mon-Sat; noon-9.30pm Sun. **Main courses** £8.95-£13.50. **Set lunches** £9.95 2 courses, £11.95 3 courses. **Credit** MC, V.
A textbook example of how to maintain an old pub while moving seamlessly into the 21st century. The Finch's Arms is a pub in name alone: decor is a tasteful, slyly modish set-up with a restaurant at the back with views over Rutland Water (you can eat from the same menu in the not-especially-pubby pub bit). Beers come from the Grainstore brewery, and the food from an inventive chef: grilled mackerel with stir-fried veg, shark with sushi rice, or a divine chicken breast salad. The welcome is warm and the ambience a delight. A winning enterprise.

Hambleton Hall

Hambleton, Oakham, LE15 8TH (01572 756991/ www.hambletonhall.com). **Food served** noon-1.30pm, 7-9.30pm daily. **Main courses** £25-£39. **Set meal** £35 3 courses. **Credit** AmEx, DC, MC, V.
Imperiously overlooking Rutland Water from land-scaped grounds on the central peninsula, Hambleton Hall is an English country hotel par excellence. Tim and Stefa Hart manage to uphold an atmosphere of relaxation amid the chintz and Regency stripes. This really is a temple to food and any sensation of stuffiness drops away as soon as the gourmet treats arrive: sweetmeats and veal or intimate cuts of the newest baby lamb drizzled with jus and chef Aaron Patterson's secret alchemical sauces. Service is expert, unobtrusive and friendly. If you fancy staying, bedrooms are individually themed, and stocked with elegant antique furniture.

King's Arms

13 Top Street, Wing, LE15 8SE (01572 737634/ www.thekingsarms-wing.co.uk) **Food served** noon-2pm, 6.30-9pm daily. **Main courses** £6.95-£14.95. **Credit** MC, V.

Sites, rites and local legends

While the thriving post-Rutland Water tourism industry has opened up the county to appreciation by a whole new group of visitors, it is important to remember that Rutland's links with its past – dating as far back as pre-Christian times – are still very visible.

The turf maze at **Wing** is one of only a handful of similar surviving pre-Christian sites dotted around the country. Adopted by the church in medieval times, when penitents were instructed to crawl around the snaking pattern of shallow trenches, the maze's original use and meaning can now only be guessed at. However, like the holy well near the church at **Ryhall**, it's a fair bet the maze was related to fertility. Likewise, the small carved stone figure set by the wall of **Braunston** church: used for years as a doorstep, this curvy earth mother was only rediscovered very recently in her lengthy lifespan.

Coming slightly closer to the present, the tiny honey-stone church at **Stoke Dry** has links to the Knights Templar, and features very unusual wall paintings and Norman carvings depicting devilry and martyrdom. Pagans here are portrayed with feathered headgear, which has led to speculation that they are native Americans – a theory which, if true, would turn accepted history on its head, as they

were painted centuries before Columbus. The parvis above the church door is reputedly haunted by a witch once locked away and forgotten by the local pastor: there's still a sign that warns you not to spread rumours. Folklore assures us that the Gunpowder Plot was hatched in the same stone cell by Guy Fawkes and entombed resident Everard Digby, who was hung, drawn and quartered for his troubles.

At **Pickworth**, a rutted field and a single arch is all that's left of a church that, along with three-quarters of the original village, was destroyed by rampaging Lancastrians searching for fleeing locals after the Battle of Losecoat Field in the War of the Roses. By the early 1800s, the arch was already a relic and an inspiration to poet John Clare.

More disappearances can be traced to Rutland Water. Walking towards the church of **St Andrew**, salvaged from the great flood, you'll find yourself strolling down a country road that slopes directly into the water. You can see it appear again on the peninsula a mile away, near Hambleton – formerly known as Upper Hambleton. Spare a thought, then, for the lost village of Nether Hambleton, which languishes 150 feet below the five-mile expanse of water.

Wing is best known for its unusual turf maze, but a recent makeover at the 17th-century King's Arms has given another reason to visit this small, peaceful village near Rutland Water. An airy lightness now infuses the once-dreary dining room, and the menu reflects the transformation. Locally sourced fish and meat are presented simply – such as a main course fillet of salmon or crushed new potatoes with a zesty lemon and prawn hollandaise, or fillet of pork with a roast red pepper and foie gras terrine as a colourful and flavour-packed starter. You'll also find exotica like crocodile and ostrich alongside imaginative vegetarian options such as roasted artichoke and wild mushroom risotto. Desserts might include a warm chocolate fondant with Turkish delight ice-cream. The wine list is short but well thought-out.

King's Cliffe House

31 West Street, King's Cliffe, Northamptonshire, PE8 6XB (01780 470172). **Food served** 7-9.15pm Wed-Sat. **Main courses** £15.50. **No credit cards.**
King's Cliffe is within easy travelling distance of anywhere in Rutland. Andrew Wilshaw and Emma Jessop have a touch of *The Good Life* here: the walled garden provides seasonal vegetables, fruit and herbs used in the

flower-decked restaurant. They do their own hot-smoking, charcuterie and salting, and there are wonderful local supplies of additive-free meat, chicken and duck. Dinner is a gentle affair. The cooking is skilled and the flavours well balanced, with an imaginative choice on the short menu: Southorpe asparagus in tempura batter with sorrel hollandaise; guinea fowl with muscat and parma ham sauce; rhubarb in honey saffron custard.

Olive Branch

Main Street, Clipsham, LE15 7SH (01780 410355). **Food served** noon-2pm, 7-9.30pm Mon-Sat; noon-3pm Sun. **Main courses** £8.25-£17. **Set lunches** (Mon-Sat) £10.50 2 courses, £12.50 3 courses; (Sun) £15 3 courses. **Credit** MC, V.
A gorgeous country boozer that takes food seriously, the Olive Branch is always buzzing. From the shabby chic interior to its location in a lovely village, with friendly service and a menu that makes the most of local ingredients, the Olive Branch hits all the right notes. Char-grilled fish and meat feature strongly, with appetising accompaniments such as sage mash or crispy sweet potatoes, and grand real ales. Puddings, including treacle tart with yoghurt ice-cream, are unmissable.

The Chilterns to York

Lincoln

An ancient city with masses of monuments to explore.

At first glance, Lincoln may not be an obvious choice for a weekend break, but look a little closer and you'll find plenty of reasons to visit. And while there is no direct train link with London, its relative obscurity on the tourist trail means you're less likely to be crowded out by coach parties.

Founded by the Romans in AD 48, Lincoln was one of Europe's most important cities right up until the 17th century, a status that leaves it with a treasure trove of Roman and medieval architecture to equal York or Canterbury.

Uphill and downhill

The city is dominated by the magnificent cathedral, a towering Gothic precipice perched upon the only hill for miles around. At night it is floodlit quite spectacularly and if you arrive by train or car across the region's flat plains, it looks rather surreal. Its companion is the medieval castle, which was built just after the Norman conquest. Surrounding the cathedral and castle is the uphill area. Crammed with cobbled streets and ancient houses, it's largely car-free and has plenty of quirky and traditional shops (including lots of bookshops) and pubs. It's in this area that you'll find most of the city's visitor attractions.

The residential bulk of the city is downhill, including a busy pedestrianised High Street with extensive – if predictable – shopping possibilities and a vibrant covered market (there's also a **farmers' market** on the first Friday of every month). Here you'll also find the **Brayford Pool**, a regenerated waterside area with shops and restaurants.

Past

Lincoln started life as a Roman garrison, and later grew into a thriving Roman community. There are plenty of remnants of the era, including **Newport Arch**, the only surviving Roman arch in Britain that still has traffic driving through it. After the Romans left in around AD 500, Lincoln became part of the Anglo-Saxon community of Lindsey, and later one of the principal burghs of the Danelaw established by the invading Vikings. The city received its charter in 1071 from William the Conqueror, who ordered the building of both the castle and the cathedral. By 1086 it was a walled metropolis of 5,000 people.

Medieval Lincoln can be seen best on the aptly named **Steep Hill**, the picturesque link between uphill and down. Here you'll see such ancient dwellings as the **Norman House** and the **Jews House**. The latter dates back to the 1170s and is Britain's oldest continuously occupied domestic building.

Other later examples include the half-timbered houses on **High Bridge** – the nation's oldest bridge to have buildings over it – and the three surviving city gates, at **Pottergate**, **Minster Yard** and the **Stonebow**.

Lincoln's later prosperity was based on the fertile agricultural region surrounding the city, and it was agriculture that led it to become a centre of heavy industry. From the manufacture of steam tractors and threshing machines grew a series of foundries and engineering works.

Present and future

In 1996 Lincoln became a university town, and it plays its new academic role to the full. The rapidly growing campus now fills the wasteland left by the city's industrial past, bringing new life to the area around the Brayford Pool, and energising the city with an influx of young people.

Lincoln is looking increasingly towards tourism for its income, and its million annual visitors are well catered for, with a wealth of places to stay and a growing number of good restaurants to visit. However, there is, as yet, mercifully little of the intensive tourism and sightseeing-by-numbers you'll find in many similar British cities. Make the most of it while you can.

What to see & do

Think of Lincoln in two parts, uphill and down, so you minimise the number of times you have to walk up **Steep Hill**. That one obstacle apart, it's a very walkable city, with the major attractions close to each other. However, there's a useful hop-on-hop-off sightseeing bus, **Guide Friday**, that covers all the major sights and runs from mid April to mid September.

If you fancy a trip along the local waterways (the **River Witham** and the **Roman Foss Dyke Canal**), there are boat services from the **William IV** pub by the Brayford and from the Waterside shopping centre.

Lincoln Cathedral seen from the gardens of the **Bishop's Palace**.

Tourist Information Centres

21 The Cornhill (High Street), LN5 7HB (01522 873256/www.lincoln.gov.uk). **Open** 9.30am-5.30pm Mon-Thur; 9.30am-5pm Fri; 10am-5pm Sat.

9 Castle Hill (Castle Square), LN1 3AA (01522 873213/www.lincoln.gov.uk). **Open** 9.30am-5.30pm Mon-Thur; 9.30am-5pm Fri; 10am-5pm Sat, Sun.
Ask about guided tours (£3-£3.50 adults, £1.50-£2 children) – they start outside the Castle Square and Cornhill offices. Ghost walks (no need to book) also start from here every Wednesday, Friday and Saturday. For more information phone 01522 874056.

Bishop's Palace

Minster Yard, LN2 1PU (01522 527468/www. english-heritage.org.uk). **Open** *Apr-Sept* 10am-6pm daily. *Oct* 10am-5pm daily. *Nov-Mar* 10am-4pm Sat, Sun. **Christmas market days** 4-7 Dec 10am-9pm. **Admission** (EH) £3.20; £1.60-£2.40 concessions. **Credit** MC, V.
Said to have once been Britain's most luxurious residence, with banqueting halls, apartments and offices, the Bishop's Palace was always an important building. Not much of the original splendour survives today except the restored Alnwick Tower, but displays show just how well the medieval bishops lived as they entertained monarchs and ran much of the city. The ruins are very atmospheric, the site is pretty, the views are splendid and there's even a small vineyard clinging to the side of the hill.

Christmas Market

Castle Square. **Dates** 4-7 Dec. Thur evening, then all day Fri-Sun. Check with Tourist Office for exact times and details.
Lincoln is twinned with Neustadt an der Weinstrasse, a German wine-producing town, which provided the inspiration for a Christmas market in the late 1980s. Today, the market is a mix of food and drink (mulled wine and roast chestnuts through to sausages and chips), fairground rides (the more sedate kind) and a mass of stalls

(some tacky, some charming). It's a popular event, and also very festive – not least because of the dramatic location, against the backdrop of the castle and cathedral.

Ellis Mill

Mill Road (01522 523870/528448). **Open** *May-Sept* 2-6pm Sat, Sun. *Oct-Apr* 2pm-dusk Sun. Weekday bookings by arrangement. **Admission** 70p; 30p concessions. **No credit cards**.
In days gone by, the long ridge on which Lincoln is built was peppered with windmills. Now there's just one, built in 1798 and restored in 1981. If the wind's blowing and they're grinding corn, it's a fascinating place to visit; fresh stoneground flour is for sale too.

Greyfriars Exhibition Centre

Broadgate, LN1 1HQ (01522 530401/www. lincolnshire.gov.uk/greyfriars). **Open** 10am-1pm, 2-4pm Tue-Sat. **Admission** free.
Housed in a 13th-century building, this centre is a good starting point for a tour through Lincoln's long history. Its changing displays are drawn from the collection of the old City and County Museum and they cover aspects of Lincoln from its prehistory until around 1750. Exhibits also include many objects retrieved from local archaeological excavations.

By train from London

There are, alas, no direct trains from London to Lincoln, but the service from **King's Cross** to **Newark Northgate** (one train every 30mins to 1hr) takes just under 1hr 30mins; from there trains to **Lincoln Central** take just under 30mins (although you may have a wait between the two services). Info: www.gner.co.uk and www.centraltrains.co.uk.

Lincoln Castle

Castle Hill, LN1 3AA (01522 511068/www.
lincolnshire.gov.uk/lincolncastle). **Open** *Apr-Oct*
9.30am-5.30pm Mon-Sat; 11am-5.30pm Sun. *Nov-Mar*
9.30am-4pm Mon-Sat; 11am-4pm Sun (last entry 1hr
before closing). **Admission** £3.50; £2 concessions;
free under-5s. **Credit** MC, V.

On a cobbled square, facing the cathedral, is the entrance
to Lincoln Castle. Built immediately after the Norman
conquest, this was a key defence for an important and
wealthy town. It saw action in the 1140s during the
Battle of Lincoln between King Stephen and the invading Matilda, when it was besieged several times, and
then in 1644 when Cromwell's Parliamentary soldiers
stormed it in less than an hour and booted the king's soldiers out of the city. In more peaceful times the castle
has been the site of a Victorian prison and a Crown
Court, which is still in operation. These days, its grounds
are the site of a busy programme of events throughout
the year, from plays, classical concerts and brass bands,
to re-enactments, medieval jousting and archery, and a
vintage car rally. There's a coffee shop here too. Walk
around the perimeter walls for some great views of the
city and surrounding countryside (especially from the
Observatory Tower). Round to the east, Cobb Tower
contains some grisly dungeons, complete with manacles
and prisoners' 13th-century carved graffiti. In the southern part of the grounds, the prison is worth a look, not
least for its chapel, the only surviving example of the
'Pentonville separate system', a maze of interlocking
doors, which kept prisoners completely isolated even
while they were sitting next to each other. Also housed
in the prison building is the Magna Carta, the foundation of the nation's civil liberties and rule of law. This is
one of the four surviving originals that King John signed
in 1215. It has been kept in Lincoln ever since.

Lincoln Cathedral

Minster Yard, LN2 1PX (01522 544544/www.
lincolncathedral.com). **Open** *June-Aug* 7.15am-8pm
Mon-Sat; 7.15am-6pm Sun. *Sept-May* 7.15am-6pm
Mon-Sat; 7.15am-5pm Sun. **Admission** £4; £3
concessions; free under-14s. **Credit** MC, V.

For several centuries, when its three Gothic towers were
capped by enormous spires, Lincoln Cathedral was (at
540ft) the tallest building in the world. Today, it remains
among the most beautiful, described by John Ruskin as
'out and out the most precious piece of architecture in
the British Isles'. It is visible from almost anywhere in
the city and now that much of the exterior restoration is
complete, its imposing west front is free of the scaffolding that obscured it for a decade. The diocese of Lincoln
once stretched from the Thames to the Humber, the
largest in the country, so it was only appropriate that
such a grand cathedral should be here. Most of what
stands today was built by St Hugh, a French monk who
became Bishop of Lincoln in 1186. Hugh brought to the
building an elegant continental style previously
unknown in England, and this style was followed
throughout the four centuries of the building's construction. However, the lower parts of the west front are
the remnants of a much earlier cathedral, a 1072 Norman
structure built by Remigius, the first Bishop of Lincoln.
The rest of this structure was destroyed by an earth-
quake in 1141. The 900-year-old cathedral boasts some
of the finest medieval architecture and craftsmanship to
be found anywhere. There's the beautiful Early English
Angel Choir, where you'll find the Lincoln Imp, the city's
devilish mascot; the fine wood carving (especially the
hidden designs under the Bishops' perches), the fine
stained glass throughout, and the library, designed by
Sir Christopher Wren. In the cathedral garden stands a
huge statue of Tennyson by George Frederick Watts.

Museum of Lincolnshire Life

Burton Road, LN1 3LY (01522 528448/www.
lincolnshire.gov.uk). **Open** *May-Oct* 10am-5.30pm
daily. *Nov-Apr* 10am-5.30pm Mon-Sat; 2-5.30pm Sun.
Last admission 4.30pm. **Admission** £2; £1.20
concessions; free under-5s. **No credit cards.**

A gem of a museum if you like a little bit of everything.
All aspects of Lincolnshire's social and economic history
are represented here. Period interiors (a printer's, a wheel-
wright's, a chemist shop, a school room), agricultural
implements, period costumes and scores of beautifully
restored traction engines and horse-drawn carriages vie
for attention. Modern Lincoln was built on heavy engineering, so there are plenty of iron giants, including the
world's first tank (built in the city's foundries). The museum hosts frequent talks and other events.

The Stonebow & Guildhall

Saltergate, LN2 1DH (01522 873507/873294/www.
lincoln.org.uk). **Open** (guided tours) 10.30am, 1.30pm
Mon, Wed, Fri, Sat. Other times by arrangement.
Admission phone for details. **No credit cards.**

In the 15th and 16th centuries the Stonebow – a limestone archway that spans the pedestrianised High Street
– was the southern gateway into the walled city. A
replacement for one that the Romans erected (its companion gates exist in Pottergate and in Minster Yard
between castle and cathedral). Now it's mostly a landmark for rendezvous that take place under its clock.
Inside is the council chamber and a room displaying a
wealth of civic insignia: swords, seals and mayoral chains.

Usher Gallery

Lindum Road, LN2 1NN (01522 527980). **Open**
10am-5.30pm Tue-Sat; 2.30-5pm Sun. Last entry
4.30pm. **Admission** phone for details. **Credit** MC, V.

A handsome provincial art gallery housing an acclaimed
collection of coins, jewellery and timepieces, in keeping
with the profession of its founder, James Ward Usher, a
local jeweller. There are also watercolours by Turner
and a collection of work by Peter de Wint, as well as
paintings by LS Lowry, John Piper and Walter Sickert.
There's a fine collection of memorabilia relating to the
Lincolnshire-born Alfred Lord Tennyson. The café is a
pleasant, sun-filled spot.

Where to stay

Lincoln lacks much truly characterful
accommodation, but is teeming with B&Bs,
especially in the West End area of the city (try
along Yarborough Road or West Parade). Most
hotels are part of a chain; the ones listed below
are chosen for reasons of location, style and
price – and not every one has all three attributes.
If you don't want an early wake-up call, avoid
those within earshot of the cathedral bells.

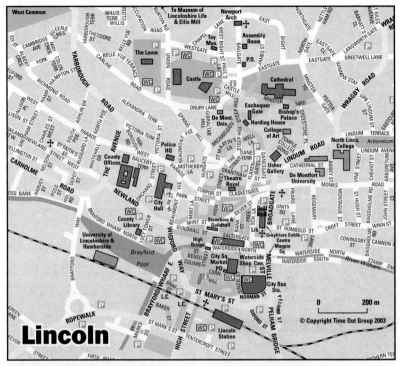

Lincoln

Courtyard by Marriott OFFER

Brayford Wharf North, LN1 1YW (01522 544244/fax 01522 560805/www.marriott.co.uk). **Rates** £65-£89 single; £90-£99 double/twin. **Rooms** (all en suite) 51 single; 26 double; 20 twin. **Credit** AmEx, DC, MC, V.

The Marriott was a major part of the regeneration of Lincoln's Brayford Pool area, and is built in a vaguely wharf-style design. The rooms are clean predictable and air-conditioned; the bathrooms all boast power showers and underfloor heating. A buffet breakfast is served in a room overlooking the water. It's a business-oriented hotel, but families are made very welcome.

D'Isney Place Hotel

Eastgate, LN2 4AA (01522 538881/fax 01522 511321/www.disneyplacehotel.co.uk). **Rates** £66.50 single occupancy; £89 double/twin; £99 family room; £109 deluxe double. **Rooms** (all en suite) 1 single; 12 double/twin; 3 deluxe double; 3 family. **Credit** AmEx, DC, MC, V.

There are no public rooms in this charming red-brick Georgian townhouse, but the guest rooms are all very pleasant (and the larger ones positively luxurious – one even has a jacuzzi). As well as being close to the historic side of the city, there's a piece of it in the delightfully secluded garden: a 700-year-old tower, part of the old wall that once surrounded the cathedral. Breakfast is served in your room. Children and dogs welcome.

Edward King House

The Old Palace, Minster Yard, LN2 1PU (01522 528778/fax 01522 527308/www.ekhs.org.uk). **Rates** £21 single; £41 twin; £62 family room. Breakfast £2 (Eng). **Rooms** 5 single; 11 twin; 1 family. **Credit** AmEx, MC, V.

The former official residence of the Bishop of Lincoln, this large guesthouse is still run by the Church. It has one of the best (and most peaceful) locations in the city, being close to the cathedral while overlooking the ruins of the medieval Bishop's Palace (the breakfast room has a beautiful view). Small, modestly decorated rooms lend the place an air of a religious retreat – especially as there are no en suite rooms. However, the bathrooms are spotlessly clean and, for the price, Edward King House is hard to beat. Children welcome. No smoking throughout. Pets by arrangement.

The Lincoln Hotel

Eastgate, LN2 1PN (01522 520348/fax 01522 510780/www.thelincolnhotel.com). **Rates** £75-£92 single/single occupancy; £75-£99 double/twin/family room (under-15s free if sharing parents' room). **Rooms** (all en suite) 15 single; 26 double; 5 executive; 22 twin; 4 family. **Credit** AmEx, DC, MC, V.

This rather brutal-looking modern hotel makes a startling contrast to the cathedral across the road, but has the twin attributes of great location and value for money. Currently undergoing a refurbishment, it aims to have modernised all its rooms by 2004; the new look is modern, with minimal designs in lighting and furniture. The rooms are a decent size, and there are even a few Roman remains in the grounds. Children and dogs welcome.

St Clements Lodge

21 Langworth Gate, LN2 4AD (tel/fax 01522 521532). **Rates** £38 single occupancy; £56 double/twin; £70-£85 family room. **Rooms** 3 double/twin/family (2 en suite). **No credit cards.**

A small but immaculate B&B close to all the uphill attractions. The rooms are large, comfortable and decorated in cosy cottage style. The owners are welcoming and it's the kind of place that gets a lot of repeat bookings. Children welcome. No smoking throughout.

The White Hart Hotel

Bailgate, LN1 3AR (01522 526222/central office 0870 4009090/fax 01522 531798/www.macdonald hotels.co.uk). **Rates** £45-£133 single; £90-£133 double/twin; £110-£153 deluxe double/twin; £120-£163 suite; £145-£183 four-poster. **Rooms** (all en suite) 6 single; 31 double/twin; 9 suites; 2 four-poster/king suites. **Credit** AmEx, DC, MC, V.

A large historic coaching inn that dates back to the 1400s, the White Hart is part of Forte's Heritage Hotels chain and is situated smack in between the castle and the cathedral. All the rooms (some of which feel a bit cramped) are of a high standard and the hotel is filled with antique porcelain, paintings and furnishings. Dogs welcome (£10 charge).

Where to eat & drink

There's not a huge amount of choice in Lincoln. Hotel restaurants are generally dependable, especially the **White Hart** (*see above*), as are many of the pubs – try the **Duke William Hotel** (44 Bailgate, 01522 533351). The **Victoria** (6 Union Road, 01522 536048) has Lincoln's best range of real ales and no music. For the best fish and chips in town, try the **Elite Fish & Chip Shop** (Moorland Shopping & Industrial Complex, Tritton Road, (01522 509505), a restaurant as well as a takeaway.

Gradually, modern bars are joining the more traditional pubs and chain pubs in the city centre, but weekend visitors after a quiet pint should be warned that Saturday nights can get very rowdy around the streets at the bottom of Steep Hill. Students, you see.

Brown's Pie Shop

33 Steep Hill, Lincoln, LN2 1LU (01522 527330). **Food served** 11.45am-3pm, 5-10pm Mon-Fri; 10am-10pm Sat, Sun. **Main courses** £7.95-£16. **Set lunch** £6.50 2 courses. **Credit** AmEx, MC, V.

Don't be misled by the name of this place – it's a bona fide restaurant and a good venue for an evening meal as well as lunch. Modestly decorated but well lit, its upstairs room is lined with tables that are spaced to allow a relative amount of privacy. Diners tuck into an extensive menu that offers steaks and dishes such as seared sea bass or Cumberland sausages alongside a full range of pies. These deserve to be tried: choices include local rabbit with Dorset scrumpy, steak and kidney, a three cheese veggie option and a game one.

The Cheese Society

1 St Martin's Lane, LN2 1HY (01522 511003/www.thecheesesociety.co.uk). **Meals served** 10am-4.30pm Mon-Sat. **Main courses** £4.95-£8.95. **Set lunch** £7.95 2 courses, £9.95 3 courses. **Credit** AmEx, MC, V.

Handily situated just off the tourist drag of Steep Hill, this is a little shop and café. Dishes – many of which have cheese as the star turn – run from salads (feta, couscous and roast veg), sandwiches (Swiss cheese with grapes and mayo or roast ham with beetroot and horseradish relish) and melts (blue cheese and bacon) to more sizeable offerings. You could order sirloin steak with frites, but melted raclette over hot new potatoes or fondue (for two) are hard to resist. Save room for the yellow belly tart (lemon curd) with ice-cream. Booking is advisable for lunch; at other times it's easy to pop in for one of the many varieties of tea and a slice of Lincolnshire plum bread. Service is charming.

The Jews House

15 The Strait, LN2 1JD (01522 524851). **Food served** 11.30am-2.30pm, 6.30-9.30pm Tue-Sat. **Main courses** £12.75-£18.95. **Set lunch** £12.95 2 courses, £14.95 3 courses. **Credit** DC, MC, V.

Possibly the oldest inhabited house in the country (it dates back to 1190), the Jews House plays host to the most upmarket restaurant in Lincoln. It may ask you to pay for the privilege but offers immaculate service and Modern European food of a decent calibre in return. A small, peaceful room overlooking the street on Steep Hill, it typically attracts smartly dressed older couples enjoying muted conversation and background classical music. A typical meal here might be baked figs with goat's cheese and a watercress and dill salad, followed by braised pork belly and seared loin of pork with steamed pak choi and coriander foam. Finish with glazed lemon tart with lime muffin or white chocolate and passion fruit mousse with chocolate shortbread. Staff are pleasant.

Wig & Mitre

30 Steep Hill, LN2 1TL (01522 535190/www.wig andmitre.com). **Meals served** 8am-11pm Mon-Sat; 8am-10.30pm Sun. **Main courses** £9.50-£16.50. **Set meals** (noon-6pm daily) £9.50 1 course, £11 2 courses, £13.95 3 courses. **Credit** AmEx, DC, MC, V.

If you're after somewhere for a leisurely Sunday lunch with the newspapers, then look no further than the Wig & Mitre, whose several floors host real ales, an impressive wine list and very acceptable food. Breakfast options include a wonderfully creamy porridge; sandwiches run from cheddar and red onion to pan-fried fillet steak with mushrooms and caramelised onions; more substantial offerings might be roast Lincolnshire sausage with garlic and black pudding mash and apple cream sauce or roast tomato and basil risotto with aged balsamic and parmesan crackling. This music-free venue offers a variety of seating arrangements from pub trestle tables to more formal table service dining. There's nowhere else like this (relaxed, civilised, open all day) in the city.

York

A historical treasure.

With soaring church towers and bristling castle defences, York is a fairytale city. Its winding medieval roads – perfect for walking tours – take you past half-timbered buildings, colourful markets and one of the country's truly great architectural masterpieces, York Minster. This is one of Britain's few remaining walled cities and in it you can wander among Norman ruins, drink in 400-year-old pubs and stand in the footsteps of Roman centurions. Best of all, it's usually less than two hours from London by train.

York is not unaware of its charms. Far from it. Like the prettiest girl at the school dance, it knows exactly what it's got. Quaint tea shops abound, along with historic pubs, restaurants and hotels, all with (hand-painted and wooden) signs reminding you exactly how long they've been in operation. Still, despite the touristy overtones, this is a great place to visit.

Eboracum to Jorvik

Roman soldiers are believed to have been the first to discover the strategic usefulness of York's location. While conquering the north of England, Roman soldiers camped where York is now, and found the site to be so well located for defence purposes that they built a permanent fort there and named it **Eboracum** – believed to mean 'the place of the yew trees'. Within a century of their arrival, Eboracum was a thriving Roman village, home to 6,000 soldiers and the de facto headquarters for all troops in northern England. While very little remains of the structures that housed the troops, Roman artefacts have been discovered that give a clear indication that as early as AD 180, York was a bustling city. Most central streets, including Stonegate and Petergate, follow the routes of the Roman streets.

Future invaders included Saxons and then Vikings, both of whom left their mark on the city. The Vikings modified the Saxon name for the settlement (**Eoforwic**), calling it **Jorvik**.

By train from London

Two to three trains an hour go to **York** direct from **King's Cross**. The journey time is between 1hr 50mins and just over 2hrs. Info: www.gner.co.uk.

Some of York's current street names are clearly descended from Viking words – the term 'gate' was used to mean 'street' in Viking dialects.

Modern invaders are largely tourists, who come in droves, drawn by the city's well-preserved architecture, multifarious museums and good restaurants. That means that, especially in the summer, it can seem like a tourist-choked open-air heritage theme park, as its population of 200,000 is augmented by four million annual visitors. But don't let that stop you. It's only crowded in the high season, and even then, its ancient layout means that you can easily escape the crowds. It is criss-crossed by a spiderweb of narrow medieval alleyways known as 'ginnels' or 'snickleways'. These make quick short cuts between the streets, and you can get wonderfully lost down the longest of them. Coffee Yard, the covered passageway linking Stonegate with Grape Lane, is only five foot ten inches high in places. **Grape Lane** itself was, it's worth mentioning, never the home of York's vintners. Those down-to-earth medieval folk had other vices to celebrate. 'Grap' meant 'grope' – this was once the city's red-light district. In fact, street names throughout the city delight and baffle. Like Grape Lane, many date back to the town's early days. Some of the street names may refer to individuals (Goodramgate, for instance), while many refer to the trades carried out there (Coppergate was home to the carpenters, Skeldergate to the shield-makers). At the edge of the city centre is the wonderfully named Whip-ma-whop-ma-gate. Don't believe what anybody tells you about the name of this street – nobody remembers what it really means.

Further down from Stonegate, you can get even more lost in the narrow, winding lanes around the **Shambles**, perhaps York's best-known street. The crazily teetering houses that line it were once home to the city's butchers; reputedly, they were built with overhanging storeys to keep direct sunlight off the meat. Now the overhanging eaves shield crowds of visitors searching for ceramic teddy bears and coats of arms in the very touristy shops that line either side.

Luckily, there is much more to shopping in York than twee teddies and handmade Yorkshire wool jumpers. Coney Street has all the high-street names, while Swinegate and

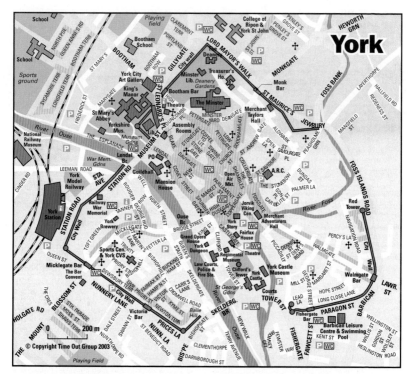

Daveygate contain more upmarket boutiques along with some designer fashion outlets. There's also an ugly purpose-built shopping centre on Coppergate, not far from the **Castle Museum** and **Clifford's Tower**. The pleasant, open-air **Newgate Market** is the place to head for local produce, from herbs and fresh fish to batteries or bars of soap.

First Stop York by Train

If you visit York by train you can take advantage of the 'First Stop York by Train' scheme that entitles rail travellers to half-price admission to all the major sights plus discounts at a number of restaurants and the York Theatre Royal. In addition, special rates are available at 30 of the city's hotels and guesthouses. Phone York Tourist Information Centre (*see below*) for more information.

What to see & do

York is packed with museums and other visitor attractions, although some of them are rather insubstantial and unashamedly aimed squarely at the tourist market. We list the best sights

below, but you can head to the Tourist Information Centre for information on many more. The main sights tend to be clustered either to the north of the centre of town around the Minster, or, alternatively, to the south around the castle area.

Tourist Information Centre

De Grey Rooms, Exhibition Square, YO10 7HB (01904 621756/www.york.gov.uk). **Open** 9am-6pm Mon-Sat; 10am-5pm Sun.
There's also a branch inside York railway station and at 20 George Hudson Street.

Bike hire

Bob Trotter's *13 Lord Mayor's Walk, YO31 7HB (01904 622868).*
A ten-minute walk from the train station.

ARC

St Saviourgate, Y01 8NN (01904 654324/ www.yorkarchaeology.co.uk). **Open** 10am-3pm daily. **Admission** £4.50; £4 concessions.
Credit AmEx, MC, V.
The Archaeological Resource Centre, located within the old church of St Saviour, is an admirable attempt to make archaeology accessible. Its hands-on exhibits, mainly aimed at children, illuminate York's history.

Barley Hall

2 Coffee Yard, off Stonegate, YO1 8AR (01904 610275/www.barleyhall.org.uk). **Open** *Mar-Oct* 10am-4pm Tue-Sun. *Nov-Feb* noon-4pm Tue-Sun. **Admission** £3.50; £2.50 concessions; free under-10s. **No credit cards.**

This splendid medieval townhouse has been lovingly restored by the Archaeological Trust to something resembling its former glory. It occasionally has volunteers dressed in period garb playing games of the time, or doing tasks such as weaving or sewing.

Castle Museum

Off Tower Street, YO1 9RY (01904 650333/ www.york.gov.uk). **Open** 9.30am-5pm daily. **Admission** £6; £3.50 concessions; £16 family. **Credit** MC, V.

York's best museum, this inspired collection of everyday objects from the past 300 years was started by Dr John Kirk, who wanted to preserve evidence of a vanishing way of life. There are carefully reconstructed period rooms, a plethora of vintage domestic appliances and tons of old toys. Its best section is the one housing extraordinary and extensive re-created Victorian and Edwardian streets and shops. Kids love it, particularly the entertaining part on loos through the ages. Among the exhibits representing everyday life in the 19th and 20th centuries is one ancient artefact: an Anglo-Saxon helmet, the oldest found in Britain.

City walls

One of the greatest pleasures of any visit to York is a stroll along the extensive sections of its medieval (13th- and 14th-century) walls. Stretching for three miles, they are punctuated by four bars (gates) – Micklegate Bar (on the original road to London), Bootham Bar, Monk Bar and Walmgate Bar (unique in the UK in still retaining its defensive barbican). There's a small museum in Micklegate Bar and an exhibition on Richard III in Monk Bar, but both are museums in name only – with few if any artefacts and largely jokey displays. However, entrance is cheap (under two quid) and the museums do provide the opportunity to roam in the ancient gateways.

Clifford's Tower

Tower Street, YO1 9SA (01904 646940/www. english-heritage.org.uk). **Open** *Apr-July, Sept* 10am-6pm daily. *Aug* 10am-6pm daily. *Oct* 10am-5pm daily. *Nov-Mar* 10am-4pm daily. **Admission** (EH) £2.50; £1.30-£1.90 concessions. **Credit** MC, V.

One of York's most immediately recognisable landmarks, the bluff white stone tower sits on a mound raised by William the Conqueror to allow him to keep an eye on the troublesome citizens. The Norman keep was destroyed by the locals in 1109 when the city's Jews used it to shelter from a mob and committed suicide rather than face the rabble. The current structure dates from 1245. There's nothing much more than a shell here, but it's an evocative shell, and there are good views. However, it's in a drab area of town and surrounded by a car park.

Fairfax House

Castlegate, YO1 9RN (01904 655543/www.fairfax house.co.uk). **Open** *Late Feb-early Jan* 11am-4.30pm Mon-Thur, Sat; 1.30-4.30pm Sun. *Guided tours* 11am, 2pm Fri. Closed early Jan-late Feb. **Admission** £4.50; £1.50-£3.75 concessions. **No credit cards.**

If furniture is your thing, this is the place for you. This fine Georgian house was designed by John Carr for the ninth Viscount Fairfax of Emley in 1750. It was rescued from obscurity as an office and cinema and meticulously restored during the 1980s and is now home to the splendid Noel Terry (of chocolate fame) collection of Georgian furniture.

Guildhall

St Helen's Square, YO1 9QN (01904 551010/ www.york.gov.uk). **Open** *May-Oct* 9am-5pm Mon-Fri; 10am-5pm Sat; 2-5pm Sun. *Nov-Apr* 9am-5pm Mon-Fri. **Admission** free.

The one-time administrative centre of the city is best viewed from the south side of Lendal Bridge. The medieval riverside building, sitting on the site of the first Roman bridge across the Ouse, was all but obliterated by German bombs during World War II. However, it has been beautifully restored, and the interior can be toured.

Jorvik Viking Centre

Coppergate, YO1 9WT (info line 01904 643211/ advance booking 01904 543403/www.vikingjorvik. com). **Open** *Apr-Oct* 9am-5.30pm daily. *Nov-Mar* 10am-4.30pm daily. **Admission** £7.20; £5.10-£6.10 concessions; £21.95 family. **Credit** MC, V.

The locals are hugely proud of this place and it is advertised everywhere in the city. It remains the city's top tourist draw and confidently expects to pull in around 500,000 punters a year. When it opened in the 1980s, it was a pioneer of the time-car-ride-through-history type of visitor attraction. The idea is that time has stopped one October day in 948, and you are able to pass through the sights, sounds and smells (there is a man who creates these choice aromas especially) of Viking York, before disembarking in the 21st century and examining some of the actual finds that were excavated from Coppergate between 1976 and 1981. Be prepared for a queue. However, if you've read a bit about the Vikings, and you're a grown-up, it's less than exciting. This one is largely for the kids.

Merchant Adventurers' Hall

Fossgate, YO1 9XD (01904 654818/www.theyork company.co.uk). **Open** *Easter-Sept* 9am-5pm Mon-Thur; 9am-3.30pm Fri, Sat; noon-4pm Sun. *Oct-Easter* 9am-3.30pm Mon-Sat. **Admission** (EH) £2; 70p-£1.70 concessions. **No credit cards.**

Once home to the city's most powerful guild, this massive medieval building (completed in 1362) has been wonderfully preserved.

National Railway Museum

Leeman Road, YO26 4XJ (01904 621261/ www.nmsi.ac.uk/nrm). **Open** 10am-6pm daily. **Admission** free.

The two huge halls that make up the NRM are heavily geared towards children (rides on Thomas the Tank Engine, stories from the Fat Controller) and railway junkies. The whole history of the railway is here, including such locomotive icons as Stephenson's stumpy 1829 *Rocket* and the undeniably beautiful *Mallard*. There are rows of old engines, plus racks of memorabilia. One for established train lovers only; others may find the exhibits begin to pall. Note also that the car park costs £4.50 per car.

The Chilterns to York

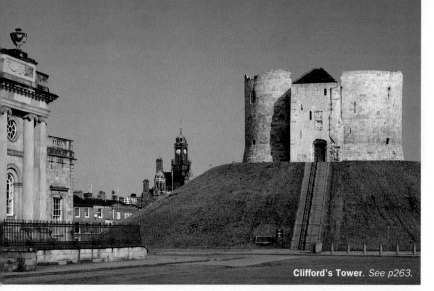
Clifford's Tower. *See p263.*

St William's College

College Street, opposite Minster, YO1 7GF (01904 557233/www.yorkminster.org). **Open** 9am-5pm daily. **Admission** £1; 50p concessions.
No credit cards.

Built around 1475, this fine half-timbered building was once home to 23 priests and a provost. The modest restaurant within the building spills out into the lovely interior courtyard in summer. Some of the medieval rooms can be viewed.

Treasurer's House

Chapter House Street, YO1 7JH (01904 624247/ www.nationaltrust.org.uk). **Open** Apr-Oct 11am-5pm daily (last admission 4.30pm). Closed Nov-Mar. **Admission** (NT) £4; £2 concessions.
No credit cards.

One of the architectural gems of York, built on the site of the 11th-century house of the Treasurer of York Minster, this beautiful late 16th- and early 17th-century building contains some fine furniture and collections of china and glass. However, the gorgeous gardens out front are the biggest attraction for those who are not furniture fanatics, and they're free.

York Brewery

12 Toft Green, YO1 6JT (01904 621162/www. yorkbrew.co.uk). **Tickets** 12.30pm, 2pm, 3.30pm, 5pm Mon-Sat. **Cost** £4.25; £3-£3.80; free under-14s.
Credit AmEx, MC, V.

This tiny independent brewery has only been operational since 1996, bringing brewing back within the city walls for the first time in 40 years. Sample a half of its Stonewall bitter before an entertaining and informative half-hour tour that's capped with another half, this time of the admirably sharp Yorkshire Terrier.

York City Art Gallery

Exhibition Square, YO1 7EW (01904 551861/ www.york.gov.uk). **Open** 10am-5pm daily.
Admission free (except for special exhibitions).

This easily digestible municipal collection spans 600 years (though large swathes of that are only covered very sketchily) and is a little too heavy on workaday British 19th-century paintings. It is notable, however, for a large number of works by York-born William Etty, and for its imaginative temporary exhibitions.

York Minster

Deangate, YO1 7JA (01904 557216/www.york minster.org). **Open** Apr-Oct 9am-4.45pm Mon-Sat; noon-3.45pm Sun. Nov-Mar 10am-4.45pm/dusk Mon-Sat; noon-3.45pm Sun. **Admission** Minster & Chapterhouse £4.50; £3 concessions; free under-16s. Undercroft, Treasury & Crypt £2.50; £1-£1.50 concessions. Tower £2.50; £1 concessions.
Credit MC, V.

This is the largest Gothic church north of the Alps and the sheer scale of the honey-coloured building's soaring towers lets you know just how important it was to the Church in medieval England. Begun in the 1220s by Archbishop Walter de Grey, the building took 250 years to complete, employing a variety of architectural styles. Broadly speaking, the transepts are in Early English style (1220-60), the nave is Decorated Gothic (1280-1350) and the chancel is Perpendicular (1361-1472). The nave is the widest of its type in Europe, but it is, perhaps, the proliferation of wonderful medieval stained glass that impresses most of all. The Great West Window (1338), with its sweetly heart-shaped tracery, is known as the 'Heart of Yorkshire'; the Great East Window (1405-8) at the far end of the chancel contains the world's largest surviving piece of medieval stained glass, while the Five Sisters' Window in the north transept is the oldest complete window in the Minster (1260).

The harmonious chapterhouse is a gem. Built in the 1270s and 1280s, it has no central supporting pillar, and is lined all around its circular walls by detailed and extraordinary carvings. The church's crypt and the foundations together form the city's best museum. The crypt contains a variety of Roman, Viking and medieval architectural fragments, but the foundations are even more extraordinary. In the late 1960s excavation work to secure the foundations of the central tower (which was threatening to collapse) uncovered not just parts of the Norman cathedral but also an Anglo-Saxon and Anglo-Scandinavian cemetery and evidence of the original Roman basilica. It was within this building that, in all probability, Constantine the Great was proclaimed Roman Emperor by his troops on the death of his father in AD 306. The church has done a wonderful job in displaying the architecture and artefacts that were discovered, including pieces such as a Saxon baby's coffin. There is nothing else in the city so fascinating.

Finally, the (tough) climb to the top of the tower is rewarded by fine views (although, strangely, York actually looks more impressive from the ground than above).

York Model Railway
York station, YO24 1AY (01904 630169). **Open** *Apr-Oct* 9am-6pm daily (last admission 5.30pm). *Nov-Mar* 10am-5pm daily (last admission 4.30pm). **Admission** £3.40; £2.80-£2 concessions; free under-4s. **Credit** MC, V.
One for little boys of all ages. The scale of the display (incorporating 600 buildings, 1,000 vehicles and 2,500 tiny people) certainly impresses.

Yorkshire Museum
Museum Gardens, YO1 7FR (01904 551800/www.york.gov.uk). **Open** 10am-5pm daily. **Admission** £4; £2.50 concessions (additional charge for special exhibitions). **Credit** MC, V.
This small museum is worth a visit, especially for history buffs, with its enlightening displays on the city and region dating back to Roman times. There's a welter of facts, but they're imaginatively presented, with displays on the daily life of monks and some of the oddities of Roman cuisine (larks' tongues, otters' noses, and so on) to ensure that kids don't get bored. The reconstructed vestibule of the chapter house of the Abbey of St Mary (the ruins of which can be seen outside the museum in Museum Gardens), complete with monkish chanting, is particularly well done and very atmospheric. Another of the museum's prize exhibits is the tiny but exquisite 15th-century pendant known as the Middleham Jewel.

Where to stay

York may have a surfeit of splendid sights and no end of teashops, but it's surprisingly lacking in noteworthy accommodation. There are few hotels or B&Bs within the city walls. However, there are plenty of options on the main roads leading into the city. Most B&Bs are clustered on Bootham, just down the road from Bootham Bar. This is a very walkable town, and, with the exception of Middlethorpe Hall, none of the hotels mentioned below is more than a 15-minute walk from the city centre.

Dairy Guesthouse
3 Scarcroft Road, YO23 1ND (01904 639367/www.dairyguesthouse.freeserve.co.uk). **Rates** £32-£50 single occupancy; £55-£60 double; £27.50 per person four-poster; £67.50 family room. **Rooms** 1 standard twin; 1 standard family; 1 double (en suite); 1 four-poster (en suite); 1 family cottage (en suite). **Credit** AmEx, MC, V (5% surcharge).
The milk of human kindness runs deep at this former dairy on the southern edge of town. Converted into one of the more laid-back B&Bs around, the owners live in a house at the back of a small flower-filled courtyard and give their guests free range of the five-bedroomed Victorian terrace at the front. There's a well-stocked kitchen where guests are encouraged to help themselves to snacks from the fridge or share their takeaways, and the rather garishly decorated rooms are equally well equipped. Next door to Melton's (*see p269*) and about a 15-minute walk from the Minster, the Dairy has recently come under new ownership, but so far the high standards have been maintained. Children welcome. No smoking throughout.

Dean Court Hotel
Duncombe Place, YO1 7EF (01904 625082/fax 01904 620305/www.deancourt-york.co.uk). **Rates** £85 single; £140-£170 double; £185 four-poster; £160-£180 family room. **Rooms** (all en suite) 8 small doubles; 19 doubles; 1 four-poster; 4 family. **Credit** AmEx, DC, MC, V.
Run by a chain (Great Western) and popular with business travellers as well as American and Japanese tourists – but don't let that put you off. It also boasts the best location in York – so close to the Minster that the rooms have double-glazing to muffle the sound of tolling bells (as well as traffic noise). It's a smart 1850 red-brick hotel with a well-maintained country house look, and includes a formal restaurant and a casual café. Children welcome.

Easton's
90 Bishopthorpe Road, YO23 1JS (01904 626646). **Rates** £32-£62 single occupancy; £42-£69 double/twin; £65-£78 family. **Rooms** (all en suite) 10 double/twin/family. **No credit cards.**
With a breakfast menu that includes forgotten gems such as kedgeree and devilled kidneys, and swathes of rich William Morris wallpapers and fabrics, this is manna from heaven for any Victorian gentlemen pining for the past. A lovely sitting room and good-sized bedrooms add to the appeal. There's a minimum stay of two nights at the weekend, and three over bank holidays. Children over five welcome. No smoking throughout.

Friars Rest Guesthouse
81 Fulford Road, YO10 4BD (01904 629823/www.friarsrest.co.uk). **Rates** £38 double; £55 triple. **Rooms** (all en suite) 4 double; 3 triple. **Credit** V.
This small and friendly B&B is a good, centrally located budget option. Its setting is the main draw, as it's located inside a former monastery less than 10 minutes' walk downriver from the city centre. The seven guestrooms are simply furnished and small, but very clean and bright. The owners are friendly and the breakfast room, while a tad flowery, is pleasant enough. Breakfasts themselves are excellent. Best of all, the price is right, especially when you remember that location…

The Golden Fleece
16 Pavement, YO1 7NP (01904 625171). **Rates** £55 single; £45 per person double; £40 per person twin. **Rooms** 2 twin; 2 double. **Credit** MC, V.

The Chilterns to York

This is a tiny place – little more than four attractive rooms above a historic old pub – but the staff couldn't be nicer, and the rooms are ideal. The fact that it is located inside the city walls with views of the Minster and the Shambles makes it attractive to some guests, while others prefer the fact that every inch of the place is said to be haunted. Ghosts have been seen throughout the place, and it is believed to be regularly visited by its original medieval owners. Sleep tight.

Grange Hotel

1 Clifton, YO30 6AA (01904 644744/fax 01904 612453/www.grangehotel.co.uk). **Rates** £100-£165 single; £100-£220 double; £200 four-poster; £240 suite. **Rooms** (all en suite) 3 single (with shower); 23 double/twin; 2 four-poster; 1 suite. **Credit** AmEx, DC, MC, V.

The grand old Regency building housing this excellent hotel stands out, even on a street of handsome red-brick Georgian terraced houses (W H Auden was born a few doors down). The well-decorated Grange has an impressive entrance, a series of relaxing public rooms decorated with period art and 30 luxurious bedrooms, with plenty of four-posters, antiques and chintz. All rooms have en suite bathrooms and satellite TV. This is where you stay if you want to splurge. It's also where you eat if you want to splash out: its three upscale restaurants – each of which confusingly blurs into the next – are all worth visiting, even if you're not staying in the hotel. The more expensive and formal is the Ivy (*see p269*), serving French and Modern British dishes, but there's also the basement Brasserie and a seafood bar. Children and small pets welcome.

Holmwood House

114 Holgate Road, YO24 4BB (01904 626183/fax 01904 670899/www.holmwoodhousehotel.co.uk). **Rates** £45-£65 single; £65-£75 double; £85 twin; £85-£110 four-poster; £75 triple; £130-£140 family suite. **Rooms** (all en suite) 11 double/twin/family suites; 2 four-poster (1 with spa bath); 1 triple. **Credit** MC, V.

A bit of a trek from the centre of town, but handy for the railway station, Bill Pitts' and Rosie Blanksby's B&B is spread over two Victorian terraced houses on a main road. The floral rooms are all slightly different, mostly embracing Victoriana. The plushest room has a four-poster bed and twin TVs. Breakfast – including kippers or croissants – is served in a basement restaurant. Children welcome. No smoking throughout.

Middlethorpe Hall

Bishopthorpe Road, YO23 2GB (01904 641241/ fax 01904 620176/www.middlethorpe.com). **Rates** £109-£115 single; £160-£210 double/twin; £265 four-poster; £220-£325 suite. **Rooms** (all en suite) 4 single; 18 double/twin; 2 four-poster; 7 suites. **Credit** MC, V.

Along with the Grange (*see above*), this place to blow the budget in York. Middlethorpe Hall lies a couple of miles south of the city opposite the racecourse. The fabulous building, begun in 1699 and set in 26 acres of grounds, has been restored to its full country house splendour by Historic House Hotels. Rooms vary greatly in size and decor, but all are in keeping with the classically restrained mood of the house. Some are in a courtyard block. The formal wood-panelled restaurant

offers classic French-based cuisine (*see p269*). There's also a popular health spa with a lovely indoor swimming pool and whirlpool, steam room, sauna, solarium and beauty treatment rooms (book treatments well in advance). The tranquillity of the beautiful, extensive park and gardens is, alas, marred by the streaming traffic on the adjacent A-road, but the views are still fabulous. Children over eight welcome.

Mount Royale Hotel

117-19 The Mount, YO24 1GU (01904 628856/ fax 01904 611171/www.mountroyale.co.uk). **Rates** £85-£115 single; £97.50 double/twin; £115 deluxe double/twin; £115 four-poster; £150 suite. **Rooms** (all en suite) 9 double/twin; 5 deluxe double/twin; 3 four-poster; 6 suites. **Credit** AmEx, MC, V, DC.

The horsey memorabilia is a reminder that the once grand Mount Royale is close to the racecourse. It's also only about a 15-minute walk from the city centre. The eccentric surroundings are gloriously mismatched, including a carpeted semi-tropical garden corridor, kidney-shaped (outdoor) swimming pool, and a cosy bar for late-night post mortems of the day's racing events. Rooms are large, staff are charming and the breakfasts are huge. Children and pets welcome.

York Backpackers

Micklegate House, 88-90 Micklegate, YO1 6JX (01904 627720/fax 01904 339350/www.yorkback packers.co.uk). **Rates** £13-£15 per person. Group rate from £16 per person. **Rooms** (140 beds) 1 double; 7 dorms (sleep 8-20); 3 family (sleep 4-6). **Credit** MC, V.

Housed in a beautiful listed Georgian mansion on the main road leading into town, this brightly decorated hostel maintains a jolly atmosphere. Accommodation is in dormitories, double or family rooms, and there's a bar, café, TV, laundry and pool table, as well as internet facilities. Popular with large groups, including stag and hen parties.

Where to eat & drink

Unlike its modern new restaurants, so many of York's pubs are historic and quaint that it's hard to believe they're real. The **Black Swan** (Peasholme Green, 01904 686911) is one of these. In a distinguished medieval timber-frame house, the pub dates back to 1417. It is believed to be haunted, so ask the bartender to point out the chair where a forlorn ghost girl is said to sit, gazing into the fireplace. The sign for the **Olde Starre Inne** (40 Stonegate, 01904 623 063), is one of the easiest to spot in town, as it stretches clear across Stonegate. The sign dates to 1733, but the tavern in fact preceded it by a couple of hundred years. Although this old pub is smack bang in the middle of the tourist path, it's still a lovely boozer with lots of wood panelling, open fireplaces and etched glass. One of the largest pubs in town, **Old White Swan** (Goodramgate, 01904 540911), spreads over a warren of nine medieval, timber-framed buildings. Its lunches are particularly good.

York Minster. *See p264.*

CONSTANTINE BY THIS SIGN CONQUER

Further down Goodramgate, the **Snickleway Inn** (01904 656138) not only has an adorable name, but also an interesting history. It dates back to the 15th century, and when you enter its historic rooms with open fireplaces, it won't surprise you that this is reputed to be one of the most haunted pubs in York. Probably not haunted at all is the **Roman Bath** (St Sampson's Square, 01904 620455), an ancient pub with a thoroughly modern interior; the fruit machines alone would be noisy enough to send any ghost back to whence it came. The attraction, though, is that in 1930, during renovations, Roman baths were discovered in its cellar. The baths are so well preserved that footprint indentations from its centurion users can be seen, along with the insignia of a Roman legion. Finally, try the tiny and adorable **Blue Bell** pub on Fossgate (01904 654904), where two itsy rooms surround the little bar.

Betty's Café Tea Rooms
6-8 St Helen's Square, YO1 8QP (01904 659142). **Food served** 9am-9pm daily. **Credit** MC, V.
Ahh… Betty's. No trip to York would be complete without stopping in for a scone and a cuppa in these revered surroundings. But the world's most famous tearoom is

resting on its laurels. It's overpriced and under-serviced, and oh so very touristy. Still, nobody comes here for the cakes or even for a warm 'fat rascal' scone (£2.95, and you pay 35p extra for a dish of ordinary jam to accompany it). No, you come here for the nostalgia value. But however charming their 1940s-style uniforms, the waitresses can seem too dour and too busy to care whether or not you want anything. It's a shame. This could be one of the best tearooms in the world. Instead, it's just one of the most famous.

The Blue Bicycle
34 Fossgate, YO1 9TA (01904 673990/www. bluebicyclerestaurant.com). **Food served** noon-2.30pm, 6-10pm Mon-Sat; noon-2.30pm, 6-9pm Sun. **Main courses** £12.90-£20. **Credit** MC, V.
Ask just about anybody in town and they'll tell you this is York's most exciting young restaurant. With a colourful, vibrant atmosphere, excellent food, personable staff and an attention to detail that would please even the most savvy urban diner, it satisfies on every level. Candlelit, with wood floors and a bistro feel, the menu changes seasonally and even simple dishes such as prawn cocktail are given new twists: prawns were layered with rich mayonnaise, and moulded into a perfect rich circle. For mains, a thick Aberdeen Angus fillet with chorizo cream filled the plate and was cooked precisely to order, while another main of creamy prawn and monkfish chowder was really more of a stew, with large

Spook city

Somehow it doesn't come as a surprise that York was voted the most haunted city in Europe in 2002 (by the Ghost Research Foundation International). If ever there were a town that should be haunted, it's this one. With its long winding medieval snickleways and ancient half-timbered buildings, if you didn't come across a transparent women in a grey dress every now and then, it would be disappointing. Indeed, in York there are entire battalions of such spirits wandering the streets.

The biggest ghost spotting, perhaps in the world, happened in 1953, when a plumber's apprentice working in the Treasurer's House (*see p264*) reported seeing a complete Roman legion of 100 men led by a centurion on horseback marching through the building's basement. His detailed description of their uniforms was at first used to discredit him, since archaeologists said they had never heard of uniforms that looked like that. In later years, however, evidence of uniforms in the style he described was uncovered, giving his story a new lease of life.

That's not all. Patrons in the Olde Starre Inne on Stonegate (*see p266*) have reported hearing the groans of wounded cavaliers who were brought to the stables behind the inn during the Civil War. Also resident is a ghost of an old woman who climbs the stairs, plus two spectral black cats.

Elsewhere, a decapitated Thomas Percy is said to wander blindly around the Church of the Holy Trinity on Goodramgate in search of his head; he was executed in 1572 for treason against Elizabeth I and his head was impaled on a pike above Mickelgate Bar.

If you choose to stay at the Snickleway Inn on Goodramgate (*see p267*), you might encounter a whole houseful of ghosts. Among them is one that has never actually been seen, but that wafts past guests, leaving the scent of lavender in its path (lavender was used to hide the stench of death during the plague). There's also a ghost of a Victorian child who sits morosely on the stairs.

So keep an eye out as you wander round this otherwise perfectly pleasant city, it might not only be other tourists that you pass in the night.

prawns and big chunks of fish in a hearty sauce. Puddings are exceptional – the delicate blueberry and lemon crème will not be forgotten easily.

19 Grape Lane
19 Grape Lane, YO1 7HU (01904 636366). **Food served** 6-10pm Tue, Wed; noon-2pm, 6-10pm Thur-Sat. **Main courses** £12.50-£17. **Credit** MC, V.
Tucked away on one of York's winding medieval lanes, this romantic, quiet restaurant is housed in a lovely building – a medieval timbered structure with low, beamed ceilings and many original fittings. At night, with candles on the tables, the effect is beautiful, if a bit cramped. The food veers from traditional to contemporary, with well-produced mains such as entrecôte steak or trout stuffed with crab meat. Starters similarly offer the mundane – chicken and grape salad – and the unusual: prawn cockail with banana and pineapple. It's a popular place with local foodies, so it's a good idea to book at weekends.

Café Concerto

21 High Petergate, YO1 7EN (01904 610478).
Food served 10am-10pm daily. **Main courses**
£9.95-£15. **Credit** MC, V.

This sweet, sunny restaurant/coffee shop has a laid-back
attitude and an eclectic menu, and walls papered with
yellowed sheet music. Starters tend towards fusion; typical dishes include oriental chicken breast salad in spicy
sesame dressing, though there are traditional items too
(chicken liver pâté with toasted ciabatta, for example).
The house special is gratin dauphinoise, a kind of posh
shepherd's pie with a filling that changes daily – on our
visit it was tuna. Again, simpler dishes (the likes of
grilled salmon) are also available. Desserts continue the
fusion motif: strawberry cheesecake with chocolate
mint, for example.

The Ivy

*Grange Hotel, 1 Clifton, YO30 6AA (01904 644744/
www.grangehotel.co.uk).* **Food served** 7-10pm Mon-
Sat; noon-2pm Sun. **Main courses** £13-£21. **Set
lunches** £9.95 2 courses, £12.95 3 courses. **Set
dinner** £28 3 courses. **Credit** AmEx, DC, MC, V.

One of York's more conservative restaurants, the Ivy –
inside the swanky Grange Hotel (*see p266*) – is the sort
of place people take their grandparents for a posh dinner. It's also popular with honeymooning couples
splashing out on starters such as seared scallops with
parma ham and parmesan crisp, or quail and watercress
ravioli. Mains are of the heavy and traditional variety,
albeit with elegant twists: duo of Gressingham duck
with white bean and truffle purée, for instance. Puddings
are especially gorgeous. The iced rum and raisin tim-
bale with banana fritters and a little jug of butterscotch
sauce was almost too pretty (and too rich) to eat. The
service is consistently exceptional and the Sunday
lunches are legendary.

Melton's Too

*25 Walmgate, YO1 9TX (01904 629222/www.melt
onstoo.co.uk).* **Food served** 10.30am-10.30pm Mon-
Sat; 10.30am-9.30pm Sun. **Main courses** £6.90-
£11.90. **Credit** MC, V.

You feel the buzz as soon as you walk in. A youngish
crowd can be found talking over coffee in the ground-
floor café/bar, while the pleasantly casual bistro-style
dining space on the first and second floors is often completely filled. Starters include a constantly changing
slate of tapas selections, as well as choices such as pasta
with rocket, red pepper and parmesan. Mains include
hearty portions of steak with red wine and shallot sauce,
cassoulet of duck and Toulouse sausage, or corn-fed
chicken with garlic and seasonal vegetables. Desserts
are a speciality, and include zucotta – hazelnuts and
chocolate on liqueur-soaked sponge cake). Add in the
friendly service and the result is a restaurant you'll never
want to leave.

Middlethorpe Hall

Bishopthorpe Road, YO23 2QB (01904 641241).
Food served 12.30-1.45pm, 7-9.30pm daily.
Set lunches £16.95 2 courses, £19.50 3 courses.
Set dinner £37.95 3 courses. **Credit** MC, V.

If you enjoy jacket-and-tie dining, this may be the place
for you. Set inside a hotel that was once a country house,
the vast gardens are overlooked by this classic restaurant with wood panelling, white linen and a marble fire-

place. The menu changes regularly, but features starters
such as civet of rabbit with mustard, bacon and lettuce,
and mains such as roast corn-fed chicken with cep custard, roast garlic and parsley, or loin of veal with sweet-
bread tortellini and hazelnut butter. There are always
good fish dishes available, plus a short vegetarian menu.
Puddings include aniseed parfait with roast pears and
blueberries, or passionfruit jelly with lime ice-cream and
poppyseed tuille. Service is as formal as the building
itself. For hotel, *see p266*.

St William's College Restaurant

5 College Street, YO1 7JF (01904 634830). **Food
served** noon-2.30pm, 6-10pm daily. **Main courses**
£10-£15. **Credit** AmEx, DC, MC, V.

Directly across the street from the cathedral, this restu-
arant sits in one of the city's most impressive medieval
timber-framed buildings, built in 1462. The name harks
back to the structure's original purpose as a school for
Minster priests; today, it's a popular tourist restaurant
serving British cuisine with modern touches. The interior is a disappointment, with simple pine tables and
little decoration. The food has its moments, though, with
starters such as cured salmon and dill frittata with
honey mustard dressing, and mains like roast loin of
lamb with sweet potato sauté and aubergine confit.
Puddings include marsala-poached peaches with vanilla
marscapone, and strawberry and elderflower jelly with
lavender biscuits. Staff are efficient and the view of the
cathedral is extraordinary.

Rubicon

*5 Little Stonegate, YO1 8AX (01904 676076/
www.rubiconrestaurant.co.uk).* **Food served**
11.30-10pm daily. **Main courses** £6-£9. **Set
meals** (11.30am-6.30pm) £8.50 2 courses, £11.50
3 courses; (6.30-10pm) £17 2 courses, £18 3 courses.
Credit MC, V.

Rubicon is not your typical vegetarian restaurant. It's
modern, elegant and cool, and you'll only notice the lack
of meat once you look at the menu. It attracts a cross-
section of locals and tourists who linger over starters
like the divine rapini (roasted aubergine, garlic, ricotta
cheese and mushrooms) or the diabolically good stilton
pâté (a blend of stilton, cream cheese, walnuts and port).
Mains such as roasted Mediterranean vegetable tart,
veggie lasagne and a Turkish stuffed aubergine continue the hearty theme.

The Tasting Room

*13 Swinegate Court East, YO1 8AJ (01904 627879/
www.thetastingroom.co.uk).* **Food served** 11.30am-
3.30pm Mon; 11.30am-3.30pm, 6-10pm Tue-Sun.
Main courses £9-£15.25. **Set dinner** (order
by 7pm, leave by 8pm) £12.95 2 courses, £18
3 courses. **Credit** MC, V.

Tucked away among the winding snickelways not far
from the Minster, this breezy, cheery restaurant has as
many tables outdoors as in, and it makes a lovely spot
for a lazy summer lunch or dinner. The menu is basic,
with an emphasis on English dishes. It includes a wide
array of salads and sandwiches for lunch (including a
fabulous goat's cheese salad), while dinner sees the likes
of pork fillet in tomato and cider sauce with roast garlic
and crisp parsnips. It can get overcrowded on warm days
and staff can be overstretched, leading to long waits. But
if you've nothing else to do, it's a nice place to linger.

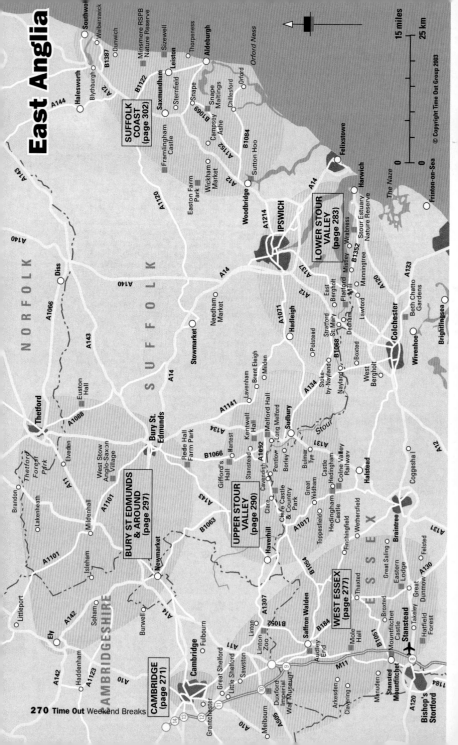

East Anglia

© Copyright Time Out Group 2003

15 miles
25 km

SUFFOLK COAST (page 302)

LOWER STOUR VALLEY (page 283)

BURY ST EDMUNDS & AROUND (page 297)

UPPER STOUR VALLEY (page 290)

WEST ESSEX (page 275)

CAMBRIDGE (page 271)

Cambridge

Colleges, commons and 'the secret of life'.

Cambridge is home to one of the two oldest English universities, with some colleges dating back to the 13th century. It's a bustling market town where the many visitors can shop for antiquarian books or fine crafts, relax on a punt down the river or experience Michelin-starred dining. It's also the place where the secret of life was discovered. Fifty years ago, two scholars, Francis Crick and Jim Watson, rushed into their local hostelry, the Eagle, to announce to bemused regulars that they'd discovered the structure of DNA. Their scientific breakthrough is commemorated at the **Whipple Museum of the History of Science**.

Most visitors to Cambridge today are happy to marvel at the town's cultural heritage while avoiding bell-ringing cyclists. Others had a more dramatic impact on the town. The Romans first settled north of the River Cam in AD 43, building a fort and creating an administrative centre. When they departed, the site was left to founder until it was revived in the eighth century by Offa the Great, who directed the building, or perhaps rebuilding, of the bridge (Grantabrycge, one of the first known uses of the word 'bridge').

The town was captured by Vikings in 1010, who subsequently razed it to the ground, but it soon recovered. When William the Conqueror arrived in 1066 he built a castle on what is now known as Castle Hill. There are still reminders of the prosperous times that followed, such as the magnificent **Church of the Holy Sepulchre** (Bridge Street, 01223 311602/ www.christianheritageuk.org.uk), which is one of only five Norman round churches in the country. Lovers of architecture can also delight in the late Gothic magnificence of **King's College Chapel**, the classicism of Christopher Wren (the **Wren Library** and **Emmanuel College**) and James Gibbs (**King's College**), as well as the more recent polychromatic

excesses of John Outram (**Judge Institute of Management Studies**). Eager historians can examine local archaeological relics that date from Neolithic times at the **Museum of Archaeology and Anthropology** (Downing Street, 01223 333516).

Cambridge first became an academic centre when some sort of incident at Oxford – apparently involving a dead woman, an arrow and a scholar holding a bow – led to some of the learned monks bidding a hasty farewell to Oxford and a hearty hello to Cambridge. The town was chosen because of its ecclesiastical connections and the first college, Peterhouse, was established in 1284.

None of which will hold out much attraction for kids, but then, so long as the weather is fine, strolling **the Backs** (the grasslands behind the colleges), splashing about in boats and picnicking in **Grantchester Meadows** will keep children (and adults) entertained.

For details of what's going on, pick up a copy of *Explorer* or *Real City* from the Tourist Information Centre, or visit www.realcity.com.

What to see & do

Tourist Information Centre
The Old Library, Wheeler Street, CB2 3QB (090658 62526/www.tourismcambridge.com). **Open** *Summer* 10am-5pm Mon-Sat; 11am-4pm Sun. *Winter* 10am-5pm Mon-Sat.
Guided walking tours are available, lasting two hours (11.30am and 1.30pm). Tickets are £7.85 per person (reductions for under-12s), which includes the entrance fee to **King's College** and **Chapel** when open. If King's is closed, the tour will visit St John's College at the reduced rate of £6.50 per person.

Bike hire
City Cycle Hire *61 Newnham Road, CB3 9EY (01223 365629/www.citycyclehire.com).* **Credit** MC, V.
A short walk from the train station.

Botanic Garden
Corey Lodge, Bateman Street, CB2 1JF (01223 336265/www.botanic.cam.ac.uk). **Open** *Feb, Mar, Oct* 10am-5pm daily. *Apr-Sept* 10am-6pm daily. *Nov-Jan* 10am-4pm daily. **Admission** £2.50; £2 concessions; free under-5s. **No credit cards**.
Opened to the public in 1846, the popular 40-acre Botanic Garden holds more than 8,000 plant species. The layout is quite formal for an English garden, with a broad avenue leading up to a fountain and terrace garden.

By train from London

Trains run direct from **King's Cross** to **Cambridge** about four times an hour and take about 50mins. Note that the railway station is a good mile's walk from the city centre. Info: www.wagn.co.uk.

East Anglia

Punting on the Cam is mandatory.

Colleges of Cambridge

All 31 colleges are independently run and have their own opening times and restrictions so it's advisable to check beforehand (www.cam.ac.uk/cambuniv/colleges.html). The most popular colleges are **Trinity**, its quadrangle immortalised in *Chariots of Fire*. The New Court of **St John's** is famous for its clock tower, familiarly known as the 'Wedding Cake' due to its extravagant design. **King's** is perhaps the best known of all, a magnificent example of neo-Gothic architecture.

Fitzwilliam Museum

Trumpington Street, CB2 1RB (01223 332900/ www.fitzmuseum.cam.ac.uk) **Open** 10am-5pm Tue-Fri, Sat; 2.15-5pm Sun **Admission** free.
Founded in 1816, this diverse and under-visited museum is home to a superb collection of painting and sculpture, as well as antiquities from Egypt, Greece and Rome. Highlights include masterpieces by Titian, Modigliani and Picasso. Tours are available at 2.45pm on Sundays (£3 per person) and there are regular lunchtime talks. The museum is closed from 21 December 2003 until summer 2004 for refurbishment.

King's College Chapel

King's Parade, CB2 1ST (01223 331250/ www.kings.cam.ac.uk). **Open** *Term-time* 9.30am-3.30pm Mon-Sat; 1.15-2.15pm Sun. *Holidays* 9.30am-4.30pm Mon-Sat; 10am-5pm Sun. **Services** (term-time) 5.30pm Mon-Sat; 10.30am, 3.30pm, 6pm Sun. **Admission** £4; £3 concessions; free under-12s. **Credit** MC, V.

Cambridge's most famous building, this long chapel was funded by many kings, among them Henry VIII, who was responsible for the ornate decoration of the antechapel and magnificent stained glass. His initials (and those of his then wife, Anne Boleyn) are carved into the dark oak screen that divides the building in two. The narrowness of the chapel emphasises its height to great effect, as do the slender, linear columns that stretch up to an explosion of fan vaulting – a Perpendicular Gothic extravagance that has no equal in Britain. Rubens's *Adoration of the Magi* (1634) stands next to the altar. If you visit in term- time, be sure to attend a service, when the choirboys' other-worldly voices provide a sublime counterpoint to the beauty of the building.

Round Church (Church of the Holy Sepulchre)

Bridge Street, CP2 1UB (01223 311602/www. christianheritageuk.org.uk). **Open** 10am-5pm daily. **Admission** free.
A 12th-century medieval church, although its Norman appearance was provided in the 19th century by some overzealous restorers. Its shape is very rare and is based upon the Church of the Holy Sepulchre in Jerusalem.

St Bene't Church

Bene't Street, CB2 3PT (01223 353903). **Open** 7.30am-6pm daily. **Admission** free.
With its Saxon tower, St Bene't (a contraction of St Benedict) is Cambridge's oldest surviving building. It was the original chapel of Corpus Christi College.

Whipple Museum of the History of Science

Department of History & Philosophy of Science on Free School Lane, off Pembroke Street, CB2 3RH (01223 330906). **Open** 1.30-4.30pm Mon-Fri. **Admission** free.

Founded in 1944, the museum houses a collection covering all branches of science. In 2003 the museum is hosting an exhibition, 'Seeing Double', to commemorate the 50th anniversary of Crick and Watson's proposal of the double helical structure of DNA.

Where to stay

Beds are in short supply in Cambridge, so book ahead. The Tourist Information Centre runs a booking service (01223 457581/accommodation bookings@cambridge.gov.uk, £3 charge).

Cambridge Garden House Moat House

Granta Place, Mill Lane, CB2 1RT (01223 259988/ www.moathousehotels.com). **Rates** £169 single; £200 double/triple. **Rooms** (all en suite) 121 twin/double. **Credit** AmEx, MC, V.

In the heart of Cambridge, this hotel is both convenient and well sited. In spite of its size (121 rooms) it is often fully booked. Rooms are clean, comfortable and inoffensively decorated, but those overlooking the river are the best. The Terrace Bar, open for non-guests, is a pleasant place for tea. Children welcome.

Hotel Felix

Whitehouse Lane, Huntingdon Road, CB3 0LX (01223 277977/www.hotelfelix.co.uk). **Rates** from £125 single; from £155 double; £260 penthouse. **Rooms** (all en suite) 20 twin; 31 double; 1 penthouse. **Credit** AmEx, DC, MC, V.

This new boutique townhouse hotel is run by Jeremy and Vivien Cassel. Two modern wings are attached to a Victorian mansion fusing original features with contemporary design. There are 52 bedrooms, plus a decent restaurant (Graffiti). All rooms have satellite TV and CD player. Dogs by arrangement. Children welcome.

Meadowcroft Hotel

16 Trumpington Road, CB2 2EX (01223 346120/ fax 01223 346138/www.meadowcrofthotel.co.uk). **Rates** £95 single; £130-£150 double/twin; £160 family room. **Rooms** (all en suite) 1 single; 13 double; 4 twin. **Credit** AmEx, MC, V.

Opened in 2000, this attractive red-brick hotel was a wel-

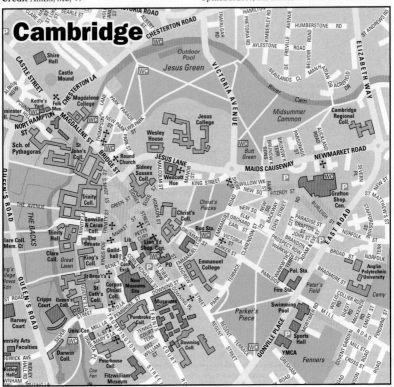

East Anglia

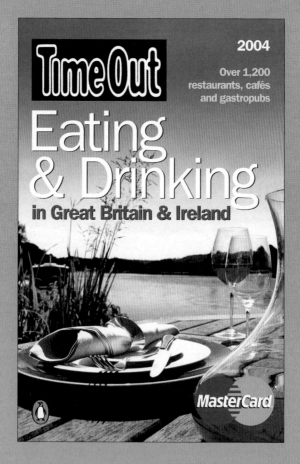

Opened in 2000, this attractive red-brick hotel was a welcome addition to Cambridge's sparse accommodation scene. With its elegant rooms, spacious lounge and bar, and original Victorian features it remains head and shoulders above much of the competition. The 12 rooms are quiet, comfortable and individually decorated. Two of the rooms have four-poster beds, and several overlook the pretty garden at the back. The well-regarded Brackenhurst restaurant is currently closed (to reopen late 2003). The Meadowcroft is about a mile from the city centre – but the walk is a pleasant one. Children welcome. Pets by arrangement. No smoking throughout.

Sleeperz Hotel

Station Road, CB1 2TZ (01223 304050/fax 01223 357286/www.sleeperz.com). **Rates** £35 single; £45 twin; £55 double; £65 triple. **Rooms** (all en suite) 4 double; 20 twin; 1 triple. **Credit** AmEx, MC, V.
Formerly a granary, bang next to the station, Sleeperz is a bit of a new concept in the hotel world: modern no-frills design, low cost – a sort of IKEA of hotels. It looks exactly how one might imagine a modern Scandinavian youth hostel: all light wood, clean design and economical use of space. Each individual room (and they're not big) has an en suite shower, small portable TV and phone. Twin rooms have space-saving bunks, while doubles have futon bases with mattresses. Sleeperz is ideal for luggage-lite visitors who will be out and about for most of the day and evening. Children are welcome. No smoking throughout.

Victoria Guest House

57 Arbury Road, CB4 2JB (01223 350086/www.vic toria-guesthouse.co.uk). **Rates** £25-£50 single; £45-£60 double. **Rooms** (3 en suite) 7 double/twin. **Credit** AmEx, MC, V.
A 20-minute walk from the centre of town, Emma and Duncan Anderson promise a warm welcome at their comfortable and reasonably priced B&B. The seven rooms available are spacious and well decorated. Breakfasts (including a vegetarian option) can be enjoyed overlooking the garden, and will certainly set you up for the day. There are no communal areas, but guests are not required to vacate the property during the day. All rooms are no smoking. Children welcome.

Where to eat & drink

Surprisingly for a town with so much wealth splashing around, there are few really good restaurants in Cambridge, though Hotel Felix's **Graffiti** has upped the quotient. In fact, if the weather is fine, a picnic assembled from the various delis, bakeries and wine merchants in the centre of town and taken to the Backs or Grantchester Meadows is a decent option.

Other recommended restaurants include **Varsity** (35 St Andrew's Street, 01223 356060) for Cypriot cooking, and **Chato Singapore Restaurant** (2-4 Lensfield Road, 01223 363129), which serves excellent Chinese and Malaysian food. Vegans can be accommodated at **Rainbow Café** (9A King's Parade, 01223 321551/www.rainbowcafe.co.uk).

Cambridge has many creaky old inns in which to enjoy the decent local ales that are served hereabouts. The **Eagle** on Bene't Street (01223 505020) is the most famous, but there are many of equal merit, including the **Pickerel Inn** at 30 Magdalene Street (01223 355068), **Fort St George** by the river on Midsummer Common (01223 354327) and **Bath Ale House** on Bene't Street (01223 350969). A pleasant walk along the Cam from Midsummer Common will take you to the **Green Dragon** (Water Street, 01223 505035), a picturesque pub with a beer garden next to the river.

Dojo Noodle Bar

1-2 Miller's Yard, Mill Lane, CB2 1RQ (01223 363471/www.dojonoodlebar.co.uk). **Food served** noon-2.30pm, 5.30-11pm Mon-Thur; noon-4pm, 5.30-11pm Fri-Sun. **Main courses** £4.30-£6.20. **Credit** MC, V.
Essentially a Japanese restaurant with an emphasis on noodles, the menu at Dojo takes in a smattering of Chinese specials and one or two Thai dishes. Portions are generous and the fresh and noodle soups are particularly good. The small interior is simple and geometric, with shared bench seating, Wagamama-style, plus some tables in the courtyard outside. A starter, main course and an Asahi shouldn't set you back more than £12.

Galleria Restaurant

33 Bridge Street, CB2 1UW (01223 362054). **Food served** noon-10.30pm daily. **Main courses** £5.95-£8.75. **Credit** AmEx, MC, V.
Overlooking the Cam, with a little balcony to make the best of its location, this continental café is clean and bright, serving reasonably priced meals, such as noodles with plenty of fresh vegetables, or good-sized portions of mushroom tagliatelle. Service copes well with sudden lunchtime rushes.

Michel's

21-4 Northampton Street, CB3 0AD (01223 353110). **Food served** noon-2.30pm, 6-10pm Mon-Sat; noon-3.30pm Sun. **Main courses** £12.50-£18. **Set lunch** (Mon-Sat) £9.45 2 courses, £11.95 3 courses. **Credit** AmEx, DC, MC, V.
The menu is short and sweet at this cosy restaurant – six starters and six mains – but the choices are interesting and generally successful. Combinations of textures and flavours include pan-fried scallops with haggis and a whisky beurre blanc or Jerusalem artichoke salad with pancetta, ceps and parmesan. Mains are a little more haphazard. Pumpkin risotto with truffles and hazelnuts was bland, while beef fillet with girolles and glazed shallots was well flavoured, but a tad overcooked. Booking is essential at weekends. Smoking is not allowed in the restaurant, though you can nip up to the wine bar if you're desperate.

Midsummer House

Midsummer Common, CB4 1HA (01223 369299/www.midsummerhouse.co.uk). **Food served** noon-2pm, 7-10pm Tue-Sat. **Set lunch** £20 2 courses, £26 3 courses. **Set dinner** £45 3 courses. **Credit** AmEx, MC, V.

With one Michelin star under his belt, Daniel Clifford, chef-patron of Midsummer House, is after another. The 'House' offers two floors and a conservatory of high-quality French dining and while the decor suffers from lurid ragged walls, they are at least hung with attractive prints. Service is formal and informative, as it needs to be with a 32-page wine list. Food is impeccably presented, perfectly cooked and marries unusual flavours – though the cep foam with coffee jelly (one of two appetisers) is one we'd like to see in the divorce courts. Starters include seared scallops with celeriac purée and truffle, and quail ravioli that looks more impressive than it tastes. Slow-cooked fillet of beef on creamed spinach with cep mousse was tender, while sea bass on white beans with chilli cream was a fine combo. Desserts include pineapple parfait. Supplements of £8.50 for a cheeseboard, £5 for the slow-cooked beef and an additional £4 for a coffee are rather less appealing, but it's still a memorable place to eat. No smoking throughout.

Venue on the Roof

Cambridge Arts Theatre, 3rd floor, 6 St Edward's Passage, CB2 3PJ (01223 367333/www.venuerestaurant.com). **Food served** 11am-11pm Mon-Sat. **Main courses** £10-£17. **Set meals** £10 2 courses (11am-7.30pm), £13.95 2 courses. **Credit** AmEx, MC, V.

This petite restaurant – recently relocated from Regent Street to the Arts Theatre – is a haven of quality contemporary food and modern decor. The regularly changing menu lists a handful of well-chosen and artistic dishes that draw on international influences. Mains might include beef fillet, lemon and tarragon roasted chicken or Moroccan lamb, while desserts range from vanilla bean crème brûlée to raspberry and sweet cheese chimichanga. A wine list covers all bases, with a heavy nod to the New World. On Fridays and Saturdays, a piano and double bass duo turn out contemporary jazz. Classy without being stuffy and with fair prices to boot.

Kettle's Yard

When he came to Cambridge in 1956, H S Ede, known as Jim, was looking for a home for himself and his wife, Helen, that would also house his collection of art and sculpture. A former curator at London's Tate, Ede's mainly 20th-century collection included paintings by artist friends such as Ben and Winifred Nicholson, Alfred Wallis, Christopher Wood and Joan Miró, as well as sculpture by Henri Gaudier-Brzeska, Constantin Brancusi, Henry Moore and Barbara Hepworth.

The area known as Kettle's Yard was a slum when Ede was offered four cottages here. With the help of architect Roland Aldridge, the houses were restored and remodelled. According to Ede, Kettle's Yard was not intended to be 'a collection of works of art reflecting my taste or the taste of a given period', but rather a place where visitors could 'find a home and a welcome, a refuge of peace and order, of the visual arts and of music… in which stray objects, stones, glass…' are arranged 'in light and space'. With this in mind, Ede kept open house every afternoon of term, guiding visitors around his home to marvel at the furniture, glass, ceramics and natural objects interspersed with the paintings and sculpture.

In 1966 Ede donated the house and its contents to the University and in 1970, three years before the Edes retired, the house was extended, and an exhibition gallery, designed by Sir Leslie Martin and David Owers, added. The gallery showcases international exhibitions of modern and contemporary art, and the house, in keeping with Ede's aim, is open every afternoon (apart from Mondays). Visitors simply ring the bell and ask to look around, helped by knowledgeable curators who can explain the provenance of many of the objects. Unlike other museums, visitors can sit in the chairs and read the books in Ede's library.

There are often lunchtime talks, while the Cambridge Modern Jazz Club (01223 362550/www.cambridgejazz.org) hosts popular regular concerts in the Yard.

Kettle's Yard

Castle Street, CB3 0AQ (01223 352124/ www.kettlesyard.co.uk). **Open** *House* Easter-Aug 1.30-4.30pm Tue-Sun. Sept-Easter 2-4pm Tue-Sun. *Gallery* 11.30am-5.30pm Tue-Sun. **Admission** free.

West Essex

Don't let the Morris dancers put you off.

The Industrial Revolution didn't really happen here. Uttlesford, as the area is known, remained agricultural through the 18th century, so the onset of modernisation had little effect on its quaint villages and winding country roads, which remain pleasantly free of the worst aspects of modern life. And that is good news for harassed Londoners looking for a pastoral break from the capital's hurly-burly.

Uttlesford radiates from the three towns of **Saffron Walden**, **Thaxted** and **Great Dunmow**, and each of these are surrounded by tiny settlements with a single street, one pub and a handful of perfect cottages. In such surroundings, it's hard to come to terms with the fact that you're just an hour or so away from London. The area is ancient and after a few days wandering past 600-year-old houses or dining in oak-beamed buildings, country life will weave its rustic magic. With innumerable public footpaths, quiet roads and large tracts of common land, it's ideal country for walking, cycling or horse riding, while those looking for more excitement can get on the trail of Dick Turpin, who plied his nefarious trade in these parts (*see p280* **Tall Turpin tales**).

Yellow is the colour...

Saffron Walden was a boom town in the Middle Ages, benefiting from its proximity to Roman trade routes. With additional wealth from saffron and cutlery, there was spare cash to throw around and evidence of those good times is still around today in its fine architecture. Saffron Walden received its name from the saffron crocus (the town was originally called Chipping Walden), which was prized for its colour, flavour and medicinal applications. Uttlesford was the national saffron centre between the 15th and 18th centuries, until explorers discovered it could be obtained abroad for a fraction of the price.

A Conservation Area, Saffron Walden's compact centre hasn't changed much since those times, consisting of a central **Market Square** (there's a market on Tuesdays and Saturdays) surrounded by narrow lanes (now dominated by antiques shops, as much of the region seems to be). Some 400 wobbly, oak-framed and wattle-and-daubed buildings survive, displaying characteristics you'll find throughout the region such as overhanging upper storeys and pastel-coloured plasterwork with ornate patterns known as pargeting. There's also late Georgian and Victorian architecture, particularly the Italianate **Corn Exchange** (now the library) in Market Square. There is an even older relic on the ancient common – the **turf maze**, said to be the largest in the country and to date back more than 800 years. It's more than a mile long in total, and not as easy to master as it looks. Nor, unfortunately, is it as dramatic a sight as one might hope. **St Mary's** church is worth a visit. It's large and imposing, and has the town's history written in its stones and interior decoration. There's also a Victorian hedge maze, modelled on Hampton Court, in the attractive **Bridge End Gardens**, though an appointment is required (contact the Tourist Information Centre, *see p279*).

Morris men and radical vicars

Thaxted has a similar history and make-up to Saffron Walden, and has been praised over the years as one of the most charming villages in the country; John Betjeman admired its 'beauty, compactness and juxtaposition of medieval and Georgian architecture', and composer Gustav Holst completed *The Planets* here (the music festival he started takes place in June and July, information from 01371 831421). A precarious three-storey **Guildhall** is the centrepiece, and one of the best surviving examples in the country. On the hill behind it, near to John Webb's windmill (not open, but worth a look), the magnificent 14th-century church is another source of local pride, with a white-painted perpendicular-arched interior and intricately carved ceiling. The light is uplifting, and even the graveyard is pretty. The vicar in the 1920s, Conrad Noel, is remembered for running up the communist and Sinn Fein flags and slashing the tyres of incensed protesters. Noel's wife,

By train from London

The nearest station to **Saffron Walden** is **Audley End**, two miles away; about four trains an hour go there direct from **Liverpool Street**. The journey takes between 50mins and 1hr. Info: www.wagn.co.uk.

East Anglia

The Art of Well-Being

 Greenwoods Estate

Welcome to Greenwoods Estate, one of the UK's premier residential retreats where customer excellence is standard and pure indulgence is compulsory. Located in the picturesque village of Stock, Greenwoods nestles amidst the surrounding countryside but lies only 30 minutes by train from Liverpool Street station. The 17th Century, Grade II listed manor house and its extensive, landscaped gardens provide the stunning focal point of the retreat while its outstanding spa and leisure facilities endow Greenwoods with the ultimate in pampering.

Relax, Refresh and Rejuvenate

Greenwoods boasts a spa, saunas, steam rooms, men's relax room, state of the art gymnasium, an aerobics studio offering personal training, pilates and yoga, as well as an enticing deep blue lap-pool.

More than 50 of the latest body and beauty treatments are also available inspired by leading names such as Carita, Elemis, Decleor and Jessica.

Our convivial cocktail lounge and bar is an ideal place to browse through a magazine over a glass of wine or settle by the fireside with a good book. A comprehensive list of fine wines, spirits and single malt whiskies are available.

For further information please call Greenwoods Estate on 01277 829990
Or visit our website : www.greenwoodsestate.com

2004 Essex

ENGLISH HERITAGE
IT'S MINE

Audley End House and Gardens

Magnificence and Beauty

A house built on the scale of a royal palace surrounded by one of Capability Brown's finest landscaped parks. Enjoy a day at Audley End House and Gardens and see how much more there is to discover.

Tea Rooms • Events Programme • Gift Shop

For further details call 01799 522399 or visit www.english-heritage.org.uk

however, was instrumental in turning the village into a Morris-dancing mecca – dancers still strut their stuff in the town every bank holiday Monday, although the chief festival is a 'Morris Weekend' on the first weekend after the Spring Bank Holiday. We thought it only fair to warn you...

Saving the bacon

Carry on heading south and you'll reach **Great Dunmow**, another ancient market town, but one lacking the cosy beauty of its neighbours. Great Dunmow's great claim to fame is the Flitch Trials, in which a flitch (side) of bacon is awarded to couples who manage not to 'quarrel, differ or dispute' for a year and a day after their marriage. They are then paraded through town on the 'bacon chair', which sits in Little Dunmow parish church. The custom dates back to the 12th century and takes place every leap year (such as 2004).

The countryside east and west of the B184 has much to offer. There are innumerable lovely villages hereabouts, most notably **Clavering**, **Manuden** and **Hazel End**, along the Stort Valley, and **Linton** and **Melbourn**, south of Cambridge. East of Thaxted, complete with duckpond, river, windmill and village green, **Finchingfield** is labelled 'the most photogenic village in Essex', if not necessarily the most peaceful. It is popular with motorcyclists, who like to congregate in the village after speeding through these otherwise serene country roads.

What to see & do

Tourist Information Centres

District Council Offices, 46 High Street, Great Dunmow, Essex CM6 1AN (01799 510490/ www.uttlesford.gov.uk). **Open** 8.30am-5pm Mon-Thur; 8.30am-4.30pm Fri.
1 Market Place, Saffron Walden, CB10 1HR (01799 510444/www.uttlesford.gov.uk). **Open** *Apr-Oct* 9.30am-5.30pm Mon-Sat. *Nov-Mar* 10am-5pm Mon-Sat.

Audley End House & Gardens

Saffron Walden, Essex CB11 4JF (01799 522399/ www.english-heritage.org.uk). **Open** *House* Apr-Sept noon-4pm Wed-Sun, bank hol Mon. Oct phone for details. Closed Nov-Mar. *Gardens* Apr-Sept 11am-5pm Wed-Sun, bank hols. Oct phone for details. Closed Nov-Mar. **Admission** (EH) *House & gardens* £8; £4-£6 concessions. *Gardens only* £4; £2-£3 concessions; free under-5s. **Credit** MC, V.
A Jacobean house on the grandest of scales and the jewel in Uttlesford's tourism crown. Audley End is brimming with accumulated wealth. Opulent furnishings, priceless books and artworks and a monumental collection of stuffed birds and animals fill the rooms, while other highlights include an elegant suite of rooms designed by Robert Adam and a magical chapel above the Great Hall. The grounds were landscaped by 'Capability'

Brown around the Cam, which runs through the lawn. A guide in each room tells you all you need to know. Phone to book a tour (October only). Opposite, there's a miniature railway through Lord Braybrooke's estate woodland (separate admission; 01799 541354).

Flitch Way

A good route for walking, cycling or riding along 15 miles of disused railway line from Hatfield Forest through Great Dunmow to Braintree. The trek takes in wild flowers and animals as well as Victorian railway architecture. Get the Tourist Information Centre at Great Dunmow (*see above*) to send you a leaflet.

Fry Art Gallery

Off Castle Street, Saffron Walden, Essex CB10 1BD (01799 513779/www.fryartgallery.org). **Open** *Easter-Oct* 2-5pm Tue, Sat, Sun, bank hols. Closed Nov-Easter. **Admission** free.
Paintings, prints and ceramics by local artists including Edward Bawden and Michael Rothstein.

The Gardens of Easton Lodge

Warwick House, Little Easton, Great Dunmow, Essex CM6 2BB (01371 876979/www.eastonlodge.co.uk). **Open** *Easter-Oct* noon-6pm Fri-Sun, bank hols; or by appointment. *Feb, Mar* times vary; phone to check. Closed Nov-Jan. **Admission** £3.80; £1.50-£3.50 concessions; free under-3s. **No credit cards.**
Since the 1970s, the Creaseys have been restoring the gardens that were originally laid out at the beginning of the 20th century by Harold Peto. There's a dovecote, a treehouse, an Italian garden and a glade, plus of course, cream teas. The place also opens for the snowdrops in February and March – phone for details.

Hatfield Forest

Off A120, Takeley, Bishop's Stortford, Hertfordshire CM22 6NE (info line 01279 874040/870678/ www.nationaltrust.org.uk). **Open** *Forest* free access throughout yr. *Lake car park* Easter-Oct 10am-5pm/dusk daily. Closed Nov-Easter. *Main car park* 24hrs daily. **Admission** (NT) *Car park* £3 per car. **No credit cards.**
A woodland and nature reserve with 400-year-old pollarded trees and ornamental lakes. The 18th-century Shell House is closed for renovation until 2004.

Imperial War Museum Duxford

Duxford Airfield, Duxford, nr Cambridge, Cambridgeshire CB2 4QR (01223 835000/ www.iwm.org.uk). **Open** *Mid Mar-mid Oct* 10am-6pm daily. *Mid Oct-mid Mar* 10am-4pm daily. **Admission** £8.50; £4.50-£6.50 concessions; free under-16s. **Credit** MC, V.
Aviation heaven with more than 150 historic aircraft from biplanes to Spitfires to Concorde. Norman Foster designed a building here for the American Air Force collection. Air shows take place throughout the summer.

Linton Zoo

Hadstock Road, Linton, Cambridgeshire CB1 6NT (01223 891308/www.lintonzoo.co.uk). **Open** *Mid May-mid Sept* 10am-6pm daily. *Mid Apr-mid May, mid Sept-Oct* 10am-5pm daily. *Nov-mid Apr* 10.30am-4pm daily. **Admission** £6; £4.50-£5.50 concessions. **Credit** MC, V.

East Anglia

Tall Turpin tales

One of Uttlesford's most famous sons is Dick Turpin. The presence of the dashing highwayman – whose legend spawned countless books and poems, as well as a TV series, an Adam Ant song and a minor industry in 'Dick Turpin slept here' plaques – can still be felt throughout the area.

In Hempstead there is a pub called the **Bluebell Inn**, which carries a plaque that reads: 'The birthplace of Dick Turpin (1705)'. Then, the pub was called the Bell and the owner was Jack Turpin, thought to be either Dick's father or brother.

A 20-minute drive brings you to **Thaxted** where Turpin is said to have served a butcher's apprenticeship in a shop that still operates under the name Ducketts. Across the road from the Guildhall is an old oak-beamed house with the plaque above the door that reads 'Dick Turpin's Cottage', one of the his many rumoured abodes in the area.

It was during his apprenticeship that young Dick fell into bad ways. He began by dealing in poached game and stolen meat. In fact, the more the details of his crimes are pieced together from legal records and newspaper reports, the less appropriate

his 'dashing' image seems. Turpin fell in with a man called Samuel Gregory and his boys, nicknamed 'the Essex Gang'. Their criminal speciality was breaking into isolated houses and terrorising the residents within until they coughed up everything they had. One unsavoury case involved an old man being badly burnt with boiling water while his maid was brutally raped. Turpin was ruthless when operating alone too. One widow refused to hand over her valuables, so he held her over an open fire until she complied.

When someone has been continually fouling their own doorstep for a period of time, they have to move on, which explains Dick's eventual demise in York. He was arrested for attacking a neighbour's prize cockerel. When the authorities did a little delving, the gallows beckoned. His most courageous act was perhaps in death. Legend has it that he climbed the ladder to the gibbet at York racecourse and had a 30-minute chat with the hangman while the noose was around his neck. Once Turpin got bored with the conversation, he threw himself off the ladder and hanged until dead.

Conservation-oriented zoo with an emphasis on breeding. There are big cats, including white tigers, snow leopards and other exotic creatures.

Mole Hall Wildlife Park

Widdington, nr Newport, Saffron Walden, Essex CB11 3SS (01799 540400/www.molehall.co.uk). **Open** 10.30am-6pm/dusk daily. **Admission** £5; £3.50-£4 concessions; free under-3s. **Credit** MC, V. Kid-friendly, family-run wildlife park in 20 acres of grounds surrounding a moated manor house. Among the species present are small monkeys, deer, otters, reptiles and a butterfly pavilion (closed in winter).

Mountfitchet Castle & House on the Hill Toy Museum

Stansted Mountfitchet, Essex CM24 8SP (01279 813237/www.gold.enta.net). **Open** *Castle* mid Mar-mid Nov 10am-5pm daily. Closed mid Nov-mid Mar. *Museum* Jan 10am-5pm Tue-Sun. Feb-Dec 10am-5pm daily. **Admission** *Castle* £6; £5-£5.50 concessions. *Museum* £4; £3.20-£3.50 concessions. **Credit** MC, V. Reconstructed Norman motte and bailey castle and village built on the site of an original. Boasts siege weapons and an adjacent toy museum with more than 50,000 exhibits, including a museum of slot machines.

Saffron Walden Museum

Museum Street, Saffron Walden, Essex CB10 1JL (01799 510333). **Open** *Mar-Oct* 10am-5pm Mon-Sat; 2-5pm Sun, bank hols. *Nov-Feb* 10am-4.30pm Mon-Sat; 2-4.30pm Sun, bank hols. **Admission** £1; 50p concessions; free under-18s. **No credit cards.** Good local history, plus anthropological, geological and costume exhibitions. The museum is next to the remains of the Norman castle keep.

Where to stay

Since the tourist board announced that there was a shortage of B&Bs in the area you can barely drive a mile through the country roads without seeing a hand-painted sign advertising a room for rent. Established places do get filled up far in advance, so early booking is advisable.

In Saffron Walden there's the centrally located and newly refurbished **Saffron Hotel** (10-12 High Street, 01799 522676, doubles £90), which also boasts a good restaurant. If you just want a bed, try the 14th-century building now run by the **Youth Hostel Association** (1 Myddylton Place, 01799 523117; £10.25 per person plus £3.50 for breakfast). In Great Dunmow, the **Starr Inn** (*see p282*) is a safe if pricey option (doubles £110).

Archway Guest House

Church Street, Saffron Walden, Essex CB10 1JW (01799 501500/fax 01799 506003). **Rates** £35 single; £55 double/twin; £70-£85 suite/family room. **Rooms** 3 single; 6 double/twin (5 en suite); 1 suite/family (en suite). **No credit cards.** This Georgian-fronted building is a quirky B&B opposite St Mary's church. There's a friendly and eccentric

atmosphere here, not least because it's decorated from top to bottom with rock memorabilia and antique toys. Rooms are spacious, particularly the suites, and the showers are so powerful that a sign in the bathrooms advises you to switch them on slowly lest you knock yourself over. Book early. Children are welcome.

Crossways Guest House

32 Town Street, Thaxted, Essex CM6 2LA (01371 830348). **Rates** £40 single occupancy; £58 double/twin. **Rooms** (all en suite) 2 double; 1 double/twin. **No credit cards.** The main attraction of this 16th-century townhouse is that it is located just opposite the Guildhall in Thaxted. There are two double rooms upstairs overlooking the High Street – smart and clean, but not especially large – and an adjoining lodge in the back garden with a twin/double, all with decor that redefines chintz. Children welcome. All bedrooms are no-smoking.

Homelye Farm

Off Braintree Road, Great Dunmow, Cambridgeshire CM6 3AW (01371 872127/fax 01371 876428/www.homelyefarm.com). **Rates** £35-£40 single/single occupancy; £60 double/twin; £75-£85 family room. **Rooms** (all en suite) 3 single; 3 double; 2 twin; 1 family. **Credit** MC, V. This motel-style B&B stands in a working farmstead on the crown of a hill just off the A120, ten minutes off Stansted Airport. The simple, clean and spacious rooms are in a converted stable block next to the house. Should you be flying from the airport, the hotel offers a package of one night's stay, up to 14 days' parking and taxis to and from the airport for £105. There's no traffic (the farm is at the end of a lane), so it's good for children, and the Pickford family will happily provide a tour of the farm. No smoking throughout.
1 mile E of Great Dunmow off A120; turn into lane opposite water tower; farm is at bottom of lane.

Springfield

16 Horn Lane, Linton, Essex CB1 6HT (01223 891383/ fax 01223 890335/www.springfield-house.co.uk). **Rates** £30 per person. **Rooms** 2 double (both en suite). **No credit cards.** This welcoming and relaxed B&B, housed in an elegant converted Victorian schoolhouse, is home to proprietor Judith Rossiter, plus her children and a dog. Two airy double bedrooms look out on to the back garden where the River Granta runs by, providing an idyllic view. Guests have their own dining room (in a plant-filled conservatory) and lounge downstairs. There is also decent food available at the Crown Inn – just around the corner. Children are welcome. No smoking throughout.
Approaching Linton along A1307 SE of Cambridge; left into High Street then first right after the Crown pub into Horn Lane; house on right next to chapel.

Whitehall Hotel

Church End, Broxted, Essex CM6 2BZ (01279 850603/fax 01279 850385/www.whitehall hotel.co.uk). **Rates** £98 single occupancy; £125 double/twin; £150 deluxe double; £195-£220 suite. Breakfast £11 (Eng); £7 (cont). **Rooms** (all en suite) 5 twin; 14 double; 5 deluxe double; 1 suite. **Credit** AmEx, DC, MC, V.

East Anglia

This sprawling Elizabethan manor provides some of the area's most luxurious accommodation. Rooms in the original house are more pleasant than those in the new extension, although they are all spacious with good views over the gardens. The restaurant, bar and lounge areas are similarly attractive, especially the double-height banquet hall with exposed studwork. Special weekend food-and-board packages are a good option, but there are plenty of weddings here in the summer so early booking is absolutely vital. Children welcome. *Take A120 E of Stansted Airport; follow signs for Broxted.*

Where to eat & drink

You won't need to drive far in this area to find a decent pub, though you might have trouble finding your way back to your hotel through the country lanes, particularly after nightfall. Fine dining, as you'd expect, is thinner on the ground, but not altogether absent.

The **White Hart** (Great Sailing, Braintree, 01371 850341) is home to the 'huffer', a traditional local triangular sandwich. Good drinking can be had at the **Flitch of Bacon** in Little Dunmow (The Street, 01371 820323) and the **Eight Bells** in Saffron Walden (18 Bridge, 01799 522790). The **Bell** in Wendens Ambo (Royston Road, 01799 540382) has a large and lovely garden and lots of pets. **Sheene Mill** (Station Road, Melbourn, 01763 261393) is 12 or so miles south-west of Cambridge and is a local destination dining spot.

Axe & Compasses

Arkesden, nr Saffron Walden, Essex CB11 4EX (01799 550272/fax 01799 550906/www.axeand compasses.co.uk). **Main courses** £12.95-£16.95. **Food served** noon-2pm, 6.45-9.30pm daily. **Set lunch** (Sun) £16 3 courses. **Credit** MC, V.
This thatched 17th-century building, divided into several spaces, with dark beams, polished brasses, horse paraphernalia and open fireplace, is a local favourite. You can eat in either the restaurant or the bar. The range is extensive. Starters run from deep-fried breaded brie to home-made chicken liver pâté; mains in the restaurant include wild Barbary duck, or prawns in cream cheese sauce.

The Cricketers

Wicken Road, Clavering, Essex CB11 4QT (01799 550442/www.thecricketers.co.uk). **Food served** noon-2pm, 7-10pm daily. **Main courses** £11-£18. **Set menu** £21.50 2 courses, £26 3 courses. **Credit** AmEx, MC, V.
The family home of celebrity chef and restaurateur Jamie Oliver offers good food at affordable prices. Jamie's mum and dad own and run this busy pub/restaurant with Oliver senior acting as maître d'. The starter of salmon nori roll with tempura batter in a sesame seed, soya and truffle oil dressing looks and tastes great and the main dish of grilled darne of halibut served on fresh runner beans and cherry tomatoes is truly tasty. The banana baked with rum, muscovado sugar and vanilla served with a rich

toffee sauce and rum and raisin ice-cream deserves special mention. Service is provided by friendly women who buzz enthusiastically around the place.

Dicken's Brasserie

The Green, Wethersfield, Essex CM7 4BS (01371 850723/fax 01371 850727/www.dickensbrasserie. co.uk). **Food served** noon-2pm, 6.30-9.30pm daily. **Main courses** £11-£16.50. **Credit** AmEx, MC, V.
This friendly restaurant beside a village green feels like a private house. John Dicken has added his personal touch to the interior – the bright and cheery decor is Shaker-style, with gastronomic quotations written along the walls. Food is traditional with a Mediterranean accent: wholesome soups; game dishes that are sumptuous without requiring a health warning; simple desserts and a respectable wine list. Good value, particularly at lunchtime where a menu offers you the same dish as a starter or a main.

Pink Geranium

Station Road, Melbourn, Cambridgeshire SG8 6DX (01763 260215/fax 01763 262110/www.pink geranium.co.uk). **Food served** noon-2pm, 7-9.30pm Tue-Sat; noon-2pm Sun. **Main courses** £17.50-£26. **Set lunch** (Tue-Fri) £14.50 2 courses, £19 3 courses. (Sat, Sun) £22.50 3 courses. **Set dinner** (Tue-Fri) £19.50 2 courses, £25 3 courses. **Credit** AmEx, MC, V.
The Pink Geranium is a converted cottage harbouring a charming dining room and a lounge with a roaring log fire. The menu matches the fine service: typical dishes include a steamed canon of lamb wrapped in leeks with tomato and tarragon jus; or ragout of wild mushrooms and asparagus with a truffle sauce. It's one of the best in the area, so expect to pay if you eat à la carte.

The Restaurant

2 Church Street, Saffron Walden, Essex (01799 526444). **Food served** 7.30-10pm Tue-Sat; 12.30-3pm Sun. **Main courses** £10-£18. **Set dinner** (Tue-Thur) £9.95 2 courses, £13.95 3 courses. **Credit** MC, V.
This basement space is divided into smoking and no-smoking rooms, with bare brick walls framed by clean colours and lines. The minimalist decor is matched by a concise menu, which includes dishes such as pan-fried pigeon breasts in a fruit jus served with green beans and garlic roasted potatoes, or grilled fillet of beef in a wild mushroom sauce with sauté potatoes, shallots and caramelised garlic. Produce is organic wherever possible and the wine cellar offers a reasonably priced range. Service is extremely relaxed bordering on indifferent.

Starr Inn

Market Place, Great Dunmow, Essex CM6 1AX (01371 874321/www.zynet.co.uk/menu/starr). **Food served** noon-1.30pm, 7-9.30pm Mon-Sat; noon-1.30pm Sun. **Set dinner** £32.50 3 courses. **Credit** AmEx, DC, MC, V.
If you're looking for an old school restaurant, this is it. The dining area is subtly lit and tables are comfortably placed to allow you to chat without the neighbours chipping in. The menu includes a mix of country classics and more up-to-date treats. The home-made tomato soup is excellent, as is the rosemary encrusted rack of new season lamb with baby vegetables and red currant jus. Service is friendly and efficient but not overbearing.

Lower Stour Valley

Constable country.

The Lower Stour Valley would stand its ground as a place of inspiring beauty without artistic representation; but it was here that John Constable found his inspiration, and this landscape that he immortalised in his paintings. A flat land with big skies, fields, locks, mill ponds, spreading oaks and willows, tumbledown cottages and giant brick waterside mills, it encapsulates a particular brand of English rural charm.

Some of the elements that contribute most to this charm – especially the massive mills, built for cleaning wool and grinding corn – are left over from the area's earlier prominence as a hub of the medieval wool trade. Such wealth means

By train from London

Eight trains an hour leave **Liverpool Street** for **Colchester** and **Ipswich**. Journey time to Colchester is 55mins. Ipswich is a further 20mins. For **Harwich Town**, change at Manningtree. Total journey time is around 1hr 30mins. Info: www.ger.co.uk and www.angliarailways.co.uk.

that nearly all the villages have grand, near cathedral-scale 15th-century churches with emphatic towers and spires, paid for by the local wool merchants of the time. Less grand but equally valuable are the numerous atmospheric country pubs that serve the delicious local brews, Adnams and Greene King.

The Stour Valley stretches roughly from **Nayland** to **Cattawade**, along the border between Essex and Suffolk. The Industrial Revolution seemed to bypass this area and the valley landscapes of the Stour still fit Constable's description, written in 1830: 'The beauty of the surrounding scenery, the gentle declivities, the luxuriant meadow flats sprinkled with flocks and herds, and well cultivated uplands, the woods and rivers, the numerous scattered villages and churches, with farmyard and picturesque cottages, all impart to their particular spot an amenity and elegance hardly anywhere else to be found.'

It's a soft, mellow landscape with a happy mixture of greenery and water – of dipping valleys and hills, with wide skyscapes and the luminescent light for which East Anglia is renowned. Villages are made up of Georgian brick houses and bulging walled half-timbered cottages, painted in white, pinks and yellows. This is an ideal area for walking. Everywhere there are excellent footpaths and the **Essex Way** runs for 81 miles from **Epping** to **Harwich**.

Dedham

As a child, Constable used to walk from his birthplace in **East Bergholt** to the grammar school in Dedham, a town made rich by the medieval wool trade. Its source of wealth is still apparent in some of the town's buildings – the timber-framed **Marlborough Head** pub was formerly the wool exchange, the **Flemish Cottages** were once a medieval cloth factory. The streets boast many elegant Georgian houses, and next to the school is the grand **St Mary's** church, with the square flint tower that featured in so many of Constable's paintings. Inside there is a tablet to a woman who died aged 35 in 1748 'in consequence of having accidentally swallowed a pin'. A newly acquired Constable, *The Ascension*, faces you as you enter the side door, but, unfortunately, it is a passionless commission.

In the low, beamed cottages on the high street you'll find antiques, gift shops and bookshops for maps and guides. As Pevsner wrote: 'There is nothing in Dedham to hurt the eye', and even to this day there are no street lights to compromise the beauty of its architecture. The home and studio of painter Sir Alfred Munnings is also here – kept as it was in the artist's heyday.

East Bergholt

The house where Constable was born in this peaceful village has long since gone, but you can still see his studio, a cream cottage with pantiled roof. His early painting tutor, John Dunthorne, lived across the road in what is now a hairdresser's. The village church has a tower that has been in ruins for centuries. A planned new spire was never built because of the Reformation; ever since, the church's bells have been housed in a unique bell cage at ground level. From the tower you can walk down the hill to **Flatford** and see the pretty riverside cottage of Willy Lott, foreman to Constable's father, Golding. Constable made sketches of the Dedham Vale from Gun Hill and the top of St Mary's church tower in Langham. **Stratford St Mary** is a pretty riverside village walkable from Flatford, with the **Priest's House**, a beautiful white and dark-timbered cottage, hanging over the main road. In **Nayland**, a large village with a striking main street, the church houses Constable's altarpiece *Christ Blessing the Bread and Wine*, which his aunt paid him to paint in 1809. Nearby, **Stoke-by-Nayland** offers spectacular views and a beautiful old Maltings and Guildhall. Constable

painted the church, with its 120-foot-tall square flint-and-brick tower. **Hadleigh** is a likeable old market town with a long high street down which sheep were once driven.

From cows to swans

Heading east towards Felixstowe, dip into the **Shotley Peninsula**, where undulating arable fields run down to the water's edge. St Mary's church (another one) at **Erwarton** has a generous view from the tombstones. Inside there are carved monuments to families who have owned the extraordinary **Erwarton Manor**. The house is not open to the public but it's worth looking over the wall to glimpse this red-brick Tudor building. In **Shotley Gate** marina, fluttering yachts tack down the Stour and run up the Orwell or head out into the open sea, while across the bay you can glimpse the massive cargo containers in Felixstowe docks.

Taking the south side of the estuary towards Harwich leads you past estuary views and through once-busy ports. **Manningtree** was a thriving port in Constable's day, but is now a small, sleepy backwater. It was the home of Matthew Hopkins, the Witchfinder General, who 'persuaded' 400 local women to confess that they were witches and then condemned them to death. He is said to have been buried in the now-demolished St Mary's church (a popular name in these parts, you may have noticed) in **Mistley**. The oddest buildings nearby are the twin **Mistley Towers** on the Manningtree Road, all that remain of a neo-classical Roman temple built by Robert Adam in 1776. At **Mistley Quay**, cargo such as coal and timber could be transferred to barges and taken up the Stour to Sudbury or into Thames sailing barges for the journey to London. There is also a secret concrete bunker at Mistley, which was used as a Cold War operations centre (currently closed for refurbishment).

Further along the estuary, **Wrabness** is a perfect starting point for marshy walks, with the **Stour Estuary Nature Reserve** providing a habitat for waterfowl and woodland birds. The ferry-port town of **Harwich** flourished in the reign of Elizabeth I, and if you head for the quay you'll find a mixture of Tudor, duckboard and brick houses in the narrow streets of the old town. The site of the 19th-century **Ha'penny Pier** was the departure point for the *Mayflower* when it set sail for the Americas in 1611 and the local MP was one Samuel Pepys.

Celts and Saxons

If you need a break from village life, you can explore **Colchester** and **Ipswich**. Colchester was the capital of Roman Britain before being burned to the ground by Boudiccea. Fragments of the walls, a Roman road and a great gate to the west remain; the Norman keep is also worth a visit. Despite the alarming spread of shopping centres, many old and quirky buildings remain.

Ipswich's streets still follow the line of those of its Saxon past (take time to look above the first storey to really appreciate the architecture), and its compact historic centre, centuries-old dock area and a string of medieval churches make it a worthwhile destination. Particularly noteworthy is the magnificent **Ancient House**, with its lavishly carved façade, and the fine art collection at **Christchurch Mansion**.

What to see & do

The best way to appreciate the Stour Valley is, naturally, to walk it. For non-strenuous strolling, one easy but enjoyable route is the path from **Dedham** to **Flatford** and back (the round trip takes around two hours). Another is the path between Dedham and East Bergholt – walked by Constable every day on his way to school – which features in *The Cornfield*. Walking maps and guides, including the handy illustrated booklet *The Essex Way* (£3), are on sale at Tourist Information Centres, bookshops in Dedham and the post office in East Bergholt.

Tourist Information Centres

1 Queen Street, Colchester, Essex CO1 2PG (01206 282920/www.colchester.gov.uk). **Open** *Easter-Sept* 9.30am-6pm Mon, Tue, Thur-Sat; 10am-6pm Wed; 10am-5pm Sun. *Oct-Easter* 10am-5pm Mon-Sat.

Flatford Lane, Flatford, East Bergholt, Colchester, Essex CO7 6UL (01206 299460/www.visit-suffolk.org.uk). **Open** *Mar-Oct* 10am-5pm daily. *Nov-Feb* 10.30am-4pm Sat, Sun.

Iconfield Park, Parkston, Harwich, Essex CO12 4EN (01255 506139/www.realessex.co.uk). **Open** *Apr-Sept* 9am-5pm Mon-Fri; 9am-4pm Sat, Sun. *Oct-Mar* 9am-5pm Mon-Fri; 9am-4pm Sat.

Bike hire

Street Life *Hamilton Road (beside bus station) Sudbury, Suffolk CO10 2UU (01787 310940/ www.streetlifecycles.co.uk).*
Close to the train station.

Action Bikes *24 Crouch Street, Colchester, Essex CO3 3ES (01206 541744).*
A mile from the train station.

Alton Water Sports Centre

Holbrook Road, Stutton, Suffolk IP9 2RY (01473 328408/www.altonwater.moonfruit.com). **Open** *Apr-Oct* 10am-8pm Mon-Fri; 10am-6pm Sat, Sun. *Nov-Mar* 10am-4pm daily. **Credit** AmEx, MC, V.
Casual day users are welcome to windsurf, canoe and sail on Ipswich's drinking water. The centre uses 25 acres of this man-made inland reservoir to let people loose in Wayfarers, canoes and windsurfers. Training sessions are also available.

Beth Chatto Gardens

Elmstead Market, nr Colchester, Essex CO7 7DB (01206 822007/www.bethchatto.co.uk). **Open** *Mar-Oct* 9am-5pm Mon-Sat. *Nov-Feb* 9am-4pm Mon-Fri.
Admission £3.50; free under-14s if accompanied.
Credit MC, V.
Before 1960 this large site was an overgrown wasteland. Over the years Beth Chatto has turned the former car park into a world-famous garden. There is a nursery adjoining, and a tearoom (though picnickers are welcome).

Blue Baker Yachts

Woolverstone Marina, Woolverstone, Ipswich, Suffolk IP9 1AS (01473 780008/www.bluebaker yachts.com). **Open** 9am-5pm Mon-Fri; 10am-3pm Sat; by appointment Sun. **Credit** AmEx, MC, V.
If you are a novice and feel like splashing out, Suffolk Yacht Charters will take you out on a day cruise (£240-£350 for the boat, plus £120 for a skipper) in the backwaters of the estuaries or out into the North Sea. If you're experienced, you can hire a boat without a skipper.

Boat hire on the Stour

Boathouse Restaurant, Mill Lane, Dedham, Suffolk CO7 6DH (01206 323153). **Open** *Apr-June, Sept* 10am-5pm Tue-Sun. *July, Aug* 10am-5pm daily. *Closed Oct-Mar.* **No credit cards.**
It costs £10 per hour, £6 for half an hour (plus a £10 deposit), to hire a rowing boat from Dedham; it takes around 90 minutes to row under the weeping willows to Flatford and back. Tickets are on sale from the boat shed or the tearooms next to the picnic area. Alternatively, try the Stour Trust (01206 393680) for a dinky electric river cruiser from Flatford; it costs £2.50 per person for a half-hour ride.

Bridge Cottage

Bridge Cottage, Flatford, Essex CO7 6OL (01206 298260/www.nationaltrust.org.uk). **Open** *Jan, Feb* 11am-3pm Sat, Sun. *Mar, Apr* 11am-5.30pm Wed-Sun. *May-Sept* 10am-5.30pm daily. *Oct* 11am-4.30pm daily. *Nov, Dec* 11am-3.30pm Wed-Sun. **Guided tours** *May-Sept, Easter, bank hols* 11am, 1pm, 2.30pm daily. **Admission** *Bridge Cottage* (NT) free. *Tours* £2, audio tapes £2 (£5 deposit). **No credit cards.**
Most of the tiny clutch of buildings at Flatford, the subject of Constable's most famous paintings, are now in the hands of the National Trust. Here are the flat ford and the mill foreman's late medieval house that feature in *The Haywain*. There's a copy of the painting in the small exhibition in Bridge Cottage, which also houses a café and a shop. You can only admire the Georgian Flatford Mill from the outside unless you pre-book a tour for a party of ten. Residential courses in arts and the environment are held in the mill, Willy Lott's house and Valley Farm, a beautiful white and timber-framed medieval farmhouse once owned by Golding Constable. There's also a Granary Museum, with eclectic rural bygones, and a dry dock where barges were built and repaired.

Castle House

Dedham, Essex CO7 6AZ (01206 322127/www. siralfredmunnings.co.uk). **Open** *Easter-July, Sept, Oct* 2-5pm Wed, Sun. *Aug* 2-5pm Wed, Thur, Sat, Sun. **Admission** £4; £1-£3 concessions. **No credit cards.**
Home to once-fashionable painter Sir Alfred Munnings, Castle House has been kept as it was in the artist's day

The Stour at **Dedham** (top) and at **Flatford Mill** (bottom). For both, *see p284*.

and is home to many of his paintings. Alongside his famous depictions of horses and horse racing there are sculptures and East Anglian landscapes on display.

Christchurch Mansion & Wolsey Art Gallery

Christchurch Park, Ipswich, Suffolk IP4 2BE (01473 433554 /www.ipswich.gov.uk/tourism/guide/ mansion.html). **Open** *Mar-Oct* 10am-5pm Tue-Sat; 2.30-4.30pm Sun. *Nov-Feb* 10am-4pm/dusk Tue-Sat; 2.30pm-4pm/dusk Sun. **Admission** free.

This Tudor house, in the shape of an 'E', was originally built as a priory for Augustinian monks. As well as chests and chairs in period rooms, you can also admire the work of Ipswich resident Thomas Gainsborough (1727-88). Among his early formal portraits of the local elite is the wooden portrait of the headmaster of Ipswich School, the Rev Robert Hingeston, and a lively later portrait of a relaxed William Woolaston playing the flute. Constable came to Ipswich to learn from Gainsborough, and if you've been trailing Constable, you'll be excited by the paintings *The Flower Garden* and *The Millstream* – among an extensive collection by the two artists considered the best outside London.

Colchester Castle Museum

Castle Park, Colchester, Essex CO1 1TJ (01206 282931/www.colchestermuseums.org.uk). **Open** 10am-5pm Mon-Sat; 11am-5pm Sun (last entry 4.30pm). **Admission** £4.25; £2.80 concessions; free under-5s. **Credit** MC, V.

Since the 16th century this castle has been a library, a jail for witches and a ruin. Today, it's a museum that tells the story of Boudicca's devastation of Colchester, life under siege during the Civil War and life in Roman Britain. Kids can try on Roman armour and togas and handle pottery. The castle stands on the site of a Roman temple to Claudius.

Harwich Habour Ferry Services

07919 911440.

Cruises from the Ha'penny Pier in Harwich. The harbour ferry takes adults (£5) and children (£4) on a half-hour tour round the harbour.

Stour Estuary RSPB Nature Reserve

Ramsey, nr Harwich, Essex (01255 886043/www. rspb.org.uk), 1 mile east of Wrabness on the B1352. **Open** free access. **Admission** free.

One of the most important estuaries in Britain for wading birds. From the reserve's three hides you can see redshanks and dunlins in the saltmarsh; from late July, black-tailed godwits from Iceland appear. Grey plovers, pintails, brent geese and shelducks also feed here. Wear your wellies.

Where to stay

There are plenty of B&Bs scattered around the Stour Valley villages. If those listed below are full, others worth considering include **May's Barn Farm** in Dedham (May's Lane, off Long Road West, 01206 323191/www.mays.barn. btinternet.co.uk, doubles £44-50), **Gladwins**

Farm in Nayland (Harpers Hill, 01206 262261/ www.gladwinsfarm.co.uk, doubles £60-£65), **Ryegate House** in Stoke-by-Nayland (01206 263679/www.ryegate.co.uk, doubles £55-£65) and the astonishingly reasonable and comfortable **Highfield** at Holbrook on the Shotley Peninsula (Harkstead Road, 01473 328250, doubles £43-£50).

Angel Inn

Polstead Street, Stoke-by-Nayland, Suffolk CO6 4SA (01206 263245/fax 01206 263373/www.horizon inns.co.uk). **Rates** £54.50 single occupancy; £69.50 double/twin. **Rooms** (all en suite) 5 double, 1 twin. **Credit** MC, V.

The Angel has been functioning as an inn in one of the most attractive Dedham Vale villages since the 16th century. Downstairs there's a tall-ceilinged dining room and a lounge with a brick fireplace (great for nestling beside with a nightcap). Rooms are smart and functional – your only worry as you head for bed will be not hitting your head on the low ceiling beams. One room available for dogs. All bedrooms are no-smoking.

From Colchester, take first exit on right as you come into Nayland; over the bridge, go past the Anchor pub, and bear right at the junction; the Angel Inn is on the crossroads as you approach the village.

Dedham Hall

Brook Street, Dedham, CO7 6AD (01206 323027/ fax 01206 323293/www.dedhamhall.demon.co.uk). **Rates** £55 single occupancy; £90 double/twin; £105-£120 family room. **Rooms** (all en suite) 1 single; 4 double/ twin; 1 family room; 12 annexe rooms. **Credit** MC, V.

Guests at Dedham Hall are treated as pampered house guests: the open kitchen, with its orange Aga and gleaming pots, is at the heart of things. Wholesome food is provided here for guests on painting courses and their art is displayed all over the house. The hotel also has an upmarket restaurant, the Fountain House. Rooms are snug and light, and there is a cosy, low-ceilinged residents' lounge with wood panelling and a bar with leather armchairs. A short walk by the river brings you to Flatford. Children welcome.

Off A12, at the far end of Dedham High Street on the left.

Edge Hall Hotel

2 High Street, Hadleigh, Suffolk IP7 5AP (01473 822458/fax 01473 827751/www.edgehall-hotel. co.uk). **Rates** £40-£50 single; £55-£95 double/twin; £70-£95 four-poster; £75-£105 family room. **Rooms** (all en suite) 2 single; 5 double/twin; 1 four-poster; 2 family. **No credit cards.**

A bright pink Georgian townhouse with a delightful walled garden and croquet lawn right in the centre of the pretty town of Hadleigh. Decor and furnishings are in keeping with the building's architecture – you can stay in an elegant four-poster in the main house or in the comfortable, modern, red-brick lodge overlooking the garden. Children welcome. Pets allowed only in the lodge. No smoking throughout.

Maison Talbooth

Stratford Road, Dedham, Essex CO7 6HN (01206 322367/ fax 01206 322752/www.talbooth.com). **Rates** £120-£150 single occupancy; £160-£220

East Anglia

double/twin; £220 suite. Breakfast £8.50 (Eng), free (cont). **Rooms** (all en suite) 8 double; 2 suites. **Credit** AmEx, DC, MC, V.

The perfect place to stay if you're into the whole country house outdoor sports thing – where else would you find a croquet lawn *and* a giant chess set? The hotel was set up so that diners at Le Talbooth (*see p289*) would have somewhere to stay after dinner. It's a big Victorian rectory decorated in grand style, with a large piano in the drawing room and French windows leading outdoors to spacious grounds. Rooms are luxurious – the Keats suite, for example, has a jacuzzi. There is no dining room in the hotel so breakfast is served in your room or on the balcony; a courtesy car takes you to and from Le Talbooth restaurant. The hotel has beautiful views of Dedham Vale. Children welcome.

From Dedham High Street, with the church on the left-hand side, drive out of the village; take first right turn after a row of houses; Maison Talbooth is 200yds up on the left.

Milsoms

Stratford Road, Dedham, Essex CO7 6HW (01206 322795/ fax 01206 323689/www.talbooth.com). **Rates** £72.50-£92.50 single occupancy; £90-£130 double/twin. Breakfast £12 (Eng), £7 (cont). **Rooms** (all en suite) 14 double/twin. **Credit** AmEx, DC, MC, V.

The Milsom dynasty of hoteliers sold this hotel in 1992 when it was the Dedham Vale Hotel, and now they've bought it back. (They also own Le Talbooth, Maison Talbooth and the Pier at Harwich.) Inside, Geraldine Milsom has applied her makeover techniques to 14 en suite bedrooms that are fresh and stylish. The atmosphere downstairs is relaxed, and excellent Modern European food is available all day (*see p289*). Children and dogs welcome. All rooms are no-smoking.

Come off A12 following signs for Dedham; cross over the bridge and take first left turn after bridge.

Old Vicarage

Higham, nr Colchester, Suffolk CO7 6JY (01206 337248). **Rates** £35-40 single occupancy; £58-£64 double; £70-£74 triple occupancy. **Rooms** (1 en suite, 2 private bathrooms) 3 double/triple. **No credit cards.**

Owner Mrs Parker treats you to afternoon tea and cake when you arrive at this 16th-century vicarage – after you've found the bell hiding beneath a creeper. Meadows, cows, the River Stour and a square church tower combine to create a stunning view from the garden or elegant drawing room. Each room exudes a quirky old world charm, in keeping with the setting, and there's a tennis court, trampoline and delightfully situated swimming pool in the garden, while a punt and canoe on the nearby river are there free of charge for the terminally restless. Children and dogs are welcome.

On A12 between Colchester and Ipswich. From Stratford St Mary, take the Higham Road; the Old Vicarage is about a mile along on the left.

Pier at Harwich Hotel

The Quay, Harwich, Essex CO12 3HH (01255 241212/fax 01255 551922/www.pieratharwich.com). **Rates** £67.50-£80 single occupancy; £90-110 double; £160 suite. Breakfast free (cont); £7.50 (Eng). **Rooms** (all en suite) 10 double/twin; 1 suite; 3 family rooms. **Credit** AmEx, DC, MC, V.

Located right on the quayside, this Victorian hotel plays strongly on the watery theme. Rooms, five of which overlook the harbour, are decorated with weatherboarding, seashells, rope and hessian floors. The former Angel Inn next door has been converted to provide more accommodation, including the luxurious Mayflower Suite with a telescope for watching harbour activity. The Pier is owned by Geraldine and Paul Milsom, who also own Le Talbooth, Maison Talbooth and Milsoms. Children welcome.

White Hart Inn

11 High Street, Nayland, nr Colchester, CO6 4JF (01206 263382/fax 01206 263638/www.whitehart-nayland.co.uk). **Rates** £69-£75 single occupancy; £82-£95 double. **Rooms** (all en suite) 6 double/twin. **Credit** AmEx, DC, MC, V.

Like the horse-drawn coaches trundling from London to Harwich in the 18th century, you, too, will have to seek out this beautiful timbered inn through the darkness – Nayland has no street lighting. Inside, the heritage interest has been developed in conjunction with modern chic to provide comfortable accommodation above the classy, fine-dining French restaurant (*see p289*). Each room is light and bright, despite ancient dark beams and curiously shaped ceilings, imposed by the eccentricity of the building. One room, 'Caroline', has two murals by Jack Gainsborough, the less famous brother, who painted them to clear his bar tab. Children welcome.

Where to eat & drink

You can stumble upon pub after pub along the old coaching routes around Dedham Vale. Many of them, such as the **Angel Inn** (*see p289*), serve restaurant meals worthy of a journey from London. For pub grub in Dedham, the **Sun** (High Street, 01206 323351) offers all-day meals and has a grassy beer garden and a restaurant. The **Cock Inn** in Polstead (01206 263150) offers upmarket food in a venerable old village pub. Formerly the Wool Exchange, the friendly **Marlborough Head** in Dedham (Mill Road, 01206 323250) is a cosy and convivial timber-beamed pub with Adnams, bar food and a restaurant. If you want something a bit more upmarket, try the **Boathouse** (Mill Lane, 01206 323153), in Dedham, which offers good food in a light airy wooden building.

In East Bergholt, the **Red Lion** (The Street, 01206 298332) is an unpretentious local with a pool table and pleasant garden. The **Swan** in Stratford St Mary was built in 1520 and at its height had stabling for 200 horses. The tiny timber-beamed bars are cosy in the winter and there is a river garden across the road for the summer. There is another **Swan** in Chappell (01787 222353), which has a garden on the River Colne.

There are fewer pubs along the Stour Estuary but the **Crown Hotel** in Manningtree (High Street, 01206 396333) and the **Thorn**

Hotel on the quay at Mistley (High Street, 01206 392821) offer good views. On the Shotley Peninsula there is a beautiful view of the Orwell from the **Butt and Oyster** at Pin Mill (01473 780764). It's so close to the water that it's said that yachts used to sail up to the hatch and get served drinks. For fine fishy food try the **Queen's Head** (The Street, 01473 787550) at Erwarton.

Angel Inn

Polstead Street, Stoke-by-Nayland, CO6 4SA (01206 263245/www.horizoninns.co.uk). **Food served** noon-2pm, 6.30-9.30pm Mon-Sat; noon-5pm, 5.30-930pm Sun. **Main courses** £9.95-£14.50. **Credit** MC, V.

You can eat in the Well Room (with a 52ft well) or at a table for two on a lovebird balcony looking down on the barn-like room. Alternatively, there are a number of timbered rooms in the pub, or, in summer, in the bricked courtyard. A wide-ranging menu offers choices such as black bacon and portobello mushroom salad, griddled sardines, chargrilled teriyaki rib eye steak and seared mackerel fillets, while vegetarians have the likes of pepper, potato and aubergine moussaka or cream risotto. A pleasant atmospheric spot with good service. Book in advance at weekends.

The Galley

25 St Nicholas Street, Ipswich, IP1 1TW (01473 281131/www.galley.uk.com). **Lunch served** noon-2pm Mon-Sat. **Dinner served** 6.30-10pm Mon-Thur; 6.30-11pm Fri, Sat. **Main courses** £13.95-£16.95. **Credit** AmEx, MC, V.

Decorated in pink and aquamarine, this leaning Elizabethan building conceals one of the best restaurants in the area. Upstairs the little rooms are open between the wall beams to create light while sloping floors add charm. Service is quick and to the point, though the owner will talk the hind legs off a donkey if asked about the food. Lobster, fresh fish and seasonal vegetables are often the order of the day and nearly all ingredients are local: Gressingham duck liver pâté, Capel St Mary flat mushrooms and Tuddenham Hall asparagus really hit the spot. Sauces are inventive, and prices are not disheartening.

Harbourside Restaurant

The Pier at Harwich, The Quay, Harwich, Essex CO12 3HH (01255 241212/www.pier@harwich. com). **Food served** noon-2pm, 6-9.30pm daily. **Main courses** £9.95-£30. **Set lunches** £16 2 courses, £19 3 courses. **Credit** AmEx, DC, MC, V.

A comfortable first-floor restaurant with stunning views over the harbour. A ship's wheel and brass compass stand give an inkling of the theme, confirmed by the toll of a ship's bell whenever a vessel passes. Main courses include fish and chips and grilled lobster, or (more adventurously) poached halibut fillet with bubble and squeak, and an all-encompassing Chef's Pic (*sic*) of cod, salmon, prawns, scampi and scallops in a saffron and white wine sauce. Non-fishy options and one vegetarian choice are available along with a flotilla of reasonably priced wines. Children are welcome at the jolly Ha'penny Bistro downstairs.

Milsoms

Stratford Road, Dedham, Essex CO7 6HW (01206 322795). **Food served** noon-2.15pm, 6-9.30pm Mon-Thur; noon-2.15pm, 6-10pm Fri, Sat; noon-2.15pm Sun. **Main courses** £8.95-£14.95. **Credit** AmEx, DC, MC, V.

This groovy restaurant/bar with a sail-covered outdoor eating area has a Mediterranean/New World vibe and first-come first-served policy. Perched on farmhouse tables are menus and order sheets – customers complete them and leave them at the bar – while a specials blackboard has good-value alternatives. Food is inventive, eclectic and bistro-style. Starters might include Asian duck tacos and hoi sin sauce, while mains could be shepherd's pie (made with Suffolk mutton) or baked field mushrooms with ratatouille and appenzellar cheese. Desserts are a high point; we loved peppered pineapple tart with vanilla pod ice-cream.

Stour Bay Café

39-43 High Street, Manningtree, Essex CO11 1AH (01206 396687). **Food served** 12.30-2pm, 7-9.30pm Wed-Sun. **Main courses** £10-£16. **Credit** AmEx, MC, V.

Intimate, atmospheric and constantly busy, the Stour Bay Café offers a mouth-watering combination of local ingredients (including basketloads of excellent fish) enhanced with Mediterranean flair. Grilled sardines with basil butter and a tapas of fishy bits top the starters menu while the cataplana – a large brass-looking bowl full of lobster, crab, langoustine, mussels, haddock and mullet in a tomato fondue – is a culinary event.

Le Talbooth

Gun Hill, Dedham, Essex CO7 6HP (01206 323150/ www.talbooth.com). **Food served** noon-2pm, 7-9.30pm Mon-Sat; noon-2pm Sun. **Set lunch** £21.50 2 courses, £24 3 courses. **Credit** AmEx, DC, MC, V.

This much-refurbished, picturesque 16th-century house overlooking a pretty-as-a-postcard section of the river provides an extraordinary dining experience and exceptional food. The family-owned Talbooth propounds the virtues of low-lit, high-priced, high-class, luxurious dining with hovering 'stealth' waiters, dressed all in black, to fulfil every request, spoken or not. The menu reads like a Who's Who of classic dishes with a few surprises – fricassée of monkfish and lobster with broad beans, herbs and tomato vermouth sauce or basmati rice and seared gnocchi with gâteaux of vegetables and goat's cheese. For the hotel, *see p287*.

White Hart Inn

11 High Street, Nayland, nr Colchester, Suffolk CO6 4JF (01206 263382/www.whitehart-nayland. co.uk). **Food served** noon-2pm, 6.30-9.30pm Tue-Fri; noon-2.30pm, 6.30-10pm Sat; 6.30-9pm Sun. **Main courses** £9.90-£16. **Set lunch** £12.95 3 courses. **Set dinner** £21.50 3 courses. **Credit** AmEx, DC, MC, V.

The whole of this former pub is now a restaurant, with a small bar area. The quality of the traditional French cookery is sublime: chilled Andalucia gazpacho and cucumber sorbet is lively and refreshing, while roast rolled loin of suckling pig with calvados sauce melts in the mouth. There's also a wonderful selection of French farmhouse cheeses. Service is impeccable and friendly, and accommodation is also available (*see p288*).

East Anglia

Upper Stour Valley

Go misty-eyed in rural Suffolk.

The pace of life in rural Suffolk – and the part of Essex that follows the Stour Valley, which runs along the border between the two counties – is sleepy and slow. For at least 100 years Suffolk has been a refuge for holidaymakers and weekenders – people who need to slow down – but in the past ten years even greater numbers of commuters have burst across the banks of the Stour (which roughly rhymes with brewer) in search of nirvana, making some villages appear more like London suburbs than East Anglian rural . But these are exceptions. On the whole Suffolk remains somnambulant, a three-toed sloth among counties, seamlessly absorbing all comers without outward signs of change. Perhaps the big skies are what give the impression that it's never overpopulated.

The Upper Stour Valley indulges life's simpler pleasures: meandering in pretty, gently undulating countryside dotted with whispering villages full of crooked Suffolk-pink cottages; eating well – the local ingredients are world class, explaining the large number of high-class restaurants; and drinking fine beer – Suffolk has two great in Adnams and Greene King. As for the resident population, they walk a reasonable line between being welcoming, and getting on with their own business.

The Stour Valley is a 60-mile stretch that flows from south of Newmarket, past Haverhill and then west to east, forming the Essex/Suffolk border, through the lovely Suffolk villages of Clare, Cavendish and Long Melford, past Dedham and Flatford Mill to its estuary in the east at the Cattawade Marshes. This break concentrates on the river's upper reaches, from Haverhill to Sudbury and up to Lavenham. (For the **Lower Stour Valley**, see p280.)

Peace in the valley

A fire swept through **Haverhill** (pronounced 'Ave-rill) in 1665, and there has been little of interest in this unlovely former wool town

since. But to the east and north, the cluster of villages within a ten-mile radius around Sudbury represents some of the best that Suffolk has to offer. Here is the grand medieval architecture of unmissable **Lavenham**, a village that grew rich on the wool trade; the thriving market town of **Sudbury** itself; and the idyllic English scene set by **Cavendish**.

Much of Suffolk's beauty is in the detail: look for cottages covered with decorated plasterwork known as pargeting (a house beside **Clare** churchyard offers a fine example). Many of the villages – especially Cavendish, with its village green and thatched cottages – have entered the collective folk memory as the very image of what an English village should look like. Indeed, it was the East Anglian understated undulations and villages that caused Cambridge-based war poet Rupert Brooke to go so misty-eyed over England.

It is also an area that wears its history in its place names: Latin, Saxon, Scandinavian and Norman French tongues inform whole clusters of village names. History is also reflected in the area's architecture: the Romans, who made their capital 30 miles to the south-east at Colchester, have left their mark in roads and numerous archaeological sites along the routes; the Saxon, and especially Norman, influence can be seen clearly in ruined castles and churches. The splendour of Elizabethan England is evident in such great manor houses as **Melford Hall** (Elizabeth I stayed here) and **Kentwell Hall**, both in Long Melford. Many of the region's churches are chronicles of its fortunes as well as its religious and architectural preferences.

That the area was once rich and powerful is not in doubt: the Domesday Book recounts numerous manors and holdings in Suffolk. In the days when ecclesiastical and state office and money were inextricably linked, Simon Theobald, also known as Simon of Sudbury, became Archbishop of Canterbury and then Chancellor to the court of Richard II. He suffered a bloody end at the hands of rioters during the Peasants' Revolt of 1381, but his head finally found its way back to the theological college he founded at **St Gregory's** in Sudbury, where it became the object of pilgrimages. His teeth were stolen as relics, and the head is now held in a little wall cupboard (if you want to see it, contact a church official on 01787 372611).

By train from London

Trains depart from **Liverpool Street** about once every hour (changing at **Marks Tey**) to **Sudbury**. The total journey takes about 1hr 10mins.
Info: www.ger.co.uk.

East Anglia

You will find, too, that history has left a trace on the landscape itself. At **Great Yeldham**, a 1,000-year-old oak still stands, even if it is encircled by iron bands; and at Clare there is a huge man-made mound topped with a few ruins, which are all that remain of a Norman castle. (Incidentally, during the Hundred Years' War, the Lord of Clare was presented with lands in France, and the local wine – claret – still bears his name.)

Long Melford – so called because it is a 'ribbon' village of about two miles in length – shows an insatiable appetite for expansion. The village, now closing in on the town boundaries of Sudbury itself, contains a wonderful church, two noble halls and close to a surely excessive 40 antiques shops, which made it an apt location for the TV series *Lovejoy*. In the unlikely event that the shops don't have the item you're after, the old village school (situated by the bridge and opposite a house once owned by another World War I poet, Edmund Blunden) hosts very popular antiques fairs on bank holidays.

A few miles from Melford, over the Essex border, lies the village of **Borley**, famous in the earlier part of last century for its numerous ghosts. Once known as the 'most haunted house in Britain', the rectory – built on the site of an old convent – had the lot: ghostly nuns, carriages drawn by coal-black horses, wailings and all kinds of nasty noises, until a careless poltergeist burnt the place down in 1939. Or at least, that's the story. Even now, spookologists stake out Borley church trying to capture a glimpse of anything that goes bump in the night. The site of the former rectory is now private land and thus unvisitable, unless of course you're returning from the dead.

Situated in a loop in the River Stour, **Sudbury** is still, more than 1,000 years after its foundation, a thriving market town. Every Thursday and Saturday, a lively market takes place in the town square, just at the foot of painter Thomas Gainsborough's statue. Author Dodie Smith uses this statue as a meeting place for the dogs in *The Starlight Barking*, her sequel to *101 Dalmatians*. Dickens modelled the rotten borough of Eatanswill in *The Pickwick Papers* on Sudbury. It's a fine town in which to spend a few hours: you can go rowing (the boathouse is at Ballingdon Hill) or take in an exhibition at **Gainsborough's House**, the birthplace of the distinguished artist.

Finally, the villages of Suffolk are renowned for their churches and numerous pubs, the latter supplied with ales by Adnams and Greene King. You can get them in London, sure, but they're still best savoured close to their home in one of the fantastic pubs in the area.

What to see & do

See also the Essex and Suffolk County Council websites (www.essexcc.gov.uk and www.suffolkcc.gov.uk) for information and full local transport timetables.

Melford Hall. *See p293.*

A portrait from **Gainsborough's House**.

Tourist Information Centres

Lady Street, Lavenham, Suffolk CO10 9RA (01787 248207/www.visit-suffolk.org.uk). **Open** *Easter-June, Sept, Oct* 10am-4.45pm daily. *July, Aug* 10am-4.45pm Mon-Thur, Sun; 10am-5.45pm Fri, Sat. *Nov-Dec, Mar* 10am-3pm Sat, Sun.

Town Hall, Market Hill, Sudbury, Suffolk CO10 1TL (01787 881320/www.babergh-south-suffolk.gov.uk). **Open** *Apr-Oct* 9am-5pm Mon-Fri; 10am-4.45pm Sat. *Nov-Mar* 9am-5pm Mon-Fri; 10am-2.45pm Sat.

Bike hire

Street Life Bus station, Hamilton Road, Sudbury, Suffolk CO10 2UU (01787 310940).
Close to the train station.

Clare Castle & Country Park

Maltings Lane, Clare, Suffolk CO10 8NW (rangers 01787 277491/www.suffolkcc.gov.uk). **Open** *Park* free access. **Visitors' centre** *Easter-Sept* 9.30am-5pm daily. Closed Oct-Easter. **Admission** *Park* free; car park 50p for 2hrs, £1 all day. **No credit cards**.
Don't let the name fool you: all that is left of Richard de Bienfait's 11th-century castle is a motte, encircled by a spiralling path, and the ruins of the old walls that once protected the inner bailey. The view from the motte's top is pleasant enough, but there really is little to see of the castle. There's also a nature trail, but this is no more than a short walk though the woods. Also within the park borders are two old platforms, the remnants of Clare railway station. In Clare itself, the parish church of St Peter and St Paul (built 1450) is worth a visit.

Colne Valley Railway

Yeldham Road, Castle Hedingham, Essex CO9 3DZ (01787 461174/www.colnevalleyrailway.co.uk). **Open** *Mar-Oct, Dec* weekends & school hols; phone or see website for timetable. Closed Jan, Feb, Nov. **Admission** *Tickets* steam trains £6, £3-£5 concessions; heritage diesel trains £5, £2.50-£4 concessions. *Historic days* phone for details. **Credit** MC, V.
Run by the Colne Valley Railway Preservation Society, the restored Pullman carriages of this working steam and diesel railway will shunt you into the past. Now in its 27th year since its inception, the railway complex has been built up lovingly by steam-keen enthusiasts. The railway offers various diversions beyond looking at old engines, including train-driving courses; there is a selection of snacks and refreshments available in the buffet car – when the trains are running – and parents and children, as well as hardened train spotters, will find something to amuse. Entrance to the complex also gives admission to the 30 acres of the Colne Valley Farm Park, where sheep, cattle and goats graze in the water-meadows. Steam or diesel train tickets allow you to have as many rides as you like during the day.

Gainsborough's House

46 Gainsborough Street, Sudbury, Suffolk CO10 2EU (01787 372958/www.gainsborough.org). **Open** 10am-5pm Mon-Sat; 2-5pm bank hol Sun & Mon. **Admission** £3.50; £1.50-£2.80 concessions. **Credit** MC, V.
Part museum, part gallery, the birthplace of painter Thomas Gainsborough (1727-88) is unusual in that it manages to combine both roles well. The house, older than its Georgian façade suggests, is a roomy, winding affair and each room highlights a different aspect of the artist's work. There are etchings, a bronze of a horse (his only known sculpture) and more paintings from throughout his career than anywhere else in the world, including *A Wooded Landscape with Cattle by a Pool* (1782). There are also regular visiting exhibitions of contemporary art and crafts. A print workshop in the old coach house offers courses to the public. The lavender walk and a mulberry tree in the garden provide the ideal space for a breather.

Gifford's Hall

Hartest, Suffolk IP29 4EX (01284 830464/ www.giffordshall.co.uk). **Open** *Easter-Sept* 11am-6pm daily. Closed Oct-Easter. Open some weekends in Dec, phone for details. **Admission** £3.50; £3.25 concessions; free under-16s. **Credit** AmEx, DC, MC, V.
The Good Life made flesh? This 33-acre smallholding, centred on a Georgian homestead, is a self-sufficient farm with gardens, vineyards, meadows filled with wild flowers and animals ranging from a flock of St Kilda sheep to a posse of Rhode Island Red hens. Bees from the hall's ten hives buzz about the sweet peas and fruits of their labours can be bought at the farm shop. Gifford's Hall also has tearooms and offers B&B accommodation (doubles from £46.50), with a glorious breakfast of sausages, bacon, eggs and tomatoes, all home grown, to get you going in the morning.

Hedingham Castle

Castle Hedingham, Halstead, Essex CO9 3DJ (01787 460261/www.hedinghamcastle.co.uk). **Open** *Apr-Oct* 11am-4pm Thur, Fri, Sun. Also open school hols. Closed Nov-Feb. **Admission** (EH) £4; £3-£3.50 concessions. **Credit** MC, V.

This solid Norman castle, rising 110ft, was built by the Earl of Oxford, Aubrey de Vere, in 1140. It was besieged by King John, and Henry VII, Henry VIII and Elizabeth I all paid it a visit. Local builders plundering for stone proved to be the downfall of nearby Clare Castle but, for-tunately, they didn't get their mitts on Hedingham. A Tudor bridge over the dry moat is a (relatively) recent addition to the castle. Inside, the great arched banqueting hall with minstrel's gallery and dormitory are simply presented and highly evocative of a lifestyle far removed from ours. The view offers a sweeping vista of the area's rolling hills. On bank holidays and other festive occasions, jousting tournaments are organised with mounted knights in full gear. Leave time to wander the impossibly picturesque village as well.

Kentwell Hall

Long Melford, Suffolk CO10 9BA (01787 310207/ www.kentwell.co.uk). **Open** *Mar-June* 11am-5pm Sun, school hols. *Mid July-early Sept* noon-5pm daily. *Sept-Oct* noon-5pm Sun. **Great annual re-creations** *End June-mid July* 11am-5pm Sat, Sun. Closed Nov-Feb. Phone for special events & to confirm opening. **Admission** £6.75; £4.25-£5.75 concessions; free under-5s. **Credit** AmEx, MC, V.
Twenty-five years ago, this magnificent brick Tudor mansion, once seat to the Clopton family, was a ramble of neglect and decrepitude. Slowly, Kentwell's new own-ers – barrister Patrick Phillips and his family – have brought about the hall's resurrection. It is not a stately home in the mould of neighbouring Melford Hall (*see below*); this is a working house where Elizabethan kitchens, gardens and animals are still maintained. The hall regularly holds historical re-creations that are immensely popular with visitors and the out-of-work actors who hey-nonny-nonny from morning till night. A recent addition to the re-creations are World War II days full of dowdy costumes and duller food. There are also open-air performances of Shakespeare and various con-certs in July and August. Phone to check when these events are taking place. If all this artifice is not for you, then the rose garden maze and various outhouses – brewery, dairy and stables, with heavy Suffolk Punch horses – are fun to walk around.

Lavenham

The village of Lavenham is the jewel in Suffolk's crown. It first got a market charter in 1257 and for four cen-turies grew rich on the wool trade – it was the 14th wealthiest town in England in the 17th century, with 33 cloth-making businesses. Since 1930 Lavenham has been without a cloth factory but its appearance and char-acter are still defined by the wealth the industry brought. Many of its timbered buildings and halls date from the 14th and 15th centuries and its most famous building, the Guildhall, was built in 1529. The church, while lack-ing some of the charisma of smaller village churches nearby, is a magnificent, imposing and martial-looking structure that rises up black and grey against the fields behind. It's possible to meander through the town won-dering at its remarkably untouched exposed beams and crooked angles. David Dymond's excellent *A Walk Around Lavenham* (£1.50) is worth getting from the Tourist Information Centre on Lady Street (*see p292*), as are many of the informative free pamphlets. There are also 'Blue-Badge' guided walks (Sat 2.30pm, Sun

11.30am and 2.30pm, £3), or pick up an audio tour (£3) from the Lavenham Pharmacy, 99 High Street (01787 247284). Head to the Market Place to look round the Guildhall of Corpus Christi (01787 247646; open Mar & Nov 11am-4pm Sat, Sun; Apr 11am-5pm Wed-Sun; May-Oct 11am-5pm daily) and Little Hall (Market Place, 01787 247179; open Apr-Oct 2-5.30pm Wed, Thur, Sat, Sun). The former is celebrated by architects as one of the finest medieval buildings in England. The neigh-bouring Little Hall, another delightfully timbered build-ing with gardens attached, offers further insight into the impact of wool money.

Melford Hall

Long Melford, Suffolk CO10 9AA (01787 880286/ www.nationaltrust.org.uk). **Open** *Apr, Oct* 2-5.30pm Sat, Sun. *May-Sept* 2-5.30pm Wed-Sun. Closed Nov-Mar. **Admission** (NT) £4.50; £2.25 concessions; free under-5s. **No credit cards.**
This turreted Tudor mansion is a well-maintained and mannered example of Suffolk's stately homes. Home to the Hyde Parker family since 1786, Melford Hall offers many set pieces: the original panelled banqueting hall, an 18th-century drawing room and a Regency library. Furniture and Chinese porcelain, captured from a Spanish galleon (the Hyde Parkers produced a number of admirals), are on display, while the gardens have a wonderful air of tranquillity; the walled garden is espe-cially beautiful. A country fair is held in the grounds each June; in November it is also the venue for a vast conflagration (with attendant explosives) in honour of Guy Fawkes' night. While you're in Melford, visit Holy Trinity church, just up the lane by the 16th-century almshouse, founded in 1573 for 12 poor men and two women. The battlemented church, with flint panelling known as flushwork, has a fine Lady Chapel.

Sue Ryder Museum

Cavendish, Suffolk CO10 8AY (01787 282591). **Open** 10am-5pm daily. **Admission** £1; 50p concessions. **No credit cards.**
Situated behind the duckpond and to the side of the Sue Ryder Care's lovely Tudor house is a tiny amateur museum that makes up for in heart what it lacks in a rigorous taxonomy. At the end of World War II, its eponymous founder was a FANY (no sniggering at the back: the Female Auxiliary Nursing Yeomanry were a top-notch outfit we'll have you know) who saw at first hand the horror of the Nazi Germany concentration camps. Sue Ryder subsequently converted her Cavendish premises into a refugee home. The museum has various uniforms, some rather ropey tableaux showing improvised hospitals, plus artefacts from the camps, including a tin of deadly Zyklon B.

Where to stay

Many pubs and restaurants in the area double up as B&Bs. The **Black Lion** (*see p296*, doubles £109.50-£146) has comfortable rooms in addition to its restaurant.

The Bull

Hall Street, Long Melford, Suffolk CO10 9JG (01787 378494/fax 01787 880307/www.old english.co.uk). **Rates** £75 single; £110 double/twin;

Lavenham: famous for its half-timbered houses. *See p293.*

£120 family room; £120-£130 suite. **Rooms** (all en suite) 3 single; 17 double/twin; 3 family; 2 suites. **Credit** AmEx, DC, MC, V.

A well-established hotel and pub situated near Melford Hall in this historic village. If you get excited by beams, you'll love it here, as both the exterior and interior feature oak and acorn beams. The place is owned by Trusthouse Forte, but the rooms have a period charm (and the two suites have separate lounge areas and king-size beds with canopies), and the bar has the dynamic duo of Adnams and Directors. The hotel was refurbished in 2003, with the bedrooms and bathrooms bearing the brunt of the modernisation, but the traditional essence hasn't changed significantly. Children and dogs welcome. Smoking is not allowed in any of the bedrooms.

Bulmer Tye House
Bulmer Tye, nr Sudbury, Essex CO10 7ED (tel/fax 01787 269315/www.bulmeressex.co.uk). **Rates** £25 single; £50 double. **Rooms** 2 single (1 en suite); 2 double. **No credit cards.**

Two miles south of Sudbury is this welcoming and eccentric B&B set in a handsome Victorian house. It's teeming with books, clavichords (the owner makes them), dolls' houses and wooden cabinets, and owners Peter and Noël Owen are happy to talk you through the stories behind them and explain their philosophy that the house is a family home not a business. The grounds, which include a grass tennis court in a glade of trees, are also great fun to explore. The village boasts a famous brickworks, which uses old methods to replicate the Tudor bricks needed for restoring old homes. Children and dogs welcome. No smoking throughout.

Lavenham Priory
Water Street, Lavenham, Suffolk CO10 9RW (01787 247404/fax 01787 248472/www.lavenhampriory. co.uk). **Rates** £68-£87 single occupancy (weekdays only); £80-£126 double/twin/four-poster; £126-£136 suite. **Rooms** (all en suite) 1 double; 1 twin; 3 four-poster; 1 suite. **Credit** MC, V.

This 13th-century house was once home to a Benedictine order, before passing into the De Vere family and then being sold on to cloth merchants. It is to the Elizabethan period of these salesmen that the present owners have restored this breathtaking building, and even in the context of one of England's most idyllic towns, it still astounds. Each of the luxurious bedrooms has oak floors and sloping gnarled beams. Slipper baths and vast beds (each bespoke for the respective rooms) add to the comfort and beauty. The three-acre gardens (with a separate walled herb garden) are as pretty as one could imagine. For weekends (you can't reserve Saturdays only), you need to book up to three months in advance. Make the effort. Children over ten welcome. No smoking throughout.

Ollivers Farm
Toppesfield, Halstead, Essex CO9 4LS (01787 237642/fax 01787 237602/www.essex-bed-breakfast. co.uk). **Rates** £23 single; £37.50-£40 single occupancy; £55-£60 double/twin. **Rooms** 2 double/twin (1 en suite), 1 single. **No credit cards.**

Adjacent to a working farm, set in two acres of landscaped gardens and recently restored, Ollivers Farm is a 1650 house set in the heart of the countryside. The three bedrooms are comfortable and downstairs there's a dining room, sitting room and terrace, all containing

East Anglia

an interesting range of local art. Mrs Blackie's full English breakfasts – including home-made brown bread, jams and locally smoked bacon from Sudbury – are sufficiently fortifying to rule out anything other than a light lunch. Historians may be interested to know that the house was built by the Symonds family, whose son emigrated to the US and became pals with John Winthrop, first governor of Massachusetts. Children over ten welcome. No smoking throughout.

A120 towards Dunmow and Braintree; follow signs to Sudbury until you get to High Garrett; straight on until Sible Hedingham; A1017 to Great Yeldham; after White Hart pub turn left at Toppesfield signpost; last proper driveway on left before you get to Toppesfield T-junction.

Red House

29 Bolton Street, Lavenham, Suffolk CO10 9RG (01787 248074/www.lavenham.co.uk/redhouse). **Rates** £40-£60 single occupancy; £60 double. **Rooms** (all en suite) 3 double. **No credit cards.**

A homely and personable B&B service is offered in this elegantly proportioned Victorian house by Diana Schofield. The three double rooms all feature subtly colour co-ordinated furnishings and the rose-filled garden is ideal for morning coffee or evening drinks. The B&B is also home to three cats. Children and dogs welcome. No smoking throughout.

Swan Hotel

High Street, Lavenham, Suffolk CO10 9QA (01787 247477/fax 01787 248286/www.macdonald-hotels.co.uk). **Rates** £90-£95 single; £120-£160 double/twin; £170-£180 four-poster; £210-£220 suite. **Rooms** (all en suite) 7 single; 34 double; 4 twin; 3 four-poster; 3 suites. **Credit** AmEx, DC, MC, V.

This sizeable and characterful 14th-century hotel holds court in the centre of Lavenham. A recent £2m refurbishment has been carefully handled, both in the bedrooms and in the modern use of natural light in the reception area. The Swan has been a hotel since at least 1667, and you'll feel the years of experience with convivial and efficient service from the moment you walk through the door. Several rooms boast four-poster beds and fireplaces big enough to set up your own hog and spit. Each room has a CD player, TV and minibar. Two bars and a restaurant add to the appeal. Children and dogs welcome.

Western House

High Street, Cavendish, Suffolk CO10 8AR (01787 280550). **Rates** £36 double/twin. **Rooms** 1 double; 2 twin. **No credit cards.**

During the 18th century Western House, whose foundations date back to the 11th century, was a staging point for carriages travelling along the Roman Way from Colchester to Bristol. Now owners Peter and Jean Marshall have made the book-lined warren of a house – which sits just inside the Suffolk border – into the most welcoming of B&Bs. Jean is a singing teacher so you may be serenaded by pupils, and Peter runs a tiny health-food store at the back. The house also has a mature one-acre organic garden. All the rooms are light and inviting, and the full breakfasts are vegetarian. No smoking throughout.

Stour lighters

Before the railways became the arteries of the British Isles, it was waterways that transported the goods that were the commercial lifeblood of England. The 24-mile River Stour was one such; one of its most common cargoes was bricks, transported from Sudbury down to the estuary and then on to London, and coal, brought back to Sudbury from the then-bustling East End docks.

Stour lighters – the boats that made these journeys – were built either in Flatford, as depicted in Constable's *Boat Building at Flatford*, or in Sudbury (adjacent to the River Stour Trust's permanent home, the Granary, in Quay Lane). Flat wooden barges, 10 feet wide and 46 feet long, they operated in pairs, the front craft permanently shackled, bow to stern, with the trailing boat, which steered both vessels. The second lighter was also the home of a small cabin behind the hold. Here the two-man crew could catch forty winks or munch their victuals. The crew consisted of a captain and a horseman – known as the 'boy' –

who would sometimes ride the horse used to pull the lighters. The horses were specially trained to jump on to the lighter's foredeck and then off the other side whenever the towpath switched from one side of the river to the other.

Each lighter carried a load of 13 tons, so each two-day trip saw 26 tons of cargo moved up or down the river. This flow of bricks and coal continued until World War I when almost the entire fleet of barges was scuttled at Ballingdon Cut, in order to prevent the Germans using them in the event of an invasion.

Luckily, two privately owned lighters survived and operated in the lower reaches of the river until 1938, when because of the huge success of the rail service, they were abandoned.

You can still see a Stour lighter in a specially built display wharf at Cornard Lock. The lighter was saved and restored by the members of the River Stour Trust. It is the bow version (the rear boat), with a bridge for steering, and is thought to be more than 100 years old.

East Anglia

Note that many of the places listed below also provide B&B. Additionally, good eating and drinking options can be found at the cheery **Bell** in Castle Hedingham (10 St James's Street, 01787 460350) and the lovely hilltop **Plough** in Hundon (Brockley Green, 01440 786789, booking essential). The **White Hart** in Great Yeldham (Poole Street, 01787 237250) does both bar snacks and grander meals. The **Swan Hotel** (*see p295*) in Lavenham has fine ales and a garden bar overlooking a sheltered courtyard.

The Angel

Market Place, Lavenham, Suffolk CO10 9QZ (01787 247388/www.lavenham.co.uk/angel). **Food served** noon-2.15pm, 6.45-9.15pm daily. **Main courses** £8.50-£14.95. **Credit** AmEx, MC, V.

Licensed premises since 1420, the Angel offers solid, rural food – steak and ale pie – with occasional inspired additions from around the world – glazed duck with spring greens and sweet and sour sauce, grilled halibut with anchovies, capers and white wine sauce. It's all aimed squarely at the upper end of the pub grub spectrum. The dark-beamed pub is full of atmosphere, the dining room is quieter and more roomy, while the tables outside, overlooking Market Square, provide an ideal spot for people-watching. Booking is essential. The Angel also has eight rooms (doubles from £70).

Black Lion

Church Walk, Long Melford, Suffolk CO10 9DN (01787 312356/www.ravenwoodhall.co.uk). **Food served** Wine bar noon-2pm, 7-9.30pm daily. *Restaurant* 7-9.30pm daily. **Set meals** £25.95 2 courses, £29.95 3 courses. **Set lunch** (Sun) £18.95 3 courses. **Credit** AmEx, MC, V.

With a comforting and comfortable interior, bar dining from a blackboard menu and (for more formal occasions), a plush classical restaurant, the Black Lion straddles two stools. Staple dishes on the restaurant menu are traditional, including grilled loin of lamb with cabbage and rich mint jus, dried smoked haddock and potato with beef tomatoes, and red pepper and butter bean cake. The blackboard offers a few more hearty options: sausage, mash and black bacon with onion gravy, or crispy battered cod with chips. Desserts such as hazelnut tart with local honey and crème fraîche tend to be light but tasty and the house wines provide enough variety to keep you clear of the otherwise expensive restaurant wine list. The Black Lion is also a comfortable B&B (doubles £95-£105).

The Bull

High Street, Cavendish, Suffolk CO10 8AX (01787 280245). **Food served** noon-2pm, 6.30-9pm Tue-Sat; noon-3pm, 6-8pm Sun. **Main courses** £5.95-£13.95. **Credit** AmEx, MC, V.

An unassuming, Tardis-like pub with a slightly dowdy, many-roomed interior that is showing signs of age. The Bull remains popular with locals and tourists primarily because the generously portioned, good-quality food comes with a manageable price tag. Old favourites such as cod or haddock with chips, grilled sirloin steak,

sausage and mash or own-made cottage pie sit comfortably alongside vegetarian stir-fried noodles and grilled swordfish. The wine list is unpretentious, the landlord keeps a good pint of Adnams, there's a snack menu if you don't want a blow-out and the dessert menu is old school and indulgent – including bread and butter pudding, spotted dick and chocolate sponge pudding. It's best to book.

Great House

Market Place, Lavenham, Suffolk CO10 9QZ (01787 247431/www.greathouse.co.uk). **Food served** noon-2.30pm, 7-9.30pm Tue-Sat; noon-2.30pm Sun. **Main courses** £10.95-£18. **Set lunches** £9.95 2 courses, £15.95 3 courses. **Set dinner** £21.95 3 courses. **Credit** AmEx, MC, V.

This was once Stephen Spender's house; now it's an elegant, formal yet relaxed French restaurant with accommodation (doubles £75-£96), run with Gallic verve and style by Régis and Martine Crépy. Fresh white tablecloths decorate the tables, and contrast with the golden wood floors. The menu, undoubtedly one of the best and most fairly priced in Suffolk, derives its strength from the use of subtle flavours, evident in dishes including pan-fried John Dory with watercress coulis, fillet of prime beef with fresh duck fois gras and cassoulette of sautéd wild mushrooms and asparagus finished with garlic and cream parsley. Among the starters, carpaccio of marinated beef with coriander dressing on a parmesan rocket salad stood out on a recent visit, while a dessert of creamy lime and lemon tart left the taste buds zinging.

Scutcher's

Westgate Street, Long Melford, Suffolk CO10 9DP (01787 310200). **Food served** noon-2pm, 7-9.30pm Tue-Sat. **Main courses** £12-£18. **Credit** AmEx, MC, V.

Within this unspectacular Grade II-listed Georgian building is what looks like a neat, informal little restaurant, but in fact it's much more than that. Vying for attention on the menu are deep-fried tiger prawns in a tempura batter, seared scallops with crab and chive mash, pan-fried halibut on tomatoes and chilli, calf's liver and bacon in a rich gravy or fillet of beef with creamy herb and shallot sauce. Veggies have to make do with a puff pastry case full of spinach, caramelised onions, mushrooms, poached egg and red pepper sauce. Poor devils. There's a broad wine list with an equally varied price range.

Tickle Manor Tearooms

17 High Street, Lavenham, Suffolk CO10 9PT (01787 248438). **Food served** 10.30am-5pm daily. **Main courses** £3-£5.95. **No credit cards.**

It's easy to miss this traditional, askew little Elizabethan (1532) teahouse. It has a modest sign by the door, and its interior embodies many comforting virtues. The rooms, both upstairs and down, are small, but the assortment of tables are a decent arm's-length apart. Service is swift and the food is simple, consisting of sandwiches, toasties, baguettes and salads, all reasonably priced, well presented and filling. For devout tea drinkers there's a broad selection to choose from and cream teas are a speciality. The cakes are worth writing home about too. There's also coffee, and a refreshing elderflower pressé.

Bury St Edmunds & Around

Clean and sedate – but there's racing at Newmarket for the wicked.

'A handsome little town of thriving and cleanly appearance.' This was how Dickens described Bury St Edmunds in The Pickwick Papers, and it's still pretty accurate today. In the early 19th century Bury made its money from textiles. Now sugar and beer are the dominant industries, but there's still a sense in which the town resembles a Victorian burgher – solid, upright and utterly intolerant of decadence and disorder. The streets positively gleam, and everything about its appearance seems to confirm Bury as a High Tory haven of snobbish insularity.

Yet in all other respects, Bury is remarkably welcoming, with a helpful Tourist Information Centre and a sedate, intelligent take on its past, which extends to the obvious efforts made to keep monuments just-so and stop modernity from encroaching on the town in too brash and inappropriate a manner. Bury grew up around the **Benedictine Abbey of St Edmund** – England's patron saint until George unseated him – in medieval times and was for centuries a place of pilgrimage. Bury's motto is 'Shrine of a king, cradle of the law', a reference to the legend that in 1214 the barons of England met in the abbey church and swore an oath to force King John to accept demands that were later enshrined in the Magna Carta. In 1539, however, the monastery was dissolved by Henry VIII and fell into ruin.

Bury has long been a busy market town. Until 1871, when the market was disbanded following complaints of 'rowdyism', it stretched all the way across **Angel Hill**, the gentle slope – now an enormous car park – that runs parallel to the Abbey Gardens, overlooked on one side by the ivy-festooned **Angel Hotel** and at the far end by the **Athenaeum** assembly rooms. The modern market, the largest of its kind in East Anglia, now takes place on Wednesdays and Saturdays in the area around Cornhill and the Butter Market, best reached via Abbeygate Street, the main shopping thoroughfare.

Around Bury

Though there's enough in Bury to keep you busy for a weekend, it's worth remembering its proximity to **Newmarket** racecourse. If a day at the races is to be the highlight of your stay, note that the July Racecourse (used in June, July and August) is prettier and more intimate

Market day in **Bury St Edmunds**.

By train from London

There are about eight trains a day to **Bury St Edmunds**, leaving from **King's Cross**. Journey time (including a change at Peterborough) is just under 2hrs. **Liverpool Street** trains leave between every 10mins and 2hrs (change at Ely or Stowmarket) and take approximately 2hrs in total. Info: www.ger.co.uk and www.angliarailways.co.uk.

than Rowley Mile. **Ely** is also worth a visit for its majestic cathedral alone, although Ely Museum and Oliver Cromwell's House are also interesting. **Thetford**, a handsome town with plenty of gardens and riverside walks, was once seat of the kings and bishops of East Anglia and more recently spawned the 18th-century radical Thomas Paine. Born in White Hart Street, he is represented in the **Ancient House Museum** (01787 277662) in the same street. Those wanting a country house experience could view **Euston Hall** (01842 766366), near Thetford, just off the A1088.

The dominating feature of this sparsely populated area is **Thetford Forest**, planted in drearily regular rows by the Forestry Commission in the 1920s. The **High Lodge Forest Centre** (off the B1107 east of Brandon, 01842 815434) has details of forest walks.

What to see & do

Tourist Information Centres

6 Angel Hill, Bury St Edmunds, Suffolk IP33 1UZ (01284 764667/www.stedmundsbury.gov.uk). **Open** *Easter-Oct* 9.30am-5.30pm Mon-Sat; 11am-4pm Sun. *Nov-Easter* 10am-4pm Mon-Fri; 10am-1pm Sat.

Ancient House Museum, White Hart Street, Thetford, Norfolk IP24 1AA (01842 752599/www. norfolk.gov.uk/tourism/museums/thetford.htm). **Open** *June-Aug* 10am-12.30pm, 1-5pm Mon-Sat; 2-5pm Sun. *Sept-May* 10am-12.30pm, 1-5pm Mon-Sat. **Admission** *Museum* July, Aug £1; 60p-80p concessions. **No credit cards.**

Abbey Ruins & Gardens

Angel Hill, Bury St Edmunds, Suffolk (01284 764667/www.stedmundsbury.gov.uk). **Open** 7.30am-dusk Mon-Sat; 9am-dusk Sun. *Guided tours* (May-Sept) 2.30pm. **Admission** free. *Guided tours* £2.50; free under-16s. **Credit** MC, V.

The Benedictine Abbey of St Edmund was destroyed in the dissolution of the monasteries in 1539, and its remains provide the focal point for Bury's tourist industry. The gardens that now surround them, with their roses, yew hedges and carefully tended beds of forget-me-nots, are great for a peaceful stroll, with the Alwyne House Tea Rooms offering sustenance (Wed-Sun). Alternatively, you could grab a picnic from the Sandwich Shop in nearby Baxter Court (just off Abbeygate Street). For some context, call the Tourist Information Centre to arrange a guided tour. In the summer months, the centre can arrange specialist tours on a variety of related subjects.

Ely Cathedral

Chapter House, The College, Ely, Cambridgeshire CB7 4DL (01353 667735/www.cathedral.ely. anglican.org). **Open** *Apr-Oct* 7am-7pm daily. *Nov-Mar* 7.30am-6pm Mon-Sat; 7.30am-5pm Sun. **Admission** £4.80; £4.20 concessions; free under-16s. Free for all Sun. **No credit cards.**

Bury may have some fine abbey ruins, better restaurants and accommodation, and a bigger market, but in the cathedral stakes, Ely wins hands down. Its roots lie in a monastery founded here in 673 by Saxon princess Etheldreda – there's a shrine to her in front of the cathedral's high altar. The current building, which dates from 1081, towers over the local landscape in imposing fashion. The inside is no less impressive; the centrepiece is the 14th-century Octagon, a stunning construction made up of eight pillars that support 200 tons of timber, glass and lead. Through the south door is a collection of medieval monastic buildings still in use today, to the north a large and lovely Lady Chapel. In addition, the South Triforium holds a Stained Glass Museum (01353 660347, admission £3.50, £2.50 concessions). A small refectory in the cathedral serves drinks and snacks, while the larger Almonry restaurant in the grounds offers more substantial fare.

Ely Museum

The Old Gaol, Market Street, Ely, Cambridgeshire CB7 4LF (01353 666655). **Open** *Nov-Feb* 10.30am-4.30pm Mon, Wed, Thur, Sat; 1-4pm Sun. *Mar-Oct* 10.30am-5pm Mon-Sat; 1-5pm Sun. **Admission** £3; £2 concessions. **No credit cards.**

Situated in the town's former prison – the museum contains some unintentionally goofy re-creations of the building's naughty history on its first floor – the capacious Ely Museum delivers a neat summation of the town's long past. Take time out and watch the wonderfully entertaining archive documentary about the local eel-catchers, on permanent repeat in one of the museum's several galleries.

Greene King Brewery

Westgate Brewery, Westgate Street, Bury St Edmunds, Suffolk IP33 1QT (01284 714297). **Open** *Museum & shop* 11am-5pm Mon-Sat; noon-4pm Sun. *Tours* 11am, 2pm, 7pm by appointment Mon-Sat. **Admission** *Museum only* £2; £1.50 concessions. *Tours* (incl museum, no under-12s daytime, no under-18s evening) £6; £7 evenings. **Credit** MC, V.

The first recorded mention of brewing in Bury came in the Domesday Book of 1086, which mentioned the abbey's 'cerevisiarii', or ale brewers. Greene King arrived on Westgate Street more than 700 years later, a fact commemorated and celebrated at the brewery's surprisingly informative museum. Greene King also offers tours of the brewhouse and fermenting room twice daily during the week; booking is essential.

Lackford Lakes

Bury Road, Lackford, Bury St Edmunds, Suffolk IP28 6HX (01284 728706). **Open** *Visitors' centre* 10am-4pm Wed-Sun. *Reserve* dawn-dusk daily. **Admission** free.

A 222-acre wetland reserve run by the Suffolk Wildlife Trust that attracts lots of tourists along with all manner of domestic and migratory birds as well as butterflies and mammals. The tranquillity of this beautiful spot belies its origins as a series of gravel excavation pits. Wildlife can be viewed from a number of hides positioned around the small lakes and marshes. A visitors' centre was opened in July 2002 by naturalist David Bellamy and houses a café, information centre and sheltered viewing gallery for colder days. No dogs or fishing allowed inside the reserve.

A cross to bear at the **Abbey Gardens**.

Manor House Museum

5 Honey Hill, Bury St Edmunds, Suffolk IP33 1HS (01284 757072). **Open** 11am-4pm Wed-Sun. **Admission** £2.50; £2 concessions. **Credit** MC, V.
Built by John Hervey, the first Earl of Bristol, this Georgian mansion has been converted into an offbeat museum full of paintings, furniture, costumes, objets d'art and lots and lots of clocks. One can, you'll rapidly discover, have too many clocks, though the touch-sensitive computer screens make fact-gleaning easy.

Moyse's Hall Museum

Cornhill, Bury St Edmunds, Suffolk IP33 1DX (01284 706183/www.stedmundsbury.gov.uk/ moyses.htm). **Open** 10.30am-4.30pm Mon-Fri; 11am-4pm Sat, Sun. **Admission** £2.50; £2 concessions; free under-5s. **Credit** MC, V.
Moyse's Hall has been many things in its 800-year history, including a tavern, a synagogue and a prison. Now it's an idiosyncratic museum of local history and archaeology that numbers among its more ghoulish exhibits a lock of Mary Tudor's hair and a book covered in the skin of William Corder, the man convicted of the notorious Red Barn murder in 1827, not to mention his flayed scalp. The museum has been refurbished with an education room, new gallery space and better visitor facilities.

St Edmundsbury Cathedral

Angel Hill, Bury St Edmunds, Suffolk IP33 1LS (01284 754933/www.stedscathedral.co.uk). **Open** *June-Aug* 8am-7pm daily. *Sept-May* 8am-6pm daily. **Admission** free; suggested donation £2.
More than 1,100 years old and still incomplete, St Edmundsbury was only granted cathedral status in 1914, and even then it was a toss-up between it and nearby St Mary's Church (also worth a peek) as to which one would get it. The Crypt Chapel and the Chapel of the Apostles are only partly built, but the most distinctive aspect of the otherwise slyly grand building is its lack of a tower. The cathedral is most of the way towards finding the £10.5 million it needs for completion; a

project is in progress to get rebuilding completed by 2004. For guided tours, call the cathedral visitor officer. The Cathedral Refectory is popular for morning coffee and light snacks (Mon-Sat), while the Landing Gallery upstairs hosts temporary exhibitions. The cathedral also has occasional classical concerts.

Theatre Royal

Westgate Street, Bury St Edmunds, Suffolk IP33 1QR (box office 01284 769505/www.theatreroyal. org). **Open** *June-Aug* (phone to check) 11am-1pm, 2-4pm Tue, Thur; 11am-1pm Sat. **Guided tours** *June-Aug* 11.30am, 2.30pm Tue, Thur; 11.30am Sat. *Sept-May* by appointment only. **Admission** free. *Tours* (NT) £2.50; £2 concessions. **Credit** AmEx, DC, MC, V.
Owned by Greene King, who used it to store hops (it's opposite the brewery, *see p298*), the delightful Theatre Royal is leased to the National Trust and is one of the smallest and oldest working theatres in the country. The programme is a mixed bag of theatre, music, comedy and dance. Opening times can be affected by rehearsals and performances, so phone to check before visiting.

West Stow Anglo-Saxon Village

Icklingham Road, West Stow, Suffolk IP28 6HG (01284 728718/www.stedmundsbury.gov.uk/ weststow.htm). **Open** 10am-5pm daily. Last entry 4pm. **Admission** £5; £4 concessions; £15 family ticket. **Credit** MC, V.
This replica village, a short drive from Bury on the A1101, is built on the site of an actual Anglo-Saxon dwelling excavated between 1965 and 1972. Wander from the Weaving House to the Living House to the Sunken House to learn about life in fifth-century East Anglia or visit the Anglo-Saxon Centre to peruse the objects on display. The Hall is currently being rebuilt and will be finished in 2004. Pigs, hens and crops (supposedly) make the place more realistic. There's also a 125-acre country park (admission is free), with nature and wild-fowl reserves and two visitors' centres.

East Anglia

Abbey Hotel

35 Southgate Street, Bury St Edmunds, Suffolk IP33 2AZ (01284 762020/fax 01284 724770/www.abbey hotel.co.uk). **Rates** £55 single occupancy; £68 double/twin; £78 suite. *St Botolph's Cottage* (sleeps 4) £78. **Rooms** (all en suite) 11 double/twin; 2 family; 1 suite. **Credit** AmEx, DC, MC, V.

Not so much one single hotel as an endearing hotchpotch of houses and extensions– Tudor, medieval, modern, you name it – all manned by Arthur and Carole Cannell. Although decor can be a little faded in some rooms, all are en suite, homely and comfortable. Everybody gathers in the friendly dining room for breakfast, although if you stay in one of the self-contained houses, you can request that breakfast be brought across. The Cannells recently bought another two adjacent houses, which they run as a separate operation. Children welcome.

Angel Hotel

3 Angel Hill, Bury St Edmunds, Suffolk IP33 1LT (01284 753926/fax 01284 714001/www.theangel. co.uk). **Rates** £85 single; £119 double/twin; £165 four-poster; £230 suite; £139-£165 family room. **Rooms** (all en suite) 8 single; 8 twin; 43 double; 4 four-poster; 4 suites; 2 family. **Credit** AmEx, DC, MC, V.

This historic coaching inn dates from 1452 and is the most famous of Bury's hotels thanks to the regular visits it received from one Charles Dickens (he wrote part of *The Pickwick Papers* here and you can still stay in his preferred room). But really, any room overlooking the Abbey Gardens and cathedral is worth having. A conversion of the ballroom a few years ago added 24 new rooms, all of them kitted out with tasteful contemporary furniture. Modern British eating options come via the respected Abbeygate Restaurant and its cosy underground sibling, the Vaults brasserie. Children and pets are welcome.

Dog & Partridge

29 Crown Street, Bury St Edmunds, Suffolk IP33 1QU (01284 764792/fax 01284 761922). **Rates** £49.50-£59.50 single; £54.50-£64.50 standard double/twin. **Rooms** (all en suite with showers) 5 twin; 4 double; 1 family. **Credit** MC, V.

Kryn and Janet Wolszczak run this welcoming Greene King-owned pub and adjacent hotel. Rooms are spacious and clean, with satellite television and plain decor that's easy on the eye. Breakfast is served in the airy pub conservatory, which doubles as a restaurant in the evening. In summer you can take breakfast, or indeed a pint of Abbot Ale, out on to the decking in the courtyard garden, where a water feature forms the focal point. No smoking throughout. Dogs (and children) accepted.

Northgate House

8 Northgate Street, Bury St Edmunds, Suffolk IP33 1HQ (01284 760469/fax 01284 724008/www.north gatehouse.com). **Rates** £55-£65 single occupancy; £90-£110 double. **Rooms** (all en suite) 3 double. **Credit** AmEx, MC, V.

This exquisitely refurbished Georgian-fronted house was once the home of author Norah Lofts. Present owners Joy and Gerard Fiennes saved this architectural gem from ruin as a labour of love, and it shows. Bedrooms combining grandiosity with restfulness are wonderfully spacious, with views across the formal gardens and filled with antique furniture. Frankly, it would be tempting to spend all day in any one of the luxurious en suite bathrooms. Piles of books and a decanter of Madeira are just part of the homely welcome. All bedrooms are no smoking. No children.

Old Egremont House

31 Egremont Street, Ely, Cambridgeshire CB6 1AE (01353 663118/ fax 01353 614516). **Rates** £41 single occupancy; £52 double/twin. **Rooms** 1 twin (en suite); 1 double (private bathroom). **No credit cards.**

This cosy B&B, run to a high standard by Sheila Friend-Smith, has a great view of Ely Cathedral from the gardens – almost worth a visit in themselves. Breakfasts use fresh local produce. Children welcome by arrangement. No smoking throughout.

Ounce House

13-14 Northgate Street, Bury St Edmunds, Suffolk IP33 1HP (01284 761779/fax 01284 768315/www. ouncehouse.co.uk). **Rates** £60-£70 single occupancy; £85-£95 double/twin; £100 family room. Special breaks. **Rooms** (all en suite) 1 twin; 2 double. **Credit** AmEx, DC, MC, V.

This genteel B&B is actually two adjacent Victorian merchant houses. Owners Simon and Jenny Pott are an excellent source of tips and gossip and offer a friendly welcome. Guests have the use of a large drawing room and a cosy, book-lined snug – which houses an honesty bar and Sky TV. Bedrooms are spacious and full of solid antique furniture that is homely rather than grand. Children welcome. No smoking throughout.

For a long time, Bury, like many of its East Anglian neighbours, was a culinary desert. Thankfully, this has changed in recent years. There are now more than enough respectable eating options with which to fill a weekend. However, be sure to book in advance, as the best places can get very busy. Pubs-wise, Greene King boozers dominate the town. If you can't fit into the tiny **Nutshell Pub** (17 The Traverse, 01284 764867) – at 16 by 7.5 feet, it's said to be the smallest pub in Britain – then try the **Masons Arms** (14 Whiting Street, 01284 753955) and **Rose & Crown** (48 Whiting Street, 01284 755934). Both pour a fine pint of the local ale and provide decent pub lunches. **No.3** (3 Risbygate Street, 01284 752716) is more bar than pub, with serviceable cocktails and funky decor, while the splendid **Old Cannon Brewery** (86 Cannon Street, 01284 768769) puts up some competition to Greene King. Of the beers brewed on site here, Gunners Daughter is particularly fine, and the food's also well worth sampling.

Bailey's Tea Rooms

5 Whiting Street, Bury St Edmunds, Suffolk IP33 1NX (01284 706198). **Food served** 8.30am-4.30pm Mon-Sat; 10.30am-2.30pm Sun. **Main courses** £2.95-£6.50. **Credit** MC, V.

Bailey's is the best tearoom in town. And you probably will want to stick to tea – coffee isn't strictly how the French or Italians make it. Most of the solid British fare on the menu is home-cooked, including imaginative salads, jacket potatoes, a good range of sandwiches and cakes and old-style pub staples for hungry horses.

The Linden Tree

7 Out Northgate, Bury St Edmunds, Suffolk IP33 1JQ (01284 754600). **Food served** noon-2pm, 6-9.30pm Mon-Fri; noon-2pm, 5-9.30pm Sat; noon-3pm, 5.30-9pm Sun. **Main courses** £6.99-£10.99. **Credit** MC, V.

If a huge plate of food and a full complement of Suffolk accents appeal, head to this pub near the station. It's very popular with the locals so book well in advance. Avoid the 'international dishes' and stick to the grill. You won't need a starter, and that's a promise.

Maison Bleue at Mortimer's

30-31 Churchgate Street, Bury St Edmunds, Suffolk 1P33 1RG (01284 760623/www.maisonbleue.co.uk). **Food served** noon-2.30pm, 7-9.30pm Tue-Sat. **Main courses** £9.95-£16.50. **Set lunches** £9.95-£12.95 2 courses, £14.95 3 courses. **Set dinner** £19.95 3 courses. **Credit** AmEx, MC, V.

If you only go to one restaurant in Bury, make it this one. Almost all of the fish is locally caught and each dish is exquisitely put together – that goes for taste as well as presentation. On a recent visit, marinated king scallops with salmon, lime and coriander in filo pastry were matched in quality by black tiger gambas in a tangy tomato salsa. Oven-baked dorado à la Provençale and whole grilled Dover sole didn't disappoint either. One tip, save room for the grand board of well-kept cheeses. Eating à la carte costs around £35 per head at dinner (with wine) and is worth every penny.

The Red Lion

High Street, Icklingham, Suffolk IP28 6PS (01638 717802). **Food served** noon-2pm, 6.15-10pm Mon-Sat; noon-2pm, 7.15-9pm Sun. **Main courses** £6-£16. **Credit** MC, V.

Owner and restaurateur Jonathan Gates has made this 16th-century inn a popular choice for evening meals and Sunday lunches in the 13 years since he took over. The large main room – all antiques and exposed beams – is split in two by a vast open fireplace. Service is friendly and portions are generous with seasonal produce and seafood featuring heavily on the à la carte menu. Bar food is also available.

Star Inn

The Street, Lidgate, Cambridgeshire CB8 9PP (01638 500275). **Food served** noon-2pm, 7-10pm Mon-Sat; noon-2.30pm Sun. **Main courses** £12.50-£15.50. **Set lunch** (Sun) £14.50 3 courses. **Credit** AmEx, MC, V.

The Catalan menu in this 16th-century inn has proved so popular that the Lidgate Star (as it's known locally) has become more of a restaurant than a pub these days, although it still serves fine ales at the bar. Indeed, on a Friday and Saturday evening, there are likely to be so many people eating fall-apart, slow-cooked Spanish lamb, tasty chorizo and bean soup, or oven-baked fish that there's barely enough elbow room to use the billiards table. Spanish landlady Teresa is never too busy to talk people through the extensive blackboard menu and her staff are friendly as can be.

La Vita é Bella

34 Abbeygate Street, Bury St Edmunds, Suffolk IP33 1LW (01284 706004). **Food served** 6-10pm Tue, Thur, Fri; noon-2.30pm, 6-10pm Wed, Sat; 6-9.30pm Sun. **Main courses** £6-£14. **Credit** AmEx, MC, V.

A friendly, old-school, family-run Italian that is a hit in the early evening for those with children. What it lacks in innovation it makes up for by doing the classics extremely well. You'll pay around £20 for three courses, excluding drinks.

A Peddar's Way of life

On the borders of Thetford Forest, in the quiet lanes that lead to the Knettishall Heath Country Park (just south of the A1066 from Thetford to Diss) lies the beginning of the Peddar's Way. Although it's probable that a track existed here in pre-Roman times, it was the Romans, in AD 61, who built it into the straight route to the north Norfolk coast it is today.

The Peddar's Way cuts straight through what was then Iceni territory; the road was intended as a security measure to subdue the disgruntled British tribes after Boudicca's rebellion. It continued to be used as a trading route throughout the prosperous medieval period enjoyed by

Suffolk and Norfolk thanks to its wool trade. These days, though, much of it is no more than a wide grass path, which makes it perfect for hearty walks through the flat countryside.

At Knettishall (where it connects to the Icknield Way leading all the way to Cornwall) the trail begins in pretty, broadleaf woodland. It runs for 46 miles to Holme-Next-the-Sea, but those not wanting to trek the whole distance can easily concoct a circular route using alternative public footpaths. Peddar is said to derive from the Latin word for 'on foot' – Pedester and the Way were first registered on a map in 1587.

Suffolk Coast

Anglo-Saxon graves and nuclear power stations make the strangest of bedfellows.

Suffolk has always retained its own distinct identity and a subtle sense of 'otherness'. Nowhere in the county is this more true than along the coast. An uneasy juxtaposition of the cosy and the bleak, the cultivated and the wild, the coast along the North Sea doesn't offer the sheltered sandy coves of the English Channel. The shoreline here is predominantly pebbly and the sea icy. Intrepid sunbathers huddle behind striped windbreaks and walkers are buffeted by stiff offshore breezes.

It's perfect Barbara Vine territory and no wonder that Ruth Rendell's darker alter ego has set several of her claustrophobic crime novels in the county. The area's brooding, atmospheric side is probably least noticeable during the height of the summer, when crowds frolic on Southwold's shingle, and music lovers attend the Proms season at Snape Maltings. But if you ever happen to be in, say, Orford, on a biting winter's day, walking in the shadow of the commanding castle keep, past the fulminating fug of the blackened smokehouse, and down to the quayside as the mist rolls slowly and silently in from the River Alde, you'll know you're somewhere pretty special.

A shore thing

There's plenty to explore along the Suffolk coast. **Woodbridge**, a few miles north-east of Ipswich, may be inland now, but this lively one-time ship-building port makes an agreeable introduction to the area. Stretching back up a hill from the River Deben, you'll find a scattering of minor sights (Woodbridge Tide Mill, the Suffolk Horse Museum, Woodbridge Museum), plus antiques shops, and the occasional pub and restaurant. On the opposite bank of the river nearby is the site of probably the most celebrated archaeological find made in Britain, **Sutton Hoo** – the fabulous treasure-stuffed ship of a seventh-century East Anglian king.

Between Woodbridge and the coast, the wind-whipped Rendlesham and Tunstall forests provide a barrier that only adds to the invigorating feeling of isolation in little **Orford**. Overlooked by a 12th-century keep, it offers walking, eating and drinking, and the opportunity to contemplate the immense expanse of Orford Ness, the largest vegetated shingle spit in Europe and a unique habitat for plants and birds. In the 12th century the then-nascent shingle spit provided a sheltered harbour for Orford. Unfortunately, it wouldn't stop growing and it now all but cuts the village off from the sea. Boat trips run from the quay. Pick up picnic supplies from Richardson's Smokehouse (Bakers Lane, 01394 450103) or the shop adjacent to the Butley Orford Oysterage (Market Hill, 01394 450277), and take a quick look at the Norman church of St Bartholomew – there's a fine font inside and a huge rosemary bush in the churchyard.

Britten and beyond

Few people are more associated with their native region than Benjamin Britten is with the Suffolk coast. Born in Lowestoft in 1913, he lived most of his life in the area. In 1947 Britten moved with the celebrated tenor (and his lifelong partner) Peter Pears to Crag House on Crabbe Street in Aldeburgh. Together with the producer and librettist Eric Crozier they came up with the idea of starting a modest musical festival. Today, the Aldeburgh Festival (actually held in Snape) is one of the world's leading classical music and opera festivals. Many of Britten's works are set in Suffolk; fans should get hold of the 'Britten Trail' leaflet available at the tourist office.

Snape Maltings, a large collection of Victorian malthouses and granaries on the reedy banks of the Alde, encompasses the famous and beautiful concert venue and music school. Less attractive is the 'unique shopping experience' that shares the same complex, consisting of a music shop, gallery, kitchen shop, crafts shop, 'period home centre', clothes store, pub and tearoom. A range of painting,

By train from London

Direct trains to **Woodbridge** are infrequent; services run about every two hours from **Liverpool Street**, with a change at **Ipswich**. The entire journey takes **1hr 35mins** to **1hr 45mins**. Info: www.angliarailways.co.uk.

The **River Blyth** runs between Southwold and Walberswick.

craft and decorative arts courses is run from here (01728 688305/www.snapemaltings.co.uk), as are regular river trips.

Aldeburgh to Southwold

The next major settlement on the coast heading north is **Aldeburgh**. It's a classy place and big enough to retain a sense of its own identity regardless of the tourists who flock here on summer weekends. The carnival in August, which ends in a torchlight procession and fireworks on the beach, is a great occasion. The wide high street, which runs parallel to the sea, is an agreeable mix of the old-fashioned (there's a traditional butcher, fishmonger, greengrocer and baker) and urbane (Palmer and Burnett sells funky gifts and homeware at No.46 and there are a couple of excellent delis; 152 – at No.152 – and the Aldeburgh Food Hall at No.183). At No.84 you'll find the **Aldeburgh Cookery School** (01728 454039/www.aldeburghcookeryschool.com), which is run by food writer Thane Prince and Sarah Fox, chef/proprietor of the Lighthouse restaurant (*see p308*), and offers day and weekend courses.

Constant erosion of the coastline means that the current seafront is something of a jumble – it was never meant to face the ocean. The oldest building in town is here – the 16th-century moot hall – as is a shiny modern lifeboat station and a popular boating pond. If you don't fancy eating at one of the town's number of excellent restaurants, then join the often considerable High Street queues at the excellent Aldeburgh Fish & Chip Shop or the Golden Galleon and then take your booty on to the pebbly beach.

Thorpeness, a couple of miles north of Aldeburgh, is a surreal little place. With its rows of black-boarded and half-timbered houses, it has the air of a Tudor theme village. The entire settlement was dreamed up as a fashionable resort by GS Ogilvie when he bought the Sizewell estate in 1910. Go for a row on the Meare, dug by hand by navvies, and sprinkled with 20 islands named after characters in *Peter Pan* in honour of Ogilvie's friend JM Barrie. Ogilvie also created a well and used a windmill to pump water to a tank on top of an 87-foot tower, which he disguised as an overgrown house, known as the 'House in the Clouds'. The windmill can be visited (01394 384948/www.suffolkcoastandheaths.org), and the Dolphin Inn (Peace Place, 01728 454994), which has rooms and a sizeable restaurant area, is good for refreshments.

A little further up the coast is the area's most controversial presence: **Sizewell** twin nuclear power stations. Apart from the legion of pylons striding across the coastal flats, the power stations are a low-key presence. The huge white dome of Sizewell B, the UK's only pressurised water reactor, is the most distinctive feature along this coast. There's a moderately popular beach by the power station for the truly blithe.

East Anglia

For whom the bell tolls

It seems hard to imagine that tiny **Dunwich** was once a thriving port. In the early Middle Ages up to 5,000 people lived within its walls, trading with the Baltic, Iceland, France and the Low Countries. Monasteries, more than a dozen churches, hospitals, palaces and even a mint reflected the town's role as a busy trading port and one of England's major ship-building towns. Continual coastal erosion, however, exacerbated by a three-day storm in 1286, meant that by the 16th century trade – along with the harbour – had dried up and medieval houses and churches dropped slowly but surely over the crumbling cliffs. On stormy nights it's said that you can hear the old church bells tolling beneath the waves. Little evidence of Dunwich's former glory now remains beyond the sparse ruins of Greyfriars Abbey and the salvaged remains of All Saints church and leper chapel in the churchyard of St James's. Don't miss the superb **Dunwich Museum**, which tells the story of this strange place and, together with a few cottages, a good pub (the Ship) and a seaside café, is all that remains of the town.

The northern extent of this area is marked by the clifftop town of **Southwold**. It's the biggest 'resort' on this stretch of coast, and although during high season holidaymakers throng the pier and picnic outside the brightly painted beach huts that stretch along the promenade, the picturesque Georgian town generally gets on with its own life. The most dominant force in Southwold is the estimable Adnams Brewery, which owns the town's best two hotels (the Crown and the Swan, behind which it is situated). There are few greater Southwold pleasures than supping an Adnams brew on one of the many greens that speckle the town.

Another must is the 20-minute walk along the seafront or cross-country to the ferry over the River Blyth to **Walberswick**. This somnolent little village was once home to painter Philip Wilson Steer and, in addition to the excellent Bell Inn, boasts a curious church-within-a-church. In the Middle Ages Walberswick was a sizeable port, and the original 15th-century St Andrew's was to be a mighty church to reflect the status of the town. But its fortunes declined before the church was finished and much of it was dismantled to build the much smaller church that lies within the older building's ruins. Another notable church close by is at Blythburgh, a tiny village rather unfortunately bisected by the A12. The huge, light-suffused Holy Trinity is known as the 'Cathedral of the Marshes'. Its hammerbeam roof is decorated with 12 glorious painted angels, which probably escaped decapitation by iconoclastic puritans in the 17th century thanks to their inaccessibility. Carvings of the seven deadly sins adorn the pew ends.

Castles in the air

The castles of **Orford** and **Framlingham** have been linked by rivalry since Henry II began Orford in 1165 to counter the considerable local power of uppity Hugh Bigod, who was based at nearby Framlingham. Now united under the stewardship of English Heritage, the two castles are among the most impressive sights in Suffolk.

Orford was the most expensive of the many castles built by Henry, who was a great castle builder and destroyer, but its short life was hastened by the silting up of Orford harbour and the decline of the town as a thriving port. Its original curtain walls are long gone, but the impressive keep – one of the best preserved in Britain – remains, and the views from the top over Orford Ness are spectacular.

While Orford Castle has its keep but no curtain walls, Framlingham has its walls but no keep. It also has 13 towers linked together by a walkway and overlooking an impressive moat. It began life in the late 12th century as the stronghold of the rebellious Earls of Norfolk and over the centuries became a prison for Catholic priests, a poorhouse, a fire station and, finally, a romantic ruin.

Framlingham Castle

Framlingham, Woodbridge, IP13 9BP (01728 724189/www.english-heritage. org.uk). **Open** *Apr-Sept* 10am-6pm daily. *Oct* 10am-5pm daily. *Nov-Mar* 10am-4pm daily. **Admission** (EH) £4; £2-£3 concessions. **Credit** MC, V.

Orford Castle

Orford, nr Woodbridge, IP12 2ND (01394 450472/www.english-heritage.org.uk). **Open** *Apr-Sept* 10am-6pm daily. *Oct* 10am-5pm daily. *Nov-Mar* 10am-4pm Wed-Sun. **Admission** (EH) £4; £2-£3 concessions; free under-5s. **Credit** AmEx, DC, MC, V.

What to see & do

See also p304 **Castles in the air**.

Tourist Information Centres

152 High Street, Aldeburgh, IP15 5AQ (01728 453637/www.suffolkcoastal.gov.uk/leisure).
Open 9am-5.30pm daily.
69 High Street, Southwold, IP18 6DS (01502 724729/www.visit-southwold.co.uk). **Open** *Apr-Sept* 10am-5pm Mon-Fri; 10am-5.30pm Sat; 11am-4pm Sun. *Oct-Mar* 11am-3.30pm Mon, Tue, Thur, Fri; 11am-3pm Wed; 10am-4.30pm Sat.
Station Buildings, Woodbridge, IP12 4AJ (01394 382240/www.suffolkcoastal.gov.uk). **Open** *Easter-Sept* 9am-5.30pm Mon-Fri; 9.30am-5pm Sat, Sun. *Oct-Easter* 9am-5.30pm Mon-Fri; 10am-4pm Sat; 10am-1pm Sun.

Aldeburgh Festival

Snape Maltings Concert Hall, Snape, IP17 1SP (box office 01728 687110/www.aldeburgh.co.uk). **Tickets** vary; phone to check. **Dates** June. **Credit** MC, V.
Founded by Benjamin Britten, Peter Pears and Eric Crozier in 1948, the annual Aldeburgh Festival is just the highlight of a busy musical year at Snape. The Britten-Pears School, based at the Maltings, puts on events throughout the year, but the big ones are the main festival in June and the Snape Proms in August. In addition, there's the annual Early Music Festival at Easter (featuring mainly baroque music) and, in October, a festival of music by Benjamin Britten. For all these events, you should check the dates with the local tourist information centre or the festival website and book well in advance (particularly for accommodation). There's also a major poetry festival here in November.

Dunwich Museum

St James Street, Dunwich, IP17 3ED (01728 648796). **Open** *Mar* 2-4.30pm Sat, Sun. *Apr-Sept* 11.30am-4.30pm daily. *Oct* noon-4.30pm daily. Closed Nov-Feb. **Admission** free; donations welcome.
The extraordinary story of how the tiny hamlet of Dunwich was once one of the region's major settlements is told with great verve in this excellent museum manned by volunteers. At its peak in the early Middle Ages, between 4,000 and 5,000 people lived within the settlement's walls, but erosion and storms had washed most of Dunwich into the sea by the 16th century.

Easton Farm Park

Easton, nr Wickham Market, IP13 0EQ (01728 746475/www.eastonfarmpark.co.uk). **Open** *mid Mar-Sept* 10.30am-6pm daily. Closed Oct-mid-Mar. **Admission** £5.25; £3.75-£4.75 concessions.
There's animal petting aplenty in the beautifully situated 35 acres of child-friendly Easton Farm Park. Watch the chicks hatching and collect the eggs, meet and feed the farm animals or take a free pony ride. The farm also opens for school half-term weeks in October and February.

Minsmere RSPB Nature Reserve

Nr Westleton, Saxmundham, IP17 3BY (01728 648281/www.rspb.org.uk/reserves/minsmere). **Open** 9am-9pm/dusk Mon, Wed-Sun. **Admission** £5; £1.50-£3 concessions; free under-5s. **Credit** MC, V.

Follow the signs from the A12 or Westleton to reach Minsmere, one of eastern England's most important reserves for wading birds. Upwards of 200 species have been recorded here in a year, including marsh harriers and bitterns. There's a shop, tearoom, nature trails, hides plus frequent guided walks and events.

Orford Ness

Quay Office, Orford Quay, Orford, Woodbridge, IP12 2NU (access info & ferry crossing 01394 450057/www.nationaltrust.org.uk/orfordness). **Ferries** *Mid Apr-June, Oct* 10am-2pm Sat (last return ferry leaves Orford Ness at 5pm). *July-Sept* 10am-2pm Tue-Sat. Closed Nov-mid Apr. **Tickets** (NT) £5.70; £2.85 concessions; free under-3s.
This desolate ten-mile stretch of shingle was a secret military site and testing ground from 1913 until the mid-1980s. Now in the hands of the National Trust, the spit has been returned to nature and is a protected rare plant and bird sanctuary. Book monthly guided walks in advance with the National Trust warden.

Southwold Sailors' Reading Room

46 East Street, Southwold (no phone). **Open** *Apr-Oct* 9am-5pm daily. *Nov-Mar* 9am-3.30pm daily. **Admission** free; donations welcome.
A stroll along the seafront should definitely include a visit to this idiosyncratic tribute to and place of rest and recreation for generations of Southwold's seafarers. Inside the tiny room the walls are adorned with a jumble of yellowing newspaper cuttings, maritime yarns and poems, model ships and faded photos of nautical characters with names such as 'Binks Popeye Palmer', 'Brushy Watson' or 'Salty Sam Jarvis'.

Sutton Hoo

Tranmer House, Sutton Hoo, Woodbridge, IP12 3DJ (01394 389700/www.nationaltrust. org.uk/places/suttonhoo). **Open** *Mid Mar-Sept* 10am-5pm daily. *Oct* 10am-5pm Wed-Sun. *Nov-mid Mar* 10am-4pm Sat, Sun. **Guided tours** daily during summer; phone for details. **Admission** £4; £2 concessions; free under-5s. **Credit** AmEx, MC, V.
From 20 grave mounds set high on a hillside by the River Deben, the richest archaeological treasure ever found in Britain was excavated in 1938 at Sutton Hoo. The centrepiece was a 90ft-long ship, the likely last resting place of the Anglo-Saxon king of East Anglia, Raedwald. The magnificent cache of treasure found here is now in the British Museum and the site, containing a small exhibition of the dig, a shop with Sutton Hoo-related items and a children's play area, puts more emphasis on café and parking facilities than archaeological history.

Where to stay

Demand for accommodation far outstrips supply on the Suffolk coast, so book as far in advance as possible. If the places listed below are full, try **Uplands** (Victoria Road, 01728 452420, doubles £87.50), the newly renovated **Brudenell Hotel** (The Parade, 01728 452071, doubles £130-£186) or the **White Lion Hotel**

East Anglia

Butley Orford Oysterage. *See p308.*

(Market Cross Place, 01728 452720, doubles
£120-£160) in Aldeburgh. There's also **Ferry
House** in Walberswick (01502 723384, doubles
£48-£50), the **Crown Inn** in Snape (Bridge
Road, 01728 688324, doubles £70), or the
Old Mill, also in Snape, where Britten
composed the opera *Peter Grimes* (01728
687477/www.oldmillsnape.co.uk, doubles/
cottage £55). If you want to stay in Orford,
there are rooms at the **King's Head** (Front
Street, 01394 450271, doubles £60) and, near
the quay, at the **Jolly Sailor** (Quay Street,
01394 450243, doubles £40-£50). In Dunwich,
the **Ship Inn** (St James Street, 01728 648219,
doubles £50-£68) has three rooms.

Acton Lodge

*18 South Green, Southwold, IP18 6HB (01502
723217).* **Rates** £35-£45 single occupancy;
£55-£75 double/twin. **Rooms** 2 double; 1 twin
(2 en suite, 1 with private bathroom).
No credit cards.

John and Brenda Smith have been running this popular
B&B since 1991. It's a substantial red-brick Italianate
villa on the edge of South Green with views over the sea
or marshes towards Walberswick and Dunwich. Inside,
many of the original features – marble fireplaces and
stripped floors – have been carefully preserved, and
rooms are spacious and well appointed. Breakfasts are
notable, and include own-made fish cakes, bread and
jams, locally caught and smoked haddock, kippers and
bloaters, as well as fresh fruit and cereals. This is a popular place, so book well in advance. Children welcome.
No smoking throughout.

Bell Inn

*Ferry Road, Walberswick, IP18 6TN (01502
723109/fax 01502 722728/www.blythweb.co.uk/
bellinn).* **Rates** £70 single occupancy; £75 double/
twin; £90-£130 family room. **Rooms** (all en suite)
4 double; 1 twin; 1 family. **Credit** MC, V.

If you want to avoid the London crowds of nearby
Southwold and Aldeburgh, then head for the tiny, waterside village of Walberswick and the 600-year-old Bell
Inn. Charming and rambling, with brick exterior and
flagstoned, beamed interior, the Bell has six rooms, sea
views and above-average pub grub. Rooms are plain but
have en suite bathrooms and tea- and coffee-making
facilities, and there's a family room for those who want
to avoid the hurly-burly of the popular bar. Book well
in advance. All bedrooms are no-smoking. Children and
dogs welcome.

Crown & Castle

*Orford, Woodbridge, IP12 2LJ (01394 450205/
www.crownandcastle.co.uk).* **Rates** £85-£135
double/twin; £95-£145 family. **Rooms** (all en suite)
14 double; 3 twin, 1 family. **Credit** MC, V.

It's well worth booking the two months in advance that
is necessary to secure a place at this sophisticated and
romantic inn, which is run by David and (food writer)
Ruth Watson. Bedrooms on the first floor of the main
building are kitted out in cool, light paints and fabrics,
with big comfy beds, plus funky tiles and massive-
headed power showers in the bathrooms. Children
and pets are both welcome. All bedrooms are no-
smoking. Another plus is the hotel's excellent Trinity
restaurant, *see p308*.
*Follow signs for Orford Castle from the Melton roundabout
on the A12; the hotel is next to the castle.*

East Anglia

Crown Hotel

90 High Street, Southwold, IP18 6DP (01502 722275/fax 01502 727263/www.adnams.co.uk). **Rates** £75 single; £110 double/twin; £130 family room; £150 suite. **Rooms** 1 single (en suite); 8 double (4 en suite); 3 twin (2 en suite); 1 suite (en suite); 2 family (en suite). **Credit** DC, MC, V.
Pub, wine bar, restaurant and small hotel, the Crown has had a chequered history, beginning life as a posting inn called the Nag's Head. Now owned and restored in pastel hues by Adnams, it's a smaller and cheaper sibling to the Swan (*see below*). There are 14 modestly sized and plainly decorated rooms, but all come with televisions, hairdryers and tea- and coffee-making facilities. For the restaurant and bar, *see p308*. Children welcome. All rooms are no-smoking.

Dunburgh

28 North Parade, Southwold, IP18 6LT (01502 723253/www.southwold.ws/dunburgh). **Rates** £40-£50 single; £65-£75 twin/double; £70-£80 superior double. **Rooms** (all en suite) 1 single; 2 double/twin; 1 superior double. **No credit cards**.
This friendly B&B is well located on a corner site overlooking the seafront and Southwold's newly renovated pier. All rooms have TV, CD player and hairdryer and decoration has a Victorian theme. Go for the double room with four-poster and balcony overlooking the sea. Children welcome. All rooms are no-smoking.

Ocean House

25 Crag Path, Aldeburgh, IP15 5BS (01728 452094). **Rates** £40-£60 single occupancy; £55-£70 double/twin. **Rooms** 1 single (private bathroom); 5 double/twin (2 en suite, 3 private bath). **No credit cards.**
Wonderfully situated overlooking Aldeburgh's pebbly beach, Ocean House is a mid-Victorian monolith that's been carefully restored to its original condition by the welcoming Phil and Juliet Brereton. The bedrooms have views out over the sea, and there's a games room in the basement. Ask for one of the first-floor rooms at the front. You'll need to book months in advance to secure a spring or summer weekend, though. No smoking throughout. Four of the rooms are available for self-catering; phone for details.

Old Rectory

Station Road, Campsea Ashe, IP13 0PU (tel/fax 01728 746524/www.theoldrectorysuffolk.com). **Rates** £55 single; £75-£85 double/twin; £85 four-poster. **Rooms** (all en suite) 1 single; 2 twin; 5 double; 2 four-poster. **Credit** MC, V.
An elegant Georgian house in the tiny inland village of Campsea Ashe near Woodbridge, the Old Rectory has just eight rooms but bags of character. Polished wood, pale furnishings and rugs all add to the tasteful impression and the excellent no-choice dinner (three courses for £19.50) is particularly recommended (compulsory if staying on a Saturday night). Children and dogs welcome. All rooms are no-smoking.
A12 N; take B1078 E to Campsea Ashe; go through village; over bridge; house is on right next to church.

Swan Hotel

Market Place, Southwold, IP18 6EG (01502 722186/fax 01502 724800/www.adnams.co.uk). **Rates** £75-£80 single; £130-£160 double/twin; £160-£170

superior double/twin; £190-£200 suite/four-poster. **Rooms** (all en suite) 3 single; 11 double/twin; 23 superior double/twin; 3 suites; 1 four-poster suite. **Credit** MC, V.
A grander and more expensive alternative to the Crown (*see above*), the self-assured Swan has always been the hub of Southwold social life. There are 26 bedrooms in the main hotel and a further 17 garden rooms, all decorated in an updated, understated version of country-house style. Bathrooms, though small, are modern and well equipped. Continental breakfast is available in your room, or you can opt for the superior full English version served in the handsome dining room overlooking Southwold's market place. Staff are particularly pleasant. Children are welcome; dogs are welcome in the garden rooms.

Wentworth Hotel

Wentworth Road, Aldeburgh, IP15 5BD (01728 452312/fax 01728 454343/www.wentworth-aldeburgh.com). **Rates** £67-£73.50 single; £120-£152 twin/double; £10 each additional child in parents' room. **Rooms** 6 single (4 en suite, 2 with private bath); 31 double/twin (all en suite). **Credit** AmEx, DC, MC, V.
The traditional and comfortable Wentworth faces the sea at the northern edge of town in Aldeburgh. A sizeable hotel with 37 well-appointed bedrooms neatly decorated in John Lewis style, it also features a sunken terrace (good for drinks on sunny days), cosy lounges, a restaurant and bar. Children and dogs welcome (there's a £2 per night charge for canine guests). All bedrooms are no-smoking.

Where to eat & drink

The best pubs in Southwold are those that allow alfresco spillover during fine weather. Try the **Lord Nelson**, situated between Market Hill and the sea (you can take your pint of Adnams to the seafront; the pub also does a mean prawn sandwich) or the **Red Lion**, where drinkers chill out on South Green. In Woodbridge, the best pub is the **King's Head** on Market Hill (01394 387750), which offers a wide range of good food, or you could also try the Thai-Malaysian dishes at **Spice Bar Restaurant & Café** (17 The Thoroughfare, 01394 382557).
In Snape, pubs that are worth a visit include the **Crown Inn** (Bridge Road, 01728 688324), which is good for food, and the **Golden Key** (Priory Road, 01728 688510). In Aldeburgh, you can try the **White Lion** (Market Cross Place), the **Mill** (Market Cross Place) or the flower-festooned **Cross Keys** (also good for food, Crab Street, 01728 452637). But the pick of the bunch is the tiny, friendly, locals-packed **White Hart** on the High Street. And don't miss out on a trip to the well-positioned **Bell Inn** (01502 723109) in pretty Walberswick, where the food is good and the welcome warm.

Butley Orford Oysterage

Market Hill, Orford, IP12 2LH (01394 450277).
Food served *Apr-Oct* noon-2.15pm, 6.30-9pm Mon-Fri, Sun; noon-2.15pm, 6-9pm Sat. *Nov-Mar* noon-2.15pm Mon-Thur, Sun; noon-2.15pm, 6.30-9pm Fri; noon-2.15pm, 6-9pm Sat. **Main courses** £6.90-£12.50. **Credit** MC, V.

Bill Pinney not only has his own small fishing fleet and oyster beds but runs a small but flourishing smokehouse as well. The family-run oysterage is small but perfectly formed, with stripped-down café surroundings and motherly service. Specials are chalked up daily on a blackboard, including fresh skate, sole, cod, herring or sprats, all served with new potatoes and a simple side salad. Freshness and simplicity are the order of the day and the place is hugely, deservedly popular as a result. Advance booking essential.

Captain's Table

3 Quay Street, Woodbridge, IP12 1BX (01394 383145/www.captainstable.co.uk). **Food served** noon-2pm, 6.30-9.30pm Tue-Thur; noon-2pm, 6.30-10pm Fri, Sat; noon-2pm Sun. **Main courses** £6.95-£15.50. **Credit** MC, V.

A bit close to a busy road for comfort, this whitewashed wayside restaurant nevertheless has a pleasant, sten-cilled interior and is close to the pretty Woodbridge estuary. The menu shows eclectic influences, with lamb kleftico or tiger prawns with a Thai curry dip alongside spaghetti bolognese, but allows room for popular classics such as char-grilled ribeye or duck leg confit with lentils and red wine. In summer, there are tables outside on a gravel terrace.

Crown Hotel

90 High Street, Southwold, IP18 6DP (01502 722275/www.adnams.co.uk). **Food served** noon-2pm, 6-8.45pm daily. **Main courses** (bar only) £8.75-£14. **Set lunch** £18.50 2 courses, £21.50 3 courses. **Set dinner** £24 2 courses, £29 3 courses. **Credit** DC, MC, V.

One of busy Southwold's most popular eating options, the Crown Hotel has a formal front room restaurant and a really buzzing bar area. Despite the overcrowding, we'd recommend opting for the more flexible, better value menu offered at the front bar, where the atmosphere's more jolly, the service is slicker and choices might include smoked haddock and mussel chowder or roast salmon with potatoes and snake beans. Booking is recommended.

The Lighthouse

77 High Street, Aldeburgh, IP15 5AU (01728 453377). **Food served** noon-2pm, 6.30-8pm daily. **Main courses** (lunch) £6.75-£9.50. **Set dinner** £14.25 2 courses, £17.50 3 courses. **Credit** AmEx, MC, V.

The menu at this bright and airy Aldeburgh bistro changes according to the daily catch. Cod or skate are bought fresh from beachside suppliers and crab, aspara-gus and smoked fish are sourced locally. Dinner is a very reasonably priced £14.25 for two or £17.50 for three courses and at lunch there's a seasonally changing menu with eight or ten choices in each course. Don't miss the potted Norfolk shrimps, hot smoked salmon with new potatoes or freshly dressed Cromer crab with herb mayonnaise. Booking recommended.

Regatta

171 High Street, Aldeburgh, IP15 5AN (01728 452011). **Food served** noon-2pm, 6-10pm daily. **Main courses** £8-£14. **Set meals** £9 2 courses, £12 3 courses. **Credit** AmEx, DC, MC, V.

A long-standing favourite, Regatta offers a flexible menu in laid-back, sunny surroundings in a prime position on Aldeburgh's High Street. Run by Robert Mabey and his wife Johanna, it opened in 1992 and has been going great guns ever since. Regatta's strengths include local game and produce, and there's a particular emphasis on fresh fish and shellfish in the spring and summer months. The place is pleasantly family-friendly during the day and also runs a series of popular gourmet evenings.

Riverside Restaurant & Theatre

Quayside, Woodbridge, Suffolk, IP12 1BH (box office 01394 382174/restaurant 01394 382587/www.theriverside.co.uk). **Food served** noon-2.15pm, 6-9.15pm Mon-Sat; noon-2.15pm Sun. **Main courses** £10-£16. **Set dinner** £24 3 courses & cinema. **Credit** AmEx, MC, V.

An old-fashioned cinema with up-to-date restaurant attached, the Riverside was originally built in 1915 and refurbished a few years ago. Try roasted red pepper and herb risotto with a parmesan and rocket salad or char-grilled pork rib with shallot and garlic cream, followed by a showing of the latest arthouse release. A fine view of the boats on the river is only slightly marred by looming Woodbridge railway station.

Swan Hotel

Market Place, Southwold, IP18 6EG (01502 722186/fax 01502 724800/www.adnams.co.uk). **Food served** noon-2.30pm, 7-9.30pm daily. **Main courses** (bar only) £10-£12. **Set lunch** (restaurant only) £18 2 courses, £22 3 courses. **Set dinner** (restaurant only) £28.50 3 courses. **Credit** MC, V.

The more grown-up of the two Adnams hotels in Southwold (the other is the Crown, *see above*), the Swan's very civilised dining room has a country-house feel and big windows overlooking the high street. Service is friendly and bustlingly efficient and dishes on the mod-ern European menu are slickly produced. Start with an agreeably powerful Bloody Mary in the bar (made the traditional way with a dash of sherry) while you make your choice from the likes of cream of celeriac soup with truffle oil, a plateful of charcuterie, pan-fried sea bass with new potatoes and saffron aïoli or risotto with mush-rooms and broad beans accompanied by a rocket and parmesan salad.

The Trinity

Crown & Castle, Orford, IP12 2LJ (01394 450205/www.crownandcastlehotel.co.uk). **Food served** *Apr-Oct* noon-2pm, 7-9pm daily. *Nov-Mar* noon-2pm, 7-9pm Mon-Sat. **Credit** MC, V.

Well worth the necessary advanced booking, a meal at the Crown & Castle's polished little bistro is always a pleasure. The short but flexible menu offers a range of mod Euro dishes such as pan-fried local skate with French beans and new potatoes, grilled salmon with pea and tarragon purée and crispy pancetta or home-potted shrimps with farmhouse toast. There's also a savvy wine list. Staff are pleasant and professional and the atmosphere invariably convivial.

Advertisers' Index

Please refer to relevant sections for
addresses/telephone numbers

Index

Photography by
pages iii, 24, 26, 31, 44, 45, 49, 68, 69, 70, 78, 81, 91, 155 Alys Tomlinson; pages 3, 85, 165, 167, 185, 187, 189, 228,
229, 232, 233, 283, 286. 294, 297, 299, 303, 306 Heloise Bergman; pages 10, 14 Lydia Evans; pages 19, 22
Canterbury Tourist Board; English Heritage Photographic Library, photographers listed: pages 30 Jonathan
Bailey, 56 Paul Hignam, 107, 120, 138 Jonathan Bailey, 253, 257 Alan Bull, 264; National Trust Photographic
Library: page 43 David Sellman, page 92 Nadia Mackenzie, page 211 Nick Meers, page 291 Rupert Truman, pages
63, 84, 101, 143, 145, 195, 199, 202, 208, 268, 272 Jonathan Perugia; page 98 Kit Burnet; pages 108, 112, 113, 115,
123, 136 Paul Carter; p158, 166, 197, 214, 224 Mike Carsley; page 171 Jonathan Cox; page 179 National Heritage
Photo Library; page 237 (left) The Natural History Museum; pages 244, 245 HMF Archive; page 267 Christi
Daugherty; page 280 Corbis.
The following images were supplied by the featured establishments/artists: pages 13, 35, 38, 40, 64, 65, 96, 104,
118, 127, 128, 129, 140, 152,161, 168, 173, 176,182, 192, 201, 219, 221, 223, 235, 236 (left), 247, 250, 292.